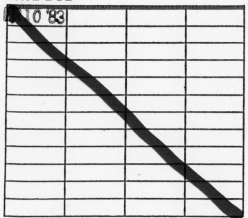

BRITISH POLITICAL FACTS
1900–1968

BRITISH
POLITICAL FACTS
1900-1968

BY

DAVID BUTLER

AND

JENNIE FREEMAN

THIRD EDITION

LONDON

MACMILLAN

NEW YORK · ST MARTIN'S PRESS

1969

© David Butler 1963, 1968, 1969

First Edition 1963
Reprinted with corrections 1964
Second Edition (completely revised) 1968
Third Edition 1969

Published by
MACMILLAN AND CO LTD
Little Essex Street London WC2
and also at Bombay Calcutta and Madras
Macmillan South Africa (Publishers) Pty Ltd Johannesburg
The Macmillan Company of Australia Pty Ltd Melbourne
The Macmillan Company of Canada Ltd Toronto
St Martin's Press Inc New York
Gill and Macmillan Ltd Dublin

Library of Congress catalog card no. 67-27323

Printed in Great Britain by
R. & R. CLARK LTD
Edinburgh

CONTENTS

INTRODUCTION TO THE FIRST EDITION

THE table of contents offers the simplest justification for this book — but inevitably it is a book that will justify itself in different ways to different readers. The scholar, the journalist, the politician and the club bore were all in the authors' minds at one point or another during its compilation. Some of those who look at this book will, we hope, be delighted to find in compact and reliable form data that might still have eluded them after searching through a dozen standard works of reference; others will at least discover from our pages where the information they seek may be found; a few, we fear, will be infuriated by our omissions and, despite all our efforts at checking, by our errors.

The idea of writing this book grew gradually in the mind of one of its authors as, in the course of twelve years as a student and a teacher at Nuffield College (which is devoted to research in contemporary subjects), he noticed the amount of time that he and others wasted in searching for seemingly obvious facts about twentieth-century Britain. If, therefore, any one reader has been especially in our minds, he is the graduate student writing a thesis on any domestic theme in the last sixty years. We hope he will find here not only an expeditious way of checking basic facts but also, if he finds time to browse through our lists and tables, a stimulating reminder of people and considerations that must have played a part, perhaps only as background, in the situations he is analysing.

But we are not concerned solely with academic needs. Experience of checking facts in newspaper offices and broadcasting studios, and the anecdotes of friends in Whitehall and Westminster have made plain to us how much elementary political data is annoyingly elusive. Many admirable works of reference exist but the right one is not always to hand; most of them, moreover, are compiled on an annual basis — which can be very frustrating for those who are trying to trace an office or a statistic over a number of years.

The compiler of any work of reference is limited by space and time. How much data shall be included? How far shall other works be duplicated? How many hours is it worth devoting to any particular compilation? In this book we have had to exclude interesting information either because it would fill a disproportionate number of pages or because it could not be obtained without more labour than we thought justified. We have consoled ourselves for setting out data in abbreviated form by giving exact references to more exhaustive sources.

Indeed, since the compilation of reference books is, even more than other research, systematised plagiarism, perhaps the most valuable part of these pages lies in these citations. We have not attempted an exhaustive bibliography — except for a compilation of bibliographies and general reference books — but we have throughout tried to list all major authorities.

The title, *British Political Facts 1900–1960*, provides a reasonably close delimitation of the scope of this book. *British* indicates that we have been concerned with the domestic history of the United Kingdom. But it is not possible to set precise boundaries to the term 'domestic' and we have perhaps strayed beyond them by listing Colonies, Governors-General, and some Ambassadors.

Political is potentially ambiguous, but we have used it to stress that our interest is in the power of the state. We have tried to list the principal people who were involved in the government of Britain at any moment in this century; we have recorded election results — as providing the basis for political authority — and major legislation — as representing its use; we have assembled, in summary form, statistical data which show some of the social and economic background to all political action.

Facts indicates that we have tried to eschew political judgements as far as possible. Some value judgements may be implicit in our selection of material, but we believe that virtually everything here would be acceptable as non-controversial evidence in debates over the nature of twentieth-century British history. It is a waste of time to argue about verifiable questions of fact. But it is also a waste of time to assemble facts except as a basis for argument. Because in this book we have stuck rigidly to facts, it does not mean that we overrate them. Analysis of our past and present situation is far more important than mere fact-gathering. Unlike Martha we are fully aware which is the better part.

1900–1960 is a somewhat arbitrary period — but any historical period must be arbitrary. Our terminal date, 31 December 1960, was determined by the availability of material in 1961–2; perhaps a second edition will carry the record forward. Our opening date was a numerological accident — but it would be hard to find a better watershed without going back at least to 1885, which because of space, and still more because of the availability of data, was impracticable. We have endeavoured to treat every one of our sixty years equally, providing as full and exact data about 1901 as about 1959. With some statistics this has proved impossible and some of our time-series are regrettably discontinuous. But in general it will be found that we have resisted the temptation to make a special favourite of the more recent past — it is not our fault that there were no Gallup polls before 1938 and that local election results cannot usefully be pursued very far back.

In compiling this book we have become very conscious of the strengths and weaknesses of other reference books — and particularly of the importance of pedantic accuracy and clear presentation. We have certainly not avoided all the pitfalls into which we have observed others falling; therefore, by way both of excuse and of warning, it may be worth describing a few of the difficulties we have faced.

The general problems of finding exact data on British politics were best exemplified in the gathering of complete lists of ministries over the last sixty years — the most time-consuming of all our operations.   There are a number of publications which purport to list all ministerial appointments — the most useful of these are the two Parliamentary handbooks, *Dod* and *Vacher*. There is also the Stationery Office publication *H.M. Ministers and Heads of Public Departments* which has appeared four or five times a year since 1946. Lists of ministers are also printed in *Hansard* once a fortnight during sessions.   But all these sources have the same disadvantage — no indication is given of the date when a minister was appointed or left office.   A man may indeed be appointed and leave office between the publication of these lists, so that there is no record whatever of his elevation.   *Keesing's Contemporary Archives* have since 1931 recorded most government appointments — but they depend solely on newspaper sources and are not altogether infallible. The *Indexes* to *The Times* are the best means of checking on ministerial changes, though here too there are problems.   *Palmer's Index to the Times* which was not superseded by the *Official Index* until 1906 is far from satisfactory; under the heading 'Official Appointments' is the depressing injunction 'See every issue'.   From 1906 the *Official Index* is much more thorough, although misprints and references to different editions of the paper do occur.   Even *The Times*, moreover, has occasionally missed a minor government change.   An additional complication lies in the range of possible days which might be considered the date of appointment: there is the announcement from Downing Street, the press report the following day, the official gazetting a week or more later, the exchange of seals and the kissing of hands.   None of these may represent the precise date on which the new minister took over his duties, but wherever possible, we have decided to use the date of *The Times* report, as being the earliest and most public announcement.   Peerages sometimes cause further confusion, since weeks usually elapse before a newly elevated minister's title is announced.   Care has also to be taken when a familiar minister disappears behind a new name — the fact that Mr Ivor Guest, Lord Ashby St Ledgers, and Viscount Wimborne were one and the same person is not immediately apparent. Another snag arises, particularly in wartime, when the titles and functions of ministries change kaleidoscopically.

In many other fields the sources of confusion were almost equally numerous.   The search for reliable and consistent evidence about newspaper circulations, religious affiliations and trade disputes caused us particular trouble and we were surprised at the difficulties involved in compiling lists of all permanent secretaries of departments and assessing the size of the various grades of the civil service.   But it would be tedious to quote all the gaps in existing works of reference which we have — with very varying success — tried to fill.   We must, however, mention the complications which arise from the structure of the United Kingdom.   The changes in Ireland in 1922 inevitably cause a break in all national statistical time-series and since then many tables have, perforce, to exclude Northern Ireland as well as

Eire; but the administrative separation of Scotland causes almost as many difficulties. Statistics are compiled independently north and south of the Border, quite often on different bases. Sometimes this arises from the different legal or administrative systems — as with education; but in the case of population and vital statistics the Registrars-General seem unnecessarily perverse in presenting their census findings in differing forms.

In preparing this book we have had assistance from many quarters — most notably from the Fellows and Students of Nuffield College, but also from officials in Parliament, in the Party Headquarters, in Government Departments and in newspaper offices, from many friends in the academic world, and from our publishers. We are also deeply indebted to anonymous compilers of the many works of reference from which we have so freely drawn. The statistical section of the book was largely prepared by Mrs Barbara Williamson with some invaluable advice from Mr Brian Mitchell and Mr Graham Pyatt of the Department of Applied Economics at Cambridge. The data for elections before 1918 was prepared by Mr Neal Blewett. The section on the courts was mainly the work of Mr Yash Ghai. Indispensable secretarial aid came from Miss Audrey Carruthers. And here is an incomplete list of others to whom we are indebted.

R. F. Allen	H. R. M. Farmer	A. MacIntyre
F. M. Barlow	Sir Edward Fellowes	A. F. Madden
Professor M. Beloff	A. Fox	G. Marshall
H. B. Berrington	Sir Michael Fraser	D. L. Munby
N. Birnbaum	S. Gordon	H. G. Nicholas
G. D. M. Block	M. Harrison	H. Pelling
P. A. Bromhead	S. C. Hawtrey	Miss M. F. Perham
Professor P. Campbell	B. Keith-Lucas	P. G. Richards
D. N. Chester	A. S. King	C. Seymour-Ure
H. A. Clegg	K. E. Kitchen	D. M. Shapiro
P. C. Collison	U. W. Kitzinger	R. J. A. Skidelsky
Miss S. J. Conwill	Professor F. Lawson	N. D. Walker
T. Evans	Sir Donald MacDougall	P. M. Williams

While we could not have completed this book without these far-flung helpers, we should stress our sole responsibility for its inevitable errors. Our readers are earnestly invited to let us know of any that they may detect.[1]

DAVID BUTLER
JENNIE FREEMAN

NUFFIELD COLLEGE, OXFORD
    June 1962

---

[1] *June 1964.* We must express our gratitude to the many people, friends and strangers, who answered this request. Several of those listed above have suggested *corrigenda* and we would like to add these names to their number: A. N. Cass, A. Deyermond, C. Driver, R. Jenkins, A. L. Lamaison, J. S. Milner, J. Morland Craig, J. Palmer, C. Pannell, M. B. Parker, J. C. Sainty, and A. H. Warren. We hope for still more suggestions of corrections and additions before the next edition.

INTRODUCTION TO THE SECOND EDITION

THE preparation of this new edition of *British Political Facts* has involved three tasks: bringing the record up to date with the facts of 1961 to 1967; incorporating new material to improve the usefulness and balance of the book; and correcting errors which have been spotted since the reprinting of the first edition.

The process of up-dating is by no means simple. The 1960's are better documented than any previous decade, but the continuity of the statistical time series which ran up to 1960 is often broken by new bases of computation. We faced the dilemma of whether to recalculate the earlier figures or not. In many cases we realised that the first edition had not made sufficiently clear what our basis of calculation had been, and we were ourselves confronted with the same difficulties that would face the ordinary reader who sought to build on our data — we had to search for what were the original criteria of selection and calculation. We hope we have remedied that failing. Another problem has been that of obtaining sufficiently up-to-date material. This affects statistics more than other kinds of fact; we have, for example, with the aid of the Addenda on p. 308, been able to incorporate all ministerial changes up to 31 December 1967, but for some of our tables the last available figures are for 1965 or even 1964.

The most challenging and rewarding part of preparing this edition has, however, lain in collecting new material. *British Political Facts* differs from the vast majority of books in the field of history and social sciences in that it is expounding no thesis of its authors but is produced entirely for the convenience of its readers. This has made us the target for all kinds of helpful criticisms and suggestions. It is the people who have found the book most useful — academics, civil servants, librarians, journalists, party officials, and officers of the Houses of Parliament—who have been its keenest — and most constructive — critics. We feel we owe them not only gratitude for the assistance they have given us but also an obligation to provide them with the material that they need in a form that will save them most time and effort.

Almost without exception the suggestions for improvement comprised ideas for additional material rather than for deletions. The only section of the first edition that we have in fact omitted is the list of constitutional cases and statutes—we felt that while it took up a considerable number of pages it was still too selective to be of much use and, more important, that the material was readily available elsewhere. The last consideration is indeed one that has loomed increasingly large in our decisions during our work on this edition. Contact with many users of *British Political Facts* has made us realise the need not just for the gathering together of facts and time series

B

from other — mainly annual — works of reference: there is also a need for material that is not available anywhere else at all. We described our first edition as 'systematised plagiarism'. But two of the major innovations in this edition — the listing of floor-crossings and the listing of Royal Commissions and other committees of inquiry — have involved an appreciable amount of original research. The more difficult and frustrating this research proved the more we became convinced that these additions were worth while and would provide short cuts for the labours of others. Other sections of the book which have been radically changed and expanded are those dealing with Social Policy, Employment and Trade Unions, and the Economy. But the sections on Parliament, on Elections, on the Armed Forces, on the British Isles, and on Local Government have also grown appreciably, and there is, indeed, no section that has not been modified in one way or another.

The correction of errors is a task in which we have had many helpers. One of the great satisfactions of publishing a book such as this is the wide range of friendly correspondence which it evokes. Misprints, omissions, and arguable points have been sent in by friends and by strangers. This edition has benefited enormously from the rigorous scrutiny which its predecessor received. It would be wrong to suggest that the first edition was riddled with errors. The percentage of mistakes in the 50,000 or more facts and figures it contained was low. In this edition, thanks to our readers, it is lower. But some undoubtedly survive, and once again we beg those who use this book to send us their corrigenda.

Even more people have assisted in the revision of this book than in its original compilation. Many of those whose names are listed in the earlier preface have given us further counsel and information. The following are only a few among the large number of others who have helped us to new material.

P. Addison	D. Jeffcock	Mrs. P. Ryan
G. S. Bain	L. Keillor	J. C. Sainty
R. Butt	T. O. Lloyd	L. J. Sharpe
T. J. M. Cartwright	A. B. Lyons	M. Steed
C. Dawson	K. MacDonald	S. Symes
N. Deakin	R. McKibbin	A. J. P. Taylor
C. Dobson	R. Neuss	Mrs I. Wagner
Miss D. Edmunds	P. Oppenheimer	R. Walford
A. Flanders	M. J. Parker	W. Wallace
A. H. Halsey	Professor A. M. Potter	Miss N. Watts
A. J. Hastings	C. Raphael	Professor T. Wilson
C. Hazlehurst	R. A. Rempel	Mrs J. Wigan
R. J. Jackson		

Among those who remain unnamed are many civil servants as well as members of the staff of the British Museum State Paper Room, the

Libraries of the House of Commons and House of Lords, and the Bodleian, who went far beyond the line of duty in gathering data for us. To all of them we owe a great debt of gratitude.

The main burden of revising and up-dating this book was borne by Mrs Anne Duncan-Jones, and I would like to pay the warmest tribute to her skill and thoroughness, and to the extraordinary zest and drive which she has brought to the tedious and often infuriating tasks that confronted her. I would also like to record my special thanks to Miss Ann Bishop for all her secretarial labours.

On this occasion while the credit for any virtues this book may have is widespread I must accept sole responsibility for any shortcomings. I hope that in due course the comments and suggestions of its users will lead to the production of new editions that will be more error-free and still more compendious.

DAVID BUTLER

NUFFIELD COLLEGE, OXFORD
December 1967

NOTE TO THE THIRD EDITION

THE third edition, by contrast to the second, involves no radical alterations. But the lapse of a few months and the helpfulness of many correspondents has made it possible for me, aided once again by Anne Duncan-Jones, to eliminate a number of misprints and minor errors. In addition the developments of another twelve months have, as far as possible, been recorded.

Many of those whose help has already been acknowledged made further suggestions, and among others who sent comments I should particularly like to thank:

R. K. Alderman	J. A. Cross
J. M. Austen	R. J. Hetherington
J. M. Bowen	S. M. Lees
F. W. S. Craig	

DAVID BUTLER

NUFFIELD COLLEGE, OXFORD
December 1968

I
MINISTRIES

The following list contains all holders of paid and political ministerial offices since 1900. It leaves out some office-holders, since various offices in the Royal Household have during the past century ceased to be political appointments. The list also omits some politicians with governmental posts, since various other offices such as the Church Estates Commissioners are at times filled by M.P.s who are not regarded as part of the Ministry. Assistant Government Whips were unpaid until the 1964 Parliament and are not listed until then. Parliamentary Private Secretaries are also unlisted.

The problems of compiling this list are discussed on p. xv. The dates are as far as possible the dates on which the announcement of the appointment appeared in *The Times*. Where more than one person holds the same title starting and finishing dates are given. In all other cases it may be assumed that the date of the new appointment represents the vacating of the office. Ministers in the cabinet are printed throughout this section in heavy type. Ministers outside the cabinet and Ministers of State are printed in capitals. Junior Ministers are in ordinary print. The seven leading offices are placed first in each Ministry; the remainder are arranged alphabetically, except the law offices and the political appointments to the Royal Household, which are placed at the end, together with the Treasury appointments which are held by Whips. In these tables (and throughout the book) titles are placed in brackets if acquired during the tenure of a particular office or on transfer to the next office. U-S. Under-Secretary; F.S. Financial Secretary; P.S. Parliamentary Secretary.

This section has been sub-divided chronologically at changes of Prime Minister, except when few other offices changed hands, as in 1902, 1923, 1937, 1955, and 1963; further subdivisions are made for the drastic reconstructions of 1915, 1931, and May 1945.

CONSERVATIVE GOVERNMENT, 1900–1905

	MINISTERS IN CABINET		JUNIOR MINISTERS ATTACHED
P.M.	**M of Salisbury (3rd)**		
		1900–11 Jul 02	
	A. Balfour	12 Jul 02–4 Dec 05	
1st Ld of[1] Treasury	**A. Balfour** *(office combined with P.M. when Balfour succeeded Salisbury)*	1900	
Ld Pres.	**D of Devonshire**	1900	
	M of Londonderry	13 Oct 03	
Ld Chanc.	**E of Halsbury**	1900	
Privy S.	**Vt Cross**	1900	
	M of Salisbury (3rd) (P.M.)		
		1 Nov 00	
	A. Balfour (P.M.)	12 Jul 02	
	M of Salisbury (4th)	11 Oct 03	

[1] The only occasion in this century when 1st Ld of Treasury was not combined with P.M.

CONSERVATIVE GOVERNMENT, 1900–1905 (contd.)

MINISTERS IN CABINET			JUNIOR MINISTERS ATTACHED		
Exch.	Sir M. Hicks Beach	1900	Treasury:		
	C. Ritchie	8 Aug 02	F.S.	R. Hanbury	1900
	A. Chamberlain	6 Oct 03		A. Chamberlain	7 Nov 00
				W. Hayes Fisher	8 Aug 02
				A. Elliott	10 Apr 03
				V. Cavendish	9 Oct 03
For. O.	M of Salisbury (3rd) (P.M.)	1900	U-S.	St J. Brodrick	1900
	M of Lansdowne	1 Nov 00		Vt Cranborne [1] (4th M of Salisbury)	
					7 Nov 00
				Earl Percy [1]	9 Oct 03
Home O.	Sir M. White Ridley	1900	U-S.	J. Collings	1900
	C. Ritchie	1 Nov 00		T. Cochrane	8 Aug 02
	A. Akers-Douglas	8 Aug 02			
Admir.	G. Goschen	1900	P. & F.S.:		
	E of Selborne	1 Nov 00		Sir W. Macartney	1900
	Earl Cawdor	5 Mar 05		H. Arnold-Forster	7 Nov 00
				E. Pretyman	11 Oct 03
			Civil Ld:		
				A. Chamberlain	1900
				E. Pretyman	7 Nov 00
				A. Lee	11 Oct 03
Bd Ag. & Fish.	W. Long	1900			
	R. Hanbury	14 Nov 00			
	E of Onslow	19 May 03			
	A. Fellowes	12 Mar 05			
Col. O.	J. Chamberlain	1900	U-S.	E of Selborne	1900
	A. Lyttelton	6 Oct 03		E of Onslow	12 Nov 00
				D of Marlborough	23 Jul 03
Bd Educ.	D of Devonshire	1900	Sec.	(office not established)	
	M of Londonderry	8 Aug 02		Sir W. Anson	8 Aug 02
				(previously Vice-President of Committee of Council on Education—Sir J. Gorst 1900–8 Aug 02)	
India O.	Ld G. Hamilton [1]	1900	U-S.	E of Onslow	1900
	St J. Brodrick	6 Oct 03		E of Hardwicke	12 Nov 00
				Earl Percy [1]	8 Aug 02
				E of Hardwicke	15 Oct 03
				M of Bath	19 Jan 05
Chief Sec. Ireland	(office not in cabinet)		V. Pres. Dept. Agric. for Ireland:		
	G. Wyndham	8 Aug 02		(Sir) H. Plunkett	1900
	W. Long	12 Mar 05			
Ld Chanc. Ireland	Ld Ashbourne	1900			
Ld Lieut. Ireland	Earl Cadogan	1900			
	(E of Dudley 8 Aug 02 & office not in cabinet)				
D. Lanc.	Ld James of Hereford	1900			
	(Sir W. Walrond 8 Aug 02 & office not in cabinet)				
Loc. Govt. Bd	H. Chaplin	1900	P.S.	T. Russell	1900
	W. Long	7 Nov 00		(Sir) J. Lawson	11 Nov 00
	G. Balfour	12 Mar 05		A. Jeffreys	27 Jun 05
Postm.-Gen.	(office not in cabinet)				
	M of Londonderry	7 Nov 00			
	A. Chamberlain	8 Aug 02			
	Ld Stanley [1]	6 Oct 03			
Scotland	Ld Balfour of Burleigh	1900			
	A. Murray	6 Oct 03			
	M of Linlithgow	2 Feb 05			

[1] Not a member of the House of Lords.

CONSERVATIVE GOVERNMENT, 1900–1905 (*contd.*)

MINISTERS IN CABINET			JUNIOR MINISTERS ATTACHED		
B.o.T.	**C. Ritchie**	1900	*P.S.*	E of Dudley	1900
	G. Balfour	7 Nov 00		A. Bonar Law	8 Aug 02
	M of Salisbury (4th)	12 Mar 05			
War O.	**M of Lansdowne**	1900	*F.S.*	J. Powell Williams	1900
	St J. Brodrick	1 Nov 00		Ld Stanley [1]	7 Nov 00
	H. Arnold-Forster	6 Oct 03		W. Bromley-Davenport	11 Oct 03
			P.S.	G. Wyndham	1900
				Ld Raglan	12 Nov 00
				E of Hardwicke	8 Aug 02
				E of Donoughmore	15 Oct 03
1st *C. Works*	**A. Akers-Douglas**	1900			
	(*Ld Windsor* 8 *Aug* 02 & *office out of cabinet*)				

MINISTERS NOT IN CABINET					
Chief Sec.	G. BALFOUR	1900	(*for Junior Ministers see above*)		
Ireland	G. WYNDHAM	7 Nov 00			
	(8 *Aug* 02 *office in cabinet*)				
D. Lanc.	(*office in cabinet*)				
	SIR W. WALROND	8 Aug 02			
Paym.-Gen.	D OF MARLBOROUGH	1900			
	SIR S. CROSSLEY	11 Mar 02			
Postm.-Gen.	D OF NORFOLK	1900			
	M OF LONDONDERRY	2 Apr 00			
	(7 *Nov* 00 *office in cabinet*)				
1st *C. Works*	(*office in cabinet*)				
	LD WINDSOR	8 Aug 02			

Law Officers:			*P.S. to Treasury:*		
Att.-Gen.	SIR R. WEBSTER	1900	Sir W. Walrond	1900	
	SIR R. FINLAY	7 May 00	Sir A. Acland Hood	8 Aug 02	
Sol.-Gen.	SIR R. FINLAY	1900	*Junior Lds of Treasury:*		
	SIR E. CARSON	7 May 00	W. Hayes Fisher	1900–8 Aug 02	
Ld Advoc.	A. MURRAY	1900	H. Anstruther	1900–11 Oct 03	
	S. DICKSON	18 Oct 03	Ld Stanley [1]	1900–7 Nov 00	
Sol.-Gen.	S. DICKSON	1900	A. Fellowes	7 Nov 00–15 Mar 05	
Scotland	D. DUNDAS	18 Oct 03	H. Forster	8 Aug 02–4 Dec 05	
	E. SALVESEN	30 Jan 05	Ld Balcarres [1]	11 Oct 03–4 Dec 05	
	J. CLYDE	16 Oct 05	Ld E. Talbot [1]	16 Jun 05–4 Dec 05	
Att.-Gen.	J. ATKINSON	1900			
Ireland					
Sol.-Gen.	D. BARTON	1900			
Ireland	G. WRIGHT	30 Jan 00			
	J. CAMPBELL	8 Jul 03			

H.M. Household:			*Lds in Waiting*		
Treas.	VT CURZON [1] (Earl Howe)	1900	E of Clarendon	1900–30 Oct 00	
	V. CAVENDISH	3 Dec 00	Ld Harris	1900–4 Dec 00	
	M OF HAMILTON [1]	11 Oct 03	Ld Churchill (Vt)	1900–4 Dec 05	
Comptr.	VT VALENTIA [1]	1900	Ld Lawrence	1900–4 Dec 05	
V. Chamb.	A. FELLOWES	1900	E of Kintore	1900–4 Dec 05	
	SIR A. ACLAND HOOD	3 Dec 00	Ld Bagot	1900–2 Jul 1901	
	LD WOLVERTON	17 Nov 02	E of Denbigh	1900–4 Dec 05	
Ld Chamb.	E OF HOPETOUN	1900	Earl Howe	30 Oct 00–1 Oct 03	
	E OF CLARENDON	12 Nov 00	Ld Kenyon	4 Dec 00–4 Dec 05	
Ld Steward	E OF PEMBROKE & MONTGOMERY		E of Erroll	19 Oct 03–4 Dec 05	
		1900			

[1] Not a member of the House of Lords.

CONSERVATIVE GOVERNMENT, 1900–1905 *(contd.)*

MINISTERS NOT IN CABINET

Capt. Gents at Arms	LD BELPER	1900
Capt. Yeomen of Guard	EARL WALDEGRAVE	1900
Master of Horse	D OF PORTLAND	1900
Master of Buckhounds	E OF COVENTRY	1900
	LD CHESHAM	2 Nov 00

(office abolished 1901*)*

LIBERAL GOVERNMENT, 1905–1908

MINISTERS IN CABINET

P.M.	**Sir H. Campbell-Bannerman**	
	5 Dec 05–5 Apr 08	
Ld Pres.	**E of Crewe**	10 Dec 05
Ld Chanc.	**Sir R. Reid**	10 Dec 05
	(Ld Loreburn)	
Privy S.	**M of Ripon**	10 Dec 05
Exch.	**H. Asquith**	10 Dec 05
For. O.	**Sir E. Grey**	10 Dec 05
Home O.	**H. Gladstone**	10 Dec 05
Admir.	**Ld Tweedmouth**	10 Dec 05
Bd Ag. & Fish.	**Earl Carrington**	10 Dec 05
Col. O.	**E of Elgin**	10 Dec 05
Bd Educ.	**A. Birrell**	10 Dec 05
	R. McKenna	23 Jan 07
India O.	**J. Morley**	10 Dec 05
Chief Sec. Ireland	**J. Bryce**	10 Dec 05
	A. Birrell	23 Jan 07
D. Lanc.	**Sir H. Fowler**	10 Dec 05
Loc. Govt. Bd.	**J. Burns**	10 Dec 05
Postm.-Gen.	**S. Buxton**	10 Dec 05
Scotland	**J. Sinclair**	10 Dec 05
B.o.T.	**D. Lloyd George**	10 Dec 05
War O.	**R. Haldane**	10 Dec 05
1st C. Works	*(office not in cabinet)*	
	L. Harcourt	27 Mar 07

JUNIOR MINISTERS ATTACHED

Treasury:

F.S.	R. McKenna		12 Dec 05
	W. Runciman		29 Jan 07
U-S.	Ld E. Fitzmaurice [1] (Ld)	18 Dec 05
U-S.	H. Samuel		12 Dec 05
P. & F.S.:			
	E. Robertson		12 Dec 05
Civil Ld:			
	G. Lambert		18 Dec 05
U-S.	W. Churchill		12 Dec 05
P.S.	T. Lough		18 Dec 05
U-S.	J. Ellis		12 Dec 05
	C. Hobhouse		29 Jan 07

Vice-Pres. Dept. Agric. for Ireland:

	Sir H. Plunkett	12 Dec 05
	T. Russell	21 May 07
P.S.	W. Runciman	18 Dec 05
	T. Macnamara	29 Jan 07
P.S.	H. Kearley	18 Dec 05
P.S.	E of Portsmouth	12 Dec 05
F.S.	T. Buchanan	14 Dec 05

MINISTERS NOT IN CABINET

Paym.-Gen.	R. CAUSTON	12 Dec 05
1st C. Works	L. HARCOURT	10 Dec 05

(27 Mar 07 office in cabinet)

[1] Not a member of the House of Lords.

LIBERAL GOVERNMENT, 1905–1908 (*contd.*)

MINISTERS NOT IN CABINET

Law Officers:

Att.-Gen.	SIR J. WALTON	12 Dec 05
	SIR W. ROBSON	28 Jan 08
Sol.-Gen.	SIR W. ROBSON	12 Dec 05
	SIR S. EVANS	28 Jan 08
Ld Advoc.	T. SHAW	12 Dec 05
Sol.-Gen. Scotland	A. URE	18 Dec 05
Att.-Gen. Ireland	R. CHERRY	20 Dec 05
Sol.-Gen. Ireland	R. BARRY	20 Dec 05

H.M. Household:

Treas.	SIR E. STRACHEY	18 Dec 05
Comptr.	MASTER OF ELIBANK	18 Dec 05
V. Chamb.	W. BEAUMONT (*Ld Allendale*)	18 Dec 05
	J. FULLER	27 Feb 07
Ld Chamb.	VT ALTHORP	18 Dec 05
Ld Steward	LD HAWKESBURY (*1st E of Liverpool*)	18 Dec 05
	EARL BEAUCHAMP	31 Jul 07
Master of Horse	E OF SEFTON	18 Dec 05
	E OF GRANARD	6 Sep 07
Capt. Gents at Arms	EARL BEAUCHAMP	18 Dec 05
	LD DENMAN	31 Jul 07
Capt. Yeomen of Guard	D OF MANCHESTER	18 Dec 05
	LD ALLENDALE	29 Apr 07

P.S. to Treasury:

G. Whiteley	12 Dec 05

Junior Lds of Treasury:

H. Lewis	18 Dec 05–5 Apr 08
J. Pease	18 Dec 05–5 Apr 08
F. Freeman-Thomas	21 Dec 05–2 Feb 06
C. Norton	21 Dec 05–5 Apr 08
J. Fuller	2 Feb 06–27 Feb 07
J. Whitley	27 Feb 07–5 Apr 08

Lds in Waiting:

Ld Denman	18 Dec 05–31 Jul 07
E of Granard	18 Dec 05–21 Aug 07
Ld Acton	18 Dec 05–5 Apr 08
Earl Granville	18 Dec 05–5 Apr 08
Ld Hamilton of Dalzell	18 Dec 05–5 Apr 08
Ld Colebrooke	20 Dec 05–5 Apr 08
Ld Herschell	31 Jul 07–5 Apr 08
Ld O'Hagan	1 Nov 07–5 Apr 08

LIBERAL GOVERNMENT, 1908–1915

MINISTERS IN CABINET

P.M.	H. Asquith	5 Apr 08–25 May 15
Ld Pres.	Ld Tweedmouth	12 Apr 08
	Vt Wolverhampton	13 Oct 08
	Earl Beauchamp	16 Jun 10
	Vt Morley	3 Nov 10
	Earl Beauchamp	5 Aug 14
Ld Chanc	Ld Loreburn (Earl)	12 Apr 08
	Vt Haldane	10 Jun 12
Privy S.	M of Ripon	12 Apr 08
	E of Crewe	9 Oct 08
	Earl Carrington	23 Oct 11
	M of Crewe	13 Feb 12
Exch.	D. Lloyd George	12 Apr 08
For. O.	Sir E. Grey	12 Apr 08

JUNIOR MINISTERS ATTACHED

Treasury:

F.S.	C. Hobhouse	12 Apr 08
	T. Wood	23 Oct 11
	C. Masterman	13 Feb 12
	E. Montagu	11 Feb 14
	F. Acland	3 Feb 15
U-S.	Ld Fitzmaurice	12 Apr 08
	T. Wood	19 Oct 08
	F. Acland	23 Oct 11
	N. Primrose	4 Feb 15

LIBERAL GOVERNMENT, 1908–1915 (*contd.*)

MINISTERS IN CABINET

JUNIOR MINISTERS ATTACHED

Home O.	H. Gladstone	12 Apr 08	*U-S.*	H. Samuel	12 Apr 08	
	W. Churchill	14 Feb 10		C. Masterman	7 Jul 09	
	R. McKenna	23 Oct 11		E. Griffith	19 Feb 12	
				C. Harmsworth	4 Feb 15	
Admir.	R. McKenna	12 Apr 08	*P. & F.S.:*			
	W. Churchill	23 Oct 11		T. Macnamara	13 Apr 08	
			Civil Ld:			
				G. Lambert	12 Apr 08	
Bd Ag. &	Earl Carrington	12 Apr 08	*P.S.*	(*post not established*)		
Fish.				Sir E. Strachey	20 Dec 09	
	W. Runciman	23 Oct 11		(*Ld Strachie*)		
	Ld Lucas	6 Aug 14		Ld Lucas	23 Oct 11	
				Sir H. Verney	10 Aug 14	
Att. Gen.	(*office not in cabinet*)					
	Sir R. Isaacs	4 Jun 12				
	Sir J. Simon	19 Oct 13				
Col. O.	E of Crewe	12 Apr 08	*U-S.*	J. Seely	12 Apr 08	
	L. Harcourt	3 Nov 10		Ld Lucas	23 Mar 11	
				Ld Emmott	23 Oct 11	
				Ld Islington	10 Aug 14	
Bd Educ.	W. Runciman	12 Apr 08	*P.S.*	T. Wood	13 Apr 08	
	J. Pease	23 Oct 11		C. Trevelyan	19 Oct 08	
				C. Addison	10 Aug 14	
India O.	J. Morley (Vt)	12 Apr 08	*U-S*	T. Buchanan	12 Apr 08	
	E of Crewe	3 Nov 10		Master of Elibank	25 Jun 09	
	Vt Morley	7 Mar 11		E. Montagu	20 Feb 10	
	E of Crewe (M)	25 May 11		C. Roberts	17 Feb 14	
Chief Sec. Ireland	A. Birrell	12 Apr 08	*V. Pres. Dept. Agric. Ireland.*			
				T. Russell	12 Apr 08	
D. Lanc.	Sir H. Fowler	12 Apr 08				
	(*Vt Wolverhampton*)					
	Ld Fitzmaurice	13 Oct 08				
	H. Samuel	25 Jun 09				
	J. Pease	14 Feb 10				
	C. Hobhouse	23 Oct 11				
	C. Masterman	11 Feb 14				
	E. Montagu	3 Feb 15				
Loc. Govt. Bd	J. Burns	12 Apr 08	*P.S.*	C. Masterman	12 Apr 08	
	H. Samuel	11 Feb 14		H. Lewis	7 Jul 09	
Postm.-Gen.	S. Buxton	12 Apr 08	*Ass.*	(*post not established*)		
	H. Samuel	14 Feb 10		Sir H. Norman	3 Jan 10	
	C. Hobhouse	11 Feb 14		C. Norton	20 Feb 10	
Scotland	J. Sinclair	12 Apr 08				
	(*Ld Pentland*)					
	T. Wood	13 Feb 12				
B.o.T.	W. Churchill	12 Apr 08	*P.S.*	(Sir) H. Kearley	12 Apr 08	
	S. Buxton	14 Feb 10		H. Tennant	10 Jan 09	
	J. Burns	11 Feb 14		J. Robertson	25 Oct 11	
	W. Runciman	5 Aug 14				
War O.	R. Haldane (Vt)	12 Apr 08	*F.S.*	F. Acland	12 Apr 08	
	J. Seely	12 Jun 12		C. Mallet	4 Mar 10	
	H. Asquith (P.M.)	30 Mar 14		F. Acland	31 Jan 11	
	Earl Kitchener	5 Aug 14		H. Tennant	25 Oct 11	
				H. Baker	14 Jun 12	
			U-S.	Ld Lucas	12 Apr 08	
				J. Seely	23 Mar 11	
				H. Tennant	14 Jun 12	
1st C. Works	L. Harcourt	12 Apr 08				
	Earl Beauchamp	3 Nov 10				
	Ld Emmott	6 Aug 14				

LIBERAL GOVERNMENT, 1908–1915 (contd.)

MINISTERS NOT IN CABINET		JUNIOR MINISTERS ATTACHED	
Paym.-Gen.	R. CAUSTON 12 Apr 08		
	(*Ld Southwark*)		
	I. GUEST 23 Feb 10		
	(*Ld Ashby St Ledgers*)		
	LD STRACHIE 23 May 12		

Law Officers:		*P.S. to Treasury:*	
Att.-Gen.	SIR W. ROBSON 12 Apr 08	G. Whiteley	12 Apr 08
	SIR R. ISAACS 7 Oct 10	J. Pease	3 Jun 08
	(4 *Jun* 12 *office in cabinet*)	Master of Elibank	14 Feb 10
Sol.-Gen.	SIR S. EVANS 12 Apr 08	P. Illingworth	7 Aug 12
	SIR R. ISAACS 6 Mar 10	J. Gulland	24 Jan 15
	SIR J. SIMON 7 Oct 10		
	SIR S. BUCKMASTER 19 Oct 13	*Junior Lds of Treasury:*	
Ld Advoc.	T. SHAW 12 Apr 08	J Pease	12 Apr 08–3 Jun 08
	A. URE 14 Feb 09	H. Lewis	12 Apr 08–7 Jul 09
	R. MUNRO 30 Oct 13	C. Norton	12 Apr 08–20 Feb 10
Sol.-Gen.	A. URE 12 Apr 08	J. Whitley	12 Apr 08–20 Feb 10
Scotland	A. DEWAR 18 Feb 09	O. Partington	6 Jul 09–19 Jan 11
	W. HUNTER 18 Apr 10	J. Gulland	7 Jul 09–24 Jan 15
	A. ANDERSON 3 Dec 11	W. Benn	20 Feb 10–25 May 15
	T. MORISON 30 Oct 13	E. Soares	20 Feb 10–16 Apr 11
Att.-Gen.	R. CHERRY 12 Apr 08	P. Illingworth	28 Feb 10–7 Aug 12
Ireland	R. BARRY 2 Dec 09	W. Jones	19 Jan 11–25 May 15
	C. O'CONNOR 26 Sep 11	F. Guest	16 Apr 11–21 Feb 12
	I. O'BRIEN 24 Jun 12	H. Webb	16 Apr 12–25 May 15
	T. MOLONY 10 Apr 13	C. Beck	3 Feb 15–25 May 15
	J. MORIARTY 20 Jun 13	W. Rea	3 Feb 15–25 May 15
	J. PIM 1 Jul 14		
Sol.-Gen.	R. BARRY 12 Apr 08		
Ireland	C. O'CONNOR 2 Dec 09		
	I. O'BRIEN 19 Oct 11		
	T. MOLONY 24 Jun 12		
	J. MORIARTY 25 Apr 13		
	J. PIM 20 Jun 13		
	J. O'CONNOR 1 Jul 14		

H.M. Household:		*Lds in Waiting:*	
Treas.	SIR E. STRACHEY 12 Apr 08	Ld O'Hagan	12 Apr 08–15 Apr 10
	W. DUDLEY WARD 20 Dec 09	Ld Hamilton	12 Apr 08–2 Oct 11
	F. GUEST 21 Feb 12	of Dalzell	
Comptr.	MASTER OF ELIBANK 12 Apr 08	Ld Colebrooke	12 Apr 08–19 Jun 11
	E OF LIVERPOOL (2nd) 12 Jul 09	Ld Herschell	12 Apr 08–25 May 15
	LD SAYE & SELE 1 Nov 12	Ld Acton	12 Apr 08–25 May 15
V. Chamb.	(SIR) J. FULLER 12 Apr 08	Earl Granville	12 Apr 08–25 May 15
	G. HOWARD 6 Feb 11	Ld Tweedmouth	15 Apr 10–4 Dec 11
Ld Chamb.	VT ALTHORP 12 Apr 08	Ld Willingdon	19 Jan 11–31 Jan 13
	(*Earl Spencer*)	Vt Allendale	2 Oct 11–25 May 15
	LD SANDHURST 14 Feb 12	Ld Loch	4 Dec 11–1 May 14
Ld Steward	EARL BEAUCHAMP 12 Apr 08	Ld Ashby St	31 Jan 13–8 Feb 15
	E OF CHESTERFIELD 22 Jun 10	Ledgers	
Master of	E OF GRANARD 12 Apr 08	(*Ld Wimborne*)	
Horse		Ld Stanmore	1 May 14–25 May 15
Capt. Gents	LD DENMAN 12 Apr 08	Ld Ranksborough	
at Arms	LD COLEBROOKE 26 Jun 11		8 Feb 15–25 May 15
Capt.	LD ALLENDALE (Vt) 12 Apr 08		
Yeomen of	E OF CRAVEN 2 Oct 11		
Guard			

COALITION GOVERNMENT, 1915–1916

MINISTERS IN CABINET			JUNIOR MINISTERS ATTACHED		
P.M.	**H. Asquith** (Lib)				
		25 May 15–5 Dec 16			
Ld Pres.	**M of Crewe** (Lib)	25 May 15			
Ld Chanc.	**Ld Buckmaster** (Lib)	25 May 15			
Privy S	**Earl Curzon** (C)	25 May 15			
Exch.	**R. McKenna** (Lib)	25 May 15	*Treasury:*		
			F.S.	E. Montagu (Lib)	26 May 15
				(also D. Lanc., in cabinet from 11 *Jan* 16*)*	
				T. Wood (Lib)	9 Jul 16
				(also D. Lanc. in cabinet)	
For. O	**Sir E. Grey** (Lib)	25 May 15	*U.-S.*	Ld R. Cecil [1] (C)	30 May 15
	(Vt)			*(also Blockade, in cabinet from* 23 *Feb* 16*)*	
			Ass.	Ld Newton (C)	18 Aug 16
Home O.	**Sir J. Simon** (Lib)	25 May 15	*U.-S.*	W. Brace (Lab)	30 May 15
	Sir H. Samuel (Lib)	10 Jan 16			
Admir.	**A. Balfour** (C)	25 May 15	*P. & F.S.:*		
				T. Macnamara (Lib)	30 May 15
			Civil Ld:		
				D of Devonshire (C)	9 Jun 15
				E of Lytton (C)	26 Jul 16
Bd Ag. &	**E of Selborne** (C)	25 May 15	*P.S.*	F. Acland (Lib)	30 May 15
Fish.	**E of Crawford** (C)	11 Jul 16			
Att.-Gen.	**Sir E. Carson** (C)	25 May 15			
	Sir F. Smith (C)	3 Nov 15			
Blockade	**Ld R. Cecil** [1] (C)	23 Feb 16			
	(also U.-S. at F.O.)				
Col. O.	**A. Bonar Law** (C)	25 May 15	*U.-S.*	A. Steel-Maitland (C)	30 May 15
Bd Educ.	**A. Henderson** (Lab)	25 May 15	*P.S.*	H. Lewis (Lib)	30 May 15
	M of Crewe (Lib)	18 Aug 16			
Health &	**W. Long** (C)	25 May 15	*P.S.*	W. Hayes Fisher (C)	30 May 15
Loc. Govt Bd					
India O.	**A. Chamberlain** (C)	25 May 15	*U.-S.*	Ld Islington (Lib)	30 May 15
Chief Sec.	**A. Birrell** (Lib)	25 May 15	*V. Pres. Dept. Agric. & Technical Instruction,*		
Ireland	**H. Duke** (C)	31 Jul 16	*Ireland:*		
				T. Russell (Lib)	30 May 15
D. Lanc.	**W. Churchill** (Lib)	25 May 15			
	H. Samuel (Lib)	25 Nov 15			
	E. Montagu (Lib)	11 Jan 16			
	(also F.S. at Treasury)				
	T. Wood (Lib)	9 Jul 16			
	(also F.S. at Treasury)				
Munitions	**D. Lloyd George** (Lib)	25 May 15	*P.S.*	C. Addison (Lib)	30 May 15–8 Dec 16
	E. Montagu (Lib)	9 Jul 16		A. Lee (C)	11 Nov 15 [2]–9 Jul 16
Paym.-Gen.	*(office not in cabinet)*				
	A. Henderson (Lab)	18 Aug 16			
Min.	**M of Lansdowne** (C)	25 May 15			
without					
Portfolio					
Scotland	**T. Wood** (Lib)	25 May 15			
	H. Tennant (Lib)	9 Jul 16			
B.o.T.	**W. Runciman** (Lib)	25 May 15	*P.S.*	E. Pretyman (C)	30 May 15
War O.	**Earl Kitchener**	25 May 15	*U.-S.*	H. Tennant (Lib)	30 May 15
	D. Lloyd George (Lib)	6 Jul 16		E of Derby (C)	6 Jul 16
			F.S.	H. Forster (C)	30 May 15
1st C. Works	**L. Harcourt** (Vt) (Lib)	25 May 15			

[1] Not a member of the House of Lords.
[2] Date of first reply in Commons as *Parliamentary (Military) Secretary to the Munitions Department.*

COALITION GOVERNMENT, 1915-1916 (contd.)

MINISTERS NOT IN CABINET			JUNIOR MINISTERS ATTACHED		

Paym.-Gen. LD NEWTON (C)   9 Jun 15
     (*A. Henderson* 18 *Aug* 16 &
        office in cabinet)

Postm.-Gen. H. SAMUEL (Lib)   26 May 15   *Ass.*   H. Pike Pease (C)   30 May 15
        J. PEASE (Lib)   18 Jan 16

    Law Officers: *P.S. to Treasury:*

Att.-Gen.   (*office in cabinet*)   J. Gulland (Lib) 30 May 15–5 Dec 16
                                      Ld E. Talbot[1] (C)

Sol.-Gen. SIR F. SMITH (C)   2 Jun 15   30 May 15–5 Dec 16
        (SIR) G. CAVE (C)   8 Nov 15   *Junior Lds of Treasury:*

Ld Advoc. R. MUNRO (Lib)   8 Jun 15   G. Howard (Lib)

Sol.-Gen. T. MORISON (Lib)   8 Jun 15   27 May 15–5 Dec 16
Scotland   G. Roberts (Lab)

Att.-Gen. J. GORDON (C)   8 Jun 15   27 May 15–5 Dec 16
Ireland   J. CAMPBELL (C)   9 Apr 16   W. Bridgeman (C)

Sol.-Gen. J. O'CONNOR (Nat)   8 Jun 15   27 May 15–5 Dec 16
Ireland   W. Rea (Lib)   27 May 15–5 Dec 16

    H.M. Household:

Treas.   J. HOPE (C)   30 May 15   *Lds in Waiting:*

Comptr. C. ROBERTS (Lib)   30 May 15   Ld Herschell (Lib) 9 Jun 15–5 Dec 16

V. Chamb. C. BECK (Lib)   30 May 15   Vt Allendale (Lib) 9 Jun 15–5 Dec 16
                               Ld Stanmore (Lib) 9 Jun 15–5 Dec 16

Ld Chamb. LD SANDHURST (Lib)   9 Jun 15   Ld Ranksborough (Lib)

Ld Steward LD FARQUHAR (C)   9 Jun 15   9 Jun 15–5 Dec 16

Master of E OF CHESTERFIELD (Lib)   9 Jun 15   Vt Valentia[1] (C)   9 Jun 15–5 Dec 16
Horse   Ld Hylton (C)   9 Jun 15–5 Dec 16

Capt. Gents LD COLEBROOKE (Lib)   9 Jun 15
at Arms

Capt.   LD SUFFIELD (C)   9 Jun 15
Yeomen of
Guard

COALITION GOVERNMENT, 1916-1922

From 6 Dec 1916 to 31 Oct 1919 there was an inner war cabinet of 5–7 ministers. **D. Lloyd George, Earl Curzon,** and **A. Bonar Law** were members throughout; the other members were,

         A. Henderson (Lab) 10 Dec 16–12 Aug 17
         Vt Milner (C) 10 Dec 16–18 Apr 18
         J. Smuts[2] 22 Jun 17–10 Jan 19
         G. Barnes (Lab) 29 May 17–3 Aug 17, 13 Aug 17–10 Jan 19
         A. Chamberlain (C) 18 Apr 18–10 Jan 19
         Sir E. Geddes (C) 10 Jan 19–31 Oct 19

MINISTERS IN CABINET			JUNIOR MINISTERS ATTACHED

P.M.   **D. Lloyd George** (Lib)
             6 Dec 16–19 Oct 22

Ld Pres.   **Earl Curzon** (C)   10 Dec 16
        A. Balfour (C)   23 Oct 19

  ιChanc.   **Ld Finlay** (C)   10 Dec 16
        Ld Birkenhead (Vt) (C) 10 Jan 19

Privy S.   **E of Crawford** (C)   15 Dec 16
        A. Bonar Law (C)   10 Jan 19
        A. Chamberlain (C)   23 Mar 21

Exch.   **A. Bonar Law** (C)   10 Dec 16   *Treasury:*
        A. Chamberlain (C)   10 Jan 19   *F.S.*   Sir H. Lever (Lib)
        Sir R. Horne (C)   1 Apr 21   15 Dec 16–19 May 19
                                  S. Baldwin (C)   18 Jun 17–1 Apr 21
                                  E. Young (Lib)   1 Apr 21–19 Oct 22

[1] Not a member of the House of Lords.
[2] Not a member of the House of Commons.

COALITION GOVERNMENT, 1916–1922 (contd.)

MINISTERS IN CABINET			JUNIOR MINISTERS ATTACHED		
For. O.	A. Balfour (C)	10 Dec 16	*U–S.*	Ld R. Cecil [1] (C)	10 Dec 16
	Earl Curzon (C)	23 Oct 19		C. Harmsworth (Lib)	10 Jan 19
	(Marquess)		*Ass. U–S.:*		
				Ld Newton (C)	10 Dec 16
				(*post abolished* 10 *Jan* 1919)	
Home O.	Sir G. Cave (Vt) (C)	10 Dec 16	*U–S.*	W. Brace (Lab)	10 Dec 16
	E. Shortt (Lib)	10 Jan 19		Sir H. Greenwood (Lib)	10 Jan 19
				(Sir) J. Baird (C)	29 Apr 19
Admir.	Sir E. Carson (C)	10 Dec 16	*P. & F.S.:*		
	Sir E. Geddes (C)	17 Jul 17		T. Macnamara (Lib)	10 Dec 16
	W. Long (C)	10 Jan 19		Sir J. Craig (C)	2 Apr 20
	Ld Lee (C)	13 Feb 21		L. Amery (C)	1 Apr 21
			P.S. Addit.:		
				E of Lytton (C)	7 Feb 17
				(*post abolished* 27 *Jan* 1919)	
			Civil Ld:		
				E. Pretyman (C)	14 Dec 16
				E of Lytton (C)	27 Jan 19
				E of Onslow (C)	26 Oct 20
				B. Eyres-Monsell (C)	1 Apr 21
			2nd Civil Ld:		
				A. Pease (C)	10 Dec 16
				(*post abolished* 10 *Jan* 1919)	
Bd Ag. &	R. Prothero (C)	10 Dec 16	*P.S.*	Sir R. Winfrey (Lib)	14 Dec 16
Fish.	(*Ld Ernle*)			D of Marlborough (C)	18 Feb 17
	Ld Lee (C)	15 Aug 19		Vt Goschen (C)	26 Mar 18
	(*Min.* 15 *Aug* 19)			Ld Clinton (C)	18 Jun 18
	Sir A. Griffith-Boscawen (C)			Sir A. Griffith-Boscawen (C)	
		13 Feb 21			10 Jan 19
				(*& Dep. Min. Fisheries* 18 *Nov* 19)	
				E of Onslow (C)	5 Apr 21
				E of Ancaster (C)	7 Apr 21
				(*& Dep. Min. Fisheries* 28 *Oct* 21)	
Att. Gen.	(*office not in cabinet*)				
	Sir G. Hewart (Lib)	7 Nov 21			
	(*Sir E. Pollock* (C) 6 *Mar* 22 &				
	office not in cabinet)				
Col. O.	W. Long (C)	10 Dec 16	*U–S*	(Sir) A. Steel-Maitland (C)	10 Dec 16
	Vt Milner (C)	10 Jan 19		W. Hewins (C)	26 Sep 17
	W. Churchill (Lib)	13 Feb 21		L. Amery (C)	10 Jan 19
				E. Wood (C)	1 Apr 21
Bd Educ.	H. Fisher (Lib)	10 Dec 16	*P.S.*	(Sir) H. Lewis (Lib)	10 Dec 16
Health	(*Dept. under Loc. Govt Bd:*		*P.S.* (*Loc. Govt Bd*):		
	see below)			W. Hayes Fisher (C)	10 Dec 16
	C. Addison (Lib)	24 Jun 19		S. Walsh (Lab)	28 Jun 17
	Sir A. Mond (Lib)	1 Apr 21		W. Astor (Vt) (C)	27 Jan 19
				E of Onslow (C)	7 Apr 21
India O.	A. Chamberlain (C)	10 Dec 16	*U–S.*	Ld Islington (Lib)	10 Dec 16
	E. Montagu (Lib)	17 Jul 17		Ld Sinha (Lib)	10 Jan 19
	Vt Peel (C)	19 Mar 22		E of Lytton (C)	22 Sep 20
				Earl Winterton [1] (C)	20 Mar 22
Chief Sec.	(Sir) H. Duke (C)	10 Dec 16	*V. Pres. Dept. Agric. & Technical Instruction*		
Ireland	E. Shortt (Lib)	5 May 18	*for Ireland:*		
	I. Macpherson (Lib)	10 Jan 19		(Sir) T. Russell (Lib)	10 Dec 16
	Sir H. Greenwood (Lib)	2 Apr 20		H. Barrie (C)	15 Jan 19
Ld Lieut.	Vt French (*E of Ypres*)	6 May 18			
Ireland	(*Not usually ministerial office. In*				
	cabinet only 28 *Oct* 19–2 *Apr* 21)				

---

[1] Not a member of the House of Lords.

COALITION GOVERNMENT, 1916–1922 (contd.)

MINISTERS IN CABINET		JUNIOR MINISTERS ATTACHED	
Lab.	**J. Hodge** (Lab) 10 Dec 16 **G. Roberts** (Lab) 17 Aug 17 **Sir R. Horne** (C) 10 Jan 19 **T. Macnamara** (Lib) 19 Mar 20	*P.S.* W. Bridgeman (C) 22 Dec 16 G. Wardle (Lab) 10 Jan 19 Sir A. Montague-Barlow (C) 2 April 20	
D. Lanc.	**Sir F. Cawley** (Lib) 10 Dec 16 **Ld Beaverbrook** (C) 10 Feb 18 (& *Min. of Propaganda/Information*) **Ld Downham** (C) 4 Nov 18 (*E of Crawford* (C) 10 *Jan* 19 & *office not in cabinet*)		
Loc. Govt. *Bd*	**Ld Rhondda** (Lib) 10 Dec 16 **W. Hayes Fisher** (C) 28 Jun 17 (*Ld Downham*) **Sir A. Geddes** (C) 4 Nov 18 **C. Addison** (Lib) 10 Jan 19 (24 *Jun* 19 *became Min. of Health*: *see above*)	(*for Junior Ministers see above,* *under Health*)	
Munitions (*Supply*)	**C. Addison** (Lib) 10 Dec 16 **W. Churchill** (Lib) 17 Jul 17 (10 *Jan* 19 *became Min. of Supply*) **Ld Inverforth** (Con) 10 Jan 19 (*office abolished* 21 *Mar* 21)	*P.S.* Sir L. Worthington-Evans (C) 14 Dec 16–30 Jan 18 F. Kellaway (Lib) 14 Dec 16–1 Apr 21 J. Seely (Lib) 18 Jul 18–10 Jan 19 J. Baird (C) 10 Jan 19–27 Jan 19 *P. & F.S.*: Sir L. Worthington-Evans (C) 30 Jan 18–13 May 18 J. Hope (C) 27 Jan 19–4 Apr 21	
Nat. S.	**N. Chamberlain** (C)[1] 19 Dec 16 (*Sir A. Geddes* 17 *Aug* 17 & *office not in war cabinet*)	*P.S.* Vt Peel (C) 15 Apr 18–Dec 18 S. Walsh (Lab) 17 Mar 17–28 Jun 17 C. Beck (Lib) 28 Jun 17–Dec 19 (*post abolished* 19 *Dec* 19)	
Min. *without* *Portfolio*	**A. Henderson** (Lab) 10 Dec 16–12 Aug 17 **Vt Milner** (C) 10 Dec 16–18 Apr 18 **Sir E. Carson** (C) 17 Jul 17–21 Jan 18 **J. Smuts**[1] 22 Jun 17–10 Jan 19 **G. Barnes** (Lab) 13 Aug 17–27 Jan 20 **A. Chamberlain** (C) 18 Apr 18–10 Jan 19 **Sir L. Worthington-Evans** (C) 2 Apr 20–13 Feb 21 **C. Addison** (Lib) 1 Apr 21–14 Jul 21		
Scotland	**R. Munro** (Lib) 10 Dec 16	*P.S. Min. of Health for Scotland:* (Sir) J. Pratt (Lib) 8 Aug 19	
B.o.T.	**Sir A. Stanley** (Lib) 10 Dec 16 **Sir A. Geddes** (C) 26 May 19 **Sir R. Horne** (C) 19 Mar 20 **S. Baldwin** (C) 1 Apr 21	*P.S.* G. Roberts (Lab) 14 Dec 16 G. Wardle (Lab) 17 Aug 17 W. Bridgeman (C) 10 Jan 19 Sir P. Lloyd-Greame (C) 22 Aug 20 Sir W. Mitchell-Thomson (C) 1 Apr 21 *Sec. Dept. Overseas Trade:* Sir A. Steel-Maitland (C) 14 Sep 17 Sir H. Greenwood (Lib) 29 Apr 19 F. Kellaway (Lib) 2 Apr 20 Sir P. Lloyd-Greame (C) 1 Apr 21 (*Director Overseas Trade Dept.*) *P.S. Mines Dept.*: W. Bridgeman (C) 22 Aug 20	

[1] Not a member of the House of Commons.

COALITION GOVERNMENT, 1916–1922 (contd.)

MINISTERS IN CABINET / JUNIOR MINISTERS ATTACHED

MINISTERS IN CABINET		JUNIOR MINISTERS ATTACHED	
Transp.	(*office not established*)	*P.S* Sir R. Williams (Lib)	23 Sep 19
	Sir E. Geddes (C) 17 Aug 19	A. Neal (Lib)	28 Nov 19
	(*Vt Peel* 7 *Nov* 21 & *office not*		
	in cabinet)		
War O.	**E of Derby** (C) 10 Dec 16	*U–S* I. Macpherson (Lib)	14 Dec 16
	Vt Milner (C) 18 Apr 18	Vt Peel (C)	10 Jan 19
	(10 *Jan* 19 *War O.* & *Air Min.*	Sir R. Sanders (C)	1 Apr 21
	combined)	*F.S.* H. Forster (Ld) (C)	10 Dec 16
	W. Churchill (Lib) 10 Jan 19	Sir A. Williamson (Lib)	18 Dec 19
	(13 *Feb* 21 *War O. only*)	G. Stanley (C)	1 Apr 21
	Sir L. Worthington-Evans (C)	*P.S.* Earl Stanhope (C)	14 Dec 16
	13 Feb 21	(*post abolished* 10 *Jan* 1919)	
1st C. Works	(*office not in cabinet*)		
	E of Crawford (C) 7 Apr 22		

MINISTERS NOT IN CABINET / JUNIOR MINISTERS ATTACHED

MINISTERS NOT IN CABINET		JUNIOR MINISTERS ATTACHED	
Air	Ld Cowdray (Lib) 3 Jan 17	*P.S Air Council:*	
	Ld Rothermere (Lib) 26 Nov 17	J. Baird (C)	14 Dec 16
	Ld Weir (Lib) 26 Apr 18	(*post abolished* 10 *Jan* 19)	
	(*War O.* & *Air Min. combined*	*U–S* J. Seely (Lib)	10 Jan 19
	10 *Jan* 19, *see above*)	G. Tryon (C)	22 Dec 19
	W. Churchill (Lib) 10 Jan 19	M of Londonderry (C)	2 Apr 20
	F. Guest (Lib) 1 Apr 21	Ld Gorell (Lib)	18 Jul 21
Blockade	Ld R. Cecil [1] (C) 10 Dec 16	*P.S* F. Leverton Harris	22 Dec 16
	(*also U. S. at F.O.*)	(*post abolished* 10 *Jan* 19)	
	Sir L. Worthington-Evans (C)		
	18 Jul 18		
	(*office abolished* 10 *Jan* 1919)		
Food Control	Vt Devonport (Lib) 10 Dec 16	*P.S.* (Sir) C. Bathurst (C)	12 Dec 16
	Ld Rhondda (Vt) (Lib) 19 Jun 17	J. Clynes (Lab)	2 Jul 17
	J. Clynes (Lab) 9 Jul 18	W. Astor (C)	18 Jul 18
	G. Roberts (Lab) 10 Jan 19	C. McCurdy (Lib)	27 Jan 19
	C. McCurdy (Lib) 19 Mar 20	Sir W. Mitchell-Thomson (C)	
	(*office abolished* 31 *Mar* 21)		19 Apr 20
Ld Chanc. Ireland	Sir I. O'Brien (Lib) 10 Dec 16		
	Sir J. Campbell (C) 4 Jun 18		
	Sir J. Ross (C) 27 Jun 21		
D. Lanc.	(*office of cabinet rank see above*)		
	E of Crawford (C) 10 Jan 19		
	Vt Peel (C) 1 Apr 21		
	Sir W. Sutherland (Lib) 7 Apr 22		
Nat. S.	(*office in cabinet*)	(*for Junior Ministers see above*)	
	Sir A. Geddes (C) 17 Aug 17		
	(*office held joint with B of Trade*		
	Jan–Aug 19 *and then abolished*)		
Paym.-Gen.	Sir J. Compton-Rickett (Lib)		
	15 Dec 16		
	Sir T. Walters (Lib) 26 Oct 19		
Pensions	G. Barnes (Lab) 10 Dec 16	*P.S.* Sir A. Griffith-Boscawen (C)	
	J. Hodge (Lab) 17 Aug 17		22 Dec 16
	Sir L. Worthington-Evans (C)	Sir J. Craig (C)	10 Jan 19
	10 Jan 19	G. Tryon (C)	2 Apr 20
	I. Macpherson (Lib) 2 Apr 20		
Min. without Portfolio	Sir E. Geddes (C)		
	10 Jan 19–19 May 19		
Postm.-Gen.	A. Illingworth (Lib) 10 Dec 16	*Ass.* H. Pike Pease (C) 10 Dec 16	
	F. Kellaway (Lib) 1 Apr 21		
Reconstruc-tion	C. Addison (Lib) 17 Jul 17	(*for Junior Ministers see above, under*	
	(*office abolished* 10 *Jan* 1919)	*National Service* & *Reconstruction*)	

[1] Not a member of the House of Lords.

COALITION GOVERNMENT, 1916–1922 (contd.)

MINISTERS NOT IN CABINET			JUNIOR MINISTERS ATTACHED		
Shipping	Sir J. Maclay (Ld) (Lib)	10 Dec 16	*P.S.*	Sir L. Chiozza Money (Lib)	22 Dec 16
	(*office abolished* 31 *Mar* 21)			L. Wilson (C)	10 Jan 19
Transp.	(*office in cabinet from* 17 *Aug* 19)			(*for Junior Ministers see above*)	
	Vt Peel (C)	7 Nov 21			
	E of Crawford (C)	12 Apr 22			
1st C. Works	Sir A. Mond (Lib)	10 Dec 16			
	E of Crawford (C)	1 Apr 21			
	(*office in cabinet* 7 *Apr* 22)				

Law Officers:			*P.S. to Treasury:*		
Att.-Gen.	Sir F. Smith (C)	10 Dec 16		Ld E. Talbot [1] (C) 14 Dec 16–1 Apr 21	
	(*Ld Birkenhead*)			N. Primrose (Lib)	
	Sir G. Hewart (Lib)	10 Jan 19			14 Dec 16–2 Mar 17
	(*office in cabinet* 7 *Nov* 21)			F. Guest (Lib) 2 Mar 17–1 Apr 21	
	Sir E. Pollock (C)	6 Mar 22		C. McCurdy (Lib)	
					1 Apr 21–19 Oct 22
Sol.-Gen.	Sir G. Hewart (Lib)	10 Dec 16		L. Wilson (C) 1 Apr 21–19 Oct 22	
	Sir E. Pollock (C)	10 Jan 19	*Junior Lds of Treasury:*		
	(Sir) L. Scott (C)	6 Mar 22		G. Howard (Lib)	
Ld Advoc.	J. Clyde (C)	10 Dec 16			10 Dec 16–27 Dec 16
	T. Morison (Lib)	25 Mar 20		G. Roberts (Lab)	
	C. Murray (C)	5 Mar 22			10 Dec 16–27 Dec 16
				W. Bridgeman (C)	
Sol.-Gen.	T. Morison (Lib)	10 Dec 16			10 Dec 16–27 Dec 16
Scotland	C. Murray (C)	25 Mar 20		W. Rea (Lib) 10 Dec 16–27 Dec 16	
	A. Briggs Constable (C)			J. Hope (C) 14 Dec 16–27 Jan 19	
		16 Mar 22		J. Pratt (Lib) 14 Dec 16–8 Aug 19	
	W. Watson (C)	24 Jul 22		S. Baldwin (C) 29 Jan 17–21 Jun 17	
Att.-Gen.	J. Campbell (C)	20 Dec 16		J. Parker (Lab) 29 Jan 17–19 Oct 22	
Ireland	J. O'Connor (Nat)	8 Jan 17		J. Towyn Jones (Lib)	
	A. Samuels (C)	7 Apr 18			29 Jan 17–4 Jul 22
	D. Henry (C)	6 Jul 19		(Sir) R. Sanders (C)	
	T. Brown (C)	5 Aug 21			5 Feb 19–1 Apr 21
	(*post vacant from* 16 *Nov* 21)			Sir G. Collins (Lib)	
					8 Aug 19–10 Feb 20
Sol.-Gen.	J. Chambers (C)	19 Mar 17		(Sir) W. Edge (Co. Lib)	
Ireland	A. Samuels (C)	12 Sep 17			8 Aug 19–24 Aug 22
	J. Powell (C)	7 Apr 18		Sir W. Sutherland (Lib)	
	D. Henry (C)	27 Nov 18			15 Feb 20–7 Apr 22
	D. Wilson (C)	6 Jul 19		Sir J. Gilmour (C)	
	T. Brown (C)	12 Jun 21			1 Apr 22–19 Oct 22
				T. Lewis (Lib) 4 Jul 22–19 Oct 22	

H.M. Household:			*Lds in Waiting:*		
Treas.	(Sir) J. Craig (C)	14 Dec 16		Ld Herschell (Lib)	
	R. Sanders (C)	10 Jun 18			14 Dec 16–11 Feb 19
	B. Eyres-Monsell (C)	5 Feb 19		Ld Stanmore (Lib)	
	G. Gibbs (C)	1 Apr 21			14 Dec 16–19 Oct 22
Comptr.	Sir E. Cornwall (Lib)	14 Dec 16		Ld Ranksborough (Lib)	
	G. Stanley (C)	28 Feb 19			14 Dec 16–4 Apr 21
	H. Barnston (C)	7 Apr 21		Vt Valentia [1] (C) 14 Dec 16–19 Oct 22	
V. Chamb.	C. Beck (Lib)	14 Dec 16		Ld Hylton (C) 14 Dec 16–18 May 18	
	W. Dudley Ward (Lib)	9 Dec 17		Ld Kenyon (C) 14 Dec 16–11 Sep 18	
Ld Chamb.	Ld Sandhurst (Vt) (Lib)	14 Dec 16		Ld Somerleyton (C)	
	D of Atholl (C)	20 Nov 21			18 May 18–19 Oct 22
Ld Steward	Ld Farquhar (Vt) (C)	14 Dec 16		E of Jersey (C) 11 Jan 19–17 Aug 19	
				E of Bradford (C)	
Master of	E of Chesterfield (Lib)	14 Dec 16			11 Feb 19–19 Oct 22
Horse				E of Onslow (C) 17 Aug 19–12 Nov 20	
Capt. Gents	Ld Colebrooke (Lib)	14 Dec 16		E of Lucan (C) 12 Nov 20–19 Oct 22	
at Arms				E of Clarendon (C)	
					7 Apr 21–19 Oct 22

[1] Not a member of the House of Lords. Viscount Valentia became a U.K. Peer (Ld Annesley) in 1917.

C

COALITION GOVERNMENT, 1916–1922 *(contd.)*

MINISTERS NOT IN CABINET		JUNIOR MINISTERS ATTACHED

H.M. Household:

Capt.	LD SUFFIELD (C)	14 Dec 16
Yeomen of Guard	LD HYLTON (C)	21 May 18

CONSERVATIVE GOVERNMENT, 1922-1924

MINISTERS IN CABINET			JUNIOR MINISTERS ATTACHED		
P.M.	A. Bonar Law				
	23 Oct 22–20 May 23				
	S. Baldwin	22 May 23–22 Jan 24			
Ld Pres.	M of Salisbury	24 Oct 22			
Ld Chanc.	Vt Cave	24 Oct 22			
Privy S.	*(office vacant)*				
	Ld R. Cecil[1]	25 May 23			
Exch.	S. Baldwin	24 Oct 22	*Treasury:*		
	(& P.M. from 22 May 23)		F.S.	J. Hills	6 Nov 22
	N. Chamberlain	27 Aug 23		A. Boyd-Carpenter	12 Mar 23
F.S. to	*(office not in cabinet)*			*(Sir W. Joynson-Hicks*	25 May 23 *&*
Treasury	Sir W. Joynson-Hicks 25 May 23			*seat in cabinet)*	
	(W. Guinness 5 Oct 23 & office			W. Guinness	5 Oct 23
	not in cabinet)				
For. O.	Marquess Curzon	24 Oct 22	U-S.	R. McNeill	31 Oct 22
Home O.	W. Bridgeman	24 Oct 22	U-S.	G. Stanley	31 Oct 22
				G. Locker-Lampson	12 Mar 23
Admir.	L. Amery	24 Oct 22	P. & F.S.:		
				B. Eyres-Monsell	31 Oct 22
				A. Boyd-Carpenter	25 May 23
			Civil Ld:		
				M of Linlithgow	31 Oct 22
Ag. & Fish.	Sir R. Sanders	24 Oct 22	*P.S. Ag. & Deputy Min. Fisheries:*		
				E of Ancaster	31 Oct 22
Air	*(office not in cabinet)*		U-S.	D of Sutherland	31 Oct 22
	Sir S. Hoare	25 May 23			
Col. O.	D of Devonshire	24 Oct 22	U-S.	W. Ormsby-Gore	31 Oct 22
Bd Educ.	E. Wood	24 Oct 22	P.S.	Ld E. Percy[1]	21 Mar 23
				E of Onslow	25 May 23
Health	Sir A. Griffith-Boscawen		P.S.	E of Onslow	31 Oct 22
		24 Oct 22		Ld E. Percy[1]	25 May 23
	N. Chamberlain	7 Mar 23			
	Sir W. Joynson-Hicks 27 Aug 23				
India O.	Vt Peel	24 Oct 22	U-S.	Earl Winterton[1]	31 Oct 22
Lab.	Sir A. Montague-Barlow		P.S.	A. Boyd-Carpenter	6 Nov 22
		31 Oct 22		H. Betterton	12 Mar 23
D. Lanc.	M of Salisbury	24 Oct 22			
	(J. Davidson & office not in				
	cabinet 25 May 23)				
Postm.-Gen.	*(office not in cabinet)*				
	Sir L. Worthington-Evans				
		28 May 23			
Scotland	Vt Novar	24 Oct 22	*P.S. Min. of Health for Scotland:*		
				J. Kidd	31 Oct 22
				W. Elliot	15 Jan 23

[1] Not a member of the House of Lords.

CONSERVATIVE GOVERNMENT, 1922–1924 (contd.)

MINISTERS IN CABINET			JUNIOR MINISTERS ATTACHED		
B.o.T.	**Sir P. Lloyd-Greame**	24 Oct 22	P.S.	Vt Wolmer[1]	31 Oct 22
			Sec. Overseas Trade Dept.:		
				Sir W. Joynson-Hicks	
					31 Oct 22–12 Mar 23
				A. Buckley	12 Mar 23–18 Nov 23
			P.S. Mines Dept.:		
				G. Lane-Fox	6 Nov 22
War O.	**E of Derby**	24 Oct 22	U.-S.	W. Guinness	31 Oct 22
				W. Ashley	8 Oct 23
			F.S.	S. Jackson	31 Oct 22
				R. Gwynne	15 Mar 23

MINISTERS NOT IN CABINET			JUNIOR MINISTERS ATTACHED		
Air	SIR S. HOARE	31 Oct 22	(for Junior Ministers see above)		
	(office in cabinet 25 May 23)				
D. Lanc.	(office in cabinet)				
	J. DAVIDSON	25 May 23			
Paym.-Gen.	(office vacant)				
	N. CHAMBERLAIN	5 Feb 23			
	SIR W. JOYNSON-HICKS	15 Mar 23			
	A. BOYD-CARPENTER	25 May 23			
Pensions	G. TRYON	31 Oct 22	P.S.	C. Craig	13 Feb 23
Postm.-Gen.	N. CHAMBERLAIN	31 Oct 22			
	SIR W. JOYNSON-HICKS	7 Mar 23			
	(Sir L. Worthington-Evans & office				
	in cabinet 28 May 23)				
Transp.	SIR J. BAIRD	31 Oct 22	P.S. Office of Works & Min. of Transp.:		
				W. Ashley	31 Oct 22
1st C. Works	SIR J. BAIRD	31 Oct 22		J. Moore-Brabazon	8 Oct 23
				(to Min. Transp. only)	
Law Officers:			P.S. to Treasury:		
Att.-Gen.	SIR D. HOGG	24 Oct 22		L. Wilson	31 Oct 22
Sol.-Gen.	SIR T. INSKIP	31 Oct 22		B. Eyres-Monsell	25 Jul 23
Ld Advoc.	W. WATSON	24 Oct 22	Junior Lds of Treasury:		
Sol.-Gen.	D. FLEMING	6 Nov 22		D. King	31 Oct 22–22 Jan 24
Scotland	F. THOMSON	5 Apr 23		A. Buckley	31 Oct 22–12 Mar 23
				F. Thomson	7 Feb 23–25 May 23
				G. Hennessy	11 Dec 22–22 Jan 24
				W. Cope	20 Mar 23–22 Jan 24
				P. Ford	25 May 23–20 Dec 23
				Sir J. Gilmour	20 Dec 23–22 Jan 24
H.M. Household:			Lds in Waiting:		
Treas.	G. GIBBS	6 Nov 22		Vt Valentia	20 Nov 22–22 Jan 24
Comptr.	H. BARNSTON	31 Oct 22		Ld Somerleyton	
V. Chamb.	D. HACKING	20 Nov 22			20 Nov 22–22 Jan 24
Ld Chamb.	E OF CROMER	20 Nov 22		E of Bradford	20 Nov 22–22 Jan 24
Ld Steward	E OF SHAFTESBURY	20 Nov 22		E of Lucan	20 Nov 22–22 Jan 24
Master of Horse	M OF BATH	20 Nov 22		E of Malmesbury	
					20 Nov 22–22 Jan 24
Capt. Gents at Arms	E OF CLARENDON	20 Nov 22		E of Albemarle	20 Nov 22–22 Jan 24
Capt. Yeomen of Guard	LD HYLTON	20 Nov 22			

---

[1] Not a member of the House of Lords.

LABOUR GOVERNMENT, 1924

MINISTERS IN CABINET			JUNIOR MINISTERS ATTACHED		
P.M.	**J. R. MacDonald**				
		22 Jan 24–3 Nov 24			
Ld Pres.	**Ld Parmoor**	22 Jan 24			
Ld Chanc.	**Vt Haldane**	22 Jan 24			
Privy S.	**J. Clynes**	22 Jan 24			
Exch.	**P. Snowden**	22 Jan 24	*Treasury:*		
			F.S.	W. Graham	23 Jan 24
For. O.	**J. R. MacDonald (P.M.)**	22 Jan 24	*U-S.*	A. Ponsonby	23 Jan 24
Home O.	**A. Henderson**	22 Jan 24	*U-S.*	R. Davies	23 Jan 24
Admir.	**Vt Chelmsford**	22 Jan 24	*P. & F.S.:*		
				C. Ammon	23 Jan 24
			Civil Ld:		
				F. Hodges	24 Jan 24
Ag. & Fish	**N. Buxton**	22 Jan 24	*P.S.*	W. Smith	23 Jan 24
Air	**Ld Thomson**	22 Jan 24	*U-S.*	W. Leach	23 Jan 24
Col. O.	**J. Thomas**	22 Jan 24	*U-S.*	Ld Arnold	23 Jan 24
Bd Educ.	**C. Trevelyan**	22 Jan 24	*P.S.*	M. Jones	23 Jan 24
Health	**J. Wheatley**	22 Jan 24	*P.S.*	A. Greenwood	23 Jan 24
India O.	**Ld Olivier**	22 Jan 24	*U-S.*	R. Richards	23 Jan 24
Lab.	**T. Shaw**	22 Jan 24	*P.S.*	Miss M. Bondfield	23 Jan 24
D. Lanc.	**J. Wedgwood**	22 Jan 24			
Postm.-Gen.	**V. Hartshorn**	22 Jan 24			
Scotland	**W. Adamson**	22 Jan 24	*U-S. Health for Scotland:*		
				J. Stewart	23 Jan 24
B.o.T.	**S. Webb**	22 Jan 24	*P.S.*	A. Alexander	23 Jan 24
			P.S. Overseas Trade Dept.:		
				W. Lunn	23 Jan 24
			P.S. Mines Dept.:		
				E. Shinwell	23 Jan 24
War O.	**S. Walsh**	22 Jan 24	*U-S.*	C. Attlee	23 Jan 24
			F.S.	J. Lawson	23 Jan 24
1st C.Works	**F. Jowett**	22 Jan 24			

MINISTERS NOT IN CABINET			JUNIOR MINISTERS ATTACHED		
Paym.-Gen.	H. Gosling	6 May 24			
Pensions	F. Roberts	23 Jan 24	*P.S.*	J. Muir	28 Jan 24
Transp.	H. Gosling	24 Jan 24	*P.S.*	(vacant)	
Law Officers:			*P.S. to Treasury:*		
Att.-Gen.	Sir P. Hastings	23 Jan 24		B. Spoor	23 Jan 24
Sol.-Gen.	Sir H. Slesser	23 Jan 24	*Junior Lds of Treasury:*		
Ld Advoc.	H. Macmillan [1]	8 Feb 24		F. Hall	2 Feb 24
Sol.-Gen.	J. Fenton [1]	18 Feb 24		T. Kennedy	2 Feb 24
Scotland				J. Robertson	2 Feb 24
				G. Warne	24 Feb 24
H.M. Household:				W. Graham	2 Feb 24
Treas.	T. Griffiths	2 Feb 24	*Lds in Waiting:*		
Comptr.	J. Parkinson	2 Feb 24		Earl De La Warr	8 Feb 24
V. Chamb.	J. Davison	2 Feb 24		Ld Muir-Mackenzie	8 Feb 24

[1] Non-political appointments.

CONSERVATIVE GOVERNMENT, 1924-1929

MINISTERS IN CABINET			JUNIOR MINISTERS ATTACHED		
P.M.	S. Baldwin	4 Nov 24–4 Jun 29			
Ld Pres.	Marquess Curzon	6 Nov 24			
	E of Balfour	27 Apr 25			
Ld Chanc.	Vt Cave	6 Nov 24			
	Ld Hailsham (Vt)	28 Mar 28			
Privy S.	M of Salisbury	6 Nov 24			
Exch.	W. Churchill	6 Nov 24	*Treasury:*		
			F.S.	W. Guinness	11 Nov 24
				R. McNeill	5 Nov 25
				(*Ld Cushendun*)	
				A. Samuel	1 Nov 27
For. O.	(Sir) A. Chamberlain	6 Nov 24	U-S.	R. McNeill	11 Nov 24
				G. Locker-Lampson	7 Dec 25
Home O.	Sir W. Joynson-Hicks	6 Nov 24	U-S.	G. Locker-Lampson	11 Nov 24
				D. Hacking	8 Dec 25
				Sir V. Henderson	9 Nov 27
Admir.	W. Bridgeman	6 Nov 24	*P. & F.S.:*		
				J. Davidson	11 Nov 24
				C. Headlam	16 Dec 26
			Civil Ld:		
				Earl Stanhope	11 Nov 24
Ag. & Fish.	E. Wood	6 Nov 24	*P.S. Ag. & Deputy Min. of Fisheries:*		
	W. Guinness	4 Nov 25		Ld Bledisloe	11 Nov 24
				E of Stradbroke	5 Feb 28
Air	Sir S. Hoare	6 Nov 24	U-S.	Sir P. Sassoon	11 Nov 24
Att.-Gen.	Sir D. Hogg (*Ld Hailsham*) 6 Nov 24 (28 Mar 28 Sir T. Inskip & office not in cabinet)				
Col. O.	L. Amery	6 Nov 24	U-S.	W. Ormsby-Gore	12 Nov 24
Dom. O.	L. Amery	11 Jun 25	U-S.	E of Clarendon	5 Aug 25
				Ld Lovat	5 May 27
				E of Plymouth	1 Jan 29
Bd Educ.	Ld E. Percy[1]	6 Nov 24	P.S.	Duchess of Atholl	11 Nov 24
Health	N. Chamberlain	6 Nov 24	P.S.	Sir K. Wood	11 Nov 24
India O.	E of Birkenhead	6 Nov 24	U-S.	Earl Winterton[1]	11 Nov 24
	Vt Peel	18 Oct 28			
Lab.	Sir A. Steel-Maitland	6 Nov 24	P.S.	H. Betterton	11 Nov 24
D. Lanc.	Vt Cecil	10 Nov 24			
	Ld Cushendun	19 Oct 27			
Scot. O.	Sir J. Gilmour (became Sec. of State for Scotland 15 Jul 26)	6 Nov 24	U-S.	W. Elliot	26 Jul 26
			P.S. Health for Scotland:		
				W. Elliot	11 Nov 24
				(*post abolished 26 Jul 26*)	
B.o.T.	Sir P. Lloyd-Greame (changed name to Sir P. Cunliffe-Lister 27 Nov 24)	6 Nov 24	P.S.	Sir B. Chadwick	11 Nov 24
				H. Williams	13 Jan 28
			P.S. Overseas Trade Dept.:		
				A. Samuel	11 Nov 24
				D. Hacking	9 Nov 27
			P.S. Mines Dept.:		
				G. Lane-Fox	11 Nov 24
				D. King	13 Jan 28
War O.	Sir L. Worthington-Evans	6 Nov 24	U-S.	E of Onslow	11 Nov 24
				D of Sutherland	2 Dec 28
			F.S.	D. King	11 Nov 24
				A. Duff Cooper	13 Jan 28
1st C. Works	Vt Peel	10 Nov 24			
	M of Londonderry	18 Oct 28			

[1] Not a member of the House of Lords.

CONSERVATIVE GOVERNMENT, 1924–1929 (contd.)

MINISTERS NOT IN CABINET			JUNIOR MINISTERS ATTACHED		
Paym.-Gen.	(office vacant)				
	D OF SUTHERLAND	28 Jun 25			
	E OF ONSLOW	2 Dec 28			
Pensions	G. TRYON	11 Nov 24	P.S.	G. Stanley	11 Nov 24
Postm.-Gen.	SIR W. MITCHELL-THOMSON		Ass.	Vt Wolmer [1]	11 Nov 24
		11 Nov 24			
Transp.	W. ASHLEY	11 Nov 24	P.S.	J. Moore-Brabazon	11 Nov 24
				(post vacant from 14 Jan 27)	
Law Officers:			P.S. to Treasury:		
Att.-Gen.	(office in cabinet)			B. Eyres-Monsell	7 Nov 24
	SIR T. INSKIP	28 Mar 28	Junior Lds of Treasury:		
Sol.-Gen.	SIR T. INSKIP	11 Nov 24		G. Hennessy	13 Nov 24–10 Dec 25
	SIR F. MERRIMAN	28 Mar 28		Ld Stanley [1]	13 Nov 24–9 Nov 27
Ld Advoc.	W. WATSON	11 Nov 24		F. Thomson	13 Nov 24–14 Jan 28
	A. MACROBERT	23 Apr 29		(Sir) W. Cope	13 Nov 24–14 Jan 28
Sol.-Gen.	D. FLEMING	11 Nov 24		Vt Curzon [1]	13 Nov 24–15 Jan 29
Scotland	A. MACROBERT	30 Dec 25		D. Margesson	28 Aug 26–4 Jun 29
	W. NORMAND	23 Apr 29		M of Titchfield [1]	13 Jan 28–4 Jun 29
				G. Bowyer	28 Dec 27–4 Jun 29
				F. Penny	13 Jan 28–4 Jun 29
				E. Wallace	1 Jan 29–4 Jun 29
H.M. Household:			Lds in Waiting:		
Treas.:	G. GIBBS	13 Nov 24		Vt Gage	1 Dec 24–4 Jun 29
	SIR G. HENNESSY	13 Jan 28		Ld Somers	1 Dec 24–23 Mar 26
Comptr.	SIR H. BARNSTON	13 Nov 24		E of Lucan	1 Dec 24–1 Jan 29
	SIR W. COPE	13 Jan 28		E of Airlie	1 Apr 26–4 Jun 29
V. Chamb.	D. HACKING	13 Nov 24		Ld Templemore	1 Jan 29–4 Jun 29
	(SIR) G. HENNESSY	10 Dec 25			
	(SIR) F. THOMSON	13 Jan 28			
Capt. Gents	E OF CLARENDON	1 Dec 24			
at Arms	E OF PLYMOUTH	26 Jun 25			
	E OF LUCAN	1 Jan 29			
Capt.	LD DESBOROUGH	1 Dec 24			
Yeomen of					
Guard					

LABOUR GOVERNMENT, 1929–1931

MINISTERS IN CABINET			JUNIOR MINISTERS ATTACHED		
P.M.	J. R. MacDonald				
		5 Jun 29–24 Aug 31			
Ld Pres.	Ld Parmoor	7 Jun 29			
Ld Chanc.	Ld Sankey	7 Jun 29			
Privy S.	J. Thomas	7 Jun 29			
	V. Hartshorn	5 Jun 30			
	T. Johnston	24 Mar 31			
Exch.	P. Snowden	7 Jun 29	Treasury:		
			F.S.	F. Pethick-Lawrence	11 Jun 29
For. O.	A. Henderson	7 Jun 29	U-S.	H. Dalton	11 Jun 29
Home O.	J. Clynes	7 Jun 29	U-S.	A. Short	11 Jun 29
Admir.	A. Alexander	7 Jun 29	P. & F.S.:		
				C. Ammon	11 Jun 29
			Civil Ld:		
				G. Hall	11 Jun 29
Ag. & Fish.	N. Buxton	7 Jun 29	P.S.	C. Addison	11 Jun 29
	C. Addison	5 Jun 30		Earl De La Warr	5 Jun 30

[1] Not a member of the House of Lords.

LABOUR GOVERNMENT, 1929–1931 *(contd.)*

MINISTERS IN CABINET			JUNIOR MINISTERS ATTACHED		
Air	Ld Thomson	7 Jun 29	U-S.	F. Montague	11 Jun 29
	Ld Amulree	14 Oct 30			
Col. O.	Ld Passfield	7 Jun 29	U-S.	W. Lunn	11 Jun 29
				D. Shiels	1 Dec 29
Dom. O	Ld Passfield	7 Jun 29	U-S.	A. Ponsonby	11 Jun 29
	J. Thomas	5 Jun 30		W. Lunn	1 Dec 29
Bd Educ.	Sir C. Trevelyan	7 Jun 29	P.S.	M. Jones	11 Jun 29
	H. Lees-Smith	2 Mar 31			
Health	A. Greenwood	7 Jun 29	P.S.	Miss S. Lawrence	11 Jun 29
India O.	W. Benn	7 Jun 29	U-S.	D. Shiels	11 Jun 29
				Earl Russell	1 Dec 29
				Ld Snell	13 Mar 31
Lab.	Miss M. Bondfield	7 Jun 29	P.S.	J. Lawson	11 Jun 29
Scot. O	W. Adamson	7 Jun 29	U-S.	T. Johnston	7 Jun 29
				J. Westwood	25 Mar 31
B.o.T.	W. Graham	7 Jun 29	P.S.	W. Smith	11 Jun 29
			P.S. *Overseas Trade Dept.:*		
				G. Gillett	7 Jul 29
			P.S. *Mines Dept.:*		
				B. Turner	1 Jun 29
				E. Shinwell	5 Jun 30
Transp.	*(office not in cabinet)*		P.S.	Earl Russell	11 Jun 29
	H. Morrison	19 Mar 31		A. Ponsonby (Ld)	1 Dec 29
				J. Parkinson	1 Mar 31
War O.	T. Shaw	7 Jun 29	U-S.	Earl De La Warr	11 Jun 29
				Ld Marley	5 Jun 30
			F.S.	E. Shinwell	11 Jun 29
				W. Sanders	5 Jun 30
1st C. Works	G. Lansbury	7 Jun 29			

MINISTERS NOT IN CABINET			JUNIOR MINISTERS ATTACHED
D. Lanc.	Sir O. Mosley	7 Jun 29	
	C. Attlee	23 May 30	
	Ld Ponsonby	13 Mar 31	
Paym.-Gen.	Ld Arnold	7 Jun 29	
Pensions	F. Roberts	7 Jun 29	P.S. *(post vacant)*
Postm.-Gen.	H. Lees-Smith	7 Jun 29	Ass. S. Viant 7 Jul 29
	C. Attlee	2 Mar 31	
Transp.	H. Morrison	7 Jun 29	*(for Junior Ministers see above)*
	(office in cabinet 19 Mar 31)		

Law Officers:

P.S. *to Treasury:*
T. Kennedy   14 Jun 29

Att.-Gen.	Sir W. Jowitt	7 Jun 29
Sol.-Gen.	Sir J. Melville	7 Jun 29
	Sir S. Cripps	22 Oct 30
Ld Advoc.	C. Aitchison	17 Jun 29
Sol.-Gen. Scotland	J. Watson	17 Jun 29

Junior Lds of Treasury:

J. Parkinson	11 Jun 29–13 Mar 31
C. Edwards	11 Jun 29–24 Aug 31
A. Barnes	11 Jun 29–23 Oct 30
W. Whiteley	27 Jun 29–24 Aug 31
W. Paling	27 Jun 29–24 Aug 31
E. Thurtle	23 Oct 30–24 Aug 31
H. Charleton	13 Mar 31–24 Aug 31

H.M. Household:

Treas.	B. Smith	24 Jun 29

Lds in Waiting:
Earl De La Warr
18 Jul 29–24 Aug 31

LABOUR GOVERNMENT, 1929–1931 (contd.)

MINISTERS NOT IN CABINET			JUNIOR MINISTERS ATTACHED
H.M. Household:			Ld Muir-Mackenzie
Comptr.	T. HENDERSON	24 Jun 29	18 Jul 29–22 May 30
V. Chamb.	J. HAYES	24 Jun 29	Ld Marley 17 Jan 30–24 Aug 31

NATIONAL GOVERNMENT, 1931–1935

	MINISTERS IN CABINET		JUNIOR MINISTERS ATTACHED		
P.M.	J. R. MacDonald (N. Lab) 24 Aug 31–7 Jun 35				
Ld Pres.	S. Baldwin (C)	25 Aug 31			
Ld Chanc.	Ld Sankey (Vt) (N. Lab)	25 Aug 31			
Privy S	*(office not in cabinet)*				
	Vt Snowden (N. Lab)	5 Nov 31			
	S. Baldwin (C)	29 Sep 32			
	(31 *Dec* 33 *A. Eden & office not in cabinet*)				
Exch.	P. Snowden (Vt) (N. Lab)	25 Aug 31	*Treasury:*		
			F.S.	W. Elliot (C)	3 Sep 31
	N. Chamberlain (C)	5 Nov 31		L. Hore-Belisha (L. Nat)	29 Sep 32
				A. Duff Cooper (C)	29 Jun 34
For. O.	M of Reading (Lib)	25 Aug 31	U.-S.	A. Eden (C)	3 Sep 31
	Sir J. Simon (L. Nat)	5 Nov 31		Earl Stanhope (C)	18 Jan 34
Home O.	Sir H. Samuel (Lib)	25 Aug 31	U.-S.	O. Stanley (C)	3 Sep 31
	Sir J. Gilmour (C)	28 Sep 32		D. Hacking (C)	22 Feb 33
				H. Crookshank (C)	29 Jun 34
Admir.	*(office not in cabinet)*		*P. & F.S.:*		
	Sir B. Eyres-Monsell (C)	5 Nov 31		Earl Stanhope (C)	3 Sep 31
				Ld Stanley [1] (C)	10 Nov 31
			Civil Ld:	*(vacant)*	
				E. Wallace (C)	10 Nov 31
Ag & Fish.	*(office not in cabinet)*		P.S.	*(vacant)*	
	Sir J. Gilmour (C)	5 Nov 31		Earl De La Warr (N. Lab)	10 Nov 31
	W. Elliot (C)	28 Sep 32			
Air	*(office not in cabinet)*				
	M of Londonderry (C)	5 Nov 31	U.-S.	Sir P. Sassoon (C)	3 Sep 31
Col. O.	J. Thomas (N. Lab)	25 Aug 31	U.-S.	Sir R. Hamilton (Lib)	3 Sep 31
	Sir P. Cunliffe-Lister (C)	5 Nov 31		E of Plymouth (C)	29 Sep 32
Dom. O.	J. Thomas (N. Lab)	25 Aug 31	U.-S.	M. MacDonald (N. Lab)	3 Sep 31
Bd Educ.	*(office not in cabinet)*		P.S.	Sir K. Wood (C)	3 Sep 31
	Sir D. Maclean (Lib)	5 Nov 31		H. Ramsbotham (C)	10 Nov 31
	Ld Irwin (*Vt Halifax*) (C)	15 Jun 32			
Health	N. Chamberlain (C)	25 Aug 31	P.S.	E. Simon (Lib)	22 Sep 31
	Sir E. Young (C)	5 Nov 31		E. Brown (L. Nat.)	10 Nov 31
				G. Shakespeare (L. Nat)	30 Sep 32
India O.	Sir S. Hoare (C)	25 Aug 31	U.-S.	*(vacant)*	
				M of Lothian (Lib)	10 Nov 31
				R. Butler (C)	29 Sep 32
Lab.	*(office not in cabinet)*		P.S.	M. Gray (Lib)	3 Sep 31
	Sir H. Betterton (C)	5 Nov 31		R. Hudson (C)	10 Nov 31
	O. Stanley (C)	29 Jun 34			
Postm.-Gen.	*(office not in cabinet)*		Ass.	G. White (Lib)	3 Sep 31
	Sir K. Wood (C)	20 Dec 33		Sir E. Bennett (N. Lab)	21 Oct 32
Scot. O.	*(office not in cabinet)*		U.-S.	N. Skelton (C)	3 Sep 31
	Sir A. Sinclair (Lib)	5 Nov 31			
	Sir G. Collins (L. Nat)	28 Sep 32			

[1] Not a member of the House of Lords.

NATIONAL GOVERNMENT, 1931–1935 (contd.)

MINISTERS IN CABINET

			JUNIOR MINISTERS ATTACHED	
B.o.T.	**Sir P. Cunliffe-Lister** (C)		P.S.	G. Lloyd-George (Lib) 3 Sep 31
		25 Aug 31		L. Hore-Belisha (L. Nat) 10 Nov 31
	W. Runciman (Ld) (L. Nat.)			L. Burgin (L. Nat) 29 Sep 32
		5 Nov 31	P.S. Overseas Trade Dept.:	
				Sir E. Young (C) 3 Sep 31
				J. Colville (C) 10 Nov 31
			P.S. Mines Dept.:	
				I. Foot (Lib) 3 Sep 31
				E. Brown (L. Nat) 30 Sep 32
War O.	(office not in cabinet)		U-S.	(vacant)
	Vt Hailsham (C)	5 Nov 31		Earl Stanhope (C) 10 Nov 31
				Ld Strathcona & Mount Royal (C)
				24 Jan 34
			F.S.	A. Duff Cooper (C) 3 Sep 31
				D. Hacking (C) 29 Jun 34
1st C. Works	(office not in cabinet)			
	W. Ormsby-Gore (C)	5 Nov 31		

MINISTERS NOT IN CABINET

			JUNIOR MINISTERS ATTACHED	
Admir.	SIR A. CHAMBERLAIN (C) 25 Aug 31		(for Junior Ministers see above)	
	(5 Nov 31 Sir B. Eyres-Monsell & office in cabinet)			
Ag. & Fish.	SIR J. GILMOUR (C) 25 Aug 31		(for Junior Ministers see above)	
	(5 Nov 31 office in cabinet)			
Air	LD AMULREE (N. Lab) 25 Aug 31		(for Junior Ministers see above)	
	(5 Nov 31 M of Londonderry & office in cabinet)			
Bd Educ.	SIR D. MACLEAN (Lib) 25 Aug 31		(for Junior Ministers see above)	
	(5 Nov 31 office in cabinet)			
Lab.	SIR H. BETTERTON (C) 25 Aug 31		(for Junior Ministers see above)	
	(5 Nov 31 office in cabinet)			
D. Lanc.	M OF LOTHIAN (Lib) 25 Aug 31			
	(SIR) J. DAVIDSON (C) 10 Nov 31			
Paym.-Gen.	SIR T. WALTERS (Lib) 4 Sep 31			
	LD ROCHESTER (N. Lab) 23 Nov 31			
Pensions	G. TRYON (C) 3 Sep 31		P.S.	(vacant)
				C. Headlam (C) 10 Nov 31
				(vacant from 29 Sep 32)
				(for Junior Ministers see above)
Postm.-Gen.	W. ORMSBY-GORE (C) 3 Sep 31			
	SIR K. WOOD (C) 10 Nov 31			
	(20 Dec 33 office in cabinet)			
Privy S.	EARL PEEL (C) 3 Sep 31			
	(5 Nov 31 Vt Snowden & office in cabinet			
	A. EDEN (C) 31 Dec 33			
Scot. O.	SIR A. SINCLAIR (Lib) 25 Aug 31		(for Junior Ministers see above)	
	(5 Nov 31 office in cabinet)			
Transp.	J. PYBUS (L. Nat) 3 Sep 31		P.S.	(Sir) G. Gillett (N. Lab) 4 Sep 31
	O. STANLEY (C) 22 Feb 33			E of Plymouth (C) 25 Nov 31
	L. HORE-BELISHA (L. Nat) 29 Jun 34			C. Headlam (C) 29 Sep 32
				(5 Jul 34 vacant)
				A. Hudson (C) 12 Apr 35
War O.	M OF CREWE (Lib) 26 Aug 31		(for Junior Ministers see above)	
	(5 Nov 31 Vt Hailsham & office in cabinet)			
1st C. Works	M OF LONDONDERRY (C) 25 Aug 31			
	(5 Nov 31 W. Ormsby-Gore & office in cabinet)			

Law Officers:			P.S. to Treasury:	
Att.-Gen.	SIR W. JOWITT (N. Lab) 3 Sep 31		Sir B. Eyres-Monsell (C) 3 Sep 31	
	SIR T. INSKIP (C) 26 Jan 32		D. Margesson (C) 10 Nov 31	

NATIONAL GOVERNMENT, 1931–1935 (contd.)

MINISTERS NOT IN CABINET			JUNIOR MINISTERS ATTACHED	
Sol.-Gen.	Sir T. Inskip (C)	3 Sep 31	*Junior Lds of Treasury:*	
	Sir F. Merriman (C)	26 Jan 32	D. Margesson (C)	
	Sir D. Somervell (C)	29 Sep 33		26 Aug 31–10 Nov 31
Ld Advoc.	C. Aitchison (N. Lab)	3 Sep 31	Sir F. Penny (C) 3 Sep 31–12 Nov 31	
	W. Normand (C)	2 Oct 33	A. Glassey (Lib) 14 Sep 31–12 Nov 31	
	D. Jamieson (C)	28 Mar 35	M of Tichfield [1] (C)	
Sol.-Gen. Scotland	J. Watson (N. Lab)	4 Sep 31		3 Sep 31–12 Nov 31
	W. Normand (C)	10 Nov 31	E. Wallace (C) 3 Sep 31–12 Nov 31	
	D. Jamieson (C)	2 Oct 33	(Sir) W. Womersley (C)	
	T. Cooper (C)	15 May 35		12 Nov 31–7 Jun 35
			Sir V. Warrender (C)	
				12 Nov 31–30 Sep 32
			G. Shakespeare (L. Nat)	
				12 Nov 31–30 Sep 32
			A. Hudson (C) 12 Nov 31–12 Apr 35	
			Sir L. Ward (C) 12 Nov 31–1 May 35	
H.M. Household:			G. Davies (C) 11 Oct 32–7 Jun 35	
Treas.:	Sir G. Hennessy (C)	3 Sep 31	J. Blindell (L. Nat)	
	Sir F. Thomson (C)	12 Nov 31		30 Sep 32–7 Jun 35
	Sir F. Penny (C)	1 May 35	J. Stuart (C) 1 May 35–7 Jun 35	
Comptr.	G. Owen (Lib)	14 Sep 31	A. Southby (C) 23 Apr 35–7 Jun 35	
	W. Rea (Lib)	12 Nov 31	*Lds in Waiting:*	
	Sir F. Penny (C)	30 Sep 32	Ld Templemore (C)	
	Sir V. Warrender (C)	1 May 35		12 Nov 31–24 Jan 34
V. Chamb.	Sir F. Thomson (C)	3 Sep 31	Vt Gage (C) 12 Nov 31–7 Jun 35	
	Sir F. Penny (C)	12 Nov 31	Vt Allendale (Lib)	
	Sir V. Warrender (C)	30 Sep 32		12 Nov 31–28 Sep 32
	Sir L. Ward (C)	1 May 35	E of Munster (C) 24 Jan 34–7 Jun 35	
Capt. Gents at Arms	E of Lucan (C)	12 Nov 31	E of Feversham (C)	
Capt. Yeomen of Guard	Ld Strathcona & Mount Royal (C)	12 Nov 31		24 Jan 34–7 Jun 35
	Ld Templemore (C)	24 Jan 34		

NATIONAL GOVERNMENT, 1935–1940

MINISTERS IN CABINET

P.M.	S. Baldwin	7 Jun 35–28 May 37
	[2] N. Chamberlain	
		28 May 37–10 May 40
Ld Pres.	J. R. MacDonald	7 Jun 35
	Vt Halifax	28 May 37
	Vt Hailsham	9 Mar 38
	Vt Runciman	31 Oct 38
	Earl Stanhope	3 Sep 39
Ld Chanc.	Vt Hailsham	7 Jun 35
	Ld Maugham	9 Mar 38
	Vt Caldecote	3 Sep 39
Privy S.	M of Londonderry	7 Jun 35
	Vt Halifax	22 Nov 35
	Earl De La Warr	28 May 37
	Sir J. Anderson	31 Oct 38
	[2] Sir S. Hoare	3 Sep 39
	Sir K. Wood	3 Apr 40

[1] Not a member of the House of Lords.
[2] Denotes member of the War Cabinet. Following the British declaration of war against Germany on 3 Sep 39, all members of the cabinet formally surrendered their portfolios to the P.M.; in the evening of the same day the formation of a war cabinet was announced.

NATIONAL GOVERNMENT, 1935–1940 (contd.)

MINISTERS IN CABINET			JUNIOR MINISTERS ATTACHED		
Exch.	N. Chamberlain	7 Jun 35	*Treasury:*		
	[2] Sir J. Simon	28 May 37	F.S.	A. Duff Cooper	18 Jun 35
				W. Morrison	22 Nov 35
				J. Colville	29 Oct 36
				E. Wallace	16 May 38
				H. Crookshank	21 Apr 39
For. O.	Sir S. Hoare	7 Jun 35	U-S.	Earl Stanhope 18 Jun 35–16 Jun 36	
	A. Eden	22 Dec 35		Vt Cranborne [1] 6 Aug 35–20 Feb 38	
	[2] Vt Halifax	21 Feb 38		(for League of Nations Affairs)	
				E of Plymouth 30 Jul 36–May 39	
				R. Butler 25 Feb 38–10 May 40	
Home O.	Sir J. Simon	7 Jun 35	U-S.	E. Wallace	18 Jun 35
	Sir S. Hoare	28 May 37		G. Lloyd	28 Nov 35
	Sir J. Anderson	3 Sep 39		O. Peake	21 Apr 39
			P.S. Min. Home Security:		
				A. Lennox-Boyd	6 Sep 39
				W. Mabane	24 Oct 39
Admir.	Sir B. Eyres-Monsell	7 Jun 35	P. & F.S.:		
	(Vt Monsell)			Sir V. Warrender	18 Jun 35
	Sir S. Hoare	5 Jun 36		Ld Stanley [1]	28 Nov 35
	A. Duff Cooper	28 May 37		G. Shakespeare	28 May 37
	Earl Stanhope	27 Oct 38		Sir V. Warrender	3 Apr 40
	[2] W. Churchill	3 Sep 39	Civil Ld:		
				K. Lindsay	18 Jun 35
				J. Llewellin	28 May 37
				A. Hudson	14 Jul 39
Ag. & Fish.	W. Elliot	7 Jun 35	P.S.	Earl De La Warr	18 Jun 35
	W. Morrison	29 Oct 36		H. Ramsbotham	28 Nov 35
	Sir R. Dorman-Smith	29 Jan 39		E of Feversham	30 Jul 36
				Ld Denham	19 Sep 39
Air	Sir P. Cunliffe-Lister		U-S.	Sir P. Sassoon	18 Jun 35
	(Vt Swinton)			A. Muirhead	28 May 37
	[2] Sir K. Wood	7 Jun 35		H. Balfour	16 May 38
	Sir S. Hoare	16 May 38			
		3 Apr 40			
Col. O.	M. MacDonald	7 Jun 35	U-S.	E of Plymouth	18 Jun 35
	J. Thomas	22 Nov 35		Earl De La Warr	30 Jul 36
	W. Ormsby-Gore	28 May 36		M of Dufferin & Ava	28 May 37
	M. MacDonald	16 May 38			
Min. for Co-ordination of Defence	(office not established)				
	Sir T. Inskip	13 Mar 36			
	[2] Ld Chatfield	29 Jan 39			
	(office abolished 3 Apr 40)				
Dom. O.	J. Thomas	7 Jun 35	U-S.	Ld Stanley [1]	18 Jun 35
	M. MacDonald	22 Nov 35		D. Hacking	28 Nov 35
	Ld Stanley [1]	16 May 38		M of Hartington [1]	4 Mar 36
	M. MacDonald	31 Oct 38		(D of Devonshire)	
	Sir T. Inskip	29 Jan 39			
	(Vt Caldecote)				
	A. Eden	3 Sep 39			
Bd Educ.	O. Stanley	7 Jun 35	P.S.	H. Ramsbotham	18 Jun 35
	Earl Stanhope	28 May 37		Earl De La Warr	28 Nov 35
	Earl De La Warr	27 Oct 38		G. Shakespeare	30 Jul 36
	H. Ramsbotham	3 Apr 40		K. Lindsay	28 May 37
Food	(combined with D. Lanc. 4 Sep 39)		P.S.	A. Lennox-Boyd	11 Oct 39
	Ld Woolton	3 Apr 40			
Health	Sir K. Wood	7 Jun 35	P.S.	G. Shakespeare	18 Jun 35
	W. Elliot	16 May 38		R. Hudson	30 Jul 36
				R. Bernays	28 May 37
				Miss F. Horsbrugh	14 Jul 39

[1] Not a member of the House of Lords.
[2] Denotes member of the War Cabinet. Following the British declaration of war against Germany on 3 Sep 39, all members of the cabinet formally surrendered their portfolios to the P.M.; in the evening of the same day the formation of a war cabinet was announced.

NATIONAL GOVERNMENT, 1935–1940 (contd.)

MINISTERS IN CABINET			JUNIOR MINISTERS ATTACHED		
India O. (& Burma O. 1937–)	M of Zetland	7 Jun 35	U.-S.	R. Butler	18 Jun 35
				Ld Stanley [1]	28 May 37
				A. Muirhead	16 May 38
				Sir H. O'Neill	11 Sep 39
Information	(office not established)		P.S.	Sir E. Grigg	19 Sep 39
	Ld Macmillan	4 Sep 39		(office vacant 3 Apr 40)	
	Sir J. Reith	5 Jan 40			
Lab.	E. Brown	7 Jun 35	P.S.	A. Muirhead	18 Jun 35
	(3 Sep 39 Lab. & Nat S.)			R. Butler	28 May 37
				A. Lennox-Boyd	25 Feb 38
				R. Assheton	6 Sep 39
D. Lanc.	(office not in cabinet)				
	Earl Winterton [1]	11 Mar 38			
	W. Morrison	29 Jan 39			
	(4 Sep 39–3 Apr 40 combined with Min. of Food)				
	G. Tryon	3 Apr 40			
Min. without Portfolio for League of Nations Affairs	A. Eden	7 Jun 35–22 Dec 35			
Min. without Portfolio	Ld E. Percy [1]	7 Jun 35–31 Mar 36			
	L. Burgin	21 Apr 39–14 Jul 39			
	[2] Ld Hankey	3 Sep 39–10 May 40			
Scot. O.	Sir G. Collins	7 Jun 35	U.-S.	N. Skelton	18 Jun 35
	W. Elliot	29 Oct 36		J. Colville	28 Nov 35
	J. Colville	16 May 38		H. Wedderburn	29 Oct 36
				J. McEwen	6 Sep 39
Shipping	(office not established)		P.S.	Sir A. Salter	13 Nov 39
	Sir J. Gilmour	13 Oct 39			
	R. Hudson	3 Apr 40			
Supply	(office not established)		P.S.	J. Llewellin	14 Jul 39
	L. Burgin	14 Jul 39			
B.o.T.	Ld Runciman (Vt)	7 Jun 35	P.S.	L. Burgin	18 Jun 35
	O. Stanley	28 May 37		E. Wallace	28 May 37
	Sir A. Duncan	5 Jan 40		R. Cross	16 May 38
				G. Lloyd-George	6 Sep 39
			P.S. Overseas Trade Dept.:		
				J. Colville	18 Jun 35
				E. Wallace	28 Nov 35
				R. Hudson	28 May 37
				G. Shakespeare	3 Apr 40
			P.S. Mines Dept.:		
				H. Crookshank	18 Jun 35
				G. Lloyd	21 Apr 39
Transp.	(office not in cabinet)		P.S.	A. Hudson	18 Jun 35
	L. Hore-Belisha	29 Oct 36		R. Bernays	14 Jul 39
	L. Burgin	28 May 37			
	E. Wallace	21 Apr 39			
War O.	Vt Halifax	7 Jun 35	U.-S.	Ld Strathcona & Mount Royal	
	A. Duff Cooper	22 Nov 35			18 Jun 35
	[2] L. Hore-Belisha	28 May 37		E of Munster	29 Jan 39
	O. Stanley	5 Jan 40		Vt Cobham	19 Sep 39
			F.S.	D. Hacking	18 Jun 35
				Sir V. Warrender	28 Nov 35
				Sir E. Grigg	3 Apr 40

[1] Not a member of the House of Lords.
[2] Denotes member of the War Cabinet. Following the British declaration of war against Germany on 3 Sep 39, all members of the cabinet formally surrendered their portfolios to the P.M.; in the evening of the same day the formation of a war cabinet was announced.

NATIONAL GOVERNMENT, 1935–1940 (*contd.*)

MINISTERS IN CABINET			JUNIOR MINISTERS ATTACHED

1st *C. Works* **W. Ormsby-Gore**   7 Jun 35
    Earl Stanhope   16 Jun 36
    (28 *May* 37 *Sir P. Sassoon &*
    office out of cabinet)

MINISTERS NOT IN CABINET

Econ.   R. Cross   3 Sep 39
Warfare

D. Lanc.   Sir J. Davidson   18 Jun 35
     Earl Winterton[1]   28 May 37
     (*office in cabinet* 11 *Mar* 38)

Paym.-Gen.   Ld Rochester   18 Jun 35
     Ld Hutchison   6 Dec 35
     E of Munster   2 Jun 38
     Earl Winterton[1]   29 Jan 39
     (*office vacant from Nov* 39)

Pensions   R. Hudson   18 Jun 35
     H. Ramsbotham   30 Jul 36
     Sir W. Womersley   7 Jun 39

Postm.-Gen.   G. Tryon   7 Jun 35
     W. Morrison   3 Apr 40

Ass.   Sir E. Bennett   18 Jun 35
     Sir W. Womersley   6 Dec 35
     W. Mabane   7 Jun 39
     C. Waterhouse   24 Oct 39

Transp.   L. Hore-Belisha   18 Jun 35
     (*office in cabinet* 29 *Oct* 36)

1st *C. Works*   (*office in cabinet*)
     Sir P. Sassoon   28 May 37
     H. Ramsbotham   7 Jun 39
     Earl De La Warr   3 Apr 40

Law Officers:

P.S. to Treasury:
     D. Margesson   18 Jun 35

Att.-Gen.   Sir T. Inskip   18 Jun 35
     Sir D. Somervell   18 Mar 36

Junior Lds of Treasury:
     J. Stuart   18 Jun 35–10 May 40

Sol.-Gen.   Sir D. Somervell   18 Jun 35
     Sir T. O'Connor   19 Mar 36
     (Sir) A Southby
              18 Jun 35–28 May 37

Ld Advoc.   D. Jamieson   18 Jun 35
     T. Cooper   25 Oct 35
     Sir W. Womersley
              18 Jun 35–6 Dec 35
     G. Davies   18 Jun 35–6 Dec 35

Sol.-Gen.   T. Cooper   18 Jun 35
Scotland   A. Russell   29 Nov 35
     J. Reid   25 Jun 36
     (Sir) J. Blindell
              18 Jun 35–28 May 37
     A. Hope   6 Dec 35–28 May 37
     (Sir) H. Morris-Jones
              6 Dec 35–28 May 37
     C. Kerr   28 May 37–4 Apr 39
     T. Dugdale   28 May 37–12 Feb 40
     C. Waterhouse
              28 May 37–18 Oct 37
     R. Cross   28 May 37–18 Oct 37
     P. Munro   18 Oct 37–10 May 40
     R. Grimston   18 Oct 37–18 May 38
     S. Furness   20 May 38–10 May 40
     Sir J. Edmondson
              4 Apr 39–13 Nov 39
     P. Buchan-Hepburn
              13 Nov 39–10 May 40
     W. Boulton   12 Feb 40–10 May 40

[1] Not a member of the House of Lords.

NATIONAL GOVERNMENT, 1935–1940 *(contd.)*

MINISTERS NOT IN CABINET			JUNIOR MINISTERS ATTACHED		
H.M. Household:			*Lds in Waiting:*		
Treas.	SIR F. PENNY	18 Jun 35	Vt Gage	18 Jun 35–11 Apr 39	
	SIR L. WARD	28 May 37	E of Munster	18 Jun 35–2 Jun 38	
	A. HOPE	18 Oct 37	E of Feversham	18 Jun 35–30 Jul 36	
	C. WATERHOUSE	4 Apr 39	M of Dufferin & Ava		
	R. GRIMSTON	12 Nov 39		29 Oct 36–28 May 37	
Comptr.	SIR G. BOWYER	21 Jun 35	E of Erne	29 Oct 36–25 Jul 39	
	SIR L. WARD	6 Dec 35	Earl Fortescue		
	SIR G. DAVIES	28 May 37		26 Aug 37–10 May 40	
	C. WATERHOUSE	18 Oct 37	E of Birkenhead		
	C. KERR	4 Apr 39		12 Jul 38–10 May 40	
V. Chamb.	SIR L. WARD	18 Jun 35	Vt Bridport	11 Apr 39–10 May 40	
	(SIR) G. DAVIES	6 Dec 35	Ld Ebury	25 Jul 39–10 May 40	
	A. HOPE	28 May 37			
	R. CROSS	18 Oct 37			
	R. GRIMSTON	18 May 38			
	SIR J. EDMONDSON	12 Nov 39			
Capt. Gents at Arms	E OF LUCAN	18 Jun 35			
Capt. Yeomen of Guard	LD TEMPLEMORE	18 Jun 35			

COALITION GOVERNMENT, 1940–1945

MINISTERS IN WAR CABINET			JUNIOR MINISTERS ATTACHED		
P.M.	**W. Churchill** (C)				
		10 May 40–23 May 45			
Ld Pres.	**N. Chamberlain** (C)	11 May 40			
	Sir J. Anderson (Nat)	3 Oct 40			
	C. Attlee (Lab)	24 Sep 43			
Ld Chanc.	*(office not in war cabinet)*				
Privy S.	**C. Attlee** (Lab)	11 May 40			
	Sir S. Cripps (Lab)	19 Feb 42			
	(Vt Cranborne 22 Nov 42 & office not in war cabinet)				
Exch.	*(office not in war cabinet)*		*Treasury:*		
	Sir K. Wood (C)	3 Oct 40	F.S.	H. Crookshank (C)	15 May 40
	(19 Feb 42 office not in war cabinet)			R. Assheton (C)	7 Feb 43
	Sir J. Anderson (Nat)	24 Sep 43		O. Peake (C)	29 Oct 44
For. O.	**Vt Halifax** (C)	11 May 40	*Min. of State:*		
	A. Eden (C)	22 Dec 40		R. LAW (C)	24 Sep 43
Min. of State	**Ld Beaverbrook** (C)	1 May 41	U-S.	R. Butler (C)	15 May 40
	O. Lyttelton (C)	29 Jun 41		R. Law (C)	20 Jul 41
	(became Min. of Production) 12 Mar 42 & remained in war cabinet)			G. Hall (Lab)	25 Sep 43
Home O. & Home Security	*(office not in war cabinet)*		U-S.	O. Peake (C)	15 May 40
	H. Morrison (Lab)	22 Nov 42		E of Munster (C)	31 Oct 44
			P.S. Home Security:		
				W. Mabane (L. Nat)	
				15 May 40–3 Jun 42	
				Miss E. Wilkinson (Lab)	
				8 Oct 40–23 May 45	
Aircraft Production	*(office not in war cabinet)*		*(for Junior Ministers see below)*		
	Ld Beaverbrook (C)	2 Aug 40			
	(J. Moore-Brabazon 1 May 41 & office not in war cabinet)				
Def.	**W. Churchill (P.M.)** (C)				
		10 May 40			

COALITION GOVERNMENT, 1940–1945 *(contd.)*

MINISTERS IN WAR CABINET			JUNIOR MINISTERS ATTACHED		
			(for Junior Ministers see below)		
Dom. O.	*(office not in war cabinet)*				
	C. Attlee (Lab)	19 Feb 42			
	(Vt Cranborne 24 Sep 43 & office not in war cabinet)				
Lab. &	*(office not in war cabinet)*		*P.S.*	R. Assheton (C) 15 May 40–4 Feb 42	
Nat. S.	E. Bevin (Lab)	3 Oct 40		G. Tomlinson (Lab)	
				8 Feb 41–23 May 45	
				M. McCorquodale (C)	
				4 Feb 42–23 May 45	
Min.	*(office not in war cabinet)*		*Deputy Min. of State:*		
resident in	O. Lyttelton (C)	19 Feb 42		Ld Moyne (C) 27 Aug 42–28 Jan 44	
Mid. East	R. Casey[1]	19 Mar 42			
	(office not in war cabinet 23 Dec 43)				
Min.	A. Greenwood (Lab)				
without		11 May 40–22 Feb 42			
Portfolio	*(Sir W. Jowitt appointed 30 Dec 42 not in war cabinet)*				
Reconstruc-	*(office not established)*				
tion	Ld Woolton (C)	11 Nov 43			
Supply	*(office not in war cabinet)*		*(for Junior Ministers see below)*		
	Ld Beaverbrook (C)	29 Jun 41			
	(Sir A. Duncan & office not in war cabinet 4 Feb 42)				
(War)	*(office not established)*		*P.S.*	G. Garro-Jones (Lab)	10 Sep 42
Production	Ld Beaverbrook (C)	4 Feb 42			
	(office vacant 19 Feb 42)				
	O. Lyttelton (C)	12 Mar 42			
	(Minister of Production)				

MINISTERS NOT IN WAR CABINET			JUNIOR MINISTERS ATTACHED		
Admir.	A. Alexander (Lab)	11 May 40	*P. & F.S.:*		
				Sir V. Warrender (C)	17 May 40
				(Ld Bruntisfield)	
			Civil Ld:		
				A. Hudson (C)	15 May 40
				R. Pilkington (C)	4 Mar 42
			F.S.	G. Hall (Lab)	4 Feb 42
				J. Thomas (C)	25 Sep 43
Ag. & Fish.	R. Hudson (C)	14 May 40	*P.S.*	Ld Moyne (C) 15 May 40–8 Feb 41	
				T. Williams (Lab)	
				15 May 40–23 May 45	
				D of Norfolk (C)	
				8 Feb 41–23 May 45	
Air	Sir A. Sinclair (Lib)	11 May 40	*P.S.*	H. Balfour (C) 15 May 40–21 Nov 44	
				Ld Sherwood (Lib)	
				20 Jul 41–23 May 45	
				R. Brabner (C) 21 Nov 44–27 Mar 45	
				Q. Hogg (C) 12 Apr 45–23 May 45	
Aircraft	Ld Beaverbrook (C)	14 May 40	*P.S.*	J. Llewellin (C)	15 May 40
Production	*(office in war cabinet 2 Aug 40)*			F. Montague (Lab)	1 May 41
	J. Moore-Brabazon (C)	1 May 41		B. Smith (Lab)	4 Mar 42
	J. Llewellin (C)	22 Feb 42		A. Lennox-Boyd (C)	11 Nov 43
	Sir S. Cripps (Lab)	22 Nov 42			
Civil Av.	*(office not established)*		*P.S.*	R. Perkins (C)	22 Mar 45
	Vt Swinton (C)	8 Oct 44			
Col. O.	Ld Lloyd (C)	12 May 40	*U-S.*	G. Hall (Lab)	15 May 40
	Ld Moyne (C)	8 Feb 41		H. Macmillan (C)	4 Feb 42
	Vt Cranborne (C)	22 Feb 42		D of Devonshire (C)	1 Jan 43
	O. Stanley (C)	22 Nov 42			

[1] Not a member of the House of Commons.

COALITION GOVERNMENT, 1940–1945 *(contd.)*

MINISTERS NOT IN WAR CABINET			JUNIOR MINISTERS ATTACHED		
Dom. O.	Vt Caldecote (C)	14 May 40	*U–S.*	G. Shakespeare (L. Nat)	15 May 40
	Vt Cranborne[1] (C)	3 Oct 40		P. Emrys-Evans (C)	4 Mar 42
	(C. Attlee 19 Feb 42 & office in war cabinet)				
	Vt Cranborne (C)	24 Sep 43			
Economic	H. Dalton (Lab)	15 May 40	*P.S.*	D. Foot (Lib)	17 May 40
Warfare	Vt Wolmer[1]	22 Feb 42			
	(E of Selborne)				
Bd Educ.	H. Ramsbotham (C)	14 May 40	*P.S.*	C. Ede (Lab)	15 May 40
	R. Butler (C)	20 Jul 41			
	(3 Aug 44 becomes Min. of Educ.)				
Exch.	Sir K. Wood (C)	12 May 40	*(for Financial Secretary to Treasury see above)*		
	(3 Oct 40 office in war cabinet, 19 Feb 42 out of war cabinet again)				
	(24 Sep 43 Sir J. Anderson & office in war cabinet)				
Food	Ld Woolton (C)	13 May 40	*P.S.*	R. Boothby (C)	15 May 40
	J. Llewellin (C)	11 Nov 43		G. Lloyd-George (Ind. L)	22 Oct 40
				W. Mabane (L. Nat)	3 Jun 42
Fuel, Light	*(office not established)*		*P.S.*	G. Lloyd (C)	3 Jun 42–23 May 45
& Power	G. Lloyd-George (Ind L.)			T. Smith (Lab)	3 Jun 42–23 May 45
		3 Jun 42			
Health	M. MacDonald (N. Lab)	13 May 40	*P.S.*	Miss F. Horsbrugh (C)	15 May 40
	E. Brown (L. Nat)	8 Feb 41			
	H. Willink (C)	11 Nov 43			
Home O.	Sir J. Anderson (C)	12 May 40	*(for Junior Ministers see above)*		
& Home	H. Morrison (Lab)	3 Oct 40			
Security	*(22 Nov 42 office in war cabinet)*				
India &	L. Amery (C)	13 May 40	*P.S.*	D of Devonshire (C)	17 May 40
Burma O.				E of Munster (C)	1 Jan 43
				E of Listowel (Lab)	31 Oct 44
Information	A. Duff Cooper (C)	12 May 40	*P.S.*	H. Nicolson (N. Lab)	17 May 40
	(attended war cabinet from 28 May 40)			E. Thurtle (Lab)	20 Jul 41
	B. Bracken (C)	20 Jul 41			
Lab. &	E. Bevin (Lab)	13 May 40	*(for Junior Ministers see above)*		
Nat. S.	*(office in war cabinet 3 Oct 40)*				
D. Lanc.	Ld Hankey (Ind)	14 May 40			
	A. Duff Cooper (C)	20 Jul 41			
	E. Brown (L. Nat)	11 Nov 43			
Ld Chanc.	Vt Simon (L. Nat)	12 May 40			
Min. resident at Allied H.Q. in N.W. Africa	H. Macmillan (C)	30 Dec 42			
Min. resident in Washington for Supply	J. Llewellin (C)	22 Nov 42			
	B. Smith (Lab)	11 Nov 43			
Min. resident in W. Africa	Vt Swinton (C)	8 Jun 42			
	H. Balfour (C)	21 Nov 44			
Min. of State in Mid. East	*(office in war cabinet)*		*(for Junior Ministers see above)*		
	Ld Moyne (C)	28 Jan 44			
	Sir E. Grigg (C)	21 Nov 44			

[1] Not a member of the House of Lords. Viscount Wolmer was moved to the House of Lords by writ of acceleration in October 1940. The same was done for Viscount Cranborne in January 1941.

COALITION GOVERNMENT, 1940–1945 (contd.)

MINISTERS NOT IN WAR CABINET		JUNIOR MINISTERS ATTACHED	
Paym.-Gen.	VT CRANBORNE [1] (C) 15 May 40		
	(*office vacant* 3 Oct 40)		
	LD HANKEY (Ind) 20 Jul 41		
	SIR W. JOWITT (Lab) 4 Mar 42		
	LD CHERWELL (C) 30 Dec 42		
Pensions	SIR W. WOMERSLEY (C) 15 May 40		Miss E. Wilkinson (Lab) 17 May 40
			Ld Tryon (C) 8 Oct 40
			W. Paling (Lab) 8 Feb 41
Min. without Portfolio	(*in war cabinet* 11 *May* 40–22 *Feb* 42)		
	SIR W. JOWITT (Lab) 30 Dec 42–8 Oct 44		
Postm.-Gen.	W. MORRISON (C) 15 May 40	*Ass.*	C. Waterhouse (C) 17 May 40
	H. CROOKSHANK (C) 30 Dec 42		A. Chapman (C) 1 Mar 41
			R. Grimston (C) 4 Mar 42
Privy S.	(*office in war cabinet*)		
	VT CRANBORNE (C) 22 Nov 42		
	LD BEAVERBROOK (C) 24 Sep 43		
Scot. O.	E. BROWN (L. Nat) 14 May 40	*P.S.*	J. Westwood (Lab) 17 May 40–23 May 45
	T. JOHNSTON (Lab) 8 Feb 41		H. Wedderburn (C) 8 Feb 41–4 Mar 42
			A. Chapman (C) 4 Mar 42–23 May 45
Shipping	R. CROSS (C) 14 May 40	*P.S.*	Sir A. Salter (Ind) 15 May 40
	(1 *May* 41 *combined with Min. of Transport, as Min. of War Transport see below*)		
Soc. Insur.	(*office not established*)	*P.S.*	C. Peat (C) 22 Mar 45
	SIR W. JOWITT (Lab) 8 Oct 44		
	(*renamed National Insurance* 17 *Nov* 44)		
Supply	H. MORRISON (Lab) 12 May 40	*P.S.*	H. Macmillan (C) 15 May 40–4 Feb 42
	SIR A. DUNCAN (C) 3 Oct 40		Ld Portal (C) 4 Sep 40–4 Mar 42
	(*Ld Beaverbrook* 29 *Jun* 41 & *office in war cabinet*)		R. Assheton (C) 4 Feb 42–30 Dec 42
	SIR A. DUNCAN (C) 4 Feb 42		C. Peat (C) 4 Mar 42–22 Mar 45
			D. Sandys (C) 30 Dec 42–21 Nov 44
			J. Wilmot (Lab) 21 Nov 44–23 May 45
			J. de Rothschild (Lib) 22 Mar 45–23 May 45
T. & C. Planning	(*office not established*)	*P.S.*	H. Strauss (C) 30 Dec 42
	W. MORRISON (C) 30 Dec 42		A. Jenkins (Lab) 22 Mar 45
	(*Minister designate until* 5 *Feb* 43)		
B.o.T.	SIR A. DUNCAN (C) 12 May 40	*P.S.*	G. Lloyd-George (Ind L.) 15 May 40
	O. LYTTELTON (C) 3 Oct 40		(& *P.S. Food* 22 Oct 40)
	SIR A. DUNCAN (C) 29 Jun 41		C. Waterhouse (C) 8 Feb 41
	J. LLEWELLIN (C) 4 Feb 42		*Sec. Bd Overseas Trade:*
	H. DALTON (Lab) 22 Feb 42		H. Johnstone (Lib) 15 May 40
			S. Summers (C) 22 Mar 45
			Mines Dept.:
			D. Grenfell (Lab) 15 May 40
			Sec. Petrol Dept.:
			G. Lloyd (C) 15 May 40–3 Jun 42
			(3 *Jun* 42 *combined in Min. of Fuel, Light & Power*)
Transp	SIR J. REITH (Nat) 14 May 40		(*for Junior Ministers see below, under War Transport*)
	J. MOORE-BRABAZON (C) 3 Oct 40		
	(1 *May* 41 *became Min. of War Transport, see below*)		

[1] Not a member of the House of Lords.

D

COALITION GOVERNMENT, 1940–1945 *(contd.)*

MINISTERS NOT IN WAR CABINET			JUNIOR MINISTERS ATTACHED		

War O.   A. EDEN (C)   11 May 40
         D. MARGESSON (C)   22 Dec 40
         SIR J. GRIGG (Nat)   22 Feb 42

U-S.   Sir H. Page Croft (C)
       (*Ld Croft*) 17 May 40–23 May 45
       Sir E. Grigg (C)
            17 May 40–4 Mar 42
       A. Henderson (Lab)
            4 Mar 42–30 Dec 42

F.S.   R. Law (C)   17 May 40
       D. Sandys (C)   20 Jul 41
       A. Henderson (Lab)   7 Feb 43

War   LD LEATHERS (C)   1 May 41
Transp.

P.S.   F. Montague (Lab)
            18 May 40–1 May 41
     (*renamed War Transport* 1 *May* 41)
       J. Llewellin (C)   1 May 41–4 Feb 42
       Sir A. Salter (Ind)
            29 Jun 41–4 Feb 42
       P. Noel-Baker (Lab)
            4 Feb 42–23 May 45

1st.C.Works LD TRYON (C)   18 May 40
         SIR J. REITH (LD) (Ind)   3 Oct 40
         (*Min. of Works & Buildings &*
            1st C. Works 3 Oct 40)
         LD PORTAL   22 Feb 42
         (*Min. of Works and Planning* 11 *Feb*
            42.   *Min. of Works Feb* 43)
         D. SANDYS (C)   21 Nov 44

P.S.   G. Hicks (Lab) 19 Nov 40–23 May 45
       H. Strauss (C)   4 Mar 42–30 Dec 42

Law Officers:
Att.-Gen.   SIR D. SOMERVELL (C)   15 May 40
Sol.-Gen.   SIR W. JOWITT (Lab)   15 May 40
           D. MAXWELL FYFE (C)   4 Mar 42
Ld Advoc.   T. COOPER (C)   15 May 40
           J. REID (C)   5 Jun 41
Sol.-Gen.   J. REID (C)   15 May 40
Scotland   (SIR) D. MURRAY (C)   5 Jun 41

P.S. to Treasury:
       D. Margesson (C)
            17 May 40–22 Dec 40
       Sir C. Edwards (Lab)
            17 May 40–12 Mar 42
       J. Stuart (C)   14 Jan 41–23 May 45
       W. Whiteley (Lab)
            12 Mar 42–23 May 45
Junior Lds of Treasury:
       S. Furness (L. Nat)
            12 May 40–18 May 40
       J. Stuart (C)   12 May 40–14 Jan 41
       P. Munro (C) 12 May 40–13 Mar 42
       P. Buchan-Hepburn (C)
            12 May 40–26 Jun 40
       W. Boulton (C) 12 May 40–13 Mar 42
       W. Paling (Lab) 18 May 40–8 Feb 41
       J. Thomas (C)   26 Jun 40–25 Sep 43
       T. Dugdale (C) 8 Feb 41–23 Feb 42
       W. Adamson (Lab)
            1 Mar 41–2 Oct 44
       A. Young (C)   23 Feb 42–3 Jul 44
       J. McEwen (C) 13 Mar 42–6 Dec 44
       L. Pym (C)   13 Mar 42–23 May 45
       A. Beechman (L. Nat)
            25 Sep 43–23 May 45
       C. Drewe (C)   3 Jul 44–23 May 45

       W. John (Lab)   2 Oct 44–23 May 45
       P. Buchan-Hepburn (C)
            6 Dec 44–23 May 45

H.M. Household:
Treas.   R. GRIMSTON (C)   17 May 40
         SIR J. EDMONDSON (C)   12 Mar 42
Comptr.   W. WHITELEY (Lab)   17 May 40
         W. JOHN (Lab)   12 Mar 42
         G. MATHERS (Lab)   2 Oct 44

Lds in Waiting:
       Earl Fortescue (C)
            31 May 40–22 Mar 45
       Vt Clifden (Lib) 31 May 40–23 May 45
       Ld Alness (L. Nat)
            31 May 40–23 May 45
       M of Normanby (C)
            22 Mar 45–23 May 45

COALITION GOVERNMENT, 1940–1945 (contd.)

	MINISTERS NOT IN WAR CABINET		JUNIOR MINISTERS ATTACHED
V. Chamb.	SIR J. EDMONDSON (C)	17 May 40	
	W. BOULTON (C)	12 Mar 42	
	A. YOUNG (C)	13 Jul 44	
	LD SNELL (Lab)		
		31 May 40–21 Apr 44	
	EARL FORTESCUE (C)	22 Mar 45	
Capt. Yeomen of Guard	LD TEMPLEMORE (C)	31 May 40	

CARETAKER GOVERNMENT, 1945

	MINISTERS IN CABINET		JUNIOR MINISTERS ATTACHED		
P.M.	**W. Churchill** 23 May 45–26 Jul 45				
Ld Pres.	**Ld Woolton**	25 May 45			
Ld Chanc.	(*office not in cabinet*)				
Privy S.	**Ld Beaverbrook**	25 May 45			
Exch.	**Sir J. Anderson**	25 May 45	*Treasury:*		
			F.S.	O. Peake	26 May 45
For. O.	**A. Eden**	25 May 45	*Min. of State:*		
				W. MABANE	25 May 45
			U-S.	Ld Dunglass [1]	26 May 45
				Ld Lovat	26 May 45
Home O.	**Sir D. Somervell**	25 May 45	U-S.	E of Munster	26 May 45
Admir.	**B. Bracken**	25 May 45	*P. & F.S.:*		
				Ld Bruntisfield	26 May 45
			Civil Ld:		
				R. Pilkington	26 May 45
			F.S.	J. Thomas	26 May 45
Ag. & Fish.	**R. Hudson**	25 May 45	P.S.	D of Norfolk	26 May 45
				D. Scott	26 May 45
Air	**H. Macmillan**	25 May 45	U-S.	Q. Hogg	26 May 45
				Earl Beatty	26 May 45
Col. O.	**O. Stanley**	25 May 45	U-S.	D of Devonshire	26 May 45
Def.	**W. Churchill (P.M.)**	25 May 45			
Dom. O.	**Vt Cranborne**	25 May 45	U-S.	P. Emrys-Evans	26 May 45
India & Burma O.	**L. Amery**	25 May 45	P.S.	E of Scarbrough	26 May 45
Lab. & Nat. S.	**R. Butler**	25 May 45	P.S.	M. McCorquodale	26 May 45
Production	**O. Lyttelton** (*& Pres. B.o.T.*)	25 May 45	P.S.	J. Maclay	28 May 45
Scot. O.	**E of Rosebery**	25 May 45	P.S.	A. Chapman	26 May 45
				T. Galbraith	26 May 45
B.o.T.	**O. Lyttelton** (*& Min. of Production*)	25 May 45	P.S.	C. Waterhouse	26 May 45
			Sec. Bd Overseas Trade:		
				S. Summers	26 May 45
War O.	**Sir J. Grigg**	25 May 45	U-S.	Ld Croft	26 May 45
	MINISTERS NOT IN CABINET		JUNIOR MINISTERS ATTACHED		
Aircraft Production	E. BROWN	25 May 45	P.S.	A. Lennox-Boyd	26 May 45

[1] Not a member of the House of Lords.

CARETAKER GOVERNMENT, 1945 (contd.)

MINISTERS NOT IN CABINET			JUNIOR MINISTERS ATTACHED		
Civil Av.	VT SWINTON	25 May 45	P.S.	R. Perkins	26 May 45
Educ.	R. LAW	25 May 45	P.S.	Mrs T. Cazalet-Keir	26 May 45
Food	J. LLEWELLIN	25 May 45	P.S.	Miss F. Horsbrugh	26 May 45
Fuel & P.	G. LLOYD-GEORGE	25 May 45	P.S.	Sir A. Hudson	26 May 45
Health	H. WILLINK	25 May 45	P.S.	H. Kerr	26 May 45
Information	G. LLOYD	25 May 45			
D. Lanc.	SIR A. SALTER	25 May 45			
Ld Chanc.	VT SIMON	25 May 45			
Min. resident in Mid. East	SIR E. GRIGG	25 May 45			
Min. resident in W. Africa	H. BALFOUR	25 May 45			
Nat. Ins.	L. HORE-BELISHA	25 May 45	P.S.	C. Peat	26 May 45
Paym.-Gen.	LD CHERWELL	25 May 45			
Pensions	SIR W. WOMERSLEY	25 May 45	P.S.	W. Sidney (Ld De L'Isle)	26 May 45
Postm.-Gen.	H. CROOKSHANK	25 May 45	Ass.	W. Anstruther-Gray	26 May 45
Supply	SIR A. DUNCAN	25 May 45	P.S.	R. Grimston	26 May 45
T. & C. Planning	W. MORRISON	25 May 45	P.S.	R. Tree	26 May 45
War Transp.	LD LEATHERS	25 May 45	P.S.	P. Thorneycroft	26 May 45
Works	D. SANDYS	25 May 45	P.S.	R. Manningham-Buller	26 May 45

Law Officers:

			P.S. to Treasury:		
Att.-Gen.	SIR D. MAXWELL FYFE	25 May 45		J. Stuart	26 May 45
Sol.-Gen.	SIR W. MONCKTON[1]	25 May 45	Junior Lds of Treasury:		
Advoc. Gen.	J. REID	25 May 45		A. Beechman	28 May 45
Sol.-Gen. Scotland	SIR D. MURRAY	25 May 45		C. Drewe	25 May 45
				P. Buchan-Hepburn	25 May 45
				R. Cary	28 May 45
H.M. Household:				C. Mott-Radclyffe	28 May 45
Treas.	SIR J. EDMONDSON	28 May 45	Lds in Waiting:		
Comptr.	L. PYM	28 May 45		Ld Alness	28 May 45
V. Chamb.	A. YOUNG	28 May 45		M of Normanby	28 May 45
Capt. Gents at Arms	EARL FORTESCUE	28 May 45		D of Northumberland	28 May 45
Capt. Yeomen of Guard	LD TEMPLEMORE	28 May 45			

LABOUR GOVERNMENT, 1945–1951

MINISTERS IN CABINET			JUNIOR MINISTERS ATTACHED
P.M.	**C. Attlee**	26 Jul 45–26 Oct 51	
Ld Pres.	**H. Morrison**	27 Jul 45	
	Vt Addison	9 Mar 51	
Ld Chanc.	**Ld Jowitt**	27 Jul 45	

[1] Not a member of the House of Commons.

LABOUR GOVERNMENT, 1945–1951 (contd.)

MINISTERS IN CABINET			JUNIOR MINISTERS ATTACHED		
Privy S.	A. Greenwood	27 Jul 45			
	Ld Inman	17 Apr 47			
	Vt Addison	7 Oct 47			
	E. Bevin	9 Mar 51			
	R. Stokes	26 Apr 51			
	(also Min. of Materials from 6 Jul 51)				
Exch.	H. Dalton	27 Jul 45	*Min. Econ. Affairs:*		
	Sir S. Cripps	13 Nov 47	H. GAITSKELL	28 Feb 50–19 Oct 50	
	H. Gaitskell	19 Oct 50			
Min. Econ. Affairs	*(office not established)*		*Treasury:*		
	Sir S. Cripps	29 Sep 47	*F.S.* W. Hall		4 Aug 45
	(office combined with Exch 13 Nov 47)		D. Jay		2 Mar 50
			Econ. S.:		
			D. Jay		5 Dec 47
			(post vacant 28 Feb 50)		
			J. Edwards		19 Oct 50
For. O	E. Bevin	27 Jul 45	*Min. of State:*		
	H. Morrison	9 Mar 51	P. NOEL-BAKER		3 Aug 45
			H. McNEIL		4 Oct 46
			K. YOUNGER		28 Feb 50
			U-S. H. McNeil	4 Aug 45–4 Oct 46	
			C. Mayhew	4 Oct 46–2 Mar 50	
			Ld Henderson	7 Jun 48–26 Oct 51	
			E. Davies	2 Mar 50–26 Oct 51	
Home O.	C. Ede	3 Aug 45	*U-S.* G. Oliver		4 Aug 45
			K. Younger		7 Oct 47
			G. de Freitas		2 Mar 50
Admir.	A. Alexander	3 Aug 45	*(for Junior Ministers see below)*		
	(office not in cabinet 4 Oct 46)				
Ag. & Fish.	T. Williams	3 Aug 45	*P.S.* E of Huntingdon		
				4 Aug 45–22 Nov 50	
			P. Collick	5 Sep 45–7 Oct 47	
			G. Brown	7 Oct 47–26 Apr 51	
			E of Listowel	22 Nov 50–26 Oct 51	
			A. Champion	26 Apr 51–26 Oct 51	
Air	Vt Stansgate	3 Aug 45	*(for Junior Ministers see below)*		
	(office not in cabinet 4 Oct 46)				
Civil Av.	*(office not in cabinet)*		*P.S.* I. Thomas		10 Aug 45
	Ld Pakenham	31 May 48	G. Lindgren		4 Oct 46
	(office not in cabinet 28 Feb 50)		F. Beswick		2 Mar 50
Col. O.	G. Hall	3 Aug 45	*Min.* E OF LISTOWEL		4 Jan 48
	A. Creech Jones	4 Oct 46	J. DUGDALE		28 Feb 50
	J. Griffiths	28 Feb 50	*U-S.* A. Creech Jones		4 Aug 45
			I. Thomas		4 Oct 46
			D. Rees-Williams		7 Oct 47
			T. Cook		2 Mar 50
C.R.O	*(office not established)*		*Min.* A. HENDERSON		14 Aug 47
	Vt Addison	7 Jul 47	*(office in cabinet 7 Oct 47)*		
	P. Noel-Baker	7 Oct 47	*U-S.* P. Gordon Walker		7 Oct 47
	P. Gordon Walker	28 Feb 50	Ld Holden		2 Mar 50
			D. Rees-Williams		4 Jul 50
			(Ld Ogmore)		
			E of Lucan		1 Jun 51
Def.	C. Attlee (P.M.)	27 Jul 45			
	A. Alexander (Vt)	20 Dec 46			
	E. Shinwell	28 Feb 50			
Dom. O.	Vt Addison	3 Aug 45	*U-S.* J. Parker		4 Aug 45
	(became C.R.O. 7 Jul 47 see above)		A. Bottomley		10 May 46
Educ.	Miss E. Wilkinson	3 Aug 45	*P.S.* A. Jenkins		4 Aug 45
	G. Tomlinson	10 Feb 47	D. Hardman		30 Oct 45

LABOUR GOVERNMENT, 1945–1951 *(contd.)*

MINISTERS IN CABINET

Fuel & P.	**E. Shinwell**	3 Aug 45
	(H. Gaitskell 7 Oct 47 & office	
	not in cabinet)	
Health	**A. Bevan**	3 Aug 45
	(H. Marquand 17 Jan 51 & office	
	not in cabinet)	
India O. &	**Ld Pethick-Lawrence**	3 Aug 45
Burma O.	**E of Listowel**	17 Apr 47
	(4 Jan 48 offices abolished)	
Lab. &	**G. Isaacs**	3 Aug 45
Nat. S.	**A. Bevan**	17 Jan 51
	A. Robens	24 Apr 51
D. Lanc.	*(office not in cabinet)*	
	H. Dalton	31 May 48
	Vt Alexander	28 Feb 50
Paym.-Gen.	*(office vacant)*	
	A. Greenwood	9 Jul 46
	(H. Marquand 5 Mar 47 & office	
	not in cabinet)	
	Vt Addison	2 Jul 48
	(Ld Macdonald 1 Apr 49 & office	
	not in cabinet)	
Min.	**A. Alexander** 4 Oct 46–20 Dec 46	
without	**A. Greenwood**	
Portfolio	17 Apr 47–29 Sep 47	
Scot. O.	**J. Westwood**	3 Aug 45
	A. Woodburn	7 Oct 47
	H. McNeil	28 Feb 50
T. & C.	*(office not in cabinet)*	
Planning	**H. Dalton**	28 Feb 50
	(recast as Local Government &	
	Planning 31 Jan 51)	
B.o.T.	**Sir S. Cripps**	27 Jul 45
	H. Wilson	29 Sep 47
	Sir H. Shawcross	24 Apr 51
War O.	**J. Lawson**	3 Aug 45
	(office not in cabinet 4 Oct 46)	

MINISTERS NOT IN CABINET

Admir.	*(office in cabinet)*	
	Vt Hall	4 Oct 46
	Ld Pakenham	24 May 51
Air	*(office in cabinet)*	
	P. Noel-Baker	4 Oct 46
	A. Henderson	7 Oct 47
Civil Av.	Ld Winster	4 Aug 45
	Ld Nathan	4 Oct 46
	(Ld Pakenham 31 May 48 & office	
	in cabinet)	
	Ld Pakenham	28 Feb 50
	Ld Ogmore	1 Jun 51

JUNIOR MINISTERS ATTACHED
(for Junior Ministers see below)

P.S.	C. Key	4 Aug 45
	J. Edwards	12 Feb 47
	A. Blenkinsop	1 Feb 49
U-S.	A. Henderson	4 Aug 45
P.S.	N. Edwards	4 Aug 45
	F. Lee	2 Mar 50

U-S.	G. Buchanan	4 Aug 45–7 Oct 47
	T. Fraser	4 Aug 45–26 Oct 51
	J. Robertson	7 Oct 47–2 Mar 50
	Miss M. Herbison	
		2 Mar 50–26 Oct 51
P.S.	F. Marshall	10 Aug 45
	E. King	7 Oct 47
	G. Lindgren	2 Mar 50
P.S.	E. Smith	4 Aug 45
	J. Belcher	12 Jan 46
	J. Edwards	1 Feb 49
	H. Rhodes	2 Mar 50
	Sec. Overseas Trade Dept.:	
	H. Marquand	4 Aug 45
	H. Wilson	5 Mar 47
	A. Bottomley	7 Oct 47
	(for Junior Ministers see below)	

JUNIOR MINISTERS ATTACHED

P. & F.S.:		
	J. Dugdale	4 Aug 45
	J. Callaghan	2 Mar 50
Civil Ld:		
	W. Edwards	4 Aug 45
U-S.	J. Strachey	4 Aug 45
	G. de Freitas	27 May 46
	A. Crawley	2 Mar 50
	(for Junior Ministers see above)	

LABOUR GOVERNMENT, 1945–1951 (*contd.*)

MINISTERS NOT IN CABINET			JUNIOR MINISTERS ATTACHED		
Food	Sir B. Smith	3 Aug 45	P.S.	Edith Summerskill	4 Aug 45
	J. Strachey	27 May 46		S. Evans	2 Mar 50
	M. Webb	28 Feb 50		F. Willey	18 Apr 50
Fuel & P.	(*office in cabinet*)		P.S.	W. Foster	4 Aug 45
	H. Gaitskell	7 Oct 47		H. Gaitskell	10 May 46
	P. Noel-Baker	28 Feb 50		A. Robens	7 Oct 47
				H. Neal	26 Apr 51
Health	(*office in cabinet*)		(*for Junior Ministers see above*)		
	H. Marquand	17 Jan 51			
Information	E. Williams	4 Aug 45			
	(*office wound up 31 Mar 46*)				
D. Lanc.	J. Hynd	4 Aug 45			
	Ld Pakenham	17 Apr 47			
	(*H. Dalton 31 May 48 & office in cabinet*)				
Nat. Ins.	J. Griffiths	4 Aug 45	P.S.	G. Lindgren	4 Aug 45
	Edith Summerskill	28 Feb 50		T. Steele	4 Oct 46
				H. Taylor	2 Mar 50
Paym.-Gen.	(*office in cabinet*)				
	H. Marquand	5 Mar 47			
	(*Vt Addison 2 Jul 48 & office in cabinet*)				
	Ld Macdonald of Gwaenysgor	1 Apr 49			
Pensions	W. Paling	3 Aug 45	P.S.	Mrs J. Adamson	4 Aug 45
	J. Hynd	17 Apr 47		A. Blenkinsop	10 May 46
	G. Buchanan	7 Oct 47		C. Simmons	1 Feb 49
	H. Marquand	2 Jul 48			
	G. Isaacs	17 Jan 51			
Postm.-Gen.	E of Listowel	4 Aug 45	Ass.	W. Burke	10 Aug 45
	W. Paling	17 Apr 47		C. Hobson	7 Oct 47
	N. Edwards	28 Feb 50			
Supply	J. Wilmot	3 Aug 45	P.S.	W. Leonard ⎫ A. Woodburn ⎭	4 Aug 45
	G. Strauss	7 Oct 47		J. Freeman ⎫ J. Jones ⎭	7 Oct 47
				J. Freeman	2 Mar 50
				M. Stewart	2 May 51
T. & C. Planning	L. Silkin	4 Aug 45	(*for Junior Ministers see above*)		
	(*H. Dalton 28 Feb 50 & office in cabinet*)				
Transp.	A. Barnes	3 Aug 45	P.S.	G. Strauss	4 Aug 45
				J. Callaghan	7 Oct 47
				Ld Lucas of Chilworth	2 Mar 50
War O.	(*office in cabinet*)		U-S.	Ld Nathan	4 Aug 45
	F. Bellenger	4 Oct 46		Ld Pakenham	4 Oct 46–17 Apr 47
	E. Shinwell	7 Oct 47	F.S.	F. Bellenger	4 Aug 45
	J. Strachey	28 Feb 50		J. Freeman	4 Oct 46–17 Apr 47
			U. &	J. Freeman	17 Apr 47
			F.S.	M. Stewart	7 Oct 47
				W. Wyatt	2 May 51
Works	G. Tomlinson	4 Aug 45	P.S.	H. Wilson	4 Aug 45
	C. Key	10 Feb 47		E. Durbin	5 Mar 47
	R. Stokes	28 Feb 50		Ld Morrison	26 Sep 48
	G. Brown	26 Apr 51			
Law Officers:			*P.S. to Treasury:*		
Att.-Gen.	Sir H. Shawcross	4 Aug 45		W. Whiteley	3 Aug 45
	Sir F. Soskice	24 Apr 51	*Junior Lds of Treasury:*		
				R. Taylor	4 Aug 45–26 Oct 51
Sol.-Gen.	Sir F. Soskice	4 Aug 45		J. Henderson	4 Aug 45–1 Jan 50
	Sir L. Ungoed-Thomas	24 Apr 51		M. Stewart	10 Aug 45–30 Mar 46

LABOUR GOVERNMENT, 1945-1951 (contd.)

MINISTERS NOT IN CABINET			JUNIOR MINISTERS ATTACHED	
Law Officers:			A. Blenkinsop	10 Aug 45–10 May 46
Ld Advoc.	G. THOMSON	10 Aug 45 [1]	F. Collindridge	10 Aug 45–9 Dec 46
	J. WHEATLEY	7 Oct 47	C. Simmons	30 Mar 46–1 Feb 49
Sol.-Gen.	D. BLADES	10 Sep 45 [1]	W. Hannan	10 May 46–26 Oct 51
Scotland	J. WHEATLEY	19 Mar 47	J. Snow	9 Dec 46–3 Mar 50
	D. JOHNSTON	24 Oct 47	R. Adams	1 Feb 49–23 Apr 50
			W. Wilkins	1 Jan 50–26 Oct 51
			H. Bowden	3 Mar 50–26 Oct 51
			C. Royle	23 Apr 50–26 Oct 51
H.M. Household:			*Lds in Waiting:*	
Treas.	G. MATHERS	4 Aug 45	Ld Westwood	10 Sep 45–17 Jan 47
	A. PEARSON	30 Mar 46	Ld Pakenham	14 Oct 45–4 Oct 46
Comptr.	A. PEARSON	4 Aug 45	Ld Henderson	21 Oct 45–7 Jun 48
	M. STEWART	30 Mar 46	Ld Chorley	11 Oct 46–31 Mar 50
	F. COLLINDRIDGE	9 Dec 46	Ld Morrison	17 Jan 47–26 Sep 48
V. Chamb.	J. SNOW	10 Aug 45	Ld Lucas of Chilworth	
	M. STEWART	9 Dec 46		9 Jul 48–18 Oct 49
	E. POPPLEWELL	16 Oct 47	Ld Shepherd	14 Oct 48–6 Jul 49
Capt. Gents	LD AMMON	4 Aug 45	Ld Kershaw	6 Jul 49–26 Oct 51
at Arms	LD SHEPHERD	18 Oct 49	Ld Darwen	18 Oct 49–26 Dec 50
Capt.	LD WALKDEN	4 Aug 45	Ld Burden	31 Mar 50–26 Oct 51
Yeomen of	LD SHEPHERD	6 Jul 49	Ld Haden-Guest	
Guard	LD LUCAS OF CHILWORTH	18 Oct 49		13 Feb 51–26 Oct 51
	E OF LUCAN	5 Mar 50		
	LD ARCHIBALD	8 Jun 51		

CONSERVATIVE GOVERNMENT, 1951-1957

MINISTERS IN CABINET			JUNIOR MINISTERS ATTACHED	
P.M.	**(Sir) W. Churchill**			
		26 Oct 51–5 Apr 55		
	Sir A. Eden	6 Apr 55–9 Jan 57		
Ld. Pres.	**Ld Woolton**	28 Oct 51		
	M of Salisbury	24 Nov 52		
Ld Chanc.	**Ld Simonds**	30 Oct 51		
	Vt Kilmuir	18 Oct 54		
Privy S.	**M of Salisbury**	28 Oct 51		
	H. Crookshank	7 May 52		
	R. Butler	20 Dec 55		
Exch.	**R. Butler**	28 Oct 51	*Min. Econ. Affs.*	
	H. Macmillan	20 Dec 55	SIR A. SALTER	31 Oct 51
			(24 *Nov* 52 *office abolished*)	
			Treasury:	
			F.S. J. Boyd-Carpenter	31 Oct 51
			H. Brooke	28 July 54
			Econ. S.:	
			R. Maudling	24 Nov 52
			Sir E. Boyle	7 Apr 55
			D. Walker-Smith	11 Nov 56
For. O.	**(Sir) A. Eden**	28 Oct 51	*Min. of State*	
	H. Macmillan	7 Apr 55	S. LLOYD	30 Oct 51–18 Oct 54
	S. Lloyd	20 Dec 55	M OF READING	11 Nov 53–17 Jan 57
			A. NUTTING	18 Oct 54–3 Nov 56
			A. NOBLE	9 Nov 56–9 Jan 57
			U-S. M of Reading	31 Oct 51–11 Nov 53
			A. Nutting	31 Oct 51–18 Oct 54
			A. Dodds-Parker	11 Nov 53–9 Jan 57
			R. Turton	18 Oct 54–20 Dec 55

[1] Non-political appointments.

CONSERVATIVE GOVERNMENT, 1951–1957 (contd.)

MINISTERS IN CABINET

JUNIOR MINISTERS ATTACHED

	Ld J. Hope	18 Oct 54–9 Dec 56
	D. Ormsby-Gore	9 Nov 56–9 Jan 57

Home O. & **Sir D. Maxwell-Fyfe** 28 Oct 51
Welsh Affs. **(Vt Kilmuir)**
    G. Lloyd-George 18 Oct 54

U-S. D. Llewellyn 5 Nov 51–14 Oct 52
    Sir H. Lucas-Tooth
        3 Feb 52–20 Dec 55
    Ld Lloyd 24 Nov 52–18 Oct 54
    Ld Mancroft 18 Oct 54–9 Jan 57
    W. Deedes 20 Dec 55–9 Jan 57

Ag. & Fish. *(office not in cabinet)*
    Sir T. Dugdale 3 Sept 53
    D. Heathcoat Amory 28 Jul 54
    (18 Oct 54 Min. of Ag. & Fish)
    combined with Min. of Food)

P.S. Ld Carrington 5 Nov 51–18 Oct 54
    R. Nugent 5 Nov 51–9 Jan 57
    Earl St Aldwyn 18 Oct 54–9 Jan 57
    H. Nicholls 7 Apr 55–9 Jan 57

Col. O. **O. Lyttelton** 28 Oct 51
    A. Lennox-Boyd 28 Jul 54

Min. A. LENNOX-BOYD 2 Nov 51
    H. HOPKINSON 7 May 52
    J. HARE 20 Dec 55
    J. MACLAY 18 Oct 56

U-S. E of Munster 5 Nov 51
    Ld Lloyd 18 Nov 54

C.R.O. **Ld Ismay** 28 Oct 51
    M of Salisbury 12 Mar 52
    Vt Swinton 24 Nov 52
    E of Home 7 Apr 55

U-S. J. Foster 3 Nov 51
    A. Dodds-Parker 18 Oct 54
    A. Noble 20 Dec 55
    Ld J. Hope[1] 9 Nov 56

Co-ordina- **Ld Leathers** 30 Oct 51
tion of   *(3 Sep 53 office abolished)*
Transport,
Fuel & Power

Def. **W. Churchill (P.M.)** 28 Oct 51
    Earl Alexander 1 Mar 52
    H. Macmillan 18 Oct 54
    S. Lloyd 7 Apr 55
    Sir W. Monckton 20 Dec 55
    A. Head 18 Oct 56

P.S. N. Birch 28 Feb 52
    Ld Carrington 18 Oct 54
    E of Gosford 26 May 56

Educ. *(office not in cabinet)*
    Miss F. Horsbrugh 3 Sep 53
    Sir D. Eccles 18 Oct 54

P.S. K. Pickthorn 5 Nov 51
    D. Vosper 18 Oct 54

Food *(office not in cabinet)*
    G. Lloyd George 3 Sep 53
    D. Heathcoat Amory 18 Oct 54
    (& combined with Min. of
    Ag. & Fish.)

P.S. C. Hill 31 Oct 51

Health **H. Crookshank** 30 Oct 51
    (7 May 52 office not in cabinet)

P.S. Miss P. Hornsby-Smith 3 Nov 51

Housing & **H. Macmillan** 30 Oct 51
Loc. Govt. **D. Sandys** 18 Oct 54

P.S. E. Marples 3 Nov 51
    W. Deedes 18 Oct 54
    E. Powell 20 Dec. 55

Lab. & **Sir W. Monckton** 28 Oct 51
Nat. S. **I. Macleod** 20 Dec 55

P.S. Sir P. Bennett 31 Oct 51
    H. Watkinson 28 May 52
    R. Carr 20 Dec 55

D. Lanc. *(office not in cabinet)*
    Ld Woolton (Vt) 24 Nov 52
    (3 Sep 53–15 Jul 54 also
    Min. of Materials)
    E of Selkirk 20 Dec 55

Paym.-Gen. **Ld Cherwell** 30 Oct 51
    (11 Nov 53 E of Selkirk &
    office not in cabinet)
    Sir W. Monckton 18 Oct 56

Pensions & *(office not in cabinet)*
Nat. Ins. **O. Peake** 18 Oct 54
    (20 Dec 55 J. Boyd-Carpenter &
    office not in cabinet)

(for Junior Ministers see below)

---

[1] Not a member of the House of Lords.

CONSERVATIVE GOVERNMENT, 1951–1957 (contd.)

MINISTERS IN CABINET			JUNIOR MINISTERS ATTACHED		
Scot. O.	**J. Stuart**	30 Oct 51	Min.	E OF HOME	2 Nov 51
				T. GALBRAITH	7 Apr 55
				(Ld Strathclyde)	
			U-S.	T. Galbraith	2 Nov 51–5 Apr 55
				W. Snadden	2 Nov 51–13 Jun 55
				J. Henderson Stewart	
					4 Feb 52–9 Jan 57
				N. Macpherson	13 Jun 55–9 Jan 57
B.o.T	**P. Thorneycroft**	30 Oct 51	Min.	D. HEATHCOAT AMORY	3 Sep 53
				T. Low	28 Jul 54
			P.S.	H. Strauss	3 Nov 51
				D. Kaberry	7 Apr 55
				D. Walker-Smith	19 Oct 55
				F. Erroll	11 Nov 56
			Sec. Overseas Trade:		
				H. Hopkinson	3 Nov 51
				H. Mackeson	28 May 52
				(3 Sep 53 office abolished, Min.	
Works	(office not in cabinet)			of State established)	
	P. Buchan-Hepburn	20 Dec 55		(for Junior Ministers see below)	

MINISTERS NOT IN CABINET			JUNIOR MINISTERS ATTACHED		
Admir.	J. THOMAS	31 Oct 51	P. & F.S.:		
	(Vt Cilcennin)			A. Noble	5 Nov 51
	VT HAILSHAM	2 Sep 56		G. Ward	20 Dec 55
			Civil Ld:		
				S. Wingfield Digby	5 Nov 51
Ag. & Fish.	SIR T. DUGDALE	31 Oct 51		(for Junior Ministers see above)	
	(3 Sep 53 office in cabinet)				
Air	LD DE L'ISLE AND DUDLEY		U-S.	N. Birch	3 Nov 51
		31 Oct 51		G. Ward	29 Feb 52
	N. BIRCH	20 Dec 55		C. Soames	20 Dec 55
Educ.	MISS F. HORSBURGH	2 Nov 51		(for Junior Ministers see above)	
	(3 Sept office in cabinet)				
Food	G. LLOYD-GEORGE	31 Oct 51		(for Junior Ministers see above)	
	(3 Sep 53 office in cabinet)				
Fuel & P.	G. LLOYD	31 Oct 51	P.S.	L. Joynson-Hicks	5 Nov 51
	A. JONES	20 Dec 55		D. Renton	20 Dec 55
Health	(office in cabinet)			(for Junior Ministers see above)	
	I. MACLEOD	7 May 52			
D. Lanc.	VT SWINTON	21 Oct 51–24 Nov 52			
	(also Min. of Materials, 24 Nov 52, Ld Woolton became D. Lanc. & office in cabinet)				
Materials	VT SWINTON	31 Oct 51–24 Nov 52			
	(also D. Lanc.)				
	SIR A. SALTER	24 Nov 52–1 Sep 53			
	(1 Sep 53–15 Jul 54 Ld Woolton combined Materials with D. Lanc. in cabinet. 15 Jul 54 Min. of Materials wound up)				
Min. Without Portfolio	E OF MUNSTER 18 Oct 54–5 Apr 55				
Nat. Ins.	O. PEAKE	31 Oct 51	P.S.	R. Turton	5 Nov 51–3 Sep 53
	(3 Sep 53 combined with Min. of Pensions, see below)				
Paym.-Gen.	(office in cabinet)				
	E OF SELKIRK	11 Nov 53			
	(20 Dec 55 office vacant, Sir W. Monckton 18 Oct 56 & office in cabinet)				

CONSERVATIVE GOVERNMENT, 1951–1957 (*contd.*)

MINISTERS NOT IN CABINET			JUNIOR MINISTERS ATTACHED		
Pensions	D. HEATHCOAT AMORY	5 Nov 51	*P.S.*	J. Smyth	5 Nov 51–20 Dec 55
(& Nat.	(1 *Sep* 53 *combined Min. of*			R. Turton	3 Sep 53–18 Oct 54
Ins.)	*Pensions & National Insurance*)			E. Marples	18 Oct 54–20 Dec 55
	O. PEAKE	3 Sep 53		Miss E. Pitt	20 Dec 55–9 Jan 57
	(18 *Oct* 54 *office in cabinet*)			R. Wood	20 Dec 55–9 Jan 57
	J. BOYD-CARPENTER	20 Dec 55			
Postm.-Gen.	EARL DE LA WARR	5 Nov 51	*Ass.*	D. Gammans	5 Nov 51
	C. HILL	7 Apr 55		C. Alport	20 Dec 55
Power	(*see Fuel & Power above*)				
Supply	D. SANDYS	31 Oct 51	*P.S.*	T. Low	3 Nov 51
	S. LLOYD	18 Oct 54		Sir E. Boyle	28 Jul 54
	R. MAUDLING	7 Apr 55		F. Erroll	7 Apr 55
				I. Harvey	11 Nov 56
Transp. (&	J. MACLAY	31 Oct 51			
Civil Av.)	A. LENNOX-BOYD	7 May 52	*P.S.*	J. Gurney Braithwaite	
	(*Ministries of Transport & Civil*				5 Nov 51–1 Nov 53
	Aviation merged 1 *Oct* 53)			R. Maudling	18 Apr 52–24 Nov 52
	J. BOYD-CARPENTER	7 Apr 55		J. Profumo	24 Nov 52–5 Apr 55
	H. WATKINSON	20 Dec 55		H. Molson	11 Nov 53–5 Apr 55
War O.	A. HEAD	31 Oct 51	*U-S. & F.S.*		
	J. HARE	18 Oct 56		J. Hutchison	5 Nov 51
				F. Maclean	18 Oct 54
Works	(SIR) D ECCLES	1 Nov 51	*P.S.*	H. Molson	3 Nov 51
	N. BIRCH	18 Oct 54		J. Bevins	11 Nov 53
	(20 *Dec* 55 *P. Buchan-Hepburn*				
	& office in cabinet)				
Law Officers:			*P.S. to Treasury:*		
Att.-Gen.	SIR L. HEALD	3 Nov 51		P. Buchan-Hepburn	30 Oct 51
	SIR R. MANNINGHAM-BULLER			E. Heath	30 Dec 55
		18 Oct 54	*Junior Lds of Treasury:*		
Sol.-Gen.	SIR R. MANNINGHAM-BULLER			H. Mackeson	7 Nov 51–28 May 52
		3 Nov 51		(Sir) H. Butcher	7 Nov 51–3 Jul 53
	SIR H. HYLTON FOSTER	18 Oct 54		E. Heath	7 Nov 51–20 Dec 55
Ld Advoc.	J. CLYDE	2 Nov 51		T. Galbraith	7 Nov 51–4 Jun 54
	W. MILLIGAN	30 Dec 54		D. Vosper	7 Nov 51–18 Oct 54
Sol.-Gen.	W. MILLIGAN	3 Nov 51		H. Oakshott	28 May 52–13 June 55
Scotland	W. GRANT	10 Jan 55		M. Redmayne	3 Jul 53–14 Jun 55
				R. Thompson	28 Jul 54–8 Apr 56
				G. Wills	26 Oct 54–9 Jan 57
				P. Legh	13 Jun 55–9 Jan 57
				E. Wakefield	24 Jan 56–9 Jan 57
				H. Harrison	8 Apr 56–9 Jan 57
H.M. Household:			*Lds in Waiting:*		
Treas.	(SIR) C. DREWE	7 Nov 51		E of Birkenhead	5 Nov 51–28 Jan 55
	T. GALBRAITH	13 Jun 55		E of Selkirk	5 Nov 51–11 Nov 53
Comptr.	R. CONANT	7 Nov 51		Ld Lloyd	7 Nov 51–24 Nov 52
	T. GALBRAITH	7 Jun 54		Ld Mancroft	15 Dec 52–18 Oct 54
	H. OAKSHOTT	13 Jun 55		Ld Hawke	11 Nov 53–9 Jan 57
				Ld Fairfax	18 Oct 54–9 Jan 57
V. Chamb.	H. STUDHOLME	7 Nov 51		Ld Chesham	28 Jan 55–9 Jan 57
	R. THOMPSON	8 Apr 56			
Capt. Gents at Arms	EARL FORTESCUE	5 Nov 51			
Capt. Yeomen of Guard	E OF ONSLOW	5 Nov 51			

CONSERVATIVE GOVERNMENT, 1957–1964

MINISTERS IN CABINET		JUNIOR MINISTERS ATTACHED

P.M.	**H. Macmillan** 18 Jan 57–13 Oct 63	
	Sir A. Douglas-Home	
	(*formerly E of Home*)	
	18 Oct 63–16 Oct 64	
First Sec.	**R. Butler** 13 Jul 62	
of State	(*office wound up* 18 Oct 63)	
Ld Pres.	**M of Salisbury** Jan 57	
	E of Home 29 Mar 57	
	Vt Hailsham 17 Sep 57	
	E of Home 14 Oct 59	
	Vt Hailsham (*Q. Hogg*) 27 Jul 60	
	(*also Min. for Science*)	
Ld. Chanc.	**Vt Kilmuir** 14 Jan 57	
	Ld Dilhorne 13 Jul 62	
Privy S.	**R. Butler** 13 Jan 57	
	(*also Home Sec.*)	
	Vt Hailsham 14 Oct 59	
	(*also Min. for Science*)	
	E. Heath 27 Jul 60	
	S. Lloyd 20 Oct 63	

Exch.	**P. Thorneycroft** 13 Jan 57	*Treasury:*	
	D. Heathcoat Amory 6 Jan 58	*F.S.* E. Powell	16 Jan 57
	S. Lloyd 27 Jul 60	J. Simon	6 Jan 58
	R. Maudling 13 Jul 62	Sir E. Boyle	22 Oct 59
	(*see also Paymaster-General*)	A. Barber	16 Jul 62
		A. Green	23 Oct 63
		Econ. S.:	
		N. Birch	16 Jan 57
		(*vacant 6 Jan 58*)	
		F. Erroll	23 Oct 58
		A. Barber	22 Oct 59
		E. du Cann	16 Jul 62
		M. Macmillan	21 Oct 63
For. O.	**S. Lloyd** 14 Jan 57	*Min. of State:*	
	E of Home 27 Jul 60	A. Noble	Jan 57–16 Jan 59
	R. Butler 20 Oct 63	D. Ormsby-Gore	
		16 Jan 57–27 Jun 61	
		J. Profumo	16 Jan 59–27 Jul 60
		J. Godber	27 Jun 61–27 Jun 63
		E of Dundee	9 Oct 61–16 Oct 64
		P. Thomas	27 Jun 63–16 Oct 64
		U-S. E of Gosford	18 Jan 57–23 Oct 58
		I. Harvey	18 Jan 57–24 Nov 58
		J. Profumo	28 Nov 58–16 Jan 59
		M of Lansdowne	
		23 Oct 58–20 Apr 62	
		R. Allan	16 Jan 59–7 Oct 60
		J. Godber	28 Oct 60–27 Jan 61
		P. Thomas	27 Jun 61–27 Jun 63
		(*post left vacant*)	
		P. Smithers	16 Jul 62–29 Jan 64
		R. Mathew	30 Jan 64–16 Oct 64

CONSERVATIVE GOVERNMENT, 1957–1964 *(contd.)*

MINISTERS IN CABINET			JUNIOR MINISTERS ATTACHED		
Home O.	R. Butler	13 Jan 57	*Min. Home Affs.:*		
	H. Brooke	13 Jul 62		D. VOSPER	28 Oct 60
				D. RENTON	27 Jan 61
				LD JELLICOE	17 Jul 62
				LD DERWENT	21 Oct 63
			U-S.	P. Hornsby-Smith	
					18 Jan 57–22 Oct 59
				J. Simon	18 Jan 57–6 Jan 58
				D. Renton	17 Jan 58–27 Jun 61
				D. Vosper	22 Oct 59–28 Oct 60
				Ld Bathurst	8 Feb 61–16 Jul 62
				C. Fletcher-Cooke	
					27 Jun 61–27 Feb 63
				C. Woodhouse	16 Jul 62–16 Oct 64
				Miss M. Pike	1 Mar 63–16 Oct 66
Ag. Fish.	D. Heathcoat Amory	14 Jan 57	*P.S.*	Earl St Aldwyn	Jan 57–27 Jun 58
& Food	J. Hare	6 Jan 58		J. Godber	18 Jan 57–28 Oct 60
	C. Soames	27 Jul 60		Earl Waldegrave	27 Jan 58–16 Jul 62
				W. Vane	28 Oct 60–16 Jul 62
				Ld St. Oswald	16 Jul 62–16 Oct 64
				J. Scott-Hopkins	
					16 Jul 62–16 Oct 64
Aviation	*(see Transp. & Civil Av.)*		*(for Junior Ministers see below*		
	D. Sandys	14 Oct 59	*Transp. & Civil Aviation)*		
	P. Thorneycroft	27 Jul 60	*P.S.*	G. Rippon	22 Oct 59
	J. Amery	16 Jul 62		C. Woodhouse	9 Oct 61
				B. de Ferranti	16 Jul 62
				N. Marten	3 Dec 62
Col. O.	A. Lennox-Boyd	14 Jan 57	*Min.*	E OF PERTH	16 Jan 57
	I. Macleod	14 Oct 59		M OF LANSDOWNE	20 Apr 62
	R. Maudling	9 Oct 61		*(joint minister with C.R.O. 21 Oct 63)*		
	(joint minister with C.R.O. 13 Jul 62)		*U-S.*	J. Profumo	18 Jan 57
	D. Sandys	13 Jul 62		J. Amery	28 Nov 58
				H. Fraser	28 Oct 60
				N. Fisher	16 Jul 62–16 Oct 64
				R. Hornby	24 Oct 63–16 Oct 64
				(joint with C.R.O. 21 Oct 63)	
C.R.O.	E of Home	14 Jan 57	*Min.*	C. ALPORT	22 Oct 59–8 Feb 61
	D. Sandys	27 Jul 60		D OF DEVONSHIRE	
	(joint minister with Col. O 13 Jul 62)				6 Sep 62–16 Oct 64
				(joint with Col. O. 21 Oct 63)	
			U-S.	C. Alport	18 Jan 57
				R. Thompson	22 Oct 59
				D of Devonshire	
					28 Oct 60–6 Sep 62
				B. Braine	8 Feb 61–16 Jul 62
				J. Tilney	16 Jul 62–16 Oct 64
				(joint with Col. O. 21 Oct 63)	
Defence	D. Sandys	13 Jan 57	*P.S.*	Ld Mancroft	18 Jan 57
	H. Watkinson	14 Oct 59		*(11 Jun 57 office vacant)*	
	P. Thorneycroft	13 Jul 62		*(reorganisation 1 Apr 64)*	
			Ministers of State:		
			Air	H. FRASER	1 Apr 64
			Army	J. RAMSDEN	1 Apr 64
			Navy	LD JELLICOE	1 Apr 64
			U-S. Air	J. Ridsdale	1 Apr 64
			U-S. Army	P. Kirk	1 Apr 64
			U-S. Navy	J. Hay	1 Apr 64
Educ.	Vt Hailsham	13 Jun 57	*P.S.*	Sir E. Boyle	18 Jan 57
	G. Lloyd	17 Sep 57		K. Thompson	22 Oct 59

CONSERVATIVE GOVERNMENT, 1957–1964 (contd.)

MINISTERS IN CABINET			JUNIOR MINISTERS ATTACHED		
	Sir D. Eccles	14 Oct 59		C. Chataway	16 Jul 62
	Sir E. Boyle	13 Jul 62		*(reorganisation 1 Apr 64)*	
	(Educ. & Science 1 Apr 64)		*Ministers of State:*		
	Q. Hogg	1 Apr 64		*(Sir E. Boyle, and seat in cabinet)*	
	(formerly Vt Hailsham)				1 Apr 64
Min. of	Sir E. Boyle	1 Apr 64		LD NEWTON	11 Mar 64
State Educ.			P.S.	Ld Bessborough	1 Apr 64
				C. Chataway	1 Apr 64
Health	*(office not in cabinet)*			*(for Junior Ministers see below)*	
	E. Powell	13 Jul 62			
	A. Barber	20 Oct 63			
Housing,	H. Brooke	13 Jan 57	Min.	LD BRECON	12 Dec 57
Loc. Govt.	C. Hill	9 Oct 61	P.S.	J. Bevins	18 Jun 57
& Welsh	Sir K. Joseph	13 Jul 62		Sir K. Joseph	22 Oct 59–9 Oct 61
Affs.				Ld Jellicoe	27 Jun 61–16 Jul 62
				G. Rippon	9 Oct 61–16 Jul 62
				F. Corfield	16 Jul 62–16 Oct 64
				Ld Hastings	3 Dec 62–16 Oct 64
Lab. &	I. Macleod	14 Jan 57	P.S.	R Carr	19 Jan 57
Nat. S.	E. Heath	14 Oct 59		R. Wood	14 Apr 58
	(12 Nov 59—Min. of Labour)			P. Thomas	22 Oct 59
	J. Hare	27 Jul 60		A. Green	27 Jun 61
	J. Godber	20 Oct 63		W. Whitelaw	16 Jul 62
D. Lanc.	C. Hill	13 Jan 57			
	I. Macleod	9 Oct 61			
	Ld Blakenham *(J. Hare)* 20 Oct 63				
Paym.-Gen.	*(office not in cabinet)*				
	R. Maudling	17 Sep 57			
	Ld Mills	14 Oct 59			
	(after 9 Oct 61 Chief Sec. to				
	Treasury & Paymaster-General)				
	H. Brooke	9 Oct 61			
	J. Boyd-Carpenter	13 Jul 62			
Min.	*(office not in cabinet)*				
without	Ld Dundee	23 Oct 58–9 Oct 61			
Portfolio	Ld Mills	9 Oct 61–14 Jul 62			
	W. Deedes	13 Jul 62–16 Oct 64			
	Ld Carrington				
		20 Oct 63–16 Oct 64			
Power	Ld Mills	13 Jan 57	P.S.	D. Renton	18 Jan 57
	(14 Oct 59 R. Wood & office			Sir I. Horobin	17 Jan 58
	not in cabinet)			J. George	22 Oct 59
	F. Erroll	20 Oct 63		J. Peyton	25 Jun 62
Science	Vt Hailsham	14 Oct 59	P.S.	D. Freeth	8 Feb 61
	(1 Apr 64 Educ. & Science)			Ld Bessborough	24 Oct 63
				(1 Apr 64, Educ. & Science)	
Scot. O.	J. Maclay	13 Jan 57	Min.	LD STRATHCLYDE	17 Jan 57
	M. Noble	13 Jul 62		LD FORBES	23 Oct 58
				J. BROWNE	22 Oct 59
				(Ld Craigton)	
			U-S.	J. Browne	18 Jan 57–22 Oct 59
				N. Macpherson	19 Jan 57–28 Oct 60
				Ld J. Hope	18 Jan 57–22 Oct 59
				T. Galbraith	22 Oct 59–8 Nov 62
				G. Leburn	22 Oct 59–15 Aug 63
				R. Brooman-White	
					28 Oct 60–12 Dec 63
				Lady Tweedsmuir	
					3 Dec 62–16 Oct 64
				J. Stodart	19 Aug 63–16 Oct 64
				G. Campbell	12 Dec 63–16 Oct 64

CONSERVATIVE GOVERNMENT, 1957–1964 (contd.)

MINISTERS IN CABINET			JUNIOR MINISTERS ATTACHED		
B.o.T.	**Sir D. Eccles**	13 Jan 57	*Min.*	D. WALKER-SMITH	16 Jan 57
	R. Maudling	14 Oct 59		J. VAUGHAN-MORGAN	17 Sep 57
	F. Erroll	9 Oct 61		F. ERROLL	22 Oct 59
	E. Heath	20 Oct 63		SIR K. JOSEPH	9 Oct 61
	(also Sec. of State for Industry,			A. GREEN	16 Jul 62–23 Oct 63
	Trade & Regional Development)			LD DERWENT	6 Sep 62–23 Oct 63
				LD DRUMALBYN	23 Oct 63–16 Oct 64
				(formerly N. Macpherson)	
				E. DU CANN	21 Oct 63–16 Oct 64
			P.S.	J. Rodgers	24 Oct 58
				N. Macpherson	28 Oct 60
				D. Price	17 Jul 62
Transp. &	**H. Watkinson**	13 Jan 57	*P.S.*	R. Nugent	18 Jan 57–22 Oct 59
Civil Av.	*(14 Oct 59 Min of Transp. only)*			A. Neave	18 Jan 57–16 Jan 59
	E. Marples	14 Oct 59		J. Hay	16 Jan 59–3 May 63
	(see above, Min. of Aviation)			Ld Chesham	22 Oct 59–16 Oct 64
				J. Hughes-Hallett	
					26 April 61–16 Oct 64
				T. Galbraith	3 May 63–16 Oct 64
				(for Junior Ministers see below)	
Works	*(office not in cabinet)*				
	G. Rippon	20 Oct 63			
	(Min. of Public Building & Works)				

MINISTERS NOT IN CABINET			JUNIOR MINISTERS ATTACHED		
Admir.	E OF SELKIRK	16 Jan 57	*P. &*	C. Soames	18 Jan 57
	LD CARRINGTON	16 Oct 59	*F.S.*	R. Allan	17 Jan 58
	EARL JELLICOE	22 Oct 63		C. Orr Ewing	16 Jan 59
	(1 Apr 64, reorganised			*(16 Oct 59 office vacant)*	
	under Min. of Defence)				
			Civil Ld:		
				T. Galbraith	18 Jan 57
				C. Orr Ewing	16 Oct 59
				J. Hay	3 May 63
Air	G. WARD	16 Jan 57	*U-S.*	C. Orr Ewing	18 Jan 57
	J. AMERY	28 Oct 60		A. Neave	16 Jan 59
	H. FRASER	16 Jul 62		W. Taylor	16 Oct 59
	(1 Apr 64, reorganised			J. Ridsdale	16 Jul 62
	under Min of Defence)				
Health	D. VOSPER	16 Jan 57	*P.S.*	J. Vaughan-Morgan	18 Jan 57
	D. WALKER-SMITH	17 Sep 57		R. Thompson	17 Sep 57
	E. POWELL	27 Jul 60		Miss E. Pitt	22 Oct 59
	(13 Jul 62 E. Powell & office			B. Braine	16 Jul 62–16 Oct 64
	in cabinet)			Ld Newton	6 Sep 62–11 Mar 64
				M of Lothian	24 Mar 64–16 Oct 64
Paym.-Gen.	R. MAUDLING	16 Jan 57			
	(17 Sep 57 office in cabinet)				
Pensions &	J. BOYD-CARPENTER	Jan 57	*P.S.*	Miss E. Pitt	19 Jan 57–22 Oct 59
Nat. Ins.	N. MACPHERSON	16 Jul 62		R. Wood	19 Jan 57–14 Apr 58
	R. WOOD	21 Oct 63		W. Vane	14 Apr 58–28 Oct 60
				Miss P. Hornsby-Smith	
					22 Oct 59–31 Aug 61
				B. Braine	28 Oct 60–8 Feb 61
				R. Sharples	8 Feb 61–16 Jul 62
				Mrs M. Thatcher	
					9 Oct 61–16 Oct 64
				S. Maydon	16 Jul 62–16 Oct 64
Min.	E OF MUNSTER	Jan 57–11 Jun 57			
without	LD MANCROFT	11 Jun 57			
Portfolio	E OF DUNDEE	23 Oct 58			
	(9 Oct 61 Ld Mills & office in cabinet)				

CONSERVATIVE GOVERNMENT, 1957–1964 *(contd.)*

MINISTERS NOT IN CABINET			JUNIOR MINISTERS ATTACHED		

Postm.-Gen. E. MARPLES — 16 Jan 57
R. BEVINS — 22 Oct 59

Ass. K. Thompson — 18 Jan 57
Miss M. Pike — 22 Oct 59
R. Mawby — 1 Mar 63

Power *(office in cabinet)*
R. WOOD — 14 Oct 59
(20 Oct 63, F. Erroll & office in cabinet)

(for Junior Ministers see above)

Supply A. JONES — 16 Jan 57
(office wound up 22 Oct 59)

P.S. W. Taylor — 18 Jan 57
(office wound up 22 Oct 59)

*Technical
Cooperation* *(new dept.)*
D. VOSPER — 27 Jun 61
R. CARR — 9 May 63

War O. J. HARE — Jan 57
C. SOAMES — 6 Jan 58
J. PROFUMO — 27 Jul 60
J. GODBER — 27 Jun 63
J. RAMSDEN — 21 Oct 63
(1 Apr 64, reorganised under Min. of Defence)

U-S. & F.S.:
J. Amery — 18 Jan 57
H. Fraser — 28 Nov 58
J. Ramsden — 28 Oct 60
P. Kirk — 24 Oct 63

Works H. MOLSON — 16 Jan 57
LD J. HOPE — 22 Oct 59
(16 Jul 62, Min. of Public Building & Works)
G. RIPPON — 16 Jul 62
(20 Oct 63, G. Rippon & office in cabinet)

P.S. H. Nicholls — 18 Jan 57
R. Thompson — 28 Oct 60
R. Sharples — 16 Jul 62

Law officers:
Att.-Gen. SIR R. MANNINGHAM-BULLER
17 Jan 57
SIR J. HOBSON — 16 Jul 62

P.S. to Treasury:
E. Heath — 17 Jan 57
M. Redmayne — 14 Oct 59

Sol.-Gen. SIR H. HYLTON-FOSTER — 17 Jan 57
SIR J. SIMON — 22 Oct 59
SIR J. HOBSON — 8 Feb 62
SIR P. RAWLINSON — 19 Jul 62

Junior Lds of Treasury:
M. Redmayne — 21 Jan 57–14 Oct 59
P. Legh — 21 Jan 57–17 Sep 57
E. Wakefield — 21 Jan 57–23 Oct 58
H. Harrison — 21 Jan 57–16 Jan 59
A. Barber — 9 Apr 57–19 Feb 58
R. Brooman-White
28 Oct 57–21 Jan 60

Ld. Advoc.
W. MILLIGAN — 17 Jan 57
W. GRANT — 5 Apr 60
I. SHEARER — 12 Oct 62

P. Bryan — 19 Feb 58–9 Feb 61
M. Hughes-Young
23 Oct 58–6 Mar 62
G. Finlay — 16 Jan 59–28 Oct 60
D. Gibson-Watt
22 Oct 59–29 Nov 61
R. Chichester-Clark
21 Jun 60–29 Nov 61

*Sol.-Gen.
Scotland* W. GRANT — 17 Jan 57
D. ANDERSON — 11 May 60
N. WYLIE — 27 Apr 64

J. Hill — 28 Oct 60–16 Oct 64
W. Whitelaw — 6 Mar 61–16 Jul 62
J. Peel — 29 Nov 61–16 Oct 64
M. Noble — 29 Nov 61–13 Jul 62
F. Pearson — 6 Mar 62–19 Oct 63
G. Campbell — 6 Sep 62–12 Dec 63
M. Hamilton — 6 Sep 62–16 Oct 64
M. McLaren — 21 Nov 63–16 Oct 64
I. MacArthur — 12 Dec 63–16 Oct 64

H.M. Household:
Treas. H. OAKSHOTT — 19 Jan 57
P. LEGH (Ld Newton) — 16 Jan 59
E. WAKEFIELD — 21 Jun 60
M. HUGHES-YOUNG — 6 Sep 62

Lds in Waiting:
Ld Hawke — 21 Jan 57–11 Jun 57
Ld Fairfax — 21 Jan 57–21 Jun 57
Ld Chesham — 21 Jan 57–22 Oct 59
M of Lansdowne
11 Jun 57–23 Oct 58

CONSERVATIVE GOVERNMENT, 1957–1964 *(contd.)*

MINISTERS NOT IN CABINET			JUNIOR MINISTERS ATTACHED	
Comptr.	(SIR) G. WILLS	19 Jan 57	E of Gosford	23 Oct 58–22 Oct 59
	E. WAKEFIELD	23 Oct 58	Earl Bathurst	17 Sep 57–8 Feb 61
	H. HARRISON	16 Jan 59	Ld St Oswald	22 Oct 59–16 Jul 62
	R. CHICHESTER-CLARK	29 Nov 61	Ld Jellicoe	8 Feb 61–27 Jun 61
			Ld Denham	27 Jun 61–16 Oct 64
	R. THOMPSON	21 Jan 57	M of Lothian	6 Sep 62–23 Mar 64
V.	P. LEGH	17 Sep 57	Ld Hastings	6 Mar 61–3 Dec 62
	E. WAKEFIELD	16 Jan 59	Ld Ferrers	3 Dec 62–10 Oct 64
	R. BROOMAN-WHITE	21 Jun 60		
	G. FINLAY	28 Oct 60		
Capt. Gents	EARL FORTESCUE	21 Jan 57		
at Arms	EARL ST ALDWYN	27 Jun 58		
Capt.	E OF ONSLOW	21 Jan 57		
Yeomen of	LD NEWTON	28 Oct 60		
Guard	LD GOSCHEN	6 Sep 62		

LABOUR GOVERNMENT, 1964–

MINISTERS IN CABINET			JUNIOR MINISTERS ATTACHED	
P.M.	**H. Wilson**	16 Oct 64		
First Sec. of	**G. Brown**	16 Oct 64	*Min of State*	
State &	**M. Stewart**	11 Aug 66–16 Mar 68	A. CROSLAND	20 Oct 64
Min. of	*(offices separated Aug 67 with*		*(until 22 Dec 64 nominally Econ.*	
Econ. Affs.	*M. Stewart remaining First Sec.)*		*Sec. to Treas.)*	
	P. Shore	29 Aug 67	A. ALBU	27 Jan 65–7 Jan 67
			T. URWIN	6 Apr 68
			U-S. M. Foley	21 Oct 64–7 Jan 67
			W. Rodgers	21 Oct 64–7 Jan 67
			H. Lever	7 Jan 67–29 Aug 67
			P. Shore	7 Jan 67–29 Aug 67
			A. Williams	29 Aug 67–
			E. Dell	29 Aug 67–
First Sec. of	**Mrs B. Castle**	6 Apr 68	*P.S.* E. Fernyhough	6 Apr 68–
State &			R. Hattersley	6 Apr 68–
Min. of			H. Walker	6 Apr 68–
Emp. & Prod.				
Ld Pres.	**H. Bowden**	16 Oct 64		
	R. Crossman	11 Aug 66		
	F. Peart	18 Oct 68		
Ld Chanc.	**Ld Gardiner**	16 Oct 64		
Privy S.	**E of Longford**	18 Oct 64		
	Sir F. Soskice	23 Dec 65		
	E of Longford	6 Apr 66		
	Ld Shackleton	16 Jan 68		
	F. Peart	6 Apr 68		
	Ld Shackleton	18 Oct 68		
Exch.	**J. Callaghan**	16 Oct 64	*Treasury: Chief Sec.*	
	R. Jenkins	30 Nov 67	J. Diamond	20 Oct 64
Treasury: Chief Sec. (office not in cabinet)			*(1 Nov 68 office in cabinet)*	
	J. Diamond		*Min of State*	
			D. TAVERNE	6 Apr 68
			F.S. N. MacDermot	21 Oct 64
			H. Lever	29 Aug 64
			Econ. A. Crosland	19 Oct 67
			S. *(de facto Min. of State, Econ. Affs.*	
			Office abolished 22 Dec 64)	
For. O.	**P. Gordon Walker**	16 Oct 64	*Min. of State*	
(& Comm.	**M. Stewart**	22 Jan 65	LD CARADON	16 Oct 64–
O.)	**G. Brown**	11 Aug 66	G. THOMSON	19 Oct 64–6 Apr 66
	M. Stewart	16 Mar 68		7 Jan 67–29 Aug 67
	(merged with Comm. O. 17 Oct 68)		W. PADLEY	19 Oct 64–7 Jan 67

E

LABOUR GOVERNMENT, 1964 –   *(contd.)*

MINISTERS IN CABINET			JUNIOR MINISTERS ATTACHED		
				Lᴅ Chalfont	23 Oct 64–
				Mrs E. White	11 Apr. 66–7 Jan 67
				F. Mulley	7 Jan 67
				G. Roberts	29 Aug 67
				Lᴅ Shepherd	17 Oct 68
			U-S.	Lᴅ Walston	20 Oct 64
				W. Rodgers	7 Jan 67
Home O.	**Sir F. Soskice**	18 Oct 64	*Min. of State*		
				Miss A. Bacon	19 Oct 64
				Lᴅ Stonham	29 Aug 67
	R. Jenkins	23 Dec 65	*U-S.*	Lᴅ Stonham	20 Oct 64–29 Aug 67
	J. Callaghan	30 Nov 67		G. Thomas	20 Oct 64–6 Apr 66
				M. Foley	25 Jan 66–7 Jan 67
				D. Taverne	6 Apr 66–6 Apr 68
				D. Ennals	7 Jan 67–1 Nov 68
				E. Morgan	6 Apr 68–
				M. Rees	1 Nov 68–
Ag. Fish.	**F. Peart**	18 Oct 64	*P.S.*	J. Mackie	20 Oct 64
& Food	**C. Hughes**	6 Apr 68		J. Hoy	21 Oct 64
Col. O.	**A. Greenwood**	18 Oct 64	*U-S.*	Mrs E. White	20 Oct 64–11 Apr 66
	E of Longford	23 Dec 65		Lᴅ Taylor	20 Oct 64–11 Oct 65
	F. Lee	6 Apr 66		Lᴅ Beswick	11 Oct 65–1 Jul 66
	(came under Dept of Common-			*(Lᴅ Taylor & Lᴅ Beswick were*	
	wealth Affs. 1 *Jul* 66. *Office*			*also U-S. at C.R.O.)*	
	abolished 7 *Jan* 67)			J. Stonehouse	6 Apr 66–7 Jan 67
C.R.O.	**A. Bottomley**	18 Oct 64	*Min.*	C. Hughes	19 Oct 64–6 Apr 66
	(re-named Commonwealth		*of*	Mrs J. Hart	6 Apr 66–26 Jul 67
	Affairs 1 *Aug* 66)		*State*	G. Thomas	7 Jan 67–6 Apr 68
	H. Bowden	11 Aug 66		Lᴅ Shepherd	26 Jul 67
	G. Thomson	29 Aug 67			
	(merged with For. O. 17 *Oct* 68)		*U-S.*	Lᴅ Taylor	20 Oct 64
				Lᴅ Beswick	11 Oct 65
				(held jointly with U-S. at Col. O.	
				until 1 *Jul* 66)	
				W. Whitlock	26 Jul 67
Def.	**D. Healey**	16 Oct 64	*Min.*	F. Mulley	19 Oct 64
			Army	G. Reynolds	24 Dec 65
			& Dep.	*(no Dep. Sec. of State after*	
			Sec. of	24 *Dec* 65. *Office abolished*	
			State	7 *Jan* 67)	
			U-S.	G. Reynolds	20 Oct 64
			for	M. Rees	24 Dec 65
			Army	D. Ennals	6 Apr 66
				J. Boyden	7 Jan 67
			Min.	C. Mayhew	19 Oct 64
			for	J. Mallalieu	19 Feb 66
			Navy	*(office abolished* 7 *Jan* 67)	
			U-S.	J. Mallalieu	21 Oct 64
			for	Lᴅ Winterbottom	6 Apr 66
			Navy	M. Foley	7 Jan 67
				D. Owen	3 Jul 68
			Min.	Lᴅ Shackleton	19 Oct 64
			for Air Force	*(office abolished* 7 *Jan* 67)	
			U-S.	B. Millan	20 Oct 64
			for Air	M. Rees	6 Apr 66
			Force	Lᴅ Winterbottom	1 Nov 68
			Min.	G. Reynolds	7 Jan 67
			of State (Administration)		
			Min.	R. Mason	7 Jan 67
			of State (Equipment)		
				J. Morris	6 Apr 68

LABOUR GOVERNMENT, 1964 -   (contd.)

	MINISTERS IN CABINET		JUNIOR MINISTERS ATTACHED	
Educ. &	M. Stewart	18 Oct 64	*Min.*	LD BOWDEN 19 Oct 64–11 Oct 65
Science	A. Crosland	22 Jan 65	*of*	R. PRENTICE 20 Oct 64–7 Jan 67
	P. Gordon Walker	29 Aug 67	*State*	E. REDHEAD 11 Oct 65–7 Jan 67
				G. ROBERTS 6 Apr 66–29 Aug 67
				MRS S. WILLIAMS 7 Jan 67–
				MISS J. LEE 17 Feb 67–
				MISS A. BACON 29 Aug 67–
			U-S.	J. Boyden 20 Oct 64–24 Feb 65
				D. Howell 20 Oct 64–
				Miss J. Lee 24 Feb 65–17 Feb 67
Health &	R. Crossman	1 Nov 68	*Min.*	S. SWINGLER 1 Nov 68–19 Feb 69
Soc. Sec.			*of*	D. ENNALS 1 Nov 68–
			State	Lady Serota 25 Feb 69–
			P.S.	N. Pentland 1 Nov 68–
				C. Loughlin 1 Nov 68–20 Nov 68
				J. Snow 1 Nov 68–
Housing &	R. Crossman	18 Oct 64	*Min.*	F. WILLEY 17 Feb 67
Local Govt.	A. Greenwood	11 Aug 66	*of*	N. MACDERMOT 29 Aug 67–28 Sep 68
			State	
			Min.	K. ROBINSON 1 Nov 68
			for Planning and Land	
			P.S.	R. Mellish 18 Oct 64–29 Aug 67
				J. MacColl 20 Oct 64–
				Ld Kennet 6 Apr 66–
				A. Skeffington 17 Feb 67–
Labour	R. Gunter	18 Oct 64	*P.S.*	R. Marsh 20 Oct 64–11 Oct 65
	(*6 Apr 68 reorganised as Min. of Employment & Productivity*)			E. Thornton 21 Oct 64–6 Apr 66
				Mrs S. Williams 6 Apr 66–7 Jan 67
				E. Fernyhough 7 Jan 67–6 Apr 68
				R. Hattersley 7 Jan 67–6 Apr 68
				H. Walker 6 Apr 68–
D. Lanc.	D. Houghton	18 Oct 64		
	(*G. Thompson 6 Apr 66 & office not in cabinet*)			
Overseas	Mrs B. Castle	18 Oct 64	*P.S.*	A. Oram 21 Oct 64
Development	A. Greenwood	23 Dec 65		
	A. Bottomley	11 Aug 66		
	(*29 Aug 67 office not in cabinet*)			
Paym.-Gen.	(*office not in cabinet*)			
	Ld Shackleton	6 Apr 68		
	Mrs J. Hart	1 Nov 68		
Min. with-	D. Houghton	6 Apr 66		
out Portfolio	P. Gordon Walker	7 Jan 67		
	(*office wound up 29 Aug 67*)			
Power	F. Lee	18 Oct 64	*P.S.*	J. Morris 21 Oct 64
	R. Marsh	6 Apr 66		Ld Lindgren 10 Jan 66
	R. Gunter	6 Apr 68		J. Bray 6 Apr 66
	R. Mason	1 Jul 68		R. Freeson 7 Jan 67
Scot. O.	W. Ross	18 Oct 64	*Min. of State*	
				G. WILLIS 20 Oct 64
				D. MABON 7 Jan 67
			U-S.	Ld Hughes 21 Oct 64–
				Mrs J. Hart 20 Oct 64–6 Apr 66
				D. Mabon 21 Oct 64–7 Jan 67
				B. Millan 6 Apr 66–
				N. Buchan 7 Jan 67–
Tech.	F. Cousins	18 Oct 64	*Min. of State*	
	A. Wedgwood Benn	4 Jul 66		J. STONEHOUSE 15 Feb 67
				J. MALLALIEU 1 Jul 68
			P.S.	Ld Snow 19 Oct 64–6 Apr 66
				R. Marsh 11 Oct 65–6 Apr 66
				P. Shore 6 Apr 66–7 Jan 67
				E. Dell 6 Apr 66–29 Aug 67
				J. Bray 7 Jan 67–
				G. Fowler 29 Aug 67–

LABOUR GOVERNMENT, 1964 –   (contd.)

MINISTERS IN CABINET			JUNIOR MINISTERS ATTACHED		
B. of T.	**D. Jay**	18 Oct 64	Min. of State	G. DARLING	20 Oct 64–6 Apr 68
	A. Crosland	29 Aug 67		E. REDHEAD	20 Oct 64–11 Oct 65
				R. MASON	20 Oct 64–7 Jan 67
				LD BROWN	11 Oct 65–
				J. MALLALIEU	7 Jan 67–1 Jul 68
				E. DELL	6 Apr 68–
				W. RODGERS	1 Jul 68–
			P.S.	Ld Rhodes	20 Oct 64
				Ld Walston	7 Jan 67
				Mrs G. Dunwoody	29 Aug 67
Transport	**T. Fraser**	18 Oct 64	Min. of State	S. SWINGLER	29 Aug 67
	Mrs B. Castle	23 Dec 65	P.S.	Ld Lindgren	20 Oct 64–10 Jan 66
	R. Marsh	6 Apr 68		S. Swingler	20 Oct 64–29 Aug 67
				J. Morris	10 Jan 66–6 Apr 68
				N. Carmichael	29 Aug 67–
				R. C. Brown	6 Apr 68–
Wales	**J. Griffiths**	18 Oct 64	Min. of State	G. ROBERTS	20 Oct 64
	C. Hughes	6 Apr 66		G. THOMAS	6 Apr 66
	G. Thomas	6 Apr 68		MRS E. WHITE	7 Jan 67
			U-S.	H. Finch	21 Oct 64
				I. Davies	6 Apr 66

MINISTERS NOT IN CABINET			JUNIOR MINISTERS ATTACHED		
Aviation	R. JENKINS	18 Oct 64	P.S.	J. Stonehouse	20 Oct 64
	F. MULLEY	23 Dec 65		J. Snow	6 Apr 66
	J. STONEHOUSE	7 Jan 67			
	(office abolished 15 Feb 67)				
D. Lanc.	*(office in cabinet)*				
	G. THOMSON	6 Apr 66			
	F. LEE	7 Jan 67			
Health	K. ROBINSON	18 Oct 64	P.S.	Sir B. Stross	20 Oct 64
	(office abolished 1 Nov 68)			C. Loughlin	24 Feb 65
				J. Snow	7 Jan 67
Land & Nat. Res.	F. WILLEY	18 Oct 64	P.S.	Ld Mitchison	20 Oct 64–6 Apr 66
	(office wound up 17 Feb 67)			A. Skeffington	21 Oct 64–17 Feb 67
Overseas Dev.	*(office in cabinet)*				
	R. PRENTICE	29 Aug 67			
Paym.-Gen.	G. WIGG	19 Oct 64–12 Nov 67			
	(office vacant 12 Nov 67)				
	(Ld Shackleton 6 Apr 68 & office in cabinet)				
Pensions & Nat. Ins.	MISS M. HERBISON	18 Oct 64	P.S.	H. Davies	20 Oct 64–7 Jan 67
	(6 Aug 66 became Min. of Social Security)			N. Pentland	21 Oct 64–
Min. without Portfolio	E. FLETCHER	19 Oct 64–6 Apr 66			
	LD CHAMPION	21 Oct 64–7 Jan 67			
	LD SHACKLETON	7 Jan 67–16 Jan 68			
	G. THOMSON	17 Oct 68–			
Postm.-Gen.	A. WEDGWOOD BENN	19 Oct 64	Ass.	J. Slater	20 Oct 64
	E. SHORT	4 Jul 66			
	R. MASON	6 Apr 68			
	J. STONEHOUSE	1 Jul 68			
Public Building & Works	C. PANNELL	19 Oct 64	P.S.	Miss J. Lee	20 Oct 64
	R. PRENTICE	6 Apr 66		J. Boyden	24 Feb 65
	R. MELLISH	29 Aug 67		Ld Winterbottom	7 Jan 67
				C. Loughlin	20 Nov 68
Social Security	MISS M. HERBISON	6 Aug 66	P.S.	H. Davies	6 Nov 66–7 Jan 67
	MRS J. HART	26 Jul 67		N. Pentland	6 Aug 66–1 Nov 68
	(office abolished 1 Nov 68, see Health & Social Security)			C. Loughlin	7 Jan 67–1 Nov 68

(For continuation of this Government see Addenda on p. 308)

Ministerial Offices, 1900–

Admiralty. First Lord of the Admiralty, 1900–64

Agriculture. President of the Board of Agriculture, 1900–3; President of the Board of Agriculture and Fisheries, 1903–19; Minister of Agriculture and Fisheries, 1919–1955; Minister of Agriculture, Fisheries and Food, 1955– (see Food)

Air. President of the Air Board, 1917; President of the Air Council, 1917–1918; Secretary of State, 1918–64

Aircraft Production. Minister, 1940–1946

Attorney-General, 1900–

Attorney-General for Ireland, 1900–22

Aviation. Minister, 1959–67 (see Civil Aviation)

Blockade. Minister, 1916–19

Burma. Secretary of State for India and Burma, 1937–47

Civil Aviation. Minister, 1944–53; Minister of Transport and Civil Aviation, 1953–59; Minister of Aviation, 1959–67

Colonies. Secretary of State, 1900–67

Commonwealth. Secretary of State for Dominions 1925–47; Secretary of State for Commonwealth Relations 1947–66; Secretary of State for Commonwealth Affairs 1966–68

Co-ordination of Defence. Minister, 1936–40

Co-ordination of Transport, Fuel and Power. Secretary of State, 1951–53

Defence. Minister, 1940–64[1]; Secretary of State 1964–

Dominions. Secretary of State, 1925–47

Duchy of Lancaster. Chancellor, 1900–

Economic Affairs. Minister, Sep–Nov 1947, Feb–Oct 1950; Secretary of State 1964–

Economic Warfare. Minister, 1939–45

Education. President of the Board of Education, 1900–44; Minister of Education, 1944–64; Secretary of State for Education and Science 1964–

Employment and Productivity. Secretary of State, 1968–

First Secretary of State, 1962–63, 1964–

Foreign Affairs. Secretary of State, 1900–1968

Foreign and Commonwealth Affairs. Secretary of State, 1968–

Food. Minister, 1916–21, and 1939–55 (see Agriculture)

Fuel and Power. Minister, 1944–57; Minister of Power, 1957–

Fuel, Light and Power. Minister, 1942–4 (see Fuel and Power)

Health. Minister, 1919–68

Health and Social Security. Secretary of State, 1968–

Home Affairs. Secretary of State, 1900–

Home Security. Minister, 1939–45

Housing and Local Government. Minister of Town and Country Planning, 1943–51; Minister of Local Government and Planning, 1951; Minister of Housing and Local Government, 1951–

India. Secretary of State for India, 1900–37; Secretary of State for India and Burma, 1937–47

Information. Minister, Mar–Nov 1918 and 1939–46

Ireland. Chief Secretary to the Lord Lieutenant of Ireland, 1900–22 (*Irish Office wound up 1924*).

Labour. Minister of Labour, 1916–39; Minister of Labour and National Service, 1939–59; Minister of Labour, 1959–68

Land and Natural Resources. Minister, 1964–67

Local Government. President of the Local Government Board, 1900–19 (see Housing and Local Government)

Local Government and Planning. Minister, 1951 (see Housing and Local Government)

Lord Advocate, 1900–

Lord Chancellor, 1900–

Lord Chancellor of Ireland, 1900–22

Lord President of the Council, 1900–

Lord Privy Seal, 1900–

Materials. Minister, 1951–54

Mines. Secretary for Mines Department, 1920–42

Munitions. Minister, 1915–19 (see Supply)

National Insurance. Minister, 1944–53; Minister of Pensions and National Insurance, 1953–66

National Service. Minister, 1917–19; Minister of Labour and National Service, 1939–59

Overseas Development. Minister, 1964–

Overseas Trade. Secretary for Overseas Trade, 1917–53

Paymaster-General, 1900–

Pensions. Minister of Pensions, 1916–1953; Minister of Pensions and National Insurance, 1953–66

Petroleum. Secretary for Petroleum Department, 1940–42

Portfolio. Minister without portfolio, 1915–21, 1935–36, 1939–42, 1942–1944, 1946, 1947, 1954–68, 1968–

Post Office. Postmaster-General, 1900–

Power. Minister, 1957– (see Fuel and Power)

[1] From 1940 to 1946 the office was held by the Prime Minister. A permanent department for Defence was not established until 1946.

Prime Minister, 1900–
Production. Minister, 1942–45
Public Building and Works. Minister, 1962–
Reconstruction. Minister, 1917–19 and 1944–45
Science. Minister, 1959–64
Scotland. Secretary, 1900–26; Secretary of State, 1926–
Shipping. Minister, 1916–21 and 1939–1941 (see *War Transport*)
Social Insurance. Minister, Oct–Nov 1944 (see *National Insurance*)
Social Security. Minister, 1966–68
Solicitor-General, 1900–
Solicitor-General for Ireland, 1900–22
Solicitor-General for Scotland, 1900–
Supply. Minister, 1919–21 and 1939–1959
Technology. Minister, 1964–
Town and Country Planning. Minister of Town and Country Planning, 1943–51 (see *Local Government and Planning*)

Trade. President of the Board of Trade, 1900–
Transport. Minister of Transport, 1919–41; Minister of War Transport, 1941–46; Minister of Transport, 1946–53; Minister of Transport and Civil Aviation, 1953–59; Minister of Transport, 1959–
Treasury. Chancellor of the Exchequer, 1900–
Wales. Minister for Welsh Affairs, 1954–64; Secretary of State for Wales, 1964–
War. Secretary of State, 1900–64
War Transport. Minister, 1941–46 (see *Shipping* and *Transport*)
Works. First Commissioner of Works, 1900–40; Minister of Works and Buildings, 1940–42; Minister of Works and Planning, 1942–43; Minister of Works, 1943–62, Minister of Public Building and Works, 1962–

SOURCE.—For a full table of changes within the central administration between 1914–56 see *The Organisation of British Central Government, 1914–1956*, by D. N. Chester and F. M. G. Willson (1957), especially Appendix C, pp. 385–420.

Holders of Ministerial Offices

Prime Minister
1900   M of Salisbury (3rd)
12 Jul 02   A. Balfour
5 Dec 05   Sir H. Campbell-Bannerman
5 Apr 08   H. Asquith
6 Dec 16   D. Lloyd George
23 Oct 22   A. Bonar Law
22 May 23   S. Baldwin
22 Jan 24   J. R. MacDonald
4 Nov 24   S. Baldwin
5 Jun 29   J. R. MacDonald
7 Jun 35   S. Baldwin
28 May 37   N. Chamberlain
10 May 40   W. Churchill
26 Jul 45   C. Attlee
26 Oct 51   (Sir) W. Churchill
6 Apr 55   Sir A. Eden
10 Jan 57   H. MacMillan
18 Oct 63   Sir A. Douglas-Home
16 Oct 64   H. Wilson

Lord President of the Council
1900   D of Devonshire
13 Oct 03   M of Londonderry
10 Dec 05   E of Crewe
12 Apr 08   Ld Tweedmouth
13 Oct 08   Vt Wolverhampton
16 Jun 10   Earl Beauchamp
3 Nov 10   Vt Morley
5 Aug 14   Earl Beauchamp
25 May 15   M of Crewe

10 Dec 16   Earl Curzon
23 Oct 19   A. Balfour
24 Oct 22   M of Salisbury (4th)
22 Jan 24   Ld Parmoor
6 Nov 24   Marquess Curzon
27 Apr 25   E of Balfour
7 Jun 29   Ld Parmoor
25 Aug 31   S. Baldwin
7 Jun 35   J. R. MacDonald
28 May 37   Vt Halifax
9 Mar 38   Vt Hailsham (1st)
31 Oct 38   Vt Runciman
3 Sep 39   Earl Stanhope
11 May 40   N. Chamberlain
3 Oct 40   Sir J. Anderson
24 Sep 43   C. Attlee
25 May 45   Ld Woolton
27 Jul 45   H. Morrison
9 Mar 51   Vt Addison
28 Oct 51   Ld Woolton
24 Nov 52   M of Salisbury (5th)
29 Mar 57   E of Home
17 Sep 57   Vt Hailsham (2nd)
14 Oct 59   E of Home
27 Jul 60   Vt Hailsham (2nd)(Q.Hogg)
16 Oct 64   H. Bowden
11 Aug 66   R. Crossman
18 Oct 68   F. Peart

Lord Chancellor
1900   E of Halsbury
10 Dec 05   Ld Loreburn (E)
10 Jun 12   Vt Haldane
25 May 15   Ld Buckmaster

10 Dec 16   Ld Finlay
10 Jan 19   Ld Birkenhead (Vt)
24 Oct 22   Vt Cave
22 Jan 24   Vt Haldane
6 Nov 24   Vt Cave
28 Mar 28   Ld Hailsham (Vt)
7 Jun 29   Ld Sankey (Vt)
7 Jun 35   Vt Hailsham
9 Mar 38   Ld Maugham (Vt)
3 Sep 39   Vt Caldecote
12 May 40   Vt Simon
27 Jul 45   Ld Jowitt
30 Oct 51   Ld Simonds
18 Oct 54   Vt Kilmuir
13 Jul 62   Ld Dilhorne
16 Oct 64   Ld Gardiner

Lord Privy Seal
1900   Vt Cross
1 Nov 00   M of Salisbury (3rd)
12 Jul 02   A. Balfour
11 Oct 03   M of Salisbury (4th)
10 Dec 05   M of Ripon
9 Oct 08   E of Crewe
23 Oct 11   Earl Carrington
13 Feb 12   M of Crewe
25 May 15   Earl Curzon
15 Dec 16   E of Crawford
10 Jan 19   A. Bonar Law
23 Mar 21   A. Chamberlain
24 Oct 22   (*office vacant*)
25 May 23   Ld R. Cecil
22 Jan 24   J. Clynes

6 Nov 24	M of Salisbury (4th)	
7 Jun 29	J. Thomas	
5 Jun 30	V. Hartshorn	
24 Mar 31	T. Johnston	
3 Sep 31	Earl Peel	
5 Nov 31	Vt Snowden	
29 Sep 32	S. Baldwin	
31 Dec 33	A. Eden	
7 Jun 35	M of Londonderry	
22 Nov 35	Vt Halifax	
28 May 37	Earl De La Warr	
31 Oct 38	Sir J. Anderson	
3 Sep 39	Sir S. Hoare	
3 Apr 40	Sir K. Wood	
11 May 40	C. Attlee	
19 Feb 42	Sir S. Cripps	
22 Nov 42	Vt Cranborne (5th M of Salisbury)	
24 Sep 43	Ld Beaverbrook	
27 Jul 45	A. Greenwood	
17 Apr 47	Ld Inman	
7 Oct 47	Vt Addison	
9 Mar 51	E. Bevin	
26 Apr 51	R. Stokes	
28 Oct 51	M of Salisbury (5th)	
7 May 52	H. Crookshank	
20 Dec 55	R. Butler	
14 Oct 59	Vt Hailsham	
27 Jul 60	E. Heath	
20 Oct 63	S. Lloyd	
18 Oct 64	E of Longford	
23 Dec 65	Sir F. Soskice	
6 Apr 66	E of Longford	
16 Jan 68	Ld Shackleton	
6 Apr 68	F. Peart	
18 Oct 68	Ld Shackleton	

Secretary of State for Economic Affairs

16 Oct 64	G. Brown
11 Aug 66	M. Stewart
29 Aug 67	P. Shore

Chancellor of the Exchequer

1900	Sir M. Hicks-Beach
8 Aug 02	C. Ritchie
6 Oct 03	A. Chamberlain
10 Dec 05	H. Asquith
12 Apr 08	D. Lloyd George
25 May 15	R. McKenna
10 Dec 16	A. Bonar Law
10 Jan 19	A. Chamberlain
1 Apr 21	Sir R. Horne
24 Oct 22	S. Baldwin
27 Aug 23	N. Chamberlain
22 Jan 24	P. Snowden
6 Nov 24	W. Churchill
7 Jun 29	P. Snowden
5 Nov 31	N. Chamberlain
28 May 37	Sir J. Simon
12 May 40	Sir K. Wood
24 Sep 43	Sir J. Anderson
27 Jul 45	H. Dalton
13 Nov 47	Sir S. Cripps
19 Oct 50	H. Gaitskell

28 Oct 51	R. Butler
20 Dec 55	H. Macmillan
13 Jan 57	P. Thorneycroft
6 Jan 58	D. Heathcoat Amory
27 Jul 60	S. Lloyd
13 Jul 62	R. Maudling
16 Oct 64	J. Callaghan
30 Nov 67	R. Jenkins

Secretary of State for Foreign Affairs

1900	M of Salisbury (3rd)
1 Nov 00	M of Lansdowne
10 Dec 05	Sir E. Grey (Vt)
10 Dec 16	A. Balfour
23 Oct 19	Earl Curzon (M)
22 Jan 24	J. R. MacDonald
6 Nov 24	(Sir) A. Chamberlain
7 Jun 29	A. Henderson
25 Aug 31	M of Reading
5 Nov 31	Sir J. Simon
7 Jun 35	Sir S. Hoare
22 Dec 35	A. Eden
21 Feb 38	Vt Halifax
22 Dec 40	A. Eden
27 Jul 45	E. Bevin
9 Mar 51	H. Morrison
28 Oct 51	(Sir) A. Eden
7 Apr 55	H. Macmillan
20 Dec 55	S. Lloyd
27 Jul 60	E of Home
20 Oct 63	R. Butler
16 Oct 64	P. Gordon Walker
22 Jan 65	M. Stewart
11 Aug 66	G. Brown
16 Mar 68	M. Stewart

(Secretary of State for Foreign and Commonwealth Affairs)

17 Oct 68	M. Stewart

Secretary of State for the Home Department

1900	Sir M. White-Ridley
1 Nov 00	C. Ritchie
8 Aug 02	A. Akers-Douglas
10 Dec 05	H. Gladstone
14 Feb 10	W. Churchill
23 Oct 11	R. McKenna
25 May 15	Sir J. Simon
10 Jan 16	Sir H. Samuel
10 Dec 16	Sir G. Cave (Vt)
10 Jan 19	E. Shortt
24 Oct 22	W. Bridgeman
22 Jan 24	A. Henderson
6 Nov 24	Sir W. Joynson-Hicks
7 Jun 29	J. Clynes
25 Aug 31	Sir H. Samuel
28 Sep 32	Sir J. Gilmour
7 Jun 35	Sir J. Simon
28 May 37	Sir S. Hoare
3 Sep 39	Sir J. Anderson
3 Oct 40	H. Morrison

25 May 45	Sir D. Somervell
3 Aug 45	C. Ede
28 Oct 51	Sir D. Maxwell-Fyfe
18 Oct 54	G. Lloyd-George
13 Jan 57	R. Butler
13 Jul 62	H. Brooke
18 Oct 64	Sir F. Soskice
23 Dec 65	R. Jenkins
30 Nov 67	J. Callaghan

First Lord of the Admiralty

1900	G. Goschen
1 Nov 00	E of Selborne
5 Mar 05	Earl Cawdor
10 Dec 05	Ld Tweedmouth
12 Apr 08	R. McKenna
23 Oct 11	W. Churchill
25 May 15	A. Balfour
10 Dec 16	Sir E. Carson
17 Jul 17	Sir E. Geddes
10 Jan 19	W. Long
13 Feb 21	Ld Lee
24 Oct 22	L. Amery
22 Jan 24	Vt Chelmsford
6 Nov 24	W. Bridgeman
7 Jun 29	A. Alexander
25 Aug 31	Sir A. Chamberlain
5 Nov 31	Sir B. Eyres-Monsell (Vt Monsell)
5 Jun 36	Sir S. Hoare
28 May 37	A. Duff Cooper
27 Oct 38	Earl Stanhope
3 Sep 39	W. Churchill
11 May 40	A. Alexander
25 May 45	B. Bracken
3 Aug 45	A. Alexander
4 Oct 46	Vt Hall
24 May 51	Ld Pakenham
31 Oct 51	J. Thomas (Vt Cilcennin)
2 Sep 56	Vt Hailsham
16 Jan 57	E of Selkirk
16 Oct 59	Ld Carrington
22 Oct 63	Earl Jellicoe

(office abolished 1 *Apr* 64)

President of the Board of Agriculture and Fisheries

1900	W. Long
14 Nov 00	R. Hanbury
19 May 03	E of Onslow
12 Mar 05	A. Fellowes
10 Dec 05	Earl Carrington
23 Oct 11	W. Runciman
6 Aug 14	Ld Lucas
25 May 15	E of Selborne
11 Jul 16	E of Crawford
10 Dec 16	R. Prothero (Ld Ernle)

(Minister of Agriculture and Fisheries)
(and Food, since 18 *Oct* 54*)*

15 Aug 19	Ld Lee

13 Feb 21 Sir A. Griffith-
            Boscawen
24 Oct 22 Sir R. Sanders
22 Jan 24 N. Buxton
6 Nov 24 E. Wood
4 Nov 25 W. Guinness
7 Jun 29 N. Buxton
5 Jun 30 C. Addison
25 Aug 31 Sir J. Gilmour
28 Sep 32 W. Elliot
29 Oct 36 W. Morrison
29 Jan 39 Sir R. Dorman-
            Smith
14 May 40 R. Hudson
3 Aug 45 T. Williams
31 Oct 51 Sir T. Dugdale
28 Jul 54 D. Heathcoat
            Amory
6 Jan 58 J. Hare
27 Jul 60 C. Soames
18 Oct 64 F. Peart
6 Apr 68 C. Hughes

President of the Air Board

3 Jan 17 Ld Cowdray

**President of the
Air Council**

26 Nov 17 Ld Rothermere
26 Apr 18 Ld Weir

Secretary of State for Air

10 Jan 19 W. Churchill
1 Apr 21 F. Guest
31 Oct 22 Sir S. Hoare
22 Jan 24 Ld Thomson
6 Nov 24 Sir S. Hoare
7 Jun 29 Ld Thomson
14 Oct 30 Ld Amulree
5 Nov 31 M of London-
            derry
7 Jun 35 Sir P. Cunliffe-
            Lister
            (Vt Swinton)
16 May 38 Sir K. Wood
3 Apr 40 Sir S. Hoare
11 May 40 Sir A. Sinclair
25 May 45 H. Macmillan
3 Aug 45 Vt Stansgate
4 Oct 46 P. Noel-Baker
7 Oct 47 A. Henderson
31 Oct 51 Ld De L'Isle
20 Dec 55 N. Birch
16 Jan 57 G. Ward
28 Oct 60 J. Amery
16 Jul 62 H. Fraser
  (*office abolished* 1 *Apr* 64)

**Minister of Aircraft
Production**

14 May 40 Ld Beaverbrook
1 May 41 J. Moore-Braba-
            zon
22 Feb 42 J. Llewellin
22 Nov 42 Sir S. Cripps
25 May 45 E. Brown
  (*office abolished* 26 *Jul* 45)

Attorney-General

1900 Sir R. Webster
7 May 00 Sir R. Finlay
12 Dec 05 Sir J. Walton
28 Jan 08 Sir W. Robson
7 Oct 10 Sir R. Isaacs
19 Oct 13 Sir J. Simon
25 May 15 Sir E. Carson
3 Nov 15 Sir F. Smith
10 Jan 19 Sir G. Hewart
6 Mar 22 Sir E. Pollock
24 Oct 22 Sir D. Hogg
23 Jan 24 Sir P. Hastings
6 Nov 24 Sir D. Hogg
28 Mar 28 Sir T. Inskip
7 Jun 29 Sir W. Jowitt
26 Jan 32 Sir T. Inskip
18 Mar 36 Sir D. Somervell
25 May 45 Sir D. Maxwell
            Fyfe
4 Aug 45 Sir H. Shawcross
24 Apr 51 Sir F. Soskice
3 Nov 51 Sir L. Heald
18 Oct 54 Sir R. Manning-
            ham-Buller
16 Jul 62 Sir J. Hobson
1 Oct 64 Sir E. Jones

Minister of Blockade

10 Dec 16 Ld R. Cecil
18 Jul 18 Sir L. Worthing-
            ton-Evans
  (*office abolished* 10 *Jan* 19)

Minister of Civil Aviation

8 Oct 44 Vt Swinton
4 Aug 45 Ld Winster
4 Oct 46 Ld Nathan
31 May 48 Ld Pakenham
1 Jun 51 Ld Ogmore
31 Oct 51 J. Maclay
7 May 52 A. Lennox-Boyd

**(Minister of Transport
and Civil Aviation)**

1 Oct 53 A. Lennox-Boyd
28 Jul 54 J. Boyd-Car-
            penter
20 Dec 55 H. Watkinson

(Minister of Aviation)

14 Oct 59 D. Sandys
27 July 60 P. Thorneycroft
16 Jul 62 J. Amery
18 Oct 64 R. Jenkins
23 Dec 65 F. Mulley
7 Jan 67 J. Stonehouse
  (*office absorbed into Ministry
of Technology* 15 *Feb* 67)

**Secretary of State for
the Colonies**

1900 J. Chamberlain
6 Oct 03 A. Lyttelton
10 Dec 05 E of Elgin
12 Apr 08 E of Crewe
3 Nov 10 L. Harcourt
25 May 15 A. Bonar Law

10 Dec 16 W. Long
10 Jan 19 Vt Milner
13 Feb 21 W. Churchill
24 Oct 22 D of Devonshire
22 Jan 24 J. Thomas
6 Nov 24 L. Amery
7 Jun 29 Ld Passfield
25 Aug 31 J. Thomas
5 Nov 31 Sir P. Cunliffe-
            Lister
7 June 35 M. MacDonald
22 Nov 35 J. Thomas
28 May 36 W. Ormsby-Gore
16 May 38 M. MacDonald
12 May 40 Ld Lloyd
8 Feb 41 Ld Moyne
22 Feb 42 Vt Cranborne
22 Nov 42 O. Stanley
3 Aug 45 G. Hall
4 Oct 46 A. Creech Jones
28 Feb 50 J. Griffiths
28 Oct 51 O. Lyttelton
28 Jul 54 A. Lennox-Boyd
14 Oct 59 I. Macleod
9 Oct 61 R. Maudling
13 Jul 62 D. Sandys
18 Oct 64 A. Greenwood
23 Dec 65 E of Longford
6 Apr 66 F. Lee
  (*office came under Commonwealth Affairs* 1 *Jul* 66 *and
abolished* 6 *Jan* 67)

**Minister for Co-ordination
of Defence**

13 Mar 36 Sir T. Inskip
29 Jan 39 Ld Chatfield

(Minister of Defence)

10 May 40 W. Churchill
27 Jul 45 C. Attlee
20 Dec 46 A. Alexander
28 Feb 50 E. Shinwell
28 Oct 51 W. Churchill
1 Mar 52 Earl Alexander
18 Oct 54 H. Macmillan
7 Apr 55 S. Lloyd
20 Dec 55 Sir W. Monckton
18 Oct 56 A. Head
13 Jan 57 D. Sandys
14 Oct 59 H. Watkinson
13 Jul 62 P. Thorneycroft

(Secretary of State)

16 Oct 64 D. Healey

**Secretary of State for
Dominion Affairs**

11 Jun 25 L. Amery
7 Jun 29 Ld Passfield
5 Jun 30 J. Thomas
22 Nov 35 M. MacDonald
16 May 38 Ld Stanley
31 Oct 38 M. MacDonald
29 Jan 39 Sir T. Inskip
            (Vt Caldecote)
3 Sep 39 A. Eden
14 May 40 Vt Caldecote

3 Oct 40 Vt Cranborne
19 Feb 42 C. Attlee
24 Sep 43 Vt Cranborne
3 Aug 45 Vt Addison

(Secretary of State for Commonwealth Relations)

7 Jul 47 Vt Addison
7 Oct 47 P. Noel-Baker
28 Feb 50 P. Gordon Walker
28 Oct 51 Ld Ismay
12 Mar 52 M of Salisbury
24 Nov 52 Vt Swinton
7 Apr 55 E of Home
27 Jul 60 D. Sandys
18 Oct 64 A. Bottomley

(Secretary of State for Commonwealth Affairs)

1 Aug 66 A. Bottomley
11 Aug 66 H. Bowden
29 Aug 67 G. Thomson
(17 Oct 68 office merged with Foreign Office)

Minister of Economic Warfare

3 Sep 39 R. Cross
15 May 40 H. Dalton
22 Feb 42 Vt Wolmer (E of Selborne)
(office wound up 23 May 45)

President of the Board of Education

1900 D of Devonshire
8 Aug 02 M of Londonderry
10 Dec 05 A. Birrell
23 Jan 07 R. McKenna
12 Apr 08 W. Runciman
23 Oct 11 J. Pease
25 May 15 A. Henderson
18 Aug 16 M of Crewe
10 Dec 16 H. Fisher
24 Oct 22 E. Wood
22 Jan 24 C. Trevelyan
6 Nov 24 Ld E. Percy
7 Jun 29 Sir C. Trevelyan
2 Mar 31 H. Lees-Smith
25 Aug 31 Sir D. Maclean
15 Jun 32 Ld Irwin (Vt Halifax)
7 Jun 35 O. Stanley
28 May 37 Earl Stanhope
27 Oct 38 Earl De La Warr
3 Apr 40 H. Ramsbotham
20 Jul 41 R. Butler

(Minister of Education)

3 Aug 44 R. Butler
25 May 45 R. Law
3 Aug 45 Miss E. Wilkinson
10 Feb 47 G. Tomlinson
2 Nov 51 Miss F. Horsbrugh
18 Oct 54 Sir D. Eccles
13 Jan 57 Vt Hailsham (2nd)

17 Sep 57 G. Lloyd
14 Oct 59 Sir D. Eccles
13 Jul 62 Sir E. Boyle

(Secretary of State for Education and Science)

1 Apr 64 Q. Hogg
18 Oct 64 M. Stewart
22 Jan 65 A. Crosland
29 Aug 67 P. Gordon Walker

Minister of Food Control

10 Dec 16 Vt Devonport
19 Jun 17 Ld Rhondda (Vt)
9 Jul 18 J. Clynes
10 Jan 19 G. Roberts
19 Mar 20 C. McCurdy
(office abolished 31 Mar 21)

Minister of Food

4 Sep 39 W. Morrison
3 Apr 40 Ld Woolton
11 Nov 43 J. Llewellin
3 Aug 45 Sir B. Smith
27 May 46 J. Strachey
28 Feb 50 M. Webb
31 Oct 51 G. Lloyd-George
18 Oct 54 D. Heathcoat Amory
(and combined with Minister of Agriculture and Fisheries)

Minister of Fuel, Light and Power

3 Jun 42 G. Lloyd-George

(Minister of Fuel and Power)

25 May 45 G. Lloyd-George
3 Aug 45 E. Shinwell
7 Oct 47 H. Gaitskell
28 Feb 50 P. Noel-Baker
31 Oct 51 G. Lloyd
20 Dec 55 A. Jones

(Minister of Power)

13 Jan 57 Ld Mills
14 Oct 59 R. Wood
20 Oct 63 F. Erroll
18 Oct 64 F. Lee
6 Apr 66 R. Marsh
6 Apr 68 R. Gunter
6 Jul 68 R. Mason

Minister of Health

(see below, under Local Government)

Secretary of State for India (and Burma 1937-48)

1900 Ld G. Hamilton
6 Oct 03 St J. Brodrick
10 Dec 05 J. Morley (Vt)
3 Nov 10 E of Crewe
7 Mar 11 Vt Morley
25 May 11 E of Crewe (M)
25 May 15 A. Chamberlain
17 Jul 17 E. Montagu
19 Mar 22 Vt Peel
22 Jan 24 Ld Olivier
6 Nov 24 E of Birkenhead

18 Oct 28 Vt Peel
7 Jun 29 W. Benn
25 Aug 31 Sir S. Hoare
7 Jun 35 M of Zetland
13 May 40 L. Amery
3 Aug 45 Ld Pethick-Lawrence
17 Apr 47 E of Listowel
(4 Jan 1948 India & Burma Offices wound up)

Minister of Information

10 Feb 18 Ld Beaverbrook
4 Nov 18 Ld Downham
(office abolished 10 Jan 19)
4 Sep 39 Ld Macmillan
5 Jan 40 Sir J. Reith
12 May 40 A. Duff Cooper
20 Jul 41 B. Bracken
25 May 45 G. Lloyd
4 Aug 45 E. Williams
(office abolished 31 Mar 46)

Chief Secretary for Ireland

1900 G. Balfour
7 Nov 00 G. Wyndham
12 Mar 05 W. Long
10 Dec 05 J. Bryce
23 Jan 07 A. Birrell
31 Jul 16 (Sir) H. Duke
5 May 18 E. Shortt
10 Jan 19 I. Macpherson
2 Apr 20 Sir H. Greenwood
(Irish Office wound up 1922)

Minister of Labour

10 Dec 16 J. Hodge
17 Aug 17 G. Roberts
10 Jan 19 Sir R. Horne
19 Mar 20 T. Macnamara
31 Oct 22 Sir A. Montague-Barlow
22 Jan 24 T. Shaw
6 Nov 24 Sir A. Steel-Maitland
7 Jun 29 Miss M. Bondfield
25 Aug 31 Sir H. Betterton
29 Jun 34 O. Stanley
7 Jun 35 E. Brown

(Minister of Labour and National Service)

3 Sep 39 E. Brown
13 May 40 E. Bevin
25 May 45 R. Butler
3 Aug 45 G. Isaacs
17 Jan 51 A. Bevan
24 Apr 51 A. Robens
28 Oct 51 Sir W. Monckton
20 Dec 55 I. Macleod
14 Oct 59 E. Heath

(Minister of Labour)

12 Nov 59 E. Heath
27 Jul 60 J. Hare
20 Oct 63 J. Godber
18 Oct 64 R. Gunter

Secretary of State for Employment and Productivity

6 Apr 68   Mrs B. Castle

Chancellor of the Duchy of Lancaster

1900		Ld James
8 Aug	02	Sir W. Walrond
10 Dec	05	Sir H. Fowler (Vt Wolverhampton)
13 Oct	08	Ld Fitzmaurice
25 Jun	09	H. Samuel
14 Feb	10	J. Pease
23 Oct	11	C. Hobhouse
11 Feb	14	C. Masterman
3 Feb	15	E. Montagu
25 May	15	W. Churchill
25 Nov	15	H. Samuel
11 Jan	16	E. Montagu
9 Jul	16	T. McKinnon Wood
10 Dec	16	Sir F. Cawley
10 Feb	18	Ld Beaverbrook
4 Nov	18	Ld Downham
10 Jan	19	E of Crawford
1 Apr	21	Vt Peel
7 Apr	22	Sir W. Sutherland
24 Oct	22	M of Salisbury
25 May	23	J. Davidson
22 Jan	24	J. Wedgwood
10 Nov	24	Vt Cecil
19 Oct	27	Ld Cushendun
7 Jun	29	Sir O. Mosley
23 May	30	C. Attlee
13 May	31	Ld Ponsonby
25 Aug	31	M of Lothian
10 Nov	31	(Sir) J. Davidson
28 May	37	Earl Winterton
29 Jan	39	W. Morrison
3 Apr	40	G. Tryon
14 May	40	Ld Hankey
20 Jul	41	A. Duff Cooper
11 Nov	43	E. Brown
25 May	45	Sir A. Salter
4 Aug	45	J. Hynd
27 Apr	47	Ld Pakenham
11 May	48	H. Dalton
38 Feb	50	Vt Alexander
31 Oct	51	Vt Swinton
24 Nov	52	Ld Woolton
20 Dec	55	E of Selkirk
13 Jan	57	C. Hill
9 Oct	61	I. Macleod
20 Oct	63	Ld Blakenham
18 Oct	64	D. Houghton
6 Apr	66	G. Thomson
7 Jan	67	F. Lee

President of the Local Government Board

1900		H. Chaplin
7 Nov	00	W. Long
12 Mar	05	G. Balfour
10 Dec	05	J. Burns
11 Feb	14	H. Samuel

25 May	15	W. Long
10 Dec	16	Ld Rhondda
28 Jun	17	W. Hayes Fisher
4 Nov	18	Sir A. Geddes
10 Jan	19	C. Addison

(24 *Jun* 19 *the Local Government Board became the Ministry of Health*)

Minister of Health

24 Jun	19	C. Addison
1 Apr	21	Sir A. Mond
24 Oct	22	Sir A. Griffith Boscawen
7 Mar	23	N. Chamberlain
27 Aug	23	Sir W. Joynson-Hicks
22 Jan	24	J. Wheatley
6 Nov	24	N. Chamberlain
7 Jun	29	A. Greenwood
25 Aug	31	N. Chamberlain
5 Nov	31	Sir E. Young
7 Jun	35	Sir K. Wood
16 May	38	W. Elliot
13 May	40	M. MacDonald
8 Feb	41	E. Brown
11 Nov	43	H. Willink
3 Aug	45	A. Bevan
17 Jan	51	H. Marquand
30 Oct	51	H. Crookshank
7 May	52	I. Macleod
20 Dec	55	R. Turton
16 Jan	57	D. Vosper
17 Sep	57	D. Walker-Smith
27 Jul	60	E. Powell
20 Oct	63	A. Barber
18 Oct	64	K. Robinson

(1 *Nov* 68 *combined with Ministry of Social Security. See Social Services*)

Minister of Land and Natural Resources

17 Oct 64   F. Willey
(17 *Feb* 67 *office wound up*)

Minister of Local Government and Planning

31 Jan 51   H. Dalton

(Minister of Housing and Local Government)

30 Oct	51	H. Macmillan
18 Oct	54	D. Sandys
13 Jan	57	H. Brooke
9 Oct	61	C. Hill
13 Jul	62	Sir K. Joseph
18 Oct	64	R. Crossman
11 Aug	66	A. Greenwood

Minister of Materials

6 Jul	51	R. Stokes
31 Oct	51	Vt Swinton
24 Nov	52	Sir A. Salter
1 Sep	53	Ld Woolton

(15 *Jul* 54 *office wound up*)

Minister of Munitions

25 May 15   D. Lloyd George

9 Jul	16	E. Montagu
10 Dec	16	C. Addison
17 Jul	17	W. Churchill
10 Jan	19	Ld Inverforth

(*and Minister designate for Ministry of Supply. Office abolished* 21 *Mar* 21)

Minister of Overseas Development

18 Oct	64	Mrs B. Castle
23 Dec	65	A. Greenwood
11 Aug	66	A. Bottomley
29 Aug	67	R. Prentice

Paymaster-General

1900		D of Marlborough
11 Mar	02	Sir S. Crossley
12 Dec	05	R. Causton (Ld Southwark)
23 Feb	10	I. Guest (Ld Ashby St Ledgers)
23 May	12	Ld Strachie
9 Jun	15	Ld Newton
18 Aug	16	A. Henderson
15 Dec	16	Sir J. Compton-Rickett
26 Oct	19	Sir T. Walters
24 Oct	22	(*office vacant*)
5 Feb	23	N. Chamberlain
15 Mar	23	Sir W. Joynson-Hicks
25 May	23	A. Boyd-Carpenter
6 May	24	H. Gosling
6 Nov	24	(*office vacant*)
28 Jul	25	D of Sutherland
2 Dec	28	E of Onslow
7 Jun	29	Ld Arnold
4 Sep	31	Sir T. Walters
23 Nov	31	Ld Rochester
6 Dec	35	Ld Hutchison
2 Jun	38	E of Munster
29 Jan	39	Earl Winterton
	Nov 39	(*office vacant*)
15 May	40	Vt Cranborne
3 Oct	40	(*office vacant*)
20 Jul	41	Ld Hankey
4 Mar	42	Sir W. Jowitt
30 Dec	42	Ld Cherwell
3 Aug	45	(*office vacant*)
9 Jul	46	A. Greenwood
5 Mar	47	H. Marquand
2 Jul	48	Vt Addison
1 Apr	49	Ld Macdonald
30 Oct	51	Ld Cherwell
11 Nov	53	E of Selkirk
20 Dec	55	(*office vacant*)
18 Oct	56	Sir W. Monckton
16 Jan	57	R. Maudling
14 Oct	59	Ld Mills
9 Oct	61	H. Brooke
13 Jul	62	J. Boyd-Carpenter
19 Oct	64	G. Wigg
6 Apr	68	Ld Shackleton
1 Nov	68	Mrs J. Hart

Minister of Pensions

10 Dec 16   G. Barnes

17 Aug 17   J. Hodge
10 Jan 19   Sir L. Worthing-
           ton-Evans
2 Apr 20   I. Macpherson
31 Oct 22   G. Tryon
23 Jan 24   F. Roberts
11 Nov 24   G. Tryon
7 Jun 29   F. Roberts
3 Sep 31   G. Tryon
18 Jun 35   R. Hudson
30 Jul 36   H. Ramsbotham
7 Jun 39   Sir W. Womersley
3 Aug 45   W. Paling
17 Apr 47   J. Hynd
7 Oct 47   G. Buchanan
2 Jul 48   H. Marquand
17 Jan 51   G. Isaacs
5 Nov 51   D. Heathcoat
           Amory

(Minister of Pensions and National Insurance)

3 Sep 53   O. Peake
20 Dec 55   J. Boyd-Carpen-
           ter
16 Jul 62   N. Macpherson
21 Oct 63   R. Wood
18 Oct 64   Miss M. Herbi-
           son

(*6 Aug 66 recast as Social Security*)

Minister of Social Insurance

8 Oct 44   Sir W. Jowitt

(Minister of National Insurance)

17 Nov 44   Sir W. Jowitt
25 May 45   L. Hore-Belisha
4 Aug 45   J. Griffiths
28 Feb 50   Edith Summer-
           skill
31 Oct 51   O. Peake
(*3 Sep 53 combined with Ministry of Pensions*)

Minister without Portfolio

25 May 15–5 Dec 16
   M of Lansdowne
10 Dec 16–12 Aug 17
   A. Henderson
10 Dec 16–18 Apr 18
   Vt Milner
17 Jul 17–21 Jan 18
   Sir E. Carson
29 May 17–27 Jan 20
   G. Barnes
22 Jun 17–10 Jan 19
   J. Smuts
18 Apr 18–10 Jan 19
   A. Chamberlain
2 Apr 20–13 Feb 21
   Sir L. Worthington-Evans
1 Apr 21–14 Jul 21
   C. Addison
10 Jan 19–19 May 19
   Sir E. Geddes
7 Jun 35–22 Dec 35
   A. Eden

7 Jun 35–31 Mar 36
   Ld E. Percy
21 Apr 39–14 Jul 39
   L. Burgin
3 Sep 39–10 May 40
   Ld Hankey
11 May 40–22 Feb 42
   A. Greenwood
30 Dec 42–8 Oct 44
   Sir W. Jowitt
4 Oct 46–20 Dec 46
   A. Alexander
17 Apr 47–29 Sep 47
   A. Greenwood
18 Oct 54–11 Jun 57
   E of Munster
11 Jun 57–23 Oct 58
   Ld Mancroft
23 Oct 58–9 Oct 61
   E of Dundee
9 Oct 61–14 Jul 62
   Ld Mills
13 Jul 62–16 Oct 64
   W. Deedes
20 Oct 63–16 Oct 64
   Ld Carrington
19 Oct 64–6 Apr 66
   E. Fletcher
21 Oct 64–7 Jan 66
   Ld Champion
7 Jan 66–29 Aug 67
   P. Gordon Walker
7 Jan 66–16 Jan 68
   Ld Shackleton
17 Oct 68–
   G. Thomson

Postmaster-General

1900   D of Norfolk
2 Apr 00   M of London-
           derry
8 Aug 02   A. Chamberlain
6 Oct 03   Ld Stanley
10 Dec 05   S. Buxton
14 Feb 10   H. Samuel
11 Feb 14   C. Hobhouse
26 May 15   H. Samuel
18 Jan 16   J. Pease
10 Dec 16   A. Illingworth
1 Apr 21   F. Kellaway
31 Oct 22   N. Chamberlain
7 Mar 23   Sir W. Joynson-
           Hicks
28 May 23   Sir L. Worthing-
           ton-Evans
22 Jan 24   V. Hartshorn
11 Nov 24   Sir W. Mitchell-
           Thomson
7 Jun 29   H. Lees-Smith
2 Mar 31   C. Attlee
3 Sep 31   W. Ormsby-Gore
10 Nov 31   Sir K. Wood
7 Jun 35   G. Tryon
3 Apr 40   W. Morrison
30 Dec 42   H. Crookshank
4 Aug 45   E of Listowel
17 Apr 47   W. Paling
28 Feb 50   N. Edwards
5 Nov 51   Earl De La Warr

7 Apr 55   C. Hill
16 Jan 57   E. Marples
22 Oct 59   J. Bevins
19 Oct 64   A. Wedgwood
           Benn
4 Jul 66   E. Short
6 Apr 68   R. Mason
1 Jul 68   J. Stonehouse

Minister of Public Building and Works

16 Jul 62   G. Rippon
18 Oct 64   C. Pannell
6 Apr 66   R. Prentice
29 Aug 67   R. Mellish

Minister of Reconstruction

17 Jul 17–10 Jan 19
   C. Addison
11 Nov 43–23 May 45
   Ld Woolton

Minister for Science

14 Oct 59   Vt Hailsham
(*1 Apr 64 combined with Dept. of Education*)

Secretary for Scotland

1900   Ld Balfour
6 Oct 03   A. Murray
2 Feb 05   M of Linlithgow
10 Dec 05   J. Sinclair (Ld
           Pentland)
13 Feb 12   T. Wood
9 Jul 16   H. Tennant
10 Dec 16   R. Munro
24 Oct 22   Vt Novar
22 Jan 24   W. Adamson
6 Nov 24   Sir J. Gilmour

(Secretary of State for Scotland)

15 Jul 26   Sir J. Gilmour
7 Jun 29   W. Adamson
25 Aug 31   Sir A. Sinclair
28 Sep 32   Sir G. Collins
29 Oct 36   W. Elliot
16 May 38   J. Colville
14 May 40   E. Brown
8 Feb 41   T. Johnston
25 May 45   Ld Rosebery
3 Aug 45   J. Westwood
7 Oct 47   A. Woodburn
28 Feb 50   H. McNeil
30 Oct 51   J. Stuart
13 Jan 57   J. Maclay
13 Jul 62   M. Noble
18 Oct 64   W. Ross

Minister of Shipping

10 Dec 16   Sir J. Maclay (Ld)
(*office abolished 31 Mar 21*)
13 Oct 39   Sir J. Gilmour
3 Apr 40   R. Hudson
14 May 40   R. Cross
(*1 May 41 combined with Ministry of Transport to form Ministry of War Transport*)

Minister of Social Security

6 Aug 66   Miss M. Herbison

26 Jul 67 Mrs J. Hart

(Secretary of State for Social Services)

17 Oct 68 R. Crossman

Minister of Supply

14 Jul 39 L. Burgin
12 May 40 H. Morrison
3 Oct 40 Sir A. Duncan
29 Jun 41 Ld Beaverbrook
4 Feb 42 Sir A. Duncan
3 Aug 45 J. Wilmot
7 Oct 47 G. Strauss
31 Oct 51 D. Sandys
18 Oct 54 S. Lloyd
7 Apr 55 R. Maudling
16 Jan 57 A. Jones
(office wound up 22 Oct 59)

Ministry of Technology

18 Oct 64 F. Cousins
4 Jul 66 A. Wedgwood Benn

Minister of Town and Country Planning

30 Dec 42 W. Morrison
4 Aug 45 L. Silkin
28 Feb 50 H. Dalton
(recast as Local Government and Planning 31 Jan 51)

President of the Board of Trade

1900 C. Ritchie
7 Nov 00 G. Balfour
12 Mar 05 M of Salisbury
10 Dec 05 D. Lloyd George
12 Apr 08 W. Churchill
14 Feb 10 S. Buxton
11 Feb 14 J. Burns
5 Aug 14 W. Runciman
10 Dec 16 Sir A. Stanley
26 May 19 Sir A. Geddes
19 Mar 20 Sir R. Horne
1 Apr 21 S. Baldwin
24 Oct 22 Sir P. Lloyd-Greame
22 Jan 24 S. Webb
6 Nov 24 Sir P. Lloyd-Greame (changed name to Cunliffe-Lister 27 Nov 24)
7 Jun 29 W. Graham
25 Aug 31 Sir P. Cunliffe-Lister
5 Nov 31 W. Runciman (Ld)
28 May 37 O. Stanley
5 Jan 40 Sir A. Duncan
3 Oct 40 O. Lyttelton
29 Jun 41 Sir A. Duncan
4 Feb 42 J. Llewellin
22 Feb 42 H. Dalton
25 May 45 O. Lyttelton
27 Jul 45 Sir S. Cripps
29 Sep 47 H. Wilson
24 Apr 51 Sir H. Shawcross
30 Oct 51 P. Thorneycroft
13 Jan 57 Sir D. Eccles
14 Oct 59 R. Maudling
9 Oct 61 F. Erroll

20 Oct 63 E. Heath
18 Oct 64 D. Jay
29 Aug 67 A. Crosland

Minister of Transport

17 Aug 19 Sir E. Geddes
7 Nov 21 Vt Peel
12 Apr 22 E of Crawford
31 Oct 22 Sir J. Baird
24 Jan 24 H. Gosling
11 Nov 24 W. Ashley
7 Jun 29 H. Morrison
3 Sep 31 J. Pybus
22 Feb 33 O. Stanley
29 Jun 34 L. Hore-Belisha
28 May 37 L. Burgin
21 Apr 39 E. Wallace
14 May 40 Sir J. Reith
3 Oct 40 J. Moore-Brabazon

(Minister of War Transport)

1 May 41 Ld Leathers

(Minister of Transport)

3 Aug 45 A. Barnes
31 Oct 51 J. Maclay
7 May 52 A. Lennox-Boyd

(Minister of Transport and Civil Aviation)

1 Oct 53 A. Lennox-Boyd
28 Jul 54 J. Boyd-Carpenter
20 Dec 55 H. Watkinson

(Minister of Transport)

14 Oct 59 E. Marples
Oct 64 T. Fraser
23 Dec 65 Mrs B. Castle

Secretary of State for War

1900 M of Lansdowne
1 Nov 00 St J. Brodrick
6 Oct 03 H. Arnold-Forster
10 Dec 05 R. Haldane (Vt)
12 Jun 12 J. Seely
30 Mar 14 H. Asquith
5 Aug 14 Earl Kitchener
6 Jul 16 D. Lloyd George
10 Dec 16 E of Derby
18 Apr 18 Vt Milner
10 Jan 19 W. Churchill
13 Feb 21 Sir L. Worthington-Evans
24 Oct 22 E of Derby
22 Jan 24 S. Walsh
6 Nov 24 Sir L. Worthington-Evans
7 Jun 29 T. Shaw
26 Aug 31 M of Crewe
5 Nov 31 Vt Hailsham
7 Jun 35 Vt Halifax
22 Nov 35 A. Duff Cooper
28 May 37 L. Hore-Belisha
5 Jan 40 O. Stanley
11 May 40 A. Eden
22 Dec 40 D. Margesson
22 Feb 42 Sir J. Grigg
3 Aug 45 J. Lawson
4 Oct 46 F. Bellenger
7 Oct 47 E. Shinwell

28 Feb 50 J. Strachey
31 Oct 51 A. Head
18 Oct 56 J. Hare
6 Jan 58 C. Soames
27 Jul 60 J. Profumo
27 Jun 63 J. Godber
21 Oct 63 J. Ramsden
(office abolished 1 Apr 64)

Minister of State for Welsh Affairs

28 Oct 51 Sir D. Maxwell Fyfe
18 Oct 54 G. Lloyd-George
13 Jan 57 H. Brooke
13 Jul 62 Sir K. Joseph

(Secretary of State for Wales)

18 Oct 64 J. Griffiths
6 Apr 66 C. Hughes

First Commissioner of Works

1900 A. Akers-Douglas
8 Aug 02 Ld Windsor
10 Dec 05 L. Harcourt
3 Nov 10 Earl Beauchamp
6 Aug 14 Ld Emmott
25 May 15 L. Harcourt (Vt)
10 Dec 16 Sir A. Mond
1 Apr 21 E of Crawford
31 Oct 22 Sir J. Baird
22 Jan 24 F. Jowett
10 Nov 24 Vt Peel
18 Oct 28 M of Londonderry
7 Jun 29 G. Lansbury
25 Aug 31 M of Londonderry
5 Nov 31 W. Ormsby-Gore
16 Jun 36 Earl Stanhope
28 May 37 Sir P. Sassoon
7 Jun 39 H. Ramsbotham
3 Apr 40 Earl De La Warr
18 May 40 Ld Tryon
3 Oct 40 Sir J. Reith (Ld)

(Minister of Works & Buildings and First Commissioner of Works)

23 Oct 40 Ld Reith

(Minister of Works and Planning)

11 Feb 42 Ld Reith
21 Feb 42 Ld Portal

(Minister of Works)

Feb 43 Ld Portal
21 Nov 44 D. Sandys
4 Aug 45 G. Tomlinson
10 Feb 47 C. Key
28 Feb 50 R. Stokes
26 Apr 51 G. Brown
18 Nov 51 (Sir) D. Eccles
1 Oct 54 N. Birch
20 Dec 55 P. Buchan-Hepburn
16 Jan 57 H. Molson
22 Oct 59 Ld J. Hope
(16 Jul 62 recast as Public Building and Works)

Leaders of the House of Commons

1900	A. Balfour
5 Dec 05	Sir H. Campbell-Banner-man
5 Apr 08	H. Asquith
10 Dec 16	A. Bonar Law
23 Mar 21	A. Chamberlain
23 Oct 22	A. Bonar Law
22 May 23	S. Baldwin
22 Jan 24	J. R. MacDonald
4 Nov 24	S. Baldwin
5 Jun 29	J. R. MacDonald
7 Jun 35	S. Baldwin
28 May 37	N. Chamberlain
11 May 40	C. Attlee [2]
19 Feb 42	Sir S. Cripps
22 Nov 42	A. Eden
27 Jul 45	H. Morrison
9 Mar 51	C. Ede
30 Oct 51	H. Crookshank
7 Apr 55	R. Butler
9 Oct 61	I. Macleod
20 Oct 63	S. Lloyd
16 Oct 64	H. Bowden
11 Aug 66	R. Crossman
6 Apr 68	F. Peart

Leaders of the House of Lords

1900	3rd M of Salisbury
12 Jul 02	D of Devonshire
13 Oct 03	M of Lansdowne
10 Dec 05	M of Ripon
14 Apr 08	E of Crewe (M) [1]
10 Dec 16	Earl Curzon (M)
22 Jan 24	Vt Haldane
6 Nov 24	Marquess Curzon
27 Apr 25	4th M of Salisbury
7 Jun 29	Ld Parmoor
25 Aug 31	M of Reading
5 Nov 31	1st Vt Hailsham
7 Jun 35	M of Londonderry
22 Nov 35	Vt Halifax
27 Oct 38	Earl Stanhope
14 May 40	Vt Caldecote
3 Oct 40	Vt Halifax
22 Dec 40	Ld Lloyd
8 Feb 41	Ld Moyne
21 Feb 42	Vt Cranborne (5th M of Salisbury)
3 Aug 45	Vt Addison
28 Oct 51	5th M of Salisbury
29 Mar 57	E of Home
27 Jul 60	2nd Vt Hailsham
20 Oct 63	Ld Carrington
18 Oct 64	E of Longford
16 Jan 68	Ld Shackleton

[1] During the critical summer of 1911 Vt Morley was temporarily Leader of the House of Lords in place of the M of Crewe.

[2] Although Mr Attlee fulfilled the role of Leader of the House of Commons during this period, he was technically only Deputy Leader.

Size of Cabinets and Governments

	1900	1910	1917	1920	1930	1940	1950	1960	1967
Cabinet Ministers	19	19	5	19	19	9	18	19	24
Non-Cabinet Ministers	10	7	33	15	9	25	20	20	27
Junior Ministers [a]	31	36	47	47	30	40	43	43	58
Number of M.P.s in paid Government Posts	33	43	60	58	50	58	68	65	92 [b]
Number of Peers in paid Government Posts	27	19	25	22	12	19	13	18	23
Total paid Government Posts	60	62	85	81	58	74	81	82	115 [b]
Parliamentary Private Secretaries	9	16	12	13	26	25	27	36	30
Total number of M.P.s involved in Government	42	59	72	71	76	83	95	101	122

[a] Including the political appointments of the Royal Household. In 1901 the Master of the Buckhounds ceased to be a political appointment. Since 1905 the Paymaster-General has been a non-Cabinet or Cabinet Ministerial post. Since 1924 the offices of Lord Chamberlain, Lord Steward, and Master of the House have been non-political. In 1930 the Captain Gentleman at Arms and Captain Yeoman of the Guard were non-political appointments. There have always been some non-political Lords in Waiting.

[b] From 1900 to 1964 there were 2–6 unpaid Government Whips, who were not included in this table. Since 1964 Assistant Government Whips have been paid. In the 1967 totals, 6 Assistant Government Whips have been included as paid Government posts.

SOURCES.—Members of the Government from *Hansard*, the first volume of each year. P.P.S.s from *Whitaker's Almanack* (the figures for 1900–40 are only approximate), and from *H.M. Ministers and Heads of Public Departments*, 1946–67 (H.M.S.O.).

Ministerial Resignations

Resignations from ministerial office are not easy to classify. A retirement on the ground of ill-health may always conceal a protest or a dismissal. However, there are some cases where ministers have unquestionably left office because they were not willing to continue to accept collective responsibility for some part of Government policy and some cases where the individual actions of ministers have been thought impolitic or unworthy.

16 Sep 03	J. Chamberlain (*Imperial preference*)
4–15 Sep 03	C. Ritchie, Ld Balfour of Burleigh, Ld G. Hamilton, D of Devonshire, A. Elliott (*Free Trade*)
6 Mar 05	G. Wyndham (*Ireland*)
30 Mar 14	J. Seely (*Curragh mutiny*)
2 Aug 14	Vt Morley, J. Burns (*Entry into war*)
5 Aug 14	C. Trevelyan (*Entry into war*)
19 Oct 15	Sir E. Carson (*Conduct of War in the Balkans*)
31 Dec 15	Sir J. Simon (*Compulsory National Service*)
3 May 16	A. Birrell (*Irish rebellion*)
25 Jun 16	Vt Selborne (*Irish Policy*)
12 Jul 17	A. Chamberlain (*Campaign in Mesopotamia*)
8 Aug 17	N. Chamberlain (*Ministry of National Service*)
17 Nov 17	Ld Cowdray (*Conduct of the Air Ministry*)
21 Jan 18	Sir E. Carson (*Ireland*)
25 Apr 18	Ld Rothermere (*Air Force*)
22 Nov 18	Ld R. Cecil (*Welsh disestablishment*)
12 Nov 19	J. Seely (*Role of Air Ministry*)
14 Jul 21	C. Addison (*Housing*)
9 Mar 22	E. Montagu (*Turkey*)
18 Nov 23	A. Buckley (*Abandonment of Free Trade*)
28 Aug 27	Vt Cecil (*Disarmament*)
19 May 30	Sir O. Mosley (*Unemployment*)
2 Mar 31	Sir C. Trevelyan (*Education*)
9 Oct 31	G. Lloyd George, G. Owen (*Decision to hold a General Election*)
28 Sep 32	Sir H. Samuel, Sir A. Sinclair, Vt Snowden, M of Lothian, I. Foot, Sir R. Hamilton, G. White, W. Rea, Vt Allendale (*Free Trade*)
18 Dec 35	Sir S. Hoare (*Laval Pact*)
22 May 36	J. Thomas (*Budget leak*)
20 Feb 38	A. Eden, Vt Cranborne (*Negotiations with Mussolini*)
12–16 May 38	Earl Winterton, Vt Swinton (*Criticism of Air strength*)
16 May 38	Ld Harlech (*Partition of Palestine*)
1 Oct 38	A. Duff Cooper (*Munich*)
21 Jan 41	R. Boothby (*Blocked Czechoslovakian assets*)
1 Mar 45	H. Strauss (*Treatment of Poles by Yalta Conference*)
26 May 46	B. Smith (*Overwork and criticism*)
13 Nov 47	H. Dalton (*Budget leak*)
3 Feb 49	J. Belcher (*Lynskey tribunal*)
16 Apr 50	S. Evans (*Agricultural subsidies*)
23–24 Apr 51	A. Bevan, H. Wilson, J. Freeman (*Budget proposals*)
20 Jul 54	Sir T. Dugdale (*Crichel Down*)
31 Oct 56	A. Nutting (*Suez*)
5 Nov 56	Sir E. Boyle (*Suez*)

29 Mar 57   M of Salisbury (*Release of Archbishop Makarios*)
6 Jan 58   P. Thorneycroft, E. Powell, N. Birch (*Economic policy*)
8 Nov 62   T. Galbraith (*Security: Exonerated and given new office 5 May 63*)
5 Jun 63   J. Profumo (*Lying to the House of Commons*)
19 Feb 66   C. Mayhew (*Defence estimates*)
3 Jul 66   F. Cousins (*Incomes policy*)
26 Jul 67   Miss M. Herbison (*Social Services policy*)
16 Jan 68   E of Longford (*Postponement of raising School Leaving Age*)
16 Mar 68   G. Brown (*Conduct of Government business*)
1 Jul 68   R. Gunter (*General dissatisfaction*)

SOURCES.—R. C. K. Ensor, *England 1870–1914*, (1936); C. L. Mowat, *Britain Between the Wars* (1955); *The Annual Register, 1900–1966; Keesing's Archives, 1931–1966;* S. E. Finer, 'The Individual Responsibility of Ministers', *Public Administration,* Winter 1956, pp. 377–96; P. J. Madgwick, 'Resignations', *Parliamentary Affairs,* Winter 1966, pp. 59–76; R. K. Alderman and J. A. Cross, *Tactics of Resignation* (1968).

Parliamentary Private Secretaries to Prime Ministers, 1900–1960

1900–02	E. Cecil	1927–29	C. Rhys	1946–51	A. Moyle
1906–08	H. Carr-Gomm	1929–31	{ L. MacNeil Weir / R. Morrison	1952–55	C. Soames
1908–10	G. Howard			1955	R. Carr
1910–15	C. Lyell	1931–32	{ R. Glyn / F. Markham	1955–58	R. Allan
1915–16	Sir J. Barran			1958–59	A. Barber
1916–17	D. Davies	1932–35	{ (Sir) R. Glyn / J. Worthington	1959–63	S. Cunningham
1918	W. Astor			1963–64	F. Pearson
1918–20	(Sir) W. Sutherland	1935	G. Lloyd	1964–66	{ P. Shore
1920–22	Sir P. Sassoon	1935–37	T. Dugdale	1964–67	{ E. Fernyhough
1922–23	J. Davidson	1937–40	Ld Dunglass	1967–68	H. Davies
1923–24	S. Herbert	1940–41	B. Bracken	1968–	{ H. Davies
1924	L. MacNeil Weir	1941–45	G. Harvie-Watt		{ E. Varley
1924–27	S. Herbert	1945–46	G. de Freitas		

Biographical Notes

Prime Ministers, Chancellors of the Exchequer, and Foreign Secretaries.[1]

Anderson, John (Sir). 1st Vt Waverley (1952)
b. 1882. *Educ.* George Watson's Coll., Edin.; Edinburgh and Leipzig Univs. Entered Col. O., 1905. Sec. to Min. of Shipping, 1917–19. K.C.B., 1919. Addit. Sec. to Loc. Govt. Bd., 1919. 2nd Sec. to Min. of Health, 1919. Ch. of Bd. of Inland Revenue, 1919–22. Joint U.-S. to Ld. Lieut. of Ireland, 1920–22. P.U.-S. Home O., 1922–32. Gov. of Bengal, 1932–37. M.P. (Nat.) for Scottish Univs., 1938–50. Ld. Privy S., 1938–39. Home Sec. and Min. of Home Security, 1939–40. Ld. Pres. of Council, 1940–43. Chanc. of Exch., 1943–45. d. 1958.

Asquith, Herbert Henry. 1st E of Oxford and Asquith (1925)
b. 1852. *Educ.* City of London School; Oxford. Barrister, 1876, practised M.P. (Lib.) for E. Fife, 1886–1918. M.P. for Paisley, 1920–24. Home Sec., 1892–95. Chanc. of Exch., 1905–8. P.M. and Leader of Lib. party, 1908–1916. Sec. for War, 1914. Formed Coalition Govt., 1915. Resigned as P.M., became Leader of Opposition, 1916. Resigned Leadership of Lib. party, 1926. d. 1928.

---

[1] Virtually all the most eminent politicians of this century held one of these three offices. But, common sense being more important than consistency, we have added biographies of the two most outstanding exceptions — Joseph Chamberlain and Aneurin Bevan.

Attlee, Clement Richard. 1st Earl Attlee (1955)
  b. 1883. *Educ.* Haileybury; Oxford. Barrister, 1906; practised, 1906–9.
Lecturer at L.S.E., 1913–23. M.P. (Lab.) for Limehouse, Stepney, 1922–50.
M.P. for W. Walthamstow, 1950–55. P.P.S. to J. R. MacDonald, 1922–24.
U.-S. for War, 1924. Chanc. of D. of Lanc., 1930–31. Postm.-Gen., 1931.
Dep. Leader of Lab. party in Commons, 1931–35. Leader of Lab. party,
1935–55. Leader of Opposition, 1935–40. Ld. Privy S., 1940–42. Sec. for
Dominions, 1942–43. Ld. Pres. of Council, 1943–45. Dep. P.M., 1942–45.
P.M., 1945–51. Min. of Def., 1945–46. Leader of Opposition, 1951–
1955. d. 1967.

Baldwin, Stanley. 1st Earl Baldwin of Bewdley (1937)
  b. 1867. *Educ.* Harrow; Cambridge. Family business. M.P. (Con.) for
Bewdley div. of Worcs., 1908–37. Joint F.S. to Treas., 1917–21; Pres. of Bd.
of Trade, 1921–22; Chanc. of Exch., 1922–23. Leader of Con. party, 1923–37.
P.M., 1923–24 and 1924–29. Leader of Opposition, 1924, 1929–31. Ld. Pres. of
Council, 1931–35. Ld. Privy S., 1932–33. P.M., 1935–37. d. 1947.

Balfour, Arthur James. 1st Earl of Balfour (1922)
  b. 1848. *Educ.* Eton; Cambridge. M.P. (Con.) for Hertford, 1874–85. M.P.
for E. Manchester, 1885–1906. M.P. for City of London, 1906–22. P.P.S. to
Ld. Salisbury, 1878–80. Pres. of Loc. Govt. Bd., 1885. Sec. for Scotland, 1886.
(Member of Cabinet, Nov 1886.) Ch. Sec. for Ireland, 1887–91. Leader
of Commons and 1st Ld. of Treas., 1891–92 and 1895–1902. P.M.,
1902–5. Leader of Con. party, 1902–11. Member of Committee of Imperial
Defence, 1914. Attended war cabinet meetings, 1914–15. 1st Ld. of Admir.,
1915–16. For. Sec., 1916–19. Ld. Pres. of Council, 1919–22 and 1925–29.
d. 1930.

Bevan, Aneurin
  b. 1897. *Educ.* Elem.; Central Labour College. Miner. M.P. (Lab.) for Ebbw
Vale, 1929–60. Deputy Leader of Lab. party, 1959–60. Min. of Health, 1945–51.
Min. of Lab. and Nat. Service, 1951. Resigned, 1951. Treasurer of Lab. party,
1956–60. d. 1960.

Bevin, Ernest
  b. 1881. *Educ.* Elem. National Organiser of Dockers' Union, 1910–21. Gen.
Sec. of T. & G.W.U., 1921–40. Member of General Council of T.U.C., 1925–40.
M.P. (Lab.) for C. Wandsworth, 1940–50. M.P. for E. Woolwich, 1950–51.
Min. of Lab. and Nat. Service, 1940–45. For. Sec., 1945–51. Ld. Privy S.,
Mar–Apr 1951. d. 1951.

Bonar Law, Andrew
  b. 1858. *Educ.* Canada and Glasgow H.S. Family business. M.P. (Con.) for
Blackfriars, Glasgow, 1900–6. M.P. for Dulwich, 1906–10. M.P. for Bootle,
1911–18. M.P. for C. Glasgow, 1918–23. P.S. to Bd. of Trade, 1902–5. Leader
of Con. party in Commons, 1911–21. Col. Sec., 1915–16. Chanc. of Exch.,
1916–18. Ld. Privy S. and Leader of Commons, 1919–21. Resigned, 1921
P.M. and Leader of Con. party, 1922–23. Resigned, 1923. d. 1923.

Brown, George Alfred
  b. 1914. *Educ.* Secondary. M.P. (Lab.) for Belper since 1945. P.P.S. to Min.
of Lab. and Nat. Service, 1945–47, and to C. of Exchequer, 1947. Joint
Parliamentary Secretary, Min. of Ag. and Fish., 1947–51. Min. of Works, Apr–
Oct 1951. First Sec. of State and Sec. of State for Econ. Affairs, 1964–66. For.
Sec. 1966–68. Deputy Leader of the Labour Party since 1960.

Butler, Richard Austen. Life Peer (1965) Ld Butler of Saffron Walden.
  b. 1902. *Educ.* Marlborough; Cambridge. M.P. (Con.) for Saffron Walden,
1929–65. U.-S. India O., 1932–37. P.S. Min. of Lab., 1937–38. U.-S.
For. O., 1938–41. Pres. Bd. of Educ., 1941–44. Min. of Educ., 1944–45.
Min. of Lab., 1945. Chanc. of Exch., 1951–55. Leader of Commons, 1955–61.
Ld. Privy S., 1955–59. Hom. Sec., 1957–62. First Sec. of State and Min. in
charge of C. African O., 1962–63. For. Sec., 1963–64. Ch. of Con. party
organisation 1959–61. Master of Trinity College, Cambridge, 1965.

Callaghan, (Leonard) James
b. 1912. *Educ.* Elem. and Portsmouth Northern Secondary Schools. M.P. (Lab.) for S. Cardiff, 1945–50. M.P. for S.E. Cardiff since 1950. P.S. Min. of Transport, 1947–50. P.S. and F.S. Admiralty, 1950–51. Chanc. of the Exch., 1964–67. Home Sec. since 1967.

Campbell-Bannerman, Henry (Sir)
b. 1836. *Educ.* Glasgow H.S. ; Glasgow Univ. and Cambridge. Family business. M.P. (Lib.) for Stirling Burghs, 1868–1908. F.S. to War O., 1871–74 and 1880–82. Sec. to Admir., 1882–84. Ch. Sec. for Ireland (without seat in cabinet), 1884–85. Sec. for War, 1886 and 1892–95. G.C.B., 1895. Leader of Lib. party in Commons, 1899–1908. P.M., 1905–8. Resigned, 1908. d. 1908.

Chamberlain, (Arthur) Neville
b. 1869. *Educ.* Rugby; Mason Science College, Birmingham. Birmingham and business career. Ld. Mayor of Birmingham, 1915–16. Dir.-Gen. of Nat. Service, 1916–17. M.P. (Con.) for Ladywood, Birmingham, 1918–29. M.P. for Edgbaston, Birmingham, 1929–40. Postm.-Gen., 1922–23. Paym.-Gen., 1923. Min. of Health, 1923. Chanc. of Exch., 1923–24. Min. of Health, 1924–29 and 1931. Ch. of Con. party organisation, 1930–31. Chanc. of Exch., 1931–37. P.M. and Leader of Con. party, 1937–40. Ld. Pres. of Council, 1940. Resigned, 1940. d. 1940.

Chamberlain, Joseph
b. 1836. *Educ.* University College School. Family business. Mayor of Birmingham, 1873–75. M.P. (Lib.) for Birmingham, 1876–85. M.P. for Birmingham W., 1885–86. M.P. (Lib. U.) for Birmingham W., 1886–1914. Pres. of Bd. of Trade, 1880–85. Pres. of Loc. Govt. Bd., 1886. Col. Sec., 1895–1903. d. 1914.

Chamberlain, (Joseph) Austen (Sir)
b. 1863. *Educ.* Rugby; Cambridge. M.P. (Con.) for E. Worcs., 1892–1914. M.P. for W. Birmingham, 1914–37. Lib. U. Whip, 1892. Civil Ld. of Admir., 1895–1900. F.S. to Treas., 1900–2. Postm.-Gen., 1902–3. Chanc. of Exch., 1903–5. Sec. for India, 1915–17. Resigned, 1917. Min. without Portfolio in war cabinet, 1918–19. Chanc. of Exch., 1919–21. Ld. Privy S. and Leader of Con. party in Commons, 1921–22. For. Sec., 1924–29. K.G., 1925. 1st Ld. of Admir., 1931. d. 1937.

Churchill, Winston Leonard Spencer (Sir)
b. 1874. *Educ.* Harrow; Sandhurst. Army, 1895–1909. M.P. (Con.) for Oldham, 1900–04. M.P. (Lib.) for Oldham 1904–06. M.P. (Lib) for N.W. Manchester, 1906–08. M.P. (Lib.) for Dundee, 1908–22. M.P. (Const.) for Epping, 1924–29. M.P. (Con.) for Epping, 1929–45; M.P. (Con.) for Woodford, 1945–64. U.-S. for Col. O., 906–108. Pres. of Bd. of Trade, 1908–10. Home Sec., 1910–11. 1st Ld. of Admiralty, 1911–15. Chanc. of D. of Lanc., 1915. Min. of Munitions, 1917–19. Sec. for War and Air, 1919–21. Col. Sec., 1921–22. Chanc. of Exch., 1924–29. 1st Ld. of Admir., 1939–47. Min. of Def., and P.M., 1940–45. Leader of Con. Party, 1940–55. Leader of Opposition, 1945–51. Min. of Def., 1951–52. P.M., 1951–55. K.G., 1953. d. 1965.

Cripps, (Richard) Stafford (Sir)
b. 1889. *Educ.* Winchester; London. Barrister, 1913. M.P. (Lab.) for E. Bristol, 1931–50. M.P. for S.E. Bristol, 1950. Kt., 1930. Sol. Gen., 1930–31. Brit. Amb. to U.S.S.R., 1940–42. Ld. Privy S. and Leader of Commons, 1942. Min. of Aircraft Prod., 1942–45. Pres. of Bd. of Trade, 1945–47. Min. for Econ. Affairs, 1947. Chanc. of Exch., 1947–50. d. 1952.

Curzon, George Nathaniel. Ld Curzon (1898), 1st Earl (1911), 1st Marquess Curzon of Kedleston (1921)
b. 1859. *Educ.* Eton and Oxford. M.P. (Con.) for Southport, 1886–98. U.-S. India O., 1891–92. U.-S. For. O., 1895–98. Viceroy of India, 1899–1905. Entered H. of Lords as Irish Representative Peer, 1908. Ld. Privy Seal, 1915–16. Pres. of Air Bd., 1916. Ld. Pres. of Council, 1916–19. Member of war cabinet, Leader of Lords, 1916–24. For. Sec., 1919–24. Ld. Pres. of Council, 1924–25. Leader of Cons. party, Lords, 1916–25. d. 1925.

F

Dalton, (Edward) Hugh John Neale. (Life Peer, 1960)
b. 1887. *Educ.* Eton; Cambridge, L.S.E. Barrister, 1914. Univ. Lecturer, London, 1919–36. M.P. (Lab.) for Camberwell, 1924–29. M.P. Bishop Auckland, 1929–31 and 1935–59. U.-S. For. O., 1929–31. Min. of Econ. Warfare, 1940–42. Pres. of Bd. of Trade, 1942–45. Chanc. of Exch., 1945–47. Chanc. of D. of Lanc., 1948–50. Min. of Town and Country Planning, 1950–51. Min. of Loc. Govt. and Planning, 1951. d. 1962.

Douglas-Home, Sir Alec (Alexander Frederick). Ld Dunglass (1918–51) 14th E of Home (1951–63)
b. 1903. *Educ.* Eton; Oxford. M.P. (Con.) for S. Lanark, 1931–45. M.P. for Lanark, 1950–51. M.P. for Kinross and W. Perthshire since 1963. P.P.S. to N. Chamberlain, 1937–40. Joint U.-S. For. O., 1945. (Succ. to E. 1951) Min. of State Scottish O., 1951–55. Sec. Commonwealth Relations 1955–60. Dep. Leader of Lords, 1956–57. Ld. Pres. of Council, 1957 and 1959–60. Leader of Lords, 1957–60. For. Sec. 1960–63. P.M. 1963–64 (Renounced peerage 1963) Leader of Cons. Party, 1963–65.

Eden, (Robert) Anthony (Sir). 1st E of Avon (1961)
b. 1897. *Educ.* Eton; Oxford. M.P. (Con.) for Warwick and Leamington, 1923–57. P.P.S. to Sir A. Chamberlain (For. Sec.), 1926–29. U.-S. For. O., 1931–33. Ld. Privy S., 1934–35. Min. without Portfolio for League of Nations Affairs, 1935. For. Sec., 1935–38. Resigned, 1938. Sec. for Dominions, 1939–40. Sec. for War, 1940. For. Sec., 1940–45. Leader of Commons, 1942–45. Dep. Leader of Opposition, 1945–51. For. Sec., 1951–55. K.G., 1954. P.M. and Leader of Con. party, 1955–57.

Gaitskell, Hugh Todd Naylor
b. 1906. *Educ.* Winchester; Oxford. M.P. (Lab.) for S. Leeds 1945–63. Princ. Private Sec. to Min. of Econ. Warfare, 1940–42. Princ. Asst. Sec. Bd. of Trade, 1942–45. P.S. Min. of Fuel and Power, 1946–47. Min. of Fuel and Power, 1947–50. Min. of State for Econ. Affairs, 1950. Chanc. of Exch., 1950–51. Leader of Lab. party, 1955-63. d. 1963.

Gordon Walker, Patrick Chrestian
b. 1907. *Educ.* Wellington; Oxford. University Teacher. M.P. (Lab.) for Smethwick, 1945–64. M.P. (Lab.) Leyton since 1966. P.P.S. to H. Morrison, 1946. Parl. U.-S., Commonwealth Relations O., 1947–50. Sec. of State for Commonwealth Relations, 1950–51. For. Sec., 1964–65. Min. without Portfolio, 1967. Sec. for Educ. and Science, 1967–68.

Grey, Edward, (Sir) 1st Vt Grey of Fallodon (1916)
b. 1862. *Educ.* Winchester; Oxford. Succ. to Btcy., 1882. M.P. (Lib.) for Berwick-on-Tweed 1885–1916. U.-S. For. O., 1892–95. For. Sec., 1905–16. (For. Sec. in Lords, 1916). Leader of Liberal party, Lords 1923–24. d. 1933.

Halifax, 3rd Vt (1934), Edward Frederick Lindley Wood. 1st Ld Irwin (1925), 1st E of (1944)
b. 1881. *Educ.* Eton; Oxford. M.P. (Con.) for Ripon, 1910–25. U.-S. Col. O., 1921–22. Pres. of Bd. of Educ., 1922–24. Min. of Agric., 1924–25. Viceroy of India, 1926–31. Pres. of Bd. of Educ., 1932–35. Sec. for War, 1935. Ld. Privy S., 1935–37. Leader of Lords, 1935–38. Ld. Pres. of Council, 1937–38. For. Sec., 1938–40. Leader of Lords, 1940. Brit. Amb. to U.S.A., 1941–46. d. 1959.

Heathcoat Amory, Derick. 1st Vt Amory (1960)
b. 1899. *Educ.* Eton; Oxford. M.P. (Con.) for Tiverton, 1945–60. Min. of Pensions, 1951–53. Min. of State for Bd. of Trade, 1953–54. Min. of Ag., Fish. and Food, 1954–58. Chanc. of Exch., 1958–60. High Commissioner for the U.K. in Canada, 1961–63.

Henderson, Arthur
b. 1863. *Educ.* Elem. M.P. (Lab.) for Barnard Castle, 1903–18. M.P. for Widnes, 1919–22. M.P. for Newcastle E., 1923. M.P. for Burnley, 1924–31. M.P. for Clay Cross, 1933–35. Sec. of Lab. party, 1911–34. Treasurer of Lab. party, 1930–35. Leader of Lab. party in Commons, 1908–10 and 1914–17. Chief Whip, 1914. Pres. Bd. of Educ., 1915–16. Paym.-Gen., 1916. Min.

without portfolio and member of war cabinet, 1916–17. Resigned from cabinet, 1917. Chief Lab. party Whip, 1920–24 and 1925–27. Home Sec., 1924. For. Sec., 1929–31. Leader of Lab. Opposition, 1931–32. d. 1935.

Hicks Beach, Michael Edward (Sir). 1st Vt St Aldwyn (1906), 1st Earl (1915)
b. 1837. *Educ.* Eton; Oxford. Succ. to Btcy., 1854. M.P. (Con.) for E. Gloucs., 1864–85. M.P. for W. Bristol, 1885–1906. Sec. of Poor Law Bd., 1868. U.-S. Home O., 1868. Ch. Sec. for Ireland, 1874–78. (Seat in cabinet, 1876.) Sec. for Col., 1878–80. Chanc. of Exch. and Leader of Commons, 1885–86. Leader of Opposition in Commons, 1886. Ch. Sec. for Ireland, 1886–87. Resigned 1887, but remained in cabinet without portfolio. Pres. of Bd. of Trade, 1888–92. Chanc. of Exch., 1895–1902. Resigned 1902. d. 1916.

Hoare, Samuel John Gurney (Sir). 1st Vt Templewood (1944)
b. 1880. *Educ.* Harrow; Oxford. M.P. (Con.) for Chelsea, 1910–44. Succ. to Btcy., 1915. Sec. for Air, 1922–24 and 1924–29. Sec. for India, 1931–35. For. Sec., 1935. 1st Ld. of Admir., 1936–37. Home Sec., 1937–39. Ld. Privy S., 1939–40. Sec. for Air, 1940. Brit. Amb. to Spain, 1940–44. d. 1959.

Horne, Robert Stevenson (Sir). 1st Vt Horne of Slamannan (1937)
b. 1871. *Educ.* George Watson's Coll., Edin.; Glasgow Univ. Member of Faculty of Advocates, 1896. K.B.E., 1918. M.P. (Con.) for Hillhead, Glasgow, 1918–37. Min. of Lab., 1919–20. Pres. of Bd. of Trade, 1920–21. Chanc. of Exch., 1921–22. d. 1940.

Jenkins, Roy Harris
b. 1920. *Educ.* Abersychan G.S.; Oxford. Army, 1939–45. M.P. (Lab.) for Central Southwark, 1948–50. M.P. (Lab.) for Stechford, Birmingham, since 1950. P.P.S. Commonwealth Relations O., 1949–50. Min. of Aviation, 1964–5. Home Sec., 1965–7. Chanc. of Exch., 1967–.

Lansdowne, 5th M of (1866). Henry Charles Keith Petty-Fitzmaurice, Vt Clanmaurice (1845–63), E of Kerry (1863–66)
b. 1845. *Educ.* Eton; Oxford. Succ. to M. 1866. Junior Ld. of Treas. (Lib.), 1869–72. U.-S. for War, 1872–74. U.-S. India O., 1880. Resigned and opposed Lib. Govt. in Lords, 1880. Gov.-Gen. of Canada, 1883–88. Viceroy of India, 1888–94. Sec. for War (Con.), 1895–1900. For. Sec., 1900–5. Leader of Con. party in Lords, 1903–16. Min. without portfolio, member of war cabinet, 1915–16. Left Con. party, 1917. d. 1927.

Lloyd, (John) Selwyn Brooke
b. 1904. *Educ.* Fettes; Cambridge. Barrister, 1930. M.P. (Con.) for Wirral since 1945. Min. of State For. O., 1951–54. Min. of Supply, 1954–55. Min. of Def., 1955. For. Sec., 1955–60. Chanc. of Exch., 1960–62. Lord Privy Seal and Leader of the House of Commons, 1963–64.

Lloyd George, David. 1st Earl Lloyd George of Dwyfor (1945)
b. 1863. *Educ.* Church School. Solicitor, 1884. M.P. (Lib.) for Caernarvon Boroughs, 1890–1945 (Ind. L., 1931–35). Pres. of Bd. of Trade, 1905–8. Chanc. of Exch., 1908–15. Min. of Munitions, 1915–16. Sec. for War, 1916. Resigned, 1916. P.M., 1916–22. Leader of Lib. party, 1926–31. d. 1945.

MacDonald, James Ramsay
b. 1866. *Educ.* Drainie School. M.P. (Lab.) for Leicester, 1906–18. M.P. for Aberavon, Glamorganshire, 1922–29. M.P. for Seaham, 1929–35. (Nat. Lab., 1931–37.) M.P. for Scottish Univs., 1936–37. Sec. of L.R.C. and Lab. party, 1900–12. Treas. of Lab. party, 1912–35. Chairman of I.L.P., 1906–9. Ch. of Lab. party, 1911–14. Resigned Chairmanship, 1914. Ch. of P.L.P. and Leader of official Opposition, 1922. Leader of Lab. party, 1922–31. P.M. and For. Sec., 1924. P.M., 1929–31. P.M. of National Govt., 1931–35. Ld. Pres. of Council, 1935–37. d. 1937.

McKenna, Reginald
b. 1863. *Educ.* St. Malo, Ebersdorf and King's Coll. School; Cambridge. Barrister, 1887. M.P. (Lib.) for N. Monmouthshire, 1895–1918. F.S. to Treas., 1905–7. Pres. Bd. of Educ., 1907–8. 1st Ld. of Admir., 1908–11. Home Sec., 1911–15. Chanc. of Exch., 1915–16. Ch. of Midland Bank, 1919–43. d. 1943.

Macmillan, (Maurice) Harold

b. 1894. *Educ.* Eton; Oxford. M.P. (Con.) for Stockton-on-Tees, 1924–29 and 1931–45. M.P. (Con.) for Bromley, 1945–64. P.S. Min. of Supply, 1940–42. U.-S. Col. O., 1942. Min. resident at Allied H.Q. in N.W. Africa, 1942–45. Sec. for Air, 1945. Min. of Housing and Loc. Govt., 1951–54. Min. of Def., 1954–55. For. Sec., 1955, Chanc. of Exch., 1955–57. P.M. and Leader of Con. party, 1957–63.

Maudling, Reginald

b. 1917. *Educ.* Merchant Taylors'; Oxford. Barrister 1940. M.P. (Con.) for Barnet since 1950. P.S. Min. of Civil Aviation, 1952. Econ. Sec. to Treasury, 1953–55. Min. of Supply, 1955–57. Paym.-Gen., 1957–59. Pres. Bd. of Trade, 1959–61. Sec. of State for Colonies, 1961–62. Chanc. of Exch., 1962–64.

Morrison, Herbert Stanley. Life Peer (1959), Ld Morrison of Lambeth

b. 1888. *Educ.* Elem. Member of L.C.C., 1922–45. Leader of Council, 1934–40. M.P. (Lab.) for S. Hackney, 1923–24, 1929–31, 1935–45. M.P. for E. Lewisham, 1945–50. M.P. for S. Lewisham, 1950–59. Min. of Transport, 1929–31. Min. of Supply, 1940. Home Sec. and Min. of Home Security, 1940–45. Member of war cabinet, 1942–45. Dep. P.M., 1945–51. Ld. Pres. of Council and Leader of Commons, 1945–51. For. Sec., 1951. Dep. Leader of Opposition, 1951–55. d. 1965.

Reading, 1st M of (1926). Rufus Daniel Isaacs (Sir), 1st Ld (1914), 1st Vt (1916) 1st E of (1917)

b. 1860. *Educ.* Brussels, Anglo-Jewish Acad., London, University College Sch. Family Business. Barrister, 1887. M.P. (Lib.) for Reading, 1904–13. Kt., 1910. Sol. Gen., 1910. Att. Gen., 1910–13 (seat in cabinet, 1912). Ld. Chief Justice, 1913–21. Brit. Amb. to U.S.A., 1918–19. Viceroy of India 1921–26. For. Sec., 1931. Leader of Lords 1931; Leader of Liberal Party, Lords 1930–35. d. 1935.

Ritchie, Charles Thomson. 1st Ld Ritchie of Dundee (1905)

b. 1838. *Educ.* City of London School. M.P. (Con.) for Tower Hamlets, 1874–85. M.P. for St. George's in the East, 1885–92. M.P. for Croydon, 1895–1903. F.S. to Admir., 1885–86. Pres. of Loc. Govt. Bd., 1886–92. Pres. of Bd. of Trade, 1895–1900. Home Sec., 1900–2. Chanc. of Exch., 1902–3. Resigned, 1903. d. 1906.

Salisbury, 3rd M of (1868). Robert Arthur Talbot Gascoyne-Cecil, Vt Cranborne (1865–68)

b. 1830. *Educ.* Eton; Oxford. M.P. (Con.) for Stamford, 1853–68. Sec. for India, 1866. Resigned, 1867. Succ. to M. 1868. Sec. for India, 1874–76. For. Sec., 1878–80. Leader of Opposition in Lords, 1881–85. Leader of the Con. party, 1885–1902. P.M. and For. Sec., 1885–86. P.M. 1886. P.M. and For. Sec., 1887–92 and 1895–1900. P.M. and Ld. Privy S., 1900–2. d. 1903.

Simon, John Allsebrook (Sir). 1st Vt Simon (1940)

b. 1873. *Educ.* Fettes; Oxford. Barrister, 1899. M.P. (Lib.) for Walthamstow, 1906–18. M.P. for Spen Valley, 1922–31. M.P. (L. Nat.) for Spen Valley, 1931–40. Kt., 1910. Sol. Gen., 1910–13. Att. Gen. (with seat in cabinet), 1913–15. Home Sec., 1915–16. For. Sec., 1931–35. Leader of L. Nat. party, 1931–40. Home Sec. and Dep. Leader of Commons, 1935–37. Chanc. of Exch., 1937–40. Ld. Chanc., 1940–45. d. 1954.

Snowden, Philip. 1st Vt Snowden (1931)

b. 1864. *Educ.* Bd. School. M.P. (Lab.) for Blackburn, 1906–18. M.P. for Colne Valley, 1922–31. Ch. of ILP 1903–6 and 1917–20. Chanc. of Exch., 1924, 1929–31, and 1931. Ld. Privy S., 1931–32. Resigned, 1932. d. 1937.

Stewart, Michael

b. 1906. *Educ.* Christ's Hospital; Oxford. Teacher. M.P. (Lab.) Fulham East, 1945–55 and for Fulham since 1955. Vice-Chamberlain, H.M. Household, 1946. Comptroller, H.M. Household, 1946–47. U.-S. for War 1947–51. P.S. Min. of Supply, 1951. Min. for Educ. and Science, 1964–65. For. Sec., 1965–66. Sec. of State for Econ. Affairs, 1966–67. First Sec. of State, 1966–68. For. (and Commonwealth) Sec., 1968–.

Thorneycroft, (George Edward) Peter. Life Peer (1967), Ld Thorneycroft of Dunston
b. 1909. *Educ.* Eton; Woolwich. Barrister, 1935. M.P. (Con.) for Stafford,
1938–45. M.P. (Con.) for Monmouth 1945–1966. P.S. Min. of War Transport,
1945. Pres. of Bd. of Trade, 1951–57. Chanc. of Exch., 1957–58. Resigned,
1958. Min. of Aviation, 1960–62. Min. of Defence 1962–64. Sec. of State
for Defence 1964.

Wilson, (James) Harold
b. 1916. *Educ.* Wirral G.S.; Oxford. University teacher. Director of Economics and Statistics, Min. of Fuel and Power, 1943–44. M.P. (Lab.) for
Ormskirk, 1945–50, and for Huyton (Lab.) since 1950. P.S. Min. of Works,
1945–47. Sec. for Overseas Trade, 1947. Pres. Bd. of Trade, 1947–51.
Resigned 1951. Leader, Lab. Party, 1963. P.M., 1964–.

Wood, (Howard) Kingsley (Sir)
b. 1881. *Educ.* Central Foundation Boys' School. Solicitor, 1903. Kt., 1918.
M.P. (Con.) for W. Woolwich, 1918–43. P.P.S. to Min. of Health, 1919–22.
P.S. Min. of Health, 1924–29. P.S. Bd. of Educ., 1931. Postm.-Gen., 1931–35
(seat in cabinet, 1933). Min. of Health, 1935–38. Sec. for Air, 1938–40. Ld.
Privy S., 1940. Chanc. of Exch., 1940–43. d. 1943.

SOURCES.—*Dictionary of National Biography, 1900–1950; Who Was Who, 1900–1960; Who's Who.*

Index of Ministers

This index covers every reference to a Minister given in the Tables of Ministries, pp. 1-48, 308.
It does not cover the supplementary information on Ministers and Ministries, pp. 48-65.

The educational information is necessarily incomplete. It is not always possible to trace the
name or status of an elementary or secondary school. When several schools are recorded, the last
is normally named here. All schools that are unstarred are 'public schools' or, more precisely,
members of the Headmasters' Conference. By courtesy, we have listed the Royal Military College
(Sandhurst) and the Royal Military Academy (Woolwich) in the University column. In this index
promotion from a knighthood to a higher order of chivalry or to a baronetcy is not recorded.

† denotes a Privy Councillor.

When an individual appears more than once on a page, the number is indicated. Double entries
are given when an individual held office under different names, and where a title was acquired after
office had been held.

Name	Born	School	Univ.	Died	Page references
†Abercorn, 3rd D of (1913) J. A. E. Hamilton, M of Hamilton (1885)	1869	Eton	..	1953	3
†Acland, Sir F.D. (14th Bt 1926)	1874	Rugby	Oxford	1939	5², 6², 8
†Acland Hood, Sir A. F. (4th Bt (1892), 1st Ld St Audries (1911)	1853	Eton	Oxford	1917	3²
Acton, 2nd Ld (1902). R. M. Dalberg-Acton	1870		Oxford	1924	5, 7
Adams, (H.) R.	1912	Emanuel	London	..	36
Adamson, Mrs J. L.				1963	35
†Adamson, W.	1863	Elementary	..	1936	16, 19
Adamson, W. M.	1881	Elementary	..	1945	30
†Addison, 1st Vt (1945). C. Addison	1869	Trinity Coll., Harrogate*	London	1951	6, 8, 10, 11³, 12, 18, 32, 33³, 34, 35
†Ailwyn, 1st Ld (1921). Sir A. E. Fellowes (K.C.V.O. 1911)	1855	Eton	Cambridge	1924	2, 3²
Airlie, 12th E of (1900). D. L. G. W. Ogilvy	1893	Eton	..	..	18
Aitchison, Ld (Scot. judge 1933). C. M. Aitchison	1882	Falkirk H.S.*	Edinburgh	1941	19, 22
†Akers-Douglas, A., 1st Vt Chilston (1911)	1851	Eton	Oxford	1926	2, 3
Albemarle, 8th E of (1984). A. A. C. Keppel	1858	Eton	..	1942	15
Albu, A.	1903	Tonbridge	London	..	45
†Aldington, 1st Ld (1962). Sir T. A. R. W. Low (K.C.M.G. 1957)	1914	Winchester	Oxford	..	38, 39

Name	Born	School	Univ.	Died	Page references
†Alexander, 1st E (1952). H. R. L. G. Alexander, 1st Vt (1946)	1891	Harrow	Sandhurst	..	37
†Alexander of Hillsborough, 1st E (1963). A. V. Alexander, 1st Vt (1950)	1885	Elementary	..	1965	16, 18, 33², 34²
Allan, R. A.	1914	Harrow	Cambridge	..	40, 43
†Allendale, 1st Vt (1911). W. C. B. Beaumont, 2nd Ld Allendale (1907)	1860	Eton	Cambridge	1923	5², 7², 9
Allendale, 2nd Vt (1923). W. H. C. Beaumont	1890	Eton	Cambridge	1956	22, 31
†Alness, 1st Ld (1934). R. Munro	1868	Aberdeen G.S.*	Edinburgh	1955	7, 9, 11, 30, 32
†Alport, Ld (Life Peer 1961). C. J. Alport	1912	Haileybury	Cambridge	..	39, 41²
†Althorp, 1st Vt (1905). C. R. Spencer, Vt Althorp (1857). 6th Earl of Spencer (1910)	1857	Harrow	Cambridge	1922	5, 7
†Altrincham, 1st Ld (1945). Sir E. W. M. Grigg (K.C.V.O. 1920)	1879	Winchester	Oxford	1955	24², 28, 30, 32
†Alverstone, 1st Vt (1913). Sir R. E. Webster) G.C.M.G. 1893). 1st Ld Alverstone (1900)	1842	King's Coll. Sch. & Charter-house	Cambridge	1915	3
†Amery, J.	1919	Eton	Oxford	..	41², 43, 44
†Amery, L. S.	1873	Harrow	Oxford	1955	10², 14, 17², 28, 31
†Ammon, 1st Ld (1944). C. G. Ammon	1875	Elementary	..	1960	16, 18, 36
†Amory, 1st Vt (1960). D. Heathcoat Amory	1899	Eton	Oxford	..	37², 38, 39, 40
Amulree, 1st Ld (1929). Sir W. W. Mackenzie (K.B.E. 1918)	1860	Perth Academy*	Edinburgh & London	1942	19, 21
Amwell, 1st Ld (1947). F. Montague	1876	Elementary	..	1966	19, 27, 30
†Ancaster, 2nd E (1910). G. H. D. Willoughby	1867	Eton	Cambridge	1951	10, 14
Anderson, Ld (Scot. judge 1913). A. M. Anderson	1862	Dundee H.S.*	Edinburgh	1936	7
Anderson, D. C.	1916	Trinity Coll. Glenalmond	Oxford & Edinburgh	..	43, 44
†Anderson, Sir J. (K.C.B. 1919). 1st Vt Waverley (1952)	1882	George Watson's Coll., Edin.	Edinburgh & Leipzig	1958	22, 23, 26², 28², 31
Anson, Sir W. (3rd Bt 1873)	1843	Eton	Oxford	1914	2
Anstruther, H. T.	1860	Eton	Edinburgh	1926	3
†Anstruther-Gray, Sir W. J. (1st Bt 1956) Ld Kilmany (Life Peer 1966)	1905	Eton	Oxford	..	32
Archibald, 1st Ld (1949). G. Archibald	1898	Allan Glen's H.S. Glasg.*	..	..	36
Armstrong, E.	1915	Wolsingham G.S.	..	..	308
Arnold, 1st Ld (1924). S. Arnold	1878	Manchester G.S.	..	1945	16, 19
†Arnold-Foster, H. O.	1855	Rugby	Oxford	1909	2, 3
†Ashbourne, 1st Ld (1885). E. Gibson	1837		Dublin	1913	2
†Ashby St Ledgers, 1st Ld (1910). I. C. Guest, 2nd Ld Wimborne (1914), 1st Vt Wimborne (1918)	1873	Eton	Cambridge	1939	7²
†Ashfield, 1st Ld (1920). Sir A. H. Stanley (Kt 1914)	1874	American Schs.	..	1948	11
†Ashley, W. W. 1st Ld Mount Temple (1932)	1867	Harrow	Oxford	1939	15², 18
†Asquith, H. H. 1st E of Ox-ford & Asquith (1925)	1852	City of London	Oxford	1928	4, 5, 6, 8

Name	Born	School	Univ.	Died	Page references
†Benn, A. Wedgwood	1925	Westminster	Oxford	..	47, 48
†Benn, W. Wedgwood, 1st Vt Stansgate (1941)	1877	Secondary	London	1960	7, 19, 33
Bennett of Edgbaston, 1st Ld (1953), Sir P. F. Bennett (Kt 1941)	1880	King Edward's Birmingham	..	1957	37
Bennett, Sir E. N. (Kt 1930)	1868	Durham	Oxford	1947	20, 25
Bernays, R. H.	1902	Rossall	Oxford	1945	23, 24
Bessborough, 10th E of (1956). F. E. N. Ponsonby, Vt. Duncannon (1920)	1913	Eton	Cambridge	..	41, 42
†Beswick, Ld. F. Beswick (Life Peer 1964)	1912	Elementary	..	..	33, 46³, 308²
†Betterton, Sir H. B. (1st Bt 1929). 1st Ld Rushcliffe (1935)	1872	Rugby	Oxford	1949	14, 17, 20, 21
†Bevan, A.	1897	Elementary	..	1960	34²
†Bevin, E.	1881	Elementary	..	1951	27, 28, 33²
†Bevins, (J.) R.	1908	Liverpool Coll.	..	..	39, 42, 44
†Bingley, 1st Ld (1933). G. R. Lane-Fox	1870	Eton	Oxford	1947	15, 17
†Birch, (E.) N. C.	1906	Eton	..	..	37, 38², 39, 40
†Birkenhead, 1st E of (1922). Sir F. E. Smith (Kt 1915), 1st Ld Birkenhead (1919), 1st Vt (1921)	1872	Birkenhead	Oxford	1930	9, 13, 17
Birkenhead, 2nd E of (1930). F. W. F. Smith, Vt Furneaux (1922)	1907	Eton	Oxford	..	26, 39
Birnam, Ld (Scot. judge 1945). Sir (T.) D. K. Murray (Kt 1941)	1884	Hamilton Acad.* & Glasgow H.S.*	Glasgow	1955	30, 32
†Birrell, A.	1850	Amersham Hall*	Cambridge	1933	4², 6, 8
Bishop, E. S.	1920	S. Bristol C.S.*	Bristol	..	308
Blades, Ld (Scot. judge 1947).	1888	Berwickshire	Edinburgh	1959	36
†Blakenham, 1st Vt (1963) J. H. Hare	1911	Eton	..	..	37, 39, 41, 42³, 44
†Bledisloe, 1st Vt (1935). Sir C. Bathurst (K.B.E. 1917), 1st Ld Bledisloe (1918)	1867	Sherborne & Eton	Oxford	1958	12, 17
Blenkinsop, A.	1911	Newcastle upon Tyne Royal G.S.	..	..	34, 35, 36
Blindell, Sir J. (Kt 1936)	1884	St. Mary's, Hitchin*	..	1937	15, 22
†Bondfield, Miss M. G.	1873	Elementary	..	1953	16, 19
Boothby, Ld (Life Peer 1958). Sir R. J. G. Boothby (K.B.E. 1953)	1900	Eton	Oxford	..	28
†Bottomley, A. G.	1907	Elementary	..	..	33, 34, 46, 47
Boulton, Sir W. W. (1st Bt 1944)	1873	Privately	..	1949	30, 31
Bowden, Ld (Life Peer 1964). B. V. Bowden	1910	Chesterfield G.S.*	Cambridge	..	47
†Bowden, H. W., Ld Aylestone (Life Peer 1967)	1905	Secondary	..	..	36, 45, 46
Bowles, Ld (Life Peer 1964). F. G. Bowles	1902	Highgate	London	..	308
Bowyer, Sir G. E. W. (Kt 1929). 1st Ld Denham (1937)	1886	Eton	Oxford	1948	18, 23, 26
†Boyd, 1st Vt (1960). A. T. Lennox-Boyd	1904	Sherborne	Oxford	..	23, 24, 27, 31, 37², 39, 42
Boyd-Carpenter, Sir A. B. (Kt 1926)	1873	Harrow	Oxford	1937	4², 15
†Boyd-Carpenter, J. A.	1908	Stowe	Oxford	..	36, 37, 39², 42, 43
Boyden, H. J.	1910	Tiffin's*	London	..	46, 47, 48
†Boyle, Sir E. C. G. (3rd Bt 1945)	1923	Eton	Oxford	..	36, 39, 40, 41, 42³
†Brabazon, 1st Ld (1942). I. T. C. Moore-Brabazon	1884	Harrow	Cambridge	1964	15, 18, 26, 27, 29
Brabner, R. A.	1911	Felsted	Cambridge	1945	27

Name	Born	School	Univ.	Died	Page references
†Brace, W.	1856	Elementary	..	1947	8, 10
†Bracken, 1st Vt (1952). B. Bracken	1901	Sedbergh	..	1958	28, 31
Bradford, 5th E of (1915). O. Bridgeman, Vt Newport (1898)	1873	Harrow	Cambridge	1957	13, 15
Braine, B. R.	1914	Hendon C.S.★	..	..	41, 43[2]
Braithwaite, Sir J. G.(1st Bt 1954)	1895	Bootham	..	1958	39
Bray, J.	1930	Kingswood	Cambridge	..	47[2]
†Brecon, 1st Ld (1957) D. V. P. Lewis	1905	Monmouth★	..	..	42
†Brentford, 1st Vt (1929). Sir W. Joynson-Hicks (1st Bt 1919)	1865	Merchant Taylors' Sch.	..	1932	14[2], 15[3], 17
Brentford, 3rd Vt (1958). L. W. Joynson-Hicks	1902	Winchester	Oxford	..	38
†Bridgeman, 1st Vt (1929). W. C. Bridgeman	1864	Eton	Cambridge	1935	9, 11[3], 13, 14, 17
Bridport, 3rd Vt (1924). R. A. H. N. Hood	1911	R.N. Coll., Dart-mouth	..	..	26
†Brodrick, (W.) St J. 9th Vt Midleton (1907), 1st E of (1920)	1856	Eton	Oxford	1942	2[2], 3
Bromley-Davenport, Sir W. (K.C.B. 1924)	1862	Eton	Oxford	1949	3
†Brooke, Ld (Life Peer 1966). H. Brooke	1903	Marlborough	Oxford	..	36, 41, 42[2]
Brooman-White, R. C.	1912	Eton	Cambridge	1964	42, 43[2], 44, 45
†Brown, E.	1881	Torquay★	..	1962	20, 21, 24, 28[2], 29, 31
†Brown, G. A.	1914	Secondary	..	..	33, 35, 45[2]
Brown, R. C.	1921	Elementary	..	..	48
Brown, R. W.	1921	Elementary	..	..	308
Brown, T. W.	1879	Campbell Coll.	Belfast	1944	13[2]
Brown, Ld (Life Peer 1964). W. Brown	1908	Rossall	..	..	48
†Browne, J. N., Ld Craigton (Life Peer 1959)	1904	Cheltenham	..	..	42[2]
Bruntisfield, 1st Ld (1942). Sir V. A. G. A. Warrender (8th Bt 1917)	1899	Eton	..	..	22[3], 23[2], 24, 27, 31
Bryan, P. E. O.	1913	St John's, Leatherhead	Cambridge	..	44
†Bryce, 1st Vt (1914). J. Bryce	1838	Glasgow H.S.★	Glasgow & Oxford	1922	4
Buchan, N.	1922	Kirkwall G.S.★	Glasgow	..	47
†Buchan-Hepburn, P. G. T. 1st Ld Hailes (1957)	1901	Harrow	Cambridge	..	25, 30[2], 32, 38, 39[2]
†Buchanan, G.	1890	Elementary	..	1955	34, 35
†Buchanan, T. R.	1846	Sherborne	Oxford	1911	4, 6
Buckley, A.	1877	Merchant Tay-lors', Crosby	..	1965	15[2]
†Buckmaster, 1st Vt (1933). Sir S. O. Buckmaster (Kt 1913), 1st Ld (1915)	1861	Aldenham	Oxford	1934	7, 8
Burden, 1st Ld (1950). T. W. Burden	1885	Elementary	London Sch. of Econ.	..	36
†Burgin, (E.) L.	1887	Christ's Coll., Finchley★	Lausanne & Paris	1945	21, 24[4], 25
Burke, W. A.	1890	Secondary	..	..	35
†Burns, J.	1858	Elementary	..	1943	4, 6[2]
Butcher, Sir H. W. (Kt 1953)	1901	Hastings G.S.★	..	1966	39
†Butler, Ld (Life Peer 1965) R. A. Butler	1902	Marlborough	Cambridge	..	20, 23, 24[2], 26, 28, 31, 36, 40[3], 41
†Buxton, 1st E (1920). S. C. Buxton, 1st Vt (1914)	1853	Clifton	Cambridge	1934	4, 6[2]
†Buxton, N. E. N. 1st Ld Noel-Buxton (1930)	1869	Harrow	Cambridge	1948	16, 18

Name	Born	School	Univ.	Died	Page references
†Cadogan, 5th E (1873). Vt Chelsea (1864)	1840	Eton	Oxford	1915	2
†Caldecote, 1st Vt (1939). Sir T. W. H. Inskip (Kt 1922)	1876	Clifton	Cambridge	1947	15, 18², 21, 22, 23², 25, 28
†Callaghan, (L.) J.	1912	Portsmouth Nn★	..	..	34, 35, 45, 46
Campbell, G. T. C.	1921	Wellington	..	..	42, 44
Campbell, Sir J. H. M. (1st Bt 1916). 1st Ld Glenavy (1921)	1851	Kingstown★	Dublin	1931	3, 9, 12, 13
†Campbell-Bannerman, Sir H. (G.C.B. 1895)	1836	Glasgow H.S.★	Glasgow	1908	4
†Caradon, Ld (Life Peer 1964). Sir H. Foot (K.C.M.G. 1951)	1907	Leighton Park	Cambridge	..	45
Carmichael, N.	1921	Estbank Acad.★	..	..	48
†Carr, R.	1916	Westminster	Cambridge	..	37, 42, 44
†Carrington, 1st E (1895). C. R. Wynn-Carrington, 3rd Ld Carrington (1868), 1st M of Lincolnshire (1912)	1843	Eton	Cambridge	1928	4
†Carrington, 6th Ld (1938). P. A. R. Carington	1919	Eton	Sandhurst	..	37², 42, 43
†Carson, 1st Ld (1921). Sir E. H. Carson (Kt 1900)	1854	Portarlington★	Dublin	1935	3, 10, 11
Cary, Sir R. A. (1st Bt 1955)	1898	Ardingly	Sandhurst	..	32
†Casey, Ld (Life Peer 1960). R. G. Casey	1890	Melbourne G.S.	Melbourne & Cambridge	..	27
†Castle, Mrs B. A.	1911	Bradford G.G.S.	Oxford	..	45, 47, 48,
†Causton, R. K. 1st Ld Southwark (1910)	1843	Privately	..	1929	4, 7
†Cave, 1st Vt (1918). Sir G. Cave (Kt 1915)	1856	Merchant Taylors'	Oxford	1928	9, 10, 14, 17
Cavendish, V. C. W. 9th D of Devonshire (1908)	1868	Eton	Cambridge	1938	2, 3, 8, 14
†Cawdor, 3rd E (1898). F. A. V. Campbell, Vt Emlyn (1847)	1847	Eton	Oxford	1911	2
†Cawley, 1st Ld (1918). Sir F. Cawley (1st Bt 1906)	1850	Secondary	..	1937	11
Cazalet-Keir, Mrs T.	1899		..	..	32
†Cecil of Chelwood, 1st Vt (1923). Ld R. Cecil	1864	Eton	Oxford	1958	8, 10, 12, 14, 17
Chadwick, Sir R. Burton (Kt 1920)	1869	Birkenhead & Privately	..	1951	17
†Chalfont, Ld (Life Peer 1964). A. Gwynne-Jones	1919	W. Monmouth S.	..	..	46
†Chamberlain, (A.) N.	1869	Rugby	Birmingham	1940	11, 14², 15², 17, 20², 22, 23, 26
†Chamberlain, J.	1836	University Coll. Sch.	..	1914	2
†Chamberlain, Sir (J.) A. (K.G. 1925)	1863	Rugby	Cambridge	1937	2³, 8, 9³, 10, 11, 17, 21
Chambers, J.	1863	Royal Acad. Institution	Queen's Coll., Belfast	1917	13
†Champion, Ld (Life Peer 1962). A. J. Champion	1897	St. John's, Glastonbury★	..	..	33, 48
†Chandos, 1st Vt (1954). O. Lyttelton	1893	Eton	Cambridge	..	26, 27², 29, 31², 37
†Chaplin, 1st Vt (1916). H. Chaplin	1840	Harrow	Oxford	1923	2
Chapman, A.	1897		Cambridge	1966	29², 31
Charleton, H. C.	1870	Elementary	..	1959	19
Chataway, C. J.	1951	Sherborne	Oxford	..	42²
†Chatfield, 1st Ld (1937). Sir A. E. M. Chatfield (K.C.M.G. 1919)	1873	H.M.S. Britannia★	..	1967	23
†Chelmsford, 1st Vt (1921). F. J. N. Thesiger, 3rd Ld Chelmsford (1905)	1868	Winchester	Oxford	1933	16
Cherry, R. R.	1859	Secondary	Dublin	1923	5, 7

Name	Born	School	Univ.	Died	Page references
†Cherwell, 1st Vt (1956). F. A. Lindemann, 1st Ld Cherwell (1941)	1886	Blair Lodge* & Darmstadt	Berlin	1957	29, 32, 37
Chesham, 3rd Ld (1882)	1850	Eton	..	1907	4
†Chesham, 5th Ld (1952). J. C. C. Cavendish	1916	Eton	Cambridge	..	39, 43, 44
†Chesterfield, 10th E of (1887). E. F. S-Stanhope	1854	Eton	Oxford	1933	7, 9, 13
Chichester-Clark, R.	1928	R.N. College*	Cambridge	..	44, 45
†Chilston, 1st Vt (1911). A. Akers-Douglas	1851	Eton	Oxford	1926	2, 3
Chorley, 1st Ld (1945). R. S. T. Chorley	1895	Kendall*	Oxford	..	36
Churchill, 1st Vt (1902). V. A. F. S. Churchill, 3rd Ld (1886)	1864	Eton	Sandhurst	1934	3
†Churchill, Sir W. L. S. (K.G. 1953)	1874	Harrow	Sandhurst	1965	4, 6³, 8, 10, 11, 12², 17, 23, 26², 31², 36, 37
†Chuter-Ede, Ld (Life Peer 1964). J. C. Ede	1882	Dorking H.S.*	Cambridge	1965	28, 33
†Cilcennin, 1st Vt (1955). J. P. L. Thomas	1903	Rugby	Oxford	1960	27, 30, 31, 38²
Clarendon, 5th E of (1870). E. H. Villiers	1846	Harrow	Cambridge	1914	32
Clarendon, 6th E of (1914). G. H. H. Villiers, Ld Hyde (1877)	1877	Eton	..	1955	13, 15, 17, 18
Clifden, 7th Vt (1930). F. G. Agar-Robartes	1883	Eton	Oxford	1966	30
†Clinton, 21st Ld (1904). C. J. R. H.-S.-F.-Trefusis	1863	Eton	..	1957	10
†Clitheroe, 1st Ld (1955). R. Assheton	1901	Eton	Oxford	..	24, 26, 27, 29
†Clyde, Ld (Scot. judge 1920). J. A. Clyde	1863	Edinburgh Academy	Edinburgh	1944	3, 13
†Clyde, Ld (Scot. judge 1954). J. L. M. Clyde	1898	Edinburgh Academy	Oxford & Edinburgh	..	39
†Clydesmuir, 1st Ld (1947). Sir D. J. Colville (G.C.I.E. 1943)	1894	Charterhouse	Cambridge	1954	21, 23, 24³
†Clynes, J. R.	1869	Elementary	..	1949	12², 16, 18
Cobham, 9th Vt (1922). J. C. Lyttelton	1881	Eton	..	1949	24
Cochrane of Cults, 1st Ld (1919). T. H. A. E. Cochrane	1857	Eton	..	1951	2
†Colebrooke, 1st Ld (1906). Sir E. A. Colebrooke (5th Bt 1890)	1861	Eton	..	1939	5, 7², 9, 13
Coleraine, 1st Ld (1954). R. K. Law	1901	Shrewsbury	Oxford	..	26², 30, 32
Collick, P. H.	1897	Elementary	..	..	33
Collindridge, F.	1890	Elementary	..	1951	36²
†Collings, J.	1831	Plymouth*	..	1920	2
Collins, Sir G. P. (K.B.E. 1919)	1875	H.M.S. Britannia*	..	1936	13, 20, 24
Collins, V. J. Ld Stonham (Life Peer 1958)	1903	Secondary	London	..	45²
†Colville, Sir D. J. (G.C.I.E. 1943). 1st Ld Clydesmuir (1947)	1894	Charterhouse	Cambridge	1954	21, 23, 24³
†Colyton, 1st Ld (1955) H. L. D. Hopkinson	1902	Eton	Cambridge	..	37, 38, 40
†Compton-Rickett, Sir J. (Kt 1907)	1847	K. Edward VI, Bath*&privately	..	1919	12
Conant, Sir R. J. E. (1st Bt 1954)	1899	Eton	Sandhurst	..	39
Concannon, J. D.	1930	Rossington S.S.*	Nottingham	..	308

G

Name	Born	School	Univ.	Died	Page references
†Hailsham, 1st Vt (1929). Sir D. M. Hogg (Kt 1922), 1st Ld Hailsham (1928)	1872	Eton	..	1950	15, 17, 21², 22²
†Hailsham, 2nd Vt (1950–63). Q. M. Hogg	1907	Eton	Oxford	..	27, 31, 38, 40³, 41³, 42
†Haldane, 1st Vt (1911). R. B. Haldane	1856	Edinburgh Academy	Edinburgh & Göttingen	1928	4, 5, 6, 16
†Halifax, 1st E of (1944). E. F. L. Wood. 1st Ld Irwin (1925), 3rd Vt Halifax (1934)	1881	Eton	Oxford	1959	10, 14, 17, 20, 22², 23, 26
†Hall, 1st Vt (1946). G. H. Hall	1881	Elementary	..	1965	18, 26, 27², 33, 34
Hall, F.	1855	Elementary	..	1933	16
†Hall, W. G.	1887	Ellesmere	..	1962	33
†Halsbury, 1st E (1898). H. S. Giffard, 1st Ld Halsbury (1885)	1823	Privately	Oxford	1921	1
†Hamilton, M of (1885) J. A. E. Hamilton, 3rd D of Abercorn (1913)	1869	Eton	..	1953	3
†Hamilton, Ld G.	1845	Harrow	..	1927	2
Hamilton of Dalzell, 2nd Ld (1900). G. G. Hamilton	1872	Eton	Sandhurst	1952	5, 7
Hamilton, M.	1918	Radley	Oxford	..	44
Hamilton, Sir R. W. (Kt 1918)	1867	St Paul's	Cambridge	1946	20
Hanbury, R.	1845	Rugby	Oxford	1903	2²
†Hankey, 1st Ld (1939). M. P. A. Hankey	1877	Rugby	..	1963	24, 28, 29
Hannan, W.	1906	N. Kelvinside S.S.*	..	..	36
Hanworth, 1st Vt (1936). Sir E. M. Pollock (K.B.E. 1917), 1st Ld Hanworth (1926)	1861	Charterhouse	Cambridge	1936	13²
†Harcourt, 1st Vt (1916). L. Harcourt	1863	Eton	..	1922	4², 6², 8
Hardman, D. R.	1901	Coleraine Acad. Inst.*	Cambridge	..	33
Hardwicke, 6th E (1897). A. E. P. H. Yorke. Vt. Royston (1873)	1867	Eton	..	1904	2², 3
†Hare, J. H. 1st Vt Blakenham (1963)	1911	Eton	..	..	37, 39, 41, 42³, 44
†Harlech, 4th Ld (1938). W. G. A. Ormsby-Gore	1885	Eton	Oxford	1964	14, 17, 21³, 23, 25
†Harlech, 5th Ld (1964). Sir (W.) D. Ormsby-Gore	1918	Eton	Oxford	..	37, 40
Harmsworth, 1st Ld (1939). C. B. Harmsworth	1869	Marylebone G.S.*	Dublin	1948	6, 10
Harper, J.	1914	Elementary	..	..	308²
Harris, 4th Ld (1872). G. R. C. Harris	1851	Eton	Oxford	1932	3
†Harris, F. L.	1886	Winchester	Cambridge	1926	12
Harrison, Sir (J.) H. (1st Bt 1961)	1907	Northampton G.S.*	Oxford	..	39, 44, 45
Harrison, W.	1921	Secondary	..	..	308²
†Hart, Mrs J. C. M.	1924	Clitheroe G.S.*	London	..	46, 47², 48
Hartington, M of (1908). E. W. S. Cavendish, 10th D of Devonshire (1938)	1895	Eton	Cambridge	1950	23, 27, 28, 31
†Hartshorn, V.	1872	Elementary	..	1931	16, 18
Harvey, I. D.	1914	Fettes	Oxford	..	39, 40, 42
Hastings, 22nd Ld (1956). E. D. H. Astley	1912	Eton	..	..	42, 45
Hastings, Sir P. (Kt 1924)	1880	Charterhouse	..	1952	16
Hattersley, R.	1932	Sheffield City G.S.*	Hull	..	45, 47
Hawke, 9th Ld (1939). B. W.	1901	Winchester	Cambridge	..	39, 44

Name	Born	School	Univ.	Died	Page references
Hawkesbury, 1st Ld (1893). C. G. S. Foljambe, 1st E of Liverpool (1905)	1846	Eton	..	1907	5
Haworth, Sir A. A. (1st Bt 1911)	1865	Rugby	..	1944	6
Hay, J. E.	1919	Hove & Sussex G.S.*	..	..	41, 43[2]
Hayes, J. H.	1889	Secondary	..	1941	20
Hayes Fisher, W. 1st Ld Downham (1919)	1853	Haileybury	Oxford	1920	2, 3, 8, 10, 11[2]
†Head, 1st Vt (1960). A. H. Head	1906	Eton	Sandhurst	..	37, 39
†Headlam, Sir C. M. (1st Bt 1935)	1876	King's Sch., Canterbury	Oxford	1964	17, 21[2]
†Heald, Sir L. F. (Kt 1951)	1897	Charterhouse	Oxford	..	39
†Healey, D. W.	1917	Bradford G.S.	Oxford	..	46
†Heath, E. R. G.	1916	Chatham House*	Oxford	..	39[2], 40, 42, 43, 44
†Heathcoat Amory, D. 1st Vt Amory (1960)	1899	Eton	Oxford	..	37[2], 38, 39, 40, 41
†Henderson, 1st Ld (1945). W. W. Henderson	1891	Q. Elizabeth G.S., Darlington*	..	..	33, 36
Henderson of Ardwick, 1st Ld (1950). J. Henderson	1884	Elementary	..	1950	35
†Henderson, A.	1863	Elementary	..	1935	8[2], 9, 11, 16, 18
†Henderson, A., Ld Rowley (Life Peer 1966)	1893	Queen's Coll., Taunton*	Cambridge	1968	30[2], 33, 34[2]
Henderson, T.	1867	Elementary	..	1960	20
Henderson, Sir V. L. (Kt 1927)	1884	Uppingham	Sandhurst	1965	17
Henderson-Stewart, Sir J. (1st Bt 1957)	1897	Morrison's Acad., Crieff*	Edinburgh	1961	38, 41
Hennessy, Sir G. R. J. (1st Bt 1927). 1st Ld Windlesham (1937)	1877	Eton	..	1953	15, 18[3], 22
Henry, Sir D. S. (1st Bt 1922)	1864	Mount St Mary's Coll.	Belfast	1925	13[2]
†Herbison, Miss M. M.	1907	Bellshill Acad.*	Glasgow	..	34, 48[2]
Herschell, 2nd Ld (1899). R. F. Herschell	1878	Eton	Oxford	1929	5, 7, 9, 13
†Hewart, 1st Vt (1940). Sir G. Hewart (Kt 1916), 1st Ld (1922)	1870	Manchester G.S.	Oxford	1943	10, 13[2]
Hewins, W. A. S.	1865	Wolverhampton G.S.	Oxford	1931	10
Hicks, (E.) G.	1879	Elementary	..	1954	30
†Hicks Beach, Sir M. E. 1st Vt St Aldwyn (1906), (9th Bt 1854), 1st E (1915)	1837	Eton	Oxford	1916	1
†Hill, Ld (Life Peer 1963) C. Hill	1904	St Olave's	Cambridge	..	37, 39, 42[2]
Hill, J. E. B.	1912	Charterhouse	Oxford	..	44
†Hills, J. W.	1867	Eton	Oxford	1938	14
Hilton of Upton, Ld (Life Peer 1965). A. V. Hilton	1908	Elementary	..	..	308
†Hoare, Sir S. J. G. (2nd Bt 1915). 1st Vt Templewood (1944)	1880	Harrow	Oxford	1959	14, 15, 17, 20, 22, 23[4]
†Hobhouse, Sir C. E. H. (4th Bt 1916)	1862	Eton	Oxford	1941	4, 5, 6[2]
Hobson, Ld (Life Peer 1963) C. R. Hobson	1904	Elementary	..	1966	35, 308
†Hobson, Sir J. G. S. (Kt 1962)	1912	Harrow	Oxford	1967	44[2]
†Hodge, J.	1855	Hutchesontown G.S.*	..	1937	11, 12
Hodges, F.	1887	Elementary	..	1947	16
†Hogg, Sir D. M. (Kt 1922). 1st Ld Hailsham (1928), 1st Vt (1929)	1872	Eton	..	1950	15, 17, 21[2], 22[2]
†Hogg, Q. M. 2nd Vt Hailsham (1950–63)	1907	Eton	Oxford	..	27, 31, 38, 40[3], 41, 42[2]
Holden, 3rd Ld (1937). A. W. E. Holden	1898	Eton	Oxford	1951	33

Name	Born	School	Univ.	Died	Page references
Kerr, C. I. 1st Ld Teviot (1940)	1874	Stephen Hawtrey's, Windsor*	..	1968	25, 26
Kerr, Sir H. W. (1st Bt 1957)	1903	Eton	Oxford	..	32
Kershaw, 1st Ld (1947). F. Kershaw	1881	Elementary	..	1962	36
†Key, C. W.	1883	Chalfont St Giles*	..	1964	34, 35
Kidd, J.	1872	Carriden*	Edinburgh	1928	14
†Kilmany, Ld (Life Peer 1966). Sir W. J. Anstruther-Gray (1st Bt 1956)	1905	Eton	Oxford	..	32
†Kilmuir, 1st E (1962). D. P. Maxwell Fyfe, 1st Vt Kilmuir (1954)	1900	George Watson's Coll., Edin.	Oxford	1967	30, 32, 36, 37, 40
King, E. M.	1907	Cheltenham	Cambridge	..	34
King, (H.) D.	1877	Training ship	..	1930	15, 17[2]
†Kintore, 10th E of (1880). A. H. T. Keith-Falconer	1852	Eton	Cambridge	1930	3
Kirk, P. M.	1928	Marlborough	Oxford	..	41
†Kitchener of Khartoum, 1st E (1914). H. H. Kitchener, 1st Ld (1898), 1st Vt (1902)	1850	France	Woolwich	1916	6, 8
†Lambert, 1st Vt (1945). G. Lambert	1866	Privately	..	1958	4, 6
†Lane-Fox, G. R. 1st Ld Bingley (1933)	1870	Eton	Oxford	1947	15, 17
†Lansbury, G.	1859	Elementary	..	1940	19
†Lansdowne, 5th M of (1866). H. C. K. Petty-Fitzmaurice, Vt Clanmaurice (1845). E of Kerry (1863)	1845	Eton	Oxford	1927	2, 3, 8
†Lansdowne, 8th M of (1944). G. J. C. M. N. Petty-Fitzmaurice	1912	Eton	Oxford	..	40, 41, 43, 44
†Law, A. Bonar	1858	Glasgow H.S.*	..	1923	3, 9[3], 14
†Law, R. K. 1st Ld Coleraine (1954)	1901	Shrewsbury	Oxford	..	26[2], 30, 32
Lawrence, 2nd Ld (1879). J. H. Lawrence	1846	Wellington	Cambridge	1913	3
Lawrence, Miss (A.) S.	1871	..	Cambridge	1947	19
†Lawson, 1st Ld (1950). J. J. Lawson	1881	Elementary	..	1965	16, 19, 34
Lawson, G. M.	1906	Elementary	..	..	308
Lawson, Sir J. G. (1st Bt 1905)	1856	Harrow	Oxford	1919	2
Leach, W.	1870	Bradford G.S.	..	1949	16
†Leathers, 1st Vt (1954). F. J. Leathers, 1st Ld (1941)	1883	Elementary	..	1965	30, 32, 37
Leburn, (W.) G.	1913	Strathallan*	..	1963	41, 42
†Lee of Fareham, 1st Vt (1922). Sir A. Lee (K.C.B. 1916). 1st Ld (1918)	1868	Cheltenham	Woolwich	1947	2, 8, 10[2]
†Lee, F.	1906	Langworthy Rd.*	..	..	34, 46, 47, 48
†Lee, Miss J. (Mrs A. Bevan)	1904	Benton*	Edinburgh	..	47[2], 48
Leechman, J.	1906	Glasgow H.S.*	Glasgow	..	308
†Lees-Smith, H. B.	1878	Aldenham	..	1941	19[2]
Legh, P. R. 4th Ld Newton (1960)	1915	Eton	Oxford	..	39, 41, 42[2] 44[3], 45[2]
†Lennox-Boyd, A. T. 1st Vt Boyd (1960)	1904	Sherborne	Oxford	..	23, 24, 27, 31, 37[2], 39, 41
Leonard, W.	1887	Elementary	..	..	35
Lever, Sir (S.) H. (K.C.B. 1917)	1869	Merchant Taylors' Sch., Crosby	..	1947	9
Lever, H.	1914	Manchester G.S.	..	..	45[2]
†Lewis, Sir (J.) H. (G.B.E. 1922)	1858	Secondary	McGill & Oxford	1933	5, 6, 7, 8, 10
Lewis, T. A.	1881		Cardiff	1923	13
†Lincolnshire, 1st M of (1912). C. R. Wynn-Carrington, 3rd Ld Carrington (1868), 1st E (1895)	1843	Eton	Cambridge	1928	4, 5, 6

Name	Born	School	Univ.	Died	Page references
Lindgren, Ld (Life Peer 1961). G. S. Lindgren	1900	Elementary	..	..	33, 34, 35, 47, 48
Lindsay, K.	1897	St Olave's	Oxford	..	23[2]
†Linlithgow, 1st M of (1902). J. A. L. Hope, 7th E of Hopetoun (1873)	1860	Eton	..	1908	2, 3
Linlithgow, 2nd M of (1908). V. A. J. Hope, E of Hopetoun (1902)	1887	Eton	..	1952	14
†Listowel, 5th E of (1931). W. F. Hare, Vt Ennismore (1924)	1906	Eton	Oxford	..	28, 33[2], 34, 35
†Liverpool, 1st E of (1905). C. G. S. Foljambe, 1st Ld Hawkesbury (1893)	1846	Eton	..	1907	5
†Liverpool, 2nd E of (1907). A. W. D. S. Foljambe, Vt Hawkesbury (1905)	1870	Eton	Sandhurst	1941	7
†Llewellin, 1st Ld (1945). J. J. Llewellin	1893	Eton	Oxford	1957	23, 24, 27[2], 28, 29, 30, 32
Llewellyn, Sir D. T. (Kt 1960)	1916	Eton	Cambridge	..	37
†Lloyd, 1st Ld (1925). Sir G. A. Lloyd (G.C.I.E. 1918)	1879	Eton	Cambridge	1941	27
Lloyd, 2nd Ld (1941). A. D. F. Lloyd	1912	Eton	Cambridge	..	37[2], 39
†Lloyd, G.	1902	Harrow	Cambridge	..	23, 24, 28, 29, 32, 38, 40
†Lloyd, (J.) S. B.	1904	Fettes	Cambridge	..	36[2], 37, 38, 39, 40[3]
†Lloyd George of Dwyfor, 1st E (1945). D. Lloyd George	1863	Llanystumdwy Church Sch.★	..	1945	4, 5, 8[2], 9[2]
†Lloyd-George, G. 1st Vt Tenby (1957)	1894	Eastbourne	Cambridge	1967	21, 24, 28[2], 29, 32, 37[2], 38, 40
†Lloyd-Greame, Sir P. (K.B.E. 1920). Changed name to Sir P. Cunliffe-Lister in 1924, 1st Vt Swinton (1935). 1st E of Swinton (1955)	1884	Winchester	Oxford	..	11[2], 15, 17[2], 20, 21, 23, 27, 28, 32, 38[2]
Loch, 2nd Ld (1900). E. D. Loch	1873	Winchester	..	1942	7
†Lochee of Gowrie, 1st Ld (1908). E. Robertson	1846	Secondary	St Andrews & Oxford	1911	4
Locker-Lampson, G. L. T.	1875	Eton	Cambridge	1946	14, 17[2]
†Londonderry, 6th M of (1884). C. S. Vane-Tempest-Stewart. Vt Castlereagh (1872)	1852	Eton	Oxford	1915	2[2], 3
†Londonderry, 7th M of (1915). C. S. H. Vane-Tempest-Stewart. Vt Castlereagh (1884)	1878	Eton	Sandhurst	1949	12, 17, 20, 21, 22
†Long, 1st Vt (1921). W. H. Long	1854	Harrow	Oxford	1924	2[3], 8, 10[2]
†Longford, 7th E of (1961). F. A. Pakenham, 1st Ld Pakenham (1945)	1905	Eton	Oxford	..	33, 34[2], 35[2], 36, 45[2], 46
†Loreburn, 1st E (1911). Sir R. T. Reid (Kt 1894), 1st Ld Loreburn (1906)	1846	Cheltenham	Oxford	1923	4, 5
†Lothian, 11th M of (1930). P. H. Kerr	1882	Oratory Sch.	Oxford	1940	20, 21
Lothian, 12th M of (1940). P. F. W. Kerr	1922	Ampleforth	Oxford	..	43, 45
†Lough, T.	1850	Wesleyan Sch., Dublin★	..	1922	4
Loughlin, C. W.	1914	Elementary	..	..	47, 48[3]
Lovat, 16th Ld (1887). S. J. Fraser	1871	Fort Augustus Abbey	Oxford	1933	17
Lovat, 17th Ld (1933). S. C. J. Fraser	1911	Ampleforth	Oxford	..	31
†Low, Sir T. A. R. W. (K.C.M.G. 1957), 1st Ld Aldington (1962)	1914	Winchester	Oxford	..	38, 39

Name	Born	School	Univ.	Died	Page references
†Manchester, 9th D of (1892). W. A. D. Montagu	1877	Eton	Cambridge	1947	5
Mancroft, 1st Ld (1937). Sir A. M. Samuel (1st Bt 1932)	1872	Secondary	..	1942	17²
Mancroft, 2nd Ld (1942). S. M. S. Mancroft	1914	Winchester	Oxford	..	37, 39, 41, 43
†Manningham-Buller, Sir R. E. (Kt 1951), 1st Ld Dilhorne (1962) 1st Vt (1964)	1905	Eton	Oxford	..	32, 39², 40, 44
†Marchamley, 1st Ld (1908). G. Whiteley	1855	Abroad	Zürich	1925	5, 7
Marchwood, 1st Vt (1945). Sir F. G. Penny (Kt 1929), 1st Ld Marchwood (1937)	1876	K. Edward VI G.S., South-ampton*	..	1955	18, 22⁴, 26
†Margesson, 1st Vt (1942). (H.) D. R. Margesson	1890	Harrow	Cambridge	1965	18, 21, 22, 25, 30²
†Marlborough, 9th D of (1892). C. R. J. Spencer-Churchill, M of Blandford (1883)	1871	Winchester	Cambridge	1934	2, 3, 10
Marley, 1st Ld (1930). D. L. Aman	1884	Marlborough & R.N.C. Greenwich	..	1952	19, 20
†Marples, E.	1907	Stretford G.S.*	..	..	37, 39, 43, 44
†Marquand, H. A.	1901	Cardiff H.S.*	Cardiff	..	34², 35³
†Marsh, R. N.	1928	Elementary	..	..	47³, 48
Marshall, F.	1883	Elementary	..	1962	34
Marten, N.	1916	Rossall	..	..	41
†Mason, R.	1925	Royston*	..	..	46, 47, 48²
Masterman, C. F. G.	1873	Weymouth*	Cambridge	1927	5, 6²
†Mathers, 1st Ld (1951). G. Mathers	1886	Elementary	..	1965	31, 36
Matthew, R.	1911	Eton	Cambridge	1966	40
†Maudling, R.	1917	Merchant Taylors'	Oxford	..	36, 39², 40, 41, 42, 43²
†Maugham, 1st Vt (1939). Sir F. H. Maugham (Kt 1928), Ld (Ld of Appeal 1935)	1866	Dover Coll.	Cambridge	1958	22
Mawby, R. L.	1922	Secondary	..	..	44
†Maxwell Fyfe, D. P. 1st Vt Kilmuir (1954) 1st E (1962)	1900	George Watson's Coll., Edin.	Oxford	1967	30, 32, 36, 37, 40
Maydon, S. L. C.	1913	Twyford*	..	..	43
Mayhew, C. P.	1915	Haileybury	Oxford	..	33, 46
†Melchett, 1st Ld (1928). Sir A. M. Mond (1st Bt 1910)	1868	Cheltenham	Cambridge & Edinburgh	1930	10, 13
†Mellish, R. J.	1913	Elementary	..	..	47, 48
Melville, Sir J. B. (Kt 1929)	1885	..	..	1931	19
†Merriman, 1st Ld (1941). Sir F. B. Merriman (Kt 1928)	1880	Winchester	..	1962	18
†Merrivale, 1st Ld (1925). Sir H. E. Duke (Kt 1918)	1855	Secondary	..	1939	8, 10
†Midleton, 1st E of (1920). (W.) St. J. Brodrick, 9th Vt Midleton (1907)	1856	Eton	Oxford	1942	2²
Millan, B.	1927	Harris Acad., Dundee	..	..	46, 47
†Milligan, Ld (Scot. judge 1960). W. R. Milligan	1898	Sherborne	Oxford & Glasgow	..	39², 44
Miller, M. S.	1920	Shawlands Acad.*	Glasgow	..	308
†Mills, 1st Ld (1957). Sir P. H. Mills (Kt 1942)	1890	NE County S., Barnard Castle*	..	1968	42³, 43
†Milner, 1st Vt (1902). Sir A. Milner (K.C.B. 1895), 1st Ld (1901)	1854	German Schs.	London & Oxford	1925	9, 10, 11, 12
†Mitchell-Thomson, Sir W. (2nd Bt 1918), 1st Ld Sels-don (1932)	1877	Winchester	Oxford	1938	11, 12, 18
Mitchison, Ld (Life Peer 1964). G. R. Mitchison	1890	Eton	Oxford	..	48
Molony, Sir T. F. (1st Bt 1925	1865	Secondary	Dublin	1949	72

Name	Born	School	Univ.	Died	Page references
Neal, A.	1862	Wesley Coll., Sheffield*	..	1933	12
Neal, H.	1897	Elementary	..	..	35
Neave, A. M. S.	1916	Eton	Oxford	..	43[2]
†Newton, 2nd Ld (1899). T. W. Legh	1857	Eton	Oxford	1942	8, 9, 10
Newton, 4th Ld (1960). P. R. Legh	1915	Eton	Oxford	..	39, 41, 42, 43, 44, 45[2]
Nicholls, Sir H. (1st Bt 1960)	1912	Q. Mary's G.S., Walsall*	..	..	44
Nicolson, Sir H. G. (K.C.V.O. 1953)	1886	Wellington	Oxford	1968	28
†Noble, Sir A. H. P. (K.C.M.G. 1959)	1908	Radley	..	..	36, 37, 38, 40
†Noble, M. A. C.	1913	Eton	Oxford	..	42, 44
†Noel-Baker, P. J.	1889	Bootham	Cambridge	..	30, 33[2], 34, 35
†Noel-Buxton, 1st Ld (1930). N. E. N. Buxton	1869	Harrow	Cambridge	1948	16, 18
†Norfolk, 15th D of (1860). H. FitzAlan-Howard, E of Arundel (1847)	1847	Oratory Sch.	..	1917	3
†Norfolk, 16th D of (1917). B. M. FitzAlan-Howard, E of Arundel (1908)	1908	Oratory Sch.	..	..	27, 31
†Norman, Sir H. (Kt 1906)	1858	Privately	Harvard & Leipzig	1939	6
Normanby, 4th M of (1932). O. C. J. Phipps, E of Mulgrave (1912)	1912	Eton	Oxford	..	30, 32
†Normand, Ld (Ld of Appeal 1947). W. G. Normand	1884	Fettes	Oxford, Paris & Edinburgh	1962	18, 22[2]
Northumberland, 10th D of (1940). H. A. Percy	1914	Eton	Oxford	..	32
Norton, C. W. 1st Ld Rathcreedan (1916)	1845	Abroad	Dublin & Sandhurst	1930	5, 6, 7
†Norwich, 1st Vt (1952). A. Duff Cooper	1890	Eton	Oxford	1954	17, 20, 21, 23[2], 24, 28[2]
†Novar, 1st Vt (1920). Sir R. C. Munro-Ferguson (G.C.M.G. 1914)	1860	Privately	Sandhurst	1935	14
†Nugent of Guildford, Ld (Life Peer 1966), Sir (G.) R. H. (1st Bt 1960)	1907	Imperial Service Coll.	Woolwich	..	37, 43
†Nutting, (H.) A.	1920	Eton	Cambridge	..	36[2]
Oakshott, Ld (Life Peer 1964). Sir H. D. Oakshott (1st Bt 1959)	1904	Rugby	Cambridge	..	39[2], 44
O'Brien, Sir I. J. (1st Bt 1916). 1st Ld Shandon (1918)	1857	Secondary & Privately	Univ. of Ireland	1930	7[2], 12
O'Connor, C. A.	1854	St Stanislaus Coll.*	Dublin	1928	7[2]
O'Connor, Sir J. (Kt 1925)	1872	Blackrock Coll.	..	1931	7, 9, 13
O'Connor, Sir T. J. (Kt 1936)	1891		..	1940	25
†Ogmore, 1st Ld (1950). D. R. Rees-Williams	1903	Mill Hill	Wales	..	33[2], 34
O'Hagan, 3rd Ld (1900). M. H. T. Townley-O'Hagan	1882	Marlborough	Cambridge	1961	5, 7
Oliver, G. H.	1888	Bolton*	..	..	33
†Olivier, 1st Ld (1924). S. Olivier	1859	Lausanne & Tonbridge	Oxford	1943	16
O'Malley, B.	1930	Mexborough G.S.*	Manchester	..	308[2]
†O'Neill, Sir (R. W.) H. (1st Bt 1929). 1st Ld Rathcavan (1953)	1883	Eton	Oxford	..	24
†Onslow, 4th E of (1870). W. H. Onslow, Vt Cranley (1855)	1853	Eton	Oxford	1911	23
Onslow, 5th E of (1911). R. W. A. Onslow, Vt Cranley (1876)	1876	Eton	Oxford	1945	10[3], 13, 14[2], 17, 18

Name	Born	School	Univ.	Died	Page references
†Runciman, of Doxford 1st Vt (1937). W. Runciman, 2nd Ld Runciman (1933)	1870	S. Shields H.S.* & Privately	Cambridge	1949	4², 6², 8, 21, 22, 24
Runcorn, Ld (Life Peer 1964) D. F. Vosper	1916	Marlborough	Cambridge	1968	37, 39, 41², 43, 44
†Rushcliffe, 1st Ld (1935). Sir H. B. Betterton (1st Bt 1929)	1872	Rugby	Oxford	1949	14, 17, 20, 21
Russell, 2nd E (1878). J. F. S. Russell	1865	Winchester	Oxford	1931	19²
Russell, Ld (Scot. judge 1936). A. Russell	1884	Glasgow Acad.	Glasgow	..	25
Russell, Sir T. W. (1st Bt 1917)	1841	Madras Acad., Fife*	..	1920	2, 4, 6, 8, 10
†St Aldwyn, 1st E (1915). M. E. Hicks Beach, 1st Vt St Aldwyn (1906)	1837	Eton	Oxford	1916	1
†St Aldwyn, 2nd E (1915). M. J. Hicks Beach	1912	Eton	Oxford	..	37, 41, 45
†St Audries, 1st Ld (1911). Sir A. F. Acland Hood (4th Bt 1892)	1853	Eton	Oxford	1917	32
St. Helens, 1st Ld (1964). M. H. C. Hughes-Young	1912	Eton	Sandhurst	..	44²
St Oswald, 4th Ld (1957). R. D. G. Winn	1916	Stowe	Bonn & Freiburg	..	41, 45
†Salisbury, 3rd M of (1868). R. A. T. Gascoyne-Cecil, Vt Cranborne (1865)	1830	Eton	Oxford	1903	1², 2
†Salisbury, 4th M of (1903). J. E. H. Gascoyne-Cecil, Vt Cranborne (1868)	1861	Eton	Oxford	1947	1, 2, 3, 14², 17
†Salisbury, 5th M of (1947). R. A. J. Gascoyne-Cecil, Vt Cranborne (1903)	1893	Eton	Oxford	..	23, 26, 27, 28², 29², 31, 36², 37, 40
†Salter, 1st Ld (1953). Sir (J.) A. Salter (K.C.B. 1922)	1881	Oxford H.S.*	Oxford	..	24, 29, 30, 32, 36 38
†Salvesen, Ld (Scot. judge 1905). E. Salvesen	1857	Collegiate Sch., Edin.*	Edinburgh	1942	3
†Samuel, 1st Vt (1937). Sir H. L. Samuel (G.B.E. 1920)	1870	University Coll. Sch.	Oxford	1963	4, 6⁴, 8², 9, 20
Samuel, Sir A. M. (1st Bt 1932). 1st Ld Mancroft (1937)	1872	Norwich G.S.*	..	1942	17²
Samuels, A. W.	1852	Royal Sch., Dungannon *	Dublin	1925	13²
†Sanders, Sir R. A. (1st Bt 1920). 1st Ld Bayford (1929)	1867	Harrow	Oxford	1940	12, 13², 14
Sanders, W. S.	1871	Elementary	Berlin	1941	19
Sandford, 1st Ld (1945). Sir A. J. Edmondson (Kt 1934)	1887	University Coll. Sch.	..	1959	25, 26, 30, 31, 32
†Sandhurst, 1st Vt (1917). W. Mansfield, 2nd Ld Sandhurst (1876)	1855	Rugby	..	1921	7, 9, 13
†Sandys, D.	1908	Eton	Oxford	..	29, 30², 32, 37, 39, 41⁴
†Sankey, 1st Vt (1932). Sir J. Sankey (Kt 1914), 1st Ld (1929)	1866	Lancing	Oxford	1948	18, 20
†Sassoon, Sir P. A. G. D. (3rd Bt 1912)	1888	Eton	Oxford	1939	17, 20, 23, 25
Saye & Sele, 18th Ld (1907). G. C. T.-W.-Fiennes	1858	Eton	..	1937	7
†Scarbrough, 11th E of (1945). L. R. Lumley	1896	Eton	Sandhurst & Oxford	..	31
†Scott, Sir L. F. (Kt 1922)	1869	Rugby	Oxford	1950	13
Scott, Sir (R.) D. (Kt 1955)	1901	Mill Hill	Cambridge	..	31
Scott-Hopkins, J. S. R.	1921	Eton	Oxford	..	41

H

Name	Born	School	Univ.	Died	Page references
Taylor, Ld (Life Peer 1958). S. J. L. Taylor	1910	Stowe	London	..	46[2]
Taylor, H. B.	1895	Elementary	..	..	35
†Taylor, R. J.	1881	Elementary	..	1954	35
Taylor, Sir W. J. (1st Bt 1963)	1902	Archb. Holgate's G.S.★	Sheffield	..	43, 44
†Templemore, 4th Ld (1924). A. C. S. Chichester	1880	Harrow	Sandhurst	1953	18, 22[2], 26, 31, 32
†Templewood, 1st Vt (1944). Sir S. J. G. Hoare (2nd Bt 1915)	1880	Harrow	Oxford	1959	14, 15, 17, 20, 22, 23[4]
†Tenby, 1st Vt (1957). G. Lloyd George	1894	Eastbourne	Cambridge	1967	21, 24, 28[2], 29, 32, 37[2], 38
†Tennant, H. J.	1865	Eton	Cambridge	1935	6[3], 8[2]
Teviot, 1st Ld (1940). C. I. Kerr	1874	Stephen Hawtrey's, Windsor★	..	1968	25, 26
†Thankerton, Ld (Ld of Appeal 1929). W. Watson	1873	Winchester	Cambridge	1948	13, 15, 18
Thatcher, Mrs M. H.	1925	Grantham G.H.S.★	Oxford	..	43
Thomas, I. Bulmer	1905	W. Monmouth★	Oxford	..	33[2]
†Thomas, J. H.	1874	Elementary	..	1949	16, 18, 19, 20[2], 23[2]
†Thomas, J. P. L. 1st Vt Cilcennin (1955)	1903	Rugby	Oxford	1960	27, 30, 31, 38[2]
†Thomas, P. J. M.	1920	Epworth Coll., Rhyl★	Oxford	..	40[2], 42
†Thomas, T. G.	1909	Tonypandy★	Southampton	..	46[2], 48[2]
Thompson, Sir K. P. (1st Bt 1963)	1909	Bootle G.S.★	..	..	41, 42, 44
Thompson, Sir R. H. M. (1st Bt 1963)	1912	Malvern	..	..	39[2], 41, 43, 44, 45
†Thomson, 1st Ld (1924). C. B. Thomson	1875	Cheltenham	Woolwich	1930	16, 19
†Thomson, Ld (Scot. judge 1949). G. R. Thomson	1893	South African Sch.	Cape Town, Oxford & Edinburgh	1962	36
Thomson, Sir F. C. (1st Bt 1929)	1875	Edinburgh Academy	Oxford & Edinburgh	1935	15[2], 18[2], 22
†Thomson, G. M.	1921	Grove Academy, Dundee	..	..	45, 46, 48[2]
†Thorneycroft, 1st Ld (1967). (G. E.) P. Thorneycroft	1909	Eton	Woolwich	..	32, 38, 41[2]
Thornton, E.	1905	Elementary	..	..	47
†Thurso, 1st Vt (1952). Sir A. H. M. Sinclair (4th Bt 1912)	1890	Eton	Sandhurst	..	20, 21, 27
Thurtle, E.	1884	Elementary	..	1954	19, 28
Tilney, J.	1907	Eton	Oxford	..	41
Titchfield, M of (1893). W. A. H. Cavendish-Bentinck, 7th D of Portland (1943)	1893	Eton	Sandhurst	..	18, 22
†Tomlinson, G.	1890	Rishton Wesleyan★	..	1952	27, 33, 35
Tree, R.	1897	Winchester	..	..	32
Trefgarne, 1st Ld (1947). G. M. Garro-Jones. *Surname changed to Trefgarne in 1954*	1894	Caterham	..	1960	27
†Trevelyan, Sir C. P. (3rd Bt 1928)	1870	Harrow	Cambridge	1958	6, 16, 19
Tryon, 1st Ld (1940). G. C. Tryon	1871	Eton	Sandhurst	1940	12[2], 15, 18, 21, 24, 25, 29, 30
Turner, Sir B. (Kt 1931)	1863	Elementary	..	1942	19
†Turton, R. H.	1903	Eton	Oxford	..	36, 38, 39
†Tweedmouth, 2nd Ld (1894). E. Marjoribanks	1848	Harrow	Oxford	1909	4, 5
Tweedmouth, 3rd Ld (1909). D. C. Marjoribanks	1874	Harrow	..	1935	7
Tweedsmuir, Vtess (1948). Lady (P. J. F.) Grant	1915	Abroad	..	..	42

Name	Born	School	Univ.	Died	Page references
Ungoed-Thomas, Sir (A.) L. (Kt 1951)	1904	Haileybury	Oxford	..	35
†Ure, A. Ld Strathclyde (Ld of Appeal 1914)	1853	Secondary	Glasgow & Edinburgh	1928	5, 7[2]
Urwin, T.	1912	Elementary	..	..	45
Valentia, 11th Vt (1863). A. Annesley (U.K. Ld Annesley 1917)	1843	..	Woolwich	1927	3, 9, 13, 15
Vane, W. M. F. 1st Ld Inglewood (1964)	1909	Charterhouse	Cambridge	..	41, 43
Varley, E.	1932	Secondary	Oxford	..	308
†Vaughan-Morgan, Sir J. K. (1st Bt 1960)	1906	Eton	Oxford	..	43[2]
Verney, Sir H. C. W. (4th Bt 1910)	1881	Harrow	Oxford	..	6
Viant, S. P.	1882	Devonport*	..	1964	19
†Vosper, D. F. Ld Runcorn (Life Peer 1964)	1916	Marlborough	Cambridge	1968	37, 39, 41[2], 43, 44
Wakefield, Sir E. B. (1st Bt 1962)	1903	Haileybury	Cambridge	1969	39, 44[2], 45[2]
†Waldegrave, 9th E (1859). W. F. Waldegrave	1851	Eton	Cambridge	1930	4
Waldegrave, 12th E (1936). G. N. Waldegrave, Vt Chewton (1933)	1905	Winchester	Cambridge	..	41
†Waleran, 1st Ld (1905). Sir W. H. Walrond (2nd Bt 1889)	1849	Eton	..	1925	3[2]
Walkden, 1st Ld (1945). A. G. Walkden	1873	Merchant Taylors' Sch., Ashwell	..	1951	36
Walker, H.	1927	Secondary	..	..	45, 47, 308
†Walker-Smith, Sir D. C. (1st Bt 1960)	1910	Rossall	Oxford	..	36, 38, 43[2]
Wallace, (D.) E.	1892	Harrow	Sandhurst	1941	18, 20, 22, 23[3], 24[2]
Walrond, Sir W. H. (2nd Bt 1889). 1st Ld Waleran (1905)	1849	Eton	..	1925	3[2]
†Walsh, S.	1859	Elementary	..	1929	10, 11, 16
Walston, Ld (Life Peer 1961). H. D. L. Walston	1912	Eton	Cambridge	..	46, 48
†Walters, Sir (J.) T. (Kt 1912)	1868	Privately & Secondary	..	1933	12, 21
Walton, Sir J. L. (Kt 1905)	1852	Merchant Taylors' Sch., Great Crosby*	London	1908	5
†Ward of Witley, 1st Vt (1960). G. R. Ward	1907	Eton	Oxford	..	38[2], 43
Ward, Sir (A.) L. (1st Bt 1929)	1875	St Paul's	Paris & Darmstadt	1956	22[2], 26[3]
†Ward, W. D.	1877	Eton	Cambridge	1946	7, 13
Wardle, G. J.	1865	Elementary	..	1947	11[2]
Warne, G. H.	1881	Elementary	..	1928	16
Warrender, Sir V. A. G. A. (8th Bt 1917). 1st Ld Bruntisfield (1942)	1899	Eton	..	..	22[3], 23[2], 24, 27, 31
†Waterhouse, C.	1893	Cheltenham	Cambridge	..	25[2], 26[2], 29[2], 31
†Watkinson, 1st Vt (1964), H. A. Watkinson	1910	Queen's Coll., Taunton*	London	..	37, 39, 41, 43
Watson, Sir J. C. (Kt 1931)	1883	Neilson Instit., Paisley*	Glasgow & Edinburgh	1944	19, 22
†Watson, W., Ld Thankerton (Ld of Appeal 1929)	1873	Winchester	Cambridge	1948	13, 15, 18
†Waverley, 1st Vt (1952). Sir J. Anderson (K.C.B. 1919)	1882	George Watson's Coll., Edin.	Edin. & Leipzig	1958	22, 23, 26[2], 28[2], 31
Webb, Sir H. (1st Bt 1916)	1866	Privately	..	1940	7
†Webb, M.	1904	Christ Ch., Lancaster*	..	1956	35
†Webb, S. J. 1st Ld Passfield (1929)	1859	Switzerland & Secondary	..	1947	16, 19[2]

II

PARTIES

Conservative Party

Party Leaders

1900	M of Salisbury	31 May 37	N. Chamberlain [2]
14 Jul 02	A. Balfour	9 Oct 40	(Sir) W. Churchill
13 Nov 11	A. Bonar Law [1]	21 Apr 55	Sir A. Eden
21 Mar 21	A. Chamberlain [1]	22 Jan 57	H. Macmillan
23 Oct 22	A. Bonar Law [1]	11 Nov 63	Sir A. Douglas-Home
28 May 23	S. Baldwin	2 Aug 65	E. Heath

Deputy Leaders

4 Aug 65   R. Maudling

Leaders in the House of Lords

1900	3rd M of Salisbury	1940	Vt Caldecote
1902	D of Devonshire	1940	Vt Halifax
1903	M of Lansdowne	1941	Ld Lloyd
1916	Earl Curzon (M)	1941	Ld Moyne
1925	4th M of Salisbury	1942	Vt Cranborne
1930	1st Vt Hailsham		(5th M of Salisbury)
1935	M of Londonderry	1957	E of Home
1935	Vt Halifax	1960	2nd Vt Hailsham
1938	Earl Stanhope	1963	Ld Carrington

Principal Office-holders

Chairmen of the Party Organisation		*Principal Agents*	
Jun 1911–Dec 16	A. Steel-Maitland	Mar 1885–Jul 03	R. Middleton
Dec 1916–Mar 23	Sir G. Younger	Jul 03–Nov 05	L. Wells
Mar 23–Nov 26	S. Jackson	Nov 05–Dec 06	A. Haig
Nov 26–May 30	J. Davidson	Dec 06–Jan 12	P. Hughes
Jun 30–Apr 31	N. Chamberlain	May 12–Jun 15	J. Boraston
Apr 31–Mar 36	Ld Stonehaven	Jun 15–Apr 20	(Sir) J. Boraston
Mar 36–Mar 42	(Sir) D. Hacking		& W. Jenkins
Mar 42–Sep 44	T. Dugdale	Apr 20–Dec 20	W. Jenkins
Oct 44–Jul 46	R. Assheton	Dec 20–Mar 23	Sir M. Fraser
Jul 46–Jul 55	Ld Woolton (Vt)	Mar 23–Feb 24	Sir R. Hall
Sep 55–Sep 57	O. Poole	Mar 24–Jan 27	(Sir) H. Blain
Sep 57–Oct 59	Vt Hailsham	Jan 27–Feb 28	Sir L. Maclachlan
Oct 59–Oct 61	R. Butler	Feb 28–Feb 31	R. Topping
Oct 61–Apr 63	I. Macleod		
Apr 63–Oct 63	I. Macleod\Ld Poole /	*General Directors*	
Oct 63–Jan 65	Vt Blakenham	Feb 31–Sep 45	(Sir) R. Topping
Jan 65–Sep 67	E. du Cann	Oct 45–Aug 57	(Sir) S. Pierssené
Sep 67–	A. Barber	Aug 57–Jun 66	(Sir) W. Urton
			(office abolished Jun 66)

Deputy Chairmen			
May 24–Jan 26	M of Linlithgow		
Sep 57–Oct 59	O. Poole (Ld)	*Director of the Organisation*	
Oct 59–Oct 63	Sir T. Low	*Department*	
	(Ld Aldington)	Jun 66–	R. Webster

[1] A. Bonar Law, 1911–21, and A. Chamberlain, 1921–22, were Leaders of the Conservative Party in the House of Commons. Formerly, when the party was in opposition, there were separate Leaders in the Commons and the Lords; and the present title 'Leader of the Conservative and Unionist Party' did not officially exist. It was first conferred, in Oct 1922, on A. Bonar Law when he was selected for his second term of office.

[2] N. Chamberlain remained Leader of the Conservative party until 4 Oct 40, though he was succeeded as Prime Minister by W. Churchill on 10 May 40, and resigned from the Government on 30 Sep 40.

Deputy Chairmen (Cont.)		*Treasurers*		
Oct 64–	Sir M. Fraser	1919–	23	E. Farquhar
		1923–	29	Vt Younger
		1930–	31	Sir S. Hoare
		Jul 31–Nov	33	Ld Ebbisham
		Nov 33–Jun	38	Vt Greenwood
		Jun 38–Feb	47	Vt Marchwood
		Feb 47–Apr	60	C. Holland-Martin
		Feb 48–Mar	52	Ld De L'Isle [1]
		Mar 52–Oct	55	O. Poole
		Oct 55–Jan	62	Sir H. Studholme
		Oct 60–Nov	65	R. Allan
		Jan 62–Aug	66	R. Stanley
		Nov 65–		Ld Chelmer
		Aug 66–		Sir T. Brinton

Conservative Research Department *1929*

Director		*Chairman*	
1930–39	(Sir) J. Ball	1929	N. Chamberlain
1939–45	*vacant*	1940	Sir K. Wood
1945–51	D. Clarke (*joint from* 48)	1943	Sir J. Bell (*Acting Hon. Chairman*)
1948–50	H. Hopkinson (*joint*)		
1948–59	P. Cohen (*joint*)	1945–64	R. Butler
1951–64	(Sir) M. Fraser (*joint to* 59)		
1964–	B. Sewill		

SOURCES.—*1958–66 Annual Conference Reports of the National Union of Conservative and Unionist Associations*, and information from the Conservative Research Department.

Chief Whips in the House of Commons

1900	Sir W. Walrond
1902	Sir A. Acland Hood
1911	Ld Balcarres
1912	Ld E. Talbot
1921	L. Wilson
1923	(Sir) B. Eyres-Monsell
1931	D. Margesson
1941	J. Stuart
1948	P. Buchan-Hepburn
1955	E. Heath
1959	M. Redmayne
1964	W. Whitelaw

Chief Whips in the House of Lords

1900	Earl Waldegrave
1911	D of Devonshire
1916	Ld Hylton
1922	E of Clarendon
1925	E of Plymouth
1929	E of Lucan (5th)
1940	Ld Templemore
1945	Earl Fortescue
1958	Earl St Aldwyn

SOURCE.—*Dod's Parliamentary Companion, 1900–66.*

Chairmen of 1922 Committee [2]

Jan 23–Nov 32	(Sir) G. Rentoul	Dec 44–Jun 45	J. McEwen
Dec 32–Dec 35	W. Morrison	Aug 45–Nov 51	Sir A. Gridley
Dec 35–Jul 39	Sir H. O'Neill	Nov 51–Nov 55	D. Walker-Smith
Sep 39–Nov 39	Sir A. Somerville	Nov 55–Nov 64	J. Morrison
Dec 39–Dec 40	W. Spens	Nov 64–Mar 66	Sir W. Anstruther-Gray
Dec 40–Dec 44	A. Erskine Hill	May 66–	Sir A. V. Harvey

SOURCE.—*The Times Index, 1923–66*, information from the 1922 Committee, R. T. McKenzie, *British Political Parties* (1955), pp. 57–61.

[1] Since February 1948 the office of Treasurer has been held jointly.
[2] Or the Conservative (Private) Members' Committee. This is an organisation of the entire back-bench membership of the Conservative Party in the Commons. It acts as a sounding-board of Conservative opinion in the House, but is not authorised to formulate policy.

National Union of Conservative and Unionist Associations — Annual Conferences,[1] 1900–

Date	Place	President	Chairman
19 Dec 00	London	M of Zetland	Ld Windsor
26–27 Nov 01	Wolverhampton	Ld Llangattock	Sir A. Hickman
14–15 Oct 02	Manchester	E of Dartmouth	Sir C. Cave
1–2 Oct 03	Sheffield	E of Derby	F. Lowe
28–29 Oct 04	Southampton	D of Norfolk	H. Bowles
14–15 Nov 05	Newcastle upon Tyne	Ld Montagu of Beaulieu	Sir W. Plummer
27 Jul 06	London	D of Northumberland	H. Imbert-Terry
14–15 Nov 07	Birmingham	„	D of Rutland
19–20 Nov 08	Cardiff	E of Plymouth	Sir R. Hodge
17–18 Nov 09	Manchester	E Cawdor	Sir T. Wrightson
17 Nov 10	Nottingham	E of Derby	H. Chaplin
16–17 Nov 11	Leeds	D of Portland	Ld Kenyon
14–15 Nov 12	London	Ld Faber	Sir W. Crump
12–14 Nov 13	Norwich	Ld Farquhar	A. Salvidge
1914–16	No conference held	Sir A. Fellowes	Sir H. Samuel
1917	London	„	„
1918–19	No conference held	„	„
10–11 Jun 20	Birmingham	„	J. Williams
17–18 Nov 21	Liverpool	A. Chamberlain	Sir A. Benn
15–16 Dec 22	London	E of Derby	Sir A. Leith.
25–26 Oct 23	Plymouth	Ld Mildmay of Flete	Sir H. Nield
2–3 Oct 24	Newcastle upon Tyne	D of Northumberland	E of Selborne
8–9 Oct 25	Brighton	G. Loder	Sir P. Woodhouse
7–8 Oct 26	Scarborough	G. Lane-Fox	Dame C. Bridge-man
6–7 Oct 27	Cardiff	Vt Tredegar	Sir R. Sanders
27–28 Sep 28	Great Yarmouth	Ld Queenborough	J. Gretton
21–22 Nov 29	London	Ld Faringdon	G. Rowlands
1 Jul 30	London	N. Chamberlain	Countess of Iveagh
1931	No conference held	„	G. Herbert
6–7 Oct 32	Blackpool	Ld Stanley	Earl Howe
5–6 Oct 33	Birmingham	E of Plymouth	Sir G. Ellis
4–5 Oct 34	Bristol	Ld Bayford	Miss R. Evans
3–4 Oct 35	Bournemouth	G. Herbert	Sir W. Cope
1–2 Oct 36	Margate	Ld Ebbisham	Sir L. Brassey
7–8 Oct 37	Scarborough	Ld Bingley	Mrs C. Fyfe
1938	No conference held	M of Londonderry	Sir E. Ramsden
1939	„	„	N. Colman
1940	„	Ld Queenborough	Lady Hillingdon
1941	„	„	Sir C. Headlam
1942	„	M of Salisbury	R. Catterall
20–21 May 43	London	„	„
1944	No conference held	„	Mrs L. Whitehead
14–15 Mar 45	London	Ld Courthope	R. Butler
3–5 Oct 46	Blackpool	O. Stanley	R. Proby
2–4 Oct 47	Brighton	H. Macmillan	Mrs Hornyold-Strickland
7–9 Oct 48	Llandudno	G. Summers	Sir H. Williams
12–14 Oct 49	London	Vt Swinton	D. Graham
12–14 Oct 50	Blackpool	Sir D. Maxwell Fyfe	A. Nutting
1951	No conference held	Ld Ramsden	Mrs L. Sayers
9–11 Oct 52	Scarborough	Sir T. Dugdale	C. Waterhouse
8–10 Oct 53	Margate	M of Salisbury	Mrs J. Warde
7–9 Oct 54	Blackpool	A. Eden	Sir G. Llewellyn
6–8 Oct 55	Bournemouth	Mrs L. Sayers	Mrs E. Emmet
11–13 Oct 56	Llandudno	R. Butler	Sir E. Edwards
10–12 Oct 57	Brighton	E of Woolton	Mrs W. Elliot
8–11 Oct 58	Blackpool	Sir R. Proby	Sir S. Bell
1959	No conference held	H. Brooke	E. Brown
12–15 Oct 60	Scarborough	„	„
11–14 Oct 61	Brighton	Vt Hailsham	Sir D. Glover

[1] 1900–12, National Union of Conservative and Constitutional Associations, 1912–17 National Unionist Association of Conservative and Liberal-Unionist Associations, 1917–24 National Unionist Association, 1924– National Union of Conservative and Unionist Associations.

Date	Place	President	Chairman
10–13 Oct 62	Llandudno	Sir G. Llewellyn	Sir J. Howard
8–11 Oct 63	Blackpool	E of Home	Mrs T. Shepherd
64	*No conference held*	Vtess Davidson	Sir M. Bemrose
12–15 Oct 65	Brighton	Vtess Davidson	Sir M. Bemrose
13–16 Oct 66	Blackpool	S. Lloyd	Sir D. Mason
18–21 Oct 67	Brighton	Ld Chelmer	Mrs A. Doughty
9–12 Oct 68	Blackpool	R. Maudling	Sir T. Constantine

SOURCES.—*National Union Gleanings 1900–12, Gleanings and Memoranda 1912–33, Politics in Review 1934–39*, all published by the National Union of Conservative Associations; *National Union of Conservative and Unionist Associations, Annual Conference Reports, 1958, 1960, and 1965*, for Conservative Party Manifestoes and major recent reports, pamphlets, etc., see G. D. M. Block, *A Source Book of Conservatism* (1964). See also I. Bulmer-Thomas, *The Growth of the British Party System* (1965).

Labour Party

Party Leaders and Deputy Leaders

Chairman of the Parliamentary Party

1906	J. K. Hardie
1908	A. Henderson
1910	G. Barnes
1911	J. R. MacDonald
1914	A. Henderson
1917	W. Adamson
1921	J. Clynes

Chairman and Leader of the Parliamentary Party

1922	J. R. MacDonald [1]
1931	A. Henderson [2]
1932	G. Lansbury
1935	C. Attlee [1]
1955	H. Gaitskell
1963	H. Wilson

Vice Chairman

1906	D. Shackleton	
1908	G. Barnes	
1910	J. Clynes	
1911	W. Brace	
1912	J. Parker	
1914	A. Gill	
1915	J. Hodge	} *Acting Chairmen*
1916	G. Wardle	
1918	J. Clynes	
1921	J. Thomas	} *joint*
	S. Walsh	

Deputy Leader

1922	S. Walsh	} *joint*
	J. Wedgwood	
1923	J. Clynes	
1931	C. Attlee	
1935	A. Greenwood	
1945	H. Morrison	
1955	J. Griffiths	
1959	A. Bevan	
1960	G. Brown	

SOURCES.—*Labour Party Annual Conference Reports, Labour Year Books*; H. Pelling, *A Short History of the Labour Party* (1961; 2nd ed. 1965), p. 130.

Leaders in the House of Lords

1924	Vt Haldane		1952	Earl Jowitt
1928	Ld Parmoor		1955	Vt (Earl) Alexander of Hillsborough
1931	Ld Ponsonby			
1935	Ld Snell		1964	E of Longford
1940	Ld (Vt) Addison		1968	Ld Shackleton

Chief Whips in the House of Commons

1906	D. Shackleton	1916	J. Parker	1931	(Sir) C. Edwards
1906	A. Henderson	1919	W. Tyson Wilson	1942	W. Whiteley
1907	G. Roberts	1920	A. Henderson	1955	H. Bowden
1914	A. Henderson	1924	B. Spoor	1964	E. Short
1914	F. Goldstone	1925	A. Henderson	1966	J. Silkin
1916	G. Roberts	1927	T. Kennedy		

[1] When the Labour Party was in power in 1924, 1929–31, 1940–45, 1945–51, and 1964–, a Liaison Committee was set up. The Chairmen of these committees are listed on p. 106.
[2] A. Henderson lost his seat in the 1931 election. The acting leader of the Labour Parliamentary Party in 1931 was G. Lansbury.

Chief Whips in the House of Lords

1924	Ld Muir-Mackenzie	1945	Ld Ammon
1924	E De La Warr	1949	Ld Shepherd (1st)
1930	Ld Marley	1954	E of Lucan (6th)
1937	Ld Strabolgi	1964	Ld Shepherd (2nd)
1941	E of Listowel	1967	Ld Beswick
1944	Ld Southwood		

SOURCES.—*Dod's Parliamentary Companion, 1900–66, Labour Party Annual Conference Reports.*

Labour Representation Committee — Executive Officers

Chairman		*Treasurer*	
1900	F. Rogers	1902	F. Rogers
1902	R. Bell	1903	A. Gee
1904	D. Shackleton	1904	A. Henderson

Secretary		*National Agent*	
		(and Deputy Secretary from 1960)	
1900	J. R. MacDonald		
		1908 A. Peters	1946 R. Windle
		1919 E. Wake	1951 A. Williams
		1929 G. Shepherd	1962 Miss S. Barker

Labour Party — National Executive Committee

Chairman		*Treasurer*	
(listed as chairman of annual conferences at end of term of office see p. 106)		1906	A. Henderson
		1912	J. R. MacDonald
		1929	A. Henderson
		1936	G. Lathan
Secretary		1943	A. Greenwood
1906	J. R. MacDonald	1954	H. Gaitskell
1912	A. Henderson	1956	A. Bevan
1935	J. Middleton	1960	H. Nicholas
1944	M. Phillips	1964	D. Davies (*acting*)
1962	A. Williams	1965	D. Davies
1968	H. Nicholas	1967	J. Callaghan

SOURCES.—*Labour Representation Committee Annual Conference Reports, 1900–5,* and *Labour Party Annual Conference Reports, 1906–66.*

Parliamentary Labour Party — Parliamentary Committee

This committee was originally known as the Executive Committee of the Parliamentary Labour Party. Its name was changed in 1951 to avoid confusion with the N.E.C. The committee was first elected in 1923 to take the place of the Policy Committee of the P.L.P. It consists of twelve Commons' members, elected at the opening of every session of Parliament by members of the P.L.P. with seats in the House of Commons. There are six *ex officio* members: the Leader and Deputy Leader of the Party, the Chief Whip in the House of Commons, the Leader of the Labour Peers, the Chief Whip of the Labour Peers and their elected representative. The elected Commons' members of the Parliamentary Committee sit on the Front Bench with the Party's Leader, Deputy Leader, Chief Whip and the Assistant Whips. Ex-Labour Ministers have the right, by custom of the House, to sit on the Front Bench, but usually prefer a place on the Back Benches. The officers and the elected twelve are joined on the Front Benches by a number of other members who have been allotted the responsibility of looking after particular subjects. After 1955 it became the practice of the Leader of the P.L.P. to invite members to take charge of particular subjects, and these members included some who are not members of the Parliamentary Committee. In 1924 and 1929 when the Labour Party was in office a Consultative Committee of twelve was appointed representative of both Front and Back Benches. During the war-time coalition the P.L.P. elected an Administrative Committee of twelve, with Peers' representation, all of whom were non-Ministers. When the Labour Party was in office from 1945 to 1951, and in 1964—, the P.L.P. set up a small Liaison Committee of three elected Back Bench M.P.s, the Leader of the House, the Government Chief Whip, and an elected Back Bench Labour Peer.

Parliamentary Labour Party — Executive Committee

The figures denote the order of successful candidates in the ballot.

1923-29

	Feb 1923	Dec 1924	Dec 1925	Dec 1926	Dec 1927	1928
W. Adamson	9	..	11	11	8	There is no record of an Executive Committee election in 1928
H. Dalton	..	..	12	3	7	
R. Davies	12	..	..	..	..	
W. Graham	..	8	2	2	3	
A. Henderson	..	10	..	12	2	
T. Johnston	3	..	..	4	4	
F. Jowett	6	..	..	..	..	
G. Lansbury	2	1	10	9	10	
H. Lees-Smith	..	11	4	6	6	
J. Maxton	..	6	..	..	..	
E. Morel	5	..	..	..	..	
F. Roberts	..	12	..	..	..	
T. Shaw	11	..	7	..	12	
E. Shinwell	7	..	..	..	..	
R. Smillie	..	2	5	7	..	
P. Snowden	1	3	1	1	1	
J. Thomas	4	4	3	5	5	
C. Trevelyan	..	7	6	8	11	
S. Walsh	..	..	8	..	..	
S. Webb	10	..	9	10	9	
J. Wedgwood	..	9	..	..	..	
J. Wheatley	8	5	..	..	..	

1931-35

	Nov 1931	Nov 1932	Nov 1933	Nov 1934
Sir S. Cripps	1	1	2	1
D. Grenfell	2	2	1	2
G. Hicks	4	3	3	5
M. Jones	7	7	4	6
W. Lunn	5	4	6	4
N. Maclean	6	6	7	7
T. Williams	3	5	5	3

1935–40

	Nov 1935	Nov 1936	Nov 1937	Nov 1938	Nov 1939
A. Alexander	6	5	2	2	1
W. Wedgwood Benn	..	..	7	5	2
J. Clynes	1	6	..	..	..
H. Dalton	2	3	5	3	10
D. Grenfell	5	4	4	4	4
G. Hall	..	..	..	..	7
T. Johnston	3	2	3	6	..
M. Jones	10	8	11	12	..
J. Lawson	..	..	..	..	12
H. Lees-Smith	9	11	8	8	5
W. Lunn	11	..	..	..	..
N. Maclean	12	..	..	..	..
H. Morrison	4	1	1	1	8
P. Noel-Baker	..	10	12	10	11
F. Pethick-Lawrence	8	9	9	9	6
D. Pritt	..	12	..	..	..
E. Shinwell	..	..	10	11	9
T. Williams	7	7	6	7	3

Parliamentary Labour Party (Parliamentary Committee)
(number indicates position in ballot)

	Nov 1951	Nov 1952	Nov 1953	Nov 1954	Jun 1955	Nov 1956	Nov 1957	Nov 1958	Nov 1959	Nov 1960	Nov 1961	Nov 1962	Nov 1963
A. Bevan	..	12	9[a]	..	7	3	3	1	..	..	..	..	..
A. Bottomley	..	..	..	..	..	..	12	9	..	..	..	..	..
G. Brown	..	..	..	..	8	10	9	..	8	..	..	..	..
J. Callaghan	7	6	4	10	3	5	5	5	2	1	7	1	2
R. Crossman	..	..	..	..	..	..	..	..	13[d]	..	..	..	..
H. Dalton	8	5	5	4	..	..	..	..	..	..	..	..	..
J. Chuter Ede	5	2	6	9	..	..	..	..	..	..	..	..	..
T. Fraser	..	..	..	..	14[e]	12	8	12	7	6	9	5	6
H. Gaitskell	3	3	2	1[b]	2[e]	..	..	..	..	..	..	..	..
P. Gordon Walker	..	..	..	..	..	..	11	6	9	8	11	6	5
A. Greenwood	12	..	..	..	10	6	7	8	6[d]	..	..	..	..
J. Griffiths	1	1	1	1[b]	1[e]	..	..	..	..	..	..	..	..
R. Gunter	..	..	..	..	..	..	..	..	..	7	6	10	8
W. Glenvil Hall	2	9	12	11	..	..	..	..	..	..	..	..	..
D. Healey	..	..	..	..	..	..	..	..	12	5	4	9	7
D. Houghton	..	..	..	..	..	..	..	..	..	10	3	4	3
D. Jay	..	..	..	..	..	..	..	..	..	..	..	..	11
F. Lee	..	..	..	..	..	..	..	..	5	12	12	12	10
G. Mitchison	..	..	..	..	12	4	2	3	10	3	8	7	12
P. Noel-Baker	9	8	10	8	9	8	10	10	..	..	..	..	..
A. Robens	4	4	7	6	4	2	6	7	4	..	..	..	..
E. Shinwell	11	11	11	7	..	..	..	..	..	..	..	..	..
Sir F. Soskice	..	7	3	3	..	7	4	4	3	2	2	2	4
M. Stewart	..	..	..	..	..	..	..	..	..	4	5	8	1
R. Stokes	6	..	..	..	11	..	..	..	..	..	..	..	..
E. Summerskill	10	10	8	5	6	9	..	11	..	..	..	..	..
F. Willey	..	..	..	..	..	..	..	..	11	11	10	11	9
H. Wilson	..	..	13[a]	12	5	1	1	2	1	9	1	3	..
K. Younger	..	..	..	..	13[c]	11	..	..	..	..	..	..	..

[a] A. Bevan resigned from the Parliamentary Committee on 14 Apr 54, H. Wilson, who was 13th in order of votes obtained, took his place on the Committee on 28 Apr 54.
[b] H. Gaitskell and J. Griffiths both obtained 170 votes and tied for first place.
[c] H. Gaitskell and J. Griffiths were elected Leader and Deputy Leader of the Parliamentary Labour Party on 14 Dec 55 and 2 Feb 56, K. Younger and T. Fraser as runners-up filled the vacant places on the Parliamentary Committee.
[d] A. Greenwood resigned from the Parliamentary Committee on 13 Oct 60. R. Crossman, who was 13th in order of votes obtained, took his place on the Committee for a few weeks until the 1960–61 sessional elections in November.

Chairmen of Parliamentary Committees when Labour has been in power

1924 *Parliamentary Executive Committee*
    1924 R. Smillie

1929–31 *Consultative Committee*
    1929 H. Snell
    1930 J. Barr

1940–45 *Administrative Committee*
    1940 H. Lees-Smith (*acting*) [1]
    1941 H. Lees-Smith (*acting*) [1]
    1942 F. Pethick-Lawrence
                  (*acting*) [1]
    1942 A. Greenwood (*acting*) [1]
    1943 A. Greenwood (*acting*) [1]
    1944 A. Greenwood (*acting*) [1]

1945–51 *Liaison Committee*
    1945 N. Maclean
    1946 M. Webb
    1947 M. Webb
    1948 M. Webb
    1949 M. Webb
    1950 W. Glenvil Hall

1964– *Liason Committee*
    1964 E. Shinwell
    1967 D. Houghton

SOURCES.—1923–29, *Daily Herald* and *Directory for National Council of Labour, TUC General Council, Labour Party and the Parliamentary Labour Party* (published annually by the Labour Party); 1931–, *Labour Party Annual Conference Reports; The Times;* and *Labour Party Directory.*

Labour Representation Committee — Annual Conferences, 1900–1905

Date	Place	Chairman
27–28 Feb 00	London	W. Steadman
1 Feb 01	Manchester	J. Hodge
20–22 Feb 02	Birmingham	W. Davis
19–21 Feb 03	Newcastle upon Tyne	J. Bell
4–5 Feb 04	Bradford	J. Hodge
26–29 Jan 05	Liverpool	A. Henderson

Labour Party — Annual Conferences, 1906–

Date	Place	Chairman
15–17 Feb 06	London	A. Henderson
24–26 Jan 07	Belfast	J. Stephenson
20–22 Jan 08	Hull	W. Hudson
27–29 Jan 09	Portsmouth	J. Clynes
9–11 Feb 10	Newport	J. Keir Hardie
1–3 Feb 11	Leicester	W. Robinson
24–26 Jan 12	Birmingham	B. Turner
29–31 Jan 13	London	G. Roberts
27–30 Jan 14	Glasgow	T. Fox
1915	*No conference held*	
26–28 Jan 16	Bristol	W. Anderson
23–26 Jan 17 [2]	Manchester	G. Wardle
23–25 Jan 18	Nottingham	W. Purdy
26–28 Jun 18	London	W. Purdy
25–27 Jun 19	Southport	J. McGurk
22–25 Jun 20	Scarborough	W. Hutchinson
21–24 Jun 21	Brighton	A. Cameron
27–30 Jun 22	Edinburgh	F. Jowett
26–29 Jun 23	London	S. Webb
7–10 Oct 24	London	J. Ramsay MacDonald
29 Sep–2 Oct 25	Liverpool	C. Cramp
11–15 Oct 26	Margate	R. Williams
3–7 Oct 27	Blackpool	F. Roberts
1–5 Oct 28	Birmingham	G. Lansbury
30 Sep–4 Oct 29	Brighton	H. Morrison
6–10 Oct 30	Llandudno	Susan Lawrence
5–8 Oct 31	Scarborough	S. Hirst
3–7 Oct 32	Leicester	G. Lathan
2–6 Oct 33	Hastings	J. Compton
1–5 Oct 34	Southport	W. Smith
30 Sep–4 Oct 35	Brighton	W. Robinson
5–9 Oct 36	Edinburgh	Jennie Adamson

[1] During C. Attlee's membership of the war-time Coalition, the Labour Party appointed an Acting Chairman each session.
[2] Adjourned for one month. Resumed 26 Feb 18 in London

4–8 Oct 37	Bournemouth	H. Dalton
1938	*No conference held*	
29 May–2 Jun 39	Southport	G. Dallas
13–16 May 40	Bournemouth	Barbara Gould
2–4 Jun 41	London	J. Walker
25–28 May 42	London	W. Green
14–18 Jun 43	London	A. Dobbs
11–15 Dec 44	London	G. Ridley
21–25 May 45	Blackpool	Ellen Wilkinson
10–14 Jun 46	Bournemouth	H. Laski
26–30 May 47	Margate	P. Noel-Baker
17–21 May 48	Scarborough	E. Shinwell
6–10 Jun 49	Blackpool	J. Griffiths
2–6 Oct 50	Margate	S. Watson
1–3 Oct 51	Scarborough	Alice Bacon
29 Sep–3 Oct 52	Morecambe	H. Earnshaw
28 Sep–2 Oct 53	Margate	A. Greenwood
27 Sep–1 Oct 54	Scarborough	W. Burke
10–14 Oct 55	Margate	Edith Summerskill
1–5 Oct 56	Blackpool	E. Gooch
30 Sep–4 Oct 57	Brighton	Margaret Herbison
29 Sep–3 Oct 58	Scarborough	T. Driberg
28–29 Nov 59	Blackpool	Barbara Castle
3–7 Oct 60	Scarborough	G. Brinham
2–6 Oct 61	Blackpool	R. Crossman
2–5 Oct 62	Brighton	H. Wilson
30 Sep–4 Oct 63	Scarborough	D. Davies
12–13 Dec 64	Brighton	A. Greenwood
27 Sep–1 Oct 65	Blackpool	R. Gunter
3–7 Oct 66	Brighton	W. Padley
2–6 Oct 67	Scarborough	J. Boyd
30 Sep–4 Oct 68	Blackpool	Jennie Lee

SOURCES.—*1900–5 Reports of the Labour Representation Committee Annual Conferences, 1906 Report of the Labour Party Annual Conference.*

Labour Party — Membership Statistics

Year	No. Constit. & Central Parties	Total Indiv. Members ('000s)	T.U.s		Soc. & Co-op. Socs.		Total Member-ship ('000s)
			No.	Members ('000s)	No.	Members ('000s)	
1900–01	7	..	41	353	3	23	376
1901–02	21	..	65	455	2	14	469
1902–03	49	..	127	847	2	14	861
1903–04	76	..	165	956	2	14	970
1904–05	73	..	158	855	2	15	900
1905–06	73	..	158	904	2	17	921
1906–07	83	..	176	975	2	21	998
1907	92	..	181	1,050	2	22	1,072
1908	133	..	176	1,127	2	27	1,159
1909	155	..	172	1,451	2	31	1,486
1910	148	..	151	1,394	2	31	1,431
1911	149	..	141	1,502	2	31	1,539
1912	146	..	130	1,858	2	31	1,895
1913	158	..	a	a	2	33	a
1914	179	..	101	1,572	2	33	1,612
1915	177	..	111	2,054	2	33	2,093
1916	199	..	119	2,171	3	42	2,220
1917	239	..	123	2,415	3	47	2,465
1918	389	b	131	2,960	4	53	3,013
1919	418	..	126	3,464	7	47	3,511
1920	492	..	122	4,318	5	42	4,360

a Owing to the operation of the Osborne Judgement it was made impossible to compile membership statistics for 1913.
b Individual membership statistics were not compiled 1918–27.

Year	No. Constit. & Central Parties	Total Indiv. Members ('000s)	T.U.s		Soc. & Co-op. Socs.		Total Member-ship ('000s)
			No.	Members ('000s)	No.	Members ('000s)	
1921	456	..	116	3,974	5	37	4,010
1922	482	..	102	3,279	5	32	3,311
1923	503	..	106	3,120	6	36	3,156
1924	529	..	108	3,158	7	36	3,194
1925	549	..	106	3,338	8	36	3,374
1926	551	..	104	3,352	8	36	3,388
1927	532	..	97	3,239	6	55[a]	3,294
1928	535	215	91	2,025[b]	7	52	2,292[b]
1929	578	228	91	2,044	6	59	2,331
1930	607	277	89	2,011	7	58	2,347
1931	608	297	80	2,024	7	37	2,358
1932	608	372	75	1,960	9	40	2,372
1933	612	366	75	1,899	9	40	2,305
1934	614	381	72	1,858	8	40	2,278
1935	614	419	72	1,913	9	45	2,378
1936	614	431	73	1,969	9	45	2,444
1937	614	447	70	2,037	8	43	2,528
1938	614	429	70	2,158	9	43	2,630
1939	614	409	72	2,214	6	40	2,663
1940	614	304	73	2,227	6	40	2,571
1941	585	227	68	2,231	6	28	2,485
1942	581	219	69	2,206	6	29	2,454
1943	586	236	69	2,237	6	30	2,503
1944	598	266	68	2,375	6	32	2,673
1945	649	487	69	2,510	6	41	3,039
1946	649	645	70	2,635[b]	6	42	3,322[b]
1947	649	608	73	4,386	6	46	5,040
1948	656	629	80	4,751	6	42	5,422
1949	660	730	80	4,946	5	41	5,717
1950	661	908	83	4,972	5	40	5,920
1951	667	876	82	4,937	5	35	5,849
1952	667	1,015	84	5,072	5	21	6,108
1953	667	1,005	84	5,057	5	34	6,096
1954	667	934	84	5,530	5	35	6,498
1955	667	843	87	5,606	5	35	6,484
1956	667	845	88	5,658	5	34	6,537
1957	667	913	87	5,644	5	26	6,583
1958	667	889	87	5,628	5	26	6,542
1959	667	848	87	5,564	5	25	6,437
1960	667	790	86	5,513	5	25	6,328
1961	667	751	86	5,550	5	25	6,326
1962	667	767	86	5,503	5	25	6,296
1963	667	830	83	5,507	6	21	6,358
1964	667	830	83	5,502	6	21	6,353
1965	659	817	79	5,602	6	21	6,440
1966	658	776	79	5,539	6	21	6,336
1967	657	734	75	5,540	6	21	6,295

[a] The Royal Arsenal Co-operative Society, through its Political Purposes Committee, continued its affiliation with the Labour Party; its membership is included in the 1927–60 totals.

[b] From 1928 to 1946 inclusive, trade unionist members of the Labour Party had to 'contract in' to payment to party political funds.

SOURCE.—*Labour Party Annual Conference Report.*

The Labour Party — Organisation and Constitutions

The Labour Representation Committee was formed on 27 Feb 1900 to promote a distinct Labour group in Parliament, representing the affiliated trade unions and socialist societies. After the General Election of 1906 the L.R.C. group of M.P.s decided to assume the title of 'Labour Party' and elected their first officers and whips. Policy was determined by the Labour Party through the annual conference and its executive authority, the National Executive Committee. There was no official party leader, but an annually elected chairman of the parliamentary party. There were scarcely any official Labour Party constituency organisations (except for those provided by local trades councils, groups of miners' lodges, and local branches of the I.L.P.). In 1914 there were only two constituency associations with individual members: Woolwich and Barnard Castle, which Will Crooks and Arthur Henderson had built up on their own.

The Reorganisation of the Labour Party, 1918

The reorganisation of the Labour Party was projected by Arthur Henderson in collaboration with Sidney Webb. Their main aims were to provide local Labour Parties in every constituency or group of constituencies. These local Labour Parties were to be based fundamentally on individual subscribing membership, though representation was provided for trades councils, trade union branches, and socialist societies. The members of the N.E.C. were to be elected by the annual conference as a whole (though eleven were to be elected from candidates nominated by the trade unions and socialist societies as a single group, five were to represent the local Labour Parties, and four were to be women). The scheme also involved an increase in affiliation fees.

The original plan was amended, so that the N.E.C. was increased to a membership of 23 (adding two to the number specified for affiliated organisations). It was agreed that the election programme should be produced by the N.E.C. and P.L.P. jointly — subject to the aims of the Party and the decisions of the annual conferences. The object of the pre-war Party had been to 'organise and maintain in Parliament and in the country a political Labour Party'. In 1918 this was changed to a new formula: 'to secure for the producers by hand and by brain the full fruits of their industry, and the most equitable distribution thereof that may be possible, upon the basis of the common ownership of the means of production and the best obtainable system of popular administration and control of each industry and service'.[1]

The 1918 constitution was modified in 1937 in favour of the local constituency Labour Parties, which had repeatedly demanded a greater share in the control of party affairs. Representation of the constituency parties on the N.E.C. was increased from five to seven. The seven were to be elected by the vote of the constituency delegates alone. The twelve trade union representatives and one representative of the socialist societies were to be elected separately by their respective conference delegations. The five

[1] The 1914 and 1918 Labour Party constitutions are set out and compared in G. D. H. Cole, *A History of the Labour Party from 1914* (1948), pp. 71–81.

I

Trades Union-sponsored M.P.s, 1918–1966 (Labour)

No figures for Trades Union-sponsored M.P.s are available before 1918. Unions are here listed under their 1960 titles. M.P.s from 1918 to 1924 sponsored by Unions which subsequently amalgamated with other Unions and adopted other titles are listed under their present titles.

Trades Unions	1918	1922	1923	1924	1929	1931	1935	1945	1950	1951	1955	1959	1964	1966
National Union of Mineworkers (Miners' Federation of Great Britain, 1918–45)	25	41	43	40	42	26	32	34	37	36	34	31	28	26
Transport and General Workers' Union	3	7	10	10	13	1	7	17	16	14	14	14	21	25
National Union of Railwaymen	1	3	4	3	8	..	5	12	10	9	8	5	6	7
Transport Salaried Staffs Association (Railway Clerks' Association, 1918–50)	..	..	..	..	7	..	6	9	7	7	5	5	7	6
National Union of General and Municipal Workers	4	5	5	4	6	2	6	10	6	6	4	4	9	11
Associated Society of Woodworkers	1	1	3	2	6	1	2	3	3	3	2	1	..	..
Union of Shop, Distributive and Allied Workers	..	1	4	4	4	1	6	8	8	9	9	9	10	8
British Iron, Steel and Kindred Trades Association	..	2	1	3	4	1	1	2	2	2	2	2	1	1
United Textile Factory Workers' Association	4	3	3	3	4	..	..	3	2	2	1	1	1	1
Amalgamated Engineering Union (Amalgamated Society of Engineers, 1918–20)	1	7	4	4	3	2	3	4	8	8	6	8	18	18
National Union of Boot and Shoe Operatives	1	2	1	..	2	..	..	4	1	1	..	..	..	..
Associated Society of Locomotive Engineers and Firemen	..	..	..	1	1	..	1	2	2	2	2	3	1	..
United Society of Boilermakers, etc.	1	1	2	2	1	..	1	..	..	..	..	..	..	..
Union of Post Office Workers	..	2	3	2	..	..	..	1	2	2	1	2	2	3
National Union of Agricultural Workers	..	..	1	..	..	..	..	1	1	1	1	2	1	1
Electrical Trades Union	..	..	..	..	..	..	..	1	1	..	..	..	1	1
Others	8	11	18	11	13	..	8	9	6	8	6	5	14	18
Total T.U. M.P.s	49	86	102	88	114	35	78	120	111	108	95	92	120	127
Co-operative Party M.P.s	1	4	6	5	9	1	9	23	18	16	18	16	20	18
Total unsponsored M.P.s	7	52	83	58	164	10	67	250	186	171	164	150	177	218
Total Labour M.P.s	57	142	191	151	287	46	154	393	315	295	277	258	317	363

Sources.—1918–24, *Labour Party Annual Conference Reports*; 1929–66, *Trade Unions and the Labour Party since 1945*, by M. Harrison (1960) (these figures are also based on the Labour Party Conference Reports but modified by examination of union accounts); J. Bailey, *The British Co-operative Movement* (1955); and information from Transport House.

women members may be nominated by any affiliated organisation and are elected by a vote of the whole party conference. The Leader (since 1929) and the Deputy Leader (since 1953) are *ex officio* members of the N.E.C. The Treasurer of the Party may be nominated by any affiliated organisation, and is elected by the vote of the whole party conference.

SOURCES.—H. Pelling, *The Origins of the Labour Party, 1880–1900* (1954); F. Bealey and H. Pelling, *Labour and Politics, 1900–1906* (1958); P. Poirier, *The Advent of the Labour Party* (1958); G. D. H. Cole, *British Working-Class Politics, 1832–1914* (1941); G. D. H. Cole, *A History of the Labour Party from 1914* (1948); R. T. McKenzie, *British Political Parties* (1955). Since 1918 complete lists of Labour Party publications have been given in the Labour Party Annual Conference Reports. See also I. Bulmer-Thomas, *The Growth of the British Party System* (1965).

Sponsored M.P.s

The table on p. 110 summarises information for sponsored Labour M.P.s.

M.P.s are also sponsored by organisations which are not members of the Trades Union Congress. The two major instances of this are the National Union of Teachers and the National Farmers' Union.

National Union of Teachers

The N.U.T. has sponsored and assisted parliamentary candidates since 1895. The number of sponsored candidates has varied, but a strict parity between the parties has always been attempted. The executive may now sponsor up to a total of four candidates from each of the Conservative, Labour and Liberal parties.

N.U.T. adopted and supported M.P.s, 1900–1966

Election	Total	Con.	Lab.	Lib.
1900	3	1	..	2
1906	2	..	..	2
1910 (Jan)	1	..	..	1
1910 (Dec)	2	..	1	1
1918	1	1	..	..
1922	3	1	2	..
1923	3	..	3	..
1924	4	1	3	..
1929	5	..	5	..
1931	3	1	2	..
1935	5	1	4	..
1945	2	..	2	..
1950	4	..	4	..
1951	4	..	4	..
1955	6	2	4	..
1959	6	2	4	..
1964	5	1	4	..
1966	4	1	3	..

SOURCE.—Information received from the National Union of Teachers. J. D. Stewart, *British Pressure Groups* (1958).

National Farmers' Union

In 1909 the N.F.U. set up a Parliamentary Fund with the object of sending two sponsored M.P.s to Parliament from each side of the House. Although sometimes 'independent on agricultural questions' all N.F.U. M.P.s have been Conservatives. Since 1945 the N.F.U. has not sponsored any candidates and has adopted a position of strict neutrality between the political parties.

N.F.U.-sponsored M.P.s, 1922–1935

Election	No. of M.P.s
1922	4
1923	3
1924	2
1929	No candidates
1931	No candidates
1935	2

SOURCES.—*National Farmers' Union Yearbooks, 1900–60*; P. Self and H. Storing, *The State and the Farmer* (1962), pp. 42–7, 204; J. D. Stewart, *British Pressure Groups* (1958), pp. 173–4.

Liberal Party

Party Leaders[1]

1900	Sir H. Campbell-Bannerman	4 Nov 31	Sir H. Samuel[4]
30 Apr 08	H. Asquith (E of Oxford and Asquith)[2]	26 Nov 35	Sir A. Sinclair
		2 Aug 45	C. Davies
14 Oct 26	D. Lloyd George[3]	5 Nov 56	J. Grimond
		18 Jan 67	J. Thorpe

Deputy Leaders

1929–31   H. Samuel
1949–51   Lady M. Lloyd George
1962–64   D. Wade

Leaders in the House of Lords

1900	Earl of Kimberley	1931	M of Reading
1902	Earl Spencer	1936	M of Crewe
1905	M of Ripon	1944	Vt Samuel
1908	E (M) of Crewe	1955	Ld Rea
1923	Vt Grey	1967	Ld Byers
1924	Earl Beauchamp		

National Liberal Federation, 1900–1936

Chairman of Committee

1900	(Sir) E. Evans
1918	Sir G. Lunn
1920	A. Brampton
1931	R. Muir
1933	R. Walker
1934	M. Gray

Treasurer

1901	W. Hart
1903	J. Massie
1907	R. Bird

1910	F. Wright
1923	Sir R. Hudson
1927	Sir F. Layland-Barratt
1934	P. Heffer

Secretary

1893	(Sir) R. Hudson
1922	F. Barter
1925	H. Oldman
1930	H. Oldman & W. Davies
1931	W. Davies

[1] All were Liberal 'Leaders in the House of Commons'. Sir H. Campbell-Bannerman from 1899 to 1908 and H. Asquith 1908 to 1926 were the only 'Leaders of the Liberal Party' from 1900 to 1960.
[2] After H. Asquith's defeat at the 1918 General Election, Sir D. Maclean was elected leader of the Parliamentary Party but relinquished this post on H. Asquith's return to the Commons in Mar 1920.
[3] D. Lloyd George was Chairman of the Parliamentary Liberal Party from Dec 1924. He assumed the leadership of the Party after Asquith's death.
[4] At the General Election in 1931 there were three Liberal groups in the House of Commons. Sir H. Samuel led the main group of Liberal M.P.s. D. Lloyd George led a small family group of Independent Liberals, and Sir J. Simon (Ld) led what was to become in 1932 the Liberal National Group (see *Minor Parties*). On 25 Nov 35 D. Lloyd George and the other Independent Liberals rejoined the Liberal Party in the House of Commons.

Liberal Party Organisation, 1936–1967

	Head		Chairman of Executive Committee
1936	W. Davies (*Secretary*)	1936	M. Gray
1952	H. Harris (*General Director*)	1946	P. Fothergill
		1949	Ld Moynihan
1960	D. Robinson (*Directing Secretary*)	1950	F. Byers
		1952	P. Fothergill
1961	P. Kemmis (*Secretary*)	1954	G. Acland
1965	T. Beaumont (*Head of Liberal Party Organisation*)	1957	D. Abel
		1959	L. Behrens
1966	P. Chitnis (*Head of Liberal Party Organisation*)	1961	D. Banks
		1963	B. Wigoder
		1965	G. Evans
		1968	J. Baker

Treasurer [1]

1937–50	Sir A. McFadyean	1955–59	P. Fothergill
1937–41	P. Heffer	1959–62	Miss H. Harvey
1941–47	Ld Rea	1959–60	P. Lort-Phillips
1942–47	H. Worsley	1961–62	J. McLaughlin
1947–53	Ld Moynihan	1962–65	R. Gardner-Thorpe
1950–58	W. Grey	1962–66	Sir A. Murray
1950–52	Vt Wimborne	1963–65	T. Beaumont
1953–62	Sir A. Suenson-Taylor (Ld Grantchester)	1966–67	J. Thorpe
		1967–68	L. Smith
		1968–	J. Pardoe

Chairman

1966	Ld Byers
1967	T. Beaumont (Ld)
1968	Ld Henley

SOURCES.—*Liberal Magazine 1900–1950*; *Liberal Year Book 1900–1939*; *Dod's Parliamentary Companion 1950–*. Annual Reports of the Liberal Party 1956–.

Chief Whips in House of Commons

1900	H. Gladstone	1930	Sir A. Sinclair		*Coalition Liberal*
1905	G. Whiteley	1931	G. Owen	1916	N. Primrose
1908	J. Pease	1932	W. Rea	1917	F. Guest
1910	Master of Elibank	1935	Sir P. Harris	1921	C. McCurdy
1912	P. Illingworth	1945	T. Horabin	1922	E. Hilton Young
1915	J. Gulland	1946	F. Byers		
1919	G. Thorne	1950	J. Grimond		
1923	V. Phillipps	1956	D. Wade		
1924	Sir G. Collins	1962	A. Holt		
1926	Sir R. Hutchinson	1963	E. Lubbock		

Chief Whips in House of Lords

1896	Ld Ribblesdale	1944	Vt Mersey
1907	Ld Denman	1949	M of Willingdon
1911–22	Ld Colebrooke	1950	Ld Moynihan
1919	Ld Denman (*Ind. Lib.*)	1950	Ld Rea
1924	Ld Stanmore	1955	Ld Amulree

SOURCE.—*Dod's Parliamentary Companion 1900–*.

National Liberal Federation — Annual Conferences, 1900–1935

Date	Place	President
27–28 Mar 00	Nottingham	R. Spence Watson
14–15 May 01	Bradford	,,
13–14 May 02	Bristol	A. Birrell
14–15 May 03	Scarborough	,,
12–13 May 04	Manchester	,,
18–19 May 05	Newcastle upon Tyne	,,
23–24 May 06	Liverpool	A. Acland
6–7 Jun 07	Plymouth	,,

[1] Until 1965 the post of Treasurer was held jointly by two or three officers.

Date	Place	President
18–19 Jun 08	Birmingham	Sir W. Angus
1–2 Jul 09	Southport	,,
25 Nov 10	Hull	,,
23–24 Nov 11	Bath	Sir J. Brunner
21–22 Nov 12	Nottingham	,,
26–27 Nov 13	Leeds	,,
1914–1918	*No conference held*	
27–28 Nov 19	Birmingham	Sir G. Lunn
25–26 Nov 20	Bradford	J. Robertson
24–25 Nov 21	Newcastle upon Tyne	,,
17–18 May 22	Blackpool	,,
30 May–1 Jun 23	Buxton	Sir D. Maclean
22–23 May 24	Brighton	,,
14–15 May 25	Scarborough	,,
17–18 Jun 26	Weston-super-Mare	J. Spender
26–27 May 27	Margate	Sir C. Hobhouse
11–12 Oct 28	Great Yarmouth	,,
3–4 Oct 29	Nottingham	,,
16–17 Oct 30	Torquay	A. Brampton
14–15 May 31	Buxton	,,
28–29 Apr 32	Clacton-on-Sea	,,
18–19 May 33	Scarborough	R. Muir
2–5 May 34	Bournemouth	,,
23–25 May 35	Blackpool	,,

Liberal Party — Annual Assemblies, 1936–

Date	Place	President
18–19 Jun 36	London	Ld Meston
27–31 May 37	Buxton	,,
19–20 May 38	Bath	,,
11–12 May 39	Scarborough	,,
1940	*No assembly held*	
18–19 Jul 41	London	,,
4–5 Sep 42	London	,,
15–17 Jul 43	London	,,
1944	*No assembly held*	
1– 3 Feb 45	London	Lady V. Bonham-Carter
9–11 May 46	London	,,
24–26 Apr 47	Bournemouth	I. Foot
22–24 Apr 48	Blackpool	E. Dodds
24–26 Mar 49	Hastings	Sir A. MacFadyean
27–28 Jan 50	London	,,
29–30 Sep 50	Scarborough	P. Fothergill
1951	*No assembly held*	
15–17 May 52	Hastings	R. Walker
9–11 Apr 53	Ilfracombe	L. Robson
22–24 Apr 54	Buxton	H. Graham White
14–16 Apr 55	Llandudno	Ld Rea
27–29 Sep 56	Folkestone	L. Behrens (*acting*)
19–21 Sep 57	Southport	,,
18–21 Sep 58	Torquay	N. Micklem
1959	*No assembly held*	Sir A. Comyns Carr
29 Sep–1 Oct 60	Eastbourne	Sir A. Murray
21–23 Sep 61	Edinburgh	Sir A. Murray
19–22 Sep 62	Llandudno	E. Malindine
10–14 Sep 63	Brighton	Sir F. Brunner
4– 5 Sep 64	London	Ld Ogmore
22–25 Sep 65	Scarborough	R. Fulford
21–24 Sep 66	Brighton	Miss N. Seear
20–23 Sep 67	Blackpool	Ld Henley
18–21 Sep 68	Edinburgh	D. Banks

SOURCES.—*Liberal Year Book 1902–1939*; *The Liberal Magazine 1900–1950*; *National Liberal Federation, Annual Reports 1900–1936*; *Keesing's Archives 1939–*.
    The Liberal Publication Department published miscellaneous collections of *Pamphlets and Leaflets, 1908–30*. The *Liberal Magazine* was published from 1893 until 1950. J. S. Rasmussen, *The Liberal Party, A Study of Retrenchment and Revival* (1965); Alan Watkins, *The Liberal Dilemma* (1966); Trevor Wilson, *The Downfall of the Liberal Party 1914–1935* (1966). See also I. Bulmer-Thomas, *The Growth of the British Party System* (1965).

Minor Parties
Common Wealth
This party was founded in 1942 by Sir Richard Acland (Liberal M.P. for Barnstaple) during the war-time electoral truce. Its immediate aim was to contest all by-elections where a 'reactionary' candidate was in the field, and was not opposed by a Labour or other 'progressive' candidate. Seats were won at Eddisbury (J. Loverseed, 1943), Skipton (H. Lawson, 1944), and Chelmsford (E. Millington, 1945). In 1943 membership of Common Wealth was proscribed by the Labour Party. In the 1945 General Election Common Wealth put up twenty-three candidates but were only successful in Chelmsford, where no Labour candidate stood: the victor there, E. Millington, joined the Labour Party. Sir R. Acland joined the Labour Party as soon as the 1945 results were known. Common Wealth survived as an organisation but contested no further parliamentary elections.

Communist Party
The Communist Party of Great Britain was founded in July 1920. In its early years it sought to affiliate to the Labour Party but was rebuffed. In 1922 J. T. W. Newbold (Motherwell) was elected to Parliament; S. Saklatvala (N. Battersea) was also elected in 1922 as a Labour M.P. (although a member of the Communist Party). After defeat in 1923, he was elected again in 1924 as a Communist. Since 1924 the Labour Party has ruled that no member of the Communist Party could be an individual member of the Labour Party and in 1935, 1943, and 1946 the Labour Party turned down further Communist requests for affiliation. In 1935 and again in 1945 W. Gallacher was elected as a Communist for W. Fife; and in 1945 P. Piratin was elected for the Mile End division of Stepney.

Secretaries of the Communist Party: 1920–29 A. Inkpin, 1929–56 H. Pollitt, 1956– J. Gollan.

Communist Candidates

1922	.	5	1931	.	26	1951	.	10
1923	.	8	1935	.	2	1955	.	17
1924	.	8	1945	.	21	1959	.	18
1929	.	25	1950	.	100	1964	.	36
						1966	.	57

SOURCE.—H. Pelling, *The British Communist Party* (1958).

Co-operative Party
In 1917 the Co-operative Congress agreed to organise as a political party. In the 1918 General Election one Co-operative M.P. was elected; he joined with the Labour Party in the House of Commons. Labour and Co-operative candidates never opposed each other at elections but it was not till 1926 that a formal understanding was reached and Co-operative Parties were made eligible for affiliation to divisional Labour Parties. In 1938 the Co-operative Party adopted a written constitution and in 1941 its representatives were invited to attend meetings of the National Council of Labour on equal terms with the Labour Party and the T.U.C. In 1946, the 1926 agreement

with the Labour Party was replaced; Co-operative candidates were to run formally as Co-operative and Labour Candidates,[1] and after the General Election of 1959 it was agreed that the number of Co-operative candidates should be limited to 30.[2]

In 1951 the Co-operative Party adopted a new constitution to prevent its members from joining organisations proscribed by the Labour Party.

Co-operative M.P.s and Candidates

1918	.	1 (10)	1945	.	23 (33)
1922	.	4 (11)	1950	.	18 (33)
1923	.	6 (10)	1951	.	16 (37)
1924	.	5 (10)	1955	.	18 (38)
1929	.	9 (12)	1959	.	16 (30)
1931	.	1 (18)	1964	.	19 (27)
1935	.	9 (21)	1966	.	18 (24)

SOURCES.—J. Bailey, *The British Co-operative Movement* (1955), *Reports of the Annual Co-operative Congress 1900–66, The People's Year Book 1932.*

Independent Labour Party

The Independent Labour Party, formed in 1893, was one of the founding bodies of the Labour Representation Committee in 1900. The I.L.P. was affiliated to the Labour Party but it held its own conferences, sponsored its own parliamentary candidates, and maintained its own policies, even after the 1918 revision of the Labour Party constitution. Differences with the Labour Party grew in the late 1920's and the 37 I.L.P. Members among the 288 Labour M.P.s elected in 1929 provided some of the second Labour Government's strongest critics. At the 1930 conference of the I.L.P., it was agreed that I.L.P. members should vote against the Labour Government when its actions conflicted with I.L.P. policy. The I.L.P. was disaffiliated by the 1932 Labour Party Conference. In 1935 17 I.L.P. candidates stood, all against Labour candidates, and four (all in Glasgow) were successful. In 1945 three of the five I.L.P. candidates won but, after the death of the party's leader, James Maxton in 1946, the I.L.P. M.P.s one by one rejoined the Labour Party. In the elections of 1950 and 1951 there were three I.L.P. candidates and in 1955 and 1959 two candidates. All lost their deposits. There were no candidates in 1964 and 1966.

M.P.s (since 1931)

1932–46	J. Maxton	1932–33	R. Wallhead
1932–47	J. McGovern	1935–47	C. Stephen
1932–39	G. Buchanan	1946–47	J. Carmichael
1932–33	D. Kirkwood		

SOURCE.—R. E. Dowse, *Left in the Centre* (1966).

Irish Nationalist Party up to 1922

From the days of Parnell until the First World War between 80 and 86 Irish Nationalists sat in the House of Commons — at times divided by internal frictions but with a safe control of more than three-quarters of the seats in Ireland. Divisions over support for the war and the Easter Rebellion broke the party's hold and in 1918 only 7 of its 58 candidates were elected, (while Sinn Fein candidates won 73 seats). T. P. O'Connor, from 1885 the solitary Irish Nationalist Member representing an English constituency,

[1] *L.P. Annual Report*, 1946, pp. 229–31.   [2] *L.P. Annual Report*, 1960, p. 24.

continued to be returned unopposed for the Scotland Division of Liverpool until his death in 1929.

Chairmen of the Irish Parliamentary Party

1900   J. Redmond   1917   J. Dillon

SOURCE.—F. S. L. Lyons, *The Irish Parliamentary Party 1890–1910* (1951).

Irish Parties since 1922

Since 1922 candidates under the label 'Irish Nationalist' have fought only two or three of the Northern Ireland seats, but from 1922 to 1924 they held one of the two Fermanagh and Tyrone Seats (the other was held by Sinn Fein) and from 1929 to 1955 they held both. T. P. O'Connor continued to represent the Scotland division of Liverpool until 1929 and one or two Liverpool seats were fought by Nationalists.

Sinn Fein reappeared as a political force in 1955 and 1959, contesting all 12 Northern Ireland seats. In 1955 Sinn Fein candidates won Mid-Ulster and Fermanagh and South Tyrone but they were disqualified as felons.

From 1943 to 1950, from 1951 to 1955 and from 1966 onwards Belfast West was held by candidates using the label 'Eire Labour' or 'Republican Labour'.

Nationalist M.P.s

1922–29	T. P. O'Connor	1929–34	J. Devlin
1922–24	T. Harbison	1934–35	J. Stewart
1922–24⎫		1935–50	P. Cunningham
1931–35⎬	(S.F.) C. Healy	1935–51	A. Mulvey
1950–55⎭		1951–55	M. O'Neill

Sinn Fein M.P.s

1955–55	P. Clarke	1955–56	T. Mitchell

Eire Labour M.P.

1943–50⎫
1951–55⎭ J. Beattie

Republican Labour M.P.

1966–   G. Fitt

Liberal National Party (National Liberal Party since 1948)

In October 1931 23 Liberal Members broke with the party and formed the Liberal National Group. The subsequent electoral history of the Liberal National Party falls into three periods: at the 1931 General Election some of the Liberal National candidates were opposed by Conservatives but none of them were by Liberals. After 1931, a Conservative only once opposed a Liberal National (Scottish Universities 1946) but they were not opposed by Liberals (except in Denbigh 1935 and St. Ives 1937) until 1945. Of 41 candidates in 1931, 35 were returned as Members of Parliament and when the 'Samuelite' Liberals left the government over the Ottawa Agreements in 1932, the 'Simonite' Liberal Nationals remained. In 1935 33 of 44 candidates were returned, and in 1945 13 of 51 candidates. E. Brown, however, who had succeeded Sir J. Simon as leader on 4 December 1940 was defeated. In May 1947 the Woolton-Teviot agreement was signed, which urged the combination of Conservative and Liberal National Constituency

Associations, and in 1948 the party was renamed the National Liberal Party. Since the 1966 General Election only two M.P.s style themselves Conservative and National Liberal. Two other members of the Group were elected as Conservatives by Joint Associations. In 1966 these four M.P.s relinquished the room assigned to them in the House of Commons to the Liberal Party. The Group is now an integral part of the Conservative Party.

Chairmen of the Parliamentary Party		*Chief Whips*	
1931	Sir J. Simon	1931	A. Glassey
1940	E. Brown	1931	G. Shakespeare
1945	(Sir) J. Henderson-Stewart	1932	(Sir) J. Blindell
1946	Sir S. Holmes	1937	C. Kerr
1947	J. Maclay	1940	H. Holdsworth
1956	(Sir) J. Duncan	1945–66	(Sir) H. Butcher
1959	Sir J. Henderson-Stewart		
1961	Sir C. Thornton Kemsley		

SOURCES.—Information from the National Liberal Party, and *Dod's Parliamentary Companion, 1931–66.*

Liberal Unionist Party

The Liberal Unionist Party was based upon those Liberals who, under J. Chamberlain and the M of Hartington, broke with the party over Irish Home Rule in 1886. After they accepted office in Ld Salisbury's 1895 government, they became increasingly fused with the Conservative Party and, although they had preserved a separate organisation with separate funds, the final merger in 1912 was to some extent a recognition of a *fait accompli.* The President between 1886 and 1904 was M of Hartington (D of Devonshire) and between 1904 and 1912 J. Chamberlain. The Organising Secretary between 1895 and 1912 was J. Boraston.

Liberal Unionist M.P.s

1900	.	68	.	Jan 1910	.	31
1906	.	23	.	Dec 1910	.	35

National Party

A small group of dissident Conservatives led by H. Page Croft, formed this party in September 1917, with a programme described by one historian as of 'xenophobic imperialism'. Most of its members drifted back to the Conservative fold and fought under the Conservative label in 1918: only Sir H. Page Croft and Sir R. Cooper survived the election (when they made a special point of attacking the sale of honours) and in 1921 it was decided not to maintain a separate parliamentary party.

SOURCES. Ld Croft, *My Life of Strife* (1948). M. Foot, 'Henry Page Croft, Baron Croft', *Dictionary of National Biography 1941–50.*

National Democratic Party

The National Democratic Party was formed in 1918 to unite support amongst the Labour Movement for the Lloyd George Government. The N.D.P. had its origins in the dispute within the Labour Movement during the war and its greatest strength in the jingoist trade unions — the Liverpool Dockers, the Musicians' Union, some of the Textile Workers, and parts of the Miners' Federation. It was also, in part, the successor to the projected

anti-socialist Trade Union Labour Party and included among its members
the Labour Ministers who refused to resign from the Government in 1918.
G. Barnes, Labour member of the War Cabinet, was its accepted leader. In
the 1918 Election the Party put up 28 candidates, all for working-class constituencies, and returned 15 to Parliament. Before the 1922 Election the
surviving N.D.P. M.P.s joined the National Liberal Party, but only one
(G. Roberts) was re-elected. The Party ceased to exist in 1923.

SOURCES.—G. D. H. Cole, *A History of the British Labour Party from 1914* (1945); G. N. Barnes,
From Workshop to War Cabinet (1924); *Labour Party Annual Conference Reports*, 1916–18; *Trades
Union Congress Reports*, 1916–18.

National Labour Party

The party was formed in 1931 from the small group of Labour M.P.s
who supported the National Government under Ramsay MacDonald. In
the 1931 General Election 13 of its 20 candidates were elected. In 1935 8
of its 20 candidates were elected. The party wound itself up just before
the 1945 election and in 1945 of the 7 surviving National Labour members
3 retired, 2 stood unsuccessfully as National candidates, and 2 as Independents (one, K. Lindsay, successfully — but in a new constituency, English
Universities).

New Party, British Union of Fascists, Union Movement

Sir Oswald Mosley (Conservative, then Independent M.P. 1918–24,
Labour M.P. 1926–31) resigned from the Labour Government in May 1930
after his *Memorandum* for dealing with unemployment had been rejected
by the Cabinet. In October 1930 a resolution calling upon the National
Executive to consider the Memorandum was narrowly defeated at the
Labour Party Conference. On 6 December 1930 the *Mosley Manifesto*
summarising the main proposals in the Memorandum was published, signed
by 17 Labour M.P.s. Six of the 17 signatories of the Manifesto resigned
from the Labour Party to form the New Party in February 1931 (Sir Oswald
and Lady Cynthia Mosley, O. Baldwin, W. J. Brown, R. Forgan, and J.
Strachey), but Baldwin and Brown remained members for only one day
and Strachey resigned in June. The New Party received two further
recruits before the 1931 General Election, W. E. D. Allen (Conservative)
and R. Dudgeon (Liberal). In the Election the New Party contested 24
seats but failed to win a single one, the New Party M.P.s all losing their
seats, and, apart from Sir Oswald Mosley, their deposits.

In 1932 the New Party was renamed the British Union of Fascists after
Mosley had been to Italy to study the 'modern movements'. The Director
of Organisation and Deputy Leader was R. Forgan. In the 1935 General
Election, the B.U.F. put up no candidates and, with the slogan 'Fascism
next Time', advised their supporters not to vote. The B.U.F. fought a
number of by-elections in 1939 and 1940, before it was proscribed by the
Government on 30 May 1940.

In 1948, Sir Oswald Mosley formed the Union Movement. Its first
Parliamentary contest was in the 1959 General Election, when he fought
North Kensington, losing his deposit. The Union Movement fought two

by-elections in the 1959 Parliament and in the 1966 General Election Sir
Oswald Mosley and 3 other candidates stood; they gained only on average
3·7% of the vote.

SOURCE.—Colin Cross, *The Fascists in Britain* (1961).

Scottish National Party

The party was formed in 1928 as the National Party of Scotland. In
1933 it merged with a body called the Scottish Party (founded 1930) and
the name was then changed to the Scottish National Party. Its first success
was in the Motherwell by-election of April 1945; but the victor, R. D.
McIntyre, was defeated in the General Election three months later. In
November 1967 Mrs W. Ewing won another seat for the party in the
Hamilton by-election.

Scottish National Party Candidates

1929	. 2		1951	. 1
1931	. 4		1955	. 2
1935	. 6		1959	. 5
1945	. 8		1964	. 15
1950	. 4		1966	. 23

Welsh Nationalist Party — Plaid Cymru

The party was founded in 1925 and has fought elections consistently
since then, but without any success at the parliamentary level until in a
by-election in 1966 its President, G. Evans, won Carmarthen.

Welsh Nationalist Candidates

1929	. 1		1951	. 4
1931	. 2		1955	. 11
1935	. 1		1959	. 20
1945	. 8		1964	. 23
1950	. 7		1966	. 20

Minor Parties — Representation in the House of Commons

	Total	Ir. Nat.	Comm.	I.L.P.	Ind. Con.	Other
1900	82	82	..	..	..	..
1906	83	83	..	..	..	..
1910	82	82	..	..	..	..
1910	84	84	..	..	..	..
1918	83	80[a]	..	..	..	3
1922	12	3	1	..	3	5
1923	7	3	..	..	..	4
1924	5	1	1	..	..	3
1929	8	3	..	..	1	4
1931	5	2	..	..	..	2
1935	9	2	1	4	..	2
1945	22	3	2	3	2	12
1950	3	2	..	..	..	1[b]
1951	3	3	..	..	..	..
1955	3	2	..	..	..	1[b]
1959	1	..	..	..	1	..
1964	1	..	..	..	..	1[b]
1966	2	1	..	..	..	1[b]

[a] There were 73 Sinn Fein candidates elected in Ireland who never took their seats. There were also
7 Nationalists elected.
[b] The 'other' candidate listed in 1950, 1955, 1964 and 1966, was, in fact, the Speaker.

SOURCES.—*The Constitutional Year Book, 1919*; D. E. Butler, *The Electoral System in Britain since
1918* (1963); G. Thayer, *The British Political Fringe* (1965).

Independent M.P.s

The number of Independent M.P.s has been small and, even among those few elected without the label of one of the parties already listed, a substantial proportion were in fact elected with the tacit support of a major party or in default of its candidate. M.P.s elected as Independents fall into six broad categories.

Independents in University Seats

J. Butler	1922	Miss E. Rathbone	1929	Sir A. Salter	1937
G. Davies	1923		1934		1945
(Sir) E. Graham-Little	1924		1935	T. Harvey	1937
	1929		1945	A. Hill	1940
	1931	(Sir) A. Herbert	1935	K. Lindsay	1945
	1935		1945	Sir J. Boyd Orr	1945
	1945			W. Harris	1945

Independents emerging from war-time situations

N. Billing	1917	W. Kendall	1941	W. Brown	1942
	1918		1945		1945
H. Bottomley	1918	G. Reakes	1942	C. White	1944
R. Barker	1918	T. Driberg	1942		

Dissident Conservatives

T. Sloan	1902	J. Erskine	1921	E. Taylor	1930
	1906		1922	D. Lipson	1937
E. Mitchell	1903	H. Becker	1922		1945[1]
C. Palmer	1920	G. Hall Caine	1922	Sir C. Headlam	1940
Sir C. Townshend	1920	O. Mosley	1922	J. McKie	1945
Sir T. Polson	1921		1923[1]	J. Little	1945
		Sir R. Newman	1929	Sir D. Robertson	1959

Dissident Liberal

J. Wason	1902	A. Hopkinson	1929[1]
G. Roberts	1922		1931[1]
A. Hopkinson	1922		1935[1]
	1923	Sir T. Robinson	1929
	1924[1]		

Dissident Labour

C. Stanton	1915	Sir O. Thomas	1922	D. Pritt	1945

Supported by the Left

E. Scrymgeour	1922	E. Scrymgeour	1929
	1923	V. Bartlett	1938
	1924		1945[1]

These later candidacies might be put into a different category.

III
PARLIAMENT
House of Commons

Speaker of the House of Commons

1895	W. Gully (Vt Selby)	Lib.
20 Jun 05	J. Lowther (Vt Ullswater)	Con.
28 Apr 21	J. Whitley	Co. Lib.
21 Jun 28	E. Fitzroy [1]	Con.
9 Mar 43	D. Clifton Brown (Vt Ruffside)	Con.
1 Nov 51	W. Morrison (Vt Dunrossil)	Con.
21 Oct 59	Sir H. Hylton-Foster [1]	Con.
26 Oct 65	Dr. H. King	Lab.

Chairman of Ways and Means Committee

1900	J. Lowther	Con.
1905	G. Lawson	Con.
1906	A. Emmott	Lib.
1911	J. Whitley	Lib.
1921	J. Hope	Con.
1924	R. Young	Lab.
1929	R. Young	Lab.
1931	Sir D. Herbert	Con.
1943	D. Clifton Brown	Con.
1943	J. Milner	Lab.
1945	C. Williams	Con.
1945	J. Milner	Lab.
1951	Sir C. MacAndrew	Con.
1959	Sir G. Touche	Con.
1962	Sir W. Anstruther-Gray	Con.
1964	Dr. H. King	Lab.
1965	Sir S. Storey	Con.
1966	Sir E. Fletcher	Lab.
1968	S. Irving	Lab.

Deputy Chairman of Ways and Means Committee
(office created 1902)

1902	A. Jeffreys	Con.
1905	L. Hardy	Con.
1906	J. Caldwell	Lib.
1910	J. Whitley	Lib.
1911	D. Maclean	Lib.
1919	Sir E. Cornwall	Lib.
1922	E. Fitzroy	Con.
1924	C. Entwistle	Lib.
1928	D. Herbert	Con.
1929	H. Dunnico	Lab.
1931	R. Bourne [1]	Con.
1938	D. Clifton Brown	Con.
1943	J. Milner	Lab.
1943	C. Williams	Con.
1945	Sir C. MacAndrew	Con.
1945	H. Beaumont [1]	Lab.
1948	F. Bowles	Lab.
1950	Sir C. MacAndrew	Con.
1951	R. Hopkin Morris [1]	Lib.
1956	Sir G. Touche	Con.
1959	Sir W. Anstruther-Gray	Con.
1962	Sir R. Grimston	Con.
1964	Sir S. Storey	Con.
1965	R. Bowen	Lib.
1966	S. Irving	Lab.
1968	H. Gourlay	Lab.

Officers of the House of Commons

	Clerk		*Librarian*
1900	(Sir) A. Milman	1887	R. Walpole
1902	Sir C. Ilbert	1908	A. Smyth
1921	(Sir) T. Webster	1937	V. Kitto
1930	(Sir) H. Dawkins	1946	H. Saunders
1937	(Sir) G. Campion	1950	S. Gordon
1948	(Sir) F. Metcalfe	1968	D. Holland
1954	(Sir) E. Fellowes		
1962	(Sir) B. Cocks		

[1] Died in office.

Fathers of the House of Commons

Name	Member of Parliament until	Length of service			
		as M.P.		as Father	
		y.	m.	y.	m.
W. Bramston Beach	August 1901	44	4	2	4
Sir M. Hicks Beach	January 1906	41	6	4	5
G. Finch	May 1907	39	6	1	4
Sir H. Campbell-Bannerman	April 1908	39	6		11
Sir J. Kennaway	January 1910	39	9	1	9
T. Burt	December 1918	44	10	8	11
T. P. O'Connor	November 1929	49	7	10	11
D. Lloyd George	December 1944	54	8	15	1
Earl Winterton	October 1951	46	11	6	10
Sir H. O'Neill	October 1952	37	8	1	0
D. Grenfell	September 1959	37	2	6	11
Sir W. Churchill	September 1964	62	0ᵃ	5	0
R. Butler	January 1965	35	8		
R. Turton	(first elected May 29)	—			4

ᵃ By tradition, the title of Father of the House of Commons is conferred on that member who has the longest *continuous* service in the House in point of time. Churchill's service was broken in 1908 and again 1922–24. His length of continuous service was therefore 40 years.

SOURCE.—J. F. S. ROSS, *Elections and Electors*, p. 470 (up to 1952).

Parliamentary Sessions

In 1900 sessions of Parliament lasted from February to July or August. Occasionally Parliament sat through the summer. In 1930 both Houses agreed that they should adjourn between July and October, and that the session should last from September or October to the September or October of the following year. During the adjournments the Speaker or the Lord Chancellor has the power to give notice of an earlier meeting of Parliament if it is in the national interest.

Parliamentary Hours of Sitting

In 1902 the House of Commons met from 2 until 11.30 p.m., but this was altered in 1906 to 2.45 until 11.30, to allow more time for lunch. During the 1939–45 war the time for rising in the evening was changed to 10.30 p.m. Since 1945 the normal hours for sitting have been 2.30 until 10.30 p.m. on every weekday except Friday although the House often sits later than this. From 1900 to 1939 the House met on Fridays from 12 a.m. to 5.30 p.m. Since 1939 the House meets on Fridays at 11 a.m. and adjourns for the week-end at 4.30 p.m. In 1967 the normal hours for sitting were fixed as a sessional experiment as follows:

Monday and Wednesday: 10 a.m.–1 p.m.; 2.30–10 p.m.

Tuesday and Thursday: 2.30–10 p.m.

Friday: 11 a.m.–4.30 p.m.

but morning sittings were discontinued, as a regular practice, in October of that year.

Government and Private Members' Time

Until 1939 Government business had precedence at every sitting of the House of Commons except certain Wednesdays and Fridays and Tuesday evenings after 8.15 p.m. until Easter. This generally gave Private Members about 8 Wednesdays and 13 Fridays on which they had precedence. This

House of Commons

Sessions		Allocation of Parliamentary Time			Parliamentary Bills		Questions to Ministers		
Parliament Met	Parliament Prorogued	Total Days on which House sat	Average length of Day	Private Members' Days[a]	Total Bills Introduced	Total Bills Receiving Royal Assent	Daily Average Starred[b] Questions	Daily Average Unstarred Questions	Session Total of all Questions
3 Dec 00	15 Dec 00	11	5h 38m	3	..	..	..	..	31.
23 Jan 01	17 Aug 01[e]	121	9h 5m	14	303	127	69	..	6,44.
16 Jan 02	18 Dec 02	181	8h 51m	17	300	121	..	..	7,168
17 Feb 03	14 Aug 03	115	9h 8m	14	311	311	28	18	4,530
2 Feb 04	15 Aug 04	124	9h 19m	13	308	121	38	18	5,93.
14 Feb 05	11 Aug 05	114	9h 12m	12	309	86	47	19	6,24.

Date of Dissolution 8 Jan 06. Duration of Parliament 5 yrs, 2 mths, 7 days.

13 Feb 06	21 Dec 06	156	8h 32m	16	346	121	70	22	11,86.
12 Feb 07	28 Aug 07	131	8h 28m	13	294	116	72	21	10,14.
29 Jan 08	19 Dec 08	171	7h 39m	18	364	129	75	21	13,81.
16 Feb 09	3 Dec 09	179	8h 38m	14	325	110	62	19	12,25.

Date of Dissolution 10 Jan 10. Duration of Parliament 3 yrs, 10 mths, 28 days.

15 Feb 10	28 Nov 10	103	6h 36m	9	289	101	81	24	8,20.

Date of Dissolution 28 Nov 10. Duration of Parliament 9 mths, 3 days

31 Jan 11	16 Dec 11	172	7h 49m	11	373	134	87	21	15,43.
14 Feb 12	7 Mar 13	206	8h 1m	14	343	101	97	19	19,91.
10 Mar 13	15 Aug 13	102	7h 55m	10	315	108	88	18	8,93.
10 Feb 14	18 Sep 14	130	7h 14m	16	391	168	55	16	7,70.
11 Nov 14	27 Jan 16	155	6h 40m	..	162	152	72	16	12,97.
15 Feb 16	22 Dec 16	127	7h 11m	..	112	105	108	20	15,74.
7 Feb 17	6 Feb 18	181	7h 21m	..	102	91	92	16	19,14.
12 Feb 18	21 Nov 18	119	7h 16m	..	99	86	89	15	12,02.

Date of Dissolution 25 Nov 18. Duration of Parliament 7 yrs, 9 mths, 25 days.

4 Feb 19	23 Dec 19	163	7h 16m	16	203	152	126	27	20,523
10 Feb 20	23 Dec 20	167	8h 20m	17½	215	138	110	22	18,652
15 Feb 21	10 Nov 21	141	8h 0m	11¾	202	125	} 101[d]	} 19[d]	14,133
14 Dec 21	19 Dec 21	4	6h 5m	..	..	..			
7 Feb 22	4 Aug 22	113	8h 3m	11	196	105	..[e]	..[e]	..[e]

Date of Dissolution 26 Oct 22. Duration of Parliament 3 yrs, 9 mths, 5 days.

20 Nov 22	15 Dec 22	20	7h 54m	..	10	10	103[e]	18[e]	12,86.
13 Feb 23	16 Nov 23	114	8h 34m	17¼	181	78	107	21	12,37.

Date of Dissolution 16 Nov 23. Duration of Parliament 11 mths, 27 days.

8 Jan 24	9 Oct 24	129	7h 50m	21½	248	79	101	25	13,092

Date of Dissolution 9 Oct 24. Duration of Parliament 9 mths, 1 day.

2 Dec 24	22 Dec 25	148	8h 17m	22½	247	145	91	23	14,03.
2 Feb 26	15 Dec 26	151	7h 55m	21	180	105	71	17	10,71.
8 Feb 27	22 Dec 27	144	7h 53m	19¾	195	91	74	14	10,53.
7 Feb 28	3 Aug 28	115	7h 34m	24½	168	79	67	13	7,55.
6 Nov 28	10 May 29	100	7h 0m	..	115	64	68	17	7,074

Date of Dissolution 10 May 29. Duration of Parliament 4 yrs, 7 mths, 2 days.

25 Jun 29	1 Aug 30	189	7h 57m	31	237	132	93	24	18,327
28 Oct 30	7 Oct 31	187	7h 47m	21¼	212	106	78	15	14,373

Date of Dissolution 8 Oct 31. Duration of Parliament 2 years, 4 mths, 28 days.

[a] 'Notional' days on which Private Members' business had precedence. The idea of parliamentary 'days' must be treated [with] caution since actual days vary in length. In recent years Private Members' days have usually been Fridays and only 5 hours [long] whereas Government 'days' are usually at least 6½ hours long and are frequently extended by suspension of the ten o'clock [rule] and by the practice of taking the affirmative and negative resolutions after ten o'clock.

[b] Including oral questions receiving a written reply.

[e] Although the session of 1901 was not due to begin until 14 Feb, Parliament sat for three days between 23 and 25 Jan to dis[pose of] business arising out of the death of Queen Victoria.   [d] For both sessions in 1921.   [e] For both sessions in 1922.

House of Commons

Sessions		Allocation of Parliamentary Time			Parliamentary Bills		Questions to Ministers		
Parliament Met	Parliament Prorogued	Total Days on which House sat	Average length of Day	Private Members' Days[a]	Total Bills Introduced	Total Bills Receiving Royal Assent	Daily Average — Starred Questions[b]	Daily Average — Unstarred Questions	Sessional Total of all Questions
3 Nov 31	17 Nov 32	155	7h 32m	I	125	103	69	10	9,667
2 Nov 32	17 Nov 33	143	7h 33m	26½	147	92	58	8	7,559
1 Nov 33	16 Nov 34	156	7h 49m	22¼	173	111	58	9	8,768
0 Nov 34	25 Oct 35	151	7h 36m	..	116	98	59	9	8,449

Date of Dissolution 25 Oct 35. Duration of Parliament 3 yrs, 11 mths, 21 days.

6 Nov 35	30 Oct 36	137	7h 55m	19½	149	111	82	13	10,215
3 Nov 36	22 Oct 37	157	7h 47m	24	170	126	79	11	11,769
6 Oct 37	4 Nov 38	168	7h 42m	26¼	179	113	85	14	13,787
8 Nov 38	23 Nov 39	200	7h 34m	14	227	171	92	17	18,460
8 Nov 39	20 Nov 40	127	6h 53m	..	80	73	84	27	13,536
1 Nov 40	11 Nov 41	113	5h 50m	..	55	54	77	23	10,825
2 Nov 41	10 Nov 42	116	6h 23m	..	46	46	80	23	11,592
1 Nov 42	23 Nov 43	122	7h 1m	..	59	58	83	22	11,911
4 Nov 43	28 Nov 44	153	7h 14m	..	55	52	77	17	11,498
9 Nov 44	15 Jun 45	95	6h 51m	..	57	48	91	18	7,856

Date of Dissolution 15 Jun 45. Duration of Parliament 9 yrs, 5 mths, 20 days.

1 Aug 45	6 Nov 46	212	7h 45m	..	106	104	128	30	27,313
2 Nov 46	20 Oct 47	164	8h 38m	..	73	71	108	22	17,310
1 Oct 47	13 Sep 48	171	8h 13m	..	92	89	97	21	16,303
4 Sep 48	25 Oct 48	10	7h 2m	..	..	..	132	41	853
6 Oct 48	16 Dec 49	208	7h 48m	10½	146	125	86	18	17,334

Date of Dissolution 3 Feb 50. Duration of Parliament 4 yrs, 4 mths, 15 days.

1 Mar 50	26 Oct 50	105	7h 50m	5	58	57	105	19	9,861
1 Oct 50	4 Oct 51	153	8h 20m	19	107	81	108	18	15,720

Date of Dissolution 5 Oct 51. Duration of Parliament 1 yr, 6 mths, 4 days.

1 Oct 51	30 Oct 52	157	8h 48m	18½	113	88	99	17	14,192
4 Nov 52	29 Oct 53	162	8h 12m	20	78	62	91	16	13,878
3 Nov 53	25 Nov 54	187	8h 11m	19	113	95	89	15	15,990
0 Nov 54	6 May 55	84	7h 58m	10	72	33	90	17	7,262

Date of Dissolution 6 May 55. Duration of Parliament 3 yrs, 6 mths, 6 days.

7 Jun 55	6 Nov 56	219	7h 57m	25½	126	101	86	16	18,285
6 Nov 56	1 Nov 57	159	7h 40m	20	93	75	90	20	14,259
5 Nov 57	23 Oct 58	156	7h 54m	20	112	89	84	18	12,734
8 Oct 58	18 Sep 59	159	7h 48m	20	113	89	89	21	14,518

Date of Dissolution 18 Sep 59. Duration of Parliament 4 yrs, 3 mths, 11 days.

0 Oct 59	27 Oct 60	160	8h 2m	22	103	80	81	21	13,471
1 Nov 60	24 Oct 61	168	8h 30m	22	117	79	73	22	13,778
1 Oct 61	25 Oct 62	160	8h 23m	22	108	75	65	23	12,226
0 Oct 62	24 Oct 63	162	8h 15m	22	105	72	67	31	13,948
2 Nov 63	31 Jul 64	155	8h 14m	22	155	102	66	37	14,291

Date of Dissolution 25 Sep 64. Duration of Parliament 5 yrs, 7 days.

7 Oct 64	8 Nov 65	177	9h 0m	22	158	94	74	46	19,148
9 Nov 65	10 Mar 66	65	8h 15m	22	74	21	67	56	7,978

Date of Dissolution 10 Mar 66. Duration of Parliament 1 yr, 5 mths, 13 days.

8 Apr 66	27 Oct 67	246	9h 50m	25	210	127	69	69	33,965
1 Oct 67	25 Oct 68	176	9h 2m	22	142	76	64	77	24,910

[a] 'Notional' days on which Private Members' business had precedence. The idea of parliamentary 'days' must be treated with ...ion since actual days vary in length. Private Members' days are usually Fridays and only 5 hours long whereas Government ...s' are usually at least 6½ hours long and are frequently extended by suspension of the ten o'clock rule and by the practice of ...g the affirmative and negative resolutions after ten o'clock. [b] Including oral questions receiving a written reply.

SOURCES.—Information from the 'Black Book', a compilation of Parliamentary statistics at the House of Commons, and the ...onal Returns of the House of Commons. Questions to Ministers taken from D. N. Chester and N. Bowring, Questions in Parliament ...2), pp. 87-8, and 316; and information from the Journal Office, House of Commons.

was always subject to the possibility that the House, or Government, might direct that the time was needed for Government business. Between 1914 and 1918 and between 1939 and 1948 Private Members' time was abolished completely. When Private Members' time was restored, the Government retained precedence on all days except for 20 Fridays. In the nine sessions 1950–51 to 1958–59 an average of ten days was allotted to Private Members' bills and 9 days to Private Members' motions. Since 22 February 1960 four extra half-days (two Mondays and two Wednesdays) have been allotted for consideration of Private Members' motions, in addition to the 20 Fridays. Friday sittings are shorter in length than the average day. Since 1 November 1967 there have been 16 Fridays per session allotted for Private Members' bills, and 4 Fridays for Private Members' motions.

SOURCES.—Sir I. Jennings, *Parliament* (2nd ed., 1957), pp. 95–9, 121–2; Sir T. Erskine May, *Parliamentary Practice* (17th ed.); Sir G. Campion, *An Introduction to the Procedure of the House of Commons* (1950); *Report of the Select Committee on the Hours of Meeting and Rising of the House*, H.C. 126 of 1930; 'The Times of Sittings of the House', *Report by Select Committee on Procedure*, Aug 1966, H.C. 153 of 1966–67.

Regnal Years

Until 1962 the dates of Acts of Parliament were recorded in terms of the regnal years during the session in which they were passed. Regnal years date from the accession of the sovereign. Thus the act listed as *11 & 12 Geo. VI, c. 65* was passed in the parliamentary session during the eleventh and twelfth regnal year of George VI (1948). The parliamentary session of 1948–49 covered three regnal years, and its acts appear under the style *12, 13 & 14 Geo. VI*. Since 1963 Acts of Parliament have been recorded by the calendar year and the chapter number, e.g. *Finance Act 1963, c. 25.*

Sovereign	Regnal Year	Date
Victoria	63	20 Jun 1899–19 Jun 1900
	64	20 Jun 1900–22 Jan 01
Edward VII	1	22 Jan 01–21 Jan 02
	10	22 Jan 10–6 May 10
George V	1	6 May 10–5 May 11
	26	6 May 35–20 Jan 36
Edward VIII	1	20 Jan 36–11 Dec 36
George VI	1	11 Dec 36–10 Dec 37
	16	11 Dec 51–6 Feb 52
Elizabeth II	1	6 Feb 52–5 Feb 53
	10	6 Feb 61–5 Feb 62

SOURCES.—Regnal years from 1154–1945 are listed in *Handbook of Dates*, ed. C. R. Cheney (1945), pp. 18–21; *Where to Look for Your Law* (1965).

Main Select Committees

Committee on Public Accounts, 1862

Chairmen

1896	A. O'Connor	1931	M. Jones
1901	Sir A. Hayter	1938	F. Pethick-Lawrence
1906	V. Cavendish	1941	W. Elliot
1908	(Sir) R. Williams	1943	Sir A. Pownall
1919	F. Acland	1945	O. Peake
1921	A. Williams	1948	R. Assheton
1923	F. Jowett	1950	Sir R. Cross
1924	W. Guinness	1950	C. Waterhouse
1924	W. Graham	1951	J. Edwards
1929	A. Samuel	1952	(Sir) G. Benson

| 1959 | H. Wilson | 1964 | J. Boyd-Carpenter |
| 1962 | D. Houghton | | |

The Committee is made up of no more than 15 members, including the Chairman, and meets on about 30 days each session. The Chairman is usually a member of the Opposition.

Usual Terms of Reference: 'for the examination of the accounts showing the appropriation of the sums granted by parliament to meet the public expenditure', 'and of such other accounts laid before parliament as the committee may think fit' (*added 15 Nov 34*). 'The Committee shall have power to send for persons, papers and records, and to report from time to time' (*added 14 Nov 33*).

SOURCES.—*Reports of the Select Committee on Public Accounts; Select Committee Returns, 1900–1967,* L. A. Abraham and S. C. Hawtrey, *A Parliamentary Dictionary* (1956); B. Chubb, *The Control of Public Expenditure* (1952).

Estimates Committee, 1912

Chairmen

1912	Sir F. Banbury	1935	Sir I. Salmon
1914	(suspended)	1939	(see National Expenditure
1917	(see National Expenditure		Committee)
	Committee)	1945	B. Kirby
1920	Sir F. Banbury	1950	A. Anderson
1924	Sir J. Marriott	1951	Sir R. Glyn
1926	(Sir) V. Henderson	1953	C. Waterhouse
1927	A. Bennett	1957	R. Turton
1929	H. Charleton	1961	Sir G. Nicholson
1930	H. Romeril	1964	W. Hamilton
1931	Sir V. Henderson		

The Committee originally consisted of 15 members. In 1921 this was increased to 24, and in 1924 to 28. Since 1948 it has had 36 members (1960–67 43 members). The Chairman is usually a Government supporter.

Terms of Reference: 'to examine and report upon such of the Estimates presented to the Committee as may seem fit to the Committee' (*7 Apr 12 original terms*), 'and to suggest the form in which the estimates shall be presented for examination, and to report what if any economies consistent with the policy implied in those estimates may be effected therein' (*added in 1921*). Until 1939 the estimates Committee seldom appointed sub-committees, although power to do so had been given in 1924; since 1945, however, following the example set by the Select Committee on National Expenditure, it has invariably done so. In 1956 the wording of the terms of reference was rearranged but the substance remained unchanged.

In 1960 the terms were altered to read : 'to examine such of the estimates presented to this House as may seem fit to the committee and report how, if at all, the policy implied in those estimates may be carried out more economically and, if the committee think fit, to consider the principal variations between the estimates and those relating to the previous financial year, and the form in which the estimates are presented to the House'. The committee has power to send for persons, papers, and records, and sit notwithstanding any adjournment of the House, to adjourn from place to place, and to report from time to time: to appoint sub-committees and to refer to such sub-committees any of the matters referred to the committee [each sub-committee has the same powers of sending for persons, etc., sitting and adjourning as the main committee], the committee shall have power to report from time to time the minutes of evidence taken before sub-committees and reported by them to the committee. In Sessions 1965 and 1966 the House gave the Estimates Committee the power 'to appoint persons with technical or scientific knowledge for the purpose of particular enquiries, either to supply information which is not readily available or to elucidate matters of complexity within the Committee's order of reference'. Since 1965 the practice has been to appoint sub-Committees specialising in particular fields.

SOURCE.—N. Johnson, *Parliament and Administration, The Estimates Committee, 1945-65* (1966).

Committee on National Expenditure, 1917-1920 and 1939-1945
Chairmen

1917	H. Samuel	1939-45	Sir J. Wardlaw-Milne
1919-20	Sir F. Banbury		

No Estimates were presented to Parliament during the two wars, and the Committee on Estimates lapsed. A Committee on National Expenditure was established each year. It consisted of 26 members 1917-20, and 32 members 1939-45. It met about 13 days a session between 1917-20, and about 19 days a session between 1939-45.

1939-45 Terms of Reference: 'to examine the current expenditure defrayed out of moneys provided by Parliament for the Defence Services, for Civil Defence, and for other services directly connected with the war, and to report what, if any, economies, consistent with the execution of the policy decided by the Government, may be effected therein'.

SOURCES.—*Reports of the Select Committee on Estimates; Select Committee Returns, 1900-1967;* Sir I. Jennings, *Parliament* (2nd ed., 1957), pp. 303-16; E. Taylor, *The House of Commons at Work* (7th ed., 1967).

Committee on Nationalised Industries (Reports and Accounts), 1956 [1]
Chairmen

1956	Sir P. Spens	1964	E. Popplewell
1957	Sir T. Low	1966	I. Mikardo
1961	Sir R. Nugent		

The Committee is appointed on a sessional basis; 1956-66 it consisted of 13 members, 1966- of 18 members. It has met on about 25 days each session. The Chairman has always been a Government supporter.

Terms of Reference: 'to examine the reports and accounts of the nationalised industries established by statute, whose controlling boards are wholly appointed by Ministers of the Crown and whose annual receipts are not wholly or mainly derived from moneys provided by Parliament or advanced by the Exchequer'. In the 1965-66 and 1966-67 Sessions the Committee's terms of reference were amended to enable them to inquire into the Post Office.

SOURCES.—*Reports of the Select Committee on Nationalised Industries (Reports and Accounts), 1957-1967; Select Committee Returns, 1957-1967;* D. Coombes, *The Member of Parliament and the Administration, the Case of the Select Committee on Nationalised Industries* (1966).

Statutory Instruments, 1944
(1944-1947 Statutory Rules and Orders)
Chairmen

1944	Sir C. MacAndrew	1951	E. Fletcher
1950	G. Nicholson	1964	G. Page

The Committee consists of 11 members, and meets fortnightly on about 16 days each session. The Chairman has always been an opposition member.

[1] Select Committees were set up each session from 1951 to 1956, under the Chairmanship of R. Assheton (1951-54) and Sir P. Spens (1954-56).

Terms of Reference: the original terms of 21 Jun 44 have been considerably enlarged by additional powers conferred over the last fifteen years. The Committee now has power to consider all Statutory Instruments.

The following are the principal forms of Parliamentary Control of such delegated legislation as is effected by Statutory Instruments.

1. Laying in draft,
   a) for affirmative resolution: that the instrument is to be made
   b) for negative resolution: that the instrument is not be be made
   c) without further proceedings.

2. Laying after making,
   a) subject to affirmative resolution approving instrument: *either* instrument does not come into operation until approved; *or* instrument ceases to operate after a specified period unless approved by then
   b) subject to negative resolution: instrument has immediate effect but is subject to annulment.
   c) without further proceedings.

The Committee has power to draw the attention of the House to Statutory Instruments on any of the following grounds, (i) that they involve public money (ii) that they are immune from challenge in the courts (iii) that they appear to make some unusual or unexpected use of the powers conferred by the Statute under which it is made (iv) that they have effect retrospectively (v) that there seems to have been an unjustifiable delay in publication of the S.I., laying it before Parliament, or sending notification to the Speaker and (vi) if elucidation is considered necessary (vii) that the drafting appears to be defective. The Committee has powers to sit when it wishes, to report from time to time, and to call for witnesses. It is obliged to give any government department an opportunity to explain an S.I. or other document before drawing it to the attention of the House.

Since 1890 the Statutory Rules and Orders and since 1948 the S.I.s, have been published in annual volumes. The average total of Orders made between 1894 and 1900 was just over 1,000.

The distinction between 'General' and 'Local' follows that adopted between public Acts and local and personal Acts of Parliament. The Documents registered as Statutory Instruments do *not* include rules of an executive character, rules made by other bodies, e.g. local authorities, unless confirmed by a government department. Statutory Instruments also include some rules made by statutory authorities which are not government departments, e.g. The Law Society, General Dental Council, Rule Committee of Church Assembly.

Statutory Instruments

Year	Annual Total	General	Local
1900	995	174	821
1910	1,368	218	1,150
1920	2,475	916	1,559
1929	1,262	391	871
1940	2,222	1,626	596
1950	2,144	1,211	933
1960	2,495	733	1,762
1966	1,641	790	851

The figures for the earlier years were given by Sir C. Carr in evidence before the *Committee on Ministers' Powers: Minutes of Evidence, II*, p. 205; the *Select Committee on Procedure* (H.C. 189 of 1945–46, p. 243); and the *Select Committee on Delegated Legislation* (H.C. 301 f 1953, p. 2). The figures for 1950 are based on J. E. Kersell, *Parliamentary Supervision of Delegated Legislation* (1960). The figures for 1960 and 1966 are from the Statutory Publications Office.

SOURCES.—*Select Committee Returns, 1944–67; Select Committee on Statutory Instruments (Rules and Orders, 1944–47)*; Sir I. Jennings, *Parliament* (2nd ed. 1957), pp. 489–516 (quotes Sir C. Carr's figures); Ld Hewart, *The New Despotism* (1929); G. W. Keeton, *The Passing of Parliament* (1952); L. A. Abraham and S. C. Hawtrey, *A Parliamentary Dictionary* (1956) and information from the Committee Office of the House of Commons; C. K. Allen, *Law and Orders* (3rd ed. 1965); Statutory Publications Office; H. C. Deb. 728, c. 1564; Select Committee on Statutory Instruments, *Special Report for the Session 1966–67* (No. 266).

Committee of Selection

Although the task of the Committee of Selection has for many years been predominately the selection of Members to serve on Standing Committees on Bills, the Committee was originally set up to appoint Committees on Private Bills and is still appointed under Private Business S.O. 109. It has 11 Members.

The Committee of Selection nominates:

Public Business

(1) Members of Standing Committees;
(2) Some or all members of Select Committees on hybrid Bills (if the House orders);
(3) The Commons members of Joint Committees on hybrid Bills (if the House orders);
(4) The two members whom Mr Speaker is to consult, if practicable, before giving his certificate to a money bill.

Private Business

(1) The panel of members to serve on committees on unopposed bills;
(2) Committees on unopposed bills;
(3) Members of committees on opposed bills;
(4) Eight members to serve on the Standing Orders Committee under S.O. 103;
(5) The panel of members to act as commissioners under the Private Legislation Procedure (Scotland) Act 1936;
(6) Commons Members on Joint Committees on special procedure petitions.

Terms of Reference: The Committee would appear to interpret its instructions in S.O. 60 (2) to have 'regard . . . to the composition of the House' by choosing Standing Committees as far as possible in direct ratio to the size of the parties in the House, except that the Liberal Party is given much higher representation than its size would merit on this basis — a Liberal member is usually appointed to all Committees of 30 members and above. In the three Parliaments since the war in which the size of the Government majority has been small the Committee of Selection has usually selected Members so as to give the Government a majority of one. The Committee tends to appoint those Members who spoke on the second reading of the Bill. In recent times of heavy legislation and expanding parliamentary activity it would appear that the position of the whips to offer advice as to which members are anxious, willing, or available to serve on a particular Committee has been strengthened. Although no Government whip is appointed to the Committee a senior opposition whip is always appointed.

SOURCES.—The History of the Committee is given in Erskine May, *Parliamentary Practice* (17th ed.) pp. 906–7. Details of responsibilities re. Standing Committees pp. 672–3.

House of Commons Services Committee, 1965

Chairman

1965   H. Bowden
1966   R. Crossman
1968   F. Peart

Terms of Reference: 'To advise Mr Speaker on the control of the accommodation and services in that part of the Palace of Westminster and its precincts occupied by or on behalf of the House of Commons and to report thereon to this House.' This Committee was set up as a result of a recommendation of the Select Committee on the Palace of Westminster of Sessions 1964–65 whose main task had been to consider the arrangements to be made by the Commons following the transfer on 26 Apr 1965 of control of the Palace from the Lord Great Chamberlain on behalf of the Crown to the two Houses.

The Committee consists of 17 members appointed by the House. It has power to send for persons, papers, and records, to sit notwithstanding the adjournment of the House, to report from time to time, and to appoint Sub-Committees, each of which consists of three members. Each Sub-Committee has similar powers to the main Committee (except of course power to nominate Sub-Committees). The Committee has four Sub-Committees: the Accommodation and Administration Sub-Committee, the Catering Sub-Committee, the Library Sub-Committee, and the Broadcasting Sub-Committee. The Catering Sub-Committee replaced the 'Select Committee on Kitchen and Refreshment Rooms' appointed every session since the late nineteenth century.

Committee on Agriculture, 1966

Chairman   1966   T. Watkins

Terms of Reference: 'To consider the activities in England and Wales of the Ministry of Agriculture, Fisheries and Food.' The Committee had power to send for persons, papers, and records, to sit notwithstanding any adjournment of the House, to adjourn from place to place, and to admit strangers during the examination of witnesses unless they otherwise order.

Committee on Science and Technology, 1966
Chairman   1966   A. Palmer

Terms of Reference: 'To consider Science and Technology.' The Committee has power to send for persons, papers.

Committee on Parliamentary Commissioner for Administration, 1967
Chairman   1967   H. Munro-Lucas-Tooth

Terms of Reference: 'To examine the reports laid before this House by the Parliamentary Commissioner for Administration, and matters in connection therewith.' The Committee had power to send for persons, papers.

Committee on Education and Science, 1968
Chairman   1968   F. Willey

Terms of Reference: 'To consider the activities of the Department of Education and Science and the Scottish Education Department.'

The Select Committees of Privileges

The following include all Reports of the Select Committee of Privileges and a few from *Ad Hoc* Committees.

1902	Imprisonment of a Member: C. O'Kelly.
1902	Imprisonment of a Member: P. McHugh.
1909	D of Norfolk: alleged interference in an election.
1911	E of Aberdeen and E of Roden: alleged interference in an election.
1924	*Daily Herald*: reflection on the impartiality of the Chairman of Committees.
1926	*Daily Mail*: allegations of corrupt motives against M.P.s.
1929–30	E. Sandham: allegations of drunkenness and acceptance of bribes against M.P.s.
1932–33	H. Bowles and E. Huntsman: reflections on a Private Bill Committee's impartiality.
1933–34	Sir S. Hoare and E of Derby: alleged improper pressure on witnesses to a Committee.
1937–38	D. Sandys: summons to Military court of Inquiry.
1937–38	Official Secrets Acts.
1938–39	Official Secrets Acts.
1939–40	Detention of A. Ramsay under 18B of Defence of the Realm Act.
1939–40	Conduct of R. Boothby.
1940–41	Conduct of R. Boothby.
1940–41	*Observer* publication of Secret Session debate.
1940–41	Grampian electricity supply bill: Highland Development League circular to M.P.s alleging irregularities in bill procedure.
1941–42	Disclosure of Secret Session proceedings by J. McGovern.

1942–43   H. Metcalf and J. Reid: payment of expense cheque to M.P. to attend prosecution by Board of Trade.

1943–44   N.U.D.A.W.: withdrawal of Trade Union financial support from W. Robinson on ground of refusal to resign seat.

1944–45   G. Reakes and D. Henderson. Offer to make donation to constituency association in return for M.P.s help.

1945–46   Writ of Summons served on officer of House within precincts.

1945–46   Disclosure in conversation of Secret Session information by E. Granville.

1945–46   Posters threatening publication of names of M.P.s voting for bread rationing.

1946–47   Assault on P. Piratin in precincts of the House.

1946–47   Action by Civil Service Clerical Association calculated to influence W. Brown.

1946–47   G. Schofield and S. Dobson (Editor and Political Correspondent of *Evening News*): refusal to reveal source of information to Committee.

1946–47   Article by G. Allighan alleging disclosure to newspapers of information from party meetings.

1946–47   Disclosure of party meeting information by E. Walkden in return for payment.

1947–48   H. Dalton: Budget disclosure.

1947–48   The Chairman of Ways and Means (J. Milner): personal explanation that he acted professionally as a solicitor against a Member.

1947–48   Broadcast and interview in *Daily Mail* by C. Brogan alleging that Secret Session information would be given to Russia.

1948–49   Alleged misrepresentation by *Daily Worker* of Member's speech (A. Blackburn).

1950   J. MacManaway: election of a Member, being a clergyman of the Church of Ireland.

1951   Abuse of members not related to transactions in House (S. Silverman, I. Mikardo). Comment on B.B.C. 'Any Questions' programme on matter referred to Committee.

1951   Report in *Sutton Coldfield News* of speech by Lady Mellor criticising ruling by the Chair.

1951   Obstruction of J. Lewis by the police.

1952–53   Amendment of the law relating to the disability of some clergy from sitting and voting in the House of Commons.

1953   Article by Mrs P. Ford in *Sunday Express* (Mrs Braddock).

1953   *Daily Worker* article (M.P.s vote money into their own pockets).

1955   Action by Bishop against chaplain after communication with M.P.

1956   *Sunday Graphic* advocates telephone campaign against A. Lewis.

1956   *Sunday Express* article on M.P.s' petrol rationing allowances.

1956   *Evening News* cartoon on petrol rationing.

1956–57   G. Strauss: threat of libel action by the London Electricity Board, following letter from the Member to the Paymaster General.

1957   Comment on B.B.C. 'Any Questions' programme on matter referred to Committee: report of speech in *Romford Recorder* on petrol rationing.

1957–58   Order in Council directing that the Report of the Judicial Committee on a Question of Law concerning the Parliamentary Privilege Act 1770, be communicated to the House of Commons.

1957–58   G. Strauss: recommendations of the Committee arising out of the case involving the London Electricity Board.

1958–59   Report of an Inquiry into the methods adopted by the London Electricity Board for the disposal of scrap cable.

1959–60   C. Pannell: allegation of threat in a letter from C. Jordan.

1960–61   A. Wedgwood Benn: petition for redress of grievances regarding the disqualification of peers.

1963–64   Q. Hogg: complaint by G. Wigg concerning a speech at the Town Hall, Chatham, on 19 Mar 64.

1964–65   P. Duffy: complaint concerning speech at Saddleworth on 12 Feb 65 alleging drunkenness among Conservative Members.

1964–65   F. Allaun: complaint concerning letter addressed to Members and advocating racial and anti-semitic views.

1964–65   The Chancellor of the Exchequer: complaint by Sir R. Cary concerning passages of speech reported in the *Daily Telegraph* 5 Jul 65, on Members' business interests.

1966–67   G. Fitt: complaint concerning allegations of treachery in *Protestant Telegraph*.

1967–68   E. Hooson: complaint concerning allegations of treachery in interview published in *Town* magazine.

1967–68   W. Hannan: complaint concerning letter in the *Scotsman* by Mrs W. Ewing, M.P., reflecting on the conduct of members.

1967–68   A. Palmer: complaint concerning article about biological warfare published in the *Observer* from information allegedly supplied by T. Dalyell, M.P.

Parliamentary Commissioner for Administration (Ombudsman)

The office of Parliamentary Commissioner for the Administration came into effect on 1 Apr 67. He is an Independent Officer whose status and powers are conferred by Statute. In investigating complaints of personal injustice or maladministration by the Central Government brought by individuals or companies 'lawfully resident' in the U.K. the Commissioner acts only at the instance of a Member of the House of Commons. Some fields of investigation, for example, where the safety of the State or relations with other countries are affected are excluded.

SOURCE.—H.M.S.O., *The Parliamentary Commissioner for the Administration* (Cmnd. 2767).

Payment of M.P.s

1912   M.P.s receive first salary; £400 per year paid to all members not receiving salaries as Ministers or officers of the House.

1913 £100 of M.P.s' salaries made tax-exempt in respect of parliamentary expenses. This remained in force until 1954.

1924 M.P.s allowed free rail travel between London and their constituencies.

1931 Salary cut to £360 as an economy measure.

1934 Salary restored to £380 and then to £400.

1937 Salary increased to £600.

1946 Salary increased to £1,000 and salaries of £500 authorised for M.P.s who, as Ministers or Leaders of the Opposition, had an official salary of less than £5,000. Free travel was granted between M.P.s' homes and Westminster as well as to their constituencies.

1953 A sessional allowance of £2 per day introduced for every day (except Friday) on which the House sat: this was payable to all M.P.s including Ministers.

1957 The sessional allowance (usually amounting to about £280 p.a. was replaced by an annual £750 to cover parliamentary expenses. The whole £1,750 drawn by ordinary M.P.s was subject to tax but M.P.s could claim as tax free any expenses up to £1,750 incurred in respect of parliamentary duties.

1964 Salary increased to £3,250 per year, following Lawrence Committee Report.

1965 Members Pensions Act. First comprehensive pensions scheme introduced for M.P.s and dependants. Members contribute £150 per year and the Exchequer an amount equal to the aggregate of the Members' contributions. Members receive pensions from the age of 65 or on ceasing to be an M.P. if later, provided they have served for 10 years or more. The pension of £600 per year for 10 years service increases to £900 after 15 years service and by £24 for each further year thereafter.

Sources.—H.C. 255 of 1920, *Report of the Select Committee on Members' Expenses*; Cmd. 5624, 1937–38, *Report of the Departmental Committee on an M.P.s' Pension Scheme*; H.C. 93 of 1945–46, *Report of the Select Committee on Members' Expenses*; H.C. 72 of 1954, *Report of the Select Committee on Members' Expenses, etc.*; *Ministerial Salaries Act, 1957*; *Report of the Committee on the Remuneration of Ministers and Members of Parliament* (Lawrence) Cmnd. 2516; *Ministerial Salaries and Members' Pensions Act* (1965).

Seats Forfeited

These members left or were expelled from the House before or after their conviction and imprisonment on criminal charges.

2 Mar	03	A. Lynch	Nat.	Galway
1 Aug	22	H. Bottomley	Ind.	Hackney South
31 Jul	41	Sir P. Latham	Con.	Scarborough & Whitby
16 Dec	54	P. Baker	Con.	S. Norfolk

These members have forfeited their seats as a result of being adjudged bankrupt.

Sep	03	P. McHugh	Nat.	N. Leitrim (re-elected)
15 Jul	09	N. Murphy	Nat.	S. Kilkenny
1 Oct	28	C. Homan	Con.	Ashton under Lyne

In addition, H. Bottomley resigned his seat 16 May 12 after filing his bankruptcy petition.

These members gave up their seats when under censure for some aspect of their parliamentary conduct.

26 Feb	31	T. Mardy Jones	Lab.	Pontypridd (*abuse of travel voucher*)
11 Jun	36	J. Thomas	Nat. Lab.	Derby (*Budget leak*)
11 Jun	36	Sir A. Butt	Con.	Balham & Tooting (*Budget leak*)
30 Oct	47	G. Allighan	Lab.	Gravesend (*expelled by a vote of 187–75 for breach of privilege*)
3 Feb	49	J. Belcher	Lab.	Sowerby (*following Lynskey Tribunal*)
5 Jun	63	J. Profumo	Con.	Stratford-on-Avon (*lying to the House*)

A. Ramsay, Con. Peebles and Southern, remained an M.P. from 1940 to 1945 although, being detained under Regulation 18B of the Defence of the Realm Act until Dec 1944, he was unable to sit from May 40 to Dec 44.

Various other members have resigned their seats while under the shadow of some minor private or public scandal but in almost every case it seems that they could well have remained as members had they chosen to do so.

House of Lords

Lord Chairmen of Committees

(Deputy Speaker of the House of Lords. The Lord Chancellor is the Speaker.)

1889	E of Morley	1944	Ld Stanmore
1905	4th E of Onslow	1946	E of Drogheda
1911	E of Donoughmore	1957	Ld Merthyr
1931	5th E of Onslow	1965	E of Listowel

Officers of the House of Lords

Clerk of the Parliaments		*Librarian*	
1885	(Sir) H. Graham	1897	A. Strong
1917	Sir A. Thring	1904	E. Gosse
1930	Sir E. Alderson	1914	A. Butler
1934	(Sir) H. Badeley	1922	C. Clay
1949	(Sir) R. Overbury	1956	C. Dobson
1953	(Sir) F. Lascelles		
1959	(Sir) V. Goodman		
1963	(Sir) D. Stephens		

SOURCES.—*Dod's Parliamentary Companion*; *Whitaker's Almanack*; *Hansard.*

Composition of the House of Lords
(including minors)

Year	Dukes[a]	Mar-quesses	Earls	Vis-counts	Barons	Life Peers[b]	Law Lords[c]	Repres. Scotland[d]	Repres. Ireland[d]	Archbps. and Bishops	Total
1901	32	34	165	38	248	..	4	16	28	26	591
1910	31	35	161	50	272	..	4	16	28	26	623
1919	28	40	165	71	319	..	6	16	27	26	698
1930	30	38	166	82	370	..	7	16	18	26	753
1939	30	38	159	96	389	..	7	16	13	26	781
1950	30	38	168	99	444	..	9	16	6	26	847
1960	26	26	132	111	538	24	8	16	1	26	908
1965	29	30	165	110	549	100	9	..	..	26	1,018

[a] Including Royal Dukes.
[b] Created by the Life Peers Act, 1958, and including 5 baronesses.
[c] Lords of Appeal in Ordinary.
[d] Scottish and Irish peers sitting by virtue of other titles are listed under their superior title.

SOURCES.—*Constitutional Year Books*, 1900–39; *Dod's Parliamentary Companion*, 1940– .

In 1965 the House of Lords was composed of 733 Peers by succession, 142 hereditary peers of first creation, 117 Law Lords and Life peers, 26 Bishops and Archbishops.

Creation of Peerages, 1900–

Administration[a]		New[b] Creations	Life Peers	Advanced in Rank	Total	Duration of Ministry (Yrs.)	Average Annual Creations[c]
Salisbury	1895–02	44	..	n.a.	44	7	6
Balfour	1902–05	18	..	5	23	3½	7
Campbell-Bannerman	1905–08	21	..	..	21	2⅓	9
Asquith	1908–15	67	..	13	80	7	11
Asquith	1915–16	17	..	2	19	1½	13
Lloyd George	1916–22	91	..	25	116	5¾	20
Bonar Law	1922–23	3	..	..	3	½	6
Baldwin	1923–24	8	..	1	9	⅔	14
MacDonald	1924	4	..	1	5	¾	7
Baldwin	1924–29	42	..	10	52	4½	12
MacDonald	1929–31	20	..	..	20	2¼	9
MacDonald	1931–35	44	..	6	50	3¾	13
Baldwin	1935–37	29	..	5	34	2	17
Chamberlain	1937–40	20	..	4	24	3	8
Churchill	1940–45	62	..	9	71	5¼	14
Attlee	1945–51	86	..	8	94	6¼	15
Churchill	1951–55	33	..	6	39	3½	11
Eden	1955–57	19	..	3	22	1¾	13
Macmillan	1957–63	51	47	6	14	6	7
Douglas-Home	1963–64	15	16	1	32	1	32
Wilson	1964–68	6	106	1	113	4¼	26

[a] These figures can be misleading as dissolution honours created by an outgoing ministry fall, in fact, into the following ministry. E.g., of H. Wilson's new creations 6 were those of Sir A. Douglas-Home.
[b] Including Law Lords.
[c] New Creations only.

Main landmarks in the Reform of the House of Lords, 1900–

In 1900 the legislative powers of the two Houses were in theory equal, with the exception that the privileges of the House of Commons in relation to financial measures should be initiated in that House.

1908 *Rosebery Committee's Report.* The House approved the following principal recommendations:

(1) That a strong and efficient second Chamber was necessary for the balance of Parliament;

(2) That this objective should be achieved by the reform and reconstitution of the House of Lords;

(3) That, as a necessary preliminary to reform, it should be accepted that the possession of a peerage should no longer of itself entail the right to sit and vote in the House.

No action was taken to implement these recommendations.

1911 *Parliament Act.* Provided that—

(1) Bills certified by the Speaker of the House of Commons as Money Bills were to receive the Royal Assent one month after being

sent to the House of Lords, even without the consent of the latter House; and

(2) any other Public Bill (except one for extending the life of a Parliament) passed by the House of Commons in three successive Sessions and rejected by the House of Lords was nevertheless to receive the Royal Assent, provided that 2 years had elapsed between the second reading in the first session and the third reading in the third session of the House of Commons.

1918 *Bryce Report.* Recommended that the differences between the 2 Houses should be settled by some means of joint consultation. Proposed that the House should consist of two elements. (i) 246 members elected by members of the House of Commons arranged in geographical areas and voting by Proportional Representation with a single transferable vote. (ii) 80 peers to be elected for a period of 12 years by a joint Committee of both Houses of Parliament on which all parties should be represented. No action was taken to implement this Report.

1946 *Travelling Expenses.* Agreed that regular attenders at the House of Lords should be reimbursed with their travelling expenses. In practice made to apply to peers attending at least one-third of the sittings of the House.

1948 *Agreed Statement of Party Leaders.* A statement of nine principles agreed to but not acted upon. The most important of these were:

(1) The second Chamber should be complementary to and not a rival to the lower House, and

(2) The revised constitution of the House of Lords should be such as to secure as far as practicable that a permanent majority was not assured for any one political party.

1948 *Criminal Justice Act.* Privileges of Peers in Criminal Proceedings abolished.

1949 *Parliament Act.* Reduced the delaying powers of the House to two sessions and one year.

1956 *Swinton Committee Report.* Recommended provision of official Leave of Absence. This was put into effect in 1958. There are normally about 200 members of the House who have Leave of Absence at any one time.

1957 *Expenses.* Provision made for Peers to claim a maximum of three guineas a day for expenses incurred in attendance at the House. This was additional to travelling expenses and claims were not subject to any minimum number of attendances.

1958 *Life Peerages Act.* Provided for the creation by the Sovereign, on the advice of the Prime Minister, of Life Peers and Peeresses. Women were thus for the first time enabled to become Members of the House of Lords. One of the objectives of this Act was to provide more balance of parliamentary representation in the House of Lords. This is achieved by the convention enabling recommendations for Life Peerages made by Opposition party leaders to be conveyed to the Queen through the agency of the Prime Minister.

1963 *Peerage Act.* Provided for—
(1) the option for Peers to disclaim within one year (one month in the case of Members of the House of Commons) their peerages for life without such a disclaimer affecting the subsequent devolution of the peerage;[1]
(2) the abolition of elections for Scottish Representative Peers and the admission of all Scottish Peers to membership of the House;
(3) the removal from Irish Peers of certain disabilities relating to their voting and candidature at parliamentary elections;
(4) the admission of all female holders of hereditary peerages to membership of the House of Lords.

1964 *Expenses.* Provision made for increasing the maximum expenses to which Peers were entitled from three guineas to four-and-a-half guineas per day.

1967 The Government announced their intention of introducing legislation for reform of the House of Lords.

[1] The following former peers have disclaimed their peerages: E of Home (Sir A. Douglas-Home), E of Sandwich (V. Montagu), Vt Hailsham (Q. Hogg), Vt Stansgate (A. Wedgwood Benn), Ld Altrincham (J. Grigg), Ld Beaverbrook (Sir M. Aitken), Ld Monkswell (W. Collier), Ld Southampton (C. Fitzroy), Ld Fraser of Allander (H. Fraser).

SOURCES.—1908 (H.L. 234), *Select Committee Report on the House of Lords*; Cd. 9038/1918, *The Reform of the Second Chamber* (Conference: Vt Bryce); Cmd. 7380/1948, *Report of the Inter Party Conference on the Parliament Bill*; H.M.S.O. (24 Jan 56), *Report of the Select Committee on the Power of the House in Relation to the Attendance of its Members*; Cmnd. 3779/1968, *House of Lords Reform*.
Sir T. Erskine May, *Parliamentary Practice* (16th edition, 1957); Sir G. Campion, *An Introduction to the Procedure of the House of Commons* (1950); J. Redlich, *Procedure of the House of Commons* (3 vols, 1908); P. A. Bromhead, *The House of Lords and Contemporary Politics, 1911–1957* (1958); Sir I. Jennings, *Parliament* (2nd ed., 1957). *Keesing's Archives, 1900–*.

IV

ELECTIONS

General Election Statistics

IT is impossible to present election statistics in any finally authoritative way. British law makes no acknowledgement of the existence of political parties, and in most general elections the precise allegiance of at least a few of the candidates is in doubt. This, far more than arithmetic error, explains the discrepancies between the figures provided in various works of reference.

Such discrepancies, however, are seldom on a serious scale (except, perhaps, for 1918). Election figures suffer much more from being inherently confusing than from being inaccurately reported. The complications that arise from unopposed returns, from plural voting, from two-member seats, and, above all, from variations in the number of candidates put up by each party are the really serious hazards in psephological interpretation.

In the figures which follow an attempt is made to allow for these factors by a column which shows the average vote won by each opposed candidate (with the vote in two-member seats halved, and with University seats excluded). This still gives a distorted picture, especially when, as in 1900 or 1931, there were many unopposed candidates or when, as in 1929, 1931, or 1950 there was a sharp change in the number of Liberals standing; in 1918 the situation was so complicated that any such statistics are omitted, as they are likely to confuse more than to clarify; for other elections they should be regarded as corrective supplements to the cruder percentages in the previous column rather than as substitutes for them.

The turn-out percentages are modified to allow for the distorting effect of the two-member seats which existed up to 1950.

To simplify classification, some arbitrary decisions have been made. Before 1918 candidates have been classified as Conservative, Liberal, or Irish Nationalist, even if their designation had a prefix such as Tariff Reform, or Independent but only officially sponsored candidates are classed as Labour. From 1918 onwards candidates not officially recognised by their party have been classified with 'Others' (except that in 1935 Ind. Lib. are placed with Lib.). Liberal Unionists have been listed as Conservatives throughout. Liberal National, National Labour, and National candidates are listed with Conservatives except in 1931.

General Election Results, 1900–1918

	Total Votes	M.P.s Elected	Candidates	Unopposed Returns	% Share of Total Vote	Average % Vote per Opposed Candidate
1900. 28 Sep–24 Oct						
Conservative	1,797,444	402	579	163	51·1	52·5
Liberal	1,568,141	184	406	22	44·6	48·2
Labour	63,304	2	15	..	1·8	26·6
Irish Nationalist	90,076	82	100	58	2·5	80·0
Others	544	..	2	..	0·0	2·2
Elec. 6,730,935 Turnout 74·6%	3,519,509	670	1,102	243	100·0	..
1906. 12 Jan–7 Feb						
Conservative	2,451,454	157	574	13	43·6	44·1
Liberal	2,757,883	400	539	27	49·0	52·6
Labour	329,748	30	51	..	5·9	39·9
Irish Nationalist	35,031	83	87	74	0·6	63·1
Others	52,387	..	22	..	0·9	18·8
Elec. 7,264,608 Turnout 82·6%	5,626,503	670	1,273	114	100·0	..
1910. 14 Jan–9 Feb						
Conservative	3,127,887	273	600	19	46·9	47·5
Liberal	2,880,581	275	516	1	43·2	49·2
Labour	505,657	40	78	..	7·6	38·4
Irish Nationalist	124,586	82	104	55	1·9	77·7
Others	28,693	..	17	..	0·4	15·4
Elec. 7,694,741 Turnout 86·6%	6,667,404	670	1,315	75	100·0	..
1910. 2–19 Dec						
Conservative	2,420,566	272	550	72	46·3	47·9
Liberal	2,295,888	272	467	35	43·9	49·5
Labour	371,772	42	56	3	7·1	42·8
Irish Nationalist	131,375	84	106	53	2·5	81·9
Others	8,768	..	11	..	0·2	9·1
Elec. 7,709,981 Turnout 81·1%	5,235,322	670	1,191	163	100·0	..
1918. Sat., 14 Dec [1]						
Coalition Unionist	3,504,198	335	374	42	32·6	
Coalition Liberal	1,455,640	133	158	27	13·5	
Coalition Labour	161,521	10	18	..	1·5	
(Coalition)	(5,121,259)	(478)	(550)	(69)	(47·6)	
Conservative	370,375	23	37	..	3·4	
Irish Unionist	292,722	25	38	..	2·7	
Liberal	1,298,808	28	253	..	12·1	
Labour	2,385,472	63	388	12	22·2	
Irish Nationalist	238,477	7	60	1	2·2	
Sinn Fein	486,867	73	102	25	4·5	
Others	572,503	10	197	..	5·3	
Elec. 21,392,322 Turnout 58·9%	10,766,583	707	1,625	107	100·0	

[1] Result announced 28 Dec 18

General Election Results, 1922–1931

	Total Votes	M.P.s Elected	Candidates	Unopposed Returns	% Share of Total Vote	Average % Vote per Opposed Candidate
1922. Wed., 15 Nov						
Conservative	5,500,382	345	483	42	38·2	48·6
National Liberal	1,673,240	62	162	5	11·6	39·3
Liberal	2,516,287	54	328	5	17·5	30·9
Labour	4,241,383	142	411	4	29·5	40·0
Others	462,340	12	59	1	3·2	28·3
Elec. 21,127,663 Turnout 71·3%	14,393,632	615	1,443	57	100·0	..
1923. Thu., 6 Dec						
Conservative	5,538,824	258	540	35	38·1	42·6
Liberal	4,311,147	159	453	11	29·6	37·8
Labour	4,438,508	191	422	3	30·5	41·0
Others	260,042	7	31	1	1·8	27·6
Elec. 21,281,232 Turnout 70·8%	14,548,521	615	1,446	50	100·0	..
1924. Wed., 29 Oct						
Conservative	8,039,598	419	552	16	48·3	51·9
Liberal	2,928,747	40	340	6	17·6	30·9
Labour	5,489,077	151	512	9	33·0	38·2
Communist	55,346	1	8	..	0·3	25·0
Others	126,511	4	16	1	0·8	29·1
Elec. 21,731,320 Turnout 76·6%	16,639,279	615	1,428	32	100·0	..
1929. Thu., 30 May						
Conservative	8,656,473	260	590	4	38·2	39·4
Liberal	5,308,510	59	513	..	23·4	27·7
Labour	8,389,512	288	571	..	37·1	39·3
Communist	50,614	..	25	..	0·3	5·3
Others	243,266	8	31	3	1·0	21·2
Elec. 28,850,870 Turnout 76·1%	22,648,375	615	1,730	7	100·0	..
1931. Tue., 27 Oct						
Conservative	11,978,745	473	523	56	55·2)	62·9
National Labour	341,370	13	20	..	1·6	
Liberal National	809,302	35	41	..	3·7)	28·8
Liberal	1,403,102	33	112	5	6·5	
(National Government)	(14,532,519)	(554)	(696)	(61)	(67·0)	..
Independent Liberal	106,106	4	7	..	0·5	35·8
Labour	6,649,630	52	515	6	30·6	33·0
Communist	74,824	..	26	..	0·3	7·5
New Party	36,377	..	24	..	0·2	3·9
Others	256,917	5	24	..	1·2	21·9
Elec. 29,960,071 Turnout 76·3%	21,656,373	615	1,292	67	100·0	..

General Election Results, 1935–1955

	Total Votes	M.P.s Elected	Candi-dates	Unopposed Returns	% Share of Total Vote	Average % Vote per Opposed Candidate
1935. Thu., 14 Nov						
Conservative	11,810,158	432	585	26	53·7	54·8
Liberal	1,422,116	21	161	..	6·4	23·9
Labour	8,325,491	154	552	13	37·9	40·3
Independent Labour Party	139,577	4	17	..	0·7	22·2
Communist	27,117	1	2	..	0·1	38·0
Others	272,595	4	31	1	1·2	21·3
Elec. 31,379,050 Turnout 71·2%	21,997,054	615	1,348	40	100·0	..
1945. Thu., 5 Jul [1]						
Conservative	9,988,306	213	624	1	39·8	40·1
Liberal	2,248,226	12	306	..	9·0	18·6
Labour	11,995,152	393	604	2	47·8	50·4
Communist	102,780	2	21	..	0·4	12·7
Common Wealth	110,634	1	23	..	0·4	12·6
Others	640,880	19	104	..	2·0	15·4
Elec. 33,240,391 Turnout 72·7%	25,085,978	640	1,682	3	100·0	..
1950. Thu., 23 Feb						
Conservative	12,502,567	298	620	2	43·5	43·7
Liberal	2,621,548	9	475	..	9·1	11·8
Labour	13,266,592	315	617	..	46·1	46·7
Communist	91,746	..	100	..	0·3	2·0
Others	290,218	3	56	..	1·0	12·6
Elec. 33,269,770 Turnout 84·0%	28,772,671	625	1,868	2	100·0	..
1951. Thu., 25 Oct						
Conservative	13,717,538	321	617	4	48·0	48·6
Liberal	730,556	6	109	..	2·5	14·7
Labour	13,948,605	295	617	..	48·8	49·2
Communist	21,640	..	10	..	0·1	4·4
Others	177,329	3	23	..	0·6	16·8
Elec. 34,645,573 Turnout 82·5%	28,595,668	625	1,376	4	100·0	..
1955. Thu., 26 May						
Conservative	13,286,569	344	623	..	49·7	50·2
Liberal	722,405	6	110	..	2·7	15·1
Labour	12,404,970	277	620	..	46·4	47·3
Communist	33,144	..	17	..	0·1	4·2
Others	313,410	3	39	..	1·1	20·8
Elec. 34,858,263 Turnout 76·7%	26,760,498	630	1,409	..	100·0	..

[1] Result announced 26 July 1945

General Election Results, 1959–1966

	Total Votes	M.P.s Elected	Candidates	Unopposed Returns	% Share of Total Vote	Average % Vote per Opposed Candidate
1959. Thu., 8 Oct						
Conservative	13,749,830	365	625	..	49·4	49·6
Liberal	1,638,571	6	216	..	5·9	16·9
Labour	12,215,538	258	621	..	43·8	44·5
Communist	30,897	..	18	..	0·1	4·1
Others	224,405	1	56	..	0·8	10·0
Elec. 35,397,080 Turnout 78·8%	27,859,241	630	1,536	..	100·0	..
1964. Thu., 15 Oct						
Conservative	12,001,396	304	630	..	43·4	43·4
Liberal	3,092,878	9	365	..	11·2	18·5
Labour	12,205,814	317	628	..	44·1	44·1
Communist	45,932	..	36	..	0·2	3·4
Others	302,982	..	98	..	1·1	7·9
Elec. 35,892,572 Turnout 77·1%	27,655,374	630	1,757	..	100·0	..
1966. Thu., 31 Mar						
Conservative	11,418,433	253	629	..	41·9	41·8
Liberal	2,327,533	12	311	..	8·5	16·1
Labour	13,064,951	363	621	..	47·9	48·7
Communist	62,112	..	57	..	0·2	3·0
Others	390,577	2	89	..	1·5	8·6
Elec. 35,964,684 Turnout 75·8%	27,263,606	630	1,707	..	100·0	..

General Election Results by Regions

	1900	1906	Jan 1910	Dec 1910	1918a	1922	1923	1924	1929	1931	1935	1945	1950	1951	1955	1959	1964	1966
ty of London																		
nservative	51	19	33	30	Coal.	43	29	39	24	53	39	12	12	14	15	18	10	6
eral	8	38	25	26	53	9	11	3	2	4	1	..	..	..	..	..	..	..
bour	..	2	1	3	Op.	9	22	19	36	5	22	48	31	29	27	24	32	36
hers	..	..	..	..	9	1	..	1	..	..	..	2	..	..	..	..	..	..
of S. England																		
nservative	123	45	107	103	Coal.	130	89	150	111	156	147	88	144	153	163	171	157	134
eral	32	107	46	49	149	23	48	5	18	4	3	3	1	..	..	1	3	4
bour	..	3	2	2	Op.	9	27	10	35	5	15	91	54	46	42	34	46	67
hers	..	..	..	1	16	3	1	..	1	..	..	3	..	..	1	..	..	1
'lands																		
nservative	60	27	49	50	Coal.	53	45	64	35	80	67	24	35	35	39	49	42	35
eral	27	59	31	30	67	17	17	2	5	3	1	..	..	..	..	..	..	..
bour	1	2	8	8	Op.	17	25	21	47	4	19	64	59	59	57	47	54	61
hers	..	..	..	..	20	..	..	..	..	..	..	2	..	..	..	..	..	..
thern England																		
nservative	98	31	45	50	Coal.	82	57	101	51	146	106	43	61	69	75	77	53	44
eral	55	102	86	82	121	27	48	9	10	9	5	2	1	2	2	2	..	2
bour	..	20	22	21	Op.	60	64	59	108	15	60	128	107	99	90	88	114	121
hers	1	1	1	1	50	2	2	2	2	1	..	..	..	..	..	..	..	..
es																		
nservative	6	..	2	3	Coal.	6	4	9	1	11	11	4	4	6	6	7	6	3
eral	27	33	27	26	20	10	12	10	9	8	6	6	5	3	3	2	2	1
bour	1	1	5	5	Op.	18	19	16	25	16	18	25	27	27	27	27	28	32
hers	..	..	..	..	15	1	..	..	..	..	..	..	..	..	..	..	..	..
land																		
nservative	36	10	9	9	Coal.	13	14	36	20	57	43	29	32	35	36	31	24	20
eral	34	58	59	58	54	27	22	8	13	7	3	..	2	1	1	1	4	5
bour	..	2	2	3	Op.	29	34	26	37	7	20	37	37	35	34	38	43	46
hers	..	..	..	..	17	2	1	1	1	..	5	5	..	..	..	1	..	..
and																		
nservative	19	16	19	17	Coal.	10	10	12	10	10	10	9	10	9	10	12	12	11
eral	1	3	1	1	1	..	..	..	..	..	..	..	..	..	..	..	..	..
bour	..	..	..	..	Op.	..	..	..	..	..	..	..	..	..	..	..	..	..
hers	81	82	81	83	100	2	2	..	2	2	2	3	2	3	2	..	..	1
versities																		
nservative	9	9	9	9	Coal.	8	9	8	8	8	9	4	..	..	..	..	..	..
eral	..	..	..	..	13	3	2	3	2	2	1	1	..	..	..	..	..	..
bour	..	..	..	..	Op.	..	..	..	..	..	..	..	..	..	..	..	..	..
hers	..	..	..	..	2	1	1	1	2	2	2	7	..	..	..	..	..	..
als																		
nservative	402	157	273	272	Coal.	345	258	419	260	521	432	213	298	321	344	365	304	253
eral	184	400	275	272	478	116	159	40	59	37	20	12	9	6	6	6	9	12
bour	2	30	40	42	Op.	142	191	151	288	52	154	394	315	295	277	258	317	363
hers	82	83	83	85	229	12	7	5	8	5	9	22	3	3	3	1	..	2
al seats	670	670	670	670	707	615	615	615	615	615	615	640	625	625	630	630	630	630

The heavy vertical lines indicate redistributions of seats.
Northern England includes Cheshire, Lancashire, Yorkshire, and all counties to their north.
Midlands includes Hereford, Worcs., Warwickshire, Northants, Lincs., Notts., Leics., Staffs., Salop, Derbyshire.
Southern England includes the rest of England, except for the County of London.

In 1918 all Coalition and all non-Coalition candidates are listed together. In fact a substantial number of the 48 Conservatives were elected without the Coupon worked with the Government. Virtually no Coupons were issued to Irish candidates but 23 of the 101 non-University seats in Ireland went to Unionists.

Party Changes between Elections

The party composition of the House of Commons changes continuously partly owing to Members changing their allegiance and partly owing to by-election results. The following table shows the net change due to both causes during the life of each Parliament. (Seats vacant at dissolution are included under the last incumbent's party.)

		Con.	Lib.	Lab.	Others
1895–1900	Dissolution	399	189	..	82
1900–05	Election	402	184	2	82
	Dissolution	369	215	4	82
1906–09	Election	157	400	30	83
	Dissolution	168	373	46	83
1910	Election	273	275	40	82
	Dissolution	274	274	40	82
1910–18	Election	272	271	42	85
	Dissolution	281	260	39	90
1918–22 a	Election	383	161	73	90
	Dissolution	378	155	87	87
1922–23	Election	345	116	142	12
	Dissolution	344	117	144	10
1923–24	Election	258	159	191	7
	Dissolution	259	158	193	5
1924–29	Election	419	40	151	5
	Dissolution	400	46	162	7
1929–31	Election	260	59	288	8
	Dissolution	263	57	281 b	14
1931–35	Election	521	37	52	5
	Dissolution	512	34	59	10
1935–45	Election	432	20	154	9
	Dissolution	398	18	166	33
1945–50	Election	213	12	393	22
	Dissolution	218	10	391	21
1950–51	Election	298	9	315	3
	Dissolution	298	9	314	4
1951–55	Election	321	6	295	3
	Dissolution	322	6	294	3
1955–59	Election	344	6	277	3
	Dissolution	340	6	281	3
1959–64	Election	365	6	258	1
	Dissolution	360	7	262	2
1964–66	Election	304	9	317	..
	Dissolution	304	10	316	..
1966	Election	253	12	363	2

a In this form the 1918–22 figures are highly misleading. This amplification may help:

		Co. U.	Con.	Co. Lib.	Lib.	Co. Lab.	Lab.	O.
Election	.	335	48	133	28	10	63	90
Dissolution	.	313	65	120	35	11	76	87

b This figure includes 15 National Labour M.P.s.

M.P.s' Changes of Allegiance

The difficulties in compiling an exact and comprehensive list of all floor-crossings, Whip withdrawals, Whip resignations, and Whip restorations are enormous. The list which follows is probably fairly complete as far as floor crossings go (except for 1918–22) but it certainly omits a number of Members who relinquished the Whip for a time. It also omits cases of M.P.s who stood without official party support in their constituencies but who remained in good standing with the Whips and some cases of M.P.s taking the Whip immediately before a General Election (as happened with several Members in 1918 and a few in 1945) or immediately after a General Election (as happened with the Lloyd George Group in 1935). No attempt has been made to record shifts between the various factions of Irish Nationalism. Throughout this list the test, in so far as it can be applied, is whether the M.P. was officially in receipt of the weekly documentary Whip.

Parliament of 1900–05

			from	to	
Nov 02	J. Wason	Orkney & Shetland	L.U.	Ind.	Won by-el Nov 02 took Lib. Whip by 05
Apr 03	J. W. Wilson	E. Worcs.	L.U.	Lib.	
Apr 03	Sir M. Foster	London Univ.	L.U.	Lib.	
Jan 04	W. Churchill	Oldham	Con.	Ind.⎫	Con. Whip restored after 2 weeks; Lib. Whip taken Apr 04
Jan 04	Sir J. Dickson-Poynder	Chippenham	Con.	Ind.⎭	
Feb 04	E. Hain	St Ives	L.U.	Lib.	
Feb 04	T. Russell	S. Tyrone	L.U.	Lib.	
Feb 04	J. Wilson	Falkirk Burghs	L.U.	Lib.	
Feb 04	E. Mitchell	N. Fermanagh	Ind.C.	Lib.	
Feb 04	J. Wood	E. Down	L.U.	Lib.	
Mar 04	J. Seely	I. of Wight	Con.	Ind.	Won by-el Apr 04 unop.; took Lib. Whip May 04
Apr 04	I. Guest	Plymouth	Con.	Lib.	
Aug 04	G. Kemp	Heywood	L.U.	Lib.	
Jul 04	J. Jameson	W. Clare	I. Nat.	Con.	
Nov 04	R. Rigg	Appleby	Lib.	Ind.	Resigned seat Dec 04
Mar 05	E. Hatch	Gorton	Con.	Ind.	
Mar 05	Sir E. Reed	Cardiff D	Lib.	Con.	

Parliament of 1906–09

			from	to	
Feb 06	J. W. Taylor	Chester-le-Street	Lib.	Lab.	
Feb 06	A. Taylor	E. Toxteth	Con.	Lib.	
Feb 07	R. Hunt	Ludlow	Con.	—	Whip withdrawn. Whip restored Mar 07.
Nov 07	L. Renton	Gainsborough	Lib.	Con.	
Aug 09	A. Corbett	Tradeston	L.U.	Ind.	
Mar 09	T. Kincaid Smith	Stratford-on-Avon	Lib.	Ind.	Lost by-el May 09
May 09	A. Cross	Camlachie	L.U.	Lib.	
Oct 09	C. Bellairs	King's Lynn	Lib.	L.U.	

Parliament of 1910

			from	to	
Nov 10	Sir J. Rees	Montgomery D.	Lib.	Con.	

Parliament of 1911–18

			from	to	
Jan 14	D. Mason	Coventry	Lib.	Ind.	
Feb 14	B. Kenyon	Chesterfield	Lab.	Lib.	Introduced as new M.P. by Lab. but resigned Whip after 2 weeks
Apr 14	W. Johnson	Nuneaton	Lab.	Lib.	Lab. Whip withdrawn

				from	to	
Apr	15	J. Hancock	Mid-Derbyshire	Lab.	Lib.	Lab. Whip withdrawn
Sep	17	H. Page Croft	Christchurch	Con.	Nat.P.	
Sep	17	Sir R. Cooper	Walsall	Con.	Nat.P.	
Jul	18	E. John	E. Denbigh	Lib.	Lab.	
Jul	18	J. Martin	St. Pancras S.E.	Lib.	Lab.	

In Nov 18 a number of Liberals became Independent or Labour and some Labour members accepted the label Coalition Labour or Coalition National Democratic Party shortly before the dissolution of Parliament.

Parliament of 1919-22

Throughout this parliament the confusion of party labels and the movements within and between the Coalition and non-Coalition wings of each party make it impossible to attempt any comprehensive listing of all switches. The following changes were, however, more clear cut.

Apr	19	J. Wedgwood	Newcastle-under-Lyme	Co.Lib.	Lab.	Lab. Whip granted May 19
Oct	19	E. Hallas	Duddeston	Co. N.D.P.	Lab.	
Nov	19	C. Malone	Leyton E.	Co.Lib	Ind.	Joined Communist party Jul 20
Oct	20	O. Mosley	Harrow	Co.Con.	Ind.	
Oct	20	Sir O. Thomas	Anglesey	Lab.	Ind.	
Feb	22	A. Hopkinson	Mossley	Co.Lib.	Ind.	

Parliament of 1922-23

Jul	23	A. Evans	Leicester E.	N.Lib.	Con.	
Oct	23	G. Roberts	Norwich	Ind.	Con.	

Parliament of 1923-24

Feb	24	G. Davies	Welsh Univ.	Ind.	Lab.	
May	24	O. Mosley	Harrow	Ind.	Lab.	

Parliament of 1924-29 [1]

Jan	26	Sir A. Mond	Carmarthen	Lib.	Con.	Made peer Jun 28
Feb	26	E. Hilton Young	Norwich	Lib.	Ind.	Took Con. Whip May 26
Oct	26	J. Kenworthy	Hull C.	Lib.	Lab.	Won by-el Nov 26
Nov	26	D. Davies	Montgomery	Lib.	Ind.	
Feb	27	G. Spencer	Broxtowe	Lab.	Ind.	Expelled from party
Feb	27	W. Benn	Leith	Lib	Ind.	Resigned seat Feb 27
Feb	27	L. Haden Guest	Southwark N.	Lab.	Ind.	Lost by-el Mar 27
Oct	27	Sir R. Newman	Exeter	Con.	Ind.	
Jul	28	Sir B. Peto	Barnstable	Con.	—	Whip withdrawn; restored Nov 28

[1] The 7 members, all former Liberal M.P.s, elected under the label 'Constitutional' never acted as a group. Two, W. Churchill and Sir H. Greenwood took the Conservative whip from the start and one, A. Moreing, later. Three reverted during the Parliament to their former Liberalism, J. Edwards, A. England, and J. Ward. One, Sir T. Robinson, became an Independent.

Parliament of 1929-31

Jun	29	Sir W. Jowitt	Preston	Lib.	Lab.	Won by-el Jun 29
Feb	31	Sir O. Mosley	Smethwick	Lab.	N.P.⎫	
Feb	31	Lady C. Mosley	Stoke	Lab.	N.P.⎪	
Feb	31	R. Forgan	W. Renfrew	Lab.	N.P.⎬	
Feb	31	W. Allen	Belfast W.	Con.	N.P.⎪	
Feb	31	C. R. Dudgeon	Galloway	Lib.	N.P.⎭	
Feb	31	J. Strachey	Aston	Lab.	N.P.	Became Ind. Jun 31
Feb	31	O. Baldwin	Dudley	Lab.	Ind.	
Feb	31	W. Brown	Wolverhampton W.	Lab.	Ind.	
Mar	31	Sir W. Wayland	Canterbury	Con.	—	Whip withdrawn; restored Apr 31
Jun	31	E. Brown	Leith	Lib.	Ind.⎫	
Jun	31	Sir R. Hutchison	Montrose	Lib.	Ind.⎬	Became L.Nat. Oct 31
Jun	31	Sir J. Simon	Spen Valley	Lib.	Ind.⎭	

In Oct 31 23 Liberal Members broke with the party to form the Liberal National Group. A further 6 Liberals, most notably the Lloyd George family, became Independent Liberals. 15 Labour members under R. MacDonald formed the National Labour Group.

Parliament of 1931-35

				from	to	
Nov	31	G. Buchanan	Gorbals	Lab.	ILP.	
Nov	31	J. McGovern	Shettleston	Lab.	ILP.	
Nov	31	J. Maxton	Bridgeton	Lab.	ILP.	
Nov	31	D. Kirkwood	Dumbarton	Lab.	ILP.	Returned to Lab. Aug 33
Nov	31	R. Wallhead	Merthyr	Lab.	ILP.	Returned to Lab. Sep 33
Dec	32	F. Llewellyn Jones	Flint	L.Nat.	Lib.	
Feb	33	H. Nathan	Bethnal Green N.E.	Ind.L.	Ind.	Took Lab. Whip Jun 34
Jun	34	J. Hunter	Dumfries	Lib.	L.Nat.	
Jun	34	J. Lockwood	Shipley	Con.	Ind.	
May	35	F. Astbury	Salford W.	Con.	Ind.	
May	35	L. Thorp	Nelson & Colne	Con.	Ind.	
May	35	A. Todd	Berwick-on-Tweed	Con.	Ind.	
May	35	Duchess of Atholl	Kinross E. & Perth	Con.	Ind.	Whip restored Sep 35
May	35	Sir J. Nall	Hulme	Con.	Ind.	Whip restored Nov 35

Parliament of 1935-45

				from	to	
Jun	36	H. Macmillan	Stockton-on-Tees	Con.	Ind.	Whip restored Jul 37
Sep	36	R. Bernays	Bristol N.	Lib.	L.Nat.	
Apr	38	Duchess of Atholl	Kinross & W. Perth	Con.	Ind.	Lost by-el Dec 38
Oct	38	H. Holdsworth	Bradford S.	Lib.	L.Nat.	
Nov	38	A. Hopkinson	Mossley	Nat.	Ind.	
Jan	39	Sir S. Cripps	Bristol E.	Lab.	—	Expelled from party; Whip restored Feb 45
Mar	39	A. Bevan	Ebbw Vale	Lab.	—	Expelled from party; Whip restored Dec 39
Mar	39	G. Strauss	Lambeth N.	Lab.	—	Expelled from party; Whip restored Feb 40
May	39	G. Buchanan	Gorbals	ILP.	Lab.	
Dec	39	C. Davies	Montgomery	L.Nat.	Ind.	Took Lib. Whip Aug 42
Mar	40	D. Pritt	Hammersmith N.	Lab.	—	Expelled from party
May	40	A. Ramsay	Peebles & S.	Con.	Ind.	Detained until Dec 44
Feb	42	E. Granville	Eye	L.Nat.	Ind.	Took Lib. Whip Apr 45
Feb	42	Sir M. Macdonald	Inverness	L.Nat.	Ind.	Whip restored by 45
Feb	42	L. Hore-Belisha	Devonport	L.Nat.	Ind.	
Feb	42	S. King-Hall	Ormskirk	N.Lab.	Ind.	
Feb	42	Sir H. Morris-Jones	Denbigh	L.Nat.	Ind.	Whip restored May 43
Feb	42	K. Lindsay	Kilmarnock	N.Lab.	Ind.	
May	42	C. Cunningham-Reid	St Marylebone	Con.	—	Whip withdrawn
Sep	42	Sir R. Acland	Barnstaple	Lib.	C.W.	
Mar	43	A. Maclaren	Burslem	Lab.	Ind.	
Nov	44	J. Loverseed	Eddisbury	C.W.	Ind.	Took Lab. Whip May 45
Jan	45	T. Driberg	Maldon	Ind.	Lab.	

Parliament of 1945-50

				from	to	
Apr	46	E. Millington	Chelmsford	C.W.	Lab.	
Oct	46	T. Horabin	N. Cornwall	Lib.	Ind.	Took Lab. Whip Nov 47
Mar	47	J. McGovern	Shettleston	ILP.	Lab.	
Jul	47	C. Stephen	Camlachie	ILP.	Ind.	Took Lab. Whip Oct 47
Nov	47	J. Carmichael	Bridgeton	ILP.	Lab.	
Nov	47	E. Walkden	Doncaster	Lab.	Ind.	
Mar	48	J. McKie	Galloway	Ind.Con.	Con.	
Apr	48	J. Platts-Mills	Finsbury	Lab.	—	Expelled from party
May	48	A. Edwards	Middlesbrough	Lab.	—	Expelled from party, took Con. Whip Aug 49
Oct	48	I. Bulmer-Thomas	Keighley	Lab.	Ind.	Took Con. Whip Jan 49
Nov	48	E. Gander Dower	Caithness & Sutherland	Con.	Ind.	
May	49	L. Solley	Thurrock	Lab.	—	Expelled from party
May	49	K. Zilliacus	Gateshead	Lab.	—	Expelled from party
Jul	49	L. Hutchinson	Rusholme	Lab.	—	Expelled from party

Parliament 1950-51

			from	to	
Aug 50	R. Blackburn	Northfield	Lab.	Ind.	

Parliament of 1951-55

			from	to	
Jun 54	Sir J. Mellor	Sutton Coldfield	Con.	Ind.	Whip restored Jul 54
Jul 54	H. Legge-Bourke	Isle of Ely	Con.	Ind.	Whip restored Oct 54
Nov 54	G. Craddock	Bradford S.	Lab.	—	
Nov 54	S. Davies	Merthyr	Lab.	—	
Nov 54	E. Fernyhough	Jarrow	Lab.	—	Whip withdrawn; restored Apr 55
Nov 54	E. Hughes	S. Ayrshire	Lab.	—	
Nov 54	S. Silverman	Nelson & Colne	Lab.	—	
Nov 54	V. Yates	Ladywood	Lab.	—	
Nov 54	J. McGovern	Shettleston	Lab.	—	Whip withdrawn; restored Mar 55
Mar 55	A. Bevan	Ebbw Vale	Lab.	—	Whip withdrawn; restored Apr 55
Mar 55	Sir R. Acland	Gravesend	Lab.	Ind.	Resigned seat to fight by-el; expelled from party

Parliament of 1955-59

			from	to	
Nov 56	C. Banks	Pudsey	Con.	Ind.	Whip restored Dec 58
May 57	P. Maitland	Lanark	Con.	Ind.	Whip restored Dec 57
May 57	Sir V. Raikes	Garston	Con.	Ind.	Resigned seat Oct 57
May 57	A. Maude	Ealing S.	Con.	Ind.	Resigned seat Apr 58
May 57	J. Biggs-Davison	Chigwell	Con.	Ind.	
May 57	A. Fell	Yarmouth	Con.	Ind.	
May 57	Vt Hinchingbrooke	S. Dorset	Con.	Ind.	Whip restored Jul 58
May 57	L. Turner	Oxford	Con.	Ind.	
May 57	P. Williams	Sunderland S.	Con.	Ind.	
Nov 57	Sir F. Medlicott	C. Norfolk	Con.	Ind.	Whip restored Nov 58
Jan 59	Sir D. Robertson	Caithness & Sutherland	Con.	Ind.	

Parliament of 1959-64

			from	to	
Mar 61	A. Brown	Tottenham	Lab.	Ind.	Took Con. Whip May 62
Mar 61	W. Baxter	W. Stirlingshire	Lab.	—	
Mar 61	S. Davies	Merthyr	Lab.	—	
Mar 61	M. Foot	Ebbw Vale	Lab.	—	Whip withdrawn; restored May 63
Mar 61	E. Hughes	S. Ayrshire	Lab.	—	
Mar 61	S. Silverman	Nelson & Colne	Lab.	—	
Mar 61	K. Zilliacus	Gorton	Lab.	—	Whip suspended; party membership restored Jan 62
Oct 61	Sir W. Duthie	Banff	Con.	Ind.	Whip restored Nov 63
Jan 64	D. Johnson	Carlisle	Con.	Ind.	

Parliament of 1964-66   [*None*]

Parliament of 1966-

			from	to	
Jul 66	G. Hirst	Shipley	Con.	Ind.	
Dec 66	R. Paget	Northampton	Lab.	Ind.	Whip restored Jun 67
Jan 68	D. Donnelly	Pembroke	Lab.	Ind.	Expelled from party Mar 68
Feb 68	24 M.P.s		Lab.	—	Whip suspended for one month

SOURCE.—For details of changes of allegiance in 1945-66 see R. J. Jackson, *Whips and Rebels* (1968).

In addition to the floor crossings recorded above there are the following instances of ex-M.P.s, after an interval out of parliament, returning to the House under a designation basically different from the ones under which they had previously sat.

(Sir) R. Acland	Lib. 35-42	C.W. 42-45	Lab. 47-55
C. Addison	Lib. 10-22	Lab. 29-31, 34-35	

P. Alden	Lib. 06–18	Lab. 23–24	
W. Allen	Lib. 92–00	Nat. 31–35	
(Sir) E. Bennett	Lib. 06–10	Lab. 29–31	N. Lab. 31–45
H. Bottomley	Lib. 06–12	Ind. 18–22	
W. Brown	Lab. 29–31	Ind. 42–50	
C. Buxton	Lib. 10–10	Lab 22–23, 29–31	
N. Buxton	Lib. 05–06, 10–18	Lab. 22–24, 29–30	
(Sir) W. Churchill	Con. 00–04	Lib. 04–22	Con. 24–64
(Sir) H. Cowan	Lib. 06–22	Con. 24–29	
A. Crawley	Lab. 45–51	Con. 62–67	
R. Denman	Lib. 10–18	Lab. 29–31	N. Lab. 31–45
(Sir) C. Entwhistle	Lib. 18–24	Con. 31–45	
R. Fletcher	Lib. 23–24	Lab. 35–42	
(Sir) D. Foot	Lib. 31–45	Lab. 57–	
G. Garro-Jones	Lib. 24–29	Lab. 35–47	
Sir E. Grigg	Lib. 22–25	Con. 33–45	
C. Guest	Lib. 10–18, 22–23	Con. 37–45	
F. Guest	Lib. 10–22, 23–29	Con. 31–37	
O. Guest	Co.Lib. 18–22	Con. 35–45	
T. Harvey	Lib. 10–18, 23–24	Ind. 37–45	
E. Hemmerde	Lib. 06–10, 12–18	Lab. 22–24	
(Sir) B. Janner	Lib. 31–35	Lab. 45–	
E. King	Lab. 45–50	Con. 64–	
H. Lawson	Lib. 85–92, 93–95	L.U. 05–06, 10–16	
H. Lees-Smith	Lib. 10–18	Lab. 22–31, 35–42	
G. Lloyd-George	Lib. 22–24, 29–50	Con. 51–56	
(Lady) M. Lloyd-George	Lib. 29–51	Lab. 57–66	
L. Mallalieu	Lib. 31–35	Lab. 48–	
C. Malone	Co.Lib. 18–19	Ind. then Comm. 19–22 Lab. 28–31	
(Sir) F. Markham	Lab. 29–31	N. Lab. 35–45	Con. 51–64
H. Mond	Lib. 23–24	Con. 29–30	
A. Ponsonby	Lib. 08–18	Lab. 22–30	
S. Saklatvala	Lab. 22–23, Comm. 24–29		
Sir A. Salter	Ind. 37–50	Con. 52–54	
J. Seddon	Lab. 06–10, Co.N.D.P. 18–22		
(Sir) E. Spears	Lib. 22–24	Con. 31–45	
C. Stephen	Lab. 22–31	I.L.P. 35–47	Lab. 47–48
(Sir) C. Trevelyan	Lib. 99–18	Lab. 22–31	

By-elections

	Total [a] By-elections	Changes	Con.		Lib.		Lab.		Others	
			+	–	+	–	+	–	+	–
1900–05	113	30	2	26	20	4	5	..	5	..
1906–09	101	20	12	..	..	18	5	..	3	2
1910	20	..	..	..	..	..	..	..	..	..
1911–18	245	31	16	4	4	16	2	4	10	8
1918–22	108	27	4	13	5 [b]	11 [b]	14	1	4	2
1922–23	16	6	1	4	3	1	2	..	..	1
1923–24	10	3	2	1	..	1	1	1	..	..
1924–29	63	20	1	16	6	3	13	1	..	..
1929–31	36	7	4	1	..	1	2	4	1	1
1931–35	62	10	..	9	..	1	10	..	..	..
1935–45	219	30	..	29	..	..	13	1	17	..
1945–50	52	3	3	..	..	..	..	..	..	3
1950–51	16	..	..	..	..	..	..	..	..	..
1951–55	48	1	1	..	..	..	..	1	..	..
1955–59	52	6	1	4	1	1	4	..	..	1
1959–64	62	9	2	7	1	..	6	2	..	..
1964–66	13	2	1	1	1	..	..	1	..	..

[a] Up to 1918, and to a lesser extent to 1926, the number of by-elections is inflated by the necessity for Ministers to stand for re-election on appointment. In 53 such cases the returns were unopposed.

[b] In 1918–22 Opposition Liberals won 5 seats and lost 2. Coalition Liberals lost 9.

Seats Changing Hands at By-elections

Date	Constituency	General Election	By-election
26 Sep 01	N.E. Lanark.	Lib.	Con.
21 Nov 01	Galway	Con.	Nat.
10 May 02	Bury	Con.	Lib.
29 Jul 02	Leeds N.	Con.	Lib.
1 Aug 02	N.E. Lancs.	Lib.	Lab.
18 Aug 02	S. Belfast	Con.	Ind. U.
22 Oct 02	Devonport	Lib.	Con.
19 Nov 02	Orkney & Shetland	Con.	Ind. Lib.
2 Jan 03	E. Cambs.	Con.	Lib.
11 Mar 03	Woolwich	Con.	Lab.
17 Mar 03	E. Sussex	Con.	Lib.
20 Mar 03	N. Fermanagh	Con.	Ind. Con.
24 Jul 03	Barnard Castle	Lib.	Lab.
26 Aug 03	Argyll	Con.	Lib.
17 Sep 03	St. Andrews	Con.	Lib.
15 Jan 04	Norwich	Con.	Lib.
30 Jan 04	Ayr	Con.	Lib.
12 Feb 04	Mid-Herts.	Con.	Lib.
17 Mar 04	E. Dorset	Con.	Lib.
6 Apr 04	Isle of Wight	Con.	Ind. Con.
20 Jun 04	Devonport	{ Con. 02 / Lib. 00 }	Lib.
26 Jul 04	W. Shropshire	Con.	Lib.
10 Aug 04	N.E. Lanark.	{ Con. 01 / Lib. 00 }	Lib.
7 Jan 05	Stalybridge	Con.	Lib.
26 Jan 05	N. Dorset	Con.	Lib.
3 Mar 05	Bute	Con.	Lib.
5 Apr 05	Brighton	Con.	Lib.
1 Jun 05	Whitby	Con.	Lib.
29 Jun 05	Finsbury E.	Con.	Lib.
13 Oct 05	Barkston Ash	Con.	Lib.

General Election 12 Jan–7 Feb 06

Date	Constituency	General Election	By-election
3 Aug 06	Cockermouth	Lib.	Con.
31 Dec 06	Mid-Cork	Nat.	I. Nat.
30 Jan 07	N.E. Derbyshire [a]	Lib.	Lab.
26 Feb 07	Brigg	Lib.	Con.
4 Jul 07	Jarrow	Lib.	Lab.
18 Jul 07	Colne Valley	Lib.	I. Lab.
31 Jul 07	N.W. Staffs. [a]	Lib.	Lab.
17 Jan 08	Mid-Devon	Lib.	Con.
31 Jan 08	S. Hereford	Lib.	Con.
24 Mar 08	Peckham	Lib.	Con.
24 Apr 08	Manchester N.W.	Lib.	Con.
20 Jun 08	Pudsey	Lib.	Con.
1 Aug 08	Haggerston	Lib.	Con.
24 Sep 08	Newcastle-o-T.	Lib.	Con.
2 Mar 09	Glasgow C.	Lib.	Con.
1 May 09	Cork City	Nat.	I. Nat.
4 May 09	Attercliffe	Lib.	Lab.
4 May 09	Stratford-on-Avon	Lib.	Con.
15 Jul 09	Mid-Derbyshire	Lib.	Lab.
28 Oct 09	Bermondsey	Lib.	Con.

General Election 14 Jan–9 Feb 10
1910—no change

General Election 2–19 Dec 10

Date	Constituency	General Election	By-election
28 Apr 11	Cheltenham	Lib.	Con.
13 Nov 11	Oldham	Lib.	Con.
21 Nov 11	S. Somerset	Lib.	Con.
20 Dec 11	N. Ayrshire	Lib.	Con.
5 Mar 12	Manchester S.	Lib.	Con.
13 Jul 12	Hanley	Lab.	Lib.
26 Jul 12	Crewe	Lib.	Con.
8 Aug 12	Manchester N.W.	Lib.	Con.
10 Sep 12	Edinburgh	Lib.	Con.
26 Nov 12	Bow & Bromley	Lab.	Con.
30 Jan 13	Londonderry	Con.	Lib.
18 Mar 13	S. Westmorland	Con.	Ind. Con.
16 May 13	E. Cambs.	Lib.	Con.
20 Aug 13	Chesterfield	Lab.	Lib.
8 Nov 13	Reading	Lib.	Con.
12 Dec 13	S. Lanarkshire	Lib.	Con.
19 Feb 14	Bethnal Green S.W.	Lib.	Con.
26 Feb 14	Leith	Lib.	Con.
20 May 14	N.E. Derbyshire	Lab.	Con.
23 May 14	Ipswich	Lib.	Con.
9 Dec 14	Tullamore	Nat.	I. Nat.
25 Nov 15	Merthyr Tydfil	Lab.	Ind.
9 Mar 16	E. Herts.	Con.	Ind.
15 Nov 16	W. Cork	I. Nat.	Nat.
23 Dec 16	Ashton-u-Lyne	Con.	Lib. (Unop.)
3 Feb 17	N. Roscommon	Nat.	S.F.
10 May 17	S. Longford	Nat.	S.F.
10 Jul 17	E. Clare	Nat.	S.F.
10 Aug 17	Kilkenny	Nat.	S.F.
2 Nov 17	Salford N.	Lib.	Lab.
19 Apr 18	Tullamore	{ I. Nat. 14 / Nat. 10 }	S.F.
20 Jun 18	E. Cavan	Nat.	S.F.

General Election 14 Dec 18

Date	Constituency	General Election	By-election
1 Mar 19	Leyton W.	Co. U.	Lib.
29 Mar 19	Hull C.	Co. U.	Lib.
16 Apr 19	C. Aberdeen & Kincardine	Co. U.	Lib.
27 May 19	E. Antrim	Con.	Ind. U.
16 Jul 19	Bothwell	Co. U.	Lab.
30 Aug 19	Widnes	Co. U.	Lab.
20 Dec 19	Spen Valley	Co. Lib.	Lab.
7 Feb 20	Wrekin	Co. Lib.	Ind.
27 Mar 20	Dartford	Co. Lib.	Lab.
27 Mar 20	Stockport	Co. Lab.	Co. U.
3 Jun 20	Louth	Co. U.	Lib.
27 Jul 20	S. Norfolk	Lib.	Lab.
12 Jan 21	Dover	Co. U.	Ind.
2 Mar 21	Woolwich E.	Lab.	Co. U.
3 Mar 21	Dudley	Co. U.	Lab.
4 Mar 21	Kirkcaldy	Co. Lib.	Lab.
5 Mar 21	Penistone	Lib.	Lab.
7 Jun 21	Westminster, St. G.	Co. U.	Ind.
8 Jun 21	Heywood & Radcliffe	Co. Lib.	Lab.
14 Dec 21	Southwark, S.E.	Co. Lib.	Lab.
18 Feb 22	Manchester, Clayton	Con.	Lab.
20 Feb 22	Camberwell N.	Co. U.	Lab.
24 Feb 22	Bodmin	Co. U.	Lib.
30 Mar 22	Leicester E.	Co. Lib.	Lab.
25 Jul 22	Pontypridd	Co. Lib.	Lab.

[a] Miners candidates standing as Lib-Lab, who only joined the Labour Party in 1909.

Date	Constituency	General Election	By-election
18 Aug 22	Hackney S.	Ind.	Co. U.
18 Oct 22	Newport	Co. Lib.	Con.

General Election 15 Nov 22

Date	Constituency	General Election	By-election
3 Mar 23	Mitcham	Con.	Lab.
3 Mar 23	Willesden E.	Con.	Lib.
6 Mar 23	Liverpool, Edge Hill	Con.	Lab.
7 Apr 23	Anglesey	Ind.	Lib.
31 May 23	Berwick on Tweed	Nat. Lib.	Con.
21 Jun 23	Tiverton	Con.	Lib.

General Election 6 Dec 23

Date	Constituency	General Election	By-election
22 May 24	Liverpool, W. Toxteth	Con.	Lab.
5 Jun 24	Oxford	Lib.	Con.
31 Jul 24	Holland with Boston	Lab.	Con.

General Election 29 Oct 24

Date	Constituency	General Election	By-election
17 Sep 25	Stockport	Con.	Lab.
17 Feb 26	Darlington	Con.	Lab.
12 Mar 26	English Univs.	Lib.	Con.
29 Apr 26	East Ham N.	Con.	Lab.
28 May 26	Hammersmith N.	Con.	Lab.
29 Nov 26	Hull C.	Lib.	Lab.
23 Feb 27	Stourbridge	Con.	Lab.
28 Mar 27	Southwark N.	Lab.	Lib.
1 Jun 27	Bosworth	Con.	Lib.
9 Jan 28	Northampton	Con.	Lab.
9 Feb 28	Lancaster	Con.	Lib.
6 Mar 28	St. Ives	Con.	Lib.
4 Apr 28	Linlithgow	Con.	Lab.
13 Jul 28	Halifax	Lib.	Lab.
29 Oct 28	Ashton-u-Lyne	Con.	Lab.
29 Jan 29	W. Midlothian	Con.	Lab.
7 Feb 29	Battersea S.	Con.	Lab.
20 Mar 29	Eddisbury	Con.	Lib.
21 Mar 29	N. Lanark	Con.	Lab.
21 Mar 29	Holland	Con.	Lib.

General Election 30 May 29

Date	Constituency	General Election	By-election
31 Jul 29	Preston	Lib.	Lab.
14 Dec 29	Liverpool, Scotland	I. Nat.	Lab. (Unop.)
6 May 30	Fulham W.	Lab.	Con.
30 Oct 30	Paddington S.	Con	Ind.
6 Nov 30	Shipley	Lab.	Con.
26 Mar 31	Sunderland	Lab.	Con.
30 Apr 31	Ashton-u-Lyne	Lab.	Con.

General Election 27 Oct 31

Date	Constituency	General Election	By-election
21 Apr 32	Wakefield	Con.	Lab.
26 Jul 32	Wednesbury	Con.	Lab.
27 Feb 33	Rotherham	Con.	Lab.
25 Oct 33	Fulham E.	Con.	Lab.
24 Apr 34	Hammersmith N.	Con.	Lab.
14 May 34	West Ham, Upton	Con.	Lab.
23 Oct 34	Lambeth N.	Lib.	Lab.
25 Oct 34	Swindon	Con.	Lab.
6 Feb 35	Liverpool, Wavertree	Con.	Lab.

Date	Constituency	General Election	By-election
16 Jul 35	Liverpool, W. Toxteth	Con.	Lab.

General Election 14 Nov 35

Date	Constituency	General Election	By-election
18 Mar 36	Dunbartonshire	Con.	Lab.
6 May 36	Camberwell, Peckham	Con.	Lab.
9 Jul 36	Derby	Con.	Lab.
26 Nov 36	Greenock	Con.	Lab.
27 Feb 37	Oxford Univ.	Con.	Ind.Con.
19 Mar 37	English Univs.	Con.	Ind.
29 Apr 37	Wandsworth C.	Con.	Lab.
22 Jun 37	Cheltenham	Con.	Ind.Con.
13 Oct 37	Islington N.	Con.	Lab.
16 Feb 38	Ipswich	Con.	Lab.
6 Apr 38	Fulham W.	Con.	Lab.
5 May 38	Lichfield	Con.	Lab.
7 Nov 38	Dartford	Con.	Lab.
18 Nov 38	Bridgwater	Con.	Ind.
17 May 39	Southwark N.	Con.	Lab.
24 May 39	Lambeth, Kennington	Con.	Lab
1 Aug 39	Brecon & Radnor	Con.	Lab.
24 Feb 40	Cambridge Univ.	Con.	Ind.Con.
8 Jun 40	Newcastle N.	Con.	Ind.Con.
25 Mar 42	Grantham	Con.	Ind.
29 Apr 42	Rugby	Con.	Ind.
29 Apr 42	Wallasey	Con.	Ind.
25 Jun 42	Maldon	Con.	Ind.
9 Feb 43	Belfast W.	U.	Eire Lab.
7 Apr 43	Eddisbury	Con.	C.W.
7 Jan 44	Skipton	Con.	C.W.
17 Feb 44	W. Derbyshire	Con.	Ind.
12 Apr 45	Motherwell	Lab.	S. Nat.
13 Apr 45	Scottish Univs.	Con.	Ind.
26 Apr 45	Chelmsford	Con.	C.W.

General Election 5 Jul 45

Date	Constituency	General Election	By-election
18 Mar 46	English Univs.	Ind.	Con.
6 Jun 46	Down	Ind. U.	U.
29 Nov 46	Scottish Univs.	Ind.	Con.
28 Jan 48	Glasgow, Camlachie	I.L.P.	Con.

General Election 23 Feb 50

1950-51—no change

General Election 25 Oct 51

Date	Constituency	General Election	By-election
13 May 53	Sunderland, S.	Lab.	Con.

General Election 26 May 55

Date	Constituency	General Election	By-election
12 Aug 55	Mid-Ulster	S.F.	U.
8 May 56	Mid-Ulster	S.F.	Ind.U.
14 Feb 57	Lewisham N.	Con.	Lab.
28 Feb 57	Carmarthen	Lib.	Lab.
12 Feb 58	Rochdale	Con.	Lab.
13 Mar 58	Glasgow, Kelvingrove	Con.	Lab.
27 Mar 58	Torrington	Con.	Lib.

General Election 8 Oct 59

Date	Constituency	General Election	By-election
17 Mar 60	Brighouse & Spenborough	Lab.	Con.
4 May 61	ªBristol S.E.	Lab.	Con.
14 Mar 62	Orpington	Con.	Lib.

ª Seat awarded to Con. on petition.

Date	Constitueney	General Election	By-election
6 Jun 62	Middlesbrough W.	Con.	Lab.
22 Nov 62	Glasgow, Woodside	Con.	Lab.
22 Nov 62	S. Dorset	Con.	Lab.
23 Aug 63	Bristol S.E.	{Lab. 59 Con.ᵃ 62	Lab.
7 Nov 63	Luton	Con.	Lab.
14 May 64	Rutherglen	Con.	Lab.
General Election 15 Oct 64			
21 Jan 65	Leyton	Lab.	Con.
24 Mar 65	Roxburgh Selkirk & Peebles	Con.	Lib.

Date	Constituency	General Election	By-election
General Election 31 *Mar* 66			
14 Jul 66	Carmarthen	Lab.	W. Nat.
9 Mar 67	Glasgow Pollok	Lab.	Con.
21 Sep 67	Walthamstow W.	Lab.	Con.
21 Sep 67	Cambridge	Lab.	Con.
2 Nov 67	Hamilton	Lab.	S. Nat.
2 Nov 67	Leicester S.W.	Lab.	Con.
28 Mar 68	Acton	Lab.	Con.
28 Mar 68	Meriden	Lab.	Con.
28 Mar 68	Dudley	Lab.	Con.
13 Jun 68	Oldham W.	Lab.	Con.
27 Jun 68	Nelson & Colne	Lab.	Con.

ᵃ Seat awarded to Cons. on petition.

M.P.s seeking Re-election

The following M.P.s on changing their party, or for other reasons, voluntarily resigned their seats to test public opinion in a by-election:

Date of by-election	M.P.	Constituency	Former label	New label	Whether Successful
18–19 Nov 02	J. Wason	Orkney & Shetland	L.U.	Ind. L.	Yes
6 Apr 03	J. Seely	I. of Wight	Con.	Lib.	Yes (unop.)
19 Aug 04	W. O'Brien	Cork City	Nat.	Nat.	Yes
31 Dec 06	D. Sheehan	Mid-Cork	Nat.	Ind. Nat.	Yes (unop.)
21 Deb 08	C. Dolan	N. Leitrim	Nat.	Ind. Nat.	No
4 May 09	T. Kincaid-Smith	Stratford-on-Avon	Lib.	Ind.	No
26 Nov 12	G. Lansbury	Bow and Bromley	Lab.	Ind.	No
18 Feb 14	W. O'Brien	Cork City	Ind. Nat.	Ind. Nat.	Yes (unop.)
21 Jul 14	R. Hazleton	N. Galway	Nat.	Nat.	Yes (unop.)
29 Nov 26	J. Kenworthy	Hull C.	Lib.	Lab.	Yes
28 Mar 27	L. Guest	Southwark N.	Lab.	Const.	No
31 Jul 29	Sir W. Jowitt	Preston	Lib.	Lab.	Yes
21 Dec 38	Dss of Atholl	Kinross & W. Perth	Con.	Ind.	No
26 May 55ᵃ	Sir R. Acland	Gravesend	Lab.	Ind.	No

ᵃ Date of General Election which overtook the by-election.

Some members have been compelled to seek re-election because they inadvertently held a government contract of appointment, or because they voted before taking the oath. This last happened in 1925.

Until the Re-election of Ministers Acts of 1919 and 1926 there were many cases of members having to seek re-election on appointment to ministerial office. In eight instances they were unsuccessful:

5 Apr 05	G. Loder	Brighton
24 Apr 08	W. Churchill	Manchester N.W.
20 Dec 11	A. Anderson	N. Ayrshire
5 Mar 12	Sir A. Haworth	Manchester S.
19 Feb 14 } 23 May 14 }	C. Masterman	{Bethnal Green S.W. Ipswich
3 Mar 21	Sir A. Griffith-Boscawen	Dudley
15 Jul 22	T. Lewis	Pontypridd

Electoral Administration

From 1900 to 1918 electoral arrangements were governed primarily by the *Representation of the People Act, 1867*, as modified by the *Ballot Act, 1872*, the *Corrupt Practices Act, 1883*, the *Franchise Act, 1884*, the *Registration Act, 1885*, and the *Redistribution of Seats Act, 1885*. The *Representation of the People Act, 1918*, the *Equal Franchise Act, 1928*, and the *Representation of the People Act, 1948* (consolidated in 1949), constitute the only major legislation in the century. There have been five major inquiries into electoral questions:

1908-10	Royal Commission on Electoral Systems
1917	Speaker's Conference on Electoral Reform
1930	Ullswater Conference on Electoral Reform
1934-44	Speaker's Conference on Electoral Reform
1965-68	Speaker's Conference on Electoral Law

The Franchise. From 1885 the United Kingdom had a system of fairly widespread male franchise, limited however by a year's residence qualification and some other restrictions. Voting in more than one constituency was permitted to owners of land, to occupiers of business premises, and to university graduates. The *Representation of the People Act, 1918* reduced the residence qualification to six months and enfranchised some categories of men who had not previously had the vote. It also enfranchised women over 30. In 1928 the *Equal Franchise Act* lowered the voting age for women to 21. In 1948 the *Representation of the People Act* abolished the business and university votes for parliamentary elections; it also abolished the six months' residence qualification. The question of votes at 18 came before Parliament in 1968.

Electorate

Year	Population	Population over 21	Electorate	Electorate as % of Adult Population[a]	
				Male	Total
1900	41,155,000	22,675,000	6,730,935	58	27
1910	44,915,000	26,134,000	7,694,741	58	28
1919	44,599,000	27,364,000	21,755,583	..	78
1929	46,679,000	31,711,000	28,850,870	..	90
1939	47,762,000	32,855,000	32,403,559	..	97
1949	50,363,000	35,042,000	34,269,770	..	98
1959	52,157,000	35,911,000	35,397,080	..	99
1965	54,606,000	36,837,000	36,128,387	..	98

[a] This percentage makes allowance for plural voting. In the period before 1914 this amounted to about 500,000. After 1918 the business vote reached its peak in 1929 at 370,000. The university electorate rose from 39,101 in 1900 to 217,363 in 1945.

Redistribution. The *Redistribution of Seats Act, 1885*, left the House of Commons with 670 members. The 1885 Act, while removing the worst anomalies, specifically rejected the principle that constituencies should be approximately equal in size. This principle was, however, substantially accepted in the *Representation of the People Act, 1918*, on the recommendation of the Speaker's Conference of 1917, although Wales, Scotland and Ireland were allowed to retain disproportionate numbers of seats. The 1918 Act increased the size of the House of Commons to 707 but this fell to 615 in 1922 on the creation of the Irish Free State. Population movements produced substantial anomalies in representation and the *Redistribution of Seats Act, 1944*, authorised the immediate subdivision of constituencies with more than 100,000 electors, which led to 25 new seats being created at the 1945 election and raised the size of Parliament to 640. It also provided for the establishment of Permanent Boundary Commissioners to report every three to seven years. The Boundary Commissioners' first recommendations were enacted in the *Representation of the People Act, 1948* (with the controversial addition by the Government of 17 extra seats as well as the abolition of the 12 University seats), and the 1950 Parliament had 625 members. The next reports of the Boundary Commissioners, given effect by resolutions of the House in December 1954 and January 1955, increased the number of constituencies to 630. The controversy caused by these changes led to the *Redistribution of Seats Act, 1958*, which modified the rules governing the Boundary Commissioners' decisions and asked them to report only every 10 to 15 years. The Boundary Commissioners started their revision in 1965; late in 1968 their recommendations had still to be brought before Parliament.

Election Expenses

Candidates' expenses were restricted by the *Corrupt Practices Act, 1883*, on a formula based on the number of electors. Candidates still had to bear the administrative costs of the election. The *Representation of the People Act, 1918*, removed from the candidates responsibility for the Returning Officers' fees and lowered the maximum limits on expenditure. This limit was further reduced by the *Representation of the People Act, 1948*. In the following table the effect of variations in the number of unopposed candidates should be borne in mind (unopposed candidates seldom spent as

Candidates' Election Expenses

Year	Total Expenditure £	Candidates	Average per Candidate £	Con.	Lib.	Lab.
1900	777,429	1,002	776	..	..	..
1906	1,166,858	1,273	917	..	..	..
1910 Jan	1,295,782	1,315	985	..	..	..
1910 Dec	978,312	1,191	821	..	..	..
1918	No pub. returns	1,625	..	..	..	..
1922	1,018,196	1,443	706	..	..	..
1923	982,340	1,446	679	845	789	464
1924	921,165	1,428	645	..	..	..
1929	1,213,507	1,730	701	905	782	452
1931	654,105	1,292	506	..	..	..
1935	722,093	1,348	536	777	495	365
1945	1,073,216	1,682	638	780	532	595
1950	1,170,124	1,868	626	777	459	694
1951	946,018	1,376	688	773	488	658
1955	904,677	1,409	642	692	423	611
1959	1,051,219	1,536	684	761	532	705
1964	1,229,205	1,757	699	790	579	751
1966	1,130,882	1,707	667	766	501	726

much as £200). It is notable how the modifications in the law have kept electioneering costs stable despite a fivefold depreciation in the value of money and a fivefold increase in the size of the electorate.

Successful Election Petitions

In the following constituencies election petitions have led to the original result being disallowed by the courts.[1]

Jul oo	Maidstone	Dec 10	Exeter
Jul oo	Monmouth	Dec 10	C. Hull
Jan o6	Worcester	Dec 10	N. Louth
Jan o6	Bomdni	Dec 10	West Ham N.
Jan 10	E. Dorset	Nov 22	Berwick on Tweed
Jan 10	E. Kerry	Dec 23	Oxford
Jan 10	The Hartlepools	May 55	Fermanagh & S. Tyrone
Dec 10	Cheltenham	Aug 55	Mid-Ulster
Dec 10	E. Cork	May 61	Bristol S.E.

[1] On 19 Oct 50 the House of Commons decided that the seat at West Belfast stood vacant because the successful candidate was ineligible as a minister of the Church of Ireland. On 20 Jul 55 the Mid-Ulster seat was declared vacant because the successful candidate was a felon: on 6 Feb 56 it was declared vacant again because the candidate in the ensuing by-election who was declared elected on petition was found to be ineligible because he held offices of profit under the Crown.

Women Candidates and M.P.s

	Conservative		Labour		Liberal		Other		Total	
	Cands.	M.P.s	Cands.	M.P.s	Cands.	M.P.s	Cands.	M.P.s	Cands.	M.P.s
1918	1	..	4	..	4	..	8	1	17	1
1922	5	1	10	..	16	1	2	..	33	2
1923	7	3	14	3	12	2	1	..	34	8
1924	12	3	22	1	6	..	1	..	41	4
1929	10	3	30	9	25	1	4	1	69	14
1931	16	13	36	..	6	1	4	1	62	15
1935	19	6	35	1	11	1	2	1	67	9
1945	14	1	45	21	20	1	8	1	87	24
1950	28	6	42	14	45	1	11	..	126	21
1951	29	6	39	11	11	..	..	..	74	17
1955	32	10	43	14	12	..	2	..	89	24
1959	28	12	36	13	16	..	1	..	81	25
1964	23	11	33	17	25	..	8	..	89	28
1966	21	7	30	19	20	..	9	..	80	26

SOURCE: up to 1951 J. F. S. Ross, *Elections and Electors* (1955).

Official returns, listing candidates' votes and expenses, have been published as Parliamentary Papers about one year after every General Election, except 1918: *1901 (352) lix, 145; 1906 (302) xcvi, 19; 1910 (259) lxxiii, 705; 1911 (272) lxii, 701; 1924 (2) xviii, 681; 1924-5 (151) xviii, 775; 1926 (1) xxii, 523; 1929-30 (114) xxiv, 755; 1931-2 (109) xx, 1; 1935-6 (150) xx, 217; 1945-6 (128) xix, 539; 1950 (146) xviii, 311; 1951-2 (210) xxi, 841; 1955 (141) xxxii, 913; 1959-60 (173) xxiv, 1031; 1964-5 (220); 1966-7 (162).*

More usable returns, identifying candidates by party and supplying supplementary data, are to be found in the following works :

Dod's Parliamentary Companion, Vacher's Parliamentary Companion, and *Whitaker's Almanack,* all issued annually (or more often).
Parliamentary Poll Book, by F. H. McCalmont (7th ed. 1910). This gives all returns from 1832 to 1910 (Jan).
Pall Mall Gazette House of Commons, issued in paperback form after each election from 1892 to 1910 (Dec).

M

The Times House of Commons, issued after the elections of January 1910 and December 1910 and 1918 and after every election since 1929.

The Constitutional Year Book, issued annually from 1885 to 1939. Up to 1920 it gives all results from 1885. Up to 1930 it gives the results for all post-1918 contests. Thereafter it records the latest four elections.

The Daily Telegraph Gallup Analysis of Election '66 provides an exhaustive statistical comparison of the 1964 and 1966 elections.

From 1945, the results of each election have been analysed in statistical appendices to the Nuffield College series of studies, *The British General Election of 1945* (1947), by R. B. McCallum and Alison Readman, *The British General Election of 1950* (1951), by H. G. Nicholas, *The British General Election of 1951* (1952), by D. E. Butler, *The British General Election of 1955* (1955), by D. E. Butler, *The British General Election of 1959* (1960), by D. E. Butler and Richard Rose, *The British General Election of 1964* (1965), by D. E. Butler and Anthony King, *The British General Election of 1966* (1966) by D. E. Butler and Anthony King.

Further data is to be found in *The Electoral System in Britain since 1918*, by D. E. Butler (2nd ed. 1963), *Parliamentary Representation*, by J. F. S. Ross (2nd ed. 1948) and *Elections and Electors*, by J. F. S. Ross (1955); *Elections in Britain*, by R. Leonard (1968), *Parliamentary Election Statistics 1918–1968*, by F. W. S. Craig (1968), *The British Voter (1885–1966)*, by M. Kinnear (1968); and *Social Geography of British Elections 1885–1910*, by H. Pelling (1967). See also the *Report of the Royal Commission on Electoral Systems* (*Cd. 5163/1910*); evidence *Cd. 5352/1910*.

The problems of electoral administration are also dealt with in the reports of the Speaker's Conferences on Electoral Reform of 1917, 1944, 1966, and the Ullswater Conference of 1930 (*Cd. 8463/1917*; *Cmd. 3636/1930*; *Cmd. 6534/1944*; and *Cmd. 6543/1944*, *Cmnd. 2917*, and *2932/1966*), *Cmnd. 3202* and *3275/1967* and *Cmnd. 3550/1968*, and in the reports of the Boundary Commissioners (*Cmd. 7260, 7274, 7270, 7231 of 1947*, and *Cmd. 9311–4 of 1954*). See also H. L. Morris, *Parliamentary Franchise Reform in England from 1885 to 1918* (New York 1921), and *The Redistribution of Seats*, by D. E. Butler, *Public Administration*, Summer 1955, pp. 125–47.

Public Opinion Polls
Gallup Poll

The British Institute of Public Opinion was established in 1937. Its name was changed in 1952 to Social Surveys (Gallup Poll) Ltd. Its poll findings were published exclusively in the *News Chronicle* until October 1960. Since 1961 its findings have been published regularly in the *Daily Telegraph* and the *Sunday Telegraph*. As the years advanced, its questions on politics became increasingly systematic and detailed. Some of its early findings are collected in *Public Opinion, 1935–1946*, edited by H. Cantril (1951). Others may be found in the *News Chronicle*, in occasional pamphlets, in the 1959 *Gallup Election Handbook*, in the 1966 *Gallup Election Handbook*, and in the monthly *Gallup Political Index* available since 1960 from Social Surveys (Gallup Poll) Ltd. (211 Regent Street, London W.1).

The following tables show in summary form the answers to the question 'If there were a General Election tomorrow, how would you vote?'

Voting Intention (Gallup Poll)

	Government %	Opposition %	Don't Know %
1939 Feb	50	44	6
1939 Dec	54	30	16
1940 Feb	51	27	22

	Con. %	Lab. %	Lib. %	Other %	Don't Know %	Con. lead over Lab. %
1943 Jun	31	38	9	8	14	− 7
Jul	27	39	9	9	16	− 12
Dec	27	40	10	9	14	− 13
1944 Feb	23	37	10	14	16	− 14
1945 Feb	24	42	11	11	12	− 18
Jun	32	45	15	7	. .	− 13
1946 Jan	30	49	10	4	7	− 19
May	37	40	12	3	8	− 3
1947 Jan	38	41	11	2	8	− 3
Mar	38	38	9	2	13	0
Jun	38	38	11	2	11	0
Jul	38	38	11	2	11	0
Aug	37	34	9	3	17	3
Sep	39	35	10	4	12	4
Nov	44	33	8	2	13	11
1948 Jan	38	37	9	1	15	1
Feb	38	35	7	3	17	3
Mar	38	36	7	2	17	2
Apr	36	35	9	5	15	1
May	37	34	9	2	18	3
Jul	42	35	8	3	12	7
Aug	40	34	7	2	17	6
Sep	38	33	8	1	20	5
Oct	38	34	8	2	18	4
Nov	38	36	7	2	17	2

Voting Intention (Gallup Poll)

		Con. %	Lab. %	Lib. %	Other %	Don't Know %	Con. lead over Lab. %
1949	Jan	38	35	11	2	14	3
	Feb	38	37	8	2	15	1
	Mar	36	37	11	2	14	−1
	Apr	36	37	11	1	15	−1
	May	39	35	9	2	15	4
	Jun	37	34	10	1	18	3
	Jul	38	36	10	2	14	2
	Aug	38	36	10	2	14	2
	Sep	40	34	9	2	15	6
	Oct	43	34	8	1	14	9
	Nov	40	32	11	1	16	8
	—						
1950	Jan	38	38	10	2	12	0
	Feb	40	41	10	1	8	−1
	Mar	41	43	6	1	9	−2
	—						
	May	40	42	8	1	9	−2
	Jun	39	42	8	2	9	−3
	Jul	38	39	10	3	10	−1
	Aug	40	42	8	1	9	−2
	Sep	38	41	10	2	9	−3
	Oct	40	42	8	0	10	−2
	—						
	Dec	41	39	9	1	10	2
1951	Jan	44	33	9	1	13	11
	Feb	46	34	8	2	10	12
	Mar	44	33	8	1	14	11
	Apr	45	34	7	2	12	11
	May	42	34	9	2	13	8
	Jun	42	36	9	1	12	6
	Jul	43	34	9	1	13	9
	Aug	44	34	10	1	11	10
	Sep	47	36	5	1	11	11
	Oct	45	39	5	0	11	6
	—						
	Dec	43	41	6	1	9	2
1952	Jan	40	43	5	2	10	−3
	Feb	35	40	10	1	14	−5
	Mar	38	43	9	1	9	−5
	—						
	May	40	44	6	1	9	−4
	Jun	38	46	9	1	6	−8
	Jul	36	45	8	2	9	−9
	—						
	Sep	37	44	8	2	9	−7
	Oct	37	43	8	1	11	−6
	Nov	38	40	8	1	13	−2
	Dec	39	40	9	1	11	−1
1953	Jan	38	41	9	1	11	−3
	Feb	38	41	9	1	11	−3
	Mar	41	39	7	1	12	2
	Apr	41	39	7	0	13	2
	May	41	39	7	1	12	2
	Jun	41	41	6	1	11	0
	—						
	Aug	39	40	7	1	13	−1
	Sep	39	42	6	1	12	−3
	Oct	39	42	7	1	11	−3
	—						
	Dec	39	41	6	1	13	−2

Voting Intention (Gallup Poll)

		Con. %	Lab. %	Lib. %	Other %	Don't Know %	Con. lead over Lab. %
1954	Jan	39	40	6	I	14	− I
	Feb	39	40	7	I	13	− I
	Mar	41	40	6	I	12	I
	Apr	40	40	6	I	13	0
	May	40	41	6	I	12	− I
	Jun	39	40	7	I	13	− I
	Aug	38	43	7	I	11	− 5
	Sep	38	43	7	I	11	− 5
	Oct	38	38	7	I	16	0
	Nov	39	40	5	I	15	− I
	Dec	42	43	2	0	13	− I
1955	Jan	40	39	6	I	14	I
	Feb	40	39	7	I	13	I
	Mar	40	39	7	I	13	I
	Apr	41	40	4	I	14	I
	May	43	40	2	I	14	3
	Jun	42	39	2	I	16	3
	Jul	42	38	8	I	11	4
	Aug	38	41	6	I	14	− 3
	Sep	43	40	6	I	10	3
	Oct	40	39	7	I	13	I
	Nov	39	40	8	I	12	− I
	Dec	40	41	6	I	12	− I
1956	Jan	40	41	6	I	12	− I
	Feb	39	40	8	I	12	− I
	Mar	36	38	6	I	19	− 2
	Apr	36	40	6	I	17	− 4
	May	37	40	7	I	15	− 3
	Jul	36	42	7	I	14	− 6
	Aug	36	42	5	I	16	− 6
	Sep	40	42	I	I	16	− 2
	Oct	36	40	8	I	15	− 4
	Nov	38	38	7	0	17	0
	Dec	38	39	7	I	15	− I
1957	Jan	39	44	6	I	10	− 5
	Feb	34	39	7	I	19	− 5
	Mar	31	41	6	I	21	− 10
	Apr	36	43	5	I	15	− 7
	May	35	42	6	I	16	− 7
	Jul	35	42	6	I	16	− 7
	Aug	36	42	4	I	17	− 6
	Sep	26	39	10	0	25	− 13
	Oct	31	41	11	I	16	− 10
	Nov	31	40	9	I	19	− 9
	Dec	35	40	8	I	16	− 5
1958	Jan	33	39	10	I	17	− 6
	Feb	29	36	15	I	19	− 7
	Apr	31	38	12	I	18	− 7
	May	28	38	15	0	19	− 10
	Jun	34	37	13	I	15	− 3
	Aug	36	36	13	I	14	0
	Sep	37	35	11	0	17	2
	Oct	38	35	10	I	16	3
	Nov	39	36	9	I	15	3
	Dec	40	36	8	I	15	4

Voting Intention (Gallup Poll)

		Con. %	Lab. %	Lib. %	Other %	Don't Know %	Con. lead over Lab. %
1959	Jan	37	36½	7	½	19	½
	Feb	33½	36½	6½	1	22½	−3
	Mar	35½	36½	5	1	22	−1
	Apr	38	38	8½	1½	14	0
	May	38½	37½	8½	1	14½	1
	Jun	38½	37	9½	½	14½	1½
	Jul	38½	35	10½	½	15½	3½
	Aug	41	36	8½	1	13½	5
	Sep	41½	36	8	½	14	5½
	Oct	40½	39	4	½	16	1½
	Nov	43	39	6	1	11	4
	Dec	40½	37½	6	1	15	3
1960	Jan	39	35	8	1	17	4
	Feb	39½	36½	7½	½	16	3
	Mar	39	35	8½	½	17	4
	Apr	37½	35½	9½	½	17	2
	May	38½	36	9	1	15½	2½
	Jun	39	36½	9	1	14½	2½
	Jul	39	35	8	1	17	4
	Aug	40	35	8	½	16½	5
	Sep	40	34	9	1	16	6
	Oct	40½	30	10	½	19	10½
	Nov	39½	35	11½	0	14	4½
	Dec	40½	32	11½	1	15	8½
1961	Jan	36½	33½	10	1	19	3
	Feb	35½	34½	10½	1	18½	1
	Mar	38½	35	13½	1	12	3½
	Apr	35½	33	12½	1	18	2½
	May	36½	33	11½	1	18	3½
	Jun	36½	33½	12½	1	16½	3
	Jul	36	34	11½	½	18	2
	Aug	32	36	14	1	17	−4
	Sep	33½	37	10	½	19	−3½
	Oct	37	37	10½	1	14½	0
	Nov	34	34½	14½	1	16	−½
	Dec	30½	34½	14	1	20	−4
1962	Jan	34½	34½	12	½	18½	0
	Feb	33	35	14	0	18	−2
	Mar	32½	36	13	½	18	−3½
	Apr	29	35	22	½	13½	−6
	May	28½	33	21	½	17	−4½
	Jun	30½	33½	21½	½	14	−3
	Jul	31	35	19	1	14	−4
	Aug	29	34	16	1	20	−5
	Sep	31½	38½	15	1	14	−7
	Oct	30½	35	15	1	18½	−4½
	Nov	30½	37	14	½	18	−6½
	Dec	30½	38	13	1	17½	−7½
1963	Jan	28½	40	12½	1½	17½	−11½
	Feb	28	40½	14	1	16½	−12½
	Mar	28	43½	12	½	16	−15½
	Apr	28	42	12	½	17½	−14
	May	29½	38½	12½	1	18½	−9
	Jun	29	42½	12	½	16	−13½
	Jul	26½	42	10½	1	20	−15½
	Aug	28½	41	11	1	18½	−12½
	Sep	28	40½	12	1	18½	−12½
	Oct	29	40	10	½	20½	−11
	Nov	30½	41½	10	½	17½	−11
	Dec	31	39½	9	½	20	−8½

Voting Intention (Gallup Poll)

	Con. %	Lab. %	Lib. %	Other %	Don't Know %	Con. lead over Lab. %
1964 Jan	32	38	9	½	20½	−6
Feb	34	39½	9	½	17	−5½
Mar	32	41	9	½	17½	−9
Apr	32½	42	8	½	17	−9½
May	33	44½	8	0	14½	−11½
Jun	35	43½	6½	½	14½	−8½
Jul	35½	43	7½	0	14	−7½
Aug	36	42	6	0	16	−6
Sep	38	39½	6½	0	15½	−1½
Oct	38	40½	8	½	13	−2½
Nov	33	43½	10	0	13	−10½
Dec	34½	43½	8	0	13½	−9
1965 Jan	36½	40	8	1	14½	−3½
Feb	41	39	6½	0	13½	2
Mar	37	38½	7	1	16½	−1½
Apr	33½	40	9	0	17	−6½
May	36½	35	9	½	19	1½
Jun	40	35	7	1	17	5
Jul	39	36½	5½	0	18½	2½
Aug	42	33	6	1	18	9
Sep	36½	42½	6½	1	13½	−6
Oct	37	40½	7	0	15	−3½
Nov	36	41½	6½	1	15	−5½
Dec	34	40½	8	1	16½	−6½
1966 Jan	36½	40½	7	1	15	−4
Feb	36	40½	5	0	18½	−4½
Mar	34	43½	7	½	15	−9½
Apr						
May	32	47½	8	1	11½	−15½
Jun	34½	45½	6	1	13	−11
Jul	35½	42	7	1	14½	−6½
Aug	37½	37	8	1	16½	½
Sep	36	38	7½	1	17½	−2
Oct	37	38	8	1	16	−1
Nov	37½	35	9	1	17½	2½
Dec	37	40½	8½	1½	12½	−3½
1967 Jan	36	38½	8½	1	16	−2½
Feb	32	43	10½	1	13½	−11
Mar	34½	35	9	2½	19	−½
Apr	40	34	8	2	16	6
May	40	33½	10	1	15½	6½
Jun	39	34	7	1½	18½	5
Jul	37	36½	9½	1½	15½	½
Aug	36	32½	9	2	20½	3½
Sep	38	35	8	2	17	3
Oct	38½	33½	9	2½	16½	5
Nov	39	33	8½	4	15½	6
Dec	42		9	5	18	16
1968 Jan	37	31½	8½	4	19	5½
Feb	42½	23	8½	4	22	19½
Mar	38	24	8½	2½	27	18
Apr	44½	23	8	2½	22	21½
May	45	21	6½	3½	24	24
Jun	40½	21	10	4	19½	19½
Jul	42	22½	10	6	19½	19½
Aug	38	26	7	3½	25½	12
Sep	39	29	8½	3½	20	10
Oct	39½	32½	6½	3½	18	7
Nov	41½	26	10½	2	20	15½
Dec	43	23	7	4	23	20

National Opinion Polls

National Opinion Polls were established in 1957 as an affiliate of Associated Newspapers Ltd. Political findings were published in the *Daily Mail* intermittently until 1961 and regularly thereafter. In October 1963 N.O.P. switched from quota to random sampling and used larger samples (usually between 2,000 and 3,000). The monthly average of their findings in answer to the question 'How would you vote if there were a general election tomorrow?' are set out below.

Voting Intention (N.O.P.)

		Con. %	Lab. %	Lib. %	Other %	Un-decided %	Con. lead over Lab. %
1963	Oct	40·2	47·5	10·0	0·3	2·0	−7·3
	Nov	38·8	46·2	10·3	0·6	4·1	−7·4
	Dec	39·3	47·6	8·8	0·3	4·0	−8·3
1964	Jan	40·1	46·7	9·3	0·3	3·6	−6·6
	Feb	39·5	48·2	9·3	0·1	2·9	−8·7
	Mar[a]	40·6	47·9	8·2	0·4	2·9	−7·3
	Apr[a]	38·4	49·8	8·2	0·2	3·4	−11·4
	May[a]	40·2	48·0	8·1	0·4	3·3	−7·8
	June[a]	40·8	48·1	7·0	0·2	3·9	−7·3
	July[a]	43·0	46·8	7·1	0·2	2·9	−3·8
	Aug[a]	45·7	45·6	5·5	0·3	2·9	+0·1
	Sep[a]	45·4	43·8	7·9	0·3	2·6	+1·6
	Oct[a] (pre-election)	44·1	44·8	8·1	0·4	2·6	−0·7
	Oct (post-election)	34·7	48·1	11·4	0·6	5·2	−13·4
	Nov [a]	37·2	49·2	10·1	0·3	3·2	−12·0
	Dec	37·9	47·5	11·9	0·3	2·4	−9·6
1965	Jan	39·3	47·7	10·2	0·5	2·3	−8·4
	Feb	42·6	47·2	8·0	0·2	2·0	−4·6
	Mar	40·4	49·4	8·3	0·3	1·6	−9·0
	Apr[a]	38·8	46·1	11·8	0·4	2·9	−7·3
	May	41·0	45·5	10·4	0·6	2·5	−4·5
	Jun	40·5	45·8	10·1	1·0	2·6	−4·3
	Jul[a]	42·0	45·3	9·7	0·5	2·5	−3·3
	Aug	45·5	41·8	9·2	0·5	3·0	+3·7
	Sep	42·0	45·3	10·2	0·3	2·2	−3·3
	Oct[a]	38·9	49·3	7·9	0·6	3·3	−10·4
	Nov	36·4	54·9	6·4	0·3	2·0	−18·5
	Dec[a]	37·9	51·6	7·7	0·2	2·6	−13·7
1966	Jan	37·8	51·4	7·0	0·2	3·6	−13·6
	Feb[a]	37·9	52·1	6·1	0·2	3·7	−14·2
	Mar[a]	38·2	51·0	7·0	0·4	3·4	−12·8
	Apr	35·2	54·4	8·6	0·7	1·1	−19·2
	May	33·5	54·3	9·4	1·1	1·7	−21·8
	Jun	36·4	53·9	6·6	0·8	2·3	−17·5
	Jul	35·7	52·0	8·8	0·9	2·6	−16·3
	Aug	37·8	46·9	11·1	1·7	2·5	−9·1
	Sep	38·1	47·5	10·8	1·4	2·2	−9·4
	Oct	35·0	49·9	11·1	1·3	2·7	−14·9
	Nov	39·4	45·1	10·8	1·8	2·9	−5·7
	Dec	41·3	45·6	8·4	1·8	2·9	−4·3
1967	Jan[a]	38·9	46·5	11·5	1·4	1·7	−7·6
	Feb[a]	39·9	45·4	11·0	1·9	1·8	−5·5
	Mar	41·2	46·6	9·0	1·5	1·7	−5·4
	Apr[a]	41·7	46·0	9·0	1·6	1·7	−4·3
	May	44·9	42·6	8·3	2·6	1·6	+2·3
	Jun	41·7	46·1	8·4	1·8	2·0	−4·4
	Jul	42·4	43·8	9·8	2·0	2·0	−1·4
	Aug	44·6	40·2	9·8	2·6	2·8	+4·4
	Sep	45·3	39·5	10·1	1·9	3·2	+5·8
	Oct	41·8	41·8	11·2	2·4	2·8	0·0
	Nov	44·9	37·9	11·7	3·3	2·2	+7·0
	Dec	44·5	37·0	12·2	4·1	2·2	+7·5

ᵃ % The average figure when two or more surveys were carried out in a given month.

Voting Intention (N.O.P.)

	Con. %	Lab. %	Lib. %	Other %	Un-decided %	Con. lead over Lab. %
1968 Jan	52·2	33·9	9·6	1·7	2·6	+18·3
Feb	49·4	32·7	11·9	3·3	2·7	+16·7
Mar	48·6	34·9	10·1	3·7	2·7	+13·7
Apr	53·7	31·1	8·7	3·3	3·2	+22·6
May	50·8	31·1	11·1	4·2	2·8	+19·7
Jun	51·4	32·4	9·0	4·6	2·6	+19·0
Jul	49·0	34·7	10·0	3·7	2·6	+14·3
Aug	46·2	35·7	11·3	3·4	3·4	+10·5
Sep	47·3	37·4	9·6	3·4	2·3	+9·9
Oct	46·6	40·0	8·7	2·7	2·0	+6·6
Nov	49·2	36·8	8·4	2·9	2·7	+12·4
Dec	53·6	32·4	8·1	3·0	2·9	+21·2

Opinion Poll Accuracy in General Election Forecasts

In addition to the Gallup Poll and N.O.P. two other polls have at times received wide newspaper coverage — the *Daily Express* Poll of Public Opinion and Research Services Ltd. Here is a comparison of the last published figures of all Opinion Polls compared with general election results (Great Britain only, minor parties excluded).

	Actual %	Gallup	*Daily Express*	Research Services	N.O.P.
1945					
Con	39·5	+1·5			
Lab	49·0	−2·0			
Lib	9·2	+1·3			
1950					
Con	43·1	+0·4	+1·4		
Lab	46·8	−1·8	−2·8		
Lib	9·3	+1·2	+1·7		
1951					
Con	47·8	+1·7	+2·2	+2·2	
Lab	49·3	−2·3	−3·3	−6·3	
Lib	2·6	+0·4	+0·9	(+4·1)[a]	
1955					
Con	49·3	+1·7	+1·9		
Lab	47·3	+0·2	−0·1		
Lib	2·8	−1·3	−0·6		
1959					
Con	48·8	−0·3	+0·3		−0·8
Lab	44·6	+1·9	+0·8		−0·5
Lib	6·1	−1·6	−1·1		(+2·4)[a]
1964					
Con	42·9	+1·6	+1·6	+2·1	+1·4
Lab	44·8	+1·2	−1·1	+1·2	+2·6
Lib	11·4	−2·9	−0·3	−2·4	−3·5
1966					
Con	41·4	−1·4	−4·0	+0·2	+0·2
Lab	48·7	+2·3	+5·9	+1·0	+1·9
Lib	8·6	−0·6	−0·9	−0·3	−1·2

[a] Error in prediction of Liberal and Other vote combined.

V

POLITICAL PLACE-NAMES

At one time or another in the twentieth century the following place-names were sufficiently famous to be alluded to without further explanation. Any such list must necessarily be very selective. No foreign names are included here — even though that means omitting Agadir, Chanak, Munich and Suez. No venues of party conferences are included, even though that means omitting Scarborough (Labour, 1960) and Blackpool (Conservative, 1963). No constituency names are included as such, even though that means omitting some, like Bewdley or Ebbw Vale, which are indelibly associated with individuals and others where sensational elections had a lasting national impact, like Colne Valley (1907), St George's Westminster (1931), East Fulham (1933), Orpington (1962) and Smethwick (1964).

Abbey House, Victoria St., S.W.1. Conservative Party Headquarters 1946–58.

Abingdon St., S.W.1. Site of Liberal Party Headquarters 1910–34.

Aldermaston, Berkshire. Site of Atomic Weapons Research Establishment. Starting- or finishing-point of the Campaign for Nuclear Disarmament's Easter Marches 1958–63. 1967– .

Ashridge, Herts. Site of Conservative Party College, 1929–39.

Astley Hall. Worcestershire home of S. (Earl) Baldwin 1902–47.

Bachelor's Walk, Dublin. Scene (26 Jul 1914) of disturbance in which soldiers killed three rioters.

Balmoral Castle, Aberdeenshire. Summer home of the Sovereign since 1852.

Birch Grove, Sussex. Home of H. Macmillan 1906– .

Blenheim Palace, Oxfordshire. Home of Dukes of Marlborough. Birthplace of (Sir) W. Churchill.

Bowood, Wiltshire. Home of Ms of Lansdowne.

Broadstairs, Kent. Birthplace and home of Edward Heath.

Carlton Club. London meeting place of Conservatives. Scene (19 Oct 1922) of gathering which brought down the Lloyd George Coalition.

Carmelite House, E.C.4. Headquarters of the *Daily Mail* and *Evening News*.

Chartwell, Kent. Home of (Sir) W. Churchill 1923–65.

Chatsworth, Derbyshire. Home of Ds of Devonshire.

Chequers, Buckinghamshire. Country house given to the nation by Lord Lee of Fareham in 1917 and used as country residence for Prime Ministers from 1921.

Cherry Cottage, Buckinghamshire. Home of C. (Earl) Attlee 1951–61.

Cherkley Court, Surrey. Home of Ld Beaverbrook 1916–64.

Church House, S.W.1. Meeting place of the Church Assembly since 1920; and of both Houses of Parliament, Nov–Dec 1940, May–Jun 1941, Jun–Aug 1944. Scene of United Nations preparatory meeting 1945 and of many Conservative gatherings.

Churt, Surrey. Home of D. Lloyd George (E) 1921–45.

Cliveden, Buckinghamshire. Home of 2nd and 3rd Vt Astor. Alleged centre of 'Cliveden Set' in 1930's. Scene (1962) of events in the Profumo affair.

Congress House, Gt. Russell St., W.C.1. Headquarters of Trades Union Congress 1960– .

Criccieth, Caernarvonshire. Welsh home of D. Lloyd George (E) 1880–1945.

Crichel Down, Dorset. The refusal to derequisition some land here led, ultimately, to the resignation of the Minister of Agriculture in Jul 1954.

Cross St., Manchester. Headquarters of the *(Manchester) Guardian*.

Curragh, The, Co. Kildare. Military camp; scene of 'mutiny' 20 Mar 1914.

Dalmeny, Midlothian. Home of Es of Rosebery.

Dorneywood, Buckinghamshire. Country house bequeathed to the nation in 1954 by Ld Courtauld-Thomson as an official residence for any Minister designated by the Prime Minister.

Downing St., S.W.1. No. 10 is the Prime Minister's official residence. No. 11 is the official residence of the Chancellor of the Exchequer. No. 12 houses the offices of the Government Whips.

Dublin Castle. Offices of the Irish Administration until 1922.

Eccleston Square, S.W.1. Site of Headquarters of the Labour Party and of the Trades Union Congress 1918–29.

Euston Lodge, Phoenix Park, Dublin. Residence of the Ld-Lieutenant of Ireland.

Falloden, Northumberland. Home of Sir E. (Vt) Grey 1862–1933.

Fleet St., E.C.4 Location of *Daily Telegraph* and *Daily Express*. Generic name for the London press.

Fort Belvedere, Berkshire. Country home of Edward VIII 1930–36.

Great George St., S.W.1. Site of the Treasury and, since 1964, of the Department of Economic Affairs.

Hampstead. London suburb which, during H. Gaitskell's leadership of the Labour Party, provided a generic name for the set of intellectuals associated with him.

Hatfield House, Hertfordshire. Home of Ms of Salisbury.

Highbury, Birmingham. Home of J. Chamberlain 1868–1914.

Hirsel, The, Berwickshire. Home of Es of Home.

Holy Loch, Dumbartonshire. Site of U.S. atomic submarine base 1962– .

Howth, Co. Dublin. Scene of gun-running 26 Jul 1914.

Invergordon, Ross and Cromarty. Site of naval protest in Sep 1931 over proposed pay reductions.

Jarrow, Durham. Shipbuilding town where unemployment reached 73% in 1935. Start of Jarrow to London protest march Oct 1936.

Kilmainham Jail, Dublin. Scene of execution of the leaders of the 1916 rising.

King St., W.C.2. Site of Communist Party Headquarters since early 1920's.

Knowsley, Lancashire. Home of Es of Derby.

Larne, Co. Antrim. Scene of gun-running 24 Apr 1914.

Limehouse, E.14. Scene of speech by D. Lloyd George 30 Jul 1909 ; became generic name for political vituperation.

Londonderry House, W.1. London home of Ms of Londonderry until 1946.

Lossiemouth, Morayshire. Home of R. MacDonald, 1866–1937.

Notting Hill, W.11. Scene of racial disturbances in Aug 1958.

Old Queen St., S.W.1 Site of Conservative Party Headquarters 1941–46. Site of Conservative Research Department 1930– .

Olympia, W.14. Exhibition Hall; scene (7 Jun 1934) of Mosley meeting which provoked violence.

Palace Chambers, S.W.1. Headquarters of Conservative Party 1922–41.

Pembroke Lodge, W.8. Home of A. Bonar Law 1909–16.

Poplar. London borough whose Poor Law Guardians (including G. Lansbury) were imprisoned in 1921 for paying more than national rates of relief.

Portland Place, W.1. Headquarters of the British Broadcasting Corporation 1932– .

Printing House Square, E.C.4. Headquarters of *The Times* since 1785.

Relugas, Morayshire. Fishing lodge of Sir E. Grey ; scene of 'Relugas Compact' with H. Asquith and R. Haldane Sep 1905.

St. James Palace, W.1. Royal Palace. Foreign Ambassadors continue to be accredited to the Court of St. James.

St. Stephen's Chambers, S.W.1. Site of Conservative Headquarters 1900–18.

Sanctuary Buildings, S.W.1. Site of Conservative Party Headquarters 1918–22.

Sandringham House, Norfolk. Royal residence since 1861.

Scapa Flow, Orkney. Naval anchorage where German Fleet was scuttled 21 Jun 1919. Scene of trouble at the time of the Invergordon 'mutiny' Sep 1931.

Scilly Isles, Cornwall. Location of H. Wilson's country cottage 1959– .

Shanklin, Isle of Wight. Scene (Feb 1949) of meeting of Labour Party leaders.

Sidney St., E.1.   Scene of police siege of anarchists 3 Jan 1911.

Smith Square, S.W.1.   Location of the Labour Party Headquarters (Transport House) since 1928; of the Conservative Party Headquarters since 1958; and of the Liberal Party Headquarters since 1965–68.

Stormont, Belfast.   Site of Parliament of Northern Ireland.

Swinton, Yorkshire.   Home of E of Swinton.   Conservative Party College since 1948.

Taff Vale, Glamorgan.   In 1901 the Taff Vale Railway Company successfully sued a trade union for loss due to a strike.

Threadneedle St., E.C.2.   Site of the Bank of England.

Tonypandy.   Scene of violent miners' strike to which W. Churchill sent troops in Nov 1910.

Transport House, S.W.1.   Headquarters of the Transport and General Workers' Union and of the Labour Party since 1928 and of the Trades Union Congress 1928–60.

Westbourne, Birmingham.   Home of N. Chamberlain 1911–40.

Wharf, The, Sutton Courtenay, Berkshire.   Home of H. Asquith 1912–28.

Whittingehame, East Lothian.   Home of A. Balfour 1848–1930.

Windsor Castle, Berkshire.   Official royal residence since 11th century.

Wolverhampton.   Town represented by E. Powell 1950–.   Scene (20 Apr 68) of his speech attacking immigration policy.

VI

CIVIL SERVICE

Heads of Departments and Public Offices [1]

Admiralty

1884	Sir E. MacGregor
1907	Sir I. Thomas
1911	Sir G. Greene
1917	Sir O. Murray
1936	Sir R. Carter
1940	Sir H. Markham
1947	(Sir) J. Lang
1961	Sir C. Jarrett
1964	(see *Defence*)

Agriculture & Fisheries

1892	(Sir) T. Elliott
1913	Sir S. Olivier
1917	(Sir) D. Hall
1920	Sir F. Floud
1927	Sir C. Thomas
1936	(Sir) D. Fergusson
1945	Sir D. Vandepeer
1952	Sir A. Hitchman

(Agriculture, Fisheries & Food)

1955	Sir A. Hitchman
1959	Sir J. Winnifrith
1968	Sir B. Engholm

Air

1917	Sir A. Robinson
1920	(Sir) W. Nicholson
1931	(Sir) C. Bullock
1936	Sir D. Banks
1939	Sir A. Street
1945	Sir W. Brown
1947	Sir J. Barnes
1955	Sir M. Dean
1963	(Sir) M. Flett
1964	(see *Defence*)

Aircraft Production (Director-General)

1940	Sir A. Rowlands
1943	Sir H. Scott
1945 –1945	} Sir F. Tribe

Aviation

(see *Transport & Civil Aviation*)

1959	Sir W. Strath
1960	(Sir) H. Hardman
1963	Sir R. Way

1966	Sir R. Clarke
1966 –1967	} Sir R. Melville

Burma

(see *India & Burma*)

Secretary to the Cabinet

1916	Sir M. Hankey
1938	Sir E. Bridges
1947	Sir N. Brook
1963	Sir B. Trend

Civil Aviation (Director-General)

1941	Sir W. Hildred
1946	Sir H. Self
1947	Sir A. Overton
1953	(see *Transport & Civil Aviation*)

Civil Service Commission (First Commissioner)

1892	W. Courthope
1907	Ld F. Hervey
1910	(Sir) S. Leathers
1928	(Sir) R. Meiklejohn
1939	(Sir) P. Waterfield
1951	P. Sinker
1954	(Sir) L. Helsby
1959	Sir G. Mallaby
1965	Sir G. Abell
1968	J. Hunt

Civil Service Department

1968	Sir W. Armstrong

Colonial Office

1897	(Sir) E. Wingfield
1900	(Sir) M. Ommaney
1907	Sir F. Hopwood
1911	Sir J. Anderson
1916	Sir G. Fiddes
1921	Sir J. Masterton-Smith
1925	Sir S. Wilson
1933	Sir J. Maffey
1937	Sir C. Parkinson
1940	Sir G. Gater
1940	Sir C. Parkinson
1942	Sir G. Gater
1947	Sir T. Lloyd
1956	Sir J. Macpherson
1959	Sir H. Poynton
1966	(see *Commonwealth Office*)

Commonwealth Relations Office

1947	{ Sir E. Machtig { Sir A. Carter
1949	Sir P. Liesching
1955	Sir G. Laithwaite
1959	Sir A. Clutterbuck
1962 –1966	} Sir S. Garner

(Commonwealth Affairs)

1966	Sir S. Garner
1968	Sir M. James

Customs Establishment (Chairman)

1900	(Sir) G. Ryder
1903	(Sir) T. Pittar

(Board of Customs and Excise)

1909	(Sir) L. Guillemard
1919	Sir H. Hamilton
1927	Sir F. Floud
1930	J. Grigg
1930	(Sir) E. Forber
1934	Sir E. Murray
1941	Sir W. Eady
1942	Sir A. Carter
1947	Sir W. Croft
1955	Sir J. Crombie
1963	Sir J. Anderson
1965	Sir W. Morton

Defence

1947	Sir H. Wilson Smith
1948	Sir H. Parker
1956	Sir R. Powell
1960	Sir E. Playfair
1961	Sir R. Scott
1964	Sir H. Hardman
1966	Sir James Dunnett

Defence (R.N.)

1966	(Sir) Michael Cary

Defence (Army)

1966	(Sir) A. Drew

Defence (R.A.F.)

1964	(Sir) M. Flett

[1] Except where stated otherwise, all these had the title of Permanent Secretary or Permanent Under-Secretary.

Dominions Office

1925	Sir C. Davies
1930	Sir E. Harding
1940	Sir C. Parkinson
1940 -1947 }	Sir E. Machtig

Economic Affairs

1964	Sir E. Roll
1966	(Sir) D. Allen
1968	Sir W. Nield

Economic Warfare (Director-General)

1939	Sir F. Leith-Ross
1940 {	Sir F. Leith-Ross / E of Drogheda
1942 -1945 }	E of Drogheda

Education (and Science)

1900	Sir G. Kekewich
1903	Sir R. Morant
1911	Sir A. Selby-Bigge
1925	Sir A. Symonds
1931	Sir H. Pelham
1937	(Sir) M. Holmes
1945	Sir J. Maud
1952	(Sir) G. Flemming
1959	Dame M. Smieton
1967	Sir H. Andrew

Exchequer and Audit Department (Comptroller and Auditor-General) [1]

1896	R. Mills
1900	D. Richmond
1904	(Sir) J. Kempe
1911	(Sir) H. Gibson
1921	Sir M. Ramsay
1931	(Sir) G. Upcott
1946	Sir F. Tribe
1958	Sir E. Compton
1966	Sir B. Fraser

Food (Director-General)

1918	Sir C. Fielding
1919 -1921 }	F. Coller
1939	Sir H. French
1945	Sir F. Tribe
1946	Sir P. Liesching
1949	(Sir) F. Lee
1951	Sir H. Hancock
1955	(see *Agriculture, Fisheries & Food*)

Foreign Office

1894	Sir T. Sanderson (Ld)
1906	Sir C. Hardinge (Ld)
1910	Sir A. Nicolson
1916	Ld Hardinge
1920	Sir E. Crowe
1925	Sir W. Tyrrell
1928	Sir R. Lindsay
1930	Sir R. Vansittart
1938	Sir A. Cadogan
1946	Sir O. Sargent [2]
1949	Sir W. Strang [2]
1953	Sir I. Kirkpatrick
1957	Sir F. Hoyer Millar
1962	Sir H. Caccia
1966	Sir P. Gore-Booth

Forestry Commission (Chairman)

1920	Ld Lovat
1927	Ld Clinton
1929	Sir J. Stirling-Maxwell
1932	Sir R. Robinson (Ld)
1952	E of Radnor
1964	Earl Waldegrave
1966	L. Jenkins

Fuel & Power

1942	Sir F. Tribe
1945	Sir D. Fergusson
1952	Sir J. Maud

(Power)

1957	Sir J. Maud
1958	(Sir) D. Proctor
1965	Sir M. Stevenson
1966	Sir D. Pitblado

Health

1919	Sir R. Morant
1920	Sir A. Robinson
1935	Sir G. Chrystal
1940	Sir J. Maude
1945	Sir W. Douglas
1951	(Sir) J. Hawton
1960	(Sir) B. Fraser
1964 -1968 }	(Sir) A. France

Health & Social Security

1968	Sir C. Jarrett

Home Office

1895	Sir K. Digby
1903	Sir M. Chalmers
1908	Sir E. Troup
1922	Sir J. Anderson
1932	Sir R. Scott
1938	Sir A. Maxwell
1948	Sir F. Newsam
1957	Sir C. Cunningham
1966	Sir P. Allen

Home Security

1939 {	Sir T. Gardiner / Sir G. Gater

1940	Sir G. Gater
1942	Sir H. Scott
1943 -1945 }	Sir W. Brown

Housing & Local Government

(see *Town & Country Planning*, 1943–51)

1951	Sir T. Sheepshanks
1955	Dame E. Sharp
1966	Sir M. Stevenson

India

1883	Sir A. Godley
1909	Sir R. Ritchie
1912	Sir T. Holderness
1920	Sir W. Duke
1924	Sir A. Hirtzel
1930	Sir F. Stewart

(India & Burma)

1937	Sir F. Stewart
1941 -1948 }	(Sir) D. Monteath

Information (Director of Propaganda)

1918 -1919 }	A. Bennett

(Director-General)

1939	Sir K. Lee
1940	F. Pick
1941	Sir C. Radcliffe
1945 -1946 }	E. Bamford

(Central Office of Information) (Director-General)

1946	Sir E. Bamford
1946	Sir R. Fraser
1954	(Sir) T. Fife Clark

Board of Inland Revenue (Chairman)

1899	Sir H. Primrose
1907	(Sir) R. Chalmers
1911	Sir M. Nathan
1914	Sir E. Nott-Bower
1918	W. Fisher
1919	Sir J. Anderson
1922	Sir R. Hopkins
1927	Sir E. Gowers
1930	(Sir) J. Grigg
1934	Sir E. Forber
1938	Sir G. Canny
1942	Sir C. Gregg
1948	Sir E. Bamford
1955	Sir H. Hancock
1958	Sir A. Johnston
1968	Sir A. France

[1] The Comptroller and Auditor-General is appointed by the Crown by letters patent and is not in the ordinary sense a civil servant.

[2] Joint Permanent Under-Secretaries—Head of the German Section: 1947–9 Sir W. Strang, 1949–50 Sir I. Kirkpatrick, 1950–1 Sir D. Gainer.

Irish Office

1893 Sir D. Harrel
1902 Sir A. Macdonnell
1908 Sir J. Dougherty
1914 Sir M. Nathan
1916 Sir W. Byrne
1918 J. Macmahon
1920 ⌠ J. Macmahon
-1922 ⌡ Sir J. Anderson

Labour

1916 (Sir) D. Shackleton
⌠ Sir D. Shackleton
1920 ⎰ Sir J. Masterton-
⎱ Smith
1921 Sir H. Wilson
1930 Sir F. Floud
1935 Sir T. Phillips

(Labour & National Service)

1939 Sir T. Phillips
1944 (Sir) G. Ince
1956 Sir H. Emmerson

(Labour)

1959 Sir L. Helsby
1962 Sir J. Dunnett
1966 (Sir) D. Barnes
1966 ⌠
-1967 ⌡ (Sir) D. Barnes

(Employment & Productivity)

1968 Sir D. Barnes

Land & Natural Resources

1964 F. Bishop
1966 Sir B. Fraser

Secretary to the Ld Chancellor[1]

1885 Sir K. Mackenzie
1915 Sir C. Schuster
1944 Sir A. Napier
1954 Sir G. Coldstream
1968 Sir D. Dobson

Materials

1951 A. Hitchman
1952 Sir J. Helmore
1953 ⌠ Sir E. Bowyer
-1954 ⌡

Munitions

1915 Sir H. Llewellyn Smith
1916 E. Phipps
1917 Sir G. Greene
1920 ⌠ Sir S. Dannreuther
-1921 ⌡ D. Neylan

Unemployment Assistance Board (Chairman)

1934 Sir H. Betterton (Ld Rushcliffe)

(Assistance Board)

1940 Ld Rushcliffe
1941 Ld Soulbury

(National Assistance Board)

1948 G. Buchanan
1954 Sir G. Hutchinson (Ld Ilford)
1964 ⌠ Ld Runcorn
-1966 ⌡

National Insurance

1944 Sir T. Phillips
1949 Sir H. Hancock
1951 Sir G. King
1953 (see *Pensions & National Insurance*)

National Service

1917 S. Fawcett
1918 ⌠ W. Vaughan
-1919 ⌡

Overseas Development

1964 Sir A. Cohen
1968 Sir G. Wilson

Parliamentary Commissioner

1967 Sir E. Compton

Pensions

1916 Sir M. Nathan
1919 Sir G. Chrystal
1935 Sir A. Hore
1941 (Sir) A. Cunnison
1946 Sir H. Parker
1948 Sir A. Wilson

(Pensions & National Insurance)

1953 Sir G. King
1955 Sir E. Bowyer
1965 Sir C. Jarrett
1966 (see *Social Security*)

Post Office

1899 Sir G. Murray
1903 Sir H. Babington-Smith
1909 Sir M. Nathan
1911 Sir A. King
1914 (Sir) E. Murray

(Director-General)

1934 (Sir) D. Banks
1936 Sir T. Gardiner

1946 Sir R. Birchall
1949 (Sir) A. Little
1955 (Sir) G. Radley
1960 Sir R. German
1966 ⌠ (Sir) J. Wall (*Deputy*
-1968 ⎰ *Chairman of Post*
⎱ *Office Board*)

Power (see *Fuel & Power*)

Privy Council (Clerk of the Council)

1899 (Sir) A. FitzRoy
1923 Sir M. Hankey
1938 Sir R. Howorth
1942 (Sir) E. Leadbitter
1951 F. Fernau
1953 (Sir) W. Agnew

Production

1942 Sir H. Self
1943 ⌠ J. Woods
-1945 ⌡

Reconstruction

1943 ⌠ N. Brook
-1945 ⌡

General Register Office (Registrar-General for England and Wales)

1880 Sir B. Henniker
1900 R. MacLeod
1902 (Sir) W. Dunbar
1909 (Sir) B. Mallet
1921 (Sir) S. Vivian
1945 (Sir) G. North
1959 E. Firth
1964 M. Reed

Department of Scientific and Industrial Research (Secretary)

1916 (Sir) F. Heath
1927 H. Tizard
1929 (Sir) F. Smith
1939 (Sir) E. Appleton
1949 Sir B. Lockspeiser
1956 (Sir) H. Melville

(Science Research Council (Chairman))

1966 Sir H. Melville

Office of the Minister for Science

1962 F. Turnbull

Scottish Office

1892 Sir C. Scott-Moncrieff
1902 Sir R. Macleod
1909 Sir J. Dodds
1921 Sir J. Lamb
1933 Sir J. Jeffrey
1937 J. Highton
1937 Sir H. Hamilton

[1] Full title, Permanent Secretary to the Ld Chancellor and Clerk of the Crown in Chancery. The Clerk of the Crown is not in the ordinary sense a civil servant and is, among other things, an officer of both Houses of Parliament.

1946 (Sir) D. Milne
1959 Sir W. Murie
1965 (Sir) D. Haddow

Shipping
1917 (Sir) J. Anderson
1919 } T. Lodge
-1920
1939 } Sir C. Hurcomb
-1941

Social Security
1966 Sir C. Jarrett
1968 (see *Health & Social
       Security*)

Technology
1964 Sir M. Dean
1966 Sir R. Clarke

Supply
1939 Sir A. Robinson
1940 Sir G. Gater
1940 Sir W. Brown
1942 Sir W. Douglas
1945 O. Franks
1946 Sir A. Rowlands
1953 Sir J. Helmore
1956 Sir C. Musgrave
1959 } Sir W. Strath
1959-

Town & Country Planning
1943 Sir G. Whiskard
1946 Sir T. Sheepshanks

(Local Government & Planning)
1951 Sir T. Sheepshanks
1951 (see *Housing & Local
       Government*)

Board of Trade
1893 Sir C. Boyle
1901 Sir F. Hopwood
1907 (Sir) H. Llewellyn
       Smith
1913 { Sir G. Barnes
       { Sir H. Llewellyn
       { Smith
1916 { Sir H. Llewellyn
       { Smith
       { (Sir) W. Marwood
1919 { Sir S. Chapman
       { Sir W. Marwood
1919 { Sir S. Chapman
       { Sir H. Payne
1920 Sir S. Chapman
1927 Sir H. Hamilton
1937 Sir W. Brown

1941 Sir A. Overton
1945 Sir J. Woods
1951 Sir F. Lee
1960 Sir R. Powell
1968 Sir A. Part

Transport
1919 Sir F. Dunnell
1921 Sir W. Marwood
1923 Sir J. Brooke
1927 C. Hurcomb
1937 Sir L. Browett

(Director-General of War Transport)
1941 Sir C. Hurcomb

(Transport)
1946 Sir C. Hurcomb
1947 Sir G. Jenkins
1968 Sir D. Serpell

(Transport & Civil) Aviation
1953 Sir G. Jenkins

(Transport) (and see *Aviation*)
1959 Sir J. Dunnett
1962 Sir T. Padmore

Treasury
1894 Sir F. Mowatt
1902 { Sir F. Mowatt
       { Sir E. Hamilton
1903 { Sir E. Hamilton
       { Sir G. Murray
1908 Sir G. Murray
1911 Sir R. Chalmers
1913 { Sir T. Heath
       { Sir J. Bradbury
1916 { Sir T. Heath
       { Sir J. Bradbury
       { Sir R. Chalmers
1919 Sir W. Fisher
1939 Sir H. Wilson
1942 Sir R. Hopkins
1945 Sir E. Bridges
1956 { Sir N. Brook
       { Sir R. Makins
1960 { Sir N. Brook
       { Sir F. Lee
1962 { Sir N. Brook
       { W. Armstrong
1963 { Sir L. Helsby
       { (Sir) W. Armstrong
1968 { Sir W. Armstrong
       { Sir D. Allen
1968 Sir D. Allen

University Grants Committee (Chairman)
1919 Sir W. McCormick
1930 Sir W. Buchanan-
       Riddell
1935 Sir W. Moberly
1949 (Sir) A. Trueman
1953 (Sir) K. Murray
1964 Sir J. Wolfenden
1968 K. Berrill

War Office
1897 Sir R. Knox
1901 Sir E. Ward
1914 Sir R. Brade
1920 Sir H. Creedy
1939 Sir J. Grigg
1942 { Sir F. Bovenschen
       { Sir E. Speed
1945 Sir E. Speed
1949 Sir G. Turner
1956 Sir E. Playfair
1960 (Sir) R. Way
1963 (Sir) A. Drew
1964 (see *Defence*)

Welsh Office
1964 G. Daniel

Works
1895 Sir R. Brett (Vt Esher)
1902 Sir S. McDonnell
1912 Sir L. Earle
1933 Sir P. Duff
1941 Sir G. Whiskard
1943 Sir P. Robinson
1946 Sir H. Emmerson
1956 Sir E. Muir

(Public Building & Works)
1962 Sir E. Muir
1965 (Sir) A. Part
1968 Sir M. Carey

Bank of England [1] (Governor)
1899 S. Gladstone
1901 (Sir) A. Prevost
1903 S. Morley
1905 A. Wallace
1908 R. Johnston
1913 W. Cunliffe (Ld)
1918 Sir B. Cokayne (Ld
       Cullen of Ashbourne)
1920 M. Norman (Ld)
1944 Ld Catto
1949 C. Cobbold (Ld)
1964 E of Cromer
1966 (Sir) L. O'Brien

[1] Founded in 1694, the Bank of England only passed into public ownership in 1946.

Salary of Permanent Secretary to the Treasury

1900	£2,500	1940	£3,500
1910	£2,500	1950	£3,750
1920	£3,500	1960	£7,500
1930	£3,500	1965	£8,885

Size of Civil Service

Adequate statistics of the number of civil servants engaged in each branch of government activity since 1900 are not readily available. Moreover, the transfer of functions between departments makes comparisons of one year with another potentially misleading. An analysis of civil service strength for certain years is to be found in *The Organisation of British Central Government, 1914–1956,* by D. N. Chester and F. M. G. Wilson. The figures in heavy type in the following table are taken from the statement *Staffs Employed in Government Departments* which has been published annually, or more frequently, by the Treasury as a Command Paper since 1919 (with retrospective figures for 1914 included in the first issue). The other figures in the table are taken from the *Annual Estimates* presented to Parliament by the Civil Service and Revenue Departments, and the *East India Home Accounts.* These figures are liable to slight error as they are estimates and not reports of the actual staff employed. In each case they are estimates for the year ending March 31 of the following year (e.g. under the third column headed '1 Apr 1920' the estimates are for 1920–21). The figures in this table should be used with great caution because of the considerable differences in the sources.

[See Table on next page.]

N

Number of Civil Servants

	1900–01	1 Aug 1914	1 Apr 1920	1 Apr 1930	1 Apr 1938	1 Apr 1950	1 Apr 1960	1 Apr. 1966
Total Non-industrial Staff	n.a.	282,420	380,963	306,154	376,491	575,274	637,374	*827,049*
Total Industrial Staff	n.a.	497,100	n.a.	483,100	204,400	396,900	358,900	*232,144*
Total Civil Service Staff	n.a.	779,520	n.a.	789,254	580,891	972,174	996,274	*1,059,193*
Admiralty	n.a.	4,366	13,432	7,433	10,609	30,801	30,731	f
War Office	n.a.	1,636	7,434	3,872	7,323	33,493	47,244	f
Air	..	..	2,839	1,704	4,317	24,407	27,563	f
Defence (Navy)	..	..	..	..	..	..	..	*32,732*
Defence (Army)	..	..	..	..	..	..	..	*48,032*
Defence (Air Force)	..	..	..	..	..	..	..	*24,848*
Aviation	..	..	..	..	..	5,271	24,756	*24,743*
Foreign Office [a]	142	187	885	730	902	6,195	5,992	g
Diplomatic Service	..	..	..	..	..	..	..	*10,567*
Overseas Development [h]	..	..	..	..	..	..	..	*2,222*
Colonial Office	109	214	256	365	438	1,286	1,211	*603*
Dominions & C.R.O.	..	..	..	52	91	904	847	g
India Office	589	554	342	n.a.	539	..	..	..
Irish Office	559	1,007	829	..	..	..	..	..
Scottish Office	159	401	517	68	n.a.	749	887	*3,229*
Welsh Office [h]	..	..	..	..	..	..	..	*444*
Treasury [b]	120	140	291	299	344	1,396	1,322	*1,639*
Home Office	297	773	926	1,024	1,688	3,953	3,534	*16,066*
Agriculture	182	2,976	3,446	2,463	4,588	16,842	14,938	*14,721*
Education (and Science)	864	2,187	1,522	1,041	1,435	3,280	2,738	*4,185*
Food	..	..	4,142	..	..	30,785	c	c
(Fuel and) Power	..	..	..	..	..	6,358	1,768	*1,622*
Health	d	d	5,820	6,711	6,771	5,893	4,993	*5,677*
Labour	..	4,428	17,835	18,076	26,934	29,902	21,394	*22,147*
(Housing and) Local Government	425	963	d	d	d	1,312	2,802	*3,796*
Munitions	..	1,250	11,440	..	..	..	..	..
National Insurance	..	1,957	2,263	n.a.	n.a.	35,539	e	e
Pensions	..	..	24,169	6,175	3,147	10,954	36,323	e
Social Security	..	..	..	..	..	..	..	*40,954*
Post Office	79,482	208,889	209,269	194,933	224,374	249,869	254,919	*396,775*
Supply	..	..	..	..	..	13,312	..	..
Board of Trade	1,359	2,535	5,410	4,398	4,611	10,136	6,735	*9,598*
Transport	..	..	876	759	2,820	6,906	6,909	*7,062*
Works	140	679	580	2,054	3,584	17,573	10,693	*20,876*
Technology [h]	..	..	..	..	..	..	..	*4,452*
Customs and Excise	3,792	10,256	12,602	11,659	14,669	14,236	15,338	*16,793*
Exchequer and Audit Department	230	269	269	331	369	501	532	*551*
Inland Revenue Board	5,345	9,753	19,446	21,059	24,342	49,740	56,026	*59,502*
National Assistance	..	..	..	..	8,105	8,516	10,509	*14,112*
Stationery Office	100	517	728	1,660	1,947	3,241	2,903	*3,057*

[a] Home civil servants only.
[b] Not including subordinate departments (e.g. Committee of Imperial Defence, University Grants Commission).
[c] Combined with Ministry of Agriculture and Fisheries.
[d] The functions of the Local Government Board passed to the Ministry of Health in 1919. In 1943 the Ministry of Town and Country Planning (later becoming the Ministry of Housing and Local Government) took back many of these functions from the Ministry of Health.
[e] National Insurance merged with the Ministry of Pensions, and in 1966 became the Ministry of Social Security.
[f] In 1964 the Admiralty, War Office and Air Office were combined into the Ministry of Defence.
[g] In 1965 the Foreign Office, Commonwealth Relations Office, Trade Commission Service and attaches abroad were combined into the Diplomatic Service.
[h] The Ministries of Technology and Overseas Development and the Welsh Office were set up in 1964 mainly by transfers of staff from other departments.

SOURCES.—*Staffs Employed in Government Departments* (H.M.S.O., first published in 1919) figures in heavy type. *Civil Estimates, Estimates for Revenue Departments, Service Estimates,* and *East India Home Accounts*) (H.M.S.O. annually), figures in light type. Figures for 1960–1966 collected by H.M. Treasury, in italics.

VII

ROYAL COMMISSIONS, COMMITTEES OF INQUIRY AND TRIBUNALS

The public investigation of problems can take a number of forms — Royal Commissions, Tribunals, ad hoc departmental Committees and special parliamentary conferences or committees. We do not deal here with purely parliamentary bodies like the Speaker's Conferences (on Electoral Reform — see p. 155 — and on Devolution) or like the Select Committees set up from time to time by the House of Commons and/or the House of Lords. But we attempt an exhaustive listing of all domestic Royal Commissions and all Tribunals of Inquiry under the *Tribunals of Inquiry Act 1921* as well as a very arbitrary and brief selection from the 1,000 or so other Committees of Inquiry appointed since 1900. It is, however, important to remember that the decision whether to refer a problem to a Royal Commission or a Committee is not necessarily determined by the importance of the subject. Royal Commissions are listed fully here because no comprehensive list is available elsewhere and because the number is not excessive. Department Committees, which have been much more numerous, often deal with relatively narrow and limited matters; we have selected only a few which seemed plainly as important as the average Royal Commission. We have also had to omit references to committees and sub-committees appointed by Royal Commissions and by Governmental Advisory Bodies, though these cover further reports of importance such as the Report to the Central Advisory Council on Education by Lady Plowden's Committee on Primary Education (1967).

Royal Commissions 1900-

This list includes all Commissions for which a Royal Warrant was issued except for permanent and operating Commissions which are listed separately. In the absence of any single official title for Royal Commissions we have tried to select the most commonly used short title. Where a body had two or more successive chairmen we have listed them all. Where a body has been formally re-constituted we have indicated this by a fresh entry. The date of appointment is the date of the Royal Warrant. The date of Report is the date of signature of the Final Report, (or failing a dated signature, the date of presentation to the House of Commons). The Command number given is that of the final Report. In many cases there are several interim Reports, sometimes exceeding in importance the final Report. The abbreviations for Command Paper are as follows:

1900–1918	Cd. 1—Cd. 9239
1919–1956	Cmd. 1—Cmd. 9899
1956–	Cmnd. 1—

Title	Chairman	Other members	Date appointed	Date of Report	Command number
Military and Civil Expenditure of India	Ld Welby	14	Aug 96	Apr 00	131
Local Taxation	Ld Balfour	14	Aug 96	May 01	638
University of London Act	Ld Davy	8	Aug 98	Feb 00	83
Newfoundland. Operation of Certain Treaties	Sir J. Bramston	2	Aug 98	*Report not published*	
Accidents to Railway Servants	Ld Hereford	14	May 99	Jan 00	41
Salmon Fisheries	E of Elgin	9	Mar 00	Jul 02	1188
Administration of the Port of London	E Egerton Ld Revelstoke	7 7	Jun 00 ..	.. Jun 02	1151
South African Hospitals	Sir R. Romer	5	Jul 00	Jan 01	453
Poisoning by Arsenic (Arsenic in Beer and Other Articles of Diet)	Ld Kelvin	6	Feb 01	Nov 03	1848
University Education (Ireland)	Ld Robertson	11	Jul 01	Feb 03	1483
Tuberculosis	Sir M. Foster W. H. Power	5 5	Aug 01 ..	.. Jun 11	5761
Coal Supplies	Ld Allerton	15	Dec 01	Jan 05	2353
Alien Immigration	Ld James	7	Mar 02	Aug 03	1741
Physical Training (Scotland)	Ld Mansfield	9	Mar 02	Mar 03	1507
Martial Law Sentences in S. Africa	Ld Alverstone	3	Aug 02	Oct 02	136
South African War	E of Elgin	7	Sep 02	Jul 03	1789
Superannuation in the Civil Service	L. Courtney	9	Nov 02	Aug 03	1744
Locomotion and Transport in London	Sir D. Barbour	12	Feb 03	Jun 05	2597
Militia and Volunteer Forces	D of Norfolk	10	Apr 03	May 04	2061
Food Supply in Time of War	Ld Balfour of Burleigh	17	Apr 03	Aug 05	2643
Trade Disputes and Trade Combinations	A Murray (Ld Dunedin)	5	Jun 03	Jan 06	2825
Ecclesiastical Discipline	Sir M. Hicks Beach	14	Apr 04	Jun 06	3040
The Feeble-Minded	M of Bath	10	Sep 04	..	..
Churches (Scotland)	E of Elgin	3	Dec 04	Apr 05	2494
War Stores in South Africa	Sir G. Farwell	5	Jun 05	Jul 06	3127
Churches (Scotland) Act, 1905	E of Elgin	5	Aug 05	Feb 10	5060
Motor-Car	Ld Selby	7	Sep 05	Jul 06	3080
Poor Laws	Ld Hamilton	18	Dec 05	Feb 09	4498
Canals and Inland Navigation of the United Kingdom	Ld Shuttleworth	15	Mar 06	Dec 09	4979
Duties of the Metropolitan Police	D. B. Jones A. Lyttelton	5	May 06	Jun 08	4156
Registration of Title	Ld Dunedin	8	May 06	Jul 10	5316
Safety in Mines	Ld Monkswell H. Cunynghame	9	Jun 06	..	..
Trinity College Dublin	Sir E. Fry	9	Jun 06	Jan 07	3311
Coast Erosion	I. Guest	13	Jul 06	*reconstituted*	..
Congested Districts in Ireland	E of Dudley	9	Jul 06	May 08	4097
Lighthouse Administration	G. Balfour	5	Aug 06	Jan 08	3923
Vivisection	Ld Selby A. Ram	10	Sep 06	Mar 12	6114
Existence of Corrupt Practices at the last Election for the City of Worcester	E. Atkinson	3	Nov 06	Nov 06	3268
Care and Control of the Feeble-Minded	E of Radnor	12	Nov 06	Jul 08	4202
Shipping 'Rings' or Conferences generally	A. Cohen	21	Nov 06	*reconstituted*	..
Mines and Quarries	Ld Monkswell	9	May 07	Feb 11	5561
Church of England in Wales and Monmouthshire	Sir R. Vaughan-Williams	9	Jun 07	Nov 10	5432
Indian Decentralisation	Sir H. Primrose C. Hobhouse	6	Sep 07	Feb 09	4360
Whisky and other potable Spirits	Ld Hereford	8	Feb 08	Jul 09	4796
Coast Erosion and Afforestation	I. Guest	19	Mar 08	May 11	5708

Title	Chairman	Other members	Date appointed	Date of Report	Command number
Land Transfer Acts	Ld St. Aldwyn	12	Jul 08	Jan 11	5483
Systems of Election	Ld R. Cavendish	8	Dec 08	May 10	5163
University Education in London	Ld Haldane	8	Feb 09	Mar 13	6717
Mauritius	Sir F. Smettenham	3	May 09	Apr 10	5185
Trade Relations between Canada and the West Indies	Ld Balfour	5	Aug 09	Aug 10	5369
Selection of Justices of the Peace	Ld James	16	Nov 09	Jul 10	5250
Divorce and Matrimonial Causes	Ld Gorell	14	Nov 09	Nov 12	6478
Metalliferous Mines and Quarries	Sir H. Cunynghame	9	May 10	Jun 14	7476
Public Records	Sir F. Pollock	9	Oct 10	Apr 18	367
Railways Conciliation and Arbitration Scheme of 1907	Sir D. Hamel	5	Aug 11	Oct 11	5922
Malta	Sir F. Mowatt	3	Aug 11	May 12	6090
Civil Service	Ld MacDonnell H. Smith	19	Mar 12	Nov 15	7832
The Natural Resources, Trade and Legislation of the Dominions	E. Vincent	10	Apr 12	Feb 17	8462
Public Services (East Indies)	J. Dickson Poynder	12	Sep 12	Aug 15	8382
Housing of the Industrial Population of Scotland, rural and urban	G. Ballantyne	12	Oct 12	Sep 17	8731
Delay in the King's Bench Division	Ld St. Aldwyn	11	Dec 12	Nov 13	7177
Finance and Currency (East Indies)	A. Chamberlain	10	Apr 13	Feb 14	7236
Venereal Diseases	Ld Sydenham	15	Nov 13	Feb 16	8189
Meat Export Trade of Australia	P. Street	1	Jun 14	Apr 15	7896
The Circumstances connected with the Landing of Arms at Howth July 26th, 1914	Ld Shaw	3	Aug 14	Sep 14	7631
University Education in Wales	Ld Haldane	9	Apr 16	Feb 18	8991
The Rebellion in Ireland	Ld Hardinge	3	May 16	Jun 16	8729
The Arrest and subsequent treatment of Mr Francis Sheehy of Skeffington, Mr Thomas Dickson, and Mr Patrick James McIntyre	Sir J. Simon	3	Aug 16	Sep 16	8376
Dardanelles	Ld Cromer	10	Aug 16	Dec 17	371
Mesopotamia War	Ld Hamilton	7	Aug 16	May 17	8610
Allegations against Sir John Jackson, Limited	A. Chamel	3	Nov 16	Mar 17	8518
Proportional Representation	J. Lowther	5	Feb 18	Apr 18	9044
Decimal Coinage	Ld Emmott	20	Aug 18	Feb 20	628
Coal Industry	Ld Sankey		Feb 19	Jun 19	360
Income Tax	Ld Colwyn	21	Apr 19	Mar 20	615
Agriculture	H. Peat	23	Jul 19	Dec 19	473[1]
Oxford and Cambridge Universities	H. Asquith	19	Nov 19	Mar 22	1588
The University of Dublin (Trinity College)	A. Geikie	5	Mar 20	Nov 20	1078
Fire Brigades and Fire Prevention	Sir P. Laurence	14	Jan 21	Jul 23	1945
The Importation of Store Cattle	Ld Finlay	5	May 21	Aug 21	1139
Local Government of Greater London	Vt Ullswater	8	Oct 21	Feb 23	1830
Honours	Ld Dunedin	7	Sep 22	Dec 22	1789
Local Government	E of Onslow	12	Feb 23	Nov 29	3436
Mining Subsidence	Ld Blanesburgh	13	Jun 23	Jun 27	2899
Superior Civil Services India	H. Lee	9	Jun 23	Mar 24	2128
Lunacy and Mental Disorder	H. Macmillan	10	Jul 24	Jul 26	2700
National Health Insurance	Ld Lawrence	13	Jul 24	Feb 26	2596
Food Prices	Sir A. Geddes	16	Nov 24	Apr 25	2390
Indian Currency and Finance	E. Hilton Young	9	Aug 25	Jul 26	Parl. paper

[1] Interim Report only; no Final Report published.

Title	Chairman	Other members	Date appointed	Date of Report	Command number
The Coal Industry	Sir H. Samuel	4	Sep 25	Mar 26	2600
Court of Session and the Office of Sheriff Principal (Scotland)	Ld Clyde	9	Jan 26	Jan 27	2801
Agriculture in India	M of Linlithgow	10	Apr 26	Apr 28	3132
Cross-River Traffic in London	Ld Lee of Fareham	6	Jul 26	Nov 26	2772
Land Drainage in England and Wales	Ld Bledisloe	11	Mar 27	Dec 27	2993
National Museums and Art Galleries	Ld d'Abernon	11	Jul 27	Jan 30	3463
London Squares	M of Londonderry	14	Aug 27	Sep 28	3196
Indian Statutory Commission	Sir J. Simon		Nov 27	May 30	3568
Police Powers and Procedure	Ld Lee	8	Aug 28	Mar 29	3297
Transport	Sir A. Griffith-Boscowen	12	Aug 28	Dec 30	3751
Labour in India	J. Whitley	11	Jul 29	Mar 31	3583
Licensing (England and Wales)	Ld Amulree	19	Sep 29	May 31	3988
Civil Service	Ld Tomlin	16	Oct 29	Jul 31	3909
Licensing (Scotland)	Ld Mackay	14	Oct 29	May 31	3894
Unemployment Insurance	H. Gregory	7	Dec 30	Oct 32	4185
Malta	Ld Askwith	3	Apr 31	Jan 32	3993
Lotteries and Betting	Sir S. Rowlatt	12	Jun 32	Jun 33	4341
Newfoundland	Ld Amulree	3	Feb 33	Oct 33	4480
The University of Durham	Ld Moyne	8	Mar 34	Jan 35	4815
Tithe Rentcharge in England and Wales	J. Williams	4	Aug 34	Nov 35	5095
Despatch of Business at Common Law	Earl Peel	7	Dec 34	Jan 36	5065
Private Manufacture of and Trading in Arms	J. Bankes	7	Feb 35	Sep 36	5292
Local Government in the Tyneside Area	Sir A. Scott	5	May 35	Feb 37	5402
Merthyr Tydfil	Sir A. Lowry	2	May 35	Nov 35	5039
Safety in Coal Mines	Ld Rockley	10	Dec 35	Dec 38	5890
Palestine	Earl Peel	1	Aug 36	Jun 37	5479
The Distribution of the Industrial Population	Sir M. Barlow	13	Jul 37	Dec 39	6153
Rhodesia-Nyasaland	Vt Bledisloe	1	Mar 38	Mar 39	5949
West Indies	Ld Moyne	1	Aug 38	Dec 39	6607
Workmen's Compensation	Sir H. Hetherington	15	Dec 38	Dec 44	658
Population	Vt Simon	16	Mar 44	..	
	Sir H. Henderson	14	May 46	Mar 49	7695
Equal Pay	C. Asquith	9	Oct 44	Oct 46	6937
Justices of the Peace	Ld du Parcq	15	Jun 46	May 48	7463
The Press	Sir D. Ross	15	Apr 47	Jun 49	7700
Betting, Lotteries and Gaming	H. Willink	12	Apr 49	Mar 51	8190
Capital Punishment	Sir E. Gowers	11	May 49	Sep 53	8932
Taxation of Profits and Income	Ld Cohen	13	Jan 51		
	Ld Radcliffe	13	..	May 55	9474
University Education in Dundee	Ld Tedder	9	May 51	Apr 52	8514
Marriage and Divorce	Ld Morton of Henryton	20	Sep 51	Dec 55	9678
Scottish Affairs	E of Balfour	15	Jul 52	Jul 54	9212
East Africa	Sir H. Dow	8	Jan 53	May 55	9475
The Civil Service	Sir R. Priestley	12	Nov 53	Nov 55	9613
The Law Relating to Mental Illness and Mental Deficiency	Ld Percy	11	Feb 54	May 57	169
Common Land	Sir I. Jennings	12	Dec 55	Jul 58	462
Doctors' and Dentists' Remuneration	Sir H. Pilkington	9	Mar 57	Feb 60	939
Local Government in Greater London	Sir E. Herbert	7	Dec 57	Oct 60	1164
The Police	Sir H. Willink	15	Jan 60	May 62	1222
The Press	Ld Shawcross	5	Mar 61	Sep 62	1811
The Penal System in England and Wales	Vt Amory	16	Aug 64	wound up May 66	
Reform of the Trade Unions and Employers' Associations	Ld Donovan	12	Apr 65	Jun 68	3623

Title	Chairman	Other members	Date appointed	Date of Report	Command number
Medical Education	Ld Todd	17	Jun 65	Apr 68	3569
Tribunals of Inquiry	Sir C. Salmon	7	Feb 66	Nov 66	3121
The Examination of Assizes and Quarter Sessions	Ld Beeching	8	Oct 66	Apr 68	3569
Local Government, England	Sir J. Maud (Ld)	11	May 66		
Local Government, Scotland	Ld Wheatley	9	May 66		

Permanent and Operating Commissions

Certain Royal Commissions have an enduring existence:

The Royal Commission on Historical Manuscripts set up in 1869 sits under the *ex officio* Chairmanship of the Master of the Rolls. It was reconstituted with extended powers in 1959. Its task is to advise and assist in the preservation of historical manuscripts and to publish them.

The *Royal Commission on Historical Monuments* was set up for England in 1908 with similar bodies for Scotland (reconstituted 1948) and Wales and Monmouthshire. Their task is to maintain an inventory of Ancient Monuments.

The *Royal Fine Arts Commission* was set up in 1924 (re-constituted in 1933 and 1946) and the *Royal Fine Art Commission for Scotland* in 1927 (reconstituted 1948): their task is to inquire into questions of public amenity and artistic importance.

The *Royal Commission for the Exhibition of 1851*, surviving from the winding up of the affairs of the Great Exhibitions, still distributes the income from surplus funds to promote scientific and artistic education. There was also the *Royal Commission for the Patriotic Fund (1854-1904)*. In addition, there have been operating Commissions for the *Paris Exhibition of 1900*, the *St Louis Exhibition of 1904*, and for the *International Exhibitions at Brussels, Rome, and Turin in 1910 and 1911*. Another miscellaneous group of operating Royal Commissions covered *Sewage Disposal (1898-1915)*, *Horse-Breeding (1887-1911)*, and *Crofter Colonisation (1888-1906)*.

War produced another group of operating or semi-permanent Royal Commissions, *Sugar Supply* (1914-21), *Wheat Supplies* (1916-25), *Paper and Paper making materials* (1917-[1]). *Defence of the Realm Losses* (1915-20), *Compensation for Suffering Damage by Enemy Action* (1921-24), and *Awards to Inventors* (1919-35, 1946-56).

[1] No Final Report.

Irish Vice-Regal Commissions

Title	Chairman	No. of members	Date appointed	Date of Report	Command number
Irish Inland Fisheries	S. Walker	7	Aug 99	Jan 01	448
Poor Law Reform in Ireland	W. L. Micks	3	May 03	Oct 06	3202
Trinity College, Dublin, Estates Commission	G. Fitzgibbon	3	Jun 04	Apr 05	2526
Arterial Drainage (Ireland)	A. Binnie	5	Sep 05	Feb 07	3374
Irish Railways, Including Light Railways	C. Scotter	7	Jul 06	Jul 10	5247
Circumstances of the Loss of the Regalia of the Order of St. Patrick	J. Shaw	3	Jan 08	Jan 08	3936
Irish Milk Supply	P. O'Neill	9	Nov 11	Oct 13	7129
Primary Education (Ireland) System of Inspection [a]	S. Dill	8	Jan 13	Jan 14	7235
Dublin Disturbances	D. Henry	2	Dec 13	Feb 14	7269
Primary Education (Ireland)[b] 1918	Ld Killanin	17	Aug 18	Feb 19	60
Intermediate Education (Ireland)[b]	T. Molony	14	Aug 18	Mar 19	66
Under Sheriffs and Bailiffs[b] (Ireland)	T. O'Shaughnessy	5	Oct 18	May 19	190
Reorganisation and Pay of the Irish Police Forces	J. Ross	6	Oct 19	Dec 19	603
Clerk of the Crown and Peace, Etc. (Ireland)[b]	J. Wakely	7	Oct 19	Jun 20	805

[a] Vice-Regal Committee (Commission).   [b] Vice-Regal Committee.

A Select List of Departmental Committees 1900-

In the absence of any single official title for a Committee we have tried to select the most commonly used short title. The Command number given is that of the final report.

Title	Chairman	Date appointed	Date of Report	Command number
Compensation for injuries to workmen	K. Digby	Nov 03	Aug 04	2208
Motor Cars	R. Hobhouse	Jan 04	Apr 04	2069
Income Tax	C. Ritchie	..	Jun 05	2575
Company and Commercial law and Practice	C. Warmington	Feb 05	Jun 06	3052
Accounts of local authorities	W. Runciman	Jan 06	Jul 07	3614
Law of Copyright	Ld Gorell	Mar 09	Dec 09	4967
Probation of Offenders Act '07	H. Samuel	Mar 09	Dec 09	5001
Procedure of Royal Commissions	Ld Balfour of Burleigh	Apr 09	Jun 10	5235
Railway Agreements and amalgamations	R. Rea	June 09	Apr 11	5631
Alien Immigrants at the Port of London	R. Lehmann	..	Mar 11	5575
Educational Endowments	C. Trevelyan	..	Mar 11	5662
National Guarantee for the War Risks of Shipping	A. Chamberlain	..	..	7560
Local Taxation	Sir J. Kempe	Nov 12	Mar 14	7315
Retrenchment in the public expenditure	R. McKenna	Jul 15	Sep 15	8068
Royal Aircraft Factory	R. Burbridge	Mar 16	Jul 16	8191
Increase of Prices of Commodities since the beginning of the War	J. Robertson	Jun 16	Sep 16	8358
Summer Time	J. Wilson	Sep 16	Feb 17	8487
Commercial and Industrial Policy. Imperial Preference	Ld Balfour of Burleigh	..	Feb 17	8482
Currency and Foreign Exchanges	Ld Cunliffe	Jan 18	Dec 19	464
National Expenditure	Ld Geddes	Aug 21	Feb 22	1589

Title	Chairman	Date appointed	Date of Report	Command number
Broadcasting	Sir M. Sykes	Apr 23	Aug 23	1951
Imperial Wireless Telegraphy	Sir R. Donald	Jan 24	Feb 24	2060
National Debt and Taxation	H. Colwyn	Mar 24	Nov 26	2800
Broadcasting	Ld Crawford and Balcarres	Aug 25	Mar 26	2599
Ministers' Powers	E of Donoughmore	Oct 29	Apr 32	4060
Finance and Industry	H. Macmillan (Ld)	Nov 29	Jun 31	3897
Regional Development	H. Chelmsford	Jan 31	Mar 31	3915
National Expenditure	Sir G. May	Mar 31	Jul 31	3920
Depressed Areas	(3 Area Chairmen)	Apr 34	Nov 34	4728
Broadcasting	Vt Ullswater	Apr 35	Mar 36	5091
Parliamentary Pensions	Sir W. Fisher	Jul 35	Nov 37	5624
Compensation and Betterment	Sir A. Uttwatt	Jan 41	Sep 42	6291
Social Insurance and Allied Services	Sir W. Beveridge	Jun 41	Nov 42	6404
Training of Civil Servants	R. Assheton	Feb 43	Apr 44	6525
Company Law Amendment	Sir L. Cohen	Jun 43	Jun 45	6659
Television	Ld Hankey	Sep 43	Dec 44	Non-parl
Rent Control	Vt Ridley	Nov 43	Feb 45	6621
Legal Aid and Legal Advice in England and Wales	Ld Rushcliffe	May 44	May 45	6641
Gas Industry	G. Heyworth	Jun 44	Nov 45	6699
Care of Children	Miss M. Curtis	Mar 45	Jan 46	6922
National Parks (England and Wales)	Sir A. Hobhouse	Jul 45	Mar 47	7121
New Towns	Ld Reith	Oct 45	Jul 46	7876
Port Transport Industry	R. Evershed	Nov 45	Dec 45	Non-parl
Closing Hours of Shops	Sir E. Gowers	Jan 46	Jan 47	7105
Higher Civil Service Remuneration	Ld Chorley	..	Sep 48	7635
Social & Economic Research	Sir G. North	Jan 47	Oct 50	8091
Resale Price Maintenance	Sir G. Lloyd-Jacob	Aug 47	Mar 49	7696
Leasehold	Ld Uthwatt	Feb 48	Jun 50	7982
Political Activities of Civil Servants	J. Masterman	Apr 48	Apr 49	7718
Intermediaries	Sir E. Herbert D. Jenkins	Feb 49	Oct 49	7904
Broadcasting	Ld Beveridge	Jun 49	Dec 50	8116
Fuel & Power Resources	Vt Ridley	Jul 51	Jul 52	8647
Departmental Records	Sir J. Grigg	Jun 52	May 54	9163
National Health Service	C. Guillebaud	May 53	Nov 55	9663
Air Pollution	Sir H. Beaver	Jul 53	Nov 54	9322
Crichel Down	A. Clark	Nov 53	May 54	9176
Electricity Supply Industry	Sir E. Herbert	Jul 54	Dec 55	9672
Port Transport Industry	Sir P. Devlin	Jul 54	Jun 56	9813
Homosexual Law Reform	Sir J. Wolfenden	Aug 54	Aug 57	247
Crown Lands	Sir M. Trustram Eve	Dec 54	May 55	9483
Administrative Tribunals & Inquiries	Sir O. Franks	Nov 55	Jul 57	218
Children & Young Persons	Vt Ingleby	Oct 56	Oct 60	1191
Damage and Casualties at Port Said	Sir E. Herbert	Dec 56	Dec 56	47
The Youth Service in England and Wales	Ctess of Albemarle	May 57	Oct 59	929
Interception of Communications	Sir N. Birkett	Jun 57	Sep 57	283
Preservation of Downing Street	E of Crawford	Jul 57	Mar 58	457
The Structure of the Public Library Service in England and Wales	Sir S. Roberts	Sep 57	Dec 58	660
Working of the Monetary System	Ld Radcliffe	Sep 57	Jul 59	827
Consumer Protection	J. Molony	Jun 59	Apr 62	1871
Control of Public Expenditure	Ld Plowden	Aug 59	Jun 61	1432
Company Law Committee	Ld Jenkins	Jan 60	May 62	1749
Broadcasting	Sir H. Pilkington	Jul 60	Jun 62	1753
Higher Education	Ld Robbins	Feb 61	Sep 63	2154
Major Ports of Great Britain	Vt Rochdale	Mar 61	Jul 62	1824
Security Procedures in Public Service	Ld Radcliffe	May 61	Nov 61	1681
Economy of Northern Ireland	Sir R. Hall	May 61	Jun 62	1835
Sunday Observance	Ld Crathorne	Jul 61	Sep 64	2528
Decimal Currency	E of Halsbury	Dec 61	Jul 63	2145
Organisation of Civil Science	Sir B. Trend	Mar 62	Sep 63	2171
The Vassall Case	Sir C. Cunningham	Oct 62	Nov 62	1871
Lord Denning's Report	Ld Denning	Jun 63	Sep 63	2152
Remuneration of Ministers and M.P.s	Sir G. Lawrence	Dec 63	Oct 64	2516

Title	Chairman	Date appointed	Date of Report	Command number
Social Studies	Ld Heyworth	Jun 63	Feb 65	2660
Housing in Greater London	Sir M. Holland	Aug 63	Mar 65	2605
Port Transport Industry	Ld Devlin	Oct 64	Nov 64	2523 (1st Report)
Aircraft Industry	Ld Plowden	Dec 64	Dec 65	2853
Shipbuilding	R. Geddes	Feb 65	Feb 66	2939
Local Authority Personal Services	F. Seebohm	Dec 65	Jul 68	3703
Civil Service	Ld Fulton	Feb 66	Jul 68	3638
Prison Security	E Mountbatten	Oct 66	Dec 66	3175

Inquiries held under the Tribunals of Inquiry (Evidence) Act, 1921

Tribunals of Inquiry (Evidence) Act, 1921

Upon a resolution of both Houses of Parliament on a matter of urgent public importance a tribunal might be appointed by the Sovereign or a Secretary of State with all the powers of the High Court as regards examination of witnesses and production of documents, for the objective investigation of facts.

Title	Members of Tribunal	Year	Command number
Destruction of documents by Ministry of Munitions officials	Ld Cave Ld Inchape Sir W. Plender	1921	1340
Royal Commission on Lunacy and Mental Disorder given powers under the Act	H. Macmillan + 9	1924	2700
Arrest of R. Sheppard, R.A.O.C. Inquiry into conduct of Metropolitan Police	J. Rawlinson	1925	2497
Allegations made against the Chief Constable of Kilmarnock in connection with the dismissal of Constables Hill and Moore from the Burgh Police Force	W. Mackenzie	1925	2659
Conditions with regard to mining and drainage in an area around the County Borough of Doncaster	Sir H. Monro (*Ch*)	1926/8	..
Charges against the Chief Constable of St. Helens by the Watch Committee	C. Parry T. Walker	1928	3103
Interrogation of Miss Irene Savidge by Metropolitan Police at New Scotland Yard	Sir J. Eldon Banks H. Lees-Smith J. Withers	1928	3147
Allegations of bribery and corruption in connection with the letting and allocation of stances and other premises under the control of the Corporation of Glasgow	Ld Anderson Sir R. Boothby J. Hunter	1933	4361
Unauthorised disclosure of information relating to the Budget	Sir J. Porter G. Simonds R. Oliver	1936	5184
The circumstances surrounding the loss of H.M. Submarine "Thetis"	Sir J. Bucknill	1939	6190
The conduct before the Hereford Juvenile Court Justices of the proceedings against Craddock and others	Ld Goddard	1943	6485
The administration of the Newcastle upon Tyne Fire, Police and Civil Defence Services	R. Burrows	1944	6522
Bribery of Ministers of the Crown or other public servants in connection with the grant of licences, etc.	Sir J. Lynskey G. Russell Vick G. Upjohn	1948	7616
Allegations of improper disclosure of information relating to the raising of the Bank Rate	Ld Parker E. Holland G. Veale	1957	350

Title	Members of Tribunal	Year	Command number
Allegations that John Waters was assaulted on 7th December, 1957, at Thurso and the action taken by Caithness Police in connection therewith	Ld Sorn Sir J. Robertson J. Dandie	1959	718
The circumstances in which offences under the Official Secrets Act were committed by William John Christopher Vassall	Ld Radcliffe Sir J. Barry Sir E. Milner Holland	1962	2009

SOURCE.—Royal Commission on the Tribunals of Enquiry (Evidence) Act, 1921 (Cmnd. 3121) Feb 1966.

Select Examples of Tribunals and Inquiries

A large number of statutory tribunals, with jurisdiction to decide quasi-legal disputes, have been created since 1900. By 1960 there were over 2,000 tribunals within the supervisory role of the *Council on Tribunals*. The fifteen-member *Council on Tribunals* was set up under the *Tribunals and Inquiries Act, 1958*, following the report of the Franks Committee (*Cmnd. 218/1957*). Its role is purely advisory, but it has to report annually to Parliament.

The Schedule to the *Tribunals and Inquiries Act, 1958* gives the list of tribunals under the supervision of the Council on Tribunals. Others have been added by subsequent legislation, e.g. by the *Mental Health Act, 1959*, the *Finance Act, 1960*, the *Civil Aviation Licensing Act, 1960*, the *Betting, Gaming and Lotteries Act, 1963*, and the *Rent Act, 1965*.

These are some of the more important tribunals:

The National Health Service Tribunals

These hear complaints against medical practitioners and dentists under the National Health Service Acts.

Industrial Courts of Inquiry (Industrial Courts Act, 1919)

The Minister of Labour empowered to refer any matter relevant to a trade dispute to these.

The Lands Tribunal (Lands Tribunal Act, 1949)

This has varied jurisdiction, including questions relating to compulsory acquisition of land by Government Departments and local authorities, such as the value of land and compensation payable under the different compensation acts.

The Transport Tribunal (Transport Acts, 1947 and 1962)

This had jurisdiction over railway charges, road transport, harbours and canals and hears appeals from various transport licensing authorities. The tribunal's jurisdiction over railway charges were removed as far as the British Railways are concerned (but not the London Transport Commission) by the Transport Act, 1962.

National Assistance Appeal Tribunals (National Assistance Act, 1948)

These used to hear appeals against the National Assistance Board on such questions as refusal to give assistance, and the nature and amount of assistance.

Supplementary Benefits Appeals Tribunals (Social Security Act, 1965)

These hear appeals against the Supplementary Benefits Commission on such questions as refusal to pay supplementary pensions or allowances or for any decision on a claim for supplementary benefits.

National Insurance Tribunals

These decide questions concerning rights to benefit under the *National Insurance Act, 1946*, and the *National Insurance (Industrial Injuries) Act, 1946*. (These questions were determined in the first instance by insurance officers of the Ministry of National Insurance until 1966, and since 1966 of the Ministry of Social Security.)

Rent Tribunals

These determine the fair rent for furnished houses under the *Furnished Houses (Rent Control) Act*, 1946.

Pensions Appeal Tribunals (Pensions Appeal Act, 1943)

These hear appeals against the Minister of Pensions concerning war pensions.

Rent Assessment Committees (Rent Act, 1965)

These fix fair rents for houses with rateable value not exceeding £200 (£400 in London) on appeal from the decision of a Rent Officer.

SOURCES.—P. and G. Ford, *A Breviate of Parliamentary Papers* (3 vols, 1951–61); H. M. Clokie and J. W. Robinson, *Royal Commissions of Inquiry: the Significance of Investigations in British Politics* (1937); R. V. Vernon and N. Mansergh, *Advisory Bodies* (1937); C. J. Hanser, *Guide to Decision: the Royal Commission* (1966); G. W. Keeton, *Trial by Tribunal* (1960); Reports of Royal Commissions and most Reports are published as Command Papers; they will be found in the lists of H.M.S.O. publications, and in the House of Commons Sessional Papers throughout the period.

VIII

ADMINISTRATION OF JUSTICE

Major Criminal Justice Legislation 1900-1967

Poor Prisoners' Defence Act, 1903. This was the first Act which made provision for legal aid, which was limited to trials on indictment.

The Probation of Offenders Act, 1907. This extended courts' probation powers and allowed appointment of official probation officers.

The Criminal Appeal Act, 1907. This created the Court of Criminal Appeal.

The Prevention of Crime Act, 1908. This provided for 'borstal training' of young recidivists and 'preventive detention' for adult habitual criminals.

The Children Act, 1908. This created 'places of detention' (later 'Remand Homes') and Juvenile Courts; it also prohibited imprisonment of those under 14, restricted imprisonment of those from 14-17 and abolished death sentence for those under 17.

The Criminal Justice Administration Act, 1914. This required Summary Courts to give time for payment of fines.

Poor Prisoners' Defence Act, 1930. This Act provided a comprehensive system of legal aid, extending aid to preliminary inquiries and to cases heard summarily before magistrates' courts.

Summary Jurisdiction (Appeals) Act, 1933. This Act made provision for free legal aid for criminal cases, payable out of county or borough funds at the discretion of the magistrates.

The Children and Young Persons Act, 1933. This Act which followed the 1927 Report of the Cecil Committee on the treatment of young offenders, codified and extended 'care and protection' law; it also raised the age of criminal responsibility from 7 to 8.

The Administration of Justice (Miscellaneous Provisions) Act, 1933. This abolished Grand Juries.

The Criminal Justice Act, 1948. Following the lines of a 1938 Bill abandoned through the onset of war, this extended the fining powers of higher courts; it further restricted imprisonment of juveniles and abolished distinction between penal servitude, imprisonment, etc.; it also improved law on probation, introduced corrective training and a new form of preventive detention and it provided for remand centres, attendance centres, and detention centres.

Legal Aid and Advice Act, 1949. This introduced a new system of aid for civil cases. It provided for the establishment of a network of local committees, composed of solicitors and some barristers to grant legal aid under regulations made by the Lord Chancellor. By this Act, aid was extended to cover all proceedings in civil courts and civil proceedings in magistrates' courts, except for certain types of action (of which defamation and breach of promise were the most important).

Cost in Criminal Cases Act, 1952. This Act empowered the courts, in the case of an indictable offence, to order reasonable defence costs to be paid out of public funds, when the accused was discharged or acquitted.

The Homicide Act, 1957. This amended the law on murder, distinguishing capital and non-capital murder and introducing the defence of diminished responsibility.

The First Offenders Act, 1958. This restricted imprisonment of adults by Summary Courts.

Legal Aid Act, 1960. This relates financial conditions for legal aid and makes further provision for the remuneration of counsel and solicitors.

The Criminal Justice Act, 1961. This provided compulsory supervision after release from detention centres and rationalised custodial sentences for 17–21 age-group.

The Children and Young Persons Act, 1963. This raised the age of criminal responsibility from 8 to 10, and redefined the need for 'care, protection, and control'.

The Criminal Injuries Compensation Board was set up in 1964, under an ex gratia State Scheme for compensating victims of crimes of violence.

The Murder (Abolition of Death Penalty) Act, 1965. This suspended death penalty until 1970, and substituted a mandatory 'life' sentence.

The Criminal Justice Act, 1967. This introduced suspended sentence, parole, a new type of sentence for recidivists and further restricts imprisonment of first offenders. It allowed majority verdicts (10–2) by juries.

The Theft Act, 1967. This rationalised definitions of theft and other dishonesty.

The Criminal Law Act, 1967. This replaced the distinction between felonies and misdemeanours, with a distinction between arrestable and non-arrestable offences.

SOURCES.—R. M. Jackson, *Enforcing the Law* (1967); N. D. Walker, *Crime and Punishment in Britain* (1965); K. Smith and D. J. Keenan, *English Law* (1963); G. Rose, *The Struggle for Penal Reform* (1961).

Principal Judges

Lord Chief Justice

1894	Ld Russell of Killowen	1922	Ld Hewart
1900	Ld Alverstone	1940	Vt Caldecote
1913	Ld Reading (Vt) (E)	1946	Ld Goddard
1921	Ld Trevethin	1958	Ld Parker of Waddington

Master of the Rolls

1897	Sir N. Lindley (Ld)	1923	Sir E. Pollock (Ld Hanworth)
1900	Sir R. Webster (Ld Alverstone)		
1900	Sir A. Smith	1935	Ld Wright
1901	Sir R. Collins	1937	Sir W. Greene (Ld)
1907	Sir H. Cozens-Hardy (Ld)	1949	Sir R. Evershed (Ld)
1918	Sir C. Eady	1962	Ld Denning
1919	Ld Sterndale		

President of the Probate, Divorce and Admiralty Division

1892	Sir F. Jeune	1918	Ld Sterndale
1905	Sir G. Barnes	1919	Sir H. Duke (Ld Merrivale)
1909	Sir J. Bigham	1933	Sir B. Merriman (Ld)
1910	Sir S. Evans	1962	Sir J. Simon

Lord President of the Court of Session

1899	Ld Kinross	1935	Ld Normand
1905	Ld Dunedin	1947	Ld Cooper
1913	Ld Strathclyde	1955	Ld Clyde
1920	Ld Clyde		

Monopolies and Restrictive Practices Commission (Chairman) 1948–56

1948	Sir A. Carter	1954	(Sir) D. Cairns

(Monopolies Commission)

1956   R. Levy
1965   (Sir) A. Roskill

Lords of Appeal in Ordinary

1887–1910	Ld Macnaghten	1946–1949	Ld Uthwatt
1889–1900	Ld Morris	1946–1949	Ld du Parcq
1894–1907	Ld Davey	1947–1951	Ld MacDermott
1899–1909	Ld Robertson	1947–1953	Ld Normand
1900–1905	Ld Lindley	1947–1957	Ld Oaksey
1905–1928	Ld Atkinson	1947–1959	Ld Morton of
1907–1910	Ld Collins		Henryton
1909–1929	Ld Shaw	1948–	Ld Reid
1910–1912	Ld Robson	1949–1950	Ld Greene
1912–1921	Ld Moulton	1949–1964	Ld Radcliffe
1913–1918	Ld Parker	1950–1961	Ld Tucker
1913–1930	Ld Sumner (Vt)	1950–1954	Ld Asquith of
1913–1932	Ld Dunedin (Vt)		Bishopstone
1918–1922	Vt Cave	1951–1960	Ld Cohen
1921–1929	Ld Carson	1953–1965	Ld Keith of Avonholm
1923–1937	Ld Blanesburgh	1954–1960	Ld Somervell of
1928–1944	Ld Atkin		Harrow
1929–1935	Ld Tomlin	1957–1962	Ld Denning
1929–1946	Ld Russell of Killowen	1959–1963	Ld Jenkins
1929–1948	Ld Thankerton	1960–	Ld Morris of Borth-
1929–39 & 1941–47			y-Gest
	Ld Macmillan	1960–	Ld Hodson
1932–35 & 1937–47	Ld Wright	1961–	Ld Guest
1935–38 & 1939–41		1961–1962	Ld Devlin
	Ld Maugham (Vt)	1962–	Ld Pearce
1935–1938	Ld Roche	1962–1965	Ld Evershed
1938–1944	Ld Romer	1964–	Ld Upjohn
1938–1955	Ld Porter	1964–	Ld Donovan
1944–51 & 1954–62		1964–	Ld Wilberforce
	Ld Simonds (Vt)	1965–	Ld Pearson
1944–1946	Ld Goddard	1968–	Ld Diplock

and such peers of Parliament as are holding, or have held, high judicial office.

Lords Justices of Appeal

1892–1900	Sir A. Levin Smith	1907–1915	Sir W. Kennedy
1894–1901	Sir J. Rigby	1912–1913	Sir J. Hamilton
1897–1901	Sir R. Collins	1913–1918	Sir C. Eady
1897–1914	Sir R. Williams	1913–1916	Sir W. Phillimore
1899–1906	Sir R. Romer	1914–1919	Sir W. Pickford
1900–1906	Sir J. Stirling	1915–1927	Sir J. Bankes
1901–1906	Sir J. Mathew	1915–1926	Sir T. Warrington
1901–1907	Sir H. Cozens-Hardy	1916–1934	Sir T. Scrutton
1906–1912	Sir J. Moulton	1918–1919	Sir H. Duke
1906–1913	Sir G. Farwell	1919–1928	Sir J. Atkin
1906–1915	Sir H. Buckley	1919–1923	Sir R. Younger

1923–1928	Sir C. Sargant	1948–1957	Sir A. Denning
1926–1934	Sir P. Lawrence	1949–1959	Sir D. Jenkins
1927–1938	Sir F. Greer	1950–1957	Sir N. Birkett
1928–1929	Sir J. Sankey	1951–1960	Sir F. Hodson
1928–1929	F. Russell	1951–1960	Sir J. Morris
1929–1940	Sir H. Slesser	1951–1960	Sir C. Romer
1929–1938	Sir M. Romer	1954–1958	Sir H. Parker
1934–1935	Sir F. Maugham	1957–1968	Sir F. Sellers
1934–1935	Sir A. Roche	1957–1963	Sir B. Ormerod
1935–1937	Sir W. Greene	1957–1962	Sir H. Pearce
1935–1948	Sir L. Scott	1958–1968	S.r H. Willmer
1937–1946	Sir F. MacKinnon	1959–	Sir C. Harman
1938–1942	Sir A. Clauson	1960–1961	Sir P. Devlin
1938–1945	Vt Finlay	1960–1965	Sir G. Upjohn
1938–1944	Sir F. Luxmoore	1960–1963	Sir T. Donovan
1938–1944	Sir R. Goddard	1961–	Sir H. Dankwerts
1938–1946	Sir H. du Parcq	1961–	Sir W. Davies
1944–1947	Sir G. Lawrence	1961–1968	Sir K. Diplock
1944–1947	Sir F. Morton	1962–	Sir C. Russell
1945–1950	Sir F. Tucker	1964–	Sir C. Salmon
1945–1951	Sir A. Bucknill	1965–	Sir E. Winn
1946–1954	Sir D. Somervell	1966–	Sir E. Davies
1946–1951	Sir L. Cohen	1966–	Sir E. Sachs
1946–1951	Sir C. Asquith	1968–	Sir J. Widgery
1947–1948	Sir F. Wrottesley	1968–	Sir F. Atkinson
1947–1949	Sir R. Evershed	1968–	Sir H. Phillimore
1948–1957	Sir J. Singleton	1968–	Sir S. Karminski

and ex officio *the Lord High Chancellor (President), the Lord Chief Justice, the Master of the Rolls, and the President of the Probate, Divorce and Admiralty Division.*

SOURCES.—*The Law List 1900–; Who Was Who 1900–,* and *Who's Who; Whitaker's Almanack 1900–.*

Statute Law Commission (Vice-Chairman)
1965   Sir L. Scarman

Statistics of Crime in Great Britain

Years	Indictable Offences known to Police		Total tried in all Courts for Indictable Offences		Non-indictable Offences			
					Criminal		Non-criminal	
Average for years	('000s)	Rate per 100,000 of the Population	('000s)	Rate per 100,000 of the Population	('000s)	Rate per 100,000 of the Population	('000s)	Rate per 100,000 of the Population
1897–1901	79	249	53	165	103	323	629	1,973
1902–06	90	266	59	176	88	261	642	1,903
1907–11	102	288	65	184	76	216	581	1,640
1914–18	85	246	59	170	57	165	461	1,337
1920–24	107	280	59	154	65	170	491	1,293
1925–29	128	325	61	163	53	136	550	1,339
1930–34	195	484	69	173	46	113	543	1,349
1935–39	267	733	82	224	43	118	682	1,868
1940–44	363	972	111	296	42	112	317	848
1945–49	486	1,278	125	328	46	122	432	1,134
1950–54	481	1,257	128	334	45	118	579	1,510
1955–59	559	1,397	137	348	50	126	731	1,848
1960–64	899	2,255	203	508	68	171	995	2,497

Before 1935–39 the proportions are calculated on the whole population, not on the population over the age of criminal responsibility (8 years). The rise in these proportions in the 1930s is slightly exaggerated due to the use of the corrected figure. The total number of persons tried in the courts refers to the number of appearances before the courts, and not to the number of *different* persons tried in any one year.

SOURCES.—G. Rose, *The Struggle for Penal Reform* (1961), pp. 286–95. *Criminal Statistics* are published annually as Command Papers. A summary of statistics can be found in the *Annual Abstract of Statistics, 1900–.*

Police Force

	England & Wales		Scotland		Ireland (N. Ireland only from 1930)	
	No. of forces	No. of Police	No. of forces	Authorised no. of Police	No. of forces	No. of Police
1900	179	41,900	64	4,900	1	12,300
1910	190	49,600	63	5,600	1	11,900
1920	191	56,500	59	6,500	1	11,600
1930	183	58,000	49	6,600	1	2,800
1940	183	57,300	48	6,800	1	2,900
1950	129	62,600	33	7,200	1	2,800
1960	125	72,300	33	8,700	1	2,900
1965	120	83,300	31	10,200	1	3,000

SOURCES.—*The War Against Crime in England and Wales 1959–1964*, Cmnd. 2296/1964; C. Reith, *A Short History of the British Police* (1948); J. M. Hart, *The British Police* (1951); B. Whitaker, *The Police* (1965); M. Banton, *The Police and the Community* (1964); Sir F. Newsam, *The Home Office* (2nd ed. 1955); Sir J. Moylan, *New Scotland Yard* (1934); Ld Devlin, *The Criminal Prosecution in England* (1966); Sir C. Allen, *The Queen's Peace* (1953); C. Reith, *A New Study of Police History* (1954); *Royal Commission on Police Powers and Procedure*, Cmd. 3297/1929; *Royal Commission on the Police*, Cmnd. 1728/1962. Much information on the police is available in three reports from the House of Commons Estimates Committee H.C. 307 of 1957–8, H.C. 293 of 1962–3, and H.C. 145 of 1966–7. Annual Reports of H.M. Inspectors of Constabulary.

Prisoners

Daily Average Population of Prisons and Borstal Institutions, Detention Centres and Remand Centres
England and Wales

1900 . .	14,739
1910 . .	20,904
1920 . .	11,000
1930 . .	11,346
1940 . .	9,377
1950 . .	20,175
1960 . .	26,824
1965 . .	30,421

SOURCE.—*Reports of Prison Commissioners for England and Wales*, published annually.

O

IX

SOCIAL CONDITIONS

Population

U.K. POPULATION 1901–1967
(thousands)

1901	41,459	1921	47,123	1941	48,216	1961	52,816
1902	41,893	1922	44,372	1942	48,400	1962	53,341
1903	42,237	1923	44,597	1943	48,789	1963	53,678
1904	42,611	1924	44,916	1944	49,016	1964	54,066
1905	42,981	1925	45,060	1945	49,182	1965	54,436
1906	43,361	1926	45,233	1946	49,217	1966	54,744
1907	43,738	1927	45,389	1947	49,571	1967	56,068
1908	44,124	1928	45,578	1948	50,065		
1909	44,519	1929	45,672	1949	50,363		
1910	44,916	1930	45,866	1950	50,616		
1911	45,222	1931	46,038	1951	50,225		
1912	45,436	1932	46,335	1952	50,444		
1913	45,648	1933	46,520	1953	50,611		
1914	46,048	1934	46,666	1954	50,784		
1915	44,333	1935	46,869	1955	50,968		
1916	43,710	1936	47,081	1956	51,208		
1917	43,280	1937	47,289	1957	51,456		
1918	43,116	1938	47,494	1958	51,680		
1919	44,599	1939	47,762	1959	51,986		
1920	46,472	1940	48,226	1960	52,383		

SOURCES

1. Census figures for 1901, 1911, 1921, 1931 and 1951. Figures for other years are mid-year estimates. Figures for 1900–21 inclusive include S. Ireland. Figures for 1915–20 and for 1940–1950 relate to civil population only. *Annual Reports of the Registrars-General for England and Wales, Scotland, and N. Ireland.*

POPULATION OF MAIN CONURBATIONS
(thousands)

	1901	1911	1921	1931	1951	1961	1967[a]
Greater London	6,586	7,256	7,488	8,215	8,348	8,172	7,881[b]
S.E. Lancashire	2,117	2,328	2,361	2,427	2,423	2,427	2,452
W. Midlands	1,483	1,634	1,773	1,933	2,237	2,344	2,446
W. Yorkshire	1,524	1,590	1,614	1,655	1,693	1,702	1,730
Merseyside	1,030	1,157	1,263	1,347	1,382	1,386	1,369
Tyneside	678	761	816	827	835	852	849
Central Clydeside	(1,343)	(1,461)	1,638	1,690	1,760	1,802	1,764

[a] Mid-year estimate.   [b] Reconstituted to cover Great London Council Area.

SOURCES.—*Censuses of Population*, England and Wales and Scotland. Central Clydeside figures for 1901 and 1911 are estimates from B. R. Mitchell and P. Deane, *An Abstract of British Historical Statistics* (1962). 1967 figures, *Annual Abstract of Statistics.*

BIRTH RATES, DEATH RATES, AND MARRIAGES IN THE U.K.

	Total Births per 1000 Population	Total Deaths per 1000 Population	Total Marriages per 1000 Population
1900	28·2	18·4	15·1
1910	25·0	14·0	14·3
1920	25·4	12·9	19·4
1930	16·8	11·7	15·5
1940	14·6	14·4	22·2
1950	16·2	11·8	16·1
1960	17·5	11·5	15·0
1967	17·0	11·0	15·6

Figures for 1900, 1910 and 1920 include Southern Ireland. Death rate in 1940 based on civil deaths and population only.

SOURCE.—*Annual Reports of the Registrars-General.*

AGE DISTRIBUTION OF THE POPULATION OF THE U.K.
(Percentages)

Age Groups	1901	1911	1921 [a]	1931	1939	1951	1960	1966
Under 10	22·2	21·0	18·2	16·1	14·1	16·0	15·1	16·3
10–19	20·3	19·1	19·0	16·8	16·3	12·9	14·9	14·8
20–29	18·3	17·3	16·2	17·1	15·6	14·2	12·7	12·9
30–39	13·9	15·1	14·5	14·5	16·0	14·5	13·7	12·4
40–49	10·5	11·4	13·1	12·9	13·1	14·8	13·5	13·0
50–59	7·3	7·9	9·6	11·1	11·3	11·9	13·2	13·0
60–69	4·7	5·1	6·0	7·3	8·5	8·9	9·4	10 0
70–79	2·2	2·5	2·7	3·4	4·1	5·3	5·6	5·6
80 and over	0·6	0·6	0·7	0·8	1·0	1·5	1·9	2·0
Total	100·0	100·0	100·0	100·0	100·0	100·0	100·0	100·0

[a] Percentages for 1921 are for England, Wales and Scotland only.

SOURCES.—Census figures for 1901, 1911, 1921, 1931, 1951. Mid-year estimate 1939, 1960 and 1966. Registrars-General of England and Wales, and Scotland, *Censuses of Population,* and the *Annual Abstract of Statistics.*

EXPECTATION OF LIFE
England and Wales
(Average future expected lifetime at birth)

Years	Male	Female	Years	Male	Female
1900–02	46	50	1938	61	66
1910–12	52	55	1950–52	66	72
1920–22	56	60	1960–62	68	74
1930–32	59	63	1964–66	69	75

SOURCES.—*Annual Reports of the Registrar-General for England and Wales,* and the *Government Actuary's Department, Annual Abstract of Statistics.*

MAIN CAUSES OF DEATH
England and Wales
(thousands)

	1900	1910	1920	1930	1940	1950	1960	1964
Total deaths	588	483	466	455	572	510	526	611
Due to:								
Tuberculosis	61	51	43	36	27	16	3	3
Cancer	27	35	44	57	69	83	96	104
Vascular lesions of the nervous system [a]	41	30	49	41	52	65	76	74
Heart diseases	n.a.	49	53	90	136	146	153	152
Pneumonia	44	40	37	28	29	18	24	30
Bronchitis	54	34	38	19	46	28	26	29
Violent Causes	20	19	17	22	47 [b]	19	23	25

[a] All diseases of the nervous system, 1900–30.
[b] Including 22,000 deaths of civilians due to operations of war.

Infant mortality (i.e. deaths under 1 year) per 1000 live births: 1900 — 154; 1910 — 105; 1920 — 80; 1930 — 64; 1940 — 57; 1950 — 30; 1960 — 22; 1964 — 20.

SOURCE.—*Annual Reports and Statistical Reviews of the Registrars-General for England and Wales.*

AVERAGE AGE AT FIRST MARRIAGE
England and Wales

Years	Bachelors	Spinsters
1901–05	26·9	25·4
1911–15	27·5	25·8
1921–25	27·5	25·6
1931–35	27·4	25·5
1941–45	26·8	24·6
1951–55	26·5	24·2
1959–60	25·9	23·5
1964–	25·2	22·8

SOURCE.—*Annual Reports of Registrars-General for England and Wales.*

DIVORCES
Great Britain
Decrees made absolute

1910	.	.	801	1950	.	.	32,516
1920	.	.	3,747	1960	.	.	25,672
1930	.	.	3,944	1966	.	.	41,898
1940	.	.	8,396				

SOURCE.—*Annual Reports of Registrars-General for England, Wales and Scotland.*

INTERCENSAL CHANGES IN POPULATION
(thousands)

	Population at beginning of period	Actual increases	Excess of births over deaths	Net gain or loss by migration
1901–1911	38,237	3,846	4,666	− 820
1911–1921	42,082	1,945	2,863	− 919
1921–1931	44,027	2,011	2,683	− 672
1931–1951	46,038	4,187	3,751	+ 465
1951–1961	50,225	2,484	2,443	+ 12

SOURCE.—*Annual Abstract of Statistics.*

NET EMIGRATION FROM GREAT BRITAIN AND IRELAND

Commonwealth citizens travelling by the long sea routes to non-European countries,
1900–50 ; all routes 1964

	1900	1901	1920	1931	1938	1946	1950	1964
All Countries	71,188	241,164	199,047	− 39,056	− 6,467	103,504	54,153	− 60,000
U.S.A.	47,978	75,021	60,067	− 10,385	− 1,432	45,751	8,541	− 11,300
Canada	7,803	115,955	94,496	− 10,464	− 3,974	43,414	6,464	− 75,300
Australasia	6,259	34,657	28,405	− 8,760	2,204	8,443	54,581	− 22,000
S. Africa	7,417	8,314	7,844	− 1,263	2,037	2,242	1,912	− 10,600

Southern Ireland excluded from 1938 onwards.
SOURCES.—1900–1950 *External Migration 1815–1950*, N. H. Carrier and J. R. Jeffrey, *Studies on Medical and Population Subjects No. 6*, General Register Office (1953). 1964 figures are for all people travelling by all routes and are derived from the Board of Trade International Passenger Survey.

NATURALISATION

Total certificates granted by the Home Department or oaths taken in period

1901–10	.	. 7,997	1931–40	.	. 15,454
1911–20	.	. 11,293	1941–50	.	. 51,132
1921–30	.	. 9,849	1951–60	.	. 44,977

SOURCES.—N. H. Carrier and J. R. Jeffrey, *External Migration, 1815–1950, Studies on Medical and Population Subjects, No. 6*, General Register Office (H.M.S.O., 1953), and *Whitaker's Almanack*.

ALIENS IN GREAT BRITAIN
(thousands)

	1901	1931	1961
Russia, Poland, Finland	93	71	128
Austro-Hungarian group	11	5	23
Balkans	6	6	15
Germany	52	16	37
France	22	16	14
Italy	24	22	70
Low Countries	12	12	18
Sweden, Norway, Denmark	17	11	8
Spain and Portugal	3	3	19
Switzerland	9	10	9
Total Europe	249	174	337
USA	17	13	80
All other countries	4	14	30
Total	270	210	447

SOURCES.—N. H. Carrier and J. R. Jeffrey *External Migration 1815–1950* (1953). 1961 Census *Summary Tables* (1966). Statistics are also available in Annual Home Office returns (summarised in the *Annual Abstracts of Statistics*) for the number of aliens registered with the police. In 1961 this number fell from 406,000 to 125,000 when permanently resident aliens were no longer required to register.

Commonwealth Immigration

Commonwealth immigration came under systematic control under the Commonwealth Immigrants Act of 1962.   This act was strengthened by the Commonwealth Immigrants Act of 1968.   The Race Relations Acts of 1965 and 1968, making race discrimination illegal, may be seen as companion legislation.

ANNUAL NET COMMONWEALTH IMMIGRATION INTO THE UNITED KINGDOM

Year	West Indians[a]	Indians	Pakistanis[a]	Australians[b]	Others[b]	Total
1956	29,800	5,600	2,100	n.a.	n.a.	n.a.
1957	23,000	6,000	5,200	n.a.	n.a.	n.a.
1958	15,000	6,200	4,700	n.a.	n.a.	n.a.
1959	16,400	2,900	900	n.a.	n.a.	n.a.
1960	49,700	5,900	2,500	n.a.	n.a.	n.a.
1961	66,300	23,750	25,100	n.a.	n.a.	n.a.
1962						
Jan/June	31,800	19,050	25,080	n.a.	n.a.	n.a.
Jul/Dec	3,241	3,050	− 137	− 2,082	− 1,569	+2,503
1963	7,928	17,498	16,330	3,774	20,464	66,000
1964[c]	14,848	15,513	10,980	5,562	28,596	75,499
1965	13,400	18,815	7,432	6,367	17,805	63,819
1966	9,023	18,402	8,008	2,056	13,859	51,348
1967	9,109	22,638	21,176	−5,236	· 11,219	36,368

[a] Fuller statistics became available under the Commonwealth Immigrants Act, 1962.
[b] No reliable estimates for individual years prior to the Act.
[c] 1964 figures include diplomats exempt from control under the Act.

COMMONWEALTH IMMIGRANTS IN THE U.K.

according to the 1961 Census and the 1966 Sample Census

Year	W. Indians	Indians and Pakistanis	Australians	Others in British Territories	Total
1961	173,076	115,982[a]	23,390[a]	285,962[b]	596,755
1966	267,850	205,340[a]	44,480	324,640[b]	942,310

[a] Persons born in these countries but British by birth or descent have been deducted for 1961.   No nationality data were included in the 1966 Sample Census, and therefore, on the basis of past data, the estimate for those born in the Indian subcontinent has been reduced by 100,000.
[b] The largest contributors to this total are Cypriots, New Zealanders, Maltese, Canadians and South Africans.

TYPES OF COMMONWEALTH ENTRANT

since 1 Jul 1962

	Holders of Ministry of Labour Vouchers	Dependants	Students	Net balance of Commonwealth Migration
Jul-Dec 62	51,121	8,832	12,596	+ 10,937
1963	30,125	26,234	18,484	+ 66,000
1964	14,705	37,460	17,705	+ 75,499
1965	12,880	41,214	12,880	+ 63,819
1966	5,461	42,026	13,831	+ 50,348
1967	4,978	52,813	10,988	+ 50,348

SOURCE.—Home Office Statistics under the Commonwealth Immigrants Act 1962, published annually since 1963.

Housing

(a) Major Housing Acts

Housing and Town Planning Act, 1909. This amended the law relating to the housing of the working classes, and provided for town-planning schemes. It also provided for the establishment of public health and housing committees of county councils.

Housing Acts, 1919, 1923, and *1924.* These Acts provided for varying subsidies to encourage the building of new houses for the working classes.

Housing Act, 1930. This Act extended subsidies and provided wider powers for slum clearance.

Housing (Financial Provisions) Act, 1933. This reduced the general subsidies, but increased subsidies for slum clearance.

Housing (Financial Provisions) Act, 1938. This Act regulated subsidies to housing.

Housing (Financial Provisions) Act, 1958. This Act provided grants for improvements to private houses.

House Purchase and Housing Act, 1959. This extended grants for improvements.

Housing Act, 1961. Lays down regulations for landlords leasing houses for less than 7 years to keep the structure, exterior, installations, etc., of the house in repair and proper working order.

Housing Act, 1964. Sets up the Housing Corporation to assist Housing Societies to provide housing accommodation and confers powers and duties on local authorities with regard to housing improvements.

(b) Major Rent and Mortgage Interest Restriction Acts

Increase of Rent and Mortgage Interest (Restrictions) Acts, 1914 and *1920.* These acts established a limit to the rent of small houses, and protected tenants from eviction.

Rent Acts, 1919–39. These altered the exact limits on rents.

Rent Act, 1939. This extended rent restriction and security of tenure to houses which had become decontrolled and to new houses.

Furnished House Rent Control Act, 1946. This Act created rent tribunals to fix the prices of furnished lettings.

Landlord and Tenant Rent Control Act, 1949. Rent tribunals were authorised to determine 'reasonable' rents, on the application of the tenants, who could also apply for the recovery of premiums. The Act applied to unfurnished houses and flats.

Housing Repairs and Rents Act, 1954. This Act authorised landlords to increase rents where sufficient repairs to their property had been carried out. Rent could also be increased to cover the increase in cost since 1939 of other services provided by the landlord.

Rent Act, 1957. This decontrolled many houses in 1958 and permitted substantial increases on controlled rents.

Rent Act, 1965. Provides for the registration of rents, introduces controls, and provides security of tenure subject to certain conditions. A landlord cannot enforce a right to possession against a tenant without a court order.

PERMANENT DWELLINGS BUILT
England and Wales

	Private Enter-prise[a] ('000s)	Local Authorities ('000s)	Total[b] ('000s)		Private Enter-prise[a] ('000s)	Local Authorities ('000s)	Total[b] ('000s)
				1941	6·9	2·9	9·8
				1942	8·2	1·4	9·6
No figures available 1900–1919				1943	3·3	2·5	5·8
1919[c]		0·6		1944	3·2	2·4	5·6
1920	97·5	15·6	252·0	1945	0·9	0·5	1·4
1921		80·8		1946	29·9	21·2	51·1
1922		57·5		1947	40·9	86·6	127·5
1923	71·8	14·3	86·1	1948	35·6	170·8	206·4
1924	116·2	20·7	136·9	1949	30·0	141·8	171·8
1925	129·2	44·2	173·4	1950	33·0	139·4	172·4
1926	143·5	74·1	217·6	1951	30·3	141·6	171·9
1927	134·9	104·1	239·0	1952	43·4	165·6	209·0
1928	113·8	55·7	169·5	1953	76·3	202·9	279·2
1929	140·3	61·8	202·1	1954	109·4	199·6	309·0
1930	128·0	55·9	183·9	1955	120·8	162·5	283·3
1931	130·7	70·1	200·8	1956	128·7	140·0	268·7
1932	144·5	55·9	200·4	1957	131·1	137·6	268·7
1933	210·7	56·0	266·7	1958	128·4	113·1	241·5
1934	287·5	40·2	327·7	1959	149·9	99·5	249·4
1935	271·9	53·5	325·4	1960	166·0	103·2	269·2
1936	275·2	71·8	347·0	1961	175·9	92·9	268·8
1937	259·7	78·0	337·7	1962	173·4	105·3	278·7
1938	230·6	100·9	331·5	1963	173·6	97·0	270·7
1939	145·5	50·5	196·0	1964	217·0	119·5	336·5
1940	27·1	15·4	42·5	1965	133·0	314·2	347·2
				1966	206·0	142·4	346·4
				1967	203·5	162·3	372·8

[a] Including houses built for families of police, prison staff, armed services and other services.
[b] Flats are included, and each is counted as one unit.
[c] 1919–44 years ending 31 Mar of following year. 1945 Apr–Dec. 1946 onwards calendar years.

SOURCES.—1919–38 M. E. Bowley, *Housing and the State, 1919–44* (1945); 1939 onwards *Annual Abstract of Statistics*. For conflicting figures for G.B. see B. Weber, 'A New Index of Residential Construction, 1838–1950', *Scottish Journal of Political Economy*, No. 2, June 1955.

NUMBER OF HOUSES
England and Wales

Occupied and Unoccupied (to nearest '000)			
1901 . .	6,710	1939 . .	11,263
1911 . .	7,550	1951 . .	12,389
1921 . .	7,979	1961 . .	14,648 [a]
1931 . .	9,400		

[a] Excluding vacant dwellings.

SOURCES.—1901, 1911, 1921, 1931, 1951, 1961 *Population Censuses*; 1939 estimates in M. E. Bowley, *Housing and the State, 1919–1944* (1945).

Education

Education Act, 1902. This abolished school boards, gave powers to local authorities to provide secondary education, and made provisions for rate aid to voluntary schools (see Local Government section).

Education (Provision of Meals) Act, 1906. By this Act cheap school meals for children attending public elementary schools were given statutory recognition. Local authorities were to use voluntary organisations, contributing only to the cost of administration. In 1914 half the cost of the meals was provided by the Exchequer.

Education (Administrative Provisions) Act, 1907. This provided for medical inspection for elementary schools. In 1912 the Board of Education made grants to Local Education Authorities to make the treatment of children possible.

Education Act, 1918. Compulsory attendance was made universal until the age of 14. Day continuation (part-time compulsory) education was introduced for children between school-leaving age and 18. This almost disappeared under the economies proposed by Geddes but was revived in 1944.

Free milk was supplied to children in need in 1921. In 1934 it was subsidised by the Milk Marketing Board. Since 1946 it has been free to all.

Education Act, 1936. Provision was made for the school-leaving age to be raised to 15 in Sep 1939 but this was not implemented. 1940–41, the school meal service was expanded and subsidised to meet war-time needs. These provisions were continued after the war, by the *Education Act, 1944.*

Education Act, 1944. This Act changed the title of the President of the Board of Education to the Minister of Education. Primary and secondary education was divided at '11 plus', and secondary education was generally provided under this Act in three types of schools, grammar, technical, and modern. Some local authorities preferred to use their powers to amalgamate these into comprehensive schools. Provision was made for compulsory part-time education between the school-leaving age and 18 in county colleges, but this has not been implemented. The minimum school-leaving age was raised to 15 (in 1947) and provision was made for raising it to 16. Powers were granted under this Act, which led to a great expansion of technical colleges. No fees were to be charged in schools which were publicly provided or aided by grants from the local authority.

School-leaving Age. It was announced in 1964 that the school-leaving age be raised to 16 in the educational year 1970–71. In 1968 this date was put back for four years.

Comprehensive Schools. In 1965 the Ministry of Education asked all local authorities to submit plans for reorganising secondary education on comprehensive lines, with a view to ending selection at 11-plus and the tripartite system.

PUPILS IN SCHOOLS
('000s)

	Public Elementary	On Grant List	Efficient Independent	Other Independent
1900	5,709	n.a.	n.a.	n.a.
1910	6,039	151	22	n.a.
1920	5,878	340	46	n.a.
1930	4,936	411	82	n.a.
	Maintained	Direct Grant		
1950	5,710	95	204	n.a.
1960	6,924	111	294	203
1967	7,335	127	307	137

SOURCES.—*Annual Abstract of Statistics.*

PERCENTAGE OF VARIOUS AGE-GROUPS IN GRANT-AIDED SCHOOLS
England and Wales

	1938	1950	1960	1965
Age 2–4	10·5	7·7	9·8	9·4
Age 5–14	86·7	92·3	94·2	94·4
Age 15–18	6·1	10·0	13·8	18·7

SOURCE.—*Annual Abstract of Statistics.*

PERCENTAGE OF VARIOUS AGES RECEIVING FULL-TIME EDUCATION
Great Britain

	10 year olds	14 year olds	17 year olds	19 year olds
1870	40	2	1	1
1902	100	9	2	1
1938	100	38	4	2
1962	100	100	15	7

SOURCE.—*Report on Higher Education* (Robbins), Cmnd. 2154/1963.

STUDENTS IN FULL-TIME HIGHER EDUCATION
Great Britain

	University	Teacher Training	Further Education
1901	20,000	5,000	—
1925	42,000	16,000	3,000
1939	50,000	13,000	6,000
1955	82,000	28,000	12,000
1963	118,000	55,000	43,000
1967–8	200,000	105,000	66,000

SOURCE.—*Report on Higher Education* (Robbins), Cmnd. 2154/1963. For 1967–8, Department of Education and Science and Scottish Education Department.

EDUCATIONAL FINANCE
£'000s

	1901	1911	1921	1931	1941	1951	1961
Exchequer Issues (G.B.) on Education and allied matters	12,536	18,744	54,046	55,116	65,600	252,900	204,100
Universities (G.B.) Total Expenditure	12,396	28,742	73,612	68,315	122,600	247,111	706,715
Income from parliamentary grants	4,006	12,711	39,587	44,178	n.a.	149,760	n.a.
Income from Local Education Authorities	6,229	14,191	30,954	35,485	n.a.	97,651	n.a.
Local Education Authorities (England & Wales) Total Expenditure	n.a.	n.a.	3,215	5,787	6,453	24,270	68,470
Income from parliamentary grants	n.a.	n.a.	1,614	1,740	2,438	15,761	49,627
Income from rates	n.a.	n.a.	281	566	599	1,040	1,578

SOURCE.—*Annual Abstract of Statistics* 1900–.

LIBRARY LOANS
United Kingdom

	('000s)
1896 . .	26,225
1911 . .	54,256
1924 . .	85,668
1935 . .	207,982
1939 . .	247,335
1948 . .	294,000
1959 . .	440,095 [a]
1962 . .	460,505 [a]

Figures relate to Public (rate supported) Libraries.

[a] Excluding loans from School libraries run by Public Libraries.

SOURCE.—Information supplied by the Library Association.

SOURCES.—The main facts on education may be found in a series of official reports from *ad hoc* committees or from sub-committees of the Consultation Committee of the Board of (Ministry of) Education.

Education of the Adolescent (Hadow)(1926); *The Primary School* (Hadow)(1931); *Secondary Education* (Spens) (1938); *The School Curriculum* (Norwood) (1943); *Education Reconstruction* (Cmd. 6458/1942–3); *Public Schools* (Flemming) (1944); *Education from 15 to 18* (Crowther) (1959); *Half Our Future* (Newsom) (1963); *Higher Education* (Robbins) (Cmnd. 2154/1963); *Primary Education* (Plowden) (1967). Since 1947 the Ministry of Education has published an *Annual Report* and *A Guide to the Educational Structure of England and Wales*. Among books on the educational system are the following: H. C. A. Barnard, *A Short History of English Education 1760–1944* (new ed. 1959); G. Baron, *A Bibliographical Guide to the English Educational System* (2nd rev. ed. 1960); H. C. Dent, *The Educational System of England and Wales* (1961); G. Kalton, *The Public Schools: a Factual Survey* (1966); R. Pedley, *The Comprehensive School* (3rd ed. 1966); J. S. McClure, *Educational Documents 1816–1963* (1965); L. Selby-Bigge, *The Board of Education* (1934); W. Taylor, *The Secondary Modern School* (1963).

Social Security

Old Age Pensions Act, 1908. This granted non-contributory pensions ranging from one to five shillings a week to be paid from national funds, subject to a means test, at the age of 70, where income was under £31 p.a.

National Insurance Act, 1911 (National Health Insurance, Pt. I). This was the first part of an act providing insurance against both ill-health and unemployment. The Act covered all those between the ages of 16 and 70 who were manual workers or earning not more than £160 p.a. (This income limit was raised in 1920 and 1942.) The self-employed, non-employed, and those already provided for by other health insurance schemes were not insurable under this Act. The scheme was administered through independent units, or 'approved societies'. Local insurance committees were set up. The insurance included benefits for sickness, maternity, and medical needs. A weekly contribution was made by the insured person, his employer, and the government. The basic weekly sickness benefit was 10s. for men, 7s. 6d. for women. It also set up general medical and pharmaceutical services.

Widows', Orphans' and Old Age Contributory Pensions Act, 1925. This provided for a contributory scheme, covering almost the same field as the national health insurance scheme. Pensions were payable to the widows of insured persons, and to insured persons and their wives over the age of 70. This age limit was reduced to 65 in 1928. The weekly rates were 10s. for widows, with additional allowances of 5s. for the first child and 3s. for each other child, 7s. 6d. for orphans and 10s. for old age pensioners.

Widows', Orphans' and Old Age Contributory Pensions Act, 1929. This Act provided a pension at age 55 for certain widows who could not satisfy the conditions of the 1925 Act.

Widows', Orphans' and Old Age Contributory Pensions (Voluntary Contributors) Act, 1937. This Act created a new scheme of voluntary insurance for old age, widows' and orphans' benefits open to certain persons who were not within the scope of the main scheme.

Old Age and Widows' Pensions Act, 1940. This reduced to 60 the age at which a woman who was herself insured or who was the wife of an insured man could become entitled to an old age pension. The Act also introduced supplementary pensions in cases of need for widow pensioners over the age of 60 and for old age pensioners. The Unemployment Assistance Board was renamed the Assistance Board and became responsible for payment of these supplementary pensions.

National Health Insurance, Contributory Pensions and Workmen's Compensation Act, 1911. This raised the income limit for compulsory insurance of non-manual workers for pensions purposes to £420 p.a.

Public Health Act, 1936. This replaced the 1875 Act, and consolidated the existing legislation.

Family Allowances Act, 1945. This granted a non-contributory allowance, to be paid to the mother, for each child other than the first. 1945–52 5s. per week; 1952– 8s. per week; 1956– 10s. per week for third and subsequent children.

National Health Service Act, 1946. By this Act, hospitals were transferred from local authorities and voluntary bodies and were to be administered by the Minister through regional hospital boards, general medical and dental services through executive councils, and other health services by county and county borough councils. Health centres were to be provided by local authorities for general, mental, dental, and pharmaceutical services, but few were built. Almost all services under the Act were to be free.

National Health Service (Amendment) Act, 1949; National Health Service Acts, 1951 and 1952, and *National Health Service Contributions Acts, 1957–1958.* These made modifications in the original scheme by imposing charges for certain parts of the scheme (prescriptions, dental treatment, etc.).

National Insurance Act, 1946. This Act provided a new scheme of insurance replacing the national health insurance and contributory pensions schemes with effect from 5 Jul 1948. All persons over school-leaving age, except certain married women, became compulsorily insurable. In addition to provisions for unemployment (see p. 206) benefits payable were retirement pension, widow's benefit, and death grant.

National Insurance Act, 1951. This Act introduced an allowance payable with widows' benefits for each dependent child in the family.

Family Allowances and National Insurance Act, 1956. Enabled allowances for dependent children to be paid in certain cases up to the age of 18; introduced new personal rate of widowed mother's allowance, reduced length of marriage condition for widow's pension, and introduced amendments to widows' pensions.

National Insurance Act, 1957. This introduced the child's special allowance for the children of divorced parents payable on the death of the father if he had been contributing towards their support and the mother had not remarried.

National Insurance Act, 1959. This introduced a state scheme of graduated pensions, requiring that both contributions and pensions should be graduated according to salary level.

Mental Health Act, 1959. The Board of Control was abolished and its functions passed to the new Mental Health Review Tribunals, local authorities, and the Minister of Health. The Act redefined the classifications of mental disorders, provided for further safeguards against improper detention, and extended the provisions for voluntary and informal treatment of patients.

Family Allowances and National Insurance Act, 1964. This increased from 18 to 19 the age limit up to which a person could be regarded as a child for the purposes of an increase of benefit or widowed mother's allowance.

Prescription Charges were ended in 1965. They were reimposed in 1968 with exemptions for some categories.

National Insurance Act, 1966. Extended the period of widow's allowance, introduced a scheme of earnings-related supplements to unemployment and sickness benefits and included a widow's supplementary allowance.

Ministry of Social Security Act, 1966 repealed and amended much previous legislation. It provided for the abolition of the Ministry of Pensions and National Insurance and the National Assistance Board and the establishment of the Ministry of Social Security. The Act also provided for a scheme of supplementary benefits to replace the system of allowances which had previously been administered by the National Assistance Board. The benefits are paid as of right to those people whose incomes are below the levels set in the Act and not according to national insurance contribution records.

OLD AGE PENSIONS
Maximum rate for a single person

Jan 1909	. .	5/–
Feb 1920	. .	10/–
Oct 1946	. .	26/–
Sep 1952	. .	32/6
Jan 1958	. .	50/–
Apr 1961	. .	57/6
Mar 1963	. .	67/6
Mar 1965	. .	81/–
Oct 1967	. .	90/–

SOURCES.—Sir E. Wilson and G. S. Mackey, *Old Age Pensions* (1941); *Keesings Contemporary Archives 1931–*; *Report on Social Insurance and Allied Services* (Beveridge), Cmd. 6404/1944, Appendix B, *National Superannuation and Social Insurance*, Cmnd 3883/1969.

Women and Children
Women's Rights

Representation of the People Act, 1918, gave women over 30 the right to vote.

The Sex Disqualification (Removal) Act, 1919, abolished disqualification by sex or marriage for entry to the professions, universities, and the exercise of any public function.

Matrimonial Causes Act, 1923, relieved a wife petitioner of necessity of proving cruelty, desertion etc. in addition to adultery as grounds for divorce. (Further acts in 1927 and 1950 extended grounds for divorce and codified the matrimonial law.)

Guardianship of Infants Act, 1924, vested guardianship of infant children in the parents jointly. If parents disagree either may apply to court, the Court's subsequent decision being guided solely by consideration of the infant's interest.

New English Law of Property, 1926, provided that both married and single women may hold and dispose of their property, real and personal, on the same terms as a man.

Representation of the People Act, 1928, gave women over 21 the right to vote.

Law Reform (Married Women and Tortfeasors) Act, 1935, empowered a married woman to dispose by will of all her property as if she were single.

British Nationality of Women Act, 1948, gave British women the right to retain British nationality on marriage to a foreigner, and ended right of alien women to acquire automatic British nationality when marrying.

Maternity and Child Welfare

Midwives Act, 1902. This Act sought to improve the standards of midwifery. It only became fully operative in 1910. Further Acts were passed in 1936 and 1951.

Notification of Births Act, 1907. This gave powers to local authorities to insist on compulsory notification of births.

Notification of Births Extension Act, 1915. This made notification universally compulsory.

Children Act, 1908. This Act consolidated the existing law and recognised the need for legal protection of children. It provided legislation covering negligence to children. Imprisonment of children was abolished, and remand homes were set up for children awaiting trial. This was to be only in special juvenile courts.

Education (Choice of Employment) Act, 1910. This empowered authorities to set up their own juvenile employment bureaux.

Maternity and Child Welfare Act, 1918. This empowered authorities to set up 'home help' schemes and clinics.

Children and Young Persons Act, 1933. This extended responsibility for children until the age of 17 and included a careful definition of the meaning of the need for care and protection. It established approved schools, and made detailed regulations about juvenile court procedure.

Children Act, 1948. This gave local authorities new responsibilities, with children's officers to administer the children's service (see *Local Government section*).

Children and Young Persons Act, 1963. This extends the power of local authorities to promote the welfare of children and deals with children and young persons in need of supervision, orders approved schools, employment of children and young persons.

Transport and Communications

CURRENT VEHICLE LICENCES [a]

	Cars[b]	Public Transport[c]	Goods Vehicles[d]	Total
1905	15,895	7,491[e]	9,000	32,386
1910	89,411	24,466[e]	30,000	143,877[e]
1915	277,741	44,480[e]	84,600	406,821[e]
1920	474,540	74,608[e]	101,000	650,148[e]
1925	1,151,453	113,267	259,341	1,524,061
1930	1,700,533	114,796	391,997	2,287,326
1935	1,973,945	96,419	490,663	2,581,027
1938	2,406,769	96,718	590,397	3,093,884
1940	1,701,500	88,200	542,200	2,331,900
1945	1,795,700	110,800	740,500	2,647,000
1946	2,232,279	110,704	769,747	3,112,930
1950	3,009,611	141,091	1,263,131	4,413,833
1955	4,781,741	104,664	1,581,814	6,468,219
1960	7,387,075	93,942	1,958,856	9,439,873
1965	10,623,900	96,500	2,219,500	12,939,900

[a] 1905–1920—Figures at 31 Mar 1925 and 1945 at 31 Aug. 1930–38 and 46–65 during quarter ending 30 Sep. [b] Cars, motor-cycles, tricycles and pedestrian controlled vehicles.
[c] Buses, coaches, and trams.
[d] Goods vehicles, haulage including agricultural vehicles, exempt including Government vehicles.
[e] These figures do not include trams. In 1920 there were 14,000 trams.

SOURCES.—*Census of mechanically propelled vehicles* (Ministry of Transport), 1926–62 *Highway Statistics* (Ministry of Transport), 1963 onwards, *The Motor Industry of Great Britain* (Soc. of Motor Manufacturers and Traders). Reports of the Steering Group appointed by the Ministry of Transport, *Traffic in Towns* (Buchanan Report), H.M.S.O. (1965).

RAILWAYS
Great Britain

	Standard Gauge Route Miles	Train Miles (million miles)	Passengers Carried (millions)	Freight[a]	
				Tons (millions)	Ton Miles (millions)
1900	18,680	379·3	962·3	461·1	n.a.
1910	19,986	386·7	936·0	504·7	n.a.
1920	20,147	355,7	1,243·2	332·2	19,173
1930	20,243	397·5	844·9	304·3	17,784
1938	19,934	420·9	1,237·2	265·7	16,266
1950	19,471	384·1	981·7	281·3	22,135
1960	18,369	375·4	1,036·7	248·5	18,650
1967	13,172	202·8[b]	837·3	200·7	—

Excluding operations of London Electric Railway, London Passenger Board, and London Transport throughout.   Standard-gauge Railways only (except 1900 and 1910).

[a] Excluding free-hauled traffic.   [b] Figures for loaded trains only, available 1967.

SOURCE.—British Railways, *Annual Report.*

SHIPPING
Tonnage registered
(United Kingdom)

	'000 gross tons	% of World tonnage
1900	11,514	51·5
1910	16,768	45·0
1920	18,111	33·6
1930	20,322	29·9
1939	17,891	26·1
1950	18,219	21·5
1960	21,131	16·3
1967	21,716	11·9

Steam and motor ships of 100 gross tons and over.

SOURCE.—*Lloyd's Register of Shipping* (Statistical Tables), published annually.

VOLUME OF POSTAL TRAFFIC

Letters, postcards, parcels, registered letters (excluding football pools). Number of inland deliveries.

1903–4	4,300 million	1939–40	7,624
1911–12	5,508	1946–7	6,601
1922–2	5,638	1951–2	7,964
1929–30	6,622	1956–7	8,753
1935–6	7,569	1959–60	9,244
		1965–6	10,461

COST OF FIRST CLASS LETTER MAIL
(inland)

6 May 1840	1d.
3 Jun 1918	1½d.
1 Jun 1920	2d.
29 May 1922	1½d.
1 May 1940	2½d.
1 Oct 1957	3d.
17 May 1965	4d.
16 Sep 1968	5d.

TELEPHONES

United Kingdom [a]	
	('000s)
1900	3
1910	122
1920	980
1930	1,996
1940	3,339
1950	5,171
1960	7,864
1967	12,112

[a] Including Southern Ireland, 1900–20.

SOURCES.—General Post Office, *Post Office Commercial Accounts*, published annually, and *Annual Abstracts of Statistics*.

P

X

EMPLOYMENT AND TRADE UNIONS

Major Employment Legislation

Factory and Workshop Act, 1901. This consolidated, with amendments, all previous Factory and Workshop Acts.

Unemployed Workmen Act, 1905. This established 'Distress Committees' to investigate needs and to provide employment or assistance. Funds were to be partly voluntary, and partly from the local rates.

Labour Exchanges Act, 1909. These were established in 1909 and renamed Employment Exchanges in 1919.

National Insurance Act, 1911. This Act covered all those between the ages of 16 and 70 years, but was limited to manual workers in industries known to be subject to severe and recurrent unemployment. (The Act covered about 2¼ million men.) Within these limits it was compulsory, and financed by a triple weekly levy, from the workman, the employer, and the government. Payment of benefit continued only for a limited period, after which responsibility for the unemployed person lapsed to the poor law. In 1916 the Act was extended to include munitions workers.

Industrial Courts Act, 1919. This provided for the establishment of an Industrial Court and Courts of Inquiry in connection with Trade disputes, and made other provisions for the settlement of such disputes.

Unemployment Insurance Act, 1920. The scheme was extended to cover the same field as the National Health Insurance scheme, and included non-manual workers with an income of under £250 p.a. Workers in agriculture or domestic service were excluded from the insurance scheme until 1936–37. It was administered through the local employment exchanges of the Ministry of Labour. The basic unemployment benefit was 7s. in 1911, increased to 15s. in 1920. It was increased in 1921, and in 1924 was 18s. It was reduced in 1928 and 1931. Additional allowances for dependants were introduced in 1921.

Unemployment Insurance Act, 1927. By this Act the original scheme was completely revised in accordance with the recommendations of the Blanesburgh Committee Report. The new scheme was to provide unlimited benefits after the insured person had satisfied certain qualifying contribution conditions.

Local Government Act, 1929. This Act abolished the Poor Law Guardians, and their responsibilities passed to county councils and county borough councils, who were so far as possible to administer the specialised branches through separate committees.

Poor Law Act, 1930. By this Act poor law was renamed Public Assistance. The existing law was consolidated.

Unemployment Insurance Act, 1930. This made qualification easier for transitional benefit, and abolished the requirement that the unemployed receiving benefits should be 'genuinely seeking work'. Transitional benefits were made to claimants in need of assistance, but unable to fulfil the usual qualifying conditions. Responsibility for the long-term unemployed was placed directly on the Exchequer in 1931, though receipt of benefit was made subject to a 'means test'. Dependants' benefits were increased.

Unemployment Act, 1934. An amended scheme was introduced distinguishing between 'unemployed benefit' paid from the Fund (at the basic rate of 17s. a week) for a limited period to those satisfying contribution conditions, and 'unemployment assistance' which was paid, subject to a 'means test', to those still needing assistance after exhausting their title to benefit, or those who were not entitled. These long-term unemployed were paid directly by the Exchequer through the newly created *Unemployment Assistance Board* (known as Assistance Board from 1940 and from 1948 until 1966 as National Assistance Board). In 1937 juveniles between the ages of 14 and 16 were brought into the scheme for medical benefits only.

Unemployment Insurance (Agriculture) Act, 1936. A separate insurance scheme was set up for agricultural workers granting lower rates of benefit than the general scheme. In 1937, the benefits of voluntary insurance for widows, orphans, etc. (see *Contributory Pensions Act, 1925*), were extended to those with small incomes, without the qualifications of insurable employment essential to insurance under the main scheme. For the first time married women could become voluntary contributors for pensions.

Control of Employment Act, 1939. This gave the government wide powers for the organisation of labour in war-time. Its aim was to make the best use of labour and to direct it to the most vital work.

Determination of Needs Act, 1941. This abolished the household ' means test '.

National Insurance (Industrial Injuries) Act, 1946. This covered all those in insurable employment against injuries and industrial diseases arising from their employment. It was financed by contributions from the insured person, his employer, and the government.

National Insurance Act, 1946. This Act covered all contributors between school-leaving age and pensionable age, for benefits for unemployment, sickness, maternity, retirement, widow's pensions, guardians' allowances, and death grants. The self-employed and non-employed were entitled to fewer benefits. The basic weekly rate for unemployment benefit was raised to 26s.

The national insurance scheme was amended by Acts in 1949, 1951, 1953, 1954, 1955, 1956, 1957, 1959, 1960, 1961, 1964, and 1965 (for rates see p. 210).

National Assistance Act, 1948. This Act repealed all the poor law still in existence and it established a comprehensive scheme to be financed from government funds, to cover all the arrangements for assistance then in force. Provision was also made for those not qualified for benefits under national insurance schemes, or where the benefits were insufficient.

Local Employment Act, 1960, makes provision for promoting employment in areas of persistent or threatened unemployment.

Payment of Wages Act, 1960 removes certain restrictions on methods of payment of wages and permits them to be paid otherwise than in cash by payment into a banking account in the name of the employee, by Postal Order, by Money Order or by Cheque.

The Contracts of Employment Act, 1963, lays down the notice required to be given by an employer to terminate the contract of a person who has been continuously employed for 26 weeks or more, the length of notice to be given varying according to the length of continuous employment.

Offices, Shops and Railway Premises Act, 1963, contains sweeping provisions relating to the health, safety, and welfare of employees, fire precautions, accidents and other matters in connection with office, shop and railway premises where they are employed.

The Industrial Training Act, 1964, gives power to establish an industrial training board for the training of persons over compulsory school age for employment in any activities of industry or commerce.

Redundancy Payments Act, 1965, obliges employers in certain industries to make payment to redundant workers and sets up a Redundancy fund to which employers must contribute.

Major Trade Union Legislation and Litigation

Taff Vale Railway Co. v. *Amalgamated Society of Railway Servants,* [1901] A.C. 426 (H.L.)

A trade union, registered under the *Trade Union Acts, 1871* and *1876,* may be sued in its registered name. Lord Hailsbury said, 'If the legislature has created a thing which can own property, which can employ servants, or which can inflict injury, it must be taken, I think, to have impliedly given the power to make it suable in a court of law, for injuries purposely done by its authority and procurement.'

The Trade Disputes Act, 1906, reversed the Taff Vale decision and freed trade unions from liability caused by the calling of a strike.

Amalgamated Society of Railway Servants v. *Osborne,* [1910] A.C. 87 (H.L.)

There is nothing in the Trade Union Acts from which it can reasonably be inferred that trade unions as defined by Parliament were meant to have the power of collecting and administering funds for political purposes. Exercise of such powers is *ultra vires* and illegal.

The Trade Union Act, 1913, reversed the Osborne judgment and laid down the conditions under which political objects could be included in the rules of a Union by its members' consent.

The Trades Disputes and Trade Unions Act, 1927, made a sympathetic strike or a lockout designed to coerce the government illegal; it also severed the connection between civil service organisations and other unions, and it imposed new restrictions on the unions' political activities and their conduct of trade disputes. The political levy could only be raised from workers who 'contracted in'.

The Trade Unions Act, 1946, repealed the 1927 Act.

Bonsor v. *Musicians' Union*, [1956] A.C. 104 (H.L.)

A member of a registered trade union wrongfully expelled from it was entitled to maintain an action for damages for breach of contract against the union in its registered name.

Rookes v. *Barnard*, [1964] A.C. 1129

Threats to strike in breach of a contractual agreement for the purpose of injuring a third party were unlawful and were, even if done in furtherance of a trade dispute, not protected by the Trade Disputes Act, 1906.

Stratford v. *Lindley*, [1964] 3 All E.R. 102

Strike Action not taken in pursuance of a trade dispute about terms of employment with the plaintiff's firm was not prima facie protected by the 1906 Trade Disputes Act.

Trades Disputes Act, 1965, reversed the Rookes v. Barnard case and disallowed actions for tort or reparation being brought in respect of some kinds of activities in the conduct of industrial disputes.

EARNINGS AND HOURS WORKED
Great Britain

Year	Average Weekly Earnings		Average Weekly Hours Worked	
	All Operatives	Men aged 21 and over	All Operatives	Men aged 21 and over
	s. d.	s. d.		
1924	47 9 [a]	56 3 [a]	n.a.	n.a.
1935	48 11	64 6	n.a.	n.a.
1938	53 3	69 0	46·5	47·7
1940	69 2	89 0	n.a.	n.a.
1941	75 10	99 5	n.a.	n.a.
1942	85 2	111 5	n.a.	n.a.
1943	93 7	121 3	50·0	52·9
1944	96 8	124 4	48·6	51·2
1945	96 1	121 4	47·4	49·7
1946	101 0	120 9	46·2	47·6
1947	108 2	128 1	45·0	46·3
1948	117 4	137 11	45·3	46·5
1949	121 9	142 8	45·3	46·6
1950	124 1	145 9	45·6	47·0

Year	Average Weekly Earnings		Average Weekly Hours Worked	
	All Operatives	Men aged 21 and over	All Operatives	Men aged 21 and over
	s. d.	s. d.		
1951	136 2	160 2	46·3	47·9
1952	147 3	173 7	45·6	47·3
1953	157 5	185 11	46·2	47·8
1954	166 6	197 8	46·5	48·3
1955	182 3	217 5	46·9	48·9
1956	197 9	235 4	46·7	48·6
1957	204 7	241 6	46·6	48·5
1958	214 2	253 2	46·2	48·0
1959	222 6	262 11	46·3	48·0
1960	n.a.	282 1	n.a.	48·0
1961	n.a.	317 10	n.a.	47·6
1962	n.a.	313 0	n.a.	47·3
1963	n.a.	323 0	n.a.	46·9
1964	n.a.	352 0	n.a.	47·8
1965	n.a.	378 0	n.a.	47·5
1966	n.a.	405 0	n.a.	46·4
1967	n.a.	411 3	n.a.	46·1
1968	n.a.	445 3	n.a.	46·2

Figures cover manufacturing industry and some non-manufacturing industries and services, but exclude coal mining, dock labour, railways, agriculture, shipping, distributive trades, catering, entertainments, and domestic services. 1935, 1938, and 1946 figures are for October, 1940–45 for July, 1947 onwards for April.

ᵃ Average of four weeks during 1924.

SOURCES.—*Ministry of Labour Gazette.* G. C. Routh, *Occupation and Pay in Great Britain 1906–60* (1966).

RATES OF UNEMPLOYMENT BENEFIT
(other than agricultural)

		Men over 18	Women over 18
15 Jan	13	7/–	Nil
25 Dec	19	11/–	Nil
8 Nov	20	15/–	12/–
3 Mar	21	20/–	16/–
30 Jun	21	15/–	12/–
14 Aug	24	18/–	15/–
19 Apr	28	17/–	15/–
8 Oct	31	15/3	13/6
26 Jul	34	17/–	15/–
1 Aug	40	20/–	18/–
2 Nov	44	24/–	22/–
3 Jun	48	26/–	26/–
24 Jul	52	32/6	26/–
19 May	55	40/–	26/–
6 Feb	58	50/–	50/–
6 Apr	61	57/6	57/6
7 Mar	63	67/6	67/6
28 Jan	65	80/–	80/–
30 Oct	67	90/–	90/–

SOURCE.—Information from Ministry of Social Security.

INDUSTRIAL ANALYSIS OF THE OCCUPIED POPULATION
Great Britain
(thousands)

	1911	1921	1931	1940	1950	1960	1965
Total Working Population	18,351	19,369	21,074	20,676	22,954	24,436	25,513
H.M. Forces	n.a.	n.a.	n.a.	2,273	697	518	423
Total in Civil Employment	n.a.	n.a.	n.a.	17,758	21,993	23,628	24,820
Agriculture & Fishing	1,493	1,373	1,259	925	1,161	983	486
Mining & Quarrying	1,308	1,469	1,385	886	852	761	625
Manufacturing Industries	6,147	6,723	7,006	7,128	8,510	8,811	8,810
Building & Contracting	950	826	1,149	1,064	1,434	1,567	1,656
Gas, Electricity & Water	117	180	246	213	353	370	411
Transport & Communications	1,260	1,359	1,443	1,146	1,781	1,662	1,628
Distributive Trades	n.a.	n.a.	n.a.	2,639	2,571	3,284	2,962
Insurance, Banking & Finance	n.a.	n.a.	n.a	370	447	555	3,045[c]
Public Administration :							
National	452[a]	706[a]	610[a]	} 1,793	619	502	545
Local	555	773	1,019		743	741	758
Professional Service	2,678[b]	2,225[b]	2,629[b]	n.a.	1,593	2,138	n.a.[c]
Miscellaneous	n.a.	n.a.	n.a.	1,594	1,929	2,154	2,186
Registered wholly unemployed	n.a.	n.a.	n.a.	645	264	290	270

The Table shows only the changes in the general pattern of industry over the period. The figures for 1911–31 are based on the Census of Population figures published by the Registrar-General. The figures for 1940–65 are compiled by the Ministry of Labour. The figures are in no cases completely comparable owing to changes in the methods of classification and changes in the age-limits.

[a] Including members of the armed forces stationed in Great Britain.   [b] Personal Service.
[c] Financial, Professional and Scientific Services calculated together.

SOURCE.—*Annual Abstract of Statistics*, 1935–46, 1938–50, 1958, 1961, and 1966.

SIZE OF LABOUR FORCE
Great Britain
(to nearest '000)

Year	Total	Male	Female
1901	16,312	11,548	4,763
1911	18,354	12,930	5,424
1921	19,357	13,656	5,701
1931	21,055	14,790	6,265
1939	19,750	14,656	5,094
1951	24,600	15,649	9,661
1960	24,436	16,239	8,197
1966	25,644	16,651	8,993
1967	25,322	16,388	8,935

1901, 1911, and 1921 figures cover persons aged 10 years and over.
1931 and 1939 figures cover persons aged 14 years and over.
1951 and 1961 figures cover persons aged 15 years and over.

SOURCES.—*Censuses of Population*, except 1939, 1960, 1966 and 1967; *Ministry of Labour Gazette*.

Trades Union Congresses 1900–1967

Date	Place	President	General Secretary	No. of Delegates
3–8 Sep 00	Huddersfield	W. Pickles	S. Woods	386
2–7 Sep 01	Swansea	C. Bowerman	,,	407
1–6 Sep 02	London	W. Steadman	,,	485
6–11 Sep 03	Leicester	W. Hornidge	,,	460
5–10 Sep 04	Leeds	R. Bell	,,	453
4–9 Sep 05	Hanley	J. Sexton	W. Steadman	457
3–8 Sep 06	Liverpool	D. Cummings	,,	491
2–7 Sep 07	Bath	A. Gill	,,	521
7–12 Sep 08	Nottingham	D. Shackleton	,,	522
6–11 Sep 09	Ipswich	,,	,,	498
12–17 Sep 10	Sheffield	J. Haslam	,,	505
4–9 Sep 11	Newcastle	W. Mullin	C. Bowerman	523
2–7 Sep 12	Newport	W. Thorne	,,	495
1–6 Sep 13	Manchester	W. Davis	,,	560
6–11 Sep 15	Bristol	J. Seddon	,,	610
4–9 Sep 16	Birmingham	H. Gosling	,,	673
3–8 Sep 17	Blackpool	J. Hill	,,	697
2–7 Sep 18	Derby	J. Ogden	,,	881
8–13 Sep 19	Glasgow	G. Stuart-Bunning	,,	851
6–11 Sep 20	Portsmouth	J. Thomas	,,	955
5–10 Sep 21	Cardiff	E. Poulton	,,	810
4–9 Sep 22	Southport	R. Walker	,,	723
3–8 Sep 23	Plymouth	J. Williams	F. Bramley	702
1–6 Sep 24	Hull	A. Purcell	,,	724
7–12 Sep 25	Scarborough	A. Swales	,,	727
6–11 Sep 26	Bournemouth	A. Pugh	W. Citrine	696
5–10 Sep 27	Edinburgh	G. Hicks	,,	646
3–8 Sep 28	Swansea	B. Turner	,,	621
2–6 Sep 29	Belfast	B. Tillett	,,	592
1–5 Sep 30	Nottingham	J. Beard	,,	606
7–11 Sep 31	Bristol	A. Hayday	,,	589
5–9 Sep 32	Newcastle	J. Bromley	,,	578
4–8 Sep 33	Brighton	A. Walkden	,,	566
3–7 Sep 34	Weymouth	A. Conley	,,	575
2–6 Sep 35	Margate	W. Kean	Sir W. Citrine	575
7–11 Sep 36	Plymouth	A. Findlay	,,	603
6–10 Sep 37	Norwich	E. Bevin	,,	623
5–9 Sep 38	Blackpool	H. Elvin	,,	650
4–5 Sep 39	Bridlington	J. Hallsworth	,,	490 [a]
7–9 Oct 40	Southport	W. Holmes	,,	667
1–4 Sep 41	Edinburgh	G. Gibson	,,	683
7–11 Sep 42	Blackpool	F. Wolstencroft	,,	717
6–10 Sep 43	Southport	Anne Loughlin	,,	760
16–20 Oct 44	Blackpool	E. Edwards	,,	730
10–14 Sep 45	Blackpool	,,	,,	762
21–25 Oct 46	Brighton	C. Dukes	V. Tewson	794
1–5 Sep 47	Southport	G. Thomson	,,	837
6–10 Sep 48	Margate	Florence Hancock	,,	859
5–9 Sep 49	Bridlington	Sir W. Lawther	,,	890
4–8 Sep 50	Brighton	H. Bullock	Sir V. Tewson	913
3–7 Sep 51	Blackpool	A. Roberts	,,	927
1–5 Sep 52	Margate	A. Deakin	,,	943
7–11 Sep 53	Douglas	T. O'Brien	,,	954
6–10 Sep 54	Brighton	J. Tanner	,,	974
5–9 Sep 55	Southport	C. Geddes	,,	984

[a] Actual attendance owing to the outbreak of war. Credentials were issued to 659 delegates.

Date	Place	President	General Secretary	No. of Delegates
3–7 Sep 56	Brighton	W. Beard	Sir V. Tewson	1,000
2–6 Sep 57	Blackpool	Sir T. Williamson	,,	995
1–5 Sep 58	Bournemouth	T. Yates	,,	993
7–11 Sep 59	Blackpool	R. Willis	,,	1,017
5–9 Sep 60	Douglas	C. Bartlett	G. Woodcock	996
4–8 Sep 61	Portsmouth	E. Hill	,,	984
3–7 Sep 62	Blackpool	B. Godwin	,,	989
2–6 Sep 63	Brighton	F. Hayday	,,	975
7–11 Sep 64	Blackpool	G. Lowthian	,,	997
6–10 Sep 65	Brighton	H. Collison	,,	1,013
5–9 Sep 66	Blackpool	J. O'Hagan	,,	1,048
4–8 Sep 67	Brighton	Sir H. Douglas	,,	1,059
2–6 Sep 68	Blackpool	Ld Wright	,,	1,054

SOURCE.—*Trades Union Congress Report, 1966.*

The Eight Largest Unions

Union	*Formed*	*Major Components*
Amalgamated Union of Engineering and Foundry Workers	1920 (1968)	Amalgamated Society of Engineers (founded 1851) merged with other unions to form the Amalgamated Engineering Union (A.E.U.) in 1920. In 1968 the A.E.U. merged with the Amalgamated Union of Foundry Workers.
Electrical Trades Union	1889	Electrical Trades Union and others. In 1968 following mergers it became the Electrical, Electronic and Telecommunications Union–Plumbing Trades Union.
National and Local Government Officers' Assocation	1905	National Association of Local Government Officers. 1930 amalgamated with National Poor Law Officers' Association and in 1963 with the British Gas Staffs Association. 1952 changed name to National and Local Government Officers' Association. Affiliated to T.U.C. in 1965.
National Union of General and Municipal Workers	1924	National Union of General Workers (founded 1889 as the National Union of Gasworkers and General Labourers of G.B. and Ireland), National Amalgamated Union of Labour (founded 1889 as Tyneside and General Labourers' Union), and Municipal Employees' Association (founded 1894).
National Union of Mineworkers	1889 (1945)	Formed as the Miners' Federation of G.B., amalgamated with specialist unions, renamed N.U.M. in 1945.
National Union of Railwaymen	1913	Amalgamated Society of Railway Servants, and General Railway Workers' Union, and others.
Transport and General Workers' Union	1922	Dock, Wharf, Riverside and General Workers' Union, National Union of Dock Labourers and other dockers' unions, United Vehicle Workers, National Union of Vehicle Workers and others. 1928 amalgamated with the Workers' Union.

Union of Shop, Distributive   1921   Co-operative Employees, and Warehouse and
and Allied Workers   (1946)   General Workers amalgamated in 1921 to
                                            form the National Union of Distributive
                                            and Allied Workers. 1946 fusion with
                                            National Amalgamated Union of Shop
                                            Assistants, Warehousemen and Clerks.

SOURCE.—*Trade Union Congress Reports, 1920–66.*

Presidents

Amalgamated Engineering Union

1920	J. Brownlie		1939	J. Tanner
1930	W. Hutchinson		1954	R. Openshaw
1933	J. Little		1956	(Sir) W. Carron (Ld)
			1967	H. Scanlon

Electrical Trades Union

1907	J. Ball		1944	F. Foulkes
1931	E. Bussey		1963	L. Cannon
1940	H. Bolton			

National and Local Government Officers' Association

1905	F. Ginn		1945	H. Corser (*Acting*)
1909	L. Hill		1946	J. Warren
1943	J. Simonds		1957	W. Anderson

National Union of General Municipal Workers Secretary

1924	W. Thorne		1946	(Sir) T. Williamson
1934	C. Dukes		1962	J. (Ld) Cooper

National Union of Mineworkers Secretary
(Miners' Federation of Great Britain, 1920–45)

1920	F. Hodges		1946	A. Horner
1924	A. Cook		1959	W. Paynter
1932	E. Edwards		1969	L. Daly

National Union of Railwaymen Secretary

1920	J. Thomas and C. Cramp		1943	J. Benstead
1931	C. Cramp		1948	J. Figgins
1933	(*Acting Secretary*)		1953	J. Campbell
1934	J. Marchbank		1958	S. Greene

Transport and General Workers Union Secretary

1921	E. Bevin		1956	F. Cousins
1940	A. Deakin[1]		1964	H. Nicholas (*Acting*)
1955	A. Tiffin		1966	F. Cousins

Union of Shop, Distributive and Allied Workers Secretary
(Union of Distributive and Allied Workers, 1921–46)

1921	J. Hallsworth and W. Robinson		1947	(*Acting Secretary*)
			1949	(Sir) A. Birch
1924	(Sir) J. Hallsworth		1962	A. Allen

[1] Acting Secretary until March 1946.

SOURCES.—*Trade Union Congress Reports, 1920–66; Amalgamated Engineering Union Monthly Journal and Report, 1920–66.*

Membership[1]

(to nearest '000)

Year	AEU	ETU	NALGO	NUGMW	NUM	NUR	T & GWU	USDAW
1920	407	57	36	..	900	458	..	..
1921	357	46	36	..	800	341	300	100
1922	256	31	33	..	750	327	300	90
1923	246	26	33	..	750	327	300	90
1924	206	28	34	327	800	327	300	93
1925	205	29	37	320	800	327	300	95
1926	162	29	40	300	800	327	300	94
1927	146	26	44	278	725	327	300	100
1928	151	26	46	258	600	313	286	109
1929	155	29	49	261	600	310	389	115
1930	154	31	61	258	600	321	384	119
1931	146	31	65	240	600	310	390	121
1932	136	31	68	220	500	285	390	127
1933	135	31	73	230	500	272	370	131
1934	146	34	79	252	500	291	403	134
1935	164	40	86	280	500	306	460	145
1936	248	48	93	340	518	338	523	158
1937	299	58	101	405	538	365	611	172
1938	334	64	106	417	584	367	635	183
1939	376	70	114	430	589	350	648	194
1940	454	80	111	441	589	362	650	223
1941	550	97	113	548	580	376	680	234
1942	645	113	121	721	599	394	806	254
1943	825	124	127	726	603	406	1,089	268
1944	811	132	133	661	605	404	1,017	272
1945	704	133	134	605	533	410	975	275
1946	723	162	146	795	538	414	1,230	374
1947	742	170	171	824	572	448	1,264	343
1948	743	182	176	816	611	455	1,271	342
1949	714	188	189	805	609	421	1,253	340
1950	716	192	197	785	602	392	1,242	343
1951	756	198	212	809	613	396	1,285	348
1952	796	203	222	808	641	397	1,277	346
1953	810	212	225	790	669	378	1,259	339
1954	823	216	230	787	675	372	1,240	344
1955	854	223	236	805	675	368	1,278	347
1956	860	228	243	808	674	369	1,264	349
1957	900	239	247	804	681	371	1,244	352
1958	888	230	252	775	674	355	1,225	353
1959	908	233	263	769	639	334	1,241	351
1960	973	243	274	769	586	334	1,302	355
1961	982	253	285	786	545	317	1,318	351
1962	986	257	295	781	529	311	1,331	356
1963	981	272	226	782	501	283	1,374	355
1964	1,011	282	338	785	479	264	1,426	352
1965	1,049	293	349	796	446	255	1,444	349
1966	1,055	293	361	793	413	220	1,428	336
1967	1,107	352	367	782	380	218	1,451	321

SOURCE.—*Trades Union Congress Reports, 1920-* (*Statistical Statements*).

[1] By 1967 two other unions had reached this level of membership. The National Union of Public Employees had 265,000 members and the Society of Graphical and Allied Trades had 229,000.

Income, Expenditure and Funds of Registered Trade Unions
(in shillings per member)

Year	Income from members	Expenditure						Funds
		Dispute benefit	Unemployment benefit	Other Welfare benefits	Political	Working Expenses	
1910	27·8	5·3	6·8	11·1	..	8·1	59·3
1920	32·4	9·3	4·5	5·1	0·5	17·2	45·8
1930	37·6	1·6	9·7	12·1	0·5	16·6	62·0
1940	36·0	0·2	3·0	10·4	0·4	14·8	92·2
1950	39·6	0·6	0·4	10·4	1·1	22·8	156·4
1960	58·8	1·1	0·4	15·5	1·2	34·9	211·6
1964	74·2	1·1	0·5	17·5	2·3	44·5	258·3

SOURCE.—A. Flanders, *Trade Unions* (1961), and *Ministry of Labour Gazette*.

Density of Union Membership in Total Labour Force
United Kingdom

1901	12·8%	1938	29·9%
1911	17·9	1948	45·1
1921	37·6	1951	44·9
1931	23·9	1956	44·0
1933	22·5	1961	42·9

SOURCE.—G. S. Bain, 'The Growth of White-Collar Unionism in Great Britain', *British Journal of Industrial Relations* IV (Nov 1966).

White-Collar Unions

Much of the expansion of union membership during the twentieth century has occurred among white-collar workers. Prior to 1900 few of these workers were unionised, but by 1920 the Webbs estimated that close to three-quarters of a million white-collar employees belonged to trade unions. More recently, there has been a further dramatic increase in union membership among white-collar employees. While union membership among manual workers increased by only 0·6 per cent between 1948 and 1964, union membership among white-collar workers increased by 33·6 per cent. In 1964 there were approximately 300 unions catering for white-collar employees with a total membership of 2·6 million. More than sixty of these organisations were affiliated to the TUC, and their 1·7 million non-manual members comprised roughly 20 per cent of total Congress membership.

SOURCE.—G. S. Bain, 'The Growth of White-Collar Unionism in Great Britain', *British Journal of Industrial Relations* IV (Nov 1966).

Major Industrial Disputes
(in which more than 500,000 working days were lost)

Dispute Began	Industrial group	Area	Numbers affected ('ooos)	Working days lost ('ooos) [a]
1900 Apr	Potters	N. Staffs.	20	640
Nov	Quarrymen	Bethesda	3	505
1902 Jul	Miners	Federated districts	103	872
1906 Oct	Shipyard workers	Clyde	15	592
1908 Feb	Shipyard workers	Humber, Barrow, Birkenhead, Clyde, E. Scotland	35	1,719
Feb	Engineers	N.E. Coast	11	1,706
Sep	Cotton operatives	Lancs., Cheshire, Derby	120	4,830
1909 Jul	Miners	S. Wales and Mon.	55	660
1910 Jan	Miners	Durham	85	1,280
Jan	Miners	Northumberland	30	1,080
Apr	Miners	Rhondda	13	2,985
Jun	Cotton operatives	Lancs. and Cheshire	102	600
Sep	Shipyard workers	N.E. Coast and Scotland	35	2,851
1911 Jun	Seamen and dockers	U.K.	120	1,020
Aug	Dockers and carters	London	22	500
Aug	Railwaymen	U.K.	145	500
Dec	Cotton weavers	N.E. Lancs.	160	2,954
1912 Feb	Miners	U.K.	1,000	30,800
Feb	Jute workers	Dundee	28	726
May	Dockers and carters	Port of London and Medway	100	2,700
1913 Jan	Cab drivers	London	11	637
Apr	Tube and metal workers	S. Staffs. and N. Worcs.	50	1,400
Aug	Transport workers	Dublin	20	1,900
1914 Jan	Builders	London	20	2,500
Feb	Miners	Yorks.	150	2,654
1915 Jul	Miners	S. Wales	232	1,400
1916 Mar	Jute workers	Dundee	30	500
1917 May	Engineers	U.K.	160	2,880
1918 May	Miners	S. Wales and Mon.	40	760
Dec	Cotton spinners	Lancs. and Cheshire	100	900
1919 Jan	Miners	Yorks.	150	1,950
Jan	Shipyard workers	N.E. Coast	40	820
Mar	Miners	Various districts	100	600
Jun	Cotton operatives	Lancs. and adjoining counties	450	7,500
Jul	Miners	Yorks.	150	4,050
Sep	Ironfounders	England, Wales, and Ireland	50	6,800
Sep	Railwaymen	U.K.	500	3,850
1920 Sep	Cotton operatives	Oldham and district	400	620
Oct	Miners	U.K.	1,100	16,000
1921 (Dec 1920)	Shipyard carpenters	U.K.	10	2,200
Apr	Miners	U.K.	1,100	72,000
Jun	Cotton operatives	Lancs. and adjoining counties	375	6,750
1922 Mar	Engineers	U.K.	250	13,650

[a] Where figures for working days lost are not given in the *Gazettes*, they have been estimated.

Dispute Began	Industrial group	Area	Numbers affected ('000s)	Working days lost ('000s)[a]
1922 Mar	Shipyard workers	Various districts	90	3,400
1923 Feb	Jute workers	Dundee	29	950
Apr	Boilermakers	Clyde, E. Scotland, N.E. Coast, Hull, Southampton, Birkenhead, Barrow	30	5,725
1924 Jan	Railwaymen	U.K.	69	500
Feb	Dockers	U.K.	110	510
Jul	Builders	U.K.	100	2,970
1925 Jul	Wool textile workers	W. Riding of Yorks. and part of Lancs.	165	3,105
1926 May	Miners	U.K.	1,050	145,200
May	General Strike	U.K.	1,580 [b]	15,000 [b]
1928 May	Cotton weavers	Nelson	17	600
1929 Jul	Cotton operatives	Lancs. and adjoining counties	388	6,596
1930 Apr	Wool textile workers	W. Riding of Yorks. and part of Lancs.	120	3,258
1931 Jan	Cotton weavers	Lancs. and adjoining counties	145	3,290
Jan	Miners	S. Wales and Mon.	150	2,030
1932 Aug	Cotton weavers	Lancs. and Yorks.	148	4,524
Oct	Cotton spinners	Lancs. and adjoining counties	130	760
1937 May	Busmen	London	24	565
1944 Mar	Miners	Wales and Mon.	100	550
Mar	Miners	Yorkshire	120	1,000
1945 Sep	Dockers	Birkenhead, Liverpool, Hull, Manchester, London	50	1,100
1953 Dec	Engineers and Shipyard workers	U.K.	1,070	1,070
1954 Sep	Dockers	Port of London and sympathy strikes	45	726
1955 May	Dockers	Various ports of England	21	673
May	Railwaymen	U.K.	70	865
1957 Mar	Engineers	U.K.	615	4,000
Mar	Shipyard workers	U.K.	165	2,150
Jul	Busmen	Provinces	100	770
1958 Apr	Dockers, transport and market workers	London	24	515
May	Busmen	Greater London	49	1,604
1959 Jun	Printing workers	U.K.	120	3,500
1962 Feb	Engineering & Shipbuilding	U.K.	1,750	1,750
Mar	Engineering & Shipbuilding	U.K.	1,750	1,750
1966 May	Shipping	U.K.	30	850
1968 May	Engineering	U.K.	1,500	1,500

[a] Where figures for working days lost are not given in the *Gazettes*, they have been estimated.
[b] Excluding Miners.

SOURCES.—*The Board of Trade Labour Gazette, 1900–17*; *The Ministry of Labour Gazette*. Published monthly, 1918–66.

Unemployment, Industrial Disputes, and Trade Union Statistics

	Unemployment[b]		Industrial Disputes[c]			Total No. of Trade Unions	Total No. of Trade Union Members ('000s)	Total No. of Trade Unions affiliated to T.U.C.	Total No. of members of Trade Unions affiliated to T.U.C. ('000s)
	Maximum ('000s)	Minimum ('000s)	Working Days Lost[d] ('000s)	No. of Stoppages beginning in year[e]	Workers involved[d] ('000s)				
1900			3,088	633	185	1,325	1,911	184	1,250
1901			4,130	631	179	1,323	2,022	191	1,200
1902			3,438	432	255	1,322	2,025	198	1,400
1903			2,320	380	116	1,297	2,013	204	1,500
1904			1,464	346	87	1,285	1,994	212	1,423
1905			2,368	349	92	1,256	1,967	205	1,541
1906			3,019	479	218	1,244	1,997	226	1,555
1907			2,148	585	146	1,282	2,210	236	1,700
1908			10,785	389	293	1,283	2,513	214	1,777
1909			2,687	422	297	1,268	2,485	219	1,705
1910			9,867	521	514	1,260	2,477	212	1,648
1911			10,155	872	952	1,269	2,565		
1912			40,890	834	1,462	1,290	3,139	202	1,662
1913			9,804	1,459	664	1,252	3,416	201	2,002
1914			9,878	972	447	1,269	4,135	207	2,232
1915			2,953	672	448	1,260	4,145	215	2,682
1916			2,446	532	276	1,229	4,359	227	2,851
1917			5,647	730	872	1,225	4,644	235	3,082
1918			5,875	1,165	1,116	1,241	5,499	262	4,532
1919			34,969	1,352	2,591	1,264	6,533	266	5,284
1920			26,568	1,607	1,932	1,360	7,926	215	6,505
1921	2,038[a]		85,872	763	1,801	1,384	8,348	213	6,418
1922	2,015 Jan	1,443 Oct	19,850	576	552	1,275	6,633	206	5,129
1923	1,525 Jan	1,229 Dec	10,672	628	405	1,232	5,625	194	4,369
1924	1,374 Jan	1,087 Jun	8,424	710	613	1,192	5,429	203	4,328
1925	1,443 Aug	1,243 Dec	7,952	603	441	1,194	5,544	205	4,351
1926	1,432 Dec	1,094 Apr	162,233	323	2,734	1,176	5,506	207	4,366
1927	1,451 Jan	1,059 May	1,174	308	108	1,164	5,219	204	4,164
1928	1,375 Aug	1,127 Mar	1,388	302	124	1,159	4,919	196	3,875
1929	1,466 Jan	1,164 Jun	8,287	431	533	1,142	4,866	202	3,673
1930	2,500 Dec	1,520 Jan	4,399	422	307	1,133	4,858	210	3,744
1931	2,880 Sep	2,578 May	6,983	420	490	1,121	4,842	210	3,719
1932	2,955 Jan	2,309 Nov	6,488	389	379	1,108	4,624	209	3,613
1933	2,407 Jan	1,858 Dec	1,072	357	136	1,081	4,444	208	3,368
1934	2,295 Jan	2,080 Sep	959	471	134	1,081	4,392	210	3,295
1935	2,333 Jan	1,888 Dec	1,955	553	271	1,063	4,590	211	3,389
1936	2,169 Jan	1,640 Aug	1,829	818	316	1,049	4,867	214	3,615
1937	1,739 Dec	1,373 Sep	3,413	1,129	597	1,036	5,295	214	4,009
1938	1,912 Dec	1,818 Apr	1,334	875	274	1,032	5,842	216	4,461
1939	2,032 Jan	1,230 Aug	1,356	940	337	1,024	6,053	217	4,669
1940	1,471 Jan	683 Dec	940	922	299	1,019	6,298	223	4,867
1941	653 Jan	151 Dec	1,079	1,251	360	1,004	6,613	223	5,079
1942	162 Jan	100 Dec	1,527	1,303	456	996	7,165	232	5,433
1943	104 Jan	..	1,808	1,785	557	991	7,867	230	6,024
1944	84 Jan	..	3,714	2,194	821	987	8,174	190	6,642
1945	111 Jan	..	2,835	2,293	531	963	8,087	191	6,576

Unemployment, Industrial Disputes, and Trade Union Statistics

	Unemployment[b]		Industrial Disputes[c]			Total No. of Trade Unions	Total No. of Trade Union Members ('000s)	Total No. of Trade Unions affiliated to T.U.C.	Total No. of members of Trade Unions affiliated to T.U.C. ('000s)
	Maximum	Minimum	Working Days Lost[d] ('000s)	No. of Stoppages beginning in year	Workers involved[e] ('000s)				
1946	408 Jan	360 Jan	2,158	2,205	526	781	7,875	192	6,671
1947	1,916 Feb	262 Sep	2,433	1,721	620	757	8,803	187	7,540
1948	359 Dec	299 Jun	1,944	1,759	424	734	9,145	188	7,791
1949	413 Jan	274 Jul	1,807	1,426	433	735	9,319	187	7,937
1950	404 Jan	297 Jul	1,389	1,339	302	726	9,274	186	7,883
1951	367 Jan	210 Jul	1,694	1,719	379	732	9,289	186	7,828
1952	468 Apr	379 Jan	1,792	1,714	415	735	9,535	183	8,020
1953	452 Feb	273 Jul	2,184	1,746	1,370	719	9,583	183	8,088
1954	387 Feb	220 Jul	2,457	1,989	448	717	9,523	184	8,094
1955	298 Jan	185 Jul	3,781	2,419	659	703	9,556	183	8,107
1956	297 Dec	223 Jun	2,083	2,648	507	694	9,726	186	8,264
1957	383 Jan	244 Jul	8,412	2,859	1,356	685	9,829	185	8,305
1958	536 Nov	395 Jan	3,462	2,629	523	675	9,639	185	8,337
1959	621 Jan	395 Jul	5,270	2,093	645	668	9,623	186	8,176
1960	461 Jan	292 Jul	3,024	2,832	817	664	9,835	184	8,128
1961	419 Jan	259 Jul	3,046	2,686	771	646	9,897	183	8,299
1962	566 Dec	397 Jun	5,795	2,449	4,420	626	9,887	182	8,313
1963	878 Feb	449 Jul	1,755	2,068	591	607	9,934	176	8,315
1964	501 Jan	318 Jul	2,277	2,524	871	598	10,079	175	8,326
1965	376 Jan	276 Jun	2,925	2,354	871	583	10,181	172	8,771
1966	465 Dec	252 Jun	2,398	1,937	530	574	10,111	168	8,787
1967	603 Feb	497 Jul	2,787	2,116	732	555	9,967	160	8,725

[a] Figures for Dec available only.
[b] 1900–20, unemployment figures for certain skilled trade unions available in *Ministry of Labour Gazettes*, figures are given as percentages. No comparable figures of total unemployed before 1921. Figures for insured workers registered as unemployed. Agricultural workers, insurable in 1936, are included from that date. Numerous changes in coverage throughout.
[c] Disputes involving less than 10 work-people and those lasting less than one day are omitted, except where aggregate duration exceeded 100 working days. [d] S. Ireland included from 1900 to 1907.
[e] Workers involved directly and indirectly. 'Indirectly' involved means those unable to work at establishments where disputes occurred, though not themselves parties to the dispute.

SOURCES.—*Annual Abstract of Statistics, Ministry of Labour Gazette* and *Abstract of Labour Statistics. T.U.C. Congress Reports.*

For a general introductory survey of industrial relations see: A. Flanders, *Trade Unions* (1967) (contains a useful bibliography); A. Flanders and H. A. Clegg (eds.), *The System of Industrial Relations in Great Britain* (1956); B. C. Roberts (ed.), *Industrial Relations: Contemporary Problems and Perspectives* (1962); Ministry of Labour, *Industrial Relations Handbook* (HMSO, 1961); Ministry of Labour, *Evidence to the Royal Commission on Trade Unions and Employers' Associations* (HMSO, 1965); and G. D. H. Cole, *An Introduction to Trade Unionism* (1953).

A comprehensive study of the whole field is to be found in the *Report* of the Royal Commission on Trades Unions and Employers' Associations (Cmnd. 3623/1968) and the eleven *Research Papers* which were published in connection with it.

For a discussion of contemporary problems see: A. Flanders, *Industrial Relations: What Is Wrong With the System?* (1965); A. Flanders, *Collective Bargaining: Prescription for Change* (1967); PEP, 'Trade Unions in a Changing Society', *Planning*, No. 472 (1963); J. Hughes, *Change in the Trade Unions*, Fabian Research Series 244 (1964); W. E. J. McCarthy, *The Future of the Unions*, Fabian Tract No. 339 (1962); E. Wigham, *What's Wrong With the Unions?* (1961); and the research papers currently being published by the Royal Commission on Trade Unions and Employers' Associations.

The definitive history of British trade unionism is H. A. Clegg *et al.*, *A History of British Trade Unions Since 1889* (Vol. 1, 1889–1910 (1964), Vols 2 and 3 are still to be published). For the period prior to 1889 see S. and B. Webb, *The History of Trade Unionism* (1920). The most useful short history is H. Pelling, *A History of British Trade Unionism* (1963) (contains an excellent bibliography, including references to the histories of individual unions).

For the legal aspects of trade unionism and industrial relations see: K. W. Wedderburn, *The Worker and the Law* (1965) (contains a very comprehensive bibliography); C. Grunfeld, *Modern Trade Union Law* (1966); and O. Kahn-Freund, 'Report on the Legal Status of Collective Bargaining and Collective Agreements in Great Britain', *Labour Relations and the Law: A Comparative Study*, O. Kahn-Freund, ed. (1965), pp. 21–39.

The most extensive work on trade union government and administration is B. C. Roberts, *Trade Union Government and Administration* (1956). See also: H. A. Clegg *et al.*, *Trade Union Officers* (1961); V. L. Allen, *Power in Trade Unions* (1954); PEP, 'The Structure and Organisation of British Trade Unions', *Planning*, No. 477 (1963); PEP, 'Trade Union Membership', *Planning*, No. 463 (1962); and TUC, *Written Evidence to the Royal Commission on Trade Unions and Employers' Associations* (1966).

For the relations between trade unions and the government see: D. F. Macdonald, *The State and the Trade Unions* (1960); V. L. Allen, *Trade Unions and the Government* (1960); and M. Harrison, *Trade Unions and the Labour Party Since 1945* (1960).

Other useful books include: W. E. J. McCarthy, *The Closed Shop* (1964); F. J. Bayliss, *British Wages Councils* (1962); and K. G. J. C. Knowles, *Strikes* (1952); B. Wootton, *The Social Foundations of Wage Policy* (1955); J. Corina, *Incomes Policy — Problems and Prospects*, Institute of Personnel Management (1966), Parts 1 and 2. A Marsh, *Industrial Relations in Engineering* (1965); E. H. Phelps Brown, *The Growth of Industrial Relations* (1959); H. A. Turner, *Trade Union Growth, Structure and Policy* (1962).

Bibliographies and details of current work on labour history and industrial relations may be found in the *Bulletin* of the Society for the Study of Labour History. Useful articles on various aspects of industrial relations as well as a chronicle of events may be found in the *British Journal of Industrial Relations*. Most of the basic statistics of industrial relations are to be found in the *Ministry of Labour Gazette*.

XI

THE ECONOMY

Some Landmarks in British Economic Policy

1 Aug	14	War emergency measures, including temporary increase in Bank Rate to 10%.
Dec	16	Exchange rate pegged at $4·77 to £.
15 Aug	18	Report of Cunliffe Committee on Currency and Foreign Exchanges (Cd. 9182) recommended eventual return to an effective gold standard at pre-war par value.
20 Mar	19	Withdrawal of official peg from sterling–dollar exchange ; exchange rates allowed to fluctuate.
Jan	21	Post-war trade slump. Unemployment exceeded 1 million (it remained above that level until 1939).
28 Apr	25	Return to fixed gold parity, at pre-1914 level ($4·86=£1). Britain now on gold bullion standard.
May	26	General Strike.
23 Jun	31	Report of Macmillan Committee on Finance and Industry (Cmd. 3897).
24 Jul	31	Report of May Committee on National Expenditure (Cmd. 3920), recommended big cuts in Government expenditure.
21 Sep	31	Gold Standard suspended ; sterling on fluctuating rate.
29 Feb	32	Import Duties Act set up Import Duties Advisory Council.
25 Apr	32	Exchange Equalisation Fund established to smooth variations in exchange rates.
30 Jun	32	Bank rate reduced to 2% and held at this level until 1939.
21 Aug	32	Ottawa Agreements on Imperial Preference.
21 Dec	33	Agricultural Marketing Act authorises quota controls on agricultural imports.
21 Dec	34	Special Areas (Development and Improvement) Act recognised problems of distressed areas.
12 Oct	36	Tripartite Agreement between Britain, France, and the U.S.A. to promote greater exchange stability by inter-Treasury Co-operation.
4 Sep	39	War emergency measures including imposition on exchange control with formal definition of the Sterling Area. Exchange rates fixed at $4·03=£.
21 Aug	41	Start of Lend-Lease.
26 Aug	44	White Paper on Employment Policy (Cmd. 6527) accepts Government responsibility for 'maintenance of a high and stable level of employment'.
21 Aug	45	End of Lend-Lease followed by U.S. and Canadian loans to Britain.
1 Jan	46	Nationalisation of Bank of England.
Feb	47	Fuel Crisis.
5 Jun	47	Gen. Marshall's speech leading to establishment of Marshall Aid (Jul 48) and of Organisation for European Economic Co-operation (Apr 48).
15 Jul	47	Sterling made convertible. Convertibility suspended 20 Aug.
4 Oct	47	Agriculture Act put the policy of agricultural subsidy and protection on a permanent basis.
4 Feb	48	'Wage Freeze' and dividend restraint.
30 Jul	48	Monopolies and Restrictive Practices (Inquiry and Control) Act established Monopolies Commission.
18 Sep	49	Devaluation of £ from $4·03 to $2·80.
13 Dec	50	Marshall Aid suspended as no longer necessary.
7 Nov	51	Bank rate increase from 2% to 2½% signals the revival of monetary policy. Import liberalisation rescinded to check record dollar drain.
25 Oct	55	Autumn budget following balance-of-payments crisis.
2 Aug	56	Restrictive Trade Practices Act established Restrictive Trade Practices Court.
11 Dec	56	Stand-by credits arranged following post-Suez balance-of-payments crisis.
12 Aug	57	Council on Prices Productivity and Incomes ('Three Wise Men') set up. (Disbanded 1961.)
19 Sep	57	Bank rate raised to 7% to meet sterling crisis.
27 Dec	57	Convertibility announced for non-resident sterling on current account.
20 Aug	59	Report of Radcliffe Committee on the working of the monetary system (Cmnd. 827).

Q

20 Nov 59   European Free Trade Area Treaty signed.
4 Dec 60   O.E.E.C. reconstituted and broadened to include U.S.A. and Canada and retitled O.E.C.D.
20 Jul 61   Plowden Report on Control of Public Expenditure.
25 Jul 61   'Pay Pause' measures of S. Lloyd following balance-of-payments crisis. Establishment of National Economic Development Council.
10 Aug 61   Britain applies to join European Economic Community (negotiations terminated Jan 63).
16 Jul 64   Resale Prices Act greatly limits resale price maintenance.
26 Oct 64   New Government meets balance-of-payments deficit by imposing 15% import surcharge (reduced to 10% in Apr 65 and ended Nov 66).
18 Mar 65   Establishment of Prices and Incomes Board.
5 Aug 65   Monopolies and Mergers Act extended 1948 Monopolies Act to cover services as well as goods.
16 Sep 65   Publication of first National Economic Plan (Cmnd. 2764).
25 Jan 66   Industrial Reorganisation Corporation established to encourage 'concentration and nationalisation and to promote the greater efficiency and international competitiveness of British Industry'. (Cmnd. 2889.)
6 Mar 66   Announcement that Decimal Currency would be adopted in 1971 (White paper, Cmnd. 3164, published 12 Dec 66).
20 Jul 66   Sterling crisis leads to Bank rate 7%, tax increases, credit restraints, and prices and incomes standstill (Cmnd. 3073).
12 Aug 66   Prices and Incomes Act becomes law (Part IV actuated 6 Oct 66).
11 May 67   Britain applies (for second time) to join European Economic Community.
18 Nov 67   Devaluation of £ from $2.80 to $2.40. Bank Rate 8%.
19 Jan 68   Major cuts in Government expenditure announced, followed up in 19 Mar Budget.
17 Mar 68   Two-tier gold standard announced by World Central Banks.
30 Mar 68   Agreement on Special Drawing Rights in International Monetary Fund.

SOURCES.—A. Shonfield, *British Economic Policy Since The War* (1958); J. C. R. Dow, *The Management of the British Economy 1945-60* (1964); A. C. Pigou, *Aspects of British Economic History 1918-1925* (1948); E. V. Morgan, *Studies in British Financial Policy 1914-1925*; S. Brittan, *The Treasury under the Tories* (1966); R. S. Sayers, 'Co-operation between Central Banks', *The Three Banks Review* (Sep 1963); R. S. Sayers, *Central Banking after Bagehot* (1959).

Select Statistics

	Net National Income (at factor cost)[a] (£m.)	Income Tax (Standard Rate in £)	Amount Retained of Bachelor's £10,000 earned income after Income Tax and Surtax	Wholesale Price Index Number[b]	Retail Price Index Number	Annual Purchasing Power of £ 1900-1965	
						1900 =20/-	1965 =20/-
	1	2	3	4	5	6	7
				(1900=100)	(1914=100)		
1900	1,750	8	9,667	100	91	20/-	119/7
1901	1,727	1/-	9,500	97	90	19/9	118/5
1902	1,740	1/2	9,417	96	90	19/7	117/3
1903	1,717	1/3	9,375	97	91	19/4	116/1
1904	1,704	11	9,542	98	92	19/1	114/11
1905	1,776	1/-	9,500	98	92	19/4	113/3
1906	1,874	1/-	9,500	101	93	19/4	114/11
1907	1,966	1/-	9,500	106	95	18/8	114/11
1908	1,875	1/-	9,500	103	93	18/4	112/2
1909	1,907	1/-	9,500	104	94	18/4	108/7
1910	1,984	1/2	9,242	109	96	18/1	108/7
1911	2,076	1/2	9,242	109	97	17/11	107/7
1912	2,181	1/2	9,242	115	100	17/3	106/7
1913	2,265	1/2	9,242	117	102	17/3	102/5
1914	2,209	1/2	9,242	117	100	17/5	102/5
1915	(2,591)	1/8	8,669	144	n.a.	14/2	83/10

	Net National Income (at factor cost)[a] (£m.)	Income Tax (Standard Rate in £)	Amount Retained of Bachelor's £10,000 earned income after Income Tax and Surtax	Wholesale Price Index Number[b]	Retail Price Index Number	Annual Purchasing Power of £ 1900–1965	
						1900 =20/-	1965 =20/-
	1	2	3	4	5	6	7
1916	(3,064)	3/-	7,721	187	n.a.	11/11	70/9
1917	(3,631)	5/-	6,721	243	n.a.	9/11	58/7
1918	(4,372)	5/-	6,721	268	n.a.	8/7	50/11
					(1938=100)		
1919	(5,461)	6/-	5,813	296	139	8/1	48/-
1920	5,664	6/-	5,813	369	159	7/-	41/6
				(1938=100)	(1938=100)		
1921	4,460	6/-	5,672	163	144	7/8	45/8
1922	3,856	6/-	5,672	131	117	9/6	56/4
1923	3,844	5/-	6,150	131	112	10/-	59/4
1924	3,919	4/6	6,389	137	112	9/11	59/-
1925	3,980	4/6	6,389	131	112	9/11	58/7
1926	3,914	4/-	6,968	122	110	10/1	59/11
1927	4,145	4/-	6,968	117	107	10/5	61/8
1928	4,154	4/-	6,968	116	106	10/6	61/8
1929	4,178	4/-	6,968	113	105	10/7	62/2
1930	3,957	4/-	6,968	99	101	11/-	63/-
1931	3,666	4/6	6,487	87	94	11/10	69/11
1932	3,568	5/-	6,103	84	92	12/1	71/7
1933	3,728	5/-	6,103	85	90	12/5	73/10
1934	3,881	5/-	6,103	87	90	12/4	73/2
1935	4,109	4/6	6,340	88	92	12/2	72/3
1936	4,388	4/6	6,341	93	94	11/10	70/4
1937	4,616	4/9	6,222	107	99	11/4	67/1
1938	4,671	5/-	6,103	100	100	11/2	66/2
1939	5,037	5/6	5,867	101	103	10/10	64/2
1940	5,980	7/-	4,965	135	117	8/11	53/1
1941	6,941	8/6	3,921	151	129	8/-	47/7
1942	7,664	10/-	3,138	157	137	7/5	44/-
1943	8,171	10/-	3,138	161	142	7/2	42/4
1944	8,366	10/-	3,138	164	145	7/-	41/3
1945	8,340	10/-	3,138	167	148	6/10	40/3
1946	7,974	10/-	3,138	173	154	6/7	39/1
1947	8,587	9/-	3,637	189	163	6/2	36/7
1948	9,669	9/-	3,501	216	175	5/9	33/11
1949	10,240	9/-	3,587	227	180	5/7	33/2
				(1954=100)			
1950	10,784	9/-	3,587	85	185	5/5	32/3
1951	11,857	9/-	3,598	99	203	5/-	29/7
1952	12,769	9/6	3,361	102	221	4/8	27/11
1953	13,773	9/6	3,411	100	228	4/8	27/6
1954	14,583	9/-	3,646	100	232	4/7	27/-
1955	15,513	9/-	3,646	103	242	4/5	26/-
1956	16,831	8/6	3,873	107	254	4/2	25/-
1957	17,842	8/6	3,873	110	264	4/1	24/3
1958	18,605	8/6	4,341	111	272	4/-	23/7
1959	19,554	8/6	4,341	111	273	4/-	23/5
1960	20,857	7/9	4,648	113	276	3/11	23/3

	Net National Income (at factor cost)a (£m.)	Income Tax (Standard Rate in £)	Amount Retained of Bachelor's £10,000 earned income after Income Tax and Surtax	Wholesale Price Index Numberb	Retail Price Index Number	Annual Purchasing Power of £ 1900-1965	
						1900 =20/-	1965 =20/-
	1	2	3	4	5	6	7
1961	22,327	7/9	4,648	116	286	3/10	22/1
1962	23,353	7/9	4,648	119	298	3/8	21/9
1963	24,845	7/9	4,648	120	304	3/7	21/6
1964	26,821	7/9	4,845	124	314	3/6	20/11
1965	28,613	8/3	5,922	130	329	3/5	20/-
1966	29,921	8/3	5,922	133	339	3/3	19/5
1967	31,148	8/3	5,715	135	347	3/2	19/1

( ) = Estimated figures.

a Changes in sources at 1914 and 1947.

b 1900–20 on different basis from later figures. 1913–49 covers materials, semi-manufactures and finished products, and is not comparable with later figures (1938 = 100 . . . 1913 = 83, 1950 = 259). 1950–3, new series based on 1948 weight and covers output of manufactured products other than fuel, food and tobacco. 1954 onwards, based on 1954 weights and covers home market sales of all manufactured products.

SOURCES—
1. 1900–14, C. H. Feinstein, 'Income and Investment in the U.K. 1856–1914', *Economic Journal*, June 1961. 1914–46, A. R. Prest, 'National Income of the U.K. 1870–1946', *Economic Journal*, March 1948. 1947 onwards, *National Income and Expenditure* Annual Blue Books.
2. *Reports of the Commissioners for Inland Revenue.*
3. *Reports of the Commissioners for Inland Revenue* and information received from the Inland Revenue.
4. Board of Trade and *London and Cambridge Economic Service.* (Supplements in '*Times*' *Review of Industry.*)
5. 1900–14, E. L. Bowley, *Wages and Income in the U.K. since 1860* (1937), p. 30. 1919 onwards based on the official indices of retail prices as published in *London and Cambridge Economic Service.* (Supplements in '*Times*' *Review of Industry.*)
6 and 7. 1900–14 based on unofficial price index compiled by G. H. Wood, in W. T. Layton and G. Crowther, *An Introduction to the Study of Prices* (1938); 1914–38 based on Ministry of Labour *Cost of Living Index* (*Min. of Labour Gazette*); 1938 onwards based on figures in *Annual Abstract of Statistics.*

	Index Number of Industrial Production (1924= 100)	Steel Productiona ('000 tons)	Coal Productionb (million tons)	Raw Cotton Consumptionc U.K. (million lbs.)	Agriculture			Price of 2½% Consols (Average for year)	Bank Rate % (Maximum and Minimum for year)	
					Cultivated Areasd ('000 acres)	Cattle ('000s)	Sheep ('000s)			
	1	2	3	4	5	6	7	8	9	
1900	73·9		225	1,737	47,795	11,455	31,055	99·6	6	3
1901	73·6		219	1,569	47,761	11,478	31,830	94·3	5	3
1902	76·4		227	1,633	47,753	11,367	30,057	94·4	4	3
1903	76·4		230	1,617	47,708	11,409	29,659	90·8	4	3
1904	75·7		232	1,486	47,671	11,576	29,105	88·3	4	3
1905	78·3		236	1,813	47,673	11,674	29,077	89·8	3	2½
1906	80·2		251	1,855	47,193	11,692	29,210	88·3	6	3½
1907	81·6		268	1,985	46,998	11,630	30,011	84·1	7	4
1908	77·1		262	1,917	47,002	11,739	31,332	86·0	7	2½
1909	78·9		264	1,824	46,888	11,762	31,840	83·9	5	2½
1910	80·6		264	1,632	46,932	11,765	31,165	81·1	5	3
1911	83·0		272	1,892	46,927	11,866	30,480	79·3	4½	3
1912	84·2		260	2,142	46,794	11,915	28,967	76·2	5	3
1913	90·5	7,664	287	2,178	46,741	11,937	27,629	73·6	5	4½
1914	84·8	7,835	266	2,077	46,643	12,145	27,886	74·8	10	3
1915	86·4	8,550	253	1,931	46,554	12,132	28,198	65·5	5	
1916	81·8	8,992	256	1,972	46,564	12,413	28,777	58·0	6	5
1917	76·4	9,717	249	1,800	46,212	12,346	27,788	54·7	6	5
1918	73·8	9,539	228	1,499	46,142	12,274	26,981	56·9	5	
1919	81·3	7,894	230	1,526	46,206	12,454	25,048	54·1	6	5
1920	90·3	9,067	230	1,726	45,953	11,735	23,329	47·0	7	6
1921	73·5	3,703	163	1,066	45,581	11,857	24,198	48·0	7	5
1922	85·0	5,881	250	1,409	45,458	12,026	23,689	56·5	5	3
1923	90·0	8,482	276	1,362	33,106	7,764	21,085	58·0	4	3
1924	100·0	8,201	267	1,369	33,057	7,794	22,239	57·0	4	
1925	103·9	7,385	243	1,609	32,920	8,035	23,578	56·3	5	4

	Index Number of Industrial Production (1924 = 100)	Steel Production[a] ('000 tons)	Coal Production[b] (million tons)	Raw Cotton Consumption[c] U.K. (million lbs.)	Agriculture Cultivated Areas[d] ('000 acres)	Cattle ('000s)	Sheep ('000s)	Price of 2½% Consols (Average for year)	Bank Rate % (Maximum and Minimum for year)
	1	2	3	4	5	6	7	8	9
1926	98·4	3,596	126	1,509	32,830	8,177	24,591	55·0	5
1927	113·4	9,097	251	1,557	32,724	8,183	25,208	54·8	5 4½
1928	110·2	8,520	238	1,520	32,617	7,978	24,602	55·9	4½
1929	115·2	9,636	258	1,498	32,547	7,890	24,315	54·3	6 4½
1930	110·8	7,326	244	1,272	32,459	7,759	24,669	55·8	5 3
1931	103·7	5,203	220	985	32,374	7,955	26,374	56·9	6 2½
1932	103·2	5,261	209	1,257	32,284	8,306	27,204	66·8	6 2
1933	110·1	7,024	207	1,177	32,193	8,647	26,651	73·7	2
1934	121·1	8,850	221	1,322	32,096	8,742	24,944	80·6	2
1935	130·3	9,859	222	1,261	32,024	8,659	25,062	86·6	2
1936	142·0	11,785	228	1,366	31,932	8,623	25,040	85·1	2
1937	150·5	12,984	240	1,431	31,827	8,639	25,541	76·3	2
1938	146·4	10,398	227	1,109	31,755	8,762	26,775	74·1	2
1939	n.a.	13,221	231	1,317	31,679	8,872	26,887	67·2	4 2
1940	n.a.	12,975	224	1,389	31,430	9,903	26,316	73·5	2
1941	n.a.	12,312	206	965	31,353	8,940	22,257	80·0	2
1942	n.a.	12,942	205	939	31,204	9,075	21,506	82·6	2
1943	n.a.	13,031	199	885	31,058	9,259	20,383	80·7	2
1944	n.a.	12,142	193	804	31,008	9,501	20,107	79·6	2
1945	n.a.	11,824	183	717	31,023	9,616	20,150	85·5	2
1946	149·4	12,695	190	813	31,010	9,629	20,358	96·3	2
1947	158·7	12,725	197	815	31,022	9,567	16,713	90·7	2
1948	171·7	14,877	209	977	31,062	9,806	18,164	78·0	2
1949	182·5	15,553	215	979	31,056	10,244	19,493	75·9	2
1950	195·1	16,293	216	1,017	31,126	10,620	20,430	70·5	2
1951	201·2	15,639	223	1,024	31,131	10,473	19,984	66·1	2½ 2
1952	195·9	16,418	227	686	31,163	10,244	21,655	59·1	4 2½
1953	207·9	17,609	224	831	31,177	10,444	22,455	61·3	4 3½
1954	222·5	18,520	224	892	31,128	10,718	22,873	66·6	3½ 3
1955	234·5	19,791	222	778	31,103	10,688	22,949	60·0	4½ 3
1956	234·4	20,659	222	714	31,092	10,907	23,594	52·8	5½ 4½
1957	237·6	21,699	224	744	31,030	10,881	24,796	50·2	7 5½
1958	236·1	19,566	216	628	31,001	10,956	26,105	50·2	7 4
1959	248·1	20·186	206	623	30,873	11,291	27,612	51·8	4
1960	265·6	24,305	194	599	30,854	11,771	27,871	46·1	6 4
1961	268·9	22,086	192	536	30,637	11,936	28,967	46·1	7 5
1962	271·7	20,491	199	473	30,655	11,859	28,498	40·2	6 4½
1963	280·9	22,520	197	483	30,644	11,716	29,344	44·8	4½ 4
1964	302·6	26,230	194	508	30,686	11,627	29,657	41·5	7 4
1965	311·3	27,006	183	492	30,660	11,943	29,911	39·0	7 6
1966	320·0	24,315	173	454	30,683	12,206	29,957	36·7	7 6
1967	319·7	23,875	171	384	30,653	12,342	28,885	37·4	8 5½

...... Change in basis of calculation.

[a] Great Britain only.   [b] Including S. Ireland, 1900–21 inclusive.
[c] From 1958 a revised bale weight was used in calculations.
[d] Total area under all crops and grass. For Great Britain excluding all holdings under one acre, for N. Ireland excluding all holdings under ¼ acre until 1953, and under one acre from 1954.

SOURCES—
1. K. S. Lomax, 'Production and Productivity Movements in the U.K. since 1900', *Journal of the Royal Statistical Society*. Series A, 1959. 1958 onwards *National Income and Expenditure* Annual Blue Books.
2. British Iron and Steel Federation, *Annual Abstract of Statistics*.
3. Ministry of Power, *Annual Abstract of Statistics*.
4. R. Robson, *The Cotton Industry in Britain* (1957), p. 332, Statistics table 1, and information supplied by the Cotton Board
5, 6 and 7. Figures for June each year. 1900–13 including Isle of Man and Channel Islands. 1914 onwards excluding Isle of Man and Channel Islands. 1900–22 including S. Ireland. *Annual Abstract of Statistics*, Agricultural Departments.
8 and 9. Bank of England *Annual Abstract of Statistics*.

	Net Balance of Payments of the U.K. on current account[a] (£m.)	Terms of Trade[b] Index No. (1938 =100)	Imports and Exports of the U.K.			Imports and Exports of the U.K. Volume Indices		Foreign Exchange Rates		
			Imports[c] c.i.f. (£m.)	Exports of U.K. Products[c] f.o.b. (£m.)	Re-exports[c] f.o.b. (£m.)	Im-ports[d]	Ex-ports[d]	U.S.A. ($ to £)	France (Francs to £)	Germany (Marks to £)
	1	2	3	4	5	6	7	8	9	10
						(1880 = 100)				
1900			523	291	63	n.a.	140·0	4·84	25·1	20·4
1901			522	280	68	176·7	141·4	4·85	25·2	20·4
1902			528	283	66	182·2	150·0	4·85	25·2	20·5
1903			543	291	70	183·8	154·1	4·85	25·1	20·4
1904			551	301	70	185·9	157·4	4·85	25·2	20·4
1905			565	330	78	187·7	173·0	4·85	25·2	20·5
1906			608	376	85	193·2	186·0	4·82	25·1	20·5
1907			646	426	92	195·8	201·1	4·84	25·1	20·5
1908			593	377	80	188·5	185·1	4·85	25·1	20·4
1909			625	378	91	193·8	192·8	4·86	25·2	20·4
1910			678	430	104	197·6	210·3	4·84	25·2	20·4
1911			680	454	103	203·6	218·0	4·84	25·3	20·4
1912			745	487	112	219·2	230·0	4·85	25·2	20·5
1913	194	143	769	525	110	227·1	238·9	4·83	25·2	20·4
1914			697	431	95	n.a.	n.a.	4·87	25·2	20·5
1915			852	385	99	n.a.	n.a.	4·77	26·3	··
1916			949	506	98	n.a.	n.a.	4·76	28·2	··
1917			1,064	527	70	n.a.	n.a.	4·76	27·4	··
1918			1,316	501	31	n.a.	n.a.	4·76	27·2	··
						(1938 = 100)				
1919		124	1,626	799	165	78	95	4·60	29·7	··
1920	210	114	1,933	1,334	223	78	123	3·97	47·9	145
1921		101	1,086	703	107	65	86	3·73	46·7	268
1922	151	109	1,003	720	104	76	119	4·41	52·8	1,654
1923	140	113	1,096	767	119	82	129	4·58	75·2	720,000
1924	72	117	1,277	801	140	92	132	4·33	81·8	18 billion
1925	46	121	1,321	773	154	94	130	4·86	106·1	20·4
1926	− 15	117	1,241	653	125	97	116	4·87	167·5	20·4
1927	82	118	1,218	709	123	99	134	4·85	124·0	20·5
1928	123	120	1,196	724	120	96	137	4·87	124·2	20·4
1929	103	120	1,221	729	110	101	141	4·84	124·0	20·4
1930	28	110	1,044	571	87	98	115	4·86	123·7	20·4
1931	− 104	99	861	391	64	100	88	4·86	124·2	20·5
1932	− 51	98	702	365	51	87	88	3·58	91·1	15·0
1933	0	96	675	368	49	88	89	4·30	86·2	14·3
1934	− 7	99	731	396	51	91	95	5·04	76·6	13·3
1935	32	100	756	426	55	93	102	4·94	74·5	12·2
1936	− 18	103	848	441	61	99	104	5·01	75·7	12·4
1937	− 56	109	1,028	521	75	105	113	4·94	120	12·3
1938	− 70	100	920	471	62	100	100	4·95	178	12·3
1939	− 250	101	886	440	46	95	94	4·68	177	11·7
1940	− 804	n.a.	1,152	411	26	(85)	(70)	4·03	177	··
1941	− 816	n.a.	1,145	365	13	(70)	(50)	4·03	··	··
1942	− 663	(103)	997	271	5	(65)	(36)	4·03	··	··
1943	− 680	(109)	1,234	234	6	(70)	(29)	4·03	··	··
1944	− 659	(104)	1,309	266	16	(75)	(31)	4·03	··	··
1945	− 875	107	1,104	399	51	61	46	4·03	203·8	··

····· Change in basis of calculation.   ( ) Estimated figures.

	Net Balance of Payments of the U.K. on current account[a] (£m.)	Terms of Trade[b] No. (1938 =100)	Imports and Exports of the U.K.			Imports and Exports of the U.K. Volume Indices		Foreign Exchange Rates		
			Imports[c] c.i.f. (£m.)	Exports of U.K. Products[c] f.o.b. (£m.)	Re-exports[c] f.o.b. (£m.)	Imports[d]	Exports[d]	U.S.A. ($ to £)	France (Francs to £)	Germany (Marks to £)
	1	2	3	4	5	6	7	8	9	10
1946	−295	109	1,298	912	50	67	99	4·03	480·0	..
1947	−442	116	1,798	1,142	59	76	109	4·03	480·0	..
1948	7	118	2,075	1,578	61	78	137	4·03	f	..
1949	38	117	2,279	1,789	58	85	151	e	g	..
1950	297	125	2,609	2,174	85	85	174	2·80	980·0	..
1951	−419	139	3,905	2,582	127	96	174	2·80	979·7	..
1952	227	129	3,465	2,567	142	88	166	2·79	981·5	West Germany only
1953	179	119	3,328	2,558	103	95	169	2·81	982·8	11·7
1954	204	120	3,359	2,650	98	96	177	2·81	981·6	11·7
1955	−92	122	3,861	2,877	116	107	190	2·79	978·1	11·7
1956	192	119	3,862	3,143	144	106	201	2·80	982·7	11·7
1957	229	116	4,044	3,295	130	110	205	2·79	h	11·7
1958	345	107	3,748	3,176	141	110	197	2·81	i	11·7
1959	90	107	3,983	3,330	131	118	205	2·81	13·77j	11·7
1960	−265	106	4,557	3,536	141	133	216	2·81	13·77j	11·7
1961	−4	109	4,398	3,682	158	131	221	2·80	13·74	11·17
1962	112	112	4,492	3,792	158	135	225	2·81	13·76	11·22
1963	111	110	4,820	4,080	154	140	238	2·80	13·72	11·16
1964	−399	108	5,696	4,412	153	156	245	2·79	13·68	11·10
1965	−91	112	5,761	4,724	173	157	259	2·80	13·70	11·17
1966	15	113	5,947	5,047	194	160	267	2·79	13·72	11·17
1967	−404	115	6,442	5,026	185	173	262	2·79 k	13·68 l	11·10 m

[a] Changes in sources and methods in 1924.
[b] Import price index as a percentage of the export price index. A rise indicates an adverse movement.
[c] 1900–22 inclusive, S. Ireland is included. From 1923 direct foreign trade of S. Ireland is excluded, and Imports and exports include trade of Great Britain and N. Ireland with S. Ireland. There are small changes in coverage from time to time.
[d] 1900–23 inclusive, including S. Ireland. 1900–13 Exports of U.K. products only. 1919 onwards, Total Exports. (1938 = 100 ... 1913 Imports = 88, 1914 Exports = 173.)
[e] 4·03 to 19 Sep, 2·80 thereafter.
[f] 480 to 25 Jan, 864 from 26 Jan to 17 Oct, 1,062 thereafter.
[g] 1,062 to 26 Apr, 1,097 from 27 Apr to 20 Sep, 980 thereafter.
[h] 984·9 to 10 Aug, 1,177·1 thereafter.
[i] 1,775·5 to 24 Dec, 13·74 from 29 Dec (in units of 100 francs).
[j] In units of 100 francs (100 francs = 1 New Franc)
[k] 2·79 to 18 Nov, 2·40 thereafter.
[l] 13·68 to 18 Nov, 11·88 thereafter.
[m] 11·10 to 18 Nov, 9·50 thereafter.

SOURCES—
1. *London and Cambridge Economic Service.* (Supplements in '*Times*' *Review of Industry*) and *Balance of Payments White Papers.*
2. *London and Cambridge Economic Service.* (Supplements in '*Times*' *Review of Industry*.) Adapted from 1961 onwards from B. of Trade figures.
3, 4, and 5. *Trade and Navigation Accounts of the U.K.*, Board of Trade, annually. From 1965 *Overseas Trade Accounts of the U.K.*
6 and 7. 1900–13, A. H. Imlah, *Economic Elements in the Pax Britannica* (1958). 1919 onwards, *London and Cambridge Economic Service.* (Supplements in '*Times*' *Review of Industry*.)
8, 9, and 10. 1900–39, *The Economist*, figures for the end of June; 1940 onwards *Annual Abstract of Statistics*. Figures are average for the year.

	Total Central Government Revenue[a] (£m.)	Main Sources of Revenue				
		Income tax[b] (£m.)	Surtax (£m.)	Customs (£m.)	Excise (£m.)	Death Duties (£m.)
	1	2	3	4	5	6
1900	140	28	..	26	38	17
1901	153	35	..	31	37	19
1902	161	39	..	35	37	18
1903	151	31	..	34	37	17
1904	153	31	..	36	36	17
1905	154	31	..	35	36	17
1906	155	31	..	33	36	19
1907	157	31	..	32	36	19
1908	152	34	..	29	34	18
1909	132	13	..	30	31	22
1910	204	60	3	33	40	25
1911	185	42	3	34	38	25
1912	189	41	4	33	38	25
1913	198	44	3	35	40	27
1914	227	59	10	39	42	28
1915	337	112	17	60	61	31
1916	573	186	19	71	56	31
1917	707	216	23	71	39	32
1918	889	256	36	103	59	30
1919	1,340	317	42	149	134	41
1920	1,426	339	55	134	200	48
1921	1,125	337	62	130	194	52
1922	914	315	64	123	157	57
1923	837	269	61	120	148	58
1924	799	274	63	99	135	59
1925	812	259	69	103	135	61
1926	806	235	66	108	133	67
1927	843	251	61	112	139	77
1928	836	238	56	119	134	81
1929	815	238	56	120	128	80
1930	858	256	68	121	124	83
1931	851	287	77	136	120	65
1932	827	252	61	167	121	77
1933	809	229	53	179	107	85
1934	805	229	51	185	105	81
1935	845	238	51	197	107	88
1936	897	257	54	211	110	88
1937	949	298	57	222	114	89
1938	1,006	336	63	226	114	77
1939	1,132	390	70	262	138	78
1940	1,495	524	76	305	224	81
1941	2,175	770	75	378	326	91
1942	2,922	1,007	75	460	425	93
1943	3,149	1,184	76	561	482	100
1944	3,355	1,317	74	579	497	111
1945	3,401	1,361	69	570	541	120
1946	3,623	1,156	76	621	564	148
1947	4,011	1,189	91	791	629	172
1948	4,168	1,368	98	824	734	177
1949	4,098	1,438	115	813	706	190
1950	4,157	1,404	121	905	724	185

	Total Central Government Revenue[a] (£m.)	Main Sources of Revenue				
		Income tax[b] (£m.)	Surtax (£m.)	Customs (£m,)	Excise (£m.)	Death Duties (£m.)
	1	2	3	4	5	6
1951	4,629	1,669	130	998	753	183
1952	4,654	1,736	131	1,024	739	152
1953	4,606	1,731	132	1,042	722	165
1954	4,987	1,893	135	1,100	772	188
1955	5,160	1,943	139	1,149	865	176
1956	5,462	2,114	158	1,199	902	169
1957	5,679	2,208	157	1,207	942	171
1958	5,850	2,322	167	1,262	930	187
1959	6,016	2,243	181	1,373	909	227
1960	6,344	2,433	189	1,457	933	236
1961	6,644	2,727	224	1,616	978	262
1962	6,794	2,818	184	1,639	1,208	270
1963	6,890	2,745	177	1,723	1,043	310
1964	8,157	3,088	184	2,008	1,166	297
1965	9,144	3,678	203	3,401		292
1966	10,219	3,246	242	3,536		301
1967	11,177	3,817	232	3,690		330

[a] Total national revenue includes Ordinary and Self-Balancing Revenue. Figures relate to year ending 31 Mar of following year.
[b] 1900–10, 'Income tax' covers Property and Income tax. 1910 figure includes arrears for 1909.

SOURCES—
1, 2, 3, 4, 5, and 6. *Finance Accounts of the U.K.*, published annually by the Treasury.

	Main Heads of Expenditure				Specimen Tariffs		Excise Duty on Beer [e] (per barrel of 36 gallons)	National Debt [f]
	De-fence (£m.)	Educa-tion [a] (£m.)	Health, Labour and In-surance [b] (£m.)	Pen-sions [c] (£m.)	Sugar [d] (per cwt.)	Tea [d] (per lb.)		
	1	2	3	4	5 s. d.	6 s. d.	7 s. d.	8
1900	121	13	..	..	..	6	6/9	628·9
1901	124	13	..	..	4/2	6	7/9	689·5
1902	101	13	..	..	4/2	6	7/9	745·0
1903	72	15	..	..	4/2	6	7/9	770·8
1904	66	16	..	..	4/2	8	7/9	762·6
1905	62	16	..	..	4/2	6	7/9	755·1
1906	59	17	..	..	4/2	5	7/9	743·3
1907	58	17	..	..	4/2	5	7/9	724·5
1908	59	17	..	..	1/10	5	7/9	709·0
1909	63	18	..	..	1/10	5	7/9	702·7
1910	67	19	..	..	1/10	5	7/9	713·2
1911	70	19	..	..	1/10	5	7/9	685·2
1912	72	20	..	..	1/10	5	7/9	668·3
1913	77	17	14	1	1/10	5	7/9	656·5
1914	437	18	14	1	1/10	5	7/9	649·8
1915	1,424	19	14	1	1/10	8	23/-	1,105·0
1916	2,007	18	14	1	14/-	1/-	24/-	2,133·1
1917	2,436	22	14	1	14/-	1/-	25/-	4,011·4
1918	2,238	23	15	1	25/8	1/-	50/-	5,871·9
1919	692	39	74	100	25/8	1/-	70/-	7,434·9
1920	292	54	73	110	25/8	1/-	100/-	7,828·8
1921	189	59	73	96	25/8	1/-	100/-	7,574·4
1922	111	50	61	83	25/8	8	100/-	7,654·3
1923	105	47	59	72	25/8	8	100/-	7,742·2
1924	114	48	65	71	11/8	4	100/-	7,641·0
1925	119	48	65	70	11/8	4	100/-	7,597·8
1926	116	53	75	65	11/8	4	100/-	7,558·6
1927	117	53	73	62	11/8	4	100/-	7,554·6
1928	113	49	76	59	11/8	4	100/-	7,527·8
1929	113	50	86	56	11/8	..	100/-	7,500·3
1930	110	55	108	55	11/8	..	103/-	7,469·0
1931	107	55	121	52	11/8	..	103/-	7,413·3
1932	103	52	155	49	11/8	4	134/-	7,433·9
1933	107	51	151	49	11/8	4	24/-	7,643·8
1934	113	53	151	47	11/8	4	24/-	7,822·3
1935	136	56	162	46	11/8	4	24/-	6,763·9
1936	186	59	162	45	11/8	6	24/-	6,759·3
1937	197	60	162	44	11/8	6	24/-	6,764·7
1938	254	62	166	43	11/8	8	24/-	6,993·7
1939	626	63	167	42	11/8	8	24/-	7,130·8
1940	3,220	63	165	41	23/4	8	90/-	7,899·2
1941	4,085	66	170	41	23/4	8	90/-	10,366·4
1942	4,840	78	186	40	23/4	8	118/1½	13,041·1
1943	4,950	80	199	39	23/4	8	138/4½	15,822·6
1944	5,125	85	208	40	23/4	8	140/7½	18,562·2
1945	4,410	118	219	42	23/4	8	140/7½	21,365·9

...... Change in basis of calculation.

	Main Heads of Expenditure				Specimen Tariffs		Excise Duty on Beer[e] (per barrel of 36 gallons)	National Debt[f] (£m.)
	De-fence (£m.)	Educa-tion[a] (£m.)	Health, Labour and In-surance[b] (£m.)	Pen-sions[c] (£m.)	Sugar[d] (per cwt.)	Tea[d] (per lb.)		
	1	2	3	4	5	6	7	8
					s. d.	s. d.	s. d.	
1946	1,653	150	334	97	23/4	8	140/7½	23,636·5
1947	854	182	380	91	23/4	8	140/7½	25,630·6
1948	753	213	598	96	23/4	8	178/10½	25,620·8
1949	741	242	806	97	11/8	2	157/10½	25,167·6
1950	777	253	835	94	11/8	2	155/4½	25,802·3
1951	1,110	274	810	91	11/8	2	155/4½	25,921·6
1952	1,404	288	884	100	11/8	2	155/4½	25,890·5
1953	1,365	303	903	97	11/8	2	155/4½	26,051·2
1954	1,436	338	619	419	11/8	2	155/4½	26,583·0
1955	1,405	378	652	433	11/8	2	155/4½	26,933·7
1956	1,525	434	750	463	11/8	2	155/4½	27,038·9
1957	1,430	481	782	490	11/8	2	155/4½	27,007·5
1958	1,468	523	794	575	11/8	2	155/4½	27,232·0
1959	1,475	215	1,209	610	11/8	2	111/9½	27,376·3
1960	1,596	204	1,384	634	11/8	2	111/9½	27,732·6
1961	1,689	247	1,417	659	11/8[g]	2	111/9½	28,251·7
1962	1,767	288	1,549	705	..	2	123/-	28,674·4
1963	1,792	334	1,716	772	..	2[h]	123/-	29,847·6
1964	1,909	389	1,897	792	..	..	147/-	30,226·5
1965	2,055	..[1]	..[1]	..[1]	..	..	171/-	30,440·6
1966	2,142	..	..	..	..	..	171/-	31,340·2
1967	2,247	..	..	..	..	..	188/8	31,950

..... Change in basis of calculation.

[a] 1900–13, 'Education' includes Science and Art. From 1935 'Education' includes Broadcasting.

[b] 1900–13, the system of classification prevents entries comparable with those for later years. 1949–53, figures cover Housing, Local Government, Health, Labour, National Insurance and National Assistance. From 1954 figures cover Health, Housing and Local Government.

[c] 1900–13, the system of classification prevents entries comparable with those for later years. Before 1954, 'Pensions' equivalent to 'non-effective' charges. 1954 onwards figures cover Pensions, National Insurance and National Assistance.

[d] Full Customs duty given. In many cases preferential rates apply to Commonwealth trade. Sugar: exceeding 98° of polarisation.

[e] 1900–32 beer of 1,055° specific gravity. 1933–49 beer of 1,027° specific gravity. 1950–60 beer of 1,030° specific gravity.

[f] Debt of U.K. Exchequer, debt created by N. Ireland Exchequer excluded. Bonds tendered for death duties and held by National Debt Commissioners excluded from 1920. External debt arising out of 1914–18 war, excluded from 1935, when it was £1,035·5 m.

[g] April 1962 Excise Duty on sugar was repealed.

[h] June 1963 tariffs on tea ceased to be direct revenue and became chargeable under the Import Duties Act, 1958.

[1] From 1965 onwards figures no longer collected in this form.

SOURCES—
1, 2, 3 and 4. *Annual Abstract of Statistics.* 2, 3, 4. 1961–64 Central Statistical Office.
5 and 6. *Customs Tariff of the U.K. (Annual Reports of Commissioners for Customs and Excise.)*
7. *Reports of Commissioners for Customs and Excise.*
8. *Finance Accounts of the U.K.*

INDUSTRIAL OUTPUT OF THE U.K.

All census Industries	Value of Production (Gross Output)
1907 [a]	1,765 £million
1924	3,747 [b]
1930	3,371 [b]
1935	3,543 [b]
1948 [c]	12,961
1951	18,733
	- - - - [d]
1958	25,946
1963	32,066

[a] Including firms in the Irish Republic.
[b] Firms employing more than 10 persons only.　　　　[c] Great Britain only.
[d] Prior to 1951 classified according to the 1948 edition of the *Standard Industrial Classification*.
Figures below the line classified according to the 1958 *Standard Industrial Classification*.

SOURCE.—*Annual Abstract of Statistics 1966.*

SURTAX

Year of Change	Income Level at which Surtax Payable	Maximum Rate in £ Payable		
	Exceeding £			£
1909	5,000	6d. on amount in excess of 3,000		
1914	3,000	1/9½	,, ,,	8,000
1915	3,000	3/6	,, ,,	10,000
1918	2,500	4/6	,, ,,	10,000
1920	2,000	6/–	,, ,,	30,000
1929	2,000	7/6	,, ,,	50,000
1930	2,000	8/3	,, ,,	50,000
1938	2,000	9/6	,, ,,	30,000
1939	2,000	9/6	,, ,,	20,000
1946	2,000	10/6	,, ,,	20,000
1951	2,000	10/–	,, ,,	20,000
1965	5,000 earned	10/–	,, ,,	15,000

SOURCE.—*Annual Reports of Commissioners for Inland Revenue.*

ESTATE DUTY

Payable on estate of net capital
value £100,000

Death occurred in Period	Rate of Duty %	Duty Payable £
Before 1909	5·5	5,500
1909–1914	8	8,000
1914–1919	9	9,000
1919–1925	14	14,000
1925–1939	19	19,000
1939–1939	20·9	20,900
1939–1940	22·8	22,800
1940–1946	24·7	24,700
1946–1949	30	30,000
After 1949	45	45,000

Where death occurred before 30 Jul 49
additional legacy and succession duties
were also payable.

SOURCE.—*Annual Reports of Commissioners
of Inland Revenue.*

MAXIMUM RATES OF DEATH DUTY

Death occurred in Period	Rate of Duty	Net Capital Value of Estate
	%	£m.
1894–1907	8	1
1907–1909	15	3
1909–1914	15	1
1914–1919	20	1
1919–1925	40	2
1925–1930	40	2
1930–1939	50	2
1939–1939	55	2
1939–1940	60	2
1940–1946	65	2
1946–1949	75	2
1949 onwards	80	1

SOURCE.—*Annual Reports of Commissioner
of Inland Revenue.*

HIRE PURCHASE

Hire Purchase and other instalment credit (Finance Houses, Durable Goods, Shops and Department Stores) — total outstanding business at end of period.

£million

1961	934
1962	887
1963	959
1964	1280
1965	1386
1966	1261
1967	1226

SOURCE.—*Annual Abstract of Statistics.*

BUDGET DATES

1900	5 Mar	1918	22 Apr	1937	20 Apr	1953	14 Apr
1901	18 Apr	1919	30 Apr	1938	26 Apr	1954	6 Apr
1902	14 Apr	1920	19 Apr	1939	25 Apr	1955	19 Apr
1903	23 Apr	1921	25 Apr		27 Sep		26 Oct
1904	19 Apr	1922	1 May	1940	23 Apr	1956	17 Apr
1905	10 Apr	1923	17 Apr		23 Jul	1957	9 Apr
1906	30 Apr	1924	29 Apr	1941	7 Apr	1958	15 Apr
1907	18 Apr	1925	28 Apr	1942	14 Apr	1959	7 Apr
1908	7 May	1926	26 Apr	1943	12 Apr	1960	4 Apr
1909	29 Apr	1927	11 Apr	1944	25 Apr	1961	17 Apr
1910	30 Jun	1928	24 Apr	1945	24 Apr	1962	8 Apr
1911	16 May	1929	15 Apr		23 Oct	1963	3 Apr
1912	2 Apr	1930	14 Apr	1946	9 Apr	1964	14 Apr
1913	22 Apr	1931	27 Apr	1947	15 Apr		11 Nov
1914	4 May		10 Sep		12 Nov	1965	6 Apr
	17 Nov	1932	19 Apr	1948	6 Apr	1966	5 May
1915	4 May	1933	25 Apr	1949	6 Apr	1967	11 Apr
	21 Sep	1934	17 Apr	1950	18 Apr	1968	19 Mar
1916	4 Apr	1935	15 Apr	1951	10 Apr		
1917	3 May	1936	21 Apr	1952	11 Apr		

XII

NATIONALISATION

Main Landmarks

1908 **The Port of London Authority** was set up in 1909 under the *Port of London Act, 1908*.

1926 **The Central Electricity Board** was set up by the *Electricity (Supply) Act, 1926*, to regulate central distribution of electricity.

1926 **The British Broadcasting Corporation** was granted its first charter as a public corporation.

1933 **The London Passenger Transport Board** was established.

1946 **The Bank of England** was nationalised, and received a charter.

1946 **The Coal Industry** was nationalised by the *Coal Industry Nationalisation Act, 1946*, which set up the National Coal Board.

1946 **Civil Aviation** was formally nationalised by the *Civil Aviation Act, 1946*. This covered the British Overseas Airways Corporation (set up in 1939), and two new corporations, British European Airways and British South American Airways.

1947 **Public Transport** (and some private transport) was nationalised by the *Transport Act, 1947*. The British Transport Commission was established, and the Docks and Inland Waterways, Hotels, Railways, London Transport, Road Haulage, and Road Passenger Transport were administered by six executive boards. The *Transport Act, 1953*, denationalised Road Haulage. *The Transport Act, 1962*, reorganised nationalised transport undertakings and provided for the establishment of separate Boards for Railways, London Transport, Docks and Waterways, and for a Transport Holding Company, as successors to the British Transport Commission.

1948 **Gas** was nationalised by the *Gas Act, 1948*, which established the Gas Council and twelve Area Gas Boards.

1949 **Iron and Steel** were nationalised by the *Iron and Steel Act, 1949*, and the Iron and Steel Corporation of Great Britain was established. The vesting date of the Act was 1 Jan 51. The *Iron and Steel Act, 1953*, denationalised the industry, and set up the Iron and Steel Board. In 1967 the *Iron and Steel Act* renationalised the industry, as from 28 Jul 67.

1954 **The U.K. Atomic Energy Authority** was established by the *U.K. Atomic Energy Authority Act, 1954*.

1957 **Electricity** was nationalised by the *Electricity Act, 1947*, which set up the British Electricity Authority in place of the Central Electricity

Board. The *Electricity Act, 1957*, set up the Electricity Council and the Central Electricity Generating Board. The twelve area boards became financially autonomous.

1968 **The Post Office** was to become a Public Corporation under legislation before Parliament during 1968–69.

Nationalised Industries — Board Chairmen

United Kingdom Atomic Energy Authority 1954

The Chairman and members of the A.E.A. are appointed by the Lord President of the Council

Chairman

1 Aug 54	Sir E. Plowden (Ld)
1 Jan 60	Sir R. Makins
10 Feb 64	Sir W. Penney (Ld)
16 Oct 67	J. Hill

SOURCE.—*United Kingdom Atomic Energy Authority Annual Reports 1954–.*

Civil Aviation

The Chairman, Deputy Chairman and members of all three corporations are appointed by the appropriate Minister

British European Airways Corporation, 1946-

Chairman

1 Aug 46	Sir H. Hartley
1 Apr 47	G. d'Erlanger
14 Mar 49	Ld Douglas
3 May 56	(Sir) A. Milward

Deputy Chairman

1 Aug 46	W. Straight
1 Apr 47	(Sir) J. Keeling [1]
1 Oct 65	K. Keith

[1] Part-time.

SOURCE.—*B.E.A. Annual Reports and Accounts, 1947–.*

British Overseas Airways Corporation, 1939-

This was established in 1939, and became one of the three corporations under the Civil Aviation Act, 1946

Chairman

26 May 43	Vt Knollys
1 Jul 47	Sir H. Hartley
1 Jul 49	Sir M. Thomas
1 May 56	(Sir) G. d'Erlanger
29 Jul 60	Sir M. Slattery
1 Jan 64	Sir G. Guthrie
1 Jan 69	C. Hardie

Deputy Chairman

1 Aug 46	Sir H. Howitt
1 Apr 48	Sir M. Thomas

1 Jul 49	W. Straight
(1 Aug 49–30 Apr 50, *additional Deputy Chairman*, J. Booth)	
21 Nov 55	Ld Rennell [1]
1 May 56	Sir G. Cribbett
20 Jun 60	Sir W. Neden [1]
3 Apr 64	K. Granville
3 Apr 64	C. Hardie

[1] Part-time.

SOURCE.—*B.O.A.C. Annual Reports and Accounts, 1946–.*

British South American Airways Corporation, 1946–49

The B.S.A.A.C. was merged with B.O.A.C. by the Airways Incorporation Act, 1949

Chairman

1 Aug 46	J. Booth
1 May 50	Sir M. Thomas

Deputy Chairman

1 Aug 46	(Sir) J. Stephenson
1 Apr 49	Sir F. Brake

SOURCE.—*B.S.A.A.C. Annual Reports an Accounts, 1947–49.*

National Coal Board, 1946-

The Chairman, Deputy Chairman and members of the Board are all appointed by the Minister

Chairman

15 Jul 46	Ld Hyndley (Vt)
1 Aug 51	Sir H. Houldsworth
1 Feb 56	(Sir) J. Bowman
7 Feb 61	A. Robens (Ld)

Deputy Chairman

15 Jul 46	Sir A. Street
1 Aug 51	W. Drummond & Sir E. Coates
21 Feb 55	J. Bowman
1 Feb 56	(Sir) J. Latham
1 Sep 60	E. Browne
1 Oct 60	A. Robens
1 Feb 61	E. Browne
8 May 67	D. Ezra

SOURCE.—*National Coal Board Annual Reports and Statement of Accounts, 1946–.*

British Electricity Authority, 1947–55 (Central Electricity Authority, 1955–57)

The Chairman and from four to six other members are appointed by the Minister. Four other members are appointed by the Minister from among the Area Board chairmen, the appointments being made from the boards in rotation

Chairman

15 Aug 47–	Ld Citrine
31 Dec 57	

Deputy Chairman

15 Aug 47–31 Aug 57	Sir H. Self
15 Aug 47–16 Dec 53	Sir J. Hacking
1 Jan 54–31 Aug 57	J. Eccles

Electricity Council, 1957–

The Council consists of a Chairman, Deputy Chairman, and two other independent members appointed by the Minister, together with the Chairman and two other members of the Generating Board, and the Chairmen of the 12 Area Boards ex officio

Chairman

1 Sep 57	Sir H. Self
1 Sep 59	(Sir) R. King
1 Jan 66	Sir R. Edwards
1 Nov 68	Sir N. Elliott

Deputy Chairman

1 Sep 57	Sir J. Eccles
1 Sep 57	R. Edwards [1] (*whole-time from 1 Oct 59*)
1 Jan 66	N. Marsh
1 Jan 66	Sir A. Wilson[1]

[1] Part-time.

SOURCES.—*British (Central) Electricity Authority Annual Reports 1947–58; Electricity Council Annual Reports 1958–.*

Gas Council, 1948–

The Chairman, Deputy Chairman and members (the Chairmen of the 12 Area Boards) are all appointed by the Minister

Chairman

23 Nov 48	Sir E. Sylvester
1 Jan 52	(Sir) H. Smith
1 Jan 60	Sir H. Jones

Deputy Chairman

25 Nov 48	H. Smith
1 Feb 52	(Sir) H. Jones
1 Jan 60	(Sir) K. Hutchison

SOURCE.—*Gas Council Annual Reports and Accounts 1948–.*

Iron and Steel Corporation, 1950–53

The Chairman, Deputy Chairman and members of the Corporation were all appointed by the Minister, as are their successors following the 1967 Act

Chairman

2 Oct 50	S. Hardie
25 Feb 52	Sir J. Green

Deputy Chairman

2 Oct 50	Sir J. Green
25 Feb 52	(*vacant*)

SOURCE.—*Iron and Steel Corporation Reports and Accounts 1951–52.*

British Steel Corporation, 1967–

Chairman

28 Jul 67	Ld Melchett

Deputy Chairmen

28 Jul 67	H. Finniston
28 Jul 67	M. Milne-Watson
28 Jul 67	A. Peach

British Transport Commission, 1947–62

The Chairman, Deputy Chairman, Members of the Commission, and Chairmen of the British Transport Executives and their successors established in 1963 are all appointed by the Minister

Chairman

8 Sep 47	Sir C. Hurcomb (Ld)
15 Sep 53	Sir B. Robertson
1 Jun 61	R. Beeching

Deputy Chairman

1 Jan 49	(Sir) J. Benstead
1 Oct 61	Sir P. Warter

Chairmen of Executives of BTC

Docks and Inland Waterways Executive [2]

1947–53	Sir R. Hill

Hotels Executive [2]

1948–51	Ld Inman (*part-time from 1950*)
1951–53	Sir H. Methven (*part-time*)

Railway Executive [2]

1947–51	Sir E. Missenden
1951–53	J. Elliot

Road Haulage Executive [2]

1948–53	G. Russell

[2] By the British Transport Commission (Executives) Order made by the Minister on 19 Aug 1953 (coming into effect on 1 Oct 1953) the Railway, Road Haulage, Docks and Inland Waterways, and Hotels Executives were abolished and their functions became directly exercisable by the Commission.

London Transport Executive

1947–53   Ld Latham
1953–59   (Sir) J. Elliot
1959–62   A. Valentine

Road Passenger Service

1948–52   G. Cardwell
(*1 Oct 52, executive abolished by British Transport Commission (Executives) Order 1952*)
SOURCE—*British Transport Commission Reports and Accounts 1948–.*

British Railways Board,[1] 1963–

Chairman

1 Jan 63   R. Beeching (Ld)
1 Jun 65   (Sir) S. Raymond
1 Jan 68   (Sir) H. Johnson

Vice-Chairman

1 Aug 64   Sir S. Mitchell
1 Aug 64   S. Raymond (Sir)
1 Aug 64   P. Shirley
SOURCE.—*British Railways Board Annual Reports and Accounts 1963–.*

London Transport Board,[1] 1963–

Chairman

1 Jan 63   (Sir) A. Valentine
1 Apr 65   M. Holmes

Vice-Chairman

1 Jan 63   A. Grainger
1 Oct 65   A. Bull
SOURCE.—*London Transport Board Annual Reports and Accounts 1964–.*

British Transport Docks Board,[1] 1962–

Chairman

3 Dec 62   Sir A. Kirby
15 Jun 67   S. Finnis

Vice-Chairman

10 Dec 62   Sir A. Crichton
1 Jan 68   R. Wills
SOURCE.—*British Transport Docks Board Annual Reports and Accounts, 1963–.*

British Waterways Board,[1] 1963–

Chairman

1 Jan 63   F. Arney
1 Jul 63   Sir J. Hawton
1 Jul 68   Sir F. Price

Vice-Chairman

1 Jan 63   Sir J. Hawton
11 Aug 63   Sir F. Parham
1 Jul 68   Sir J. Horton
SOURCE.—*British Waterways Board Annual Reports and Accounts, 1963–.*

Transport Holding Company,[1] 1962–

Chairman

15 Nov 62   Sir P. Warter
15 Nov 67   Sir R. Wilson

Deputy Chairman

16 Nov 62   Sir R. Wilson
SOURCE.—*Transport Holding Company Annual Reports 1963–.*

National Freight Corporation,[1] 1969

Chairman

1 Jan 69   Sir R. Wilson

National Bus Company,[1] 1969

Chairman

1 Jan 69   A. Todd

[1] The Transport Act, 1962, reorganised nationalised transport undertakings and provided for the establishment of the public corporations listed here to replace the B.T.C. and its executives. The Transport Act, 1968, created the National Freight Corporation to take over the Road Haulage and Shipping interests of the Transport Holding Company and the Sundries and Freight-Liner interests of the Railways Board. It also created the National Bus Company to take over responsibility for state-owned bus companies and bus manufacturing interests from the Transport Holding Company. A Bill before Parliament at the beginning of 1969 provides for the transfer of the London Transport Board to the control of the Greater London Council.

R

Other Public Bodies

There are a large number of public bodies set up by statute which are neither branches of the government departments listed on pages 169–72, nor nationalised industries as listed above.   They have been established in the fields of industry, commerce, the social sciences and research to carry out a variety of administrative, regulatory, and executive or managerial functions. Important examples of such bodies classified loosely by their main functions are as follows:

Advisory:

Computer Board for Universities and Research Councils
Law Commission
Monopolies Commission
National Board for Prices and Incomes
National Economic Development Council
Water Resources Board

Regulatory:

Air Transport Licensing Board
Race Relations Board
Independent Television Authority
British Board of Film Censors

Executive or Managerial:

Agricultural Marketing Boards (Egg, Wool, Hops, Milk, Potato)
British Airports Authority
British Sugar Corporation Ltd.
Cable and Wireless Ltd.
Commonwealth Development Corporation
Forestry Commission
Herring Industry Board
Land Commission
National Dock Labour Board
National Research Development Corporation
New Towns Development Corporations
Sugar Board
White Fish Authority

SOURCES.—For an analysis of the statutory provisions of the nationalised industries, see D. N. Chester, *The Nationalised Industries* (1951).   Other studies of the nationalised industries include: The Acton Society Trust, *Twelve Studies on Nationalised Industries* (1950–53); H. A. Clegg and T. E. Chester, *The Future of Nationalisation* (1953); W. A. Robson, ed., *Problems of Nationalised Industries* (1952); W. A. Robson, *Nationalised Industry and Public Ownership* (1960). D. Coombes, *The Member of Parliament and the Administration. The Case of the Select Committee on Nationalised Industries* (1966).
See also the *Annual Reports and Accounts* of the nationalised industries and the *Reports of the Select Committee on Nationalised Industries*, October 1952, July 1953, and since 1957.   The *Committee Report on the Coal Industry* (Reid), Cmd. 6610/1945;   the *Committee Report on the Gas Industry* (Heyworth), Cmd. 6699/1945–6;   the *Report of the Advisory Committee on the Organisation of the National Coal Board* (Fleck), N.C.B., 18 Jan 1955;   the *Report of the Committee of Inquiry into the Electricity Supply Industry* (Herbert), Cmd. 9672/1956.
A list of Public Bodies is to be found each year in *Whitaker's Almanack*.   See also D. N. Chester, 'Public Corporations and the Classification of Administrative Bodies', *Political Studies*, p. 34 (1953); J. F. Garner, *New Public Corporations' Public Law*, p. 324 (1966).

XIII

LOCAL GOVERNMENT

Local Government Structure

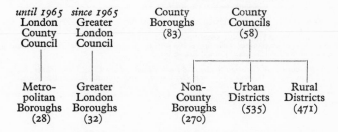

| London | | England & Wales (1968) | | |

London

until 1965
London
County
Council

since 1965
Greater
London
Council

Metro-
politan
Boroughs
(28)

Greater
London
Boroughs
(32)

England & Wales (1968)

County
Boroughs
(83)

County
Councils
(58)

Non-
County
Boroughs
(270)

Urban
Districts
(535)

Rural
Districts
(471)

Scotland (1968)

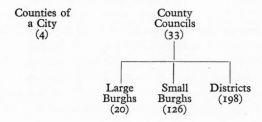

Counties of
a City
(4)

County
Councils
(33)

Large
Burghs
(20)

Small
Burghs
(126)

Districts
(198)

Number of Councils: England & Wales

	County Councils inc. London	County Boroughs[a]	Non-County Boroughs	London Boroughs[b]	Urban District Councils	Rural District Councils
1900	62	67	250	28[b]	800	663
1910	62	75	249	28[b]	812	657
1920	62	82	246	28[b]	799	649
1930	62	83	300	28[b]	780	638
1940	61	83	256	28[b]	581	476
1950	61	83	309	28[b]	572	475
1960	62	83	319	28[b]	564	473
1966	59	82	270	32[b]	535	471

[a] The figures in this column are deceptively constant. In the 1960s a few County Boroughs disappeared through local government amalgamation (almost all in Greater London), while a few more non-County Boroughs were promoted to county status.
[b] Until 1965, Metropolitan Boroughs. Excluding the City of London.
No exact figures for the number of Parish Councils are available. In 1900 there were approximately 8,000, in 1920 approximately 7,000 and in 1966 approximately 7,700.

Local Government Finance — England and Wales

Year (ending 31 Mar)	Total Receipts from Rates £000s	Assessable Value of all Rateable Property £000s	Average Rates collected per £ of Assessable Value	Government Grants (£000s) [b]	Total Expenditure (£000s)
1900	40,734	175,623	4s. 11·8d.	12,249	100,862
1910	63,261	215,310	6s. 2·8d.	20,915	166,105
1920	105,590	220,714	9s. 6·8d.	48,263	289,353
1930	156,312	284,937	11s. 6·8d.	107,828	423,655 [c]
1940	200,567	318,834	12s. 7·5d.	181,900	578,798 [c]
1950	280,195	325,262	17s. 3·0d.	294,358	849,099 [c]
1960	646,608	687,618	18s. 10·0d.	705,590	1,865,718 [c]
1965	988,054	2,099,034	9s. 6·0d. [a]	1,102,989	2,902,829 [c]

[a] Spectacular fall partly due to re-rating of Industry and partly to general revaluation 1 Apr 63.
[b] Consisting partly of grants in aid, and partly of receipts from Local Taxation Account and from the local Taxation Licence Duties, not including capital receipts.
[c] Expenditure other than out of loans for capital works. Including the repayment of loans by various local authorities to the L.C.C. Consolidated Loans Fund.

SOURCES.—*Annual Local Taxation Returns*; *Annual Reports of the Local Government Board, Ministry of Health, and Ministry of Housing and Local Government*; also summarised in the *Annual Abstract of Statistics, 1900–1966*. *Rates and Rateable Values in England and Wales* (annually from the Ministry of Health, 1919–43, Town and Country Planning, 1943–51, Local Government and Planning, 1951, Housing and Local Government, 1951–66).

Major Legislation Affecting Local Government

Education Act, 1902. This transferred the responsibility for education from school boards and school attendance committees to county councils, county borough councils, and some of the larger county districts.

Local Government Act, 1929. This abolished the guardians of the poor, and transferred their responsibilities for poor law and registration to county councils and county borough councils. It also reorganised the system of grants in aid, creating the general grant, partly as compensation for the complete de-rating of agriculture and the de-rating of industry to 25 per cent.

Local Government Act, 1933. This was a codifying Act covering the structure and constitution of local authorities of all sorts, but making no fundamental change in the law.

Local Government Act, 1948. This Act replaced the block grant by the Exchequer Equalisation grant. It transferred responsibility for valuation from local authorities to Inland Revenue and it provided for revaluation: small houses being valued on pre-war building costs, other houses by reference to pre-war rents.

Local Government Act, 1958. This Act abolished most percentage grants and the Exchequer Equalisation grant, substituting a general grant and a rate deficiency grant. It established Local Government Commissions to recommend alteration of boundaries of local authorities (see below, *Local Government Boundary Commission Act, 1945*). It provided for greater delegation of functions by county councils.

Housing Acts. A series of acts between 1919–67 provided for the building of houses by local authorities with varying rates of subsidy from the Exchequer and from the rates, the Housing Subsidies Act, 1967, being the most recent.

Town and Country Planning Act, 1932. This established a general system of planning control which could be adopted by second tier local authorities.

Town and Country Planning Act, 1947. This applied planning control to the whole country, transferred responsibility to county councils and county borough councils, and introduced development charges balanced by a compensation fund of £300 m.

Town and Country Planning Act, 1953. This abolished development charges and the £300 m. fund.

Town and Country Planning Act, 1959. This Act altered the basis of compensation for compulsory acquisition.

Town and Country Planning Act, 1962. This consolidates enactments for England and Wales from 1944 onwards and incorporates planning sections of other Acts.

New Towns Act, 1946. This provided for the establishment of new towns to be built by development corporations appointed by the Ministry, and was succeeded by further Acts which were consolidated in the *New Towns Act, 1965.*

Local Government (Boundary Commission) Act, 1945. This provided for the establishment of a local government boundary commission.

Local Government Boundary Commission (Dissolution) Act, 1949. This abolished the Local Government Boundary Commission (see *Local Government Act, 1958*).

Children Act, 1948. After the Curtis Committee Report, this Act made counties and county boroughs responsible for all children without proper homes.

National Health Service Act, 1946. This Act transferred local authority hospitals to the Ministry of Health. It made counties and county boroughs responsible for ambulance service, maternity and child welfare, health visiting, home helps, prevention of illness, and after-care, etc.

National Assistance Act, 1948. This repealed the existing poor law. It made counties and county boroughs responsible for accommodation of the aged and those temporarily homeless, also for welfare services for the blind, deaf, dumb, etc. Financial assistance and residual responsibilities were passed to the National Assistance Board.

Local Government Boundary Commission Act, 1958. This set up local boundary commissions, produced a number of reports before being wound up in 1966. The main recommendations put into effect were in the Black Country and Tees-side.

Rating and Valuation Act, 1961. This Act ended the derating of industrial and freight-transport property, empowered the Minister to reduce by order the rateable value of dwellings in valuation lists, offered 50% relief from rates on property occupied by charities, and introduced a new method of rating statutory water undertakings. Industry and Commerce re-rated to 100% values.

London Government Act, 1963. This Act replaced the old LCC with a Greater London Council which covered, in addition to the old LCC area, almost all of Middlesex and some suburban portions of Surrey, Kent, Essex, and Hertfordshire. All the existing 85 local authorities in the GLC area were merged into 32 new boroughs (the City of London alone preserved its complete independence). The first GLC election took place on 9 Apr 64, two, three and four councillors being chosen *en bloc* from each of the 32 boroughs. The GLC formally took over from the LCC on 1 Apr 65.

Local Government (Financial Provision) Act, 1963. This extends the powers of local authorities to defray expenses incurred by their members and officers, and to contribute to other local authorities and to bodies having activities connected with local government, and makes further provision with respect to borrowing by local authorities; the management of local authority debt, the application by local authorities of capital funds, renewal and repair funds, unexpended balances of loans, and capital money received by way of financial adjustment.

Housing Act, 1964. This set up a new Housing Corporation to assist Housing Societies, conferred new compulsory powers on local authorities to secure improvement of houses, amended the improvement grant system and strengthened the powers of local authorities in dealing with houses in multi-occupation.

Protection from Eviction Act, 1964. This Act prevents a landlord of residential premises from recovering possession without an order of the county court. The court is given power to suspend an order for possession.

Rating Act, 1966. This confers on rateable occupiers of dwellings the right to pay rates in monthly instalments and provides for the granting of rebates in respect of such rates.

Local Government Elections

Since the Second World War the results of Local Government Elections have increasingly been accepted as barometers to the national political mood. They can be misleading. The custom of fighting under national party labels has spread only gradually and sporadically. The fact that, under the triennial system, only a third of the seats on borough and district councils are fought each year causes much confusion (a party may claim a great trend in its favour because it is gaining compared to three years before, even though it is losing compared to the previous year). Moreover the results are very patchily reported and no altogether satisfactory statistics are available. However, the results in the boroughs of England and Wales (excluding London), both county and non-county, do provide some pointer to the national mood (even though the smaller non-county boroughs introduce a very distorting element). Between 3,300 and 3,500 seats used to be fought each year, usually on a party basis; since 1964 the number of seats at risk has been between 3,000 and 3,200 owing to the merging of councils under the London Government Act. Since 1946 the outcome of these borough contests has been fairly accurately reported, although it was not until 1965 that the first really detailed analyses of the voting figures appeared (see *The Economist* 22 May 65 and 21 May 66).

Party politics in many cities goes back to the first half of the nineteenth century but, although in most sizeable towns (practically all over 50,000) councillors have worn political labels throughout this century, in only a few larger councils did a majority of councillors of one party mean that that party exercised control. Labour successes after the first World War introduced a more organised form of party politics into some councils. After the Second World War, the local government franchise was extended to practically the same basis as that for parliamentary elections (it had hitherto been confined to ratepayers) and, with sweeping Labour successes in the 1945 municipal elections and an organised Conservative counter-attack in the succeeding years, party politics extended their hold to most urban authorities, including practically all those with more than 20,000 inhabitants. Here is the record since 1945 of the party control in cities which in 1967 had more than 250,000 inhabitants: 'Citizen' in Bristol and 'Progressive' (also called 'Moderate') in Scottish cities and Newcastle refers to local anti-Socialist, Conservative-supported parties.

Borough Council Election Results

	Conservative and Conservative-supported Independent	Independent without Conservative Support	Labour	Liberal	Total
1949	1,749	426	1,091	79	3,345
1950	1,610	510	1,132	72	3,324
1951	1,893	548	883	79	3,403
1952	1,138	488	1,718	53	3,397
1953	1,571	447	1,448	60	3,526
1954	1,498	511	1,438	74	3,521
1955	1,604	514	1,470	56	3,644
1956	1,358	454	1,614	72	3,498
1957	1,292	435	1,642	89	3,458
1958	1,307	460	1,705	118	3,590
1959	1,545	441	1,399	103	3,488
1960	1,750	449	1,137	130	3,466
1961	1,453	470	1,387	196	3,506
1962	995	465	1,571	454	3,485
1963	973	524	1,733	255	3,485
1964	967	474	1,494	149	3,084
1965	1,140	476	1,027	154	2,797
1966	1,107	467	1,259	151	2,984
1967	1,690	466	846	148	3,150
1968	2,184	436	450	152	3,222

SOURCE.—Information supplied by Conservative Central Office.

Belfast. 1945– Unionist.
Birmingham.
1945 No clear majority.[1] 1946–7 Labour. 1947–9 No majority. 1949–52 Conservative. 1952–66 Labour. 1966– Conservative.

[1] 'No clear majority' is shown wherever no party had a clear overall majority of seats; frequently a party holding half the seats was able to exercise some control in this situation with the aid of the mayoral vote and in other cases a party exercised control in alliance with a minor group.

Bradford
1945–51 Labour. 1951–2 No clear majority. 1952–59 Labour. 1959–61 No clear majority, 1961–2 Conservative and National Liberal. 1962–3 No clear majority. 1963–67 Labour. 1967– Conservative.

Bristol
1945–9 Labour. 1949–51 No clear majority. 1951–2 Citizen. 1952–60 Labour 1960–3 Citizen. 1963–67 Labour. 1967– Citizen.

Cardiff
1945–58 anti-Labour coalition. 1958–61 Labour. 1961–63 No clear majority. 1963–65 Labour. 1965–6 No clear majority. 1967– Conservative.

Coventry
1945–67 Labour. 1967– Conservative.

Edinburgh
1945–62 Progressive. 1962–65 No clear majority. 1965– Progressive.[1]

Glasgow
1945–7 Labour. 1947–50 No clear majority. 1950–52 Progressive. 1952–68 Labour.[1] 1968– No clear majority.

Leeds
1945–51 Labour. 1951–53 Conservative. 1953–67 Labour. 1967– Conservative.

Leicester
1945–49 Labour. 1949–52 Conservative. 1952–61 Labour. 1961–2 Conservative. 1962–3 No clear majority. 1963–66 Labour. 1966–67 No continuous majority. 1967– Conservative.

Liverpool
1945–54 Conservative. 1954–55 Conservative with Protestant support. 1955–61 Labour. 1961–63 Conservative. 1963–67 Labour. 1967– Conservative.

Manchester
1945–47 Labour. 1947–49 No clear majority. 1949–52 Conservative. 1952–3 No clear majority. 1953–67 Labour. 1967– Conservative.

Newcastle
1945–49 Labour. 1949–58 Progressive. 1958–67 Labour. 1967– Conservative.

Nottingham
1945–50 Labour. 1950–51 No clear majority. 1951–52 Conservative. 1952–3 No clear majority. 1953–60 Labour. 1960–61 No clear majority. 1961–63 Conservative. 1963–67 Labour. 1967– Conservative.

Sheffield
1945–68 Labour. 1968– Conservative.

Stoke-on-Trent
1945– Labour.

Tees-side (Created 1967)
1967– Conservative.

[1] The position in Edinburgh and Glasgow is complicated by two ex-officio councillors who make clear definition of overall majority difficult.

Party Representation on the London County Council, 1898–1961

Year	Councillors (elected)				Total	Aldermen				Total	Majority
	Pr.	MRM	Lab.	Ind.		Pr.	MRM	Lab.	Ind.		
1898	84	34	..	..	118	13	6	..	..	137	Pr.
1901	87	31	..	..	118	14	5	..	..	137	Pr.
1904	83	35	..	..	118	15	4	..	..	137	Pr.
1907	38	79	..	I	118	9	10	..	..	137	MRM
1910	55	60	3	..	118	2	15	..	2	137	MRM
1913	50	67	I	..	118	3	14	..	2	137	MRM
1919	40	68	15	I	124	6	12	2	..	144	MRM
1922	25	82	17	..	124	5	12	3	..	144	MRM
1925	6	83	35	..	124	3	13	4	..	144	MRM
1928	5	77	42	..	124	I	12	6	I	144	MRM
1931	6	83	35	..	124	..	13	6	I	144	MRM
1934	..	55	69	..	124	..	9	11	..	144	Lab.
1937	..	49	75	..	124	..	8	12	..	144	Lab.
	Lib.	Con.	Lab.	Comm.		Lib.	Con.	Lab.	Comm.		
1946	2	30	90	2	124	..	6	14	..	144	Lab.
1949	I	64	64	..	129	..	5	16	..	150 [a]	Lab.
1952	..	37	92	..	129	..	6	15	..	150	Lab.
1955	..	52	74	..	126	..	8	13	..	147	Lab.
1958	..	25	101	..	126	..	7	14	..	147	Lab.
1961	..	42	84	..	126	..	7	14	..	147	Lab.

[a] Plus Chairman, an outsider and Labour nominee.

Pr.—Progressives (Lib).   Ind.—Independent.
MRM—Municipal Reform Moderates (Con).   Comm.—Communist.
Lab.—Labour.   Lib.—Liberal.

SOURCES.—Sir G. Gibbon and R. W. Bell, *History of the London County Council, 1889–1939* (1939); *General Election of County Councillors* (published after each election by the L.C.C.), 1919–61.

Party Representation in the Greater London Council 1964-

Year	Councillors		Aldermen	
	Con.	Lab.	Con.	Lab.
1964	36	64	5	11
1967	82	18	10	6

SOURCES —J. Redlich and F. W. Hirst (ed. B. Keith-Lucas), *The History of Local Government in England* (1958); *Report of Royal Commission on Local Taxation 1901*, XXIV; *Report of Royal Commission on the Poor Law 1909*, XXXVII; *Report of Royal Commission on Local Government 1924–25*, XIV; *1928–29*, VIII, *1929–30*, XV; *Proposals for Reform in Local Government 1928*, XIX; *Social Insurance and Allied Services 1942–43* (The Beveridge Report); *A National Health Service 1943–44*, VIII; *Report of Interdepartmental Committee on the Care of Children 1945–46*, X (The Curtis Report); *Report of the Local Government Boundary Commission for the year 1947, 1947–48*, XIII; *Local Government: Areas and Status of Local Authorities in England and Wales, 1956*, Cmd. 9831; *Local Government: Functions of County Councils and County District Councils in England and Wales 1957*, Cmnd. 161; *Local Government Finance (England and Wales) 1957*, Cmnd. 209. T. W. Freeman, *The Conurbations of Great Britain* (1966). *Report of the Royal Commission on Local Government in Greater London* (1960) Cmnd. 1164. *Staffing of Local Government* (Mallaby) (1967); *Management of Local Government* (Maud) (5 vols 1967).

XIV

ROYALTY

British Kings and Queens, 1900-1960

Name	Accession		Coronation		Died		Age	Reigned
Victoria	20 Jun 1837		28 Jun 1838		22 Jan 1901		81	63 yrs
Edward VII	22 Jan 1901		9 Aug 1902		6 May 10		68	9 yrs
George V	6 May 10		22 Jun 11		20 Jan 36		70	25 yrs
Edward VIII	20 Jan 36		..		(Abdicated)		..	325 days
George VI	11 Dec 36		12 May 37		6 Feb 52		56	15 yrs
Elizabeth II	6 Feb 52		2 Jun 53		..		..	..

Use of Royal Power

Throughout this century great efforts have been made to avoid involving the Crown in politics. But there have been a few occasions when, unavoidably or deliberately, the Sovereign has been involved in decision making. No list of such occasions can be very satisfactory. It may omit times when in private audience the Sovereign expressed strong views to the Prime Minister. It may include times when, despite all the formality of consultation, the Sovereign had no real opportunity of affecting the outcome. The following list of incidents is compiled primarily from *Cabinet Government*, by Sir Ivor Jennings, *King George V*, by Sir Harold Nicolson, and *King George VI*, by Sir J. W. Wheeler-Bennett.

Dec 1909   Edward VII's refusal to promise to create peers until after a second general election.

Jul 1910   George V's sponsorship of the Constitutional Conference.

Nov 1910   George V's secret pledge to create peers, if necessary.

Jul 1914   George V's sponsorship of Buckingham Palace Home Rule Conference.

Mar 1917   George V's support for General Haig, when in danger of being dismissed.

May 1923   George V's summons of S. Baldwin as Prime Minister.

Jan 1924   George V's request to J. R. MacDonald to form government.

Aug 1931   George V's invitation to J. R. MacDonald to form National Government.

May 1940   George VI's invitation to W. Churchill to form Coalition Government.

Jul 1945   George VI's advice on switching appointment of Bevin and Dalton (a disputed allegation).

Jan 1957   Elizabeth II's summons of H. Macmillan as Prime Minister.

Oct 1963   Elizabeth II's invitation to E of Home to form a Government.

Nov 1965   Elizabeth II's award of G.C.V.O. to Governor of Rhodesia.

Regency Acts, 1937 and 1953

These Acts provide that if the Sovereign is under 18 years of age, the royal functions shall be exercised by a Regent appointed under the provisions of the Acts. (Formerly the appointment of a Regent was *ad hoc*.) The Regent may not give assent to Bills altering the succession to the throne or repealing the Acts securing the Scottish Church.

The Acts provide for Counsellors of State to be appointed during the Monarch's absence from the U.K., or infirmity; and empower certain high officials of the state to declare that 'the Sovereign is by infirmity of mind or body incapable for the time being of performing the royal function'.

(Much of the law regarding Regency is found in these Acts.)

The Royal Family

Children of Queen Victoria

1. H.R.H. Princess Victoria (Princess Royal). Born 21 Nov 1840, married Prince Frederick of Prussia (1858), afterwards Kaiser Frederick III, died 5 Aug 1901.
2. **H.M. King Edward VII.** Born 9 Nov. 1841, married H.R.H. Princess Alexandra (eldest daughter of King Christian IX of Denmark), 10 Mar 1863, succeeded to the throne 22 Jan 1901, crowned at Westminster Abbey 9 Aug 1902, died 6 May 1910 (*for children, see below*).
3. H.R.H. Princess Alice. Born 25 Apr 1843, married Prince Louis (1862), afterwards Grand Duke of Hesse, died 14 Dec 1878.
4. H.R.H. Prince Alfred, D of Edinburgh. Born 6 Aug 1844, married Marie Alexandrovna (1874) only daughter of Alexander II, Emperor of Russia. Succeeded as D of Saxe-Coburg and Gotha 22 Aug 1893, died 30 Jul 1900.
5. H.R.H. Princess Helena. Born 25 May 1846, married H.R.H. Prince Christian of Schleswig-Holstein (1866), died 9 Jun 1923.
6. H.R.H. Princess Louise. Born 18 Mar 1848, married M of Lorne (1871), afterwards 9th D of Argyll, died 3 Dec 1939.
7. H.R.H. Prince Arthur, D of Connaught. Born 1 May 1850, married H.R.H. Princess Louisa of Prussia (1879), died 16 Jan 1942.
8. H.R.H. Prince Leopold, D of Albany. Born 7 Apr 1853, married Princess Helena of Waldeck (1882), died 28 Mar 1884.
9. H.R.H. Princess Beatrice. Born 14 Apr 1857, married H.R.H. Prince Henry of Battenberg (1885), died 26 Oct 1944.

Children of Edward VII

1. H.R.H. Prince Albert, D of Clarence and Avondale (1891). Born 8 Jan 1864, died 14 Jan 1892.
2. **H.M. King George V.** H.R.H. Prince George, D of York (1893), Prince of Wales (1901–1910). Born 3 Jun 1865, married (6 July 1893) H.S.H. Princess Mary of Teck (Queen Mary, died 24 Mar 1953), succeeded to

the throne 6 May 1910, crowned at Westminster Abbey 22 Jun 1911, assumed by Royal Proclamation (17 Jun 1917) the name of Windsor for his House and family, died 20 Jan 1936 (*for children, see below*).

3. H.R.H. Princess Louise (Princess Royal). Born 20 Feb 1867, married to 1st D of Fife (1889), died 4 Jan 1931. Children: (i) H.H. Princess Alexandra, Duchess of Fife. Born 17 May 1891, married H.R.H. Prince Arthur of Connaught (1913), died 26 Feb 1959. Child: Alastair, D of Connaught, born 9 Aug 1914, died 26 Apr 1943. (ii) H.H. Princess Maud. Born 3 Apr 1893, married to 11th E of Southesk (1923), died 14 Dec 1945. Child: D of Fife, born 23 Sep 29, married (1956) Hon. Caroline Dewar.

4. H.R.H. Princess Victoria. Born 6 Jul 1868, died 2 Dec 1935.

5. H.R.H. Princess Maud. Born 26 Nov 1869, married Prince Charles of Denmark (1896), afterwards King Haakon VII of Norway, died 20 Nov 1938. Child: H.M. Olaf V, King of Norway. Born 2 Jul 1903, married (1929) H.R.H. Princess Marthe of Sweden. Children: (i) H.R.H. Princess Ragnhild, born 9 Jun 1930, married (1953) to E. Lorentzen. (ii) H.R.H. Princess Astrid, born 12 Feb 1932. (iii) H.R.H. Harald, Crown Prince of Norway, born 21 Feb 1937, married (1968) Miss S. Haraldsen.

Children of George V

1. H.R.H. Prince Edward, D of Windsor (1936), Prince of Wales (1910–36). Born 23 Jun 1894, succeeded to the throne as **King Edward VIII** on 20 Jan 1936, abdicated 11 Dec 1936. Married Mrs W. Simpson on 3 Jun 1937.

2. **H.M. King George VI.** H.R.H. Prince Albert, D of York (1920). Born 14 Dec 1895, married Lady Elizabeth Bowes-Lyon, daughter of 14th E of Strathmore and Kinghorne on 26 Apr 1923, succeeded to the throne on 11 Dec 1936, crowned at Westminster Abbey 12 May 1937, died 6 Feb 1952 (*for children, see below*).

3. H.R.H. Princess Victoria (Princess Royal). Born 25 Apr 1897, married (1922) to 6th E of Harewood, died 28 Mar 1965. Children: (i) George, 7th E of Harewood. Born 7 Feb 1923, married (1949) Marion, daughter of E. Stein. Divorced, 7 Jul 1967. Married (1967) Patricia Tuckwell. Children: David, Vt Lascelles, born 21 Oct 1950; J. Lascelles, born 5 Oct 1953; R. Lascelles, born 14 Feb 1955; M. Lascelles, born 5 Jul 1964. (ii) G. Lascelles, born 21 Aug 1924, married (1952) Miss A. Dowding. Child: H. Lascelles, born 19 May 1953.

4. H.R.H. Prince Henry, D of Gloucester (1928). Born 31 Mar 1900, married (1935) Lady A. Montagu-Douglas-Scott, daughter of 7th D of Buccleuch. Children: (i) H.R.H. Prince William, born 18 Dec 1941. (ii) H.R.H. Prince Richard, born 26 Aug 1944.

5. H.R.H. Prince George, D of Kent (1934). Born 20 Dec 1902, married (1934) H.R.H. Princes Marina of Greece and Denmark, killed on active service 25 Aug 1942. Children: (i) H.R.H. Prince Edward, D of Kent,

born 9 Oct 1935, married (1961) Katherine, daughter of Sir W. Worsley. Children: George, E of St Andrews, born 26 Jun 1962; Lady Helen Windsor, born 28 April 1964. (ii) Princess Alexandra, born 25 Dec 1936, married (1963) Hon. Angus Ogilvy. Children: James Ogilvy, born 29 Feb 1964, Marina Ogilvy, born 31 Jul 1966. (iii) H.R.H. Prince Michael, born 4 July 1942.

6. H.R.H. Prince John. Born 12 Jul 1905, died 18 Jan 1919.

Children of George VI

1. **H.M. Queen Elizabeth II.** Born 21 Apr 1926, married to Philip, D of Edinburgh on 20 Nov 1947, succeeded to the throne 6 Feb 1952, crowned at Westminster Abbey 2 Jun 1953. Children: (i) H.R.H. Prince Charles, Prince of Wales (26 Jun 1958), D of Cornwall, born 14 Nov 1948. (ii) H.R.H. Princess Anne, born 15 Aug 1950. (iii) Prince Andrew, born 19 Feb 1960. (iv) Prince Edward, born 10 Mar 1964.

2. H.R.H. Princess Margaret. Born 21 Aug 1930, married on 6 May 1960 to Antony Armstrong-Jones (created E of Snowdon, 1961). Children: (i) David, Vt Linley, born 3 Nov 1961. (ii) Lady Sarah Armstrong-Jones, born 1 May 1964.

Private Secretaries to the Sovereign

1895–1901	Sir A. Bigge (Ld Stamfordham)	1936–43	Sir A. Hardinge
1901–13	Sir F. Knollys (Ld) (Vt) [1]	1943–52	Sir A. Lascelles
1910–31	Ld Stamfordham [1]	1953–	Sir M. Adeane
1931–36	Sir C. Wigram (Ld)		

[1] Ld Stamfordham and Ld Knollys were joint private secretaries 1910–13 to King George V.

Lord Chamberlains

1898	E of Hopetoun	1922	E of Cromer
1900	5th E of Clarendon	1938	6th E of Clarendon
1905	Vt Althorp (Earl Spencer)	1952	E of Scarbrough
1912	Ld Sandhurst (Vt)	1961	Ld Cobbold
1921	D of Atholl		

Civil List of the Crown

The annuities payable to the Sovereign and Members of the Royal Family are known as the Civil List which is granted by Parliament upon the recommendation of a Select Committee.

Year	Privy Purse	Total
1900	£60,000	£385,000
1901	£110,000	£470,000
1931[a]	£97,000	£420,000
1938	£110,000	£410,000
1952	£60,000	£475,000

[a] By Command of the King the Civil List was reduced by £50,000 p.a. as from 1 Oct, 1931, in view of the national economic situation.

SOURCES.—*Imperial Calendar*; *Whitaker's Almanack*; *Dictionary of National Biography*; *Who Was Who*; *Who's Who*.

XV
THE BRITISH ISLES

Scotland

UNTIL 1885, when the post of Secretary for Scotland was re-created (becoming Secretary of State for Scotland in 1926), the Lord Advocate was the principal Officer of State for Scotland, assisted by the Solicitor-General for Scotland. In 1900 there were Scottish boards for local government, fisheries, in 1912 agriculture, and in 1919 health, (the functions of the Board of Education had already devolved in 1877 on to the Scottish Education Department) but the majority were theoretically responsible to the Home Secretary, or another appropriate Minister at Westminster. In practice, even after the creation of the Scottish Secretary the Boards had a statutory life independent of any Minister. The Boards were recognised as an anachronism by the Reports of the Royal Commission on the Civil Service in 1914,[1] and the Haldane Committee on the Machinery of Government in 1918.[2] Both reports suggested that there was inadequate ministerial responsibility for the activities of these boards. In 1928 the Boards of Agriculture and Health and the Prison Commission for Scotland were abolished and their duties were assigned to statutory departments under the responsibility of the Secretary of State for Scotland. As the result of a general review of the Scottish administration by the Gilmour Committee,[3] the functions of the Departments of Agriculture, Education, Health, Prisons, and the Fisheries Board were vested directly in the Secretary of State for Scotland, by the *Reorganisation of Offices (Scotland) Act, 1939*. The Scottish Home Department was established at the same time. During and after the Second World War some additional administrative responsibilities were allocated to the Scottish Office. As a result of the Royal Commission Report on Scottish Affairs[4] published in 1954, there were further transfers to Scottish Departments of functions such as the responsibility for roads. Most 'United Kingdom' Departments (i.e. those whose responsibilities embrace Scotland) in the field of home affairs have regional offices in Scotland. The Home Office, though not counted as a United Kingdom Department has certain responsibilities for what happens in Scotland e.g. over dangerous drugs and aliens as do the Ministries of Agriculture, Fisheries and Food and Departments of Education and Science. The headquarters of the four Scottish Departments are in Edinburgh, with small liaison offices in Whitehall. Scottish Ministers divide their time between their Edinburgh headquarters and Whitehall, especially while Parliament is sitting. The Secretary of State, the Scottish Law officers, and the Parliamentary Under-Secretaries

[1] Cd. 7338/1914. [2] Cd. 9320/1918. [3] Cmd. 5563/1936–37. [4] Cmd. 9212/1953–54.

have usually been members of the House of Commons, but since the appointment of the first Minister of State to the Scottish Office in 1951 either this
appointment or that of one or two Parliamentary Under-Secretaries has been
held by members of the House of Lords.   Scotland has its separate system
of law courts and its bar, its own established church, and its own Heraldic
authority, Lord Lyon King at Arms.

SOURCES.—Sir D. Milne, *The Scottish Office* (1957).   Sir R. Coupland, *Welsh and Scottish Nationalism* (1954).

Wales

The only significant devolution of administrative responsibility to Wales
has taken place since 1950, and this to a much more limited extent than in
Scotland.   In 1907 a Welsh Department of the Board of Education (now part
of the Ministry of Education) was established.   A Welsh Board of Health
was set up in 1919, but was only to exercise such powers in Wales as the
Minister thought fit.   A Welsh Office in the Ministry of Housing and Local
Government was also established.   In 1951 a Minister for Welsh Affairs
was appointed, holding the office jointly with the Home Office from 1951
to 1957.   From 1957 to 1964 the Minister for Welsh Affairs was also the
Minister of Housing and Local Government.   A second parliamentary
secretary was appointed at the Home Office from 1951 to 1957 to be responsible for Welsh Affairs; in 1957 a Minister of State for Welsh Affairs was
appointed and in 1964 a Welsh Office was established with a Secretary of
State for Wales.   In 1960 a Welsh Grand Committee analagous to the
Scottish Grand Committee was appointed to consider all Bills and other
parliamentary business relating exclusively to Wales.

Welsh national or separatist feeling has, however, expressed itself in
forces other than the movement for home rule or devolution.   The most
important aspects of this have been the campaigns on such matters as the
Church, education, land and temperance reform.   The 1881 Welsh Sunday
Closing Act and the 1889 Intermediate Education (Wales) Act were the
beginning of separate legislation for Wales.   In the twentieth century the
most conspicuous milestone here was the act to Disestablish the Church of
England in Wales which finally came into force in 1920 after being suspended
during World War I.

SOURCES.—Sir R. Coupland, *Welsh and Scottish Nationalism* (1954).   J. F. Rees, 'The Problem of
Wales,' *Nineteenth Century and After*, (1949) also in *The Problem of Wales and other Essays* (1963).

Ireland 1900-1922

From 1900 to 1921 the Lord-Lieutenant[1] of Ireland was responsible for the
administration of Irish affairs, with an office in Dublin.   His Chief Secretary[2]
was a member of the House of Commons, and assisted him in carrying on the
parliamentary business of the department, for which he was the responsible
minister.   At the same time there were several departments in Dublin,
working under the presidency of the Chief Secretary: the Department of
Agriculture and Technical Instruction, the Irish Congested Districts Board,

[1] See p. 252.   [2] See p. 49.

and the Local Government Board for Ireland. There were three boards of education commissioners, all of whom were appointed by the Lord-Lieutenant or the Government, and there was the Irish Land Commission. The Irish Public Works Board was controlled by the Treasury in London, and not by the Irish Government. There was scarcely any further devolution of administrative authority to Ireland between 1900 and 1922.

The Irish Office remained in existence until 1924 after the partition of Ireland, though the posts of Chief Secretary and Lord-Lieutenant lapsed in 1922, with the recognition of the Irish Free State. The functions previously exercised by the Irish Office became the responsibility of the Home Office (for Northern Ireland) and the Colonial Office handled relations with Eire. When Ireland became a republic in 1949, the Commonwealth Relations Office continued to be the department responsible for relations with her. In 1966 this responsibility was transferred to the Commonwealth Affairs Office.

Lord-Lieutenants of
Ireland 1900–22

1895	Ld Cadogan
18 Aug 02	E of Dudley
3 Feb 06	E of Aberdeen
19 Feb 15	Ld Wimborne
12 May 18	Vt French
2 May 21	Vt FitzAlan

Northern Ireland 1922-

The Northern Ireland Parliament was created by the *Government of Ireland Act, 1920*. The powers of the Crown are exercised by the Governor,[1] who is appointed by the Crown. Provision was made in the Act for the continued representation of Northern Ireland constituencies in the House of Commons of the United Kingdom. The constitutional position of Northern Ireland is thus unique in that it is part of the United Kingdom and sends representatives to the United Kingdom Parliament but is subject in most internal matters to the jurisdiction of a Parliament and Government of its own. The Government of Ireland Act confers on that Parliament extensive powers for the regulation of the affairs of Northern Ireland, but excludes a number of specified matters from its jurisdiction. In respect of these excluded matters executive power remains with the United Kingdom Government, and only the United Kingdom Parliament can legislate. Consequently Northern Ireland is subject to two jurisdictions, and although most of Northern Ireland's public services are administered by Ministers who are members of the Northern Ireland Government, there are some public services, such as, for example, the Post Office services, the Customs and Excise service, and the Inland Revenue service, for which Ministers of the United Kingdom Government are responsible.

In respect of all matters on which the Northern Ireland Parliament is empowered to make laws, executive powers are exercisable by the Government of Northern Ireland. At the head of this Government is the Governor

[1] See p. 254.

appointed by the Crown who summons, prorogues and dissolves the Parliament, appoints the members of the Privy Council, organises the Civil Service, and appoints Ministers to administer such Government departments as the Northern Ireland Parliament may establish. The present departments are the Prime Minister's Department, the Ministry of Finance, the Ministry of Home Affairs, the Ministry of Development, the Ministry of Education, the Ministry of Agriculture, the Ministry of Commerce, and the Ministry of Health and Social Services. The Ministers in charge of these eight departments (together in 1967, with the Minister in the Senate, the Minister of State in the Ministry of Development, and the Minister who is Leader of the House) form an Executive Committee of the Privy Council which aids and advises the Governor in the exercise of his executive powers.

The Parliament of Northern Ireland consists of a Senate and a House of Commons. The House of Commons has 52 members, Proportional Representation was used in the elections of 1921 and 1925 but since 1929, except for 4 members for Queen's University, Belfast, they are now chosen directly by single-member constituencies. The Senate has 26 members, 24 being elected by the House of Commons by proportional representation, and two being *ex officio*, the Lord Mayor of Belfast and the Mayor of Londonderry. The main differences between the Northern Ireland law relating to elections to the Northern Ireland Parliament and the United Kingdom law relating to elections to the United Kingdom Parliament are that the Northern Ireland law retains the University seats, retains the 'business premises' qualification for a vote, and requires qualified electors either to have been born in Northern Ireland or to have been resident in the UK for seven years and to possess the requisite residence, business premises or service qualification. The Parliament of Northern Ireland may legislate on all matters except certain fields that were permanently excepted by the 1920 Act, such as the succession to the Crown, making of peace or war, the armed forces of the Crown, the making of treaties, honours, naturalisation and aliens, and certain functions that were reserved such as postal and telegraph services, the Supreme Court, and the important forms of taxation. It was also prohibited from making laws which would interfere with religious freedom or might discriminate against any religious body, and until 1961, from taking property without compensation. All United Kingdom bills apply to Northern Ireland unless there is express provision to the contrary. In general, legislation at Stormont has followed very closely legislation in Westminster. The revenue of the Government of Northern Ireland is derived partly from taxes imposed by the United Kingdom Parliament (known as 'reserved' taxes) and partly from taxes imposed by the Northern Ireland Parliament (known as 'transferred taxes'). The powers of the Northern Ireland Parliament are similar to those of the United Kingdom Parliament as regards the appropriation of revenue. The Treasury is responsible for financial relations with Northern Ireland, and other departments are concerned with trade, commerce, and employment, but the Home Office retains the major responsibility for Northern Ireland.

S

Governors of Northern Ireland 1922–		Prime Ministers of Northern Ireland 1921–	
11 Dec 22	D of Abercorn	7 Jun 21	Sir J. Craig
7 Sep 45	Earl Granville		(1927 Vt Craigavon)
1 Dec 52	Ld Wakehurst	26 Nov 40	J. Andrews
1 Dec 64	Ld Erskine	6 May 43	Sir B. Brooke
2 Dec 68	Ld Grey		(1952 Vt Brooke- borough)
		25 Mar 63	T. O'Neill

General Elections of Northern Ireland

Date	Unionist	Ind. Unionist	Lib.	Lab.	Nat.	Sinn Fein Republican Abstentionist	Eire Lab. Rep. Lab. Soc. Rep. Ind. Lab.	Ind. & Other
24 May 21	40	..	..	..	6	6	..	..
28 Apr 25	32	4	..	3	10	2	..	1
22 May 29	37	3	..	1	11	..	..	..
30 Nov 33	36	2	..	2	9	2	..	1
9 Feb 38	39	3	..	1	8	..	1	..
14 Jun 45	33	2	..	2	9	..	3	3
10 Feb 49	37	2	..	..	9	..	2	2
22 Oct 53	38	1	..	..	7	2	3	1
20 Mar 58	37	..	..	4	8	..	2	1
31 May 62	34	..	1	4	9	..	3	1
25 Nov 65	36	..	1	2	9	..	2	2

SOURCES.—N. Mansergh, *The Government of Northern Ireland* (1936); T. Wilson (ed.), *Ulster under Home Rule* (1955); Sir F. Newsam, *The Home Office* (1954), pp. 167–70; R. J. Lawrence, *The Government of Northern Ireland* (1965).

The Channel Islands

The Channel Islands which were originally part of the Duchy of Normandy have been associated with England since 1066. They have their own legislative assemblies, systems of local administration, fiscal systems, and courts of law. The Islanders have general responsibility for the regulation of their local affairs subject to the prerogative of the Crown over appointment to the chief posts in the local administrations and the necessity of Royal Assent to legislative measures passed by the insular assemblies. Most of the laws by which they are governed emanate from their representative assemblies and although they cannot be regarded as local authorities most of their public services are provided by these assemblies in the same way as local government services are provided and administered in Great Britain.

The Channel Islands are divided into 2 Bailiwicks, one comprising Jersey and the other, Alderney, Sark, and Guernsey with its dependants, Herm and Jethou. Each Bailiwick has a Lieutenant Governor appointed by the Crown for a period of 5 years, through whom all official communications between the U.K. Government and the Islands pass, and in whom certain executive functions are vested. A Bailiff also appointed by the Crown presides over the local legislatures, the States, and over the sittings of the Royal Court. Since 1948 all members of the States who have the right to vote are elected directly or indirectly by the electorate. The Islands have their own Courts of Law, but there remains leave to appeal to the Judicial Committee of the Privy Council.

The Island Assemblies may initiate legislation but they must then petition the Sovereign in Council to give these measures force of law. Acts of the UK Parliament do not apply to the Channel Islands unless by express provision or necessary application. As a general rule Parliament refrains from legislating on matters with which these assemblies can deal unless for some special reason a U.K. act must be preferred to local legislation.

The public revenues of the Islands are raised by duties on imported goods, by income taxes and other taxes. Proposals made by the States for raising revenue require authorisation by Order in Council but responsibility for determining how the revenue shall be spent is, in practice, left to the States. Immunity from taxation for Crown purposes has been a privilege of the Islanders since the time of Edward VI.

The Isle of Man

This island was successively under the rule of Norway, of Scotland, of the Stanley family and of the Dukes of Atholl before it became a Crown Colony in 1765. Since 1886 the internal affairs of the island have been regulated by the Tynwald, which has evolved from the Lord of Man's Council composed of his chief officials and other persons of importance and the House of Keys. The latter comprises 24 representatives elected by all over the age of 21 who have resided in the island for 6 months. The consent of both the Legislative Council and the Keys is requisite for any Act of Tynwald except when in three successive sessions of a Parliament the Keys pass the same Bill, or a very similar one, which is twice rejected by the Council. In that case the Bill is deemed to have been passed by the Council. All legislation by Tynwald depends for its validity on confirmation by Orders made by the Queen in Council.

Most of the public services are provided by Tynwald and administered by Boards of Tynwald, but the Lieutenant Governor is the executive authority for certain services, including the police and the administration of justice. He is also responsible under insular legislation for initiating proposals for the raising and disbursement of the public revenue. By the Isle of Man Act of 1958 the Treasury's control over the Island's finances was removed enabling the Tynwald to regulate its own finances and Customs, although under the Act, the Island continues to make an annual contribution to the Exchequer for defence and common services. There is a statutory body of members of Tynwald known as the Executive Council with whom the Lieutenant Governor confers before making proposals for the raising or expenditure of money, and all such proposals subsequently require the assent of Tynwald.

XVI

THE COMMONWEALTH

Main Territories under British Rule since 1900

Commonwealth Status 1 Jan 1969		Original entry into British rule and Status in 1900	Changes of Status
—	Aden	Colony (1839) and adjacent Protectorate	Acceded to South Arabian Federation 1963. Became People's Republic of South Yemen 1967
Ass. State	Antigua	Colony (1663)	*See* Leeward Isles
—	Ascension	Admiralty administered territory (1815)	Became dependency of Colony of St Helena 1922
Member	Australia	First settled 1788 6 self-governing colonies (1855 and later)	Federal government formed 1901. Dominion status recognised 1907
Colony	Bahamas	First settled 1646 Colony (1783)	
Member	Barbados	Settled 1627 Colony (1662)	Part of West Indies Federation 1958–62; Independence granted 1966
—	Basutoland	Protectorate (1871) Colony (1884)	Independence granted 1966. Now Lesotho
—	Bechuanaland	Protectorate (1885)	Independence granted 1966. Now Botswana
Colony	Bermuda	First settled 1609 Colony (1684)	
Member	Botswana	—	Formerly Bechuanaland Protectorate. Independence granted 1966 as Republic
—	British Guiana	Ceded Colony (1814)	Independence granted 1966. Now Guyana
Colony	British Honduras	First settled 1638 Colony (separated from Jamaica 1884)	
Dependency	British Indian Ocean Territory	Dependencies of Mauritius or Seychelles	The Chagos, Archipeligo and Aldabra, Farqhar and Desroches Islands were formed into a single British Dependency in 1965
—	British North Borneo	Protectorate (1888)	Administered by Chartered Company 1882–1946. Became part of North Borneo Colony 1946. Entered Malaysian Federation as Sabah 1963
Protected State	British Solomon Islands	Protectorate (1893)	
—	British Somaliland	Protectorate (1887)	Independence granted 1960 when it became part of Somalia, a Republic outside the Commonwealth
—	British Togoland	—	Administered by Britain under League of Nations mandate 1922–46 and under U.N. Trusteeship 1946–57. Merged with Ghana 1957
Protectorate	Brunei	Protectorate (1888)	
—	Burma	Indian Province (1852)	Separated from India 1937. Independence granted in 1948 when it became a Republic outside the Commonwealth

256

Commonwealth Status 1 Jan 1969		Original entry into British rule and Status in 1900	Changes of Status
—	Cameroons (British)	—	Administered as part of Nigeria under League of Nations mandate 1922. Northern Cameroons incorporated in Nigeria 1961. Southern Cameroons joined Cameroon Republic, outside the Commonwealth
Member	Canada	Ceded Colonies from 1714 onwards. Self-governing Federation (1867)	Dominion status recognised 1907
—	Cape of Good Hope	Ceded Colony (1814)	Dominion status recognised 1907. Province of Union of South Africa
Colony	Cayman, Turks, and Caicos Islands	Ceded (1670) Dependencies of Jamaica (1848)	Separate dependencies under Colonial Office following Jamaican Independence 1962
Member —	Ceylon	Ceded Colony (1802)	Independence granted 1948
	Christmas Island	Annexed (1888)	Part of Straits Settlements 1900 by incorporation with Singapore. Separate Colony Jan 1958. Transferred to Australia Oct 1958
—	Cocos-Keeling Islands	Annexed (1857)	Part of Straits Settlement 1903. Incorporated in Singapore Colony 1946. Transferred to Australia 1958
Protectorate	Cook Islands	Protectorate (1888)	Annexed 1900. Administered by New Zealand since 1901
Member	Cyprus	British administered territory (1878)	Annexed by Britain 1914. Colony 1925. Independence granted as Republic 1960
Ass. State	Dominica	Colony (1763)	See Leeward Isles
—	East African Protectorate	Protectorate (1895)	Became a Colony and protectorate of Kenya 1920. See Kenya
—	Egypt	Occupied by British since 1882	British Protectorate 1914–22
—	Eire	Part of U.K. (1801)	Part of Ireland. Independence granted as Irish Free State 1922 with Dominion status. Took name of Eire 1937. Independent Republic outside the Commonwealth 1949
Colony	Falkland Islands	Colony (1833)	
Colony	Fiji	Colony (1874)	
Member	Gambia	Settlement began 1618 Colony (1843) and adjacent Protectorate (1888)	Independence granted 1965
Member	Ghana	—	Formerly Gold Coast. Independence granted 1957. Republic 1960
Colony	Gibraltar	Ceded Colony (1713)	
Colony	Gilbert and Ellice Islands	Protectorate (1892)	Colony 1915
—	Gold Coast	Settlement began 1750. Colony (1821 and 1874)	Independence granted 1957. Now Ghana
Ass. State	Grenada	Ceded Colony (1763)	See Leeward Isles
Member	Guyana	—	Formerly British Guiana. Independence granted 1966
Colony	Hong Kong	Ceded Colony (1843)	
Member	India	Settlement began 1601. Indian Empire (1876)	Independence granted 1947. Republic 1950

Commonwealth Status 1 Jan 1969		Original entry into British rule and Status in 1900	Changes of Status
—	Ireland	Union with Great Britain (1801)	Independence granted to 26 counties. Known as Eire since 1937.
Member	Jamaica	Colony (seized 1655 and ceded 1670)	Part of West Indies Federation 1958–62. Independence granted 1962
Member	Kenya	—	Formerly East African Protectorate. Colony and Protectorate of Kenya (1920). Independence granted 1963. Republic 1964
—	Labuan	Colony (1848) governed by North Borneo Company (1890)	Administered by Straits Settlement 1907. Became separate Straits Settlement 1912. Part of North Borneo (1946) now Sabah (1963)
—	Lagos	Colony (1861)	Amalgamated with protectorate of Southern Nigeria 1906
Ass. State and Colony	Leeward Isles	Colonies federated (1871)	Federated Colony dissolved 1956. (Antigua, Montserrat, St Kitts–Nevis and until 1940 Dominica and Virgin Is.) Part of West Indies Federation (except for Virgin Is.) 1958–62. Attained Associated Statehood 1967 (except for Virgin Is.)
Member	Lesotho	—	Formerly Basutoland Colony. Independence granted 1966 with indigenous monarch
Member	Malawi	—	Formerly Nyasaland. Part of Federation of Rhodesia and Nyasaland 1953–63 Independence granted 1964. Republic 1966
—	Malay States	9 Protectorates, 4 of which were federated	
—	Malaya	—	Formerly Malay States (federated and unfederated) and Straits Settlements. Independence granted in 1957 as elective monarchy. Merged in Malaysia Federation 1963.
Member	Malaysia	—	Formed in 1963 by a federation of Malaya, Singapore, Sabah (North Borneo), and Sarawak; Singapore seceded in 1965. An indigenous elective monarchy
—	Maldive Islands	Protectorate (1887)	Independence granted 1965
Member	Malta	Ceded Colony (1814)	Independence granted 1964
Member	Mauritius	Ceded Colony (1814)	Independence granted 1968
Ass. State	Montserrat	First settled (1642) as Colony	See Leeward Isles
—	Natal	Colony (1843)	Province of South Africa 1910
Trusteeship	Nauru	—	Administered by Australia under League of Nations mandate 1920–47 and under U.N. Trusteeship since 1947
Trusteeship	New Guinea	—	Administered by Australia under League of Nations mandate 1921–46 and under U.N. Trusteeship since 1946. United with Papua 1946
Condominuim	New Hebrides	—	Administered as Anglo-French condominium since 1906
Member	New Zealand	Self-governing Colony (1854)	Dominion status recognised 1907
—	Newfoundland	Settlement began 1623. Self-governing Colony (1855)	Dominion status recognised 1907. Under U.K. Commission of government 1933–1949. Acceded to Canada 1949

Commonwealth Status 1 Jan 1969		Original entry into British rule and Status in 1900	Changes of Status
Member	Nigeria	Protectorates (1900)	Colony of Lagos joined Southern Nigeria 1906. Protectorates of Northern and Southern Nigeria joined 1914. Independence granted 1960. Republic 1963
—	Norfolk Island	Settled 1788. Under New South Wales (1896)	Became dependency of Australian Government 1914
—	North Borneo	—	Colony created in 1946 mainly from British North Borneo. Entered Malaysian federation as Sabah 1963
—	Northern Rhodesia	Chartered Company territory (1889)	Administered by British South Africa Company. Became Protectorate 1924. Part of Federation of Rhodesia and Nyasaland 1953–63. Independence granted 1964. Now Zambia
—	Nyasaland	Protectorate (1891)	Part of Federation of Rhodesia and Nyasaland 1953–63. Independence granted 1964. Now Malawi
—	Orange Free State	—	Colony 1902. Province of Union of South Africa 1910
Member	Pakistan	—	Part of Indian Empire. Independence granted 1947. Republic 1950
—	Palestine	—	Administered by Britain under League of Nations mandate 1922–48. Achieved Independence as State of Israel 1948
—	Papua	Protectorate (1884) Colony (1888)	Administered by Australia since 1906 United with New Guinea 1940
Colony	Pitcairn	Settled 1790 Colony (1898)	
Colony	Rhodesia	—	Formerly Southern Rhodesia. Part of Federation of Rhodesia and Nyasaland 1953–63. Resumed status as a self-governing colony with name of Rhodesia 1964. Unilateral declaration of 'independence' 1965
—	Rhodesia and Nyasaland	—	Federation of Northern Rhodesia, Nyasaland, and Southern Rhodesia established in 1953 and dissolved in 1963
—	Sabah	—	Formerly North Borneo. Part of Malaysian Federation since 1963
Ass. State	St Christopher (St Kitts) and Nevis	Colony (1625)	See Leeward Isles
Colony	St Helena	Administered by E. India Co. 1673 Colony (1833)	
Ass. State	St Lucia	Ceded Colony (1814)	See Windward Isles
Ass. State	St Vincent	Ceded Colony (1763)	See Windward Isles
—	Sarawak	Protectorate (1888)	Ceded to Britain in 1946 as Colony. Part of Malaysian Federation since 1963
Colony	Seychelles	Dependency of Mauritius (1810)	Separate Colony 1903
Member	Sierra Leone	Colony (1808) and adjacent Protectorate (1896)	Independence granted 1961
Member	Singapore	Under Indian government 1824 Became Independent Colony (1946)	Separate Colony 1946. Part of Malaysian Federation 1963–65. Seceded to form Republic 1965
—	Straits Settlements (Singapore, Penang, Malacca)	Colonies (1867)	Part of Straits Settlements. Malacca, Labuan added 1912. Labuan and Penang joined Malay States 1948.

260 THE COMMONWEALTH

Commonwealth Status 1 Jan 1969		Original entry into British rule and Status in 1900	Changes of Status
			Singapore joined Malaysian Federation 1963
—	South Africa, Union of	—	Formed 1910 from the Colonies of Cape of Good Hope, Natal, Orange Free State, and Transvaal. Dominion status 1910. Became Republic 1961 and left the Commonwealth
Protectorate	South Arabia	—	Federation formed in 1959 from 6 states or sheikhdoms. A further 16 subsequently acceded together with (1963) the Colony of Aden
—	South-West Africa	—	Administered by South Africa under League of Nations mandate 1920–46 and under U.N. Trusteeship since 1946. Unilaterally incorporated in South Africa 1949
—	South Yemen	—	Formerly Aden Protectorate
—	Southern Rhodesia	Chartered Company (1889)	Administered by British South Africa Company. Self-governing Colony 1923. Part of Federation of Rhodesia and Nyasaland 1953–63. Now Rhodesia.
—	Sudan	Condominium with Egypt (1899)	Independence granted 1956 when it became Republic outside the Commonwealth
Member	Swaziland	—	British Protectorate 1903. Independence granted 1968
—	Tanganyika	—	Administered by Britain under League of Nations mandate 1920–46 and under U.N. Trusteeship 1946–61. Independence granted 1961. Republic 1962. Merged with Zanzibar to form Tanzania 1964
Member	Tanzania	—	Formed by merging Tanganyika and Zanzibar 1964
Prot. State	Tonga	Protectorate (1900)	
—	Transjordan	—	Administered by Britain under League of Nations mandate 1922–28. Full independence recognised 1946
—	Transvaal	Annexed 1902	Responsible Government 1966. Province of Union of South Africa 1910
Member	Trinidad Tobago	Ceded (1802 and 1814) Colony (combined 1889)	Part of West Indies Federation 1958–62. Independence granted 1962
—	Tristan da Cunha	British settlement (1815)	Dependency of Colony of St Helena 1938. (Evacuated 1961–63)
Member	Uganda	Protectorate (1894)	Independence granted 1962. Sovereign State 1963
Colony	Virgin Islands	Colonies (1666)	See Leeward Isles
—	West Indies Federation	—	Independence was granted in 1958 to a Federation of the colonies of Jamaica, Trinidad and Tobago, Barbados, the Leeward Isles (except for the Virgin Isles) and the Windward Isles. The Federation broke up in 1962 when Jamaica and Trinidad and Tobago became Independent. Some common institutions were continued by the other members of the Federation
—	Western Samoa	—	Administered by New Zealand under League of Nations mandate 1920–46 and under U.N. Trusteeship 1946–62. Independent Republic 1962
Ass. States	Windward Isles	Colonies (1763 and 1814 federated in 1885)	The colonies Grenada, Dominica, St Lucia, and St Vincent. Part of West Indies Federation 1958–62. Attained Associated Statehood 1967

Commonwealth Status 1 Jan 1969	Original entry into British rule and Status in 1900	Changes of Status
Member Zambia	—	Formerly Northern Rhodesia. Part of Federation of Rhodesia and Nyasaland 1953–63. Independence granted as Republic 1964
— Zanzibar	Protected State (1890)	Independence granted 1963. Republic 1964. Merged with Tanganyika as Tanzania 1964

Independent Self-Governing Members of the Commonwealth

New Zealand [1] 1852
Canada [1] 1867
Australia [1] 1901
South Africa [1] 1909–61
Newfoundland [1, 2] 1907–33
Ireland (Eire) 1922–48
India [3] 1947 (Republic 1950)
Pakistan 1947 (Republic 1956)
Ceylon 1948
Ghana 1957 (Republic 1960)
Malaya 1957 (Malaysia, 1963) (Elective Monarchy)
Nigeria 1960 (Republic 1963)
Cyprus 1961 (Republic 1960)
Sierra Leone 1961
Tanganyika 1961 (Republic 1962) became Tanzania 1965
Jamaica 1962

Trinidad 1962
Uganda 1962 (Republic 1963)
Zanzibar 1963–64
Kenya 1963 (Republic 1964)
Zambia 1964 (Republic 1964)
Malta 1964
Malawi 1964 (Republic 1966)
Gambia 1965
Singapore 1965 (Republic 1965)
Guyana 1966
Botswana 1966 (Republic 1966)
Lesotho 1966 (Indigenous Monarchy)
Barbados 1966
Mauritius 1968
Swaziland 1968 (Indigenous Monarchy)
Federation of Rhodesia and Nyasaland 1953–63 [4]

[1] These were recognised as having 'Dominion Status', in 1907.
[2] From 1933 to 1949 Newfoundland was governed by a U.K. Commission of Government. In 1949 Newfoundland joined the Canadian confederation as the tenth Province.
[3] Indian representatives were invited to attend Imperial Conferences and Prime Ministers' Meetings 1917–47.
[4] Although the Central African Federation, set up in 1953, and composed of N. Rhodesia, S. Rhodesia, and Nyasaland, was not a fully independent member of the Commonwealth, her Prime Ministers were invited to the Prime Ministers' Meetings 1955–62 and the Prime Minister of Rhodesia was invited 1962–1965.
[5] Barbados, Jamaica, Trinidad, Tobago, the Leeward and the Windward Islands all formed the West Indies Federation between 1958 and 1962.

Commonwealth Prime Ministers' Meetings, 1900–
(All have taken place in London)

30 Jun–11 Aug 02	Colonial Conference
15 Apr–9 May 07	Colonial Conference
23 May–20 Jun 11	Imperial Conference
Mar–May 17	Imperial War Conference
Jun–Aug 18	Imperial War Conference
1 Oct–8 Nov 23	Imperial Conference
19 Oct–23 Nov 26	Imperial Conference
1 Oct–14 Nov 30	Imperial Conference
14 May–15 Jun 37	Imperial Conference
1–16 May 44	Commonwealth Prime Ministers' Meeting
23 Apr–23 May 46	Commonwealth Prime Ministers' Meeting
11–22 Oct 48	Commonwealth Prime Ministers' Meeting
21–28 Apr 49	Commonwealth Prime Ministers' Meeting
4–12 Jan 51	Commonwealth Prime Ministers' Meeting
3–9 Jun 53	Commonwealth Prime Ministers' Meeting
31 Jan–8 Feb 55	Commonwealth Prime Ministers' Meeting
27 Jun–6 Jul 56	Commonwealth Prime Ministers' Meeting
26 Jun–5 Jul 57	Commonwealth Prime Ministers' Meeting
3–13 May 60	Commonwealth Prime Ministers' Meeting
8–17 Mar 61	Commonwealth Prime Ministers' Meeting
10–19 Sep 62	Commonwealth Prime Ministers' Meeting
8–13 Jul 64	Commonwealth Prime Ministers' Meeting
17–25 Jan 65	Commonwealth Prime Ministers' Meeting
6–15 Sep 66	Commonwealth Prime Ministers' Meeting
7–15 Jan 69	Commonwealth Prime Ministers' Meeting

SOURCES.—*Commonwealth Relations Office List 1951*, pp. 56–58, and *C.R.O. List 1960*; *Annual Register 1900–*; *Keesing's Archives 1945–*.

Certain other meetings of comparable status have been held

20 Jun–5 Aug 21	Conference of Prime Ministers and London Representatives of the United Kingdom, the Dominions, and India	London
Jul–Aug 32	Imperial Economic Conference	Ottawa
4–13 Apr 45	British Commonwealth Meeting	London
27 Nov–11 Dec 52	Commonwealth Economic Conference	London
11–12 Jan 66	Commonwealth Prime Ministers' Meeting	Lagos

Commonwealth Secretariat

As a result of the Commonwealth Prime Ministers' Meeting of Jul 1964 a Commonwealth Secretariat was established in London with its own civil servants seconded from Commonwealth Governments.

Secretary-General
Aug 65   A. Smith (Canada)

Viceroys and Governors-General

Australia 1901
1 Jan	01	E of Hopetoun
9 Jan	03	Ld Tennyson
21 Jan	04	Ld Northcote
9 Sep	08	E of Dudley
31 Jun	11	Ld Denman
18 May	14	Sir R. Munro-Ferguson
6 Oct	20	Ld Forster
8 Oct	25	Ld Stonehaven
22 Jan	31	Sir I. Isaacs
23 Jan	36	Ld Gowrie
30 Jan	45	D of Gloucester
11 Mar	47	Sir W. McKell
8 May	53	Sir W. Slim
2 Feb	60	Vt Dunrossil
3 Aug	61	Vt de L'Isle
22 Sep	65	Ld Casey

Barbados
30 Nov 66	Sir J. Stow	

Canada 1900
	1898	E of Minto
10 Dec	04	Earl Grey
13 Oct	11	D of Connaught
11 Nov	16	D of Devonshire
11 Aug	21	Ld Byng
2 Oct	26	Vt Willingdon
4 Apr	31	E of Bessborough
2 Nov	35	Ld Tweedsmuir
21 Jun	40	E of Athlone
12 Apr	46	Vt Alexander
28 Feb	52	V. Massey
15 Sep	59	G. Vanier
4 Apr	67	D. Michener

Ceylon 1948–
4 Feb	48	Sir H. Moore
6 Jul	49	Ld Soulbury
17 Jul	54	Sir O. Goonetilleke
2 Mar	62	W. Gopallawa

Gambia 1965–
18 Feb 65	Sir F. Singhateh	

Ghana 1957–60
6 Mar	57	E of Listowel

1 Jul 60 Declared Republic with Ghanain Presidents

Guyana 1966–
26 May 66	Sir R. Luyt	
16 Dec 66	Sir D. Rose	

Viceroys of India 1900–47
	1899	Ld Curzon
30 Apr	04	Ld Ampthill) *(officiating)*
13 Dec	04	Ld Curzon
18 Nov	05	E of Minto
23 Nov	10	Ld Hardinge of Penshurst
4 Apr	16	Ld Chelmsford
2 Apr	21	E of Reading
10 Apr	25	E of Lytton *(officiating)*
3 Apr	26	Ld Irwin
29 Jun	29	Vt Goschen *(officiating)*
24 Oct	29	Ld Irwin
18 Apr	31	E of Willingdon
16 May	34	Sir G. Stanley *(officiating)*
18 Apr	36	M of Linlithgow
25 Jun	38	Ld Brabourne *(officiating)*
25 Oct	38	M of Linlithgow
20 Oct	43	Vt Wavell
24 Mar	47	Vt Mountbatten (Earl)

Dominion of India— Governors-General 1947–50
15 Aug	47	Earl Mountbatten
21 Jun	48	Chakravarty Rajagopalachari

26 Jan 50 Declared Republic with Indian presidents

Jamaica 1962
6 Aug 62	Sir C. Campbell	

Kenya 1963–64
12 Dec	63	M. Macdonald

12 Dec 64 Declared Republic with Kenyan Presidents

Malawi 1964–66
6 Jul	64	Sir G. Jones

6 Jul 66 Declared Republic with Malawi Presidents

Malta 1964–
21 Sep	64	Sir M. Dorman

Mauritius 1968–
1 Sep	68	Sir A. Williams

New Zealand 1900
(Governors)
	1897	E of Ranfurly
20 Jun	04	Ld Plunkett
22 Jun	10	Ld Islington
19 Dec	12	E of Liverpool

Governors-General
28 Jun	17	E of Liverpool
27 Sep	20	Earl Jellicoe
13 Dec	24	Sir C. Fergusson
18 Mar	30	Ld Bledisloe
12 Apr	35	Vt Galway
21 Feb	41	Ld Newall
16 Jun	46	Ld Freyberg
1 Dec	52	Sir C. Norrie (Ld)
3 Sep	57	Vt Cobham
9 Nov	62	Sir B. Fergusson
19 Oct	67	Sir A. Porritt

Nigeria 1960–63
1 Oct	60	N. Azikiwe

1 Oct 63 Declared Republic with Nigerian Presidents

Dominion of Pakistan—1947-56

15 Aug 47 M. Jinnah
14 Sep 48 Khwaja Nazi-
              muddin
19 Oct 51 Ghulam Moham-
              med
6 Oct 55 Iskander Mizra
*23 Mar 56 Republic of Paki-
stan with Pakistani Presidents*

Federation of Rhodesia and Nyasaland 1957-60

8 Oct 57 E of Dalhousie
*31 Dec 63 Federation
dissolved*

Sierra Leone 1961-67

27 Apr 61 Sir H. Boston

South Africa 1910-61

31 May 10 Vt Gladstone
8 Sep 14 Vt Buxton
20 Nov 20 Prince Arthur of
              Connaught
21 Jan 24 E of Athlone
26 Jan 31 E of Clarendon
5 Apr 37 Sir P. Duncan
1 Jan 46 G. van Zyl
1 Jan 51 E. Jansen
25 Nov 59 C. Swart

*The Union of South Africa
became an independent republic
outside the British Commonwealth on 31 May 61.   C.
Swart was sworn in as the first
president.*

Tanganyika 1961-62

9 Dec 61 Sir R. Turnbull
*9 Dec 62 Declared Republic
with Tanganyikan Presidents*

Trinidad and Tobago 1962-

31 Aug 62 Sir S. Hochoy

Uganda 1962-63

9 Oct 62 Sir F. Crawford
*9 Oct 63 Declared Republic
with Ugandan Presidents*

West Indies 1957-62

10 May 57 Ld Hailes
Feb 62 Federation dissolved

XVII

INTERNATIONAL RELATIONS

Major Treaties and Documents subscribed to by Britain since 1900[1]

30 Jan 02	Anglo-Japanese Alliance	13 Apr 39	British Guarantee to Roumania and Greece
8 Apr 04	Anglo-French Entente	12 May 39	British Guarantee to Turkey
31 Aug 07	Anglo-Russian Entente		
18 Mar 15	Anglo-Russian Agreement over Constantinople	25 Aug 39	Anglo-Polish Agreement of Mutual Assistance
25 Apr 15	Treaty of London (Italy)	14 Aug 41	Atlantic Charter
May 16	Sykes-Picot Agreement (Middle East)	23 Feb 42	Anglo-American Mutual Aid Agreement (Lend-Lease 'Master Agreement')
31 Oct 17	Balfour Declaration (Palestine)		
28 Jun 19	Treaty of Versailles (Germany) and League of Nations Covenant [2]	26 May 42	Anglo-Soviet Treaty
		22 Jul 44	Bretton Woods Agreement (International Finance)
10 Sep 19	Treaty of St Germain (Austria)	11 Feb 45	Yalta Agreement
27 Nov 19	Treaty of Neuilly (Bulgaria)	26 Jun 45	United Nations Charter [3]
		2 Aug 45	Potsdam Agreement
4 Jun 20	Treaty of Trianon (Hungary)	6 Dec 45	Anglo-American Financial Agreement
10 Aug 20	Treaty of Sèvres (Turkey)	9 Feb 47	Peace Treaties with Italy, Hungary, Roumania, Bulgaria, and Finland
6 Dec 21	Articles of Agreement for an Irish Peace		
13 Dec 21	Washington Four Power Treaty (Pacific)	17 Mar 48	Brussels Treaty Organisation
6 Feb 22	Washington Nine Power Treaty (China)	16 Apr 48	Organisation for European Economic-Cooperation
6 Feb 22	Washington Five Power Treaty (Naval)	6 Jul 48	Economic-Cooperation Agreement (Marshall Aid)
23 Aug 23	Treaty of Lausanne (Middle East and the Straits)	4 Apr 49	North Atlantic Treaty Organisation (Nato)
		5 May 49	Council of Europe
15 Oct 25	Locarno Pact	4 Nov 50	Convention for the protection of Human Rights and Fundamental Freedoms
27 Aug 28	General Pact for the Renunciation of War (Briand-Kellogg)		
		28 Nov 50	Colombo Plan (South and South-East Asia)
22 Apr 30	London Naval Treaty	8 Sep 51	Treaty of Peace with Japan
18 Jun 35	Anglo-German Naval Agreement	30 Dec 53	European Organisation for Nuclear Research established
25 Mar 36	London Naval Treaty		
20 Jul 36	Montreux Agreement (Straits)	20 Jul 54	Geneva Conventions on Indo-China
7 Aug 36	Non-Intervention Agreement (Spain)	8 Sep 54	South-East Asia Defence Treaty (Seato)
26 Aug 36	Anglo-Egyptian Treaty		
29 Sep 38	Munich Agreement	3 Oct 54	London Nine Power Agreement (European security and integration)
31 Mar 39	Franco-British Guarantee to Poland		

[1] See also the section on the *Commonwealth* (pp. 256-63).

[2] The *International Labour Organisation* (I.L.O.) was created by the Treaty of Versailles, as a semi-autonomous organisation associated with the League of Nations. On 16 Dec 20 a statute was drawn up for the establishment of the *Permanent Court of International Justice* at the Hague. The Hague Court had its preliminary session on 30 Jan 22. It was dissolved by resolution of the League Assembly in Apr 1946.

[3] The Charter made provision for the continuance of the International Court of Justice at the Hague. The I.L.O. continued to function as one of the specialised agencies of the United Nations. (Among the other subsidiary organisations were F.A.O., U.N.E.S.C.O., W.H.O., I.M.F., etc. See *The Statesman's Year-Book, 1967-68*, pp. 11-19, for a brief summary of the organisations and their member countries.)

23 Oct 54	Western European Union (formerly Brussels Treaty Organisation)		21 Aug 59	Central Treaty Organisation (Cento). Formerly the the Baghdad Pact
21 Dec 54	European Coal and Steel Community (Britain made an agreement of association). Community formed on 18 Apr 51		20 Nov 59	European Free Trade Association
			31 May 60	Antarctic Treaty
			14 Dec 60	Organisation for Economic Co-operation and Development (formerly Organisation for European Economic Co-operation)
4 Apr 55	Special agreement whereby Britain joined the Baghdad Pact (defence). (Pact signed 24 Feb 55)			
15 May 55	Austrian State Treaty (occupation ended and declaration of neutrality)		29 Mar 62	European Organisation for the Development and Construction of Space Vehicle Launchers
29 Jul 57	International Atomic Energy agency		30 Sep 62	Convention on the High Seas
4 Feb 59	European Atomic Energy Community (Euratom). Britain made an agreement of association. (Euratom formed 1 Jan 58)		5 Aug 63	Test-ban Treaty
			30 Aug 63	European Space Research Organisation
			27 Jan 67	Outer Space Treaty
			1 Jul 68	Nuclear Non-Proliferation Treaty

League of Nations, 1919–1946

Britain was a founder member of the League of Nations. Between 1919 and 1922 the British Government conducted its relations with the League through its cabinet secretariat. After 1922 the Foreign Office was responsible for British representation at the League. A member of the Government was generally deputed to act as British representative at meetings of the League. No permanent national delegation stayed at Geneva. A. Eden was the only Minister appointed officially for League of Nations Affairs (7 Jun–22 Dec 35). Vt Cranborne was Parliamentary Under-Secretary at the Foreign Office with special responsibility for League of Nations Affairs from 6 Aug 35 until 20 Feb 38. The League was formally dissolved in 1946; although in practice it ceased to meet during the war.

United Nations, 1946–

Britain was one of the original signatories of the Charter of the United Nations. Since 1946 the British Government has had a permanent representative at the United Nations in New York. In addition, a Minister of State at the Foreign Office has usually been given special responsibility for United Nations affairs. Since 1964 the permanent representative has been a Minister of State at the Foreign Office.[1]

British Ambassadors to Leading Powers, 1900–

Austria-Hungary (–1914)

1896	Sir H. Rumbold
9 Sep 00	Sir F. Plunkett
7 May 05	Sir W. Goschen
1 Nov 08	Sir F. Cartwright
1 Nov 13	Sir M. de Bunsen
12 *Aug* 14	*War declared by G.B. on Austria-Hungary*

France

1896	Sir E. Monson
1 Jan 05	Sir F. Bertie (Ld)
19 Apr 18	E of Derby
27 Nov 20	Ld Hardinge of Penshurst
31 Dec 22	M of Crewe
30 Jul 28	Sir W. Tyrrell (Ld)
17 Apr 34	Sir G. Clerk
24 Apr 37	Sir E. Phipps
1 Nov 39	Sir R. Campbell
24 *Jun* 40	*Diplomatic mission withdrawn*
23 Oct 44	A. Duff Cooper
9 Jan 48	Sir O. Harvey
13 Apr 54	Sir G. Jebb

[1] Since 1964 there has also been a Minister of State at the Foreign Office with special responsibility for disarmament. This office was held by Ld Chalfont 1964–67 and F. Mulley 1967–.

11 Apr 60 Sir P. Dixon	1 May 39 Sir P. Loraine	1 Apr 08 Sir G. Barclay
11 Feb 65 Sir P. Reilly	11 *Jun* 40 *War declared by*	(*Min. plen. ad. int.*)
17 Sep 68 C. Soames	*Italy on G.B.*	1 Jul 08 Sir G. Lowther
	5 Apr 44 Sir N. Charles	10 Oct 13 Sir L. Mallet
Germany	(1944, *High Com-*	5 *Nov* 14 *War declared by*
1895 Sir F. Lascelles	*missioner*; 1945,	*G.B. on Turkey*
1 Nov 08 Sir W. Goschen	*Representative*	1 Nov 20 Sir H. Rumbold
4 *Aug* 14 *War declared by*	*of H.M. Gov-*	2 Feb 24 (Sir) R. Lindsay
G.B. on Ger-	*ernment with the*	(*H.M. Represen-*
many	*personal rank of*	*tative*)
10 Jan 20 Ld Kilmarnock	*Ambassador*)	1 Mar 25 Sir R. Lindsay
(*ch. d'aff.*)	9 Oct 47 Sir V. Mallet	(*Ambassador*)
29 Jun 20 Ld D'Abernon	12 Nov 53 Sir A. Clarke	12 Nov 26 Sir G. Clerk
12 Oct 26 Sir R. Lindsay	19 Sep 62 Sir J. Ward	16 Dec 33 Sir P. Loraine
1 Aug 28 Sir H. Rumbold	17 Dec 66 Sir C. Shuck-	25 Feb 39 Sir H. Knatch-
2 Aug 33 Sir E. Phipps	burgh	bull-Hugessen
29 Apr 37 Sir N. Henderson		29 Sep 44 Sir M. Peterson
3 *Sep* 39 *War declared by*	**Russia**	10 May 46 Sir D. Kelly
G.B. on Ger-	1898 Sir C. Scott	20 Apr 49 Sir N. Charles
many	28 Apr 04 Sir C. Hardinge	6 Dec 51 Sir K. Helm
	(Ld)	13 Jan 54 Sir J. Bowker
(*Military Governors*)	10 Feb 06 Sir A. Nicolson	15 Nov 58 Sir B. Burrows
1945 Sir B. Montgomery	23 Nov 10 Sir G. Buchanan	7 Mar 63 Sir W. Allen
1946 Sir S. Douglas	1917 *Diplomatic mission*	16 Mar 67 Sir R. Allen
1947 Sir B. Robertson	*withdrawn*	
	1 Feb 24 Sir R. Hodgson	**U.S.A.**
(*British High Commissioners*)	(*ch. d'aff.*)	1893 Sir J. Pauncefote
1949 Sir B. Robertson	3 *Jun* 27 *Suspension of dip-*	(Ld)
1950 Sir I. Kirkpatrick	*lomatic relations*	4 Jun 02 (Sir) M. Herbert
1953 Sir. F. Hoyer Millar	7 Dec 29 Sir E. Ovey	23 Oct 03 Sir M. Durand
	24 Oct 33 Vt Chilston	3 Feb 07 J. Bryce
(*Ambassadors to*	19 Jan 39 Sir W. Seeds	19 Apr 13 Sir A. Spring-
West Germany)	12 Jun 40 Sir S. Cripps	Rice
5 May 55 Sir F. Hoyer	4 Feb 42 Sir A. Kerr	1 Jan 18 E of Reading
Millar	(Ld Inverchapel)	25 Mar 20 Sir A. Geddes
7 Feb 57 Sir C. Steel	17 May 46 Sir M. Peterson	2 Feb 24 Sir E. Howard
15 Feb 63 Sir F. Roberts	22 Jun 49 Sir D. Kelly	11 Mar 30 Sir R. Lindsay
15 May 68 Sir R. Jackling	18 Oct 51 Sir A. Gascoigne	29 Aug 39 M of Lothian
	1 Oct 53 Sir W. Hayter	24 Jan 41 Vt Halifax (E of)
Italy	19 Feb 57 Sir P. Reilly	23 May 46 Ld Inverchapel
1898 Sir P. Currie (Ld)	29 Apr 60 Sir F. Roberts	22 May 48 Sir O. Franks
17 Jan 03 Sir F. Bertie	27 Nov 62 Sir H. Trevelyan	31 Dec 52 Sir R. Makins
1 Jan 05 Sir E. Egerton	27 Aug 65 Sir G. Harrison	2 Nov 56 Sir H. Caccia
1 Dec 08 Sir J. Rennell	3 Oct 68 Sir D. Wilson	18 Oct 61 Sir W. Ormsby-
Rodd		Gore (Ld Har-
21 Oct 19 Sir G. Buchanan	**Turkey**	lech)
25 Nov 21 Sir R. Graham	1898 Sir N. O'Conor	6 Apr 65 Sir P. Dean
26 Oct 33 Sir E. Drummond		21 Feb 69 J. Freeman
(E of Perth)		

British Ambassadors to Leading International Organisations
1946–1967

The United Nations	North Atlantic Council	European Communities
1946 Sir A. Cadogan	1953 Sir C. Steel	1960 Sir A. Tandy
1950 Sir G. Jebb	1957 Sir F. Roberts	1963 Sir C. O'Neill
1954 Sir P. Dixon	1960 Sir P. Mason	1965 Sir J. Marjoribanks
1960 Sir P. Dean	1963 Sir E. Shuckburgh	
1964 Ld Caradon	1966 Sir B. Burrows	

SOURCES.—*United Nations Yearbooks, 1946-. Foreign Office List 1953-. Diplomatic Service List 1967.*

Among the major works on international relations since 1900 are: A. J. P. Taylor, *Struggle for Mastery in Europe, 1848–1918* (1954); C. R. M. F. Cruttwell, *A History of the Great War, 1914–18* (1936); C. B. Falls, *The First World War* (1960); G. M. Gathorne-Hardy, *A Short History of International Affairs, 1920–39* (1950); E. H. Carr, *International Relations between the Two World Wars* (1947); E. H. Carr, *Twenty Years' Crisis* (1947); G. F. Hudson, *Far East in World Politics* (1939); W. M. Jordan, *Great Britain, France and the German Problem, 1919–39* (1943); F. S. Northedge, *British Foreign Policy: The Process of Readjustment, 1945–1961* (1962); A. J. P. Taylor, *Origins of the Second World War*

(1961); J. W. Wheeler-Bennett, *Munich: Prologue to Tragedy* (1948); A. Wolfers, *Britain and France between the two Wars* (1940); Sir L. Woodward, *British Foreign Policy in the Second World War* (1962); W. McNeill, *America, Britain and Russia. Their Co-operation and Conflict 1941–46* (1953); F. S. Northedge, *The Troubled Giant, Britain among the Great Powers 1916–1939* (1967).

Among the main works on Britain and the international organisations are: F. P. Walters, *History of the League of Nations* (2 vols, 1951); G. L. Goodwin, *Britain and the United Nations* (1957); and A. H. Robertson, *European Institutions* (1966).

The Royal Institute of International Affairs has published the *Survey of International Affairs* annually since 1920. The main British documents of the period are edited by G. P. Gooch and H. Temperley, *British Documents on the Origin of the War* (11 vols, 1927–39), and edited by R. Butler and Sir E. L. Woodward (later J. P. T. Bury), *Documents on British Foreign Policy, 1919–39* (three series, still in course of publication).

Since 1915 the texts of major public documents have been printed in the *Annual Register*. For reference only, see *The Statesman's Year-Book*, and the *Year Book of International Organisations, 1951–66*

XVIII
ARMED FORCES

Service Chiefs

Royal Navy
Chief of Naval Staff

1899	Ld W. Kerr
1904	Sir J. Fisher (Ld)
1910	Sir A. Wilson
1911	Sir F. Bridgeman
1912	Prince Louis of Battenberg

First Sea Lord

1914	Ld Fisher
1915	Sir H. Jackson
1916	Sir J. Jellicoe
1917	Sir R. Wemyss
1919	Earl Beatty
1927	Sir C. Madden
1930	Sir F. Field
1933	Sir E. Chatfield (Ld)
1938	Sir R. Backhouse
1939	Sir D. Pound
1943	Sir A. Cunningham (Ld)
1946	Sir J. Cunningham
1948	Ld Fraser of North Cape
1951	Sir R. McGrigor
1955	Earl Mountbatten
1959	Sir C. Lambe
1960	Sir C. John
1964	Sir D. Luce
1966	Sir V. Begg
1968	Sir H. Le Fanu

Army
Commander in Chief

1895	Vt Wolseley
1900	Ld Roberts (Earl)

Chief of Imperial General Staff

1904	Sir N. Lyttelton
1908	Sir W. Nicholson
1912	Sir J. French
1914	Sir C. Douglas
1914	Sir J. Wolfe-Murray
1915	Sir W. Robertson
1918	Sir H. Wilson
1922	E of Cavan
1926	Sir G. Milne
1933	Sir A. Montgomery Massingberd
1936	Sir C. Deverell
1937	Vt Gort
1939	Sir E. Ironside
1940	Sir J. Dill
1941	Sir A. Brooke (Ld Alanbrooke)
1946	Vt Montgomery
1948	Sir W. Slim
1952	Sir J. Harding
1955	Sir G. Templer
1958	Sir F. Festing
1963–4	Sir R. Hull

Chief of General Staff

1964	Sir R. Hull
1965	Sir J. Cassels
1968	Sir G. Baker

Royal Air Force
Chief of Air Staff

1918	Sir H. Trenchard
1918	Sir F. Sykes
1919	Sir H. Trenchard
1930	Sir J. Salmond
1933	Sir G. Salmond
1933	Sir E. Ellington
1937	Sir C. Newall
1940	Sir C. Portal
1946	Sir A. Tedder (Ld)
1950	Sir J. Slessor
1953	Sir W. Dickson
1956	Sir D. Boyle
1960	Sir T. Pike
1964	Sir C. Elworthy
1968	Sir J. Grandy

Defence Staff
Chief of Defence Staff

1964	Earl Mountbatten
1965	Sir R. Hull
1967	Sir C. Elworthy

Defence Organisation

Committee of Imperial Defence, 1904–1946

The committee was first established in 1902 on a temporary basis to advise the Prime Minister, as a result of British experience in the Boer War of the need for planning and co-ordination of the Empire's defence forces. The C.I.D. was established permanently in 1904, as a small flexible advisory committee to the Prime Minister. Members were usually cabinet ministers concerned with defence, military leaders, and key civil servants. The Dominions also had representatives sitting on the committee occasionally. The Prime Minister was the chairman of the committee, which had no executive power, but exercised considerable influence. A secretariat was set up to assist the C.I.D., which was later adopted by the cabinet itself. During the first world war the C.I.D. was suspended. Its functions between 1914 and 1919 were taken over by the War Council (Nov 1914), the Dardanelles Committee (May 1915), the War Committee (Nov 1916), and finally the War Cabinet (Dec 1916–Nov 1919). The C.I.D. resumed plenary sessions in 1922. In the 'thirties the membership of the C.I.D. rose from about 11 to 18, and the committee became unwieldy. This led to the establishment of a Minister for the Co-ordination of Defence (1936–40), who was without a department, but worked through the Committee Secretariat. On the outbreak of the Second World War the C.I.D. was again suspended, and its responsibilities taken over by the War Cabinet. In 1946 the decision to make the suspension permanent was published in a White Paper on the C.I.D. (Cmd. 6923).

Secretaries to the C.I.D. 1904-1946

1904	G. Clarke	1912	(Sir) M. Hankey [1]
1907	Sir C. Ottley	1938	H. Ismay

Ministry of Defence. The C.I.D. was replaced by a cabinet defence committee, with executive power, and the Ministry of Defence was set up as a regular department on 1 Jan 47. It existed as an administrative body, responsible for liaison between the Service Ministries and co-ordination of defence policy until 31 Mar 64.

On 1 Apr 64, a new unified Ministry of Defence was created which absorbed the four separate departments, the Admiralty, the War Office, the Air Ministry and the former Ministry of Defence. This Department is now responsible for the formulation of defence policy and administration of the Armed Forces. The Ministry is broadly organised into central staffs, who are concerned with general defence policy and strategy, and staffs, under the Admiralty Board, the Army Board and the Air Force Board, who are responsible for the control and administration of the three Services. The Minister in charge of the department is the Secretary of State for Defence and he is assisted by two Ministers responsible for Administration and Equipment respectively, and three Under-secretaries of State for the Royal Navy, the Army and the Royal Air Force. At the same time a new appointment of Chief of Defence Staff was created.

SOURCES.—F. A. Johnson, *Defence by Committee* (1960); D. N. Chester and F. M. G. Willson, *The Organisation of British Central Government* (1957); J. Ehrman, *Cabinet Government and War, 1890–1940* (1958). *Whitaker's Almanack 1965.*

[1] Sir M. Hankey (later Ld Hankey) became the Joint Secretary to the C.I.D. and the cabinet in 1916, and in 1923 he was also appointed Clerk to the Privy Council.

T

Total Forces Serving [a] (year ending 31 March)
(to nearest '000)

	1900	1910	1920	1930	1940 [b]	1950 [b]	1960	1965
Army	661	522	435	333	1,688	360	252	187
Royal Navy [d]	98	128	133	97	282	135	93	96
Royal Air Force	..	..	28	33	303	193	158	123
Total Forces	759 [c]	650	596	463	2,273 [e]	688	503	406

[a] Men locally enlisted abroad are excluded, except that the figures for the army include those whose documents are held in the U.K.
[b] Including Women's Auxiliaries. The figures for the war years include a number of casualties that had not been reported on the dates to which the figures relate. They also include men and women locally enlisted abroad.
[c] Including 278,000 non-regulars.
[d] Excluding the Royal Marine Police, except in 1940.
[e] The total strength of the Armed Forces reached its war-time peak in 1945 with 5,098,100 men and women serving.

Total Expenditure on Defence [a] (year ending 31 March)
(£ millions)

	1899–1900	1909–10	1919–20	1929–30	1939–40	1949–50	1959–60	1964–65
War Office	43·6	27·2	395·0	40·5	81·9	291·8	428·2	506·6
Navy	26·0	35·8	156·5	55·8	69·4	186·8	364·6	473·9
Air Force	..	..	52·5	16·8	66·6	201·6	485·1	491·8
Defence Total [b]	69·8	63·0	604·0	113·1	626·4 [c]	740·7	1,475·7	1,909·0

[a] The figures refer to the Exchequer of the U.K. and include Northern Ireland only to the extent that services, taxes, etc., are reserved to the U.K. Parliament.
[b] The discrepancies between the service votes and the totals are due to the expenditures of the Ministries of Defence and Civil Aviation (1950 and 1960), and the Army Ordnance Factories.
[c] Including votes of credit of £408·5 m. Defence expenditure reached its war-time peak in 1944–5 at £5,125·0 m.

SOURCES.—*The Annual Abstract of Statistics, 1900–*; for a brief summary of the statistics. The *Army, Navy* and *Air Estimates* giving the full figures, are published annually as government white papers up to 31 Mar 64. From 1 Apr 64 figures are those given in Ministry of Defence Estimates.

Conscription

After a long controversy about conscription, H. Asquith announced the introduction of the first *Military Service Bill* on 5 Jan 16. Military service lapsed in 1919. It was first introduced in peace time on 26 Apr 39. The period of compulsory service was to have been six months, but war intervened. Conscription was extended to women from Dec 1941 until Jan 1947, but few women were called up after Nov 1944. The *National Service Act, 1947* provided for the continuation of military service after the war. The period of service was twelve months. It was increased to eighteen months in Dec 1948, and to two years in Sep 1950. A government white paper published on 5 Apr 57 [1] announced a progressive reduction in the national service intake. No men were to be called up after the end of 1960, so that by the end of 1962 there were no national servicemen left in the forces. (This was slightly modified by the *Army Reserves Bill*, introduced in 1962.)

[1] Cmnd. 124/1957.

Rationing

The first national rationing scheme in this country came into operation on 31 Dec 17, with the rationing of sugar. This was followed in Jul 1918 by national schemes for meat, lard, bacon, ham, butter and margarine. The abolition of rationing began on 28 Jul 18 and was completed on 29 Nov 20. Butter and meat rations were most severely restricted in Apr–May 1918 and sugar in 1919. There was much controversy during the course of World War I over the form that rationing should take. National rationing was preceded by local schemes and even after Jul 1918 rationing was, in many cases, wider in extent locally than nationally. The characteristic feature of the World War I scheme was the tie to the retailer of each customer.

When World War II broke out in Sep 1939, prearranged plans for commodity control were at once put into effect. Rationing was introduced on 8 Jan 40 when bacon, butter, and sugar were put under control and extended during the following two years to meat, tea, margarine, lard, jam, marmalade, cheese, eggs, and milk. In Dec 1941 the 'points' system was introduced to ration such items as tinned meat and biscuits and from Jul 1942 sweets and chocolate were rationed under a system of 'personal points'. During the war animal feedstuffs, fertilisers, farm machinery, petrol, domestic coal, clothing and textiles were also rationed. Rationing was at its most stringent, however, in the immediate post-war years. In Jul 46, bread rationing, which in 1939 the Minister of Food had described as 'the last resort of a starving nation', was introduced for the first time ever and this was followed in Nov 1947 by the rationing of potatoes. In Dec 1947 the distribution of nearly all important foods was controlled with the exception of some fresh fruit and vegetables, fish and coffee; the bacon, butter, meat and fats rations were at their lowest ebbs and the basic petrol ration had been suspended altogether. The gradual abolition of rationing began in Apr 1948; it was not completed until the abolition of meat and butter rationing in Jul 1956, and of coal rationing in 1958.

During the Suez crisis of 1956, petrol rationing was re-introduced. It lasted from 17 Dec 56 to 14 May 57.

Principal Military Operations

Boer War, 1899–1902

Following the rejection by the British Government of the Boer ultimatum, the Transvaal and Orange Free State declared war on Britain in October 1899. Major operations against the Boers ended in the summer of 1900, but guerrilla warfare continued. Peace was finally concluded at Vereeniging on 31 May 02.

First World War, 1914–1918

Britain declared war on Germany on 4 Aug 14, when German troops invaded Belgium and on Austria-Hungary on 10 Aug 14. Turkey joined the Central Powers in Nov 1914, and Bulgaria in May 1915. On 30 Oct 18 an armistice was agreed between the Allied Powers and the Ottoman

Government. On 3 Nov 18 there was an armistice with Austria-Hungary, and on 11 Nov 18 with the German Government. The Treaty of Versailles was signed on 28 Jun 19.

Intervention in Russia, 1918–1919

British troops landed at Murmansk and Archangel in June and August of 1918. Troops also entered the Transcaucasus in August 1918. The withdrawal of troops from the Transcaucasus was completed by 5 Apr 19; and from Murmansk and Archangel by 28 Sep 19.[1]

Second World War, 1939–1945

Britain declared war on Germany on 3 Sep 39, following the German invasion of Poland. On 10 Jun 40 Italy declared war on Britain. In 1941 Bulgaria, Finland, Hungary, and Roumania joined the Axis powers. Britain declared war on Japan on 8 Dec 41. The declaration of the defeat of Germany was made on 8 May 45. On 14 Aug 45 the Japanese surrendered and the war in the Far East was officially ended. (The first atom bomb was dropped by the Americans on Hiroshima on 5 Aug 45, and the second on Nagasaki on 9 Aug 45.)

Korean War, 1950–1953

Britain declared her support for the United States' action in Korea on 28 Jun 50, following the invasion of South Korea by North Korean troops, and the call for a cease fire by an emergency session of the United Nations Security Council. The intervention of Chinese troops fighting with the North Koreans was confirmed on 6 Nov 50. An armistice was signed between the United Nations and the Communist forces on 27 Jul 53.

Suez, 1956

Following the Egyptian nationalisation of the Suez Canal on 26 Jul 56, tension grew in the Middle East. The Israeli army attacked the Egyptians on 29 Oct 56 in the Sinai peninsula. The rejection of a British and French ultimatum by Egypt resulted in a combined British and French attack on Egypt on 1 Nov 56. Operations were halted at midnight on 6–7 Nov 56. On 26 Jan 61 full diplomatic relations were resumed between Britain and Egypt.

BRITISH COSTS AND CASUALTIES IN THE MAJOR WARS [a]

War	Total Engaged ('000s)	Killed [b] ('000s)	Percentage, Col. 3 to Col. 2	Cost (£m.)
1899–1902 Boer War	448	22	4·9	217
1914–18 World War I	9,669 [c]	947 [c]	9·8	3,810
1939–45 World War II	5,896 [d]	265 [d]	4·5	34,423

[a] These figures, particularly for World War I, are open to dispute.
[b] Including those dying of wounds, of disease, and while prisoners of war.
[c] Empire figures.   [d] Great Britain

SOURCE.—*Chambers's Encyclopaedia.*

[1] C. H. Ellis, *Operations in Transcaspia, 1918–19* (St Antony's Papers, No. 6, 1959), and R. H. Ullman, *Anglo-Soviet Relations, 1917–21*, Vol. I. *Intervention and the War* (Princeton, 1961).

British casualties in the Korean war were 749 killed.[1] Casualties in the Suez attack were 21 men killed.[2] The total expenditure incurred on the Korean War by Britain was about £50 m.[3] The military expenditure incurred by the Suez operation was about £30 m.[4]

Major War Commanders

World War I

Allenby, E. 1st Vt (1919). 1861–1936
    Field-Marshal. C-in-C Egyptian Expeditionary Force 1917–19.
Beatty, D. 1st E (1919). 1871–1936
    Admiral of the Fleet. Commanded Grand Fleet 1916–19.
Fisher, J. 1st Ld (1909). 1841–1920
    Admiral of the Fleet. 1st Sea Lord 1914–15.
French, J. 1st E of Ypres. 1852–1925
    Field-Marshal. C-in-C British Expeditionary Force in France 1914–15.
    C-in-C Home Forces 1916.
Haig, J. 1st E (1919). 1861–1928
    Field-Marshal. Commanding 1st Army 1914–15. C-in-C Expeditionary Forces in France and Flanders 1915–19.
Hamilton, I. Sir (1915). 1853–1947
    General. C-in-C Mediterranean Expeditionary Force 1915.
Jellicoe, J. 1st E of (1925). 1859–1935
    Admiral of the Fleet. Commanded Grand Fleet 1914–16.
Plumer, H. 1st Vt (1929). 1857–1932
    Field-Marshal. General Officer Commanding Italian Expeditionary Force 1917–18. 2nd Army British Expeditionary Force 1918–19.
Robertson, W. Sir. 1st Bt (1919). 1860–1933
    Field-Marshal. Chief of Imperial General Staff 1915–18. C-in-C Eastern Command 1918. Great Britain 1918–19. B.A.O.R. 1919–20.
Trenchard, H. 1st Vt (1936). 1873–1956
    Marshal of the RAF. Assistant Commandant Central Flying School 1913–14. G.O.C. Royal Flying Corps in the Field 1915–17. Chief of Air Staff 1918–29.
Wilson, H. Sir. 1st Bt (1919). 1864–1922
    Field-Marshal. Assistant Chief of General Staff to Ld French 1914.
    Commanded 1st Army Corps 1915–16. Eastern Command 1917.
    British Military Representative Versailles 1917.

World War II

Alexander, H. 1st E (1952). 1891–
    Field-Marshal. C-in-C Middle East 1942–43. C-in-C North Africa 1943. C-in-C Allied Armies in Italy 1943–44. Supreme Allied Commander Mediterranean Theatre 1944–45.

[1] H.C. Deb., 1952–53, Vol. 518, Cols. *221-222.*
[2] H.C. Deb., 1956–57, Vol. 561, Col *36.*
[3] H.C. Deb., 1952–53, Vol. 517, Col. *1218.*
[4] H.C. Deb., 1956–57, Vol. 575, Col. *51.*

Auchinleck, C. Sir. 1884–
> Field-Marshal. C-in-C India 1941 and 1943–47. C-in-C Middle East 1941–42.

Brooke-Popham, H. Sir. 1878–1953
> Air Chief Marshal. C-in-C Far East 1940–41.

Cunningham, A. 1st Vt of Hindhope (1946). 1883–1962.
> Admiral of the Fleet. Ld Commissioner of the Admiralty and Deputy Chief of Naval Staff 1938–39. C-in-C Mediterranean 1939–42. Naval C-in-C Expeditionary Force North Africa 1942. C-in-C Mediterranean 1943. 1st Sea Ld and Chief of Naval Staff 1943–46.

Dill, J. Sir. 1881–1944
> Field-Marshal. Commanded 1st Corps in France 1939–40. Chief of I.G.S. 1940. British Representative on Combined Chief of Staffs' Committee in U.S. 1941.

Douglas, W. 1st Ld (1948). 1893–
> Marshal of the RAF. C-in-C Fighter Command 1940–43. Air Officer C-in-C Middle East 1943–44. Air Officer C-in-C Coastal Command 1944–45. Air C-in-C British Air Forces of Occupation in Germany 1945–46.

Dowding, H. 1st Ld (1943) 1882–
> Air Chief Marshal. Air Officer C-in-C Fighter Command 1936–1940.

Fraser, B. 1st Ld (1946). 1888–
> C-in-C Home Fleet 1943–44. C-in-C Eastern Fleet 1944–45.

Gort, J. 6th Vt Ireland (1902). 1st Vt UK (1945) 1886–1946
> Field-Marshal. C-in-C British Expeditionary Force 1939–40. Commanded B.E.F. in withdrawal towards Dunkirk 1940.

Harris, A. Sir. 1st Bt (1953). 1893–
> Marshal of the RAF. C-in-C Bomber Command 1942–45.

Ironside, W. 1st Ld (1941). 1880–1959
> Field-Marshal. C.I.G.S. 1939–40. C-in-C Home Forces 1940.

Leigh-Mallory, T. Sir. 1892–1944
> Air Chief Marshal. Air Officer C-in-C Fighter Command 1942. Air C-in-C Allied Expeditionary Force 1943–44. Lost while flying to take up appointment as Allied Air C-in-C South-East Asia.

Montgomery, B. 1st Vt of Alamein (1946). 1887–
> Field-Marshal. Commander 8th Army 1942 in N. Africa, Sicily and Italy. C-in-C British Group of Allied Armies N. France 1944. British Commander Allied Expeditionary Forces in Europe 1944–46.

Mountbatten, L. 1st E of Burma (1947). 1900–
> Admiral of the Fleet. Chief of Combined Operations 1942–43. Supreme Allied Command S.E. Asia 1943–46.

Percival, A. 1887–1966
> Lieutenant-General. G.O.C. Malaya 1941–42.

Portal C. 1st Vt (1946) 1893–
  Marshal of the RAF. Air Officer C-in-C Bomber Command 1940.
  Chief of the Air Staff 1940–45.

Pound, D. Sir. 1877–1943
  Admiral of the Fleet. C-in-C Mediterranean 1936–39.

Ramsay, B. Sir. 1883–1945
  Admiral. Flag Officer commanding Dover 1939–42. Naval Commander Eastern Task Force Mediterranean 1943.

Ritchie, N. Sir. 1897–
  General. Commander of 8th Army, Libya, 1941.

Slim, W. 1st Vt (1960) 1891–
  Field-Marshal. C-in-C Allied Land Forces S.E. Asia 1945–46.

Tedder, A. 1st Ld (1946). 1890–1967
  Marshal of the RAF. Air Officer C-in-C Middle East 1941–43. Air C-in-C Mediterranean Air Command 1943. Deputy Supreme Commander under Gen. Eisenhower 1943–45.

Wavell, A. 1st E (1947). 1883–1950
  Field-Marshal. Formed Middle East Command 1939. C-in-C India 1941. Supreme Commander S.W. Pacific 1941–43.

XIX

THE PRESS[1]

National Daily Newspapers

(British Gazette), 5–13 May 1926
Proprietors: His Majesty's Stationery Office. Printed at offices of *Morning Post.*
Policy: Strong opposition to the general strike.
Editor: W. Churchill.

(Daily Chronicle), 1869–1930
Proprietors: E. Lloyd, 1871–1918. Frank Lloyd and family trading as United Newspapers Ltd. Lloyd family parted with their interest in 1918. Incorporated with *Daily News* as the *News Chronicle,* 1930.
Policy: Liberal.
Editors: W. Fisher, 1899. R. Donald, 1902. E. Perris, 1918–30.

(Daily Citizen), 1912–Jan 1915
Proprietors: Labour Newspapers Ltd.
Policy: Official Labour.
Editor: F. Dilnot, 1912–15.

Daily Express, 1900
Proprietors: A. Pearson, Daily Express (1900) Ltd. Acquired by Ld Beaverbrook, London Express Newspaper Ltd., 1915. 1954 control relinquished by Ld Beaverbrook to Beaverbrook Newspapers Ltd. Block of shares transferred to the Beaverbrook Foundation.
Policy: Independent conservative.
Editors: A. Pearson, 1900. R. Blumenfeld, 1902. B. Baxter, 1929. A. Christiansen, 1933. E. Pickering, 1957. R. Wood, 1962. R. Edwards, 1964. D. Marks, 1965.

(Daily Graphic), 1890–1926. 1946–52
Proprietors: Founded by W. L. Thomas. Owned by H. Baines & Co. Amalgamated with *Daily Sketch* in 1926 (Kemsley Newspapers). Appeared as *Daily Sketch and Daily Graphic* 1926–46, as *Daily Graphic* 1946–52, then as *Daily Sketch.*
Policy: Independent conservative.
Editors: H. Hall, 1891. H. White, 1907. W. Ackland, 1909. A. Hutchinson, 1912. A. Netting, 1917. H. Lawton, 1919. E. Tebbutt, 1923. H. Heywood, 1925–6. A. Thornton, 1946. N. Hamilton, 1947. H. Clapp, 1948–52 (see *Daily Sketch*).

(Daily Herald), 1912–1964
Proprietors: Daily Herald Printing and Publishing Society in association with Odhams Press Ltd. Formed Daily Herald (1929) Ltd. (Chair-

---

[1] The policies of national newspapers between 1900 and 1967 have inevitably fluctuated. 'Policy' should here be taken only as a general indication of the nature of the paper. In very few cases have newspapers been the official organs of a political party.

man : Ld Southwood). 49 per cent of shares held by T.U.C., 51 per cent by Odhams Press. 1960 new agreement between Odhams Press and T.U.C. 1961 Daily Mirror Newspapers, Ltd. take over Odham's Press. T.U.C. sign agreement for the paper to be published by the Mirror Group (International Publishing Corporation). 1964 T.U.C. sold their 49% holding to I.P.C. 1964, replaced by the *Sun*.

Policy: General support to Labour Movement, 1912–23, 1960–. Official Labour 1923–60.

Editors: R. Kenny, 1912. C. Lapworth, 1913. G. Lansbury, 1913. W. Ryan, 1922. H. Fyfe, 1923. W. Mellor, 1926. W. Stevenson, 1931. F. Williams, 1937. P. Cudlipp, 1940. S. Elliott, 1953. D. Machray, 1957. J. Beavan, 1960.

(Issued as a weekly paper during 1st World War, launched again as a daily in 1919.)

Daily Mail, 1896
Proprietors: A. Harmsworth (Ld Northcliffe), Associated Newspapers Ltd.
  Policy: Independent. Right-wing Conservative.
  Editors: T. Marlowe, 1899. W. Fish, 1926. O. Pulvermacher, 1929. W. McWhirter, 1930. W. Warden, 1931. A. Cranfield, 1935. R. Prew, 1939. S. Horniblow, 1944. F. Owen, 1947. G. Schofield, 1950. A. Wareham, 1955. W. Hardcastle, 1959. M. Randall, 1963. A. Brittenden, 1966.

Daily Mirror, 1903
Proprietors: A. Harmsworth, Sir H. Harmsworth (Ld Rothermere), 1914. Pictorial Newspaper (1910) Co. Daily Mirror Newspapers Ltd. 1961, bought by International Publishing Corporation (Chairman: C. King. H. Cudlipp, 1968).
  Policy: Independent.
  Editors: Mary Howarth, 1903. H. Fyfe, 1904. A. Kinealy, 1907. E. Flynn, 1915. A. Campbell, 1919. L. Brownlee, 1931. C. Thomas, 1934. S. Bolam, 1948. J. Nener, 1953. L. Howard, 1960.

(Daily News), 1846–1930
Proprietors: Daily News Ltd., 1901 (Chairman: G. Cadbury, 1901–11). Amalgamated with *Morning Leader*, as *Daily News and Leader*, 1912. Amalgamated with *Westminster Gazette*, 1928. Amalgamated with *Daily Chronicle*, 1930. Continued as *News Chronicle* (see below).
  Policy: Liberal.
  Editors: E. Cook, 1896. R. Lehmann, 1901. A. Gardiner, 1902. S. Hodgson, 1920–30.

(Daily Paper), 1904 (32 issues only)
Proprietor: W. Stead.
  Policy: 'A paper for the abnormally scrupulous'.
  Editor: W. Stead.

Daily Sketch, 1908
Proprietors: E. Hulton and Co. Ltd. Daily Mirror Newspapers Ltd., and Sunday Pictorial Newspapers (1920) Ltd. Bought by the Berry brothers, 1926, and merged with the *Daily Graphic*. Name changed to *Daily Graphic*, 1946–52. Subsidiary of Allied

Newspapers Ltd. Kemsley Newspapers Ltd. Bought by Associated Newspapers Ltd., 1952. Renamed *Daily Sketch*, 1953.

Policy: Independent conservative.

Editors: J. Heddle, 1909. W. Robinson, 1914. H. Lane, 1919. H. Gates, 1922. H. Lane, 1923. A. Curthoys, 1928. A. Sinclair, 1936. S. Carroll, 1939. L. Berry, 1942. A. Thornton and M. Watts, 1943. A. Thornton, 1944. N. Hamilton, 1947. H. Clapp, 1948. H. Gunn, 1953. C. Valdar, 1959. H. French, 1962.

Daily Telegraph, 1855

Proprietors: Ld Burnham and family. Sold to Sir W. Berry (Ld Camrose), Sir G. Berry (Ld Kemsley) and Sir E. Iliffe (Ld) in 1928. Absorbed *Morning Post*, as *Daily Telegraph and Morning Post* in 1937. Ld Camrose acquired Ld Kemsley's and Ld Iliffe's interests in 1937. M. Berry (Ld Hartwell) succeeded him as Editor-in-Chief in 1968.

Policy: Conservative.

Editors: (Sir) J. le Sage, 1885. F. Miller, 1923. A. Watson, 1924. (Sir) C. Coote, 1950. M. Green, 1964.

(Daily Worker), 1930–1966

Proprietors: Daily Worker Cooperative Society Ltd. Descendant of the *Sunday Worker*, 1925–30. Publication suppressed 1941–42. Changed name to *Morning Star*, 1966.

Editors: W. Rust, 1930. J. Shields, 1932. I. Cox, 1935. R. Palme Dutt, 1936. W. Rust, 1939. J. Campbell, 1949. G. Matthews, 1959–1966.

(Financial News), 1884–1945

Proprietors: Financial News Ltd, 1898 (H. Marks). Incorporated with the *Financial Times* in 1945.

Policy: Finance, independent.

Editors: H. Marks, 1884. Dr Ellis, 1916. H. O'Neill, 1921. W. Dorman and W. Lang, 1921. Sir L. Worthington-Evans, 1924. Sir E. Young, 1925. O. Hobson, 1929. M. Green, 1934. H. Parkinson, 1938–45.

Financial Times, 1888

Proprietors: Financial Times Ltd. Incorporated Financier and Bullionist. Incorporated the *Financial News* in 1945. Merged with Westminster Press Ltd. as Financial and Provincial Publishers, Ltd. 1967.

Policy: Finance, independent.

Editors: W. Lawson. A. Murray, 1901. C. Palmer, 1909. D. Hunter, 1924. A. Chisholm, 1938. A. Cole, 1940. H. Parkinson, 1945. (Sir) G. Newton, 1950.

(Manchester) Guardian, 1821

Proprietors: The Manchester Guardian & Evening News Ltd. Renamed *Guardian*, 1959. The Scott Trust.

Policy: Independent liberal.

Editors: C. P. Scott, 1872. E. Scott, 1929. W. Crozier, 1932. A. Wadsworth, 1944. A. Hetherington, 1956.

(Majority), 1906 (10–14 Jul only)

Proprietors: Majority Ltd.

Policy: 'The organ of all who work for wage or salary'.

Morning Advertiser, 1794

Proprietors: Incorporated Society of Licensed Victuallers.

Policy: Defence of the interests of licensed trade.
Editors: F. Doney, 1894. H. Fyfe, 1902. G. Talbot, 1903. H. Byshe,
   1913. A. Jackson, 1924. H. Bennett, 1927. F. Millman, 193?.
   E. Hopwood, 1947. D. Quick, 1954. L. Forse, 1956.

(Morning Herald), 1892–1900
   Proprietors: Morning Newspaper Co. Became *London Morning* in 1898, and
      Morning Herald in 1899. Merged with *Daily Express* in 1900.
   Policy: Independent.
   Editor: D. Murray, 1892–1900.

(Morning Leader), 1892–1912
   Proprietors: Colman family of Norwich. Merged with *Daily News*, as *Daily
      News and Leader* in 1912 (see *Daily News*).
   Policy: Liberal.
   Editor: E. Parke, 1892–1912.

(Morning Post), 1772–1937
   Proprietors: Sir A. Borthwick (Ld Glenesk), 1876–1908. Lady Bathurst,
      1908–24. Absorbed in *Daily Telegraph* in 1937 (Ld Camrose).
   Policy: Conservative.
   Editors: J. Dunn, 1897. S. Wilkinson, 1905. F. Ware, 1905. H. Gwynne,
      1911–37.

(Morning Standard), 1857–1917
   Proprietors: Bought from Johnston family by A. Pearson, 1904. Sold to
      D. Dalziel (Ld) in 1910. Ceased, 1917.
   Policy: From 1904 supporter of tariff reform.
   Editors: W. Mudford, 1874. G. Curtis, 1900. H. Gwynne, 1904. H.
      White, 1911–17.

Morning Star, 1966
   Proprietors: Morning Star Co-operative Society. Successor to the *Daily Worker*.
   Policy: Communist.
   Editor: G. Matthews, 1966.

(New Daily), 25 Apr 1960–66
   Proprietors: The British Newspaper Trust Ltd. Sponsored by the People's
      League for the Defence of Freedom, the Free Press Society, and
      the Anti-Socialist Front.
   Policy: 'The only daily newspaper in Great Britain independent of com-
      bines and trade unions.'
   Editor: E. Martell, 1960–66.

(News Chronicle), 1930–60
   Proprietors: Amalgamation of *Daily News and Leader* and *Daily Chronicle* in
      1930 (Cadbury family). Bought by Associated Newspapers Ltd.
      in 1960, and merged with *Daily Mail*.
   Policy: Liberal.
   Editors: T. Clarke, 1930. A. Vallance, 1933. G. Barry, 1936. R. Cruik-
      shank, 1948. M. Curtis, 1954. N. Cursley, 1957.

(Recorder), 27 Oct 1953–17 May 1954
   Proprietors: The Recorder Ltd. (Managing Director: E. Martell). A weekly
      suburban newspaper 1870–1939, continued as a weekly after 1954.

Policy: Independent.   'Keynote: pride in Britain and the British Empire.'
Editor: W. Brittain, 1953–4.

Sun, 1964
Proprietors: International Publishing Corporation (Chairman: C. King. H. Cudlipp, 1968).
Policy: Labour.
Editors: S. Jacobson, 1964.   R. Dinsdale, 1965.

The Times, 1785
Proprietors: Founded as the *Daily Universal Register*, became *The Times* in 1788.   Owned by the Walter family, 1785–1908.   Bought by Ld Northcliffe in 1908.   Owned by J. Astor and J. Walter in 1922. 7 Aug 24, Times Association formed (comprising Lord Chief Justice, Warden of All Souls, Oxford, President of the Royal Society, President of the Institute of Chartered Accountants and Governor of the Bank of England).   21 Dec 66, Monopolies Commission approves common ownership of *The Times* and *The Sunday Times* by The Thomson Organisation.   Times Newspapers Ltd. formed.   President: G. Astor.   Chairman: Sir W. Haley.   1967 K. Thomson.
Policy: Independent conservative.
Editors: G. Buckle, 1884.   G. Dawson, 1912.   H. Steed, 1919.   G. Dawson, 1922.   R. Barrington-Ward, 1941.   W. Casey, 1948.   Sir W. Haley, 1952.   W. Rees-Mogg, 1967.

(Tribune), 1906 only
Proprietors: F. Thomasson.
Policy: Liberal.
Editors: W. Hill and S. Pryor, 1906.

(Westminster Gazette), 1921–8 issued as a morning paper.
(See *Evening Papers*).

National Sunday Newspapers
(excluding all those not published in London)

((Illustrated) Sunday Herald), 1915–27
Proprietors: Sir E. Hulton.   Renamed *Illustrated Sunday Herald*.   Bought by Berry family in 1926 and renamed *Sunday Graphic* in 1927 (see below).
Policy: Independent conservative.
Editors: J. E. Williams.   T. Hill, 1926–7.

(National News), 1917–18
Proprietors: Odhams Press Ltd.
Policy: Independent.
Editor: A. de Beck, 1917–18

News of the World, 1843
Proprietors: News of the World Ltd.   (Sir) G. Riddell (Ld), 1903–34.   The Carr family 1934–69.   1969–News Ltd., (R. Murdoch).
Policy: Independent conservative.
Editors: Sir E. Carr, 1891.   D. Davies, 1941.   R. Skelton, 1946.   A. Waters, 1947.   R. Cudlipp, 1953.   S. Somerfield, 1959.

Observer, 1791
Proprietors: F. Beer. Bought by Ld Northcliffe in 1905. Bought by W.
Astor (Vt) in 1911. 1945 became the Observer Trust Ltd.
Chairmen: Vt Astor, 1945. D. Foot, 1953. Sir I. Evans, 1957.
Policy: Conservative. Independent since 1942.
Editors: F. Beer, 1894. A. Harrison, 1905. J. Garvin, 1908. I. Brown,
1942. D. Astor, 1948.

People, 1881
Proprietors: W. Madge and Sir G. Armstrong. Sir W. Madge, 1914–22.
M. L. Publishing Co. Ltd. The People Ltd. Odhams Press.
1961 amalgamated with International Publishing Corporation
(Chairman: C. King. H. Cudlipp, 1968).
Policy: Independent.
Editors: J. Hatton. J. Sansome 1913. H. Swaffer 1924. H. Ainsworth
1925. S. Campbell, 1958. R. Edwards, 1966.

(Reynolds News), 1850–1967
Proprietors: Originally *Reynolds's Weekly Newspaper,* and later *Reynolds's
Illustrated News.* Owned by J. Dicks and family since 1879.
H. Dalziel (Ld)[1] appointed business manager in 1907. He
became the sole proprietor in 1914. Bought by the National
Co-operative Press Ltd. Incorporated the *Sunday Citizen,*
1962. Changed name to *Sunday Citizen and Reynolds News,*
Policy: Support for the Labour and Co-operative movements.
Editors: W. Thompson, 1894. H. Dalziel, 1907. J. Crawley, 1920.
S. Elliott, 1929. Sir W. Richardson, 1941–67

(Sunday Citizen), 1962–67. (*See above, Reynolds News.*)

(Sunday Dispatch), 1801–1961
Proprietors: Sir G. Newnes. Originally the *Weekly Dispatch* until 1928.
Bought by the Harmsworth family. Ld Northcliffe, Ld Rother-
mere from 1928. Associated Newspapers Ltd. Absorbed by
the *Sunday Express* in 1961.
Policy: Independent conservative.
Editors: M. Cotton. H. Swaffer, 1915. B. Falk, 1919. H. Lane, 1933. W.
Brittain, 1934. C. Brooks, 1936. C. Eade, 1938. H. Gunn, 1959–61.

Sunday Express, 1918
Proprietors: Sunday Express Ltd. (Ld Beaverbrook).
Policy: Independent conservative.
Editors: J. Douglas, 1920. J. Gordon, 1928. J. Junor, 1954.

(Sunday Graphic (and Sunday News)), 1915–60
Proprietors: Sir E. Hulton. Originally called the *Sunday Herald,* renamed the
Illustrated Sunday Herald. Bought by the Berry family in
1926, and renamed the *Sunday Graphic* in 1927. Daily Graphic
and Sunday Graphic Ltd., a subsidiary of Ld Kemsley's news-
papers. Incorporated the *Sunday News* in 1931. Bought by
R. Thomson in 1959. Ceased publication in 1960.
Policy: Independent.
Editors: T. Hill, 1927. A. Sinclair, 1931. R. Simpson, 1935. M. Watts,
1947. N. Hamilton, 1947. I. Lang, 1948. A. Josey, 1949.
B. Horniblow, 1950. P. Brownrigg, 1952. M. Randell, 1953.
G. McKenzie, 1953. A. Hall, 1958. R. Anderson, 1959. A.
Ewart, 1960.

[1] Ld Dalziel of Kirkcaldy, not to be confused with Ld Dalziel of Wooler, who was proprietor of the
Evening Standard 1910–15.

(Sunday Illustrated), 1921–23
Proprietor: H. Bottomley.
  Policy: Independent.
  Editor: H. Bottomley.

(Sunday (Illustrated) News), 1842–1931
Proprietors: Originally *Lloyd's Sunday News.* Sunday News Ltd. United
  Newspapers Ltd (W. Harrison). Merged with the *Sunday
  Graphic* in 1931.
  Policy: Independent liberal.
  Editors: T. Catling. W. Robinson, 1919. E. Perris, 1924. E. Wallace,
  1929–31.

Sunday Mirror, 1963
Proprietors: International Publishing Corporation.
  Policy: Independent.
  Editor: M. Christiansen, 1963.

(Sunday Pictorial), 1915–1963
Proprietors: The Harmsworth family. Taken over by Ld Rothermere in
  1922. Sunday Pictorial Newspapers (1920) Ltd. 1961 absorbed
  by International Publishing Corporation (Cecil King). 1963.
  Became *Sunday Mirror (see above).*
  Policy: Independent.
  Editors: F. Sanderson, 1915. W. McWhirter, 1921. D. Grant, 1924. W.
  McWhirter, 1928. D. Grant, 1929. H. Cudlipp, 1938. R.
  Campbell, 1940. H. Cudlipp, 1946. P. Zec, 1949. H. Cudlipp,
  1952. C. Valdar, 1953. L. Howard, 1959. R. Payne, 1960.

((Sunday) Referee), 1877–1939
Proprietors: Printed by the Daily News Ltd. Owned by I. Ostrer. Incor-
  porated in the *Sunday Chronicle* in 1939 (which was published in
  Manchester and ceased independent publication in 1955).
  Policy: Conservative.
  Editors: R. Butler. R. Donald, 1922. A. Laber, 1924. M. Joulden, 1933.

(Sunday Special), 1897–1904
Proprietor: H. Schmidt.

Sunday Telegraph, 1961
Proprietors: The Sunday Telegraph Ltd (M. Berry (Ld Hartwell)).
  Policy: Independent conservative.
  Editor: D. Maclachlan, 1961, B. Roberts, 1966.

Sunday Times, 1822
Proprietors: Mrs. F. Beer. Bought by H. Schmidt. Amalgamated with the
  Sunday Special in 1904. Bought by the Berry family in 1915.
  Bought by R. Thomson in 1959. Thomson Allied Newspapers.
  1967, Times Newspapers Ltd, formed to run *The Times* and
  Sunday Times.
  Policy: Independent conservative.
  Editors: L. Rees, 1901. W. Hadley, 1932. H. Hodson, 1950. C.
  Hamilton, 1961. H. Evans, 1967.

(Sunday Worker), 1925–30
Proprietors: The Communist Party through nominees. Published daily as
  the *Daily Worker* from 1930.
  Policy: Communist.
  Editors: W. Paul, 1925. W. Holmes, 1927.

London Evening Newspapers

(Evening Echo and Chronicle), 22 Mar–4 May 1915
Proprietor: E. Lloyd. Merged with *Star*.
  Policy: Liberal
  Editor:

(Echo), 1868–1905
Proprietors: Consolidated Newspapers. F. Pethick-Lawrence in control, 1901–5.
  Policy: Radical, progressive.
  Editors: W. Crook, 1898. T. Meech, 1900. P. Alden, 1901. F. Pethick-Lawrence, 1901–5.

Evening News, 1881
Proprietors: A. Harmsworth (Evening News Ltd.), 1894. Associated Newspapers Ltd., 1905.
  Policy: Conservative.
  Editors: W. Evans, 1896. C. Beattie, 1922. F. Fitzhugh, 1924. G. Schofield, 1943. J. Marshall, 1950. R. Willis, 1954. J. Gold, 1967.

Evening Standard, 1827
Proprietors: Bought by A. Pearson from Johnston family in 1904. Absorbed *St James's Gazette* in 1905. D. Dalziel (Ld),[1] 1910. Hulton and Co. 1915–23. Incorporated with *Pall Mall Gazette* and *Globe*, 1923. Bought by Ld Beaverbrook in 1924.
  Policy: Independent conservative.
  Editors: S. Pryor, 1897. W. Woodward, 1906. J. Kilpatrick, 1912. D. Sutherland, 1914. A. Mann, 1916. D. Phillips, 1920. E. Thompson, 1923. G. Gilliat, 1928. P. Cudlipp, 1933. R. Thompson, 1938. F. Owen, 1939. M. Foot, 1942. S. Elliott, 1943. H. Gunn, 1944. P. Elland, 1950. C. Wintour, 1959.

(Evening Times), 1910–11
Proprietors: London Evening Newspaper Co. (J. Morrison, Sir S. Scott, J. Cowley).
  Policy: Conservative.
  Editors: C. Watney, E. Wallace.

(Globe), 1803–1921
Proprietors: (Sir) G. Armstrong, 1871–1907. H. Harmsworth, 1907–11. W. Madge, 1912–14. Absorbed by *Pall Mall Gazette* in 1921, incorporated with *Evening Standard* in 1923.
  Policy: Conservative.
  Editors: Sir G. Armstrong, 1895. P. Ogle, 1907. J. Harrison, 1908. C. Palmer, 1912. W. Peacock, 1915–21.

(Pall Mall Gazette), 1865–1923
Proprietors: W. Astor (Ld), 1892. Sir H. Dalziel, 1917. Sir J. Leigh, 1923. Incorporated with *Evening Standard* in 1923.
  Policy: Conservative.
  Editors: Sir D. Straight, 1896. F. Higginbottom, 1909. J. Garvin, 1912. D. Sutherland, 1915–23.

---

[1] Ld Dalziel of Wooler, not to be confused with Ld Dalziel of Kirkcaldy who was proprietor of *Reynolds' News*, 1914–29.

(St James's Gazette), 1880–1905
Proprietors: E. Steinkopff, 1888. W. Dallas Ross. A. Pearson, 1903. Amalgamated with *Evening Standard* in 1905.
Policy: Conservative.
Editors: H. Chisholm, 1897. R. McNeill, 1900. G. Fiennes, 1903. S. Pryor, 1904–5.

(Star), 1887–1960
Proprietors: Star Newspaper Co. Owned by Daily News Ltd. Bought by Associated Newspapers Ltd, and incorporated in *Evening News*, 1960.
Policy: Liberal.
Editors: E. Parke, 1891. J. Douglas, 1908. W. Pope, 1920. E. Chattaway, 1930. R. Cruikshank, 1936. A. Cranfield, 1941. R. McCarthy, 1957–60.

(Sun), 1893–1906
Proprietors: T. P. O'Connor. H. Bottomley, 1900. Sir G. Armstrong and W. Madge, 1904–6.
Policy: Literary, non-political.
Editors: T. P. O'Connor. T. Dahle.

(Westminster Gazette), 1893–1928
Proprietors: Sir G. Newnes, 1893. Liberal Syndicate (Chairman: Sir A. Mond), 1908–15. Last issue as evening paper 5 Nov 21. First issue as morning paper 7 Nov 21. Incorporated with *Daily News* in 1928.
Policy: Liberal.
Editors: J. Spender, 1896. J. Hobman, 1921–28.

Circulations of National Newspapers, 1910–1968

National Daily Newspapers
(to nearest '000)

	1910	1930	1939	1951	1960	1965	1968
D. Express	400	1,603	2,486	4,193	4,130	3,981	3,853
D. Herald/Sun	..	750[b]	2,000	2,071	1,467	1,274	1,066
D. Mail	900	1,968	1,510	2,245	2,084	2,464	2,095
D. Mirror	630	1,071	1,367[d]	4,567	4,545	4,957	5,034
D. News	320	900	..	..			..
D. Sketch	750[a]	1,013	850[d]	777	1,152	844	915
D. Telegraph	230	222[c]	640[d]	976[e]	1,155[e]	1,351	1,407
D. Worker/ M. Star	..	n.a.	100[d]	115	73[f]	..	n.a.
Guardian	40	47	51	140	190	270	281
M. Leader	250	..	..	..	..	..	..
M. Post	n.a.	119	..	..	..	..	..
N. Chronicle	800[a]	967	1,317	1,583	1,206	..	..
Times	45	187	213	254	255	258	401

Unless otherwise stated the figures are taken from *T. B. Browne's Advertiser's ABC*, 1910–40, and 1950–65 figures are from the Audit Bureau of Circulations, published in the *Newspaper Press Directory*.

[a] Circulation figure for 1915, *T. B. Browne.*
[b] P.E.P.: *Report on the British Press* (1938) gives 1082 for 1930.
[c] From the P.E.P. *Report.*
[d] From the P.E.P. *Report.* Figure for 1938.
[e] *Daily Telegraph* audited circulation figures.
[f] ABC circulation in 1956. Latest available figure.

National Sunday Newspapers
(to nearest '000)

	1900	1910	1930	1937	1951	1960	1965	1968
Lloyd's Weekly Newspaper	1,250	1,250	1,450[b]	..	..	..	..	..
News of the World	400	1,500	3,250[b]	3,850	8,407	6,664	6,176	6,191
Observer	60	n.a.	201	208	450	738	829	903
People	n.a.	n.a.	2,535	3,406	5,181	5,468	5,538	5,533
Reynolds News	2,000[a]	2,000[a]	420	426	712	329	236	..
Sunday Dispatch	n.a.	n.a.	1,197	741	2,631	1,520	..	..
Sunday Express	..	..	958	1,350	3,178	3,706	4,187	4,238
Sunday Graphic	..	..	1,100[b]	651	1,121	890	..	..
Sunday Mirror	..	..	..	..	..	..	5,022	8,132
Sunday Pictorial	..	..	1,883	1,345	5,170	5,461	..	..
Sunday Referee	n.a.	n.a.	73	342	..	..	..	..
Sunday Telegraph	..	..	..	..	..	..	662	713
Sunday Times	n.a.	n.a.	153	270	529	1,001	1,290	1,461

Unless otherwise stated, the figures are taken from *T. B. Browne's Advertiser's ABC*, 1900–30; the figures for 1937 are from the *Report of the Royal Commission on the Press, 1947–49* (Cmd. 7700 and 7690/1949); 1951–60 are the Audit Bureau of Circulations' figures quoted in the *Newspaper Press Directory*.

[a] These figures should be treated with caution. They are from an advertisement in *T. B. Browne's Advertiser's ABC* for 1901 and 1911.
[b] From *Sell's World Press*.

London Evening Newspapers
(to nearest '000)

	1905	1910	1930	1939	1951	1960	1965	1968
E. News	300	300	667	822	1,752	1,153	1,238	1,182
E. Standard	n.a.	160	n.a.	390	862	586	680	657
Star	250	327	744	503	1,228	744	..	..

All circulation figures for evening newspapers exclude Sporting Editions. 1905–39 figures from *T. B. Browne's Advertiser's ABC*; 1951–65 figures are from the Audit Bureau of Circulations, published in the *Newspaper Press Directory*. Information on the circulations of other evening papers is not available.

Provincial Morning Daily Newspapers 1900–

Sporting newspapers and publications such as the *Hull Shipping Gazette* and the Hartlepool *Daily Shipping List* have been omitted. Bold type indicates newspapers still being published on 1 Jan 67.

BATH—*Bath Daily Argus* (1870). Merged with local evening paper, *Bath Daily Chronicle*, in Jan 1900.

BEDFORD—*Bedford Daily Circular* (1903). Merged with *Bedford Record* July 1939.

BIRMINGHAM—*Daily Argus* (1891). Merged with local evening paper, *Birmingham Evening Dispatch*, Jan 1902.
Birmingham Daily Post (1857). Changed name to *Birmingham Post* May 1918. Became **Birmingham Post and Gazette** Nov. 1956.
Birmingham Daily Gazette (1862). Merged with *Midland Express* and changed name to *Birmingham Gazette and Express* 1904. Merged with *Birmingham Post* Nov 1956.

BRADFORD—*Bradford Observer* (1834). Changed name to *Yorkshire Daily Observer* Nov 1901. Changed name to *Yorkshire Observer* Jan 1909. Merged with local evening paper, *The Telegraph and Argus*, Nov 1956.

U

BRIGHTON—*Morning Argus* (1896).   Ceased publcation as morning paper May 1926.[1]
   Sussex Daily News (1868).   Merged with *Evening Argus* Mar 1956.
BRISTOL—*Bristol Western Daily Press* (1858).   Changed name to **Western Daily Press** 1928.
   Bristol Mercury (1790).   Changed name to *Bristol Daily Mercury* Dec 1901.   Ceased publication Nov 1909.
   Bristol Times and Mirror (1713).   Merged with *Western Daily Press* 1932.
CROYDON—*Surrey Morning Echo* (1908).   Ceased publication Jan 1910.
DARLINGTON—*North Star* (1881).   Merged with *Newcastle Daily Journal* 1926.
   Northern Echo (1870).
EXETER—*Devon and Exeter Daily Gazette* (1772).   Merged with *Western Morning News* Mar 1932.
   Western Times (1827).   Became weekly paper 1922.[2]
HUDDERSFIELD—*Huddersfield Daily Chronicle* (1871).[2]   Ceased publication Dec 1915.
HULL—*Daily Mail* (1787).   Became an evening paper 1902.
   Eastern Morning News (1864).   Ceased publication Nov 1929.
IPSWICH—**East Anglian Daily Times** (1874).
LEAMINGTON—*Leamington, Warwick, Kenilworth and District Morning News* (1896).   Originally *Leamington, Warwick, Kenilworth and District Daily Circular*.   Changed name and started morning publication in 1919.
LEEDS—*Leeds Mercury* (1718).   Changed name to *Leeds and Yorkshire Mercury* Oct 1901–Nov 1907.   Merged with *Yorkshire Post* Nov 1939.
   Yorkshire Post (1754).
LEICESTER—*Leicester Daily Post* (1872).   Ceased publication Mar 1921.
LIVERPOOL—*Liverpool Courier* (1808).   Changed name to *Liverpool Daily Courier* Sep 1922.   Changed name to *Daily Courier* Oct 1922.   Ceased publication Dec 1929.
   Liverpool Mercury (1811).   Merged with *Liverpool Daily Post* Nov 1904.
   Liverpool Daily Post (1855).
   Journal of Commerce (1861).
MANCHESTER—*Manchester Courier* (1825).   Ceased publication Jan 1916.
   Daily Dispatch (1900).   Merged with *News Chronicle* Nov 1955.
   Manchester Guardian (1821).   (*See under National Daily Newspapers.*)
   Manchester Journal of Commerce.   Ceased publication 1911.
   Telegraphic News.   Ceased publication 1901.
   Daily Citizen (1912).   Ceased publication June 1915.
   Daily Sketch (1909).   Ceased publication Apr 1911.
NEWCASTLE—*Illustrated Chronicle* (1910).   Ceased publication June 1925.
   Newcastle Daily Chronicle (1858).   Merged with *North Mail* Mar 1923.
   Newcastle Daily Journal (1832).   Became *Newcastle Journal and North Mail* Sep 1939.   Changed name to **Journal** Jul 1958.
   North Mail (1901).   Incorporated *Newcastle Daily Chronicle* Mar 1923 and became *North Mail and Newcastle Daily Chronicle*.   Merged with *Newcastle Journal* in Sep 1939.
   Newcastle Morning Mail (1898).   Changed name to *Morning Mail* Feb 1901.   Ceased publication Aug 1901.
NORWICH—**Eastern Daily Press** (1870).
   Norfolk Daily Standard (1885).   Became an evening paper in 1900.
NOTTINGHAM—*Nottingham Daily Express* (1860).   Changed name to *Nottingham Journal and Express* Apr 1918.   Changed named to *Nottingham Journal* 1921.   Merged with *Nottingham Guardian* Sep 1953 to become **Nottingham Guardian Journal.**
   Nottingham Daily Guardian (1861).   Changed name to *Nottingham Guardian* Oct 1905.   Merged with *Nottingham Journal* Sep 1953.
OXFORD—*Oxford Morning Echo* (1860).   Ceased publication Jan 1900.
PLYMOUTH—*Western Daily Mercury* (1860).   Merged with *Western Morning News* Jan 1921.
   Western Morning News (1860).

   [1] Localised editions of the *Argus* were published at Battle, Chichester, Eastbourne, East Grinstead, Hastings, Horsham, Hove, Lewes, Littlehampton, Rye, Tunbridge Wells, and Worthing.   Those still publishing in 1926 were merged with the Brighton *Morning Argus* into the *Evening Argus*.
   [2] Not published on Saturdays.

PORTSMOUTH—*Southern Daily Mail* (1884). Ceased publication 1905.
SHIELDS—*Shields Morning Mail* (1889). Ceased publication Feb 1901.
SHEFFIELD—*Yorkshire Early Bird* (1899). Became morning paper in 1929. Changed name to *Early Bird* Mar 1938. Merged with local evening paper, *Chronicle Midday*, May 1950.
    Sheffield Daily Telegraph (1855). Changed name to *Sheffield Telegraph* Jun 1934; to *Sheffield Telegraph and Daily Independent* Oct 38–May 39; to *Telegraph and Independent* Jun–Jul 42; to *Sheffield Telegraph* Jul 42–Sep 65; to **Sheffield Morning Telegraph** Sep 65.
    Sheffield and Rotherham Independent (1819). Changed name to *Sheffield Independent* Jan 1901. Changed name to *Sheffield Daily Independent* Feb 01–Oct 09. Changed name to *Daily Independent* June 1922. Amalgamated with *Sheffield Telegraph* Oct 1938.
YORK—*Yorkshire Herald* (1790). Became weekly 1936.

CARDIFF—*South Wales Daily News* (1872). Changed name to *South Wales News* Apr 1928. Merged with *Western Mail* Aug 1928.
    Western Mail (1869).
    Cardiff Journal of Commerce (1904). Changed name to *Cardiff and South Wales Journal of Commerce* July 1914. Changed name to *South Wales Journal of Commerce* June 1918. Ceased publication Apr 1935.
NEWPORT—*South Wales Daily News* (1872). Changed name to *South Wales News* 1928. Merged with *Western Mail* 1928.
SWANSEA—*Swansea Gazette*. Changed name to *Swansea Daily Shipping Register* 1900. Ceased publication 1918.

ABERDEEN—*Aberdeen Daily Journal* (1746). Merged with *Aberdeen Free Press* Nov 1922 and became **Aberdeen Press and Journal.**
    Aberdeen Free Press (1853). Merged with *Aberdeen Daily Journal* Nov 1922.
GLASGOW—**Glasgow Herald** (1783).
    North British Daily Mail (1847). Became *Glasgow Daily Mail* 1901. Merged with *Glasgow Record* 1901.
    Daily Record (1895). Incorporated *Glasgow Daily Mail* 1901 and became *Daily Record and Daily Mail.* Changed name to *Daily Record and Mail* 1902. Changed name to **Daily Record** 1954.
    Bulletin (1915). Became *Bulletin and Scots Pictorial* Jan 1924. Ceased publication July 1960.
DUNDEE—*Dundee Advertiser* (1861). Merged with *Courier and Argus* 1926 and became *Dundee Advertiser and Courier.*
    Courier and Argus (1861). Merged with the daily edition of *Dundee Advertiser* 1926 and became *Dundee Advertiser and Courier.*
    Dundee Advertiser and Courier (1926). Changed named to *Dundee Courier and Advertiser* 1926. Changed name to **Courier and Advertiser** 1926.
EDINBURGH—**Scotsman** (1817).

BELFAST—**Belfast News-letter** (1737).
    Northern Whig (1824). Changed name to *Northern Whig and Belfast Post* June 1919. Ceased publication 1963.
    Irish Daily Telegraph (1904). Merged with local evening paper, *Belfast Telegraph*, Apr 1952.
    Irish News and Belfast Morning News (1881).

SOURCES.—*Willing's Press Guide 1900–1967*; the catalogue of the British Museum Newspaper Library at Colindale.

Main Political Weeklies

Economist, 1843
  Proprietors: The Economist Newspaper Limited. (Since 1928 50% of shares held by Financial Newspaper Proprietors Limited, later Financial News Ltd.)
     Policy: Independent.
    Editors: E. Johnstone, 1883. F. Hurst, 1907. H. Withers, 1916. W. Layton, 1922. G. Crowther, 1938. D. Tyerman, 1956. A. Burnet, 1965.

Nation, 1907
  Proprietors: The *Nation.* 1931 Amalgamated with the *New Statesman.*
  Policy: Independent Radical.
  Editors: H. Massingham, 1907. H. Henderson, 1923. H. Wright, 1930–
    1931.
New Statesman, 1913
  Proprietors: Statesman Publishing Company. 1931 Amalgamated with the
    Nation, The Statesman and Nation Publishing Company.
  Policy: Independent. Radical.
  Editors: C. Sharp, 1913.   K. Martin, 1931.   J. Freeman, 1961.
    P. Johnson, 1965.
The Spectator, 1828
  Proprietors: The Spectator Limited since 1898. J. St. L. Strachey, 1898.
    (Sir) E. Wrench, 1925. I. Gilmour, 1954. H. Creighton, 1967.
  Policy: Independent conservative.
  Editors: J. St. L. Strachey, 1897. (Sir) Evelyn Wrench, 1925. W. Harris,
    1932. W. Taplin, 1953. I. Gilmour, 1954. B. Inglis, 1959.
    I. Hamilton, 1962. I. Macleod, 1963. N. Lawson, 1966.
Time and Tide, 1920
  Proprietors: Lady Rhondda 1920–1958. L. Skevington, 1958. T. Beau-
    mont, 1960. W. Brittain, 1962.
  Policy: Independent.
  Editors: Lady Rhondda, 1920. A. Lejeune, 1957. L. Skevington, 1958.
    J. Thompson, 1960. W. Brittain, 1962.
Tribune, 1937
  Proprietors: Tribune Publications, Ltd.
  Policy: Left-wing.
  Editors: W. Mellor, 1937. J. Hartshorn, 1938. R. Postgate, 1940.
    A. Bevan, 1942. J. Kimche, 1945. M. Foot, 1948. R. Ed-
    wards, 1952. M. Foot, 1956. R. Clements, 1959.

Newspaper Readership
(percentage of population over the age of 16)

	National Dailies	National Sundays
1939	67	82
1947	73	89
1961	85	93

SOURCE.—*Abstract of Information,* IPA Research Dept.

The Press Council

The General Council of the Press was formed in 1953 under the chairmanship of W. (Ld) Astor. He was succeeded in 1955 by Sir L. Andrews, and in 1959 by G. Murray. In 1963 the Council was reorganised to bring in lay members and its title was changed to the Press Council. Ld Devlin became the first independent chairman. The objects of the Council were changed on the reorganisation and now include preserving the freedom of the Press; maintaining the highest professional and commercial standards in the Press; considering complaints about the conduct of the Press or the conduct of persons and organisations towards the press; watching for restrictions on the supply of information of public interest and importance; and reporting publicly on developments tending towards greater concentration or monopoly in the Press and publishing relevant statistical material.

SOURCES.—*The Cambridge Bibliography of English Literature,* Vol. III, pp. 797-8, lists all press directories, pp. 798-846 lists newspapers and magazines. *The History of the Times,* Pt II, pp. 1130-36 gives a chart of the Metropolitan morning and evening press from 1884-1947. There are several press directories which cover all or part of the period: *T. B. Browne's Advertiser's ABC, 1900-1932; Sell's*

Dictionary of the World's Press, 1900–1921 (including a *Who's Who* of notabilities of the British Press in 1914–21 editions); *Mitchell's Newspaper Press Directory* (became *Benn's* in 1946), 1900–61; *Willing's Press Guide, 1900–1961*. PEP: *Report on the British Press* (1938); *Report of the Royal Commission on the Press* (Cmd. 7700 of 1949, Minutes of Evidence, Cmd. 7317 of 1948); *Report of the Royal Commission on the Press* (Cmnd. 1811 of 1962); N. Kaldor and R. Silverman, *A Statistical Analysis of Advertising Expenditure and of the Revenue of the Press* (1948); A. P. Wadsworth, 'Newspaper Circulations' (in *Proceedings of the Manchester Statistical Society*, 1954). J. L. Hammond, *C. P. Scott of the Manchester Guardian* (1934); J. W. Robertson Scott, *The Life and Death of a Newspaper* (*The Pall Mall Gazette*) (1952); A. Gollin, *The Observer and J. L. Garvin* (1960); F. Williams, *Dangerous Estate* (1957); C. Seymour-Ure, *Politics, the Press and the Public* (1968). Press Council Annual Reports *The Press and the People*; H. P. Levy, *The Press Council* (1967). *Hulton Readership Surveys*, J. W. Hobson and Harry Henry, came out annually between 1947 and 1955. The Institute of Practitioners in Advertising *National Readership Surveys*, first published in 1947, 1954, and have been coming out continuously bi-annually since 1957. Great Britain South of the Caledonian Canal Up to 1961 field work, etc., carried out by the London Press Exchange, since then by the British Market Research Bureau.

XX

BROADCASTING AUTHORITIES

The British Broadcasting Corporation

The British Broadcasting Company Ltd. was formed by some 200 manufacturers and shareholders on 18 Oct 22, registered on 15 Dec 22, and received its licence on 18 Jan 23. A system of paid licences for owners of radio receivers was started in 1922. London, Manchester, Birmingham, and Newcastle stations began to operate in November and December, 1922. This was followed by the establishment of the *British Broadcasting Corporation* under royal charter (20 Dec 26), which came into operation on 1 Jan 27. It was to be a public service body 'acting in the national interest' and financed by licence fees paid by all owners of radio receivers. (A formal agreement with the Postmaster General had been drawn up on 9 Nov 26.) Under the royal charter the B.B.C. was granted a licence for ten years and was to be directed by a board of governors nominated by the government. The charter was renewed and modified 1 Jan 37, 1 Jan 47, 1 Jul 52, 30 Jul 64.

British Broadcasting Company, 1923–1926

Chairman: Ld Gainford

Managing Director: (Sir) J. Reith
(formerly **General Manager**)

Board members:

G. Isaacs (Marconi) [1]
B. Binyon (Radio Communication Co.)
A. McKinstry (Metropolitan Vickers)
J. Gray (British Thomson-Houston Co.)

Sir W. Noble (General Electric)
H. Pease (Western Electric)
W. Burnham (Burndept)
Sir W. Bull, M.P.

British Broadcasting Corporation, 1927–1967

Board of Governors

		Chairmen			*Vice-Chairmen*
1 Jan	27	E of Clarendon	1 Jan	27	Ld Gainford
2 Jun	30	J. Whitley	1 Jan	33	R. Norman
28 Mar	35	Vt Bridgeman	25 Oct	35	H. Brown
3 Oct	35	R. Norman	8 Jun	37	C. Millis
19 Apr	39	Sir A. Powell	1 Jan	47	Marchioness of Reading
1 Jan	47	Ld Inman	7 Jan	51	Ld Tedder
9 Jun	47	Ld Simon	1 Jul	54	Sir P. Morris
1 Aug	52	Sir A. Cadogan	1 Jul	60	Sir J. Duff
1 Dec	57	Sir A. fforde	19 Sep	65	Ld Fulton
1 Feb	64	Sir J. Duff (*acting*)	11 Jun	66	R. Lusty
14 May	64	Ld Normanbrook	31 Jul	67	Ld Fulton
1 Sep	67	Ld Hill of Luton	1 Jan	68	R. Lusty
			15 Feb	68	Ld Fulton

[1] On the death of G. Isaacs, Marconi's were represented by F. Kellaway.

Governors

1927–31	Sir G. Nairne	1950–52	Ld Clydesmuir [2]
1927–32	M. Rendall	1951–52	F. Williams
1927–32	Mrs P. Snowden (Vtess)	1950–56	Prof. Barbara Wootton
1932–36	H. Brown	1952–54	Sir P. Morris
1933–35	Vt Bridgeman	1951–55	I. Stedeford
1933–37	Mrs M. Hamilton	1952–56	Lady Rhys Williams
1935–39	Lady Bridgeman	1954–59	Ld Rochdale
1935–39	H. Fisher	1955–60	Sir E. Benthall
1937–39	Sir I. Fraser	1956–61	Mrs T. Cazalet-Keir
1937–39	J. Mallon	1956–62	Dame F. Hancock
1938–39	Miss M. Fry	1959–60	Sir J. Duff
1939–41 [1]			(*Vice-Chairman* 60–65)
1941–46	Lady V. Bonham-Carter	1960–62	E of Halsbury
1941–46	Sir I. Fraser		(*Vice-Chairman* 66–67)
1941–46	J. Mallon	1960–65	R. Lusty
1941–46	A. Mann	1961–66	G. Cooke
1941–46	H. Nicolson	1962–68	Dame A Godwin
1946–49	Miss B. Ward	1962–67	Sir A. Clarke
1946–49	G. Lloyd	1966–67	Ld Fulton
1946–49	Sir R. Peck	1966–68	J. Trower
1946–50	E. Whitfield	1967–	Sir R. Murray
1946–50	Marchioness of Reading	1968–[3]	Sir R. Bellenger
1947–52	J. Adamson	1968–[3]	P. Wilson
1950–54	Ld Tedder	1968–[3]	T. Jackson
		1968–	Sir L. Constantine (Ld)
		1968–	Dame M. Green
		1969–	Sir H. Greene

Governors appointed to represent national interests

N. Ireland

1952–58	Sir H. Mulholland
1958–62	J. McKee
1962–67	Sir R. Pim
1968–	Ld Dunleagh

Scotland

1952–55	Ld Clydesmuir
1955–56	T. Johnston
1956–60	E of Balfour
1960–65	Sir D. Milne
1965–	Lady Baird

Wales

1952–60	Ld Macdonald
1960–65	Mrs R. Jones
1965–	G. Williams

Directors-General

1 Jan	27	Sir J. Reith
1 Oct	38	F. Ogilvie
1 Jan	42	Sir C. Graves & R. Foot
24 Jun	43	R. Foot
31 Mar	44	(Sir) W. Haley
17 Jul	52	B. Nicholls (*acting*)
1 Dec	52	Sir I. Jacob
31 Dec	59	(Sir) H. Greene
1 Apr	68	C. Curran

SOURCES.—*BBC Handbooks 1928–*; *Whitaker's Almanack 1928–*.

B.B.C. Television

On 2 Nov 1936 the first scheduled public service television was started from Alexandra Palace. The service was suspended from September 1939 until June 1946. The first stations outside London, in the Midlands and the North began transmitting in 1949 and 1951 respectively. By 1966, with more than 100 transmitting stations, B.B.C. Television was within the range of more than 99 per cent of the population of the United Kingdom. In April 1964 a second B.B.C. Channel was opened in the London Area and by 1967 it was available to more than two-thirds of the population of the U.K.

Broadcast Receiving Licences and B.B.C. Expenditure

Broadcasting receiving licences were first issued for 10s. a year in 1922;

[1] 5 Sep 39, the Board was reduced to 2 members (Chairman and Vice-Chairman) by Order in Council. The Board was reconstituted to its full strength of 7 members in 1941.
[2] 1 Aug 52, appointed Governor to represent Scottish interests.
[3] In 1967 the Board's strength was increased to 12 members.

the price for sound only licences was raised to £1 in 1946 and to £1 5s. in 1965. Licences for television were introduced in 1946 when a combined radio and television licence cost £2; this was raised to £3 in 1954, to £4 in 1957 and to £5 in 1965. From 1939–45 all licence revenue went to the government and the B.B.C. was financed by an annual grant in aid. The external services have continued to be financed in this way. From 1957 to 1963 a £1 excise duty was levied from the television licence fee.

	Licences ('000s)			B.B.C. expenditure on revenue account £000s	
	Total	Sound only	Sound and Television		
1925	1,654	1,654	..	..	
1927	2,270	2,264	..	902	
1930	3,092	3,076	..	1,224	
1935	7,012	6,970	..	2,473	
1940	8,951	8,898	..	4,350	
1945	9,710	9,663	..	9,001	
				Home	External
1947	10,778	10,713	15	7,273	3,878
1950	12,219	11,819	344	9,579	4,471
1955	13,980	9,414	4,504	17,964	5,093
1960	15,005	4,480	10,470	30,560	6,408
1965	16,047	2,759	13,253	55,642	8,499

The difference between the total and other licences column is explained by the issue of free licences to the blind.

The expenditure figures from 1940 onwards are for the year ending the following 31 Mar. The figures from 1947 onwards are for operational expenditure only.

Independent Television

The Independent Television Authority was set up by the Postmaster-General under section 1 (3) of the *Television Act, 1954*, on 4 Aug 1954 for a period of ten years. The Authority was to licence programme contracting companies and to regulate their output. The whole of the finance of Independent Television was to depend on advertising revenue though the Act specifically prohibited the 'sponsoring' of programmes by advertisers. The first Commercial programmes were transmitted on 22 Sep 1955. The *Television Act, 1964*, which came into effect on 31 Jul 1964 increased the I.T.A.'s power over programmes and advertising and enlarged the membership of the authority from 10 to 13.

Members of the Independent Television Authority 1954–

Chairman		National Members
		N. Ireland
31 Mar 55	Sir K. Clarke	
8 Nov 57	Sir I. Kirkpatrick	
6 Nov 62	Sir J. Carmichael (*acting*)	1955–60 A. Chichester
1 Jul 63	Ld Hill of Luton	1960–65 Sir L. O'Brien
1 Sep 67	Ld Aylestone	1965– D. Gilliland

Deputy Chairman		
4 Aug 54	Sir C. Colston	
3 Jan 55	Sir R. Matthews	*Scotland*
22 Jun 60	Sir J. Carmichael	1955–58 T. Honeyman
29 Jul 64	Sir S. Caine	1958–64 T. Talbot-Rice
1 Jul 67	Sir R. Gould	1964– W. MacFarlane Grey

Wales		1958–61	W. Beard
1955–56	Ld Aberdare	1960–60	Sir J. Carmichael
1956–63	J. Alban Davies	1960–64	Sir S. Caine
1964–	Sir B. Bowen-Thomas	1960–65	Mrs I. Graham-Bryce
		1960–64	A. Cropper
Other Members		1961–64	Sir T. Williamson (Ld)
1955–56	Ld Layton	1961–66	Dame A. Bryan
1955–56	Miss M. Popham	1964–	Lady Burton
1955–57	Miss D. Powell	1964–	Sir P. Hamilton
1955–58	G. Thorneycroft	1964–	H. Hunt
1955–59	Sir H. Hinchliffe	1964–	Sir O. Saunders
1956–60	Miss D. Harris	1964–	Sir V. Tewson
1957–60	T. Summerson	1965–	Mrs M. Adams
1957–61	Dame F. Farrer	1965–	Lady Plummer
		1966–	Lady Sharp

SOURCE.—*Independent Television Authority Reports and Accounts 1954–*.

Programme Contracting Companies

The following programme contracting companies have been appointed by the I.T.A.

They are listed together with their original date of appointment and their major controlling interests. In 1964 all were re-appointed to provide programmes until July 1968. On 11 June 1967 new contractors were announced to operate from 30 July 1968 to 29 July 1974.[1]

A.B.C. Television. 1956–68 (Weekends North and Midlands). Chairman, 1956: Sir P. Warter. A wholly owned subsidiary of Associated British Picture Corporation (see Thames Television).

Anglia Television. 1958 (East Anglia). Chairman, 1958: Marquess Townshend of Raynam. Significant minority interests held by the (*Manchester*) *Guardian* and Romulus and Remus Films.

A.T.V. Network. (1955–1966 Associated TeleVision) 1955. (Midlands Monday to Friday, London Saturday and Sunday.) Chairman, 1955: P. Littler, 1960: Sir R. Renwick (Ld). Originally Associated Broadcasting Development Co., then renamed Associated Broadcasting Co. Now wholly controlled by Associated Television Ltd., in which substantial shareholdings are in the hands of the *Daily Mirror* and IPC group, Beaverbrook Newspapers (since 1965) and (formerly) Moss Empires.

Border Television. 1961 (Carlisle). Chairman: J. Burgess. Shares widely held.

Channel Television. 1962 (Channel Islands). Chairman, 1962: Senator G. Troy, 1963: Senator W. Krichefski. Controlling interest (formerly) held by a subsidiary of A.B.P.C. (see A.B.C. Television).

Grampian Television. 1960 (Aberdeen). Chairman, 1960: Sir A. King, 1968: I. Tennant. Shares widely held.

[1] Most of the existing contractors were reappointed for the new contract period commencing 30 Jul 68, although Harlech Television replaced T.W.W., and Rediffusion and A.B.C. Television came together to form Thames Television. The 7-day companies were appointed to serve the Midlands, Lancashire and Yorkshire.

Granada Television. 1955 (North Monday to Friday); 1968 (Lancashire all week). Chairman, 1955: S. Bernstein. A wholly owned subsidiary of the Granada group.

Harlech Television. 1968 (Wales and West of England). Chairman, 1968: Ld Harlech. Shares widely held.

London Weekend Television. 1968 (London Friday 7 p.m. to Sunday). Chairman, 1968: A. Crawley. Significant minority interests held by Bowater Paper Corporation, I.T.C. Pension Trust, Lombard Banking, G.E.C., Pearl Assurance, the *Daily Telegraph* and the *Observer*.

Rediffusion Television (Associated Rediffusion 1955–64). 1955–68 (London Monday to Friday). Chairman, 1955: (Sir) J. Wills. Majority interests held by British Electric Traction and Rediffusion (see Thames Television).

Scottish Television. 1956 (Central Scotland). Chairman, 1957: R. Thomson (Ld). Controlling interests held by The Thomson Organisation Ltd until 1968, when I.T.A. required it to divest itself of much of its holdings.

Southern Television. 1958 (South of England). Chairman, 1958: J. Davis. Main shareholders, the Rank Organisation, the Amalgamated Press, and Associated Newspapers. The Amalgamated Press holding passed to the *Daily Mirror* group when the latter acquired the Amalgamated Press in Nov 1958. The *Television Act, 1954,* requirement of 'adequate competition' forced the *Daily Mirror* holding to be sold to Associated Newspapers, the Rank Organisation and D. C. Thomson Ltd.

Thames Television. 1968 (London Monday to Friday 7 p.m.). Chairman, 1968: Sir P. Warter. Shares broadly divided between A.B.P.C. and Rediffusion, with controlling share held by A.B.P.C.

T.W.W. 1958–68 (Wales and the West of England). Chairman, 1958: E of Derby. Main shareholders *News of the World, Liverpool Daily Post*, E of Derby and J. Hylton (after 1965 his executors).

Tyne-Tees Television. 1956 (North-East). Chairman, 1956: Sir R. Pease, 1963: E. Fairburn, 1968: G. Daysh. Significant shareholdings formerly held by the *Daily News* Ltd., Black Brothers, William Baird & Co.; in 1968 by Mercantile Investment Trust.

Ulster Television. 1959 (Northern Ireland). Chairman, 1959: E of Antrim. Shares widely held.

Wales (West and North) Television. 1962–4. Chairman, 1962: H. Hayden Williams, 1963 *(acting)*: C. Traherne. Shares widely held. In 1964 this company was absorbed by T.W.W.

Westward Television. 1960 (South-West). Chairman: P. Cadbury. Shares widely held.

Yorkshire Television. 1968 (Yorkshire). Chairman, 1968: Sir R. Graham. Significant minority interests held by Telefusion and *Yorkshire Post*.

Independent Television News Ltd.

1955, Editor and chief executive: A. Crawley, 1955. (Sir) G. Cox, 1956. Managing director: D. Edwards, 1968. Editor: N. Ryan, 1968. This is an independent non-profit making company, to provide a common news service for all the contracting companies. The appointment of the managing director and the editor must have the approval of the I.T.A.

SOURCES.—*I.T.A. Annual Reports and Accounts, 1954–*; *Investing in Television* in *The Economist* 9 May 59, p. 553. *The Press Council Annual Report 1966.*

Sykes Committee Report on Broadcasting, Cmd. 1951/1923; *Crawford Committee Report on Broadcasting*, Cmd. 2599/1926; *Selsdon Committee Report on Television*, Cmd. 4793/1934–35; *Ullswater Committee Report on Broadcasting*, Cmd 5091/1935–36; *Hankey Committee Report on Television* Non-Parliamentary Papers, 1945; *Government Statement on Broadcasting Policy*, Cmd. 6852/1945–46; *Beveridge Committee Report on Broadcasting*, Cmd. 8116 and 8117/1950–51; *Government Memoranda on the Report of the Broadcasting Committee, 1949*, Cmd. 8291/1950–51, and Cmd. 8550/1951–52; *Government Memorandum on Television Policy*, Cmd. 9005/1953–54; G.P.O., *1st and 2nd Reports of the Television Advisory Committee*, 1952 (1953) and 1953 (1954); *Report from the Select Committee on Broadcasting (Anticipation of Debates)* H.M.S.O. 1966; *Pilkington Committee on Broadcasting*, Cmnd. 1753/1962; *Government Memoranda on Broadcasting*, Cmnd. 1770 & 1893/1962; *Firt Report from the Committee on Broadcasting etc. of the Proceedings of Parliament* (H.M.S.O., 1966); *Government Statement on Broadcasting*, Cmnd. 3169/1966.

Annual Reports and Accounts of the B.B.C. 1927–, *Annual Reports and Accounts of the I.T.A. 1954–*; *B.B.C. Handbook 1927–.*

Sir G. Beadle, *Television: a Critical Review* (1963); A. Briggs, *The History of Broadcasting in the United Kingdom*, Vol. I: *The Birth of Broadcasting* (1961); Vol. II: *The Golden Age of Radio* (1965); R. H. Coase, *British Broadcasting: a Study in Monopoly* (1950); B. Paulu, *British Broadcasting* (1956); B. Paulu, *British Broadcasting in Transition* (1961); Ld Reith, *Into the Wind* (1949); Ld Simon of Wythenshawe, *The B.B.C. from Within* (1953); H. H. Wilson, *Pressure Groups: the Campaign for Commercial Television* (1961).

XXI

RELIGION

Church Membership Statistics

EXTREME caution should be observed in making use of church membership statistics, as no entirely reliable sources exist giving information about membership or attendance. The last reasonably authoritative figures of religious affiliations in Britain were taken from the 1851 census, though even then there was no compulsion to answer the questions on religion. Since then no census has included questions on religious affiliation. Strictly comparable figures are impossible to obtain for church membership and church attendance between 1900 and 1966. The definition of membership varies greatly from one denomination to another, as does the minimum age for reception into the church. At one extreme, the Roman Catholic Church officially records the Roman Catholic population of all ages, regardless of church attendance. Nonconformist churches with adult baptism, and in the case of the Methodists a probationary period before baptism, are the most exclusive. These statistics give no indication how frequently 'members' of the churches attended services. Moreover even within the denominations different figures are quoted at different times and in different sources. E.g. Church of England membership can be variously defined by figures for baptised membership, those for Easter communicants, and the Electoral Roll. In a report prepared by Gallup Poll for A.B.C. Television (University of London Press, 1964), *TV and religion*, it was stated that in the three television areas of London, Midlands, and the North only 1 in 17 of those aged 16 and over, i.e., 6% say that they have no religious affiliation, yet the total of all the religious statistics available do not add up to anything like 94% of the population. A further problem is the definition of church-going. J. K. Lawton in an article in the British Council of Churches bulletin, *The Church in the World*, said that if church attendance was to be judged by the criteria of twice a month churchgoing the figure was 15%, if the criteria was one attendance in three months it rose to 40%. A Gallup survey done for the magazine *Sunday* (May 1966) suggested that about 10 million people go to church most Sundays or at least once a month. No precise information is available on the effect of religious broadcasting on attendance at church services. Some studies of church attendance and religious affiliations that have attempted to fill out these necessarily very inadequate figures are: *Religious Broadcasts and the Public*, by the B.B.C. Audience Research Department (1955); 'How Many in the Pew?' in *The Economist* of 30 Aug 58; *Puzzled People*, by Mass Observation (1948); *A Survey of Social Conditions in England and Wales*, chapter 18, by A. M. Carr-Saunders, D. C. Jones, and C. M. Moser (1958); R. F. Neuss, *Facts and Figures about the Church of England No. 3* (1966); and Gallup Poll figures for church membership and attendance.

More general works on religion in Britain in the twentieth century are: R. B. Braithwaite, *The State of Religious Belief* (1927); E. O. James, *History of Christianity in England* (1949); R. Lloyd, *The Church of England in the Twentieth Century* (2 vols, 1948–50); G. Spinks (ed.), *Religion in Britain since 1900* (1952); R. F. Wearmouth, *The Social and Political Influence of Methodism in the Twentieth Century* (1957); J. Highet, *The Scottish Churches* (1960). Maps on the strength of religion in Britain are given in *The Reader's Digest Atlas of Britain* (1965).

THE CHURCH OF ENGLAND

Principal degrees of membership for the Provinces of Canterbury and York.

(Totals for 43 dioceses) [a]

Year	Home population of the two provinces (000s)	Estimated baptised membership		Estimated confirmed membership		Membership of parochial electoral rolls	
		(000s) [d]	Per 1,000 home pop.	(000s) [d]	Per 1,000 pop. aged 13 and over [e]	(000s)	Per 1,000 pop. of appropriate age
1901	30,673 [b]	n.a.		n.a.		n.a.	
1911	33,807 [b]	n.a.		n.a.		n.a.	
1921	35,390 [b]	22,000	622	8,100	301	3,537 [f]	140
1931	37,511 [b]	23,800	634	9,000	302	3,686	145
1941	39,173 [c]	24,900	636	9,200	294	3,423 [g]	120
1951	41,330 [b]	25,800	624	9,400	284	2,923 [h]	95
1956	42,227 [c]	26,771	634	9,691	286	2,895	93
1958	42,663 [c]	27,005	633	9,748	284	2,877 [i]	91
1960	43,296 [c]	27,323	631	9,792	281	2,862	89
1962	44,185 [c]	27,384	620	9,842	277	2,793	85
1964	44,893 [c]	27,500	613	9,730	270	2,739	82
1966	45,547 [c]	27,658	607	9,957	270	2,682	81

[a] In 1910 there were 15,864 parochial churches; in 1966 there were 17,755.
[b] Enumerated in the Registrar General's censuses of ecclesiastical areas.
[c] Estimates based on the Registrar General's annual estimates of population at 30th June.
[d] Calculated by the Statistical Unit of the Central Board of Finance of the Church of England by reference to the age composition of the home population, born and resident in the two provinces, and to the respective rates of infant baptisms at Anglican fonts per 1,000 live births; and to the respective rate of Anglican confirmations per 1,000 males and females living at age 15 years. (It is not possible to include in these estimates baptised and confirmed Anglicans who were born abroad but are now resident in the two provinces.)
[e] In the Church of England very few boys and girls are confirmed before the age of 13 years.
[f g h] Figures for 1924, 1940, and 1953, respectively.
[i] 1957 was the first year that persons of 17 years and over were included in the electoral rolls. In previous years the minimum age was 18 years.

SOURCES.—*Facts and Figures about the Church of England*, Nos. 1-3. Edited by R. F. Neuss, Published by the Church Information Office (1966).

Archbishops and leading Bishops of the five principal Dioceses in the Church of England [1]

(These are the only sees automatically represented in the House of Lords)

Archbishops of Canterbury

1896	F. Temple (*Frederick Cantuar:*)
1903	R. Davidson (*Randall Cantuar:*)
1928	C. Lang (*Cosmo Cantuar:*)
1942	W. Temple (*William Cantuar:*)
1945	G. Fisher (*Geoffrey Cantuar:*)
1961	A. Ramsey (*Michael Cantuar:*)

Archbishops of York

1891	W. Maclagan (*Willem Ebor:*)
1909	C. Lang (*Cosmo Ebor:*)
1929	W. Temple (*William Ebor:*)
1942	C. Garbett (*Cyril Ebor:*)
1956	A. Ramsey (*Michael Ebor:*)
1961	F. Coggan (*Donald Ebor:*)

Bishops of London

1897	M. Creighton (*Mandell Londin:*)
1901	A. Winnington-Ingram (*A. F. London:*)
1939	G. Fisher (*Geoffrey Londin:*)
1945	J. Wand (*William Londin:*)
1956	H. Campbell (*Henry Londin:*)
1961	R. Stopford (*Robert Londin:*)

Bishops of Durham

1890	B. Westcott (*B. F. Dunelm:*)
1901	H. Moule (*Handley Dunelm:*)
1920	H. Henson (*Herbert Dunelm:*)
1939	A. Williams (*Alwyn Dunelm:*)
1952	A. Ramsey (*Michael Dunelm:*)
1956	M. Harland (*Maurice Dunelm:*)
1966	I. Ramsey (*Ian Dunelm:*)

Bishops of Winchester

1895	R. Davidson (*Randall Winton:*)
1903	H. Ryle (*Herbert E. Winton:*)
1911	E. Talbot (*Steuart Edward Winton:*)
1924	F. Woods (*Theodore Winton:*)
1932	C. Garbett (*Cyril Winton:*)
1942	M. Haigh (*Mervyn Winton:*)
1952	A. Williams (*Alwyn Winton:*)
1961	S. Allison (*Falkner Winton:*)

[1] Names in brackets are those used as signature.

THE CHURCH IN WALES

The Church in Wales was disestablished from 31 March 1920

Year	Parochial Easter Day Communicants Estimated No. (000s)	No. of Churches
1920	160	1,755
1930	167	1,774
1940	175	1,766
1950	n.a.	n.a.
1960	183	1,783
1965	165	1,777

SOURCE.—Information from the Secretary, the Representative Body of the Church in Wales.

EPISCOPAL CHURCH IN SCOTLAND

Year	Communicants ('000s)	No. of Church Buildings
1900	46	354
1910	52	404
1920	57	416
1930	60	415
1940	62	404
1950	57	397
1960	57	369
1965	55	358

SOURCES.—*The Year Book for the Episcopal Church in Scotland*; *Whitaker's Almanack* (figures for 1910 and 1920); *The Statesman's Year-Book* (figures for 1930 and 1940).

BAPTIST UNION
British Isles [a]

Year	Members ('ooos)	No. of Places of Worship [b]
1900	366	2,579
1910	419	2,889
1920	405	2,866
1930	406	2,965
1940	382	3,044
1950	338	3,110
1960	318	3,053
1965	295	3,048

[a] These are statistics actually received from the churches; no estimates are made for churches omitting to return figures.
[b] England and Wales only.

SOURCE.—*The Baptist Handbook, 1900–1966.*

CONGREGATIONAL UNION
United Kingdom [a]

Year	Members ('ooos)	No. of Places of Worship
1900	436	4,607 [b]
1910	494	4,721
1920	n.a.	n.a.
1930	490	3,556
1939	459	3,435
1950	387	3,173
1959	212	2,984
1965	198	2,799

[a] 1900 and 1910 figures for British Isles.
[b] Figure for 1901.

SOURCE.—*The Congregational Year Book, 1900–1966.*

METHODIST CHURCH [a]
Great Britain and Ireland

Year	Members and Probationers ('ooos)	Churches, etc.
1900	520	9,037
1910	544	n.a.
1920	512	9,013
1930	548	9,070
1940	823	n.a.
1950	776	n.a.
1959	729	n.a.
1965	690	n.a.

[a] Up to 1930 these figures are for the Wesleyan Methodist Church. The Methodist Church was formed in 1932 by a union of the Wesleyan, Primitive, and United Methodist Churches. The United Methodists were themselves formed by a union of three separate bodies in 1905.

SOURCE.—*The Minutes of the Methodist Conference, 1900–1966,* W. S. F. Pickering, *Anglo-Methodist Relations* (1961) gives figures (for England only) for all bodies (1906–1957).

PRESBYTERIAN CHURCH
England

Year	Members ('ooos)
1900	76
1911	87
1922	84
1930	84
1940	82
1950	82
1960	71
1965	70

SOURCES.—1900 and 1911, *The Official Handbook of the Presbyterian Church of England*; 1922–66, *The Statesman's Year-Book.*

THE CHURCH OF SCOTLAND [a]
(Presbyterian)

Year	Total Communicants on Rolls ('ooos)	No. of Places of Worship
1901	1164	n.a.
1911	1220	1,703
1921	1278	1,704
1931	1281	2,795
1941	1269	2,507
1951	1273	2,348
1959	1307	2,242
1966	1234	n.a.

[a] In 1929 the United Free Church of Scotland rejoined the Church of Scotland.

SOURCE.—*The Church of Scotland Year Book.*

THE ROMAN CATHOLIC CHURCH
Great Britain

Year	Estimated Catholic Population ('ooos) [a]	Catholic Baptisms ('ooos)	No. of Public Churches and Chapels
1900	5415	n.a.	1,536
1910	5515	n.a.	1,773
1920	5704	n.a.	1,408
1930	6024 [b]	66	1,564
1940	3444 [c]	70	1,802
1950	3884 [c]	87	1,971
1960	4818	112 [d]	3,204
1965	7982	137 [e]	3,319

[a] These figures include England and Wales, Scotland, Ireland, 1900–30, and N. Ireland, 1940–66.
[b] This figure is made up of the English estimate for 1930, the Scottish estimate for 1926, and the Irish estimate for 1911.
[c] The figures for 1940 and 1950 include the N. Irish Catholic population taken from the 1937 census.
[d] Figure for 1959.   [e] Up to 7 years.

Roman Catholic Archbishops of Westminster

1892	H. Vaughan (Cardinal, 1893)	1943	B. Griffin (Cardinal, 1946)
1903	F. Bourne (Cardinal, 1911)	1956	W. Godfrey (Cardinal, 1958)
1935	A. Hinsley (Cardinal, 1937)	1963	J. Heenan (Cardinal, 1965)

SOURCE.—*The Catholic Directory, 1900–1966.*

NORTHERN IRELAND
Religious Affiliations
(to nearest '000)

Year	Roman Catholic	Presbyterian	Protestant Episcopalian	Methodist	Others
1911	430	395	327	46	52
1937	428	391	345	55	60
1951	471	410	353	67	69
1961	498	413	345	72	98

SOURCE.—Census reports quoted in *The Statesman's Year-Books, 1900–1966.*

THE JEWISH COMMUNITY[a]
Great Britain

Year	Estimated No. of Jews ('ooos)	Approx. No. of Synagogues
1900	160	80 [d]
1910	243	200 [d]
1920	287	200 [d]
1929 [b]	297	300 [e]
1940	385 [c]	200 [e]
1950	450	240 [e]
1960	450	240 [e]
1965	450	240 [e]

[a] Statistics for 1900 for G.B. and Ireland, 1910 for the British Isles, 1920 for U.K., 1929 for G.B., 1940–60 for G.B. and N. Ireland.
[b] No Jewish statistics available, 1930–34.
[c] Including about 35,000 refugees.
[d] From *Whitaker's Almanack.*
[e] From *The Statesman's Year-Book.*

SOURCE.—*The Jewish Year Book, 1900–1966.*

x

XXII

PRESSURE GROUPS

1. Pressure Group Activities

The Scope of Pressure Group Activities. Governmental consultation with organised groups of 'affected interests' and other appropriate persons has been normal constitutional practice in the twentieth century. Indeed, statutes often make such consultations mandatory in certain executive actions such as promulgating administrative regulations. Both in these formal consultations and in the informal discussions between groups and the government there are a variety of procedures and participants. The extent and methods of pressure group activity are surveyed in the following works, S. E. Finer, *Anonymous Empire* (1958; 2nd ed. 1966), J. D. Stewart, *British Pressure Groups* (1958), and A. Potter, *Organized Groups in British National Politics* (1961). All of these general works contain useful bibliographies of pressure group studies.

Group Strategies. It is impossible here to list all of the methods for group access to the government. Nevertheless, some studies of group relations with particular political institutions are worth noting.

Legislative Strategy: H. H. Wilson, *Pressure Group: The Campaign For Commercial Television* (1961).

Executive Strategy: H. Eckstein, *Pressure Group Politics: The Case of The British Medical Association* (1960).

Political Party Relations: M. Harrison, *Trade Unions and the Labour Party Since 1945* (1960).

Participation in Government Committees: P.E.P., *Advisory Committees In British Government* (1960).

Judicial Relations: R. B. Stevens and B. S. Yamey, *The Restrictive Practices Court. A Study of the Judicial Process and Economic Policy* (1965).

Public Opinion Campaigns: H. H. Wilson, 'Techniques of Pressure', *Public Opinion Quarterly* (1951).

2. Types of Organised Interests

Trade Unions. The main association representing workers is the Trades Union Congress (founded in 1868).

Business. By far the most important organisation representing business interests is the Confederation of British Industry. The C.B.I. was formed in 1965 by a merger of the Federation of British Industries (1916), the

National Association of British Manufacturers (1915), and the British Employers' Confederation (1919). In addition to this powerful confederation most industries are also represented by their own specialised associations, many of which are affiliated with the C.B.I. It is estimated that there are now about 2,500 trade associations of which about 1,000 represent manufacturing industry. The variety of these associations, their structure and activities are discussed by Political and Economic Planning in *Industrial Trade Associations* (1957). Also important in representing industrial interests as well as commercial interests is the Association of British Chambers of Commerce (1860), the history of which is presented in A. R. Ilersic and P. F. B. Liddle, *Parliament of Commerce* (1960). There are numerous associations representing trading enterprises. The most important federation of these is the National Chamber of Trade (1897). Both the Chambers of Commerce and the Chambers of Trade are organised on the basis of affiliated local chambers representing area interests rather than commodity interests. The multitude of specialised commodity associations of merchants is discussed in H. Levy, *Retail Trade Associations*, (1942).

Finance, Insurance, and Property. The largest association representing property owners is the National Federation of Property Owners and Ratepayers (1888). This and other property organisations are discussed by the Property Council in *The Property Developer* (1964). The relations between developers and insurance organisations is explored by B. P. Whitehouse in *Partners in Property* (1964). Another important financial interest is the Building Societies Association (1869) which has extensive dealings with the Treasury. Its development is outlined in S. J. Price, *Building Societies* (1958). Little has been written about the political activities of other financial institutions, but see P. Ferris, *The City* (1965).

The Professions. Professional organisations commonly have the dual purpose of not only representing the interests of the profession in public affairs but also administering the qualifications for entrance into the profession. Examples would be the Royal Institute of British Architects (1834) and the Royal Institution of Chartered Surveyors (1868). However, there are also some associations organised to advance knowledge in the profession and to represent its interests. Outstanding examples of non-qualifying associations are the British Medical Association (1832) and the National Union of Teachers (1870). The organisation and development of the main professions are discussed in A. M. Carr-Saunders and P. A. Wilson *The Professions* (1933) and in G. Millerson, *The Qualifying Associations* (1964). In addition to these general works there are also numerous studies of particular professions which, in passing, discuss organisational relations with the government. Amongst these are A. Tropp, *The School Teachers* (1957) and B. Abel-Smith, *A History of the Nursing Profession* (1960).

Agriculture. The main organisation representing farmers is the National Farmers Union (1908). Also important are the Country Landowners Association (1907) representing large landowners and the National Union of Agricultural Workers (1920) representing farm labourers. These three main groups and some of the numerous specialised commodity associations are discussed in P. J. O. Self and H. Storing, *The State and the Farmer* (1962).

Causes and Voluntary Services. There are a large number of groups representing causes or offering voluntary services. These may seek to influence public policy by direct contact with Parliament and the Ministries or indirectly through appeals to public opinion. Many of these organisations and their work are described in *Voluntary Social Services* (National Council of Social Services, 1966). Some notable examples of these causes and their respective groups are as follows:

Family: National Citizens Advice Bureaux Council (1939).
Children: National Society for the Prevention of Cruelty to Children (1884).
Animals: Royal Society for the Prevention of Cruelty to Animals (1824).
Health: Royal National Institute for the Blind (1868).
The Elderly: National Old People's Welfare Council (1940).
Amenities: Council for the Preservation of Rural England (1926).
Prisoners: Howard League for Penal Reform (1886).
Community: National Council of Social Service (1919).
Religious: Lord's Day Observance Society (1831).
Temperance: United Kingdom Alliance (1853).
International Relations: United Nations Association (1945). Campaign for
    Nuclear Disarmament (1958).

The pressure-group activities of some 'cause' groups have been studied in considerable detail. Examples are J. B. Christoff, *Capital Punishment and British Politics* (1962) and G. Wootton, *The Politics of Influence: British Ex-Servicemen, Cabinet Decisions and Cultural Change*, 1917–1957 (1963).

Local Authorities. The interests of the local authorities are represented by two main kinds of groups. First, there are the associations of each tier of local authorities. Most powerful amongst these are the Association of Municipal Corporations (1873) and the County Councils Association (1889). In addition, there are associations representing each of the professions in local government services. Examples would be the Institution of Municipal Engineers (1873) and the Institute of Municipal Treasurers and Accountants (1885). All kinds of municipal employees are also represented by the National and Local Government Officers Association (1905), which is described by J. H. Warren the General Secretary of N.A.L.G.O. in *Local Government Service* (1952). The best guide to local authority Organisations is the *Municipal Yearbook*.

3. Sources of Information about Groups

Locating Particular Groups. To locate the groups representing any particular interest the sources are the directories of the specialised trade or locality. Some helpful guides are G. P. Henderson and I. G. Anderson, *Current British Directories* (1966), *Directory of British Associations* (1965), the H.M.S.O. *Directory of Employers Associations, Trade Unions, Trade Organisations,* &c. and *Whitaker's Almanack.*

Periodicals. Most organisations issue periodical magazines, newsletters or yearbooks. The titles and location of these publications can be found in the *British Union Catalogue of Periodicals.*

History and Organisation. Most national groups circulate handbooks or official histories in which the structure and development of the organisation are discussed. These are difficult to find through the normal bibliographical sources, as they may not be technically 'published'. Hence these are best obtained by writing directly to the group concerned.

XXIII
BIBLIOGRAPHICAL NOTE

THIS book does not attempt to provide an extensive bibliography of works on British politics since 1900. That would demand a separate volume and much of its contents would duplicate bibliographies already available. The main sources of factual data used in compiling this book are listed separately in the appropriate sections. There are, however, some works of reference of such major importance and reliability that it seems useful to collect them together as a help or reminder to those involved in research.

Many of the standard and most useful sources for reference are Stationery Office publications. Summaries, guides, and short-cuts to these publications are provided in the Stationery Office : *Catalogue of Government Publications* (annually), the *Sectional Lists of Government Publications*, published by the Stationery Office for individual departments, the *List of Cabinet Papers 1880–1914* (H.M.S.O., 1966), the *General Index to Parliamentary Papers, 1900–1949* (H.M.S.O.), the three volumes by P. and G. Ford, *Breviate of Parliamentary Papers* (1900–16, 1917–39, 1940–54), and C. Hughes, *The British Statute Book* (1957).

For reference to day-to-day political events the *Official Index to the 'Times'* is the most complete guide, though before 1906 *Palmer's Index to the 'Times'* is difficult to use successfully and is by no means complete. *Keesing's Contemporary Archives* since 1931 give a concise summary of news reported in the national Press, though they were not published in their present fuller form until 1937. Brief chronologies of the year's major events (including some very minor ones) are printed in the *Annual Register* (since 1954 the *Annual Register of World Events*), which also covers them in greater detail in the main text of the book. Still briefer summaries of the year's events are to be found in *Whitaker's Almanack*.

For biographical details of leading figures in British politics since 1900 the main sources are the *Dictionary of National Biography* (1901–11, 1912–21, 1922–30, 1931–40, 1941–50), the *Concise Dictionary of National Biography, 1901–50*, *Who Was Who* (1897–1916, 1916–28, 1929–40, 1941–50, 1951–60), and *Who's Who*, for those still alive. As supplements to these, for lesser-known figures in the Labour and Co-operative movement see also the *Labour Who's Who*, 1924 and 1927 (The Labour Publishing Company) and the *Herald Book of Labour Members* (1923, with a supplement in 1924). Appointments are recorded in many official sources. The major annual publications are : the *Imperial Calendar and Civil Service List*, *H.M. Ministers and Heads of Public Departments* (published since 1946, from four to six times a year), and the *London Gazette*, where appointments are announced officially, which appears about once a fortnight. Official appointments are also recorded in the annual *Lists* of the *Foreign Office*, the *Colonial Office*, and the *Commonwealth Relations Office*, the *Army*, *Navy* and *Air Force Lists*, the *Law List*, and the *Annual Estimates* of the civil, revenue, and service departments. There are two handbooks on Parliament, giving the names of M.P.s, details of procedure and officials : *Dod's Parliamentary Companion* (annually) and *Vacher's Parliamentary Companion* (published from four to six times a year). Extremely valuable sources of reference for the House of Commons are the books *House of Commons* published by the *Pall Mall Gazette* in 1906, 1910 and 1911, and since 1910 by the *Times* after each General Election (1922–4 excepted). Other sources of biographical information are *Debrett's* and *Burke's Peerage*, and *Burke's Dictionary of the Landed Gentry*, the *Directory of Directors*, the *Authors' and Writers' Who's Who*, and other directories devoted to the members of particular professions.

The annual almanacks are also an extremely useful source of information. Amongst these the most notable are: the *Constitutional Year Book* (published until 1939), *Whitaker's Almanack*, *The Statesman's Year-Book*, the *Yearbook of International Organisations*, the *United Nations Yearbook*, and *Britain: An Official Handbook* (published by the Central Office of Information).

The major sources for British statistics are already quoted in notes to the tables throughout the book. The most readily available is the *Annual Abstract of Statistics* (H.M.S.O.). This appears both annually, and in a form covering a ten-year period, since 1945. The *Censuses of Population, Industry* and *Production* though infrequent provide the firmest figures. Much of the information in annual publications is only estimated. The reports of the major revenue departments: the *Commissioners for Customs and Excise*, the *Commissioners for Inland Revenue*, and the *Registrars-General for England and Wales* and for *Scotland* are major sources of statistical information — as are the reports of the other Government Departments, and especially the *Ministry of Labour* with its monthly *Gazette* (until 1917 this was the *Board of Trade Labour Gazette*), and *Annual Abstract of Labour Statistics*. Other major sources of information are *The London and Cambridge Economic Service* published about three times a year in the '*Times*' *Review of Industry* and the *Abstract of British Historical Statistics* by B. R. Mitchell and P. Deane (1962).

A useful guide to works on British politics is the subject index of the British Museum Library. Bibliographical references can be checked through the *Cumulative Book Index*. For information on many aspects of British politics the *Encyclopaedia Britannica* or *Chambers's Encyclopaedia* may give a lead. Weekly journals, especially the *Economist*, may provide much additional information. Apart from the *Times*, the national dailies are not indexed, which makes reference a slow process. But newspaper libraries generally have their own index system and may be of much help.

No attempt is being made in the book to provide a bibliography for the period 1900–67. An extensive bibliography is already available for much of the period by C. L. Mowat in his book *Britain between the Wars* (1955) and in his article, 'Some Recent Books on the British Labour Movement', *Journal of Modern History*, xvii, No. 4, December 1945. He has also published *British History since 1926*, a select bibliography (The Historical Association, 1960). Another critical bibliography is supplied by A. J. P. Taylor, *English History 1914–45* (1966). Other bibliographies include J. Palmer, *Government and Parliament in Britain: a bibliography* (1964, The Hansard Society), E. J. Hobsbawm, 'Twentieth Century British Politics', *Past and Present*, No. 11, April 1957 and H. R. Winkler, 'Some Recent Writings on Twentieth Century Britain', the *Journal of Modern History*, xxxii, No. 1, March 1960.

Addenda

Insert on p. 48

LABOUR GOVERNMENT, 1964–   (*contd.*)

MINISTERS NOT IN CABINET

Law Officers:

Att.-Gen.	SIR E. JONES	18 Oct 64
Sol.-Gen.	SIR D. FOOT	18 Oct 64
	SIR A. IRVINE	24 Aug 67
Ld Advoc.	G. STOTT	20 Oct 64
Sol.-Gen.	J. LEECHMAN	20 Oct 64
Scotland	H. S. WILSON	11 Oct 65

H.M. Household:

Treas.	S. IRVING	21 Oct 64
	J. SILKIN	11 Apr 66
	C. GREY	7 July 66
Comptr.	C. GREY	21 Oct 64
	W. WHITLOCK	7 Jul 66
	W. HOWIE	1 Apr 67
	J. McCANN	29 Jul 67
	I. EVANS	6 Feb 68
V. Chamb.	W. WHITLOCK	21 Oct 64
	J. McCANN	11 Apr 66
	C. MORRIS	29 Jul 67
Capt. Gents at Arms	LD SHEPHERD	21 Oct 64
	LD BESWICK	29 Jul 67
Capt. Yeomen of Guard	LD BOWLES	

JUNIOR MINISTERS ATTACHED

P.S. to Treasury:

E. Short	18 Oct 64
J. Silkin	4 Jul 66

Junior Lds. of Treasury

G. Rogers	21 Oct 64–11 Jan 66
G. Lawson	21 Oct 64–1 Apr 67
J. McCann	21 Oct 64–11 Apr 66
	29 Jul 67–
I. Davies	21 Oct 64–6 Apr 66
Mrs H. Slater	21 Oct 64–6 Apr 66
J. Silkin	11 Jan 66–11 Apr 66
A. Fitch	16 Apr 66–
J. Harper	16 Apr 66–
W. Whitlock	11 Apr 66–7 Jul 66
	1 Apr 67–28 Jul 67
W. Howie	16 Apr 66–1 Apr 67
H. Gourlay	7 Jul 66–29 Oct 68
B. O'Malley	1 Apr 67–
W. Harrison	29 Oct 68–

Asst Govt Whips:

A. Fitch	22 Oct 64 [1]–16 Apr 66
H. Gourlay	22 Oct 64 [1]–7 Jul 66
J. Harper	22 Oct 64 [1]–16 Apr 66
W. Howie	22 Oct 64 [1]–16 Apr 66
B. O'Malley	22 Oct 64 [1]–1 Apr 67
J. Silkin	22 Oct 64 [1]–11 Jan 66
C. Morris	25 Jan 66–29 Jul 67
E. Bishop	16 Apr 66–1 Apr 67
R. W. Brown	16 Apr 66–20 Jan 67
W. Harrison	16 Apr 66–
N. McBride	16 Apr 66–
I. Evans	7 Jul 66–6 Feb 68
E. Armstrong	20 Jan 67–
H. Walker	1 Apr 67–5 Mar 68
E. Varley	29 Jul 67–30 Nov 68
E. Perry	6 Feb 68–
J. Concannon	11 Apr 68–
M. Miller	29 Oct 68–

Lds in Waiting:

Ld Hobson	21 Oct 64–17 Feb 66
Ld Beswick	28 Dec 64–11 Oct 65
Ld Sorensen	28 Dec 64–20 Apr 68
Lady Phillips	10 Dec 65–
Ld Hilton	6 Apr 66–
Lady Serota	23 Apr 68–25 Feb 69

[1] The appointment of Assistant Government Whips as paid Ministers of the Crown dates technically from 12 Nov 64.

INDEX

This index lists all major items in the book, but it is not exhaustive; it does not include individual names of people or places, the names of publications, of Bills or Acts of Parliament, or separate entries in bibliographies. References to important items are grouped together, with sub-headings. The index of Ministers on pages 65–98 supplements this index, and should be used for finding details of Ministries on pages 1–48, and p. 308.